AMERICAN
SOLDIER

AMERICAN SOLDIER

GENERAL
TOMMY FRANKS

WITH Malcolm McConnell

1❿ ReganBooks
Celebrating Ten Bestselling Years
An Imprint of HarperCollins*Publishers*

Photography credits: all photographs courtesy of Tommy Franks or from the Department of Defense except the following: p. ii, AP/Wide World Photos; p. viii, Gary Bonaccorso/DoD; p. 188, AP/Wide World Photos; p. 318, Christopher Morris/VII; Insert 1: p. 9 (bottom), government of Jordan; p. 13 (bottom), Gary Bonaccorso/DoD; pp. 14–16, Jeff Haynes; Insert 2: pp. 2–3, Christopher Morris / VII; p. 4 (top), Gary Bonaccorso/DoD; p. 5 (top), Steven Harris/Polaris; pp. 6–7, Christopher Morris / VII; p. 8 (bottom), AP/Wide World Photos; p. 9 (top), AP/Wide World Photos; p. 10 (top), AP/Wide World Photos; p. 10 (bottom), Reuters/CORBIS; p. 11, Scott Nelson/ Getty Images; pp. 12–14, Karen Ballard/Redux; p. 15 (top), the White House; p. 15 (bottom), LUKE FRAZZA/AFP/Getty Images

HarperCollins books may be purchased for educational, business, or sales promotional use. For information please write: Special Markets Department, HarperCollins Publishers Inc., 10 East 53rd Street, New York, NY 10022.

FIRST EDITION

Designer: Publications Development Company of Texas
Maps: Jason Petho, Petho Cartography

Printed on acid-free paper

Library of Congress Cataloging-in-Publication Data has been applied for.

ISBN 0-06-073158-3

04 05 06 07 08 PDC/QWF 10 9 8 7 6 5 4 3 2 1

TO ALL WHO SERVE . . .
AND THOSE WHO LOVE THEM.

CONTENTS

The art of war is of vital importance to the State.
It is a matter of life and death, a road either to safety or to ruin.
Hence under no circumstances can it be neglected.

—SUN TZU

PROLOGUE
D-DAY

I leaned forward in the leather chair, watching the blank video projection screen. After a flicker of static, the wood-paneled White House Situation Room snapped into focus.

President George W. Bush sat between Vice President Dick Cheney and Secretary of State Colin Powell at the head of the mahogany table. The five other members of the National Security Council sat along the sides, facing the screen on which our image appeared, just as theirs was displayed here.

The men's dark suits were well cut. Dr. Condoleezza Rice wore a tailored jacket. They could have been a corporate board, but the subject of this teleconference was not profit or loss. The topic was war.

If the President gave me the order, thousands of Coalition soldiers and Marines would attack across the Iraqi border in a matter of hours. Hundreds of American, British, and Australian warplanes would support the ground force.

"Can you hear me, Mr. President?" I asked.

"Yes we can, Tommy. We can hear you fine. You've got the National Security Council here."

"Sir," I began. "I would like to give a brief introduction of our component commanders and let them give you a quick status report. We'll go around the horn. I'll start with Lt. General Buzz Moseley."

I nodded to my left. Buzz wore a desert-tan U.S. Air Force flight suit with the three stars of his rank on the shoulders. Beside him at our oval table was Royal Air Force Air Vice Marshal Glenn Torpy, who commanded the Coalition's British aviators. Group Captain Geoff Brown, the commander of the Australian Air Component, sat to my right.

"Our command and control is full up, Mr. President," Buzz reported. "Our Coalition forces are in place. The Air Component is airborne, overhead Iraq right now. Mr. President, we have the best-trained, best-equipped, best-motivated people in the world, and we're well prepared to execute this task."

The people in Washington looked grave. Colin was plainly tired. Maybe even as tired as I was. My immediate boss, Secretary of Defense Donald Rumsfeld, was calm, thoughtful. Beside him, Air Force General Dick Myers, Chairman of the Joint Chiefs of Staff, appeared somber. Director of Central Intelligence George Tenet sat across the table, listening closely. They recognized the gravity of the moment.

The ultimate objective of our forces was Baghdad. Their mission was to overwhelm the enemy and topple one of the most dangerous and repressive dictatorships in the world, the Baathist regime of Saddam Hussein.

Then, as I looked at the screen, I could see President Bush speaking—but now I couldn't hear his words. Apparently the sound on the secure satellite video link had just failed. *Hope this isn't an omen.* The President spoke again, but the picture was mute. Don Rumsfeld waved, pointing a finger toward his ear and mouthing something. Then Buzz leaned over and tapped a switch on my black console.

I had inadvertently cut the audio. "Mr. Secretary, I found this thing on my machine here," I said with exaggerated contrition. "I can read you loud and clear now."

My gaffe had broken the tension. The White House Situation Room echoed with laughter.

"Don't worry, Tommy," the President said, grinning. "We haven't lost confidence. Fortunately we're dealing with pilots sitting next to you."

His tone changed. The President's words were precise. "General," he asked Buzz Moseley, "do you have everything you need to win?"

"You bet, Sir."

"Pleased with the strategy?" the President continued.

"Absolutely," Buzz answered.

Our strategy to defeat Saddam's military and free Iraq was contained in a complex and ambitious operations plan that my staff and I had hammered out over months with Don Rumsfeld, an OPLAN unique in military history. During Operation Desert Storm, which drove the Iraqis from Kuwait, the coalition had deployed 560,000 troops in fourteen divisions. The four-day ground war did not begin until an intense five-week air campaign had pounded the enemy. In Operation Iraqi Freedom, I would command fewer than half the number of troops—in only five divisions, equipped with less than half the armor and artillery—than the force that had defeated the Iraqi army in 1991. But we would not stop at the Euphrates River. We planned to go all the way to Baghdad and beyond. And under our strategy, decisive air operations would begin *after* our ground units went into combat.

This was a calculated risk. But in thirty-eight years as a soldier, I'd learned the difference between a risk and a gamble.

Next, I introduced U.S. Army Lt. General David McKiernan, our Land Component commander in Kuwait. "Mr. President, we have 170,000 American, British, and Australian soldiers and Marines that are trained and ready here."

"We're proud of the British and the Australians," the President said.

"As we speak," David continued, "we're moving into forward attack positions along the Kuwaiti border. Our logistics are in place to sustain our operations for as far north and as long as we need to go."

"General," George Bush asked him, "you got everything you need to win?"

"Yes, Sir."

"Satisfied with the strategy?"

"Yes, Sir."

Next came my Naval Component commander, Vice Admiral Tim Keating, in Bahrain. He described his 149 ships—sixty from Coalition allies—deployed in the eastern Mediterranean, the Red Sea, and the Arabian Gulf, a fleet that included five aircraft carriers. "We're ready to execute, Mr. President."

"Got everything you need?" George Bush asked again.

"We do, Sir."

President Bush tilted back in his chair and smiled. "I'm going to stop asking about the plan since you guys were the ones that developed it."

I heard laughter around the teleconference loop. The President had the natural leader's ability to put his subordinates at ease.

I moved on to our Marine Component commander, Lt. General Earl Hailston, also in Bahrain, who led our Consequence Management Task Force. "Morale is high," he stressed, then added that his forces were "ready to respond to any incident" involving biological or chemical weapons.

All across the theater of war, our young men and women were pulling on their hot, uncomfortable MOPP protective suits before "saddling up" in the rest of their combat gear. Our latest intelligence reports suggested that Iraqi frontline units and Republican Guard divisions had been armed with nerve and mustard gas—and possibly weaponized anthrax and botulinum toxins.

Neither Earl Hailston nor I could confirm the validity of this intelligence until the troops entered Iraq. But we had seen the Iraqis training to operate in a weapons of mass destruction (WMD) environment, and communications intercepts indicated their concern with "chemicals and toxins." *Since the Iraqis know we won't use WMD,* I thought, *their preparations must mean they will.* I had no doubt WMD would be used against our forces in the days ahead. The enemy had the artillery and missiles to deliver these weapons of mass destruction. It was my duty as Commander, U.S. Central Command, to make certain the Coalition forces I would order into harm's way were protected against *any* threat the enemy could present.

Indeed, I was glad that we had created Earl Hailston's task force to respond to whatever WMD threats we might encounter.

Safeguarding the kids in my command to the maximum degree possible while accomplishing the mission was a responsibility I took very seriously. But in the coming hours, no matter how well my commanders had prepared their units, some of these brave young people would be killed and wounded, an immutable aspect of war that those who had never experienced combat often forgot.

I had learned my first lessons about war's harsh reality as an Artillery forward observer in the rice paddies and mangrove swamps of Vietnam's Mekong Delta thirty-five years earlier. Tonight, as our soldiers and Marines bulldozed through the thick sand berm on the Iraqi border and rolled north into the dark fields of landmines, they would be ready to shed their blood, following the orders I would transmit to their commanders.

Even after all these years in uniform, this still amazed me. I would be seated in my air-conditioned command center in Qatar, scanning a wall of digital maps pulsing with bright symbols, but I would also be riding in those clanking Abrams tanks and Bradley fighting vehicles. In my mind, I'd choke on the dust and sooty diesel fumes and smell the bitter sweat of fear.

I continued to introduce my commanders, moving the teleconference around the region.

From a desert field site near Saudi Arabia's border with Iraq, U.S. Army Major General Dell Dailey, who commanded the elite Special Mission Units of Task Force 20, told the President his men were "ready to go to war *again*."

Dell's Joint Special Operations Command had spearheaded ground combat in Afghanistan in October 2001, less than a month after the 9/11 terrorist attacks. In Operation Enduring Freedom, Central Command and its Afghan allies had defeated the Taliban regime and destroyed Osama bin Laden's al Qaeda terrorist sanctuary in seventy-six days. Now my command was going to war for the second time in less than two years.

While the component commanders reported their readiness, I glanced at the CENTCOM logo on the conference room wall. The map of our Area of Responsibility covered twenty-five nations, spreading from Africa across the Arabian Peninsula, Iraq, Iran, Afghanistan, and Pakistan, then on through former Soviet Central Asia, right up to Kyrgyzstan's glacier frontier with China. Half a billion people, most of them young, poor, and angry at their plight, lived in this troubled area. War had plagued the region—which held 65 percent of the world's proven reserves of oil and natural gas—for decades.

I remembered the advice my predecessor, Marine General Tony Zinni, had offered before I'd assumed command in July 2000.

"Tom," he'd told me. "Your mission will be to foster peace, stability, and security. But the region is boiling over with *de*stabilizing tribal, ethnic, and religious hatred and is fertile ground for terrorism. If America gets involved in a major war in the next few years, it will probably be in this part of the world. It's a dangerous neighborhood."

When the commanders' reports ended, I spoke again, slowly and deliberately, aware of the historic moment.

"Mr. President, this force is ready. D-Day, H-Hour is 2100 hours tonight Iraqi time, 1800 hours Greenwich Mean, 1300 hours East Coast time."

President Bush nodded to the National Security Council, then turned toward me.

"All right. For the sake of peace in the world and security for our country and the rest of the free world. . . ." He paused as we listened intently. . . . "And for the freedom of the Iraqi people, as of this moment I will give Secretary Rumsfeld the order necessary to execute Operation Iraqi Freedom.

"Tommy," the President added, his voice firm. "May God bless the troops."

The seven thousand miles separating me from the White House vanished. I felt the impact of the President's invocation.

"Mr. President," I answered. "May God bless America."

I saluted, and the Commander-in-Chief returned the salute.

THE TARMAC ROARED WITH THE ENGINES OF REFUELING TANKERS and reconnaissance jets taking off.

I paused, climbing the stairs to my plane. The President had just ordered me to go to war. The troops were ready. The question in my mind was, *am I ready?*

Watching a huge gray jet lumber down the runway and climb into the desert sky, I felt a deep well of confidence. But strangely, I did not think of my seasoning in combat, my years as a commanding officer, or the military education I'd received in my career.

Instead, my thoughts cast back to the small towns of the American Southwest where I'd grown up. It was this environment, my family, my friends, and my faith that had formed my values, my character. It was these elements that had made me who I was, years before I ever put on the uniform of a soldier.

Success in the campaign ahead would depend more on character, sense of purpose, and values—the nation's, the President's, my own, and the troops'—than on raw military power.

PART I

DEEP
ROOTS

---

*Everyone who got where he is
had to begin where he was.*

—ROBERT LOUIS STEVENSON

1

PLANTING SEEDS

WYNNEWOOD, OKLAHOMA
JUNE 1950

My understanding of the world and its consequences—of right and wrong, good and evil—began when I was five in central Oklahoma. That may be hard to believe, but it's true.

It was my father, Ray Franks, who taught me those lessons.

"You pull up just as hard as you push down, Tommy Ray," Dad said. He was trimming two-by-fours for our barn roof with a hand-saw on the tailgate of the old Ford pickup. The saw blade snarled down through the board and ripped up with a thinner sound. His right arm, tanned like leather under the short sleeve of a washed-out shirt, bulged as he leaned his stocky weight into the saw.

It was summer, nice in the shade of the cottonwood trees near the barn. I was barefoot, in faded bib overalls that were getting short in the legs, sitting in the dirt, watching my father work, listening closely, as always, to his soft-spoken words. He smiled a lot and liked to josh around. But when we were alone together, my dad often took a moment to explain the things he'd learned in his life.

"Here, Tommy Ray," he said, tossing me a couple of splintery cuttings. "You can play with these blocks."

"But, Dad, they ain't *real* toys."

"*Aren't* real toys," he corrected, flipping another board end to me. "But they are, you see. A few years back, kids had to make do with toys their daddies made for them. They couldn't just drive to the five-and-dime in town and buy ready-made."

I fingered the wood, still hot from the saw blade. "How come?"

He wiped his face with a handkerchief, laid another plank across the tailgate, and lined up the saw. "Well, Tommy Ray, we had a war. Most of the countries in the whole world were fighting. America had to fight the Germans and the Japanese. Millions and millions of guys my age and younger were soldiers and sailors and flyers and had to go fight."

Fight, I thought. That was like when the barnyard chickens went rolling around, pecking and squawking. Or like when the big kids walking to school in the winter threw ice balls. But what would make a million soldiers and sailors fight?

"How come, Dad?"

"Bad people, Tommy Ray. The Japanese attacked us at a place called Pearl Harbor. It went on for years, and a lot of our boys didn't come home."

"Where'd they go?"

Father laid down the saw and smiled that soft grin he had when he needed to explain something sad, like when Ginger the cat got hit by a truck. "Well, those boys got killed. They died for America, Tommy Ray."

My mother said people went to heaven when they died. Those boys went to fight and just kept going till they got to heaven.

"Did you go fight?"

"I was in the Army Air Corps, Tommy Ray. I fixed airplanes for the boys to fly. I didn't have to fight, but I think my job was important."

In my mind's eye, I could see my father fixing airplanes with shiny propellers. He could mend anything—the electric water heater for the bathroom, the truck, the tractor, all the different plows and reapers. Folks were always bringing their broken things to the farm for Ray Franks to fix. Mother told me that Dad could never say no if people needed help.

"Did you go to Pearl Harbor?"

My father shook his head, smiling. "No, Tommy Ray. I went to a place called the Panama Canal Zone. They've got palm trees down there, and really pretty birds called parrots."

"Mother didn't have to fight, did she?"

"The ladies stayed home and worked really hard, son. Lots of men, too. The whole country went to work. People planted victory gardens for their food. The boys in my Scout troop collected tin cans and newspapers. Things were scarce. That's why children couldn't always have new toys, why their dads or uncles had to make them blocks and doll houses."

My father always explained things so I could see a picture. So many years later, I recall that afternoon clearly. This was my first appreciation of war. What I learned was clear: Bad people started wars, and Americans had to go fight. I already understood about cats getting run over. About steers going to the slaughterhouse. Now I saw that whenever wars were started, some boys didn't come home.

"Will I have to go fight?"

My father stacked the trimmed boards up against the fender and sighed. "Tommy Ray, I hope not. But you get used to playing with those blocks I just cut, because there are more bad people starting trouble again in a place called Korea. I think America is in for another trying time, son."

I set my blocks in a square and then leaned forward to scratch in the dirt between my ankles, fascinated by the little rust-colored bugs swarming up from the ground. They looked angry, like a million soldiers.

"Oh, hey . . ." I yelped. The bugs were crawling up my legs and biting. "Dad . . ."

He snatched me up with one arm and shook the flapping legs of my overalls. "Tommy Ray, you were sitting on an *anthill*. Those little devils are red ants, son. They're nasty."

We were at the garden spigot now, and Dad ran the water over my ankles. It felt cool. But in my mind I pictured crowds of soldiers with guns like my father's 12-gauge shotgun, boiling out of the ground, just like the ants.

That night, I had my bath, said my prayers, and my mother tucked me in. But I couldn't go to sleep right away. I'd learned important new information out in the shade of the cottonwoods. When there are wars, boys go to fight, mothers work hard, and kids like me go without toys.

M Y FATHER HAD BEEN A SCOUTMASTER FOR AS LONG AS I COULD remember. One of the neat things about that was that I got to tag along on field trips and campouts—big adventures to places like Robbers' Cave State Park and Turner Falls.

One November Saturday, he loaded the Wynnewood troop into an old yellow school bus and we drove a couple of hours east to McAlester State Prison. It was a raw, cloudy day, and those high concrete walls looked dark and cold when we squeaked to a stop in the parking lot.

"Okay, boys," my father called out from the front of the bus. "No horsing around today. Listen up and do what the officers tell you."

"Yes, Ray," the kids chanted. They never called my father "Mr. Franks." But they always did what he asked them to do.

The narrow tunnel through the wall echoed like a cave when the steel door slammed behind us. I held my dad's hand as we marched in. There were more clanging doors and bars with chipped gray paint. The smell of floor wax was sour. A tall man with a police hat and a shiny leather pistol belt led us into a room with school desks. There were signs with big long words printed in big black letters underlined in red.

The officer almost shouted as he read out the prison rules. I didn't understand everything he said, but I knew the words "punishment," "bread and water," and even "solitary confinement" from *The Green Hornet* on the radio. The boys were quiet.

"We can start the tour now, Mr. Franks," the officer with the shiny belt said.

We walked down a hall with a squeaky linoleum floor, and through more gates with bars. Then a steel door opened into a big room with bright lights hanging from the ceiling.

"The dining hall," the officer announced.

We stood along the wall, watching. Men in black-and-white striped uniforms, like sideways pajamas, shuffled in from another door. Their hair was clipped so short their heads looked white. They kept their hands clasped behind them until they reached the food line. Officers with long black wooden sticks watched from the corners. There was the slap of shoe leather on the floor, but not a single human voice. Each man stopped, took a metal tray, then moved ahead to get his food from fellow prisoners wearing white cooks' hats standing behind the steaming counter.

"Lunch today is beef stew, bread and margarine, and a sugar cookie. They can have water, a glass of milk, or a cup of coffee," the officer said.

From where I stood the stew being ladled into the trays looked thin, yellowy.

"What kind of sentences are these fellows serving?" my father asked.

The officer frowned. "They're mostly long-time men, Mr. Franks. Bad actors . . . bank robbers, kidnappers, a number of manslaughter and murder convictions. I guess the average sentence for this bunch is about twenty."

"Twenty years in prison, boys," my father said. "You break the law and that's what happens."

I didn't understand at first. Then I got it: *Rob a bank, and this is where they send you.*

"This is what's called the consequence of your actions, boys," my father said as we left the dining hall.

He took my hand again. "Okay," he said. "Now we're getting serious, so if anybody feels like being a wiseacre, he'd best wait back here."

Another hallway led to a green steel door. "This is the execution chamber," the officer said. "The day of the execution, we take the man through this door."

He opened the green door, and we blinked at the bright lights inside. A big chair filled the room. I could smell leather.

"All right, boys," he said. "Line up."

The kids made a straight line that led out the green door, then moved ahead, one at a time, to sit in the big wooden chair.

"This is the electric chair, Tommy Ray," my dad explained. "It's where murderers are executed."

The boys inched forward. Some sat longer in the chair than others. Executed meant killed, that much I knew.

"This is the ultimate consequence for the ultimate act of evil," my father told the troop.

When all the boys had sat in the chair, it was my turn. I reached up and felt the smooth wood, the leather straps with cold metal buckles. There was a black steel cap dangling up there like a lamp without a bulb.

"Up you go, Tommy Ray," Dad said, hoisting me into the chair.

The boys were staring at me. But I wasn't even a little bit afraid. My father stood right beside me. I could feel his warm hand next to the cool metal buckle.

As the school bus rumbled out of the prison parking lot that afternoon, I stared back at the high walls. I had learned another important lesson. A consequence was what followed what you did. If you did good things, you'd be rewarded with further good things. If you broke the law, you'd have to pay the price.

I have never forgotten that lesson.

WHEN I WAS SIX, WE MOVED TO THE SMALL TOWN OF STRATFORD, about fifteen miles northeast of Wynnewood. My father had worked as a banker, a grain farmer, a fix-it man, and a mechanic. Now he was ready for a new line of work.

When I was young, his restless streak seemed perfectly normal. A few years later, I realized that he was an optimistic dreamer, convinced that the next job or business would make us rich.

And the fact is that my dad was good at everything he took on. Maybe too good. There wasn't a refrigerator, an outboard motor, a gas or diesel engine that he couldn't repair. If somebody drove over a backfiring John Deere Model 60 tractor to have Ray Franks "take a little look at the damn timing chain," my father would rebuild the engine. And if they'd shaken hands on a price of ten dollars for the job, he would not accept a nickel more, even if he'd spent fifteen dollars on spare parts.

I LIKED LIVING IN TOWN, BEING AROUND KIDS MY OWN AGE. OUR wood frame house was only a block from the Stratford School.

When we went to live in Stratford, my father was certain that he'd found work that would set us up in style. He bought out a little water-well drilling company and set to work to make the business profitable.

My mother always supported my dad in whatever new venture he chose. She was three years older, born into a family of poor cotton farmers in eastern Oklahoma in 1911. Although she was baptized Lorene, her family nicknamed her Pete, probably the country version of "petite," because she never stood higher than four feet eleven inches on her tallest day. But she packed a lot of strength, heart, and perseverance into that small frame. She loved my dad and me with an intensity that was obvious even to strangers. Whatever job, project, or abrupt shift in life Ray Franks chose, she backed him.

Following the customs of the time, my mother thought of herself as a wife and a homemaker. She kept a spotless house; she sent my father out in the morning in hand-scrubbed and ironed work clothes, and me to school in shirts and jeans with ironed creases. My mother was a wonderful cook who took a lot of care with meals, even though we often didn't have the money for fancy food.

She canned vegetables from the garden and put up Mason jars of fruit. Pies were one of her specialties. She always found the creamiest white lard at the farmers' market for her flaky crusts. Her cherry and apple pies won prizes at local fairs, as did her chocolate and marble cakes. And later, when times were tough, Mother sold her baked goods for extra money.

Dad's new business was centered on a clanking, truck-mounted Bucyrus-Erie Model 22 "spudder" drill. The working end of the drill was raised and dropped by a cable system running off a roaring diesel engine on the truck bed. He explained that it was like a pile driver with a casehardened steel tip that could bite through mud, shale, and soft rock layers to find water. After making a little money that first year, my father invested in a modern rotary drill. Sometimes he'd have both rigs working on different jobs and hustle between them by car, making sure the shafts were sinking true.

Even though I was just a little kid, my dad patiently explained the fine points of the equipment to me. By age seven, I knew as much about diesel engines as I did about reading and arithmetic. Weekdays after school and Saturdays, I'd join Dad out in the work shed or on a farm where he was drilling a well, helping when I could, but mainly just watching, listening to him, and learning.

It was probably then that I first realized there was something wrong with my dad's left hand. Growing up as a youngster in Wynnewood, I'd accepted the fact that the fingers on that hand were different than those of his right. Now I studied his hand as he deftly spun socket wrenches and adjusted chain tensions. The first joint of his thumb was missing, the digit ending in a shiny knuckle. His index finger was also missing the end joint. And the middle finger was a stub. I now recognized that there was something strange about his left eye, too. The lid drooped a little, and the white was cloudy. The eye itself did not move.

For some reason, I never asked him about this. And he never chose to discuss the injuries. Years later, when we lived in Midland, Texas, my Uncle Bob Myers told me the story. "Your dad got hurt when he was about ten years old," Uncle Bob explained. While my father's family was living in the oilfield town of Seminole, Oklahoma, he and some other boys were walking the railroad tracks one summer afternoon. They found some shiny brass explosive caps, the kind that switchmen laid out on the tracks to warn locomotive engineers to stop for an obstacle ahead. Dad snatched up a couple of the caps and took them home. He grabbed a hammer from his father's tool chest and slammed it down on one to see what would happen. The explosion shredded his left hand and drove splinters into his left eye, half blinding him.

But through all the years I spent watching my father perform some of the trickiest, most frustrating engine repairs, flat on his back under a car or truck, groping to replace a water-pump gasket or oil seal, I never heard a word of complaint about his handicap. He just did his work. And in World War II, despite a disability that would have exempted him from military service, he enlisted and served skillfully as an Army Air Corps mechanic.

Growing up in my father's shadow, I learned a lot about perseverance and self-reliance.

O NE SPRING DAY AFTER SCHOOL WHEN I WAS IN SECOND GRADE, I came home and got a glass of milk from the refrigerator. My mother was out in the garden, fixing strings for the pole beans that were sprouting. I wandered out of the kitchen into the cool living room and sat in one of the good chairs. The afternoon sun through the window highlighted the worn leather cover of the family Bible on the cherry-wood desk Dad had refinished. My teacher, Mrs. Burnette, had mentioned that we could learn a lot about our families from reading the birth and death inscriptions in the Bible.

I put down my empty milk glass and opened the heavy book on my lap. There were dates written with neat strokes of a fountain pen, my mother and her sisters' birth dates and the dates of my grandparents' deaths. But there was also a stiff, folded paper, which I opened.

"Certificate of Birth," I read aloud. "Tommy Ray Bentley, born June 17, 1945." That was *my* birthday. I was Tommy Ray Franks. Why did this paper say "Bentley"?

I heard the kitchen screen door spring shut. "Mother," I called. "Can you come in here, please?"

She stood in the doorway, half-covered by her faded blue garden apron. "Oh, Tommy Ray," she said, her voice soft. "What have you got there?"

I held up the birth certificate. "It says Bentley, Mother. I'm not Bentley. I'm Tommy Ray Franks."

She touched her hair the way she did sometimes when she was upset. "Of course you are, Tommy Ray." Mother came over and gently lifted the Bible and birth certificate from my hands. "When you were born, they made a mistake at the hospital, and your dad and I had to have the papers changed. We just kept this old one as a souvenir." Mother replaced the Bible on the desk.

I wondered where my correct birth certificate was. Frowning a little, I started to ask.

"Tommy Ray," Mother said, reaching out to hug me. "You're my little baby, and I love you more than anything. So does your dad."

I *knew* that. I also realized something had happened to make my mother sad. "Sure," I said, hugging her back. "I love you and Dad, too."

It wasn't until I was a junior at Lee High School in Midland, Texas, that my folks finally told me I had been adopted. But I had secretly known the truth for years. And I never doubted for a minute that they were my parents, my family.

THE SPECIAL LOVE OF ADOPTIVE PARENTS DID NOT PREVENT THEM from disciplining me when I needed it. And, looking back, I needed it pretty often. Today, I guess you'd say that I learned to "press the envelope" when I was a grade school student in Stratford, Oklahoma.

Like most small town boys, I spent most of the warm weather outside, usually roaming the creek beds that fed the Washita River. My partners in these adventures were the Bells brothers, who lived next door. On a typical summer day, we'd pack a peanut butter sandwich or two and head out to the stock ponds on nearby farms to hunt frogs. For me, this represented more than just the natural meanness of a nine-year-old boy. My father's business sucked up most of our available money, so dinner often consisted of beans and cornbread. Frog legs dusted in flour and fried crisp were a welcome treat.

Basic frog-hunting technique involved gigging with a forked spear tip attached to a broom handle. The big bullfrogs congregated near the mossy earthen pond dams on hot afternoons. If we snuck up silently and didn't spook them with a shadow, we could usually gig three or four before the rest dove.

It was a harmless pursuit for a bunch of country boys—except that the Bells brothers and I often broke the rules. Rural Oklahoma etiquette required you to always ask permission to come on someone's land. We followed that rule, but we wouldn't always announce our true intentions. Once we asked a farm lady if we could gather windfall paper shell pecans from the trees near her house.

"Sure, boys," she said. "But don't go near the stock pond. It's deep and slippery."

"Yes, ma'am," we said in unison.

Half an hour later, with a dozen frogs in our sack, the Bells brothers and I decided it was too hot an afternoon to pass up a swim. We were skinny dipping, hooting and hollering, when the lady appeared on the edge of the pond.

"Get out of there right now."

No woman except my mother had ever seen me bare naked. It wasn't much fun crawling up the muddy bank with this lady glaring at us.

And it wasn't much fun getting home to find that she'd called my mother to complain. "Wait'll your father gets home."

I went to my room, not very pleased with myself. Telling lies was a really bad thing. I never knew my father to lie to anyone.

He was a firm believer that the punishment should fit the crime. I had to walk all the way back out to that farm and apologize. After I had done so, and turned for home, Dad drove up.

"Hop in, son. You lied to that lady, Tommy Ray. Have you learned your lesson?"

"Yes, Sir," I said . . . and I had, too.

WHEN BUSINESS WAS GOOD, MY FOLKS INDULGED ME. THE summer I was eight, they bought me a dapple quarter horse mare and taught me to ride. I loved old Gray. She was patient and gentle. Riding her, I could play Bob Steele, just like in the Saturday matinee cowboy serials.

The trouble was, every real cowboy had a gun. Dad was teaching me to shoot an old hex-barrel Winchester .22 pump rifle and a Remington .410 shotgun. But I wasn't yet allowed to take the guns out on my own. So one boring July afternoon, I decided to *borrow* eight silver dollars from the velvet sack in the family cedar chest. I figured I could make that much in a few weeks poaching pecans and selling them to Mr. Herbert down at the Purina feedstore.

Downtown in the general store, I laid those silver dollars down for a Daisy Red Rider pump BB-gun.

Then, armed like a real trail hand, I rode Gray over to the rodeo grounds to test my marksmanship. It was the middle of the week, and no one was around. The best targets were the big old bulbs mounted under wide tin reflectors around the grandstand. My first shot missed, pinging off the metal. The second hit dead center with a satisfying "pop." And one by one, I shot out a dozen bulbs. Gray stood still under my saddle, her strong neck bent as she nibbled dry grass.

I was washing up for dinner when the town constable knocked on our front door. Dad went outside to talk to him. *Well, this can't have anything to do with me,* I thought, and headed toward the kitchen for dinner.

I didn't make it.

"Tommy Ray," Father said, more sad than angry. "Come in here, right now."

The constable was driving off, so at least I didn't have to face him. "All right, son, are you going to tell me what happened?"

"Yes, sir."

It was not a pretty story. Theft and vandalism.

This demanded more than an apology. My father took me out the kitchen door and removed his belt. He'd only whacked me a few times before, and never really to inflict physical punishment, more to emphasize the fact that I'd been a bad boy. Today, I got three hard, quick smacks on the rear.

In the kitchen, I learned the rest of my punishment. My allowance would be stopped until both the stolen money and the cost of the rodeo grounds' lights had been repaid. I was also restricted to the yard—indefinitely. This hurt worse than the belt. No more Saturday matinees at the Stratford picture show for a long, long time. For twenty-five cents out of my dollar-a-week chore allowance, I had been able to use a dime to buy a ticket, and then spend the rest on a soda pop, a box of popcorn, and a pickle for a nickel each. Then, properly provisioned, I could sit back in the flickering dark with the Bells brothers and watch the latest installment of *Flash Gordon* or *Sergeant Preston of the Royal Mounted Police*. Now I'd be stuck at the house for at least two months.

One rainy Saturday morning in August, as I moped around my room thinking about the Bells boys chomping pickles at the picture show, I remembered that silent line of convicts in striped uniforms, shuffling into the prison dining hall.

Action and consequence. The real lesson of that Boy Scout field trip suddenly came into focus.

MY FATHER WAS NOT SATISFIED WITH HIS WELL-DIGGING BUSINESS. And Mother no longer enjoyed small-town Oklahoma. The summer between my fourth and fifth grades, we moved 350 miles southwest to Midland, Texas. Mother had family there, and we always drove to Midland for Christmas. This was great—heading off to the big city.

While we were waiting for the new house my folks were building in the suburbs to be finished, we lived with my mother's sister, Mildred, and my uncle, Bob Myers, in their big, comfortable home at 1205 West Wall Street. This was a well-to-do neighborhood, not far from downtown. And I walked every day about half a mile to West Elementary School through the section called "Old Midland," an area of two- and three-story brick houses built during the oil boom of the 1920s.

In the mid-1950s, Midland was one of the richest towns in America. The Permian Basin oilfields produced over 20 percent of America's petroleum. And the city of only 65,000 people had the largest Rolls Royce dealership in the country. A few years later, it boasted the biggest Learjet franchise as well. It was a boom-and-bust, bust-and-boom community. Wildcatters who managed by luck, skill, guile, and sometimes-questionable business practices to nail down productive oil leases were among the town's elite, along with the senior engineers and executives of Humble Oil Company—which would become Exxon. Together, they made up the membership of the Midland and Ranchland Hills Country Clubs and the Petroleum Club.

Uncle Bob had made his money in oil, starting in the field and working his way up the corporate ladder to take early retirement before age sixty. He was a jovial, affectionate man who loved having a youngster around the house. Every morning Uncle Bob drove downtown for coffee and donuts at Agnes' Café, where the new high rollers and Old Money dignitaries gathered. Bob always made a point of introducing me with a standup handshake to these wealthy gentlemen.

The wildcatters I met seemed like something out of a movie. They wore gray Stetsons and double-vented western-style suits. Their cowboy boots were handmade of exotic hides. Many of these men left Agnes' in the late morning, Uncle Bob explained, to converge on the 007 Bar, where they'd hoist their first martini by noon. "That's where they conduct their real business, Tommy Ray," he told me. They would do oil deals, buy and sell mineral leases, borrow and lend money, and throw huge parties, where the deals were passed up the line to the major oil companies.

Even in boom times, though, there was always the occasional bust. One Christmas, there was a wildcatter who laid down cash for two new Cadillac Coupes de Ville—pink for his wife and blue for himself. Three months later, flat broke, he came crawling across the lobby of Midland National Bank in search of new credit.

Aunt Mildred owned and ran a beauty shop downtown in the Petroleum Building. She had worked hard her whole life and had undergone the pain of a divorce at a time when this was a real stigma, but she always maintained her dignity . . . and she always had a smile on her face. She loved Bob probably as much as my mother loved my dad. Like Bob, Aunt Mildred treated me like one of her own children, took an active interest in my life, and was always a source of encouragement.

One of her daughters, Betty, was married to Lelland "Docie" Foster, a respected Midland banker. Like my dad, Docie had served as an enlisted man in the Army Air Corps during World War II. We took to each other from the start. It was great fun to go down and visit him at the bank. He'd escort me to the boardroom like I was a rich oilman, and a secretary would bring us Cokes and donuts. If I showed up at lunchtime, Docie would always take me to eat brisket or chicken at Johnny's Barbeque, a local landmark. One of the things I learned from Docie Foster was to treat people, no matter their social class or the size of their bank accounts, with respect. He also impressed upon me that the members of his and my father's generation—like the Roman Cincinnatus before them—had left the civilian world to serve their country during wartime, and then had returned home to get on with their lives.

Mildred's other daughter, Doris Jean, was married to Johnny Bowden, who had flown Air Force cargo planes during World War II and stayed on to become a career military officer. Having lived overseas for years, Johnny was polished and worldly. When he and Doris Jean came back to Midland, it was always in a new Oldsmobile or Buick. And when he joined the family men to go quail hunting, he always fired handmade European shotguns. Greatly influenced by my dad, Docie Foster, and Johnny Bowden, by the age of twelve I was thinking that becoming a military officer might be a pretty good deal.

My father found a job clerking in the sporting goods department at the Basin Supply Company. The huge store on the near-west side was a Midland institution that had been started by an oilman during the boom years. Basin Supply still sold drill bits and other oilfield gear, but as Midland grew, the company began to stock home furnishings and expensive appliances. They also offered a line of high-quality televisions and hi-fi record players, and a large selection of sporting goods.

For the first time since he'd worked at the bank in Wynnewood, my dad wore a white shirt and tie to work. Then, after a while, he went "Texan" and started wearing thin bolo ties with silver-and-turquoise slides. His customers bought Barbour jackets and top-of-the-line Browning, Winchester, and Remington .12-gauge shotguns—quail guns, as we called them.

Quail hunting was, and is, a way of life in Midland. Between Uncle Bob and Docie Foster, the family had access to some of the best bird shooting anywhere on the ranches and oil leases surrounding town. Bob's house was the headquarters. We would go out early in the morning to hunt, then come back to play billiards in Bob's game room or watch college football on TV. And at Christmastime, when eggnog was served, a little Jack Daniel's always found its way into the adults' cups. Hunting quail and hanging out at Midland National Bank were a lot more fun than gigging frogs in Oklahoma.

Walking back and forth to school, I'd pass the Turner Mansion, the biggest and richest house in town. Red brick with rolling lawns with automatic sprinklers, the mansion had a big swimming pool and tennis courts. I knew kids in school whose families lived in houses almost as large.

Midland was an interesting town. There were few private schools, and for the most part the children of the rich were not separated from the rest of the world. Our parents might not necessarily socialize, but we kids didn't pay much attention to money. In fact, I was absolutely ignorant. I remember thinking that it would be nice if my father joined the country club so I could ride my bike out there and swim in the pool. And some kids my age were learning to play golf. That might be fun, too.

I had no idea that Dad was struggling along on a modest salary, and helping to pay the mortgage on the new house by working weekends as a shade-tree mechanic. If I hadn't been so self-centered, I would have realized that my family was short of money. We weren't "poor off," as the local saying went, but there were times when cash was scarce.

I'll always remember one Friday evening between paychecks when I asked my father for some spending money. We were driving home to Uncle Bob's, and my dad turned around and pulled up in front of a little corner grocery store on the west side of Andrews Highway. I knew my mother sometimes shopped here, which seemed funny because the store was out of the way.

"Tommy Ray," Father said, "go in and tell the man behind the cash register who you are and ask for five dollars until next payday."

I sat in the front seat, frowning. That would be kind of a *low class* thing to do, I thought, and just too embarrassing.

"No, sir. I'd rather not."

"Why?" he asked.

"I'm not very proud of my name," I finally said.

"Okay, son," Dad said, starting the Mercury's engine and shifting into first gear. He dug in his pocket and came up with several quarters and a crumpled dollar bill, what Mother called "your father's coffee money." He handed me the change and the bill. "This'll do you for the weekend," he said.

I took the cash, not thinking at the time of how my dad would pay for coffee or tobacco the next week. When I went to the movie that night and bought a big tub of buttered popcorn, I thought it was nice we weren't poor folks. I've replayed this scene in my mind a thousand times over the course of almost fifty years, and I regret saying the words—"I'm not very proud of my name"—to this day.

THERE WERE POOR PEOPLE IN MIDLAND. AS A RETIREMENT JOB, my Uncle Bob started a little business he called the Biff Bang Construction Company. It wasn't a moneymaker, but Bob didn't care. The black and Hispanic—what we then called the Negro and Mexican—neighborhoods south of the Union Pacific tracks were run down and neglected. Bob bought and refurbished homes there and sold them on low-interest mortgages to families who couldn't qualify for a bank loan.

I started working with him during the summer and after school. I knew, of course, that the city was segregated, that Negroes and Mexicans went to different schools. And I'd just assumed this was because they were different and somehow not as good as white people. The only folks I'd ever met were white. Cutting and hanging sheetrock with Uncle Bob, I had the chance to meet Negro and Mexican kids. I was surprised to learn that they spoke English just as well as I did, that they were friendly, and that their moms cooked great food like mine did. Bob wasn't a tough boss, and I probably spent as much time tossing footballs with these neighborhood boys in vacant lots as I did swinging a hammer.

One evening I came home and told my mother, "I met the neatest kid at Uncle Bob's new house down on Camp Street. His name is LeRoy and he sure can throw the football."

"That's nice," she said. "Does he go to your school?"

"No, ma'am. He's a Negro."

The next afternoon, she looked up from rolling out pie dough. "Did you see your little nigger friend today?" she asked pleasantly.

I'd heard that word my whole life, and it had never occurred to me my parents were bigots. That was the word they'd grown up with and it seemed natural to hear them say it.

"Well," I said, "LeRoy is a *Negro* and he's probably going to play quarterback next year at Booker T. Washington High School."

"That's nice, Tommy Ray."

My mother was not a mean person. She and my father, I later realized, were ignorant, not evil. I quietly chose on that day to look at people differently.

I JOINED THE BOY SCOUTS OUT IN OUR NEW NEIGHBORHOOD. Wearing a uniform—which my mother always pressed to parade ground perfection and Dad squared away before each troop meeting—gave me a sense of pride. I loved the challenge of studying and working on projects to earn merit badges. Making rank was easy at the time—my father spent a lot of time coaching me. For a couple of years, being the best possible Boy Scout seemed a worthy goal.

Then came Alamo Junior High. No doubt about it, the girls in my class looked pretty different from the boys, and a *lot* more interesting. Scouting was still fun, but the attraction of earning marksmanship and lifesaving merit badges was fading fast.

By ninth grade, the Scouts had become a low priority in my life. A motor scooter—a five-horsepower Cushman Eagle with its high, Harley Davidson–style handlebars and teardrop gas tank—was the coolest possession any kid could own. My dad had always indulged me. So in April 1959, two months before I turned fourteen and could legally drive a scooter, he helped me buy a bright red 1952 Eagle. I was working with him after school as a mechanic's helper, so the money he added to my small savings was technically a salary advance. My folks had already given me a black horsehide James Dean jacket. Now I was all set to make waves in junior high.

That scooter was definitely cool. On the highways near town, if I found a down slope, I could crank out fifty miles an hour with the throttle wide open. But it was hard to start, which was embarrassing if I offered someone a ride home from school, stomped on the kick starter, and the motor refused to turn over. The starting gear was missing teeth. If that gear didn't line up properly, you could kick all day, and the flywheel would not turn.

At times like that, I'd go back into school and call my father. "The Eagle won't start." Ten minutes later, he'd be there. He would jiggle the starting pedal, rock the scooter back and forth, and give it a kick. The motor would come to life, with the roar of a Briggs and Stratton lawnmower. My dad was always there when I called.

The next year, again with his help, I bought a '58 Cushman Eagle, black with nice chrome. My father kept my old one and got it running much better than I had. He loved bikes. As a young man in the 1930s, he and a friend had toured the country on Indian motor-cycles, working farm harvests when they could, sleeping in the hobo jungles of the Great Depression, learning about humanity.

Other kids at school had scooters, too. And summer evenings after work, my dad would join my friends and me for rides out to the frozen custard stand, then on to the Texas League Midland Braves ballpark. We'd watch the games with Uncle Bob in his box right behind home plate. Living high, as they say, ain't half of it.

Dad always worked on my buddies' scooters, solving any problem, and often spending his own money, mailing off to Dallas for parts. The kids all loved my father. In his patient, soft-spoken way, he taught them more about life than just spark plug gaps and carburetor settings.

This was one of the happiest times of a very happy childhood. I played junior high football, because of my height more than my talent, and threw the shot put in the spring. But my focus wasn't on athletics. It was much more fun fooling around with scooters, hunting rabbits and quail, and water-skiing out on Lake Thomas. The lake was about seventy miles from Midland, but my dad would frequently take us out on Saturday after he finished work. He'd rebuilt a 16-horsepower Firestone outboard that we'd mount on the back of a rented aluminum boat. As always, he was a patient teacher and made sure each of us learned to stand up on the skis, no matter how many times we fell.

Through hard work, my father had been promoted to sporting goods manager at Basin Supply. He was earning almost $400 a month, enough to pay the mortgage on time and put meat on the table each night. Times were good.

In 1960, I entered Midland High School, which was downtown; I would stay there for a year while Robert E. Lee High, on the west side, was under construction. High school football, of course, is practically a religion in Texas, so I tried out for and made the Midland junior varsity squad. But I sure didn't have your basic God-given talent. I thought I might make a decent receiver, but running those pass patterns over and over again at practice was just plain boring. And besides, I was more interested in swimming and hunting. And girls.

The best thing about Midland High was the Youth Center across the street. It was without question the best teenage hangout in town. You could shoot pool and listen to Elvis on the jukebox. Girls in poodle skirts and ponytails would come in and stand around waiting for someone to ask them to dance. My dancing talents were about as refined as my football skills . . . but I had a lot more motivation to practice.

I spent my junior and senior high school years at Robert E. Lee, where I was in the second graduating class. I learned years later that there was a girl one year behind me named Laura Welch. I didn't know her at the time, but when I met her a few years ago as First Lady Laura Bush, we chatted about Midland in the White House.

LATE IN MY JUNIOR YEAR, I STARTED GETTING MORE INTERESTED IN cars than scooters. Midland was wealthy enough that lots of kids had Chevy convertibles; a few of them even had new Corvettes. By now I was a junior capitalist, selling Spudnut donuts door-to-door after school, and also working with Dad. He'd left his job at Basin Supply and opened Midland Marine, a boat and outboard motor shop halfway between Midland and Odessa, twenty miles west of town. He was such a great mechanic that people came from all over to get their

Evinrude and Johnson boat motors fixed. But Lake Thomas was seventy miles away, so the shop's location was far from ideal.

I wanted a car badly. And we finally found a deal on a 1958 MGA Roadster.

"She needs a little work, Tommy Ray," my dad said when we went to see the man who was selling it. "But I think she'd be a nice car for you."

"Yes, sir," I said, practically drooling. In a few weeks, all the rust spots were gone, and the small chrome grill was dazzling. Then we went to work on the four-cylinder engine and gearbox. By the time we finished, the Roadster was one of the quickest cars on the street.

I STARTED TAKING HER OUT TO THE DRAG STRIPS IN SAN ANGELO, Texas, and Hobbs, New Mexico. Quarter-mile drag racing was a highly organized, addictive kind of sport, more a cult than a hobby. After a few disappointing performances, I learned how to win. Cars were matched by horsepower, tire size, and weight, so I never raced any machine inherently more powerful than mine. The skill lay in tactics. Most kids were infatuated with the noise and energy of a high-revving engine, and couldn't wait to pop the clutch when the Christmas-tree start lights blinked from red to amber to green. But they spun their wheels in a gray cloud of burning rubber before the engine's torque fully transferred to the asphalt. They would lose a second or two—a lot of time in a quarter-mile race.

I made that mistake in the beginning. Now I learned to watch my tach, keeping revs well below the red line, forcing the "hole shot" nerves away with the blare of the other guys' rumbling tailpipes. When the light flashed green, I would accelerate smoothly, nursing optimum RPM out of each gear. I started winning trophies.

And driving that race-winning MGA to school was the best. Out at the drag strips, the officials scrawled your car's class and race number on the windows with white shoe polish. Naturally, I'd *forget* to wipe off that polish before I pulled into the Lee parking lot.

Hanging around the drag strips attracted me to "real cars." Again, with my dad's help, I found what I wanted. It was a black 1957 Chevy Bel Air two-door hardtop with a V-8. Everything about this car said power, class, and speed. The tailfins were trimmed in chrome, as were the forward-leaning hooded headlights. The grille was pure sex, about 300 pounds of high-chrome steel. With a four-on-the-floor gearshift, it was just aching to become a racing machine.

Together, my father and I made that happen. One spring evening out at the shop, I watched, amazed, as my dad whipped the old engine out with a chain hoist and deftly lowered in the 327 V-8 we had rebuilt and augmented with a supercharger. We cut a hole in the hood for the chrome air intake, and I was in business.

To save the racing tires, we towed this new car on a trailer to the drag strips. I applied the lessons I'd learned in the little MGA to the big Chevy. I kept winning trophies. But I learned not to win by too much, or the other drivers would file a formal challenge. On drag strips in the Southwest, that was a serious matter. They were saying you didn't beat them fairly, but had some illegal boost in the engine. The race officials would impound your car and take the engine apart, calipers in hand, to measure bore and stroke. Nobody won in a challenge. I used other tactics to win. Run your own race, not the other guy's. Know your car. Know yourself.

M Y SENIOR YEAR WENT BY TOO FAST. I WAS DEFINITELY LIVING the American dream. Quail hunting with the men of the family, wearing the uniform of the Lee football team, drag racing, and getting ready for college.

I had a steady girl, Shell Dougherty, a tall, brown-eyed beauty I'd met at Midland High. She liked me, and I was pretty sure we were meant for each other.

For several years, I had assumed that college would automatically follow high school: All my friends thought the same way. And Shell and I dreamed of attending the same school, away from our parents.

But our folks conspired and parental common sense prevailed. Shell's family sent her off to Texas Tech; I was accepted at the University of Texas in Austin. This was meant to be a cooling-off period eventually, and it worked: Shell married a law student a few years later, and I married Cathy Jane Carley—the best single decision I ever made, in or out of uniform.

On a hot June evening in 1963, I found myself walking across the Lee High School stage in a cap and gown, reaching out to shake Dr. Leslie Hinds's hand and accept my diploma. *Ain't this a great country,* I thought, as I pumped my fist up and down to the delight of my friends.

I was off to UT Austin for some *real* fun—or so I thought—in the summer of 1963.

2

"MAKE 'EM A HAND"

Everybody who's been a freshman at a big school has probably had a similar experience. During my first few days at the University of Texas I felt isolated, even though I was surrounded by twenty thousand students. The campus occupied a big hunk of downtown Austin. There were wide lawns, a maze of classroom buildings, a football stadium that could seat the population of Midland, and the University Tower looming over the whole place. During registration that muggy week in August 1963, with kids hurrying every which way to get signed up for classes, I might have been one of those ants boiling out of the dirt on my folks' farm back in Wynnewood.

My goal in college was to become a chemical engineer. I liked high school science well enough, and had earned good grades. But those first days on campus, I couldn't even read the map to locate my classrooms.

Soon enough, though, I did find a new home—in the Delta Upsilon fraternity house. The DU house was a four-story cube of blue aluminum and glass overlooking a circular drive on Leon Street. When I walked up that drive wearing my Madras sport coat and a starched white shirt during Rush Week, the house looked like something out of a sci-fi movie.

Pretty cool, I thought.

Known for its high academic standards, Delta Upsilon was also the fraternity of Darrell Royal, the legendary Longhorn football coach. DU's reputation as a party house was also a definite attraction. I got along fine with the brothers and moved into the house as a pledge that September.

There were no telephones in the rooms, but each floor had a phone bank. For an eighteen-year-old freshman away from home for the first time, these nicotine-yellow phones were a real temptation. It was great fun to lounge around the hall day or night in T-shirt and shorts, burning up the phone lines with girls and other guys I'd met on campus. Shooting the breeze about the next party or the football schedule was a lot better than diagramming sentences for English Comp or memorizing the Periodic Table of Elements. Odd as it sounds now, my poor study habits probably began while I was yakking away on the second-floor phones in the DU house.

One of the projects my pledge class took on was building a beer garden on the sloping backyard behind the house. It was here that I really got to know Mike Corley, Jimmy Sewell, Terry Marlatt, and Jack Slayton. Though we were from different parts of Texas, we shared a common interest in girls and parties; the job was a shared labor of love.

It was no mean feat of amateur engineering either. We had to dig into the hillside with picks and shovels to level out a dirt platform for the cinderblock-and-brick floor. And, because of the angle of the slope, we sweated through some heavy calculations to determine the correct height of the upright beams holding the lattice roof. Luckily, I could go to the trusty phones and call my dad in Midland whenever we had a problem.

The beauty of this beer garden was its ridge-top location. We would sit back in the shade drinking and watch the cars on the street below. And the garden also overlooked two girls' dorms, so we had an ideal place to scout the local talent. This was a helluva lot better than studying.

I remember a fall afternoon that first semester when Jimmy Sewell, Terry Marlatt, and I were treating some of the older brothers to a cold case of Lone Star.

One of the guys, who was taking geology, offered a recitation of Moh's mineral hardness scale, which began with "Talc, Gypsum, Calcite, Fluorite . . ." and ended up with ". . . Topaz, Corundum, and Diamond." By Longhorn tradition, he'd memorized the sequence using a time-honored technique: TGCFAOQTCD, which also stood for "Texas Girls Can Flirt And Other Quaint Things Can Do." But he replaced "Flirt" with a more suggestive "F" word. I was learning the ways of the world.

The subject briefly shifted from girls to cars, always of interest to young Texans.

"That big Olds has definitely got glass-pack pipes," Jimmy said, tilting his bottle at a blue 88.

"Does not," I argued. "That's a stock sedan straight from the dealer. Probably belongs to some preacher."

Accurately judging the features of cars was a highly regarded skill among DU brothers. But so was assessing the charms of strolling co-eds.

"The one in the pleated skirt is really stacked," Phil Ruzicka announced. He nodded at two girls walking on the sidewalk below.

"Probably falsies," Terry countered.

"I can state for a fact that they're not," Phil said, sipping beer.

We hooted our appreciation and respect. Phil was a well-experienced junior. I watched the other girl, a curvy blond with a ponytail and a cashmere sweater set done up with a little gold chain at the neck. Her name was Janet, and I'd invited her to a fraternity party on Friday night. I planned to make my move after we'd all had a couple beers.

One of the important lessons I was learning at the University of Texas was that the Sexual Revolution wasn't just something you read about in *Playboy*. During my last two years at Lee High in Midland, Shell Dougherty and I had gone steady. Now I was discovering the freedom of dating two or three different girls a week, away from their—and my own—parents' supervision. College turned out to be a whole lot more interesting than I ever imagined.

Girls weren't the only temptation. Too many weeknights when I should have been studying, we'd pile a bunch of guys into Terry Marlatt's parents' sedan—three of them hiding in the trunk with a load of six-packs—and head off to the drive-in to watch a movie. If we weren't off to the movies, we could always drive over for a cheeseburger at Dirty's, then cruise up and down Austin's main drag, Guadalupe Street—pronounced Guada-*loop* in Texas Anglo fashion.

But college wasn't nonstop hedonism. We all took President John Kennedy's assassination very hard. The university cancelled classes that Friday afternoon, and I joined about five thousand other silent, teary-eyed students jammed into the Union, watching Walter Cronkite on the big black-and-white TV. This was a sad day for Texas. President Kennedy had inspired my generation. We could all recite that part of his inauguration speech: "Ask not what your country can do for you . . ." Now the President was dead. Everybody I knew got drunk that night.

B Y THE TIME SPRING BREAK CAME AROUND, I REALIZED THAT MY second-semester grades were going to be a lot worse than they'd been in the fall. I showed up for class about half the time, but rarely did the reading assignments. And most of those test and quiz papers might just as well have been written in Mandarin Chinese.

Back home for spring break, I never opened the textbooks I'd promised myself to read each day. By the spring of 1964, bikinis had pretty well replaced one-piece swimsuits and it was much more exciting to chase girls and hang out with my high school friends than to study.

While I was occupied with these serious pursuits, though, my father and mother were confronting a crisis. Dad's business was failing. As always, being a conscientious craftsman, he spent too much time on the jobs for the money he charged. And the shop's flat-out bad location was hurting it more and more, as competing businesses sprouted up closer to the lake.

One morning that April, I sat down to breakfast surprised to find Dad still at the table. He and Mother sat close together as my father made the announcement.

"I'm selling the business, Tommy Ray. It's not working out the way I hoped, and I've got an offer."

I still didn't realize how I was connected to my folks' financial troubles. "What are you going to do, Dad?"

"We're planning to move down to Austin," Mother said. "We'll get a place and we can all live together."

"There're plenty of good jobs around Austin, son," my father added, optimistic as always.

Only later that afternoon did I realize what my parents had in mind: If I moved back in with them in Austin, it would save them the ninety dollars a month room and board they were paying to keep me at the DU house. What with tuition, books, and the fifty dollars spending money they'd sent me each month, my parents were going broke. Things had gotten so bad that my mother was selling her pies and cakes again to help keep me in college. I'd miss the late-night bull sessions with the brothers, but laying off the beer on school nights would no doubt improve my study habits. And I did like my mother's cooking.

But the reality of our new circumstances really smacked me alongside the head, as they say, when I sold my MG and my hotrod Chevy. After I used most of the money for next year's tuition, I had enough left over for a used Plymouth four-door. *A green Plymouth*, I thought, climbing into the car. *Times sure have changed.*

IN THE FIRST SEMESTER OF MY FRESHMAN YEAR, I HAD MADE A grade point average of 1.2 on UT's 3.0 point system; I even pulled off a B to class up my Cs. But the spring semester turned out a whole

lot worse. Between the girls, the beer, and the hours I spent lollygag-
ging around the DU house instead of studying, I ended up that May
with a 0.5—six hours of D or F in my unchallenging twelve-hour
course load.

My abysmal academic performance was confirmed when I got
the dreaded letter from the registrar in June 1964, two weeks after
final exams. I was placed on scholastic probation.

A S MY DAD HAD PREDICTED, THERE WAS A GOOD JOB FOR HIM IN
Austin. While I was out water skiing at Viking Marina on Lake
Austin one day that spring, I met Maurice Doke, the owner of the
marina and a state senator. A Longhorn football star in the fifties,
Mr. Doke was partial to UT students.

"If you ever need an experienced mechanic," I told him, "my father is about as good as they come."

Dad started working for Maurice Doke two weeks later.

Before the fall semester started, I moved with my parents into a
small rented house on Rosedale Avenue in northwest Austin, and actually began studying again on weeknights. Not surprisingly, my grades
went back up, rising to 1.25 after final exams that December—not
quite high enough to get me off "sco-pro," but I figured I could ease
up a little and start enjoying college life again.

Big mistake.

Late one Thursday night a few weeks into the spring '65 semester,
I found myself hunched over a pitcher of Lone Star in Scholtz's Beer
Garden discussing weighty issues with Jack Slayton and Jimmy Sewell.

"The Buddhists say all reality is illusion," Jimmy announced,
echoing his Anthropology lectures. "Maybe they're on to something."

"Let's drink to the Buddhists," I said, topping off our mugs.

"Space and time are the same thing, mathematically," Jack added.
I think he was taking Astronomy.

We had reached the Profound Insight stage of college drinking.

I chugged my beer. "Well, what about atoms? Electrons orbit the nucleus just like planets go around the sun, right? What if . . . *every* damn atom in my finger, or this mug is actually a little solar system . . ."

". . . and some guy in a bar on one of those electron planets is drinking a pitcher," Jack said, eyes gleaming. ". . . or whatever the hell he'd drink. And looking at *his* finger, and . . ."

THAT SPRING, MY GRADES WENT TO HELL IN A HAND BASKET. After I got a couple Fs on mid-term exams, I just stopped going to class. I did take my finals in May 1965 on the hope that there'd be enough multiple-choice questions to give me decent odds at making a D. False hope.

That summer I worked part-time with my father out at Viking Marina, repairing outboards and driving ski boats on Lake Austin, and spent three afternoons a week bagging groceries at an HEB Supermarket. These jobs left plenty of time to party. And my buddies and I didn't need much excuse to party.

Then I got yet another letter from the registrar. By now I'd been on scholastic probation for a year. I'd failed to make an acceptable GPA during that time—and I would not be readmitted to the university for the next semester. After six months, I could reapply. The students called this "laying out"; some saw it as a normal hazard of campus life. I saw it as an excuse to go out with Terry Marlatt and get drunk.

When I woke up before dawn the next morning with a headache, turned on the light, and read that letter again, I concluded that my parents were wasting their money trying to keep me in school. I'd abused their trust and hard work. And as tough as it was to admit this, it was obvious that I was just too spoiled, unfocused, and immature to get much out of college.

I had a lot of growing up to do.

As I was lying in bed thinking, a plan took shape in my mind. Even if I did make it back to school in six months, I'd still have to pretend to be interested in my classes. I didn't want to pretend anymore, about anything. Then I remembered my cousin Johnny Bowden's solid, respectable Air Force career. I didn't think I could be an officer, but I could serve my country as a soldier.

That summer, I started reading the newspapers and watching the TV news every night. President Johnson had sent the Marines to Vietnam and begun bombing the Communist North. But the Vietcong guerrillas hadn't gotten the message, so it looked like America would have to up the ante. I felt ready to haul my share of the load.

Besides, the idea of going to the other side of the world to fight for my country was just plain "studly." The military would probably be a more adventurous version of camping and hunting, which I'd always loved. Whatever I did in the Army would be better than bagging groceries at the supermarket or fixing outboards with my dad. I wanted to get out in the world and do something real. And being a soldier was about as real as you could get.

The U.S. Army recruiting station in Austin was downtown. On that hot Friday morning of August 20, 1965—head still throbbing, mouth cotton-dry with a beer hangover—I was the first guy through the door.

THE GREYHOUND BUS SQUEAKED TO A STOP AT THE RECEPTION center inside the main gate of Fort Leonard Wood, Missouri. It was about 95 degrees that August afternoon, with matching humidity. Outside on the ramp a husky soldier with lots of stripes on his starched fatigues and a Smokey the Bear hat stared at us. He did not look friendly.

"This ain't the ladies' garden tour, recruits," he bellowed. "Off that bus, *now!*"

I'd been on this seat for thirty hours and hadn't managed much sleep. Tired, hungry, and a little scared, I felt the first sour ache of homesickness.

When we'd managed to form a reasonably straight line, the soldier in the hat walked up and down, looking us over. The toes of his black boots were so shiny that I glimpsed my reflection as he strode by.

"Listen up, and listen good, 'cause I don't repeat myself," he said, squinting out from under his hat brim. "My name is Staff Sergeant Kittle. You *will* remember my name because I am your platoon sergeant. Do you understand?"

The guys around me shuffled. One kid actually nodded, smiling. A big mistake.

"I am not your mother," Kittle shouted. "I am not your daddy. I am *definitely* not your girlfriend. Your answer is, 'Yes, Sergeant.'"

"Yes, Sergeant."

We had to yell that reply about six times before Sergeant Kittle was satisfied.

Eventually, we stumbled into two ranks and shuffled down the street to start in-processing, passing between two-story wooden barracks with steel fire escapes. The grass was parched, brown. Dirty white rocks lined the sidewalks. This place looked like a 1940s factory.

Staff Sergeant Kittle called cadence, trying to get us to march in step. "Left. Right. . . . Yo' left, right, left . . ."

I was doing fine, but the guy behind me kept stepping on my heels.

Some joker in the middle of the platoon muttered, "Welcome to Fort Lost in the Woods."

Staff Sergeant Kittle was not amused. "You recruits will shut the fuck up or your collective ass is grass and I'm a lawnmower."

Nobody wisecracked after that.

When are they going to feed us and let us go to bed? I wondered. I was not happy to be here. But I would have been a lot less happy if I'd known the answer to that question.

INSTEAD OF FOOD AND SLEEP, WE GOT HAIRCUTS. MINE WASN'T TOO bad; I'd been expecting to be shaved bald, but the potbellied barber actually left a fuzz on the top of my head. In the stifling supply building, we moved down a gauntlet, stopping at each counter to be issued fatigues, GI underwear (with string ties on the flapping boxer shorts), an Army Class A uniform, a confusing batch of different hats, and boots.

"Shoe size?" the guy issuing the footwear asked like a robot.

"Nine, triple E. I have really wide feet, so they've gotta be triple E width."

The soldier scratched the armpit of his sweaty T-shirt and reached behind him without looking into a bin full of boots, the pairs tied together by their laces. "Nine," he said, dumping two pairs of black combat boots onto the pile of uniforms filling my arms. "Next."

I didn't move. "Triple E, right?"

"Yeah . . . sure. Next man."

In our new barracks, my bed was in a row of steel-frame double bunks that faced more bunks in the open squad bay. No sooner had we dumped our stacks of uniforms than a smiling Sergeant Kittle invited us to a "GI party."

Wonder if they'll have sandwiches, I thought.

It wasn't that kind of party. Instead, we spent the next five hours scrubbing the already clean barracks. I joined four other recruits assigned to clean the latrine. The gleaming white commodes were lined up side by side, every two toilets sharing a roll of paper—no stalls, no partitions. *They expect us to sit here out in the open?* Homesickness had become a nagging pain, like a toothache.

"Nice party," I told the guy kneeling next to me, polishing the floor tiles with a rag.

"Fuckin' straight. I shoulda gone 4-F." He spoke with an East Coast accent I could hardly understand.

"What's 4-F?"

"When you can't get drafted."

"Wasn't drafted," I said. "I enlisted."

He shook his head and slid over to the next commode.

TWO DAYS LATER, MY PLATOON DOUBLE-TIMED THROUGH THE dawn rain, draped in ponchos, gripping our rifles across our chests, what Sergeant Kittle called the High Port position. The flapping ponchos blocked the rain, but also trapped the sweat inside. Still, the heat was nothing compared to the pain in my feet. Those boots were definitely not triple E: the balls of my feet were squeezed tight as a vice in my father's shop.

"I used to date a beauty queen," Sergeant Kittle sang, counting the cadence.

". . . used to date a beauty queen," we echoed.

"Now I sleep with an M-14."

Forty right boot soles smacked the wet asphalt of the road.

"Left . . . right. Yo left . . . Gimme yo left, right, ley-eft . . ."

Forty left boots hit the pavement.

Maybe my feet would go numb in a little while. Not this morning. By the time we double-timed down to the parade ground and back to our company area, I was limping badly. As the platoon lined up outside the mess hall for breakfast, Sergeant Kittle came over.

"Franks," he said, the rain dripping off his hat. "Fall out."

"Yes, Sergeant."

"You got some kind of problem with marching?"

"No, Sergeant."

He leaned closer, his voice more quiet. "Been watching you, boy. The way you march ain't normal. Come with me."

The recruits stared as Sergeant Kittle led me toward the barracks. "You gotta have blisters, son," he said out of earshot of the others. "Why didn't you tell me? I'm your platoon sergeant. My job is to get all your sorry asses trained as soldiers, and that won't happen if you can't march."

"It's my boots, Sergeant," I admitted. "They're too tight; they're crushing my feet. I need wider boots."

He shook his head. "Too late for that, Franks." Then he grinned. "But there's ways to fix the problem. You just should have told me."

His trick was simple. Soak the boots in scalding water in the barracks washtub, then jam them full of balled up newspaper and hang them in the shower room to dry, slowly stretching the wet leather as it dries. I got a day of light duty wearing flip-flops. The next morning, I could march without pain.

Now my M-14 rifle didn't feel like a dead weight. I belted out the cadence songs with the best of them.

"If I die in a combat zone . . ."

". . . Box me up and ship me home."

"Yo ley-eft, right, left, right, left . . ."

The platoon rounded the corner to the company street. We were marching well, everybody in step. My feet didn't hurt. This was fun. I could smell the greasy bacon and soupy gray creamed beef on toast—Shit on a Shingle—that the mess hall served for breakfast. I was hungry. SOS would taste good this morning.

Sergeant Kittle trotted backwards beside the formation, somehow keeping step. He scanned our ranks. "Lookin' good, 3rd Platoon. Some of you might make soldiers yet."

As I jogged past him, Kittle nodded and shot me a quick grin.

I wasn't homesick anymore.

"READY ON THE RIGHT," THE SAFETY OFFICER'S VOICE echoed over the bullhorn. "Ready on the left. Ready on the firing line."

I lay prone, elbows on a sandbag, squinting through the peep sight of my M-14 rifle at the target, a hundred meters away.

"Twenty rounds. Commence firing."

I squeezed the trigger and the butt thumped into my shoulder. This 7.62mm NATO caliber was the biggest rifle I'd ever fired. But the kick wasn't as bad as my dad's old Remington .12 gauge that I'd first shot at age eight.

It was a cool sunny September afternoon in the Ozark foothills. I was happy to be there, actually shooting the "lightweight, air-cooled, gas-operated, magazine-fed, semiautomatic shoulder weapon" that we'd marched with and dry-fired for a month. Rifles smacked and popped all along the line as my platoon faced the challenge of Army marksmanship. The rifle kick pounded some of the guys really hard because they weren't gripping the stock tightly enough. Rounds kicked up brown dust low on the target berm. Sergeant Kittle bent over the troopers who were having trouble, raising or lowering their rifle barrels, offering quiet encouragement.

He stopped behind me to observe. I breathed in and out evenly the way he'd taught us, squeezing the trigger "like a tit." The rifle seemed to fire itself and a hot brass shell casing popped out into the sunlight to clink onto the growing pile beside the sandbag.

When we'd fired the twenty rounds and carefully cleared our rifles, Kittle watched as the trainees pulling targets marked our hits. I had managed to put all my shots inside the nine ring, with several rounds in the bull's-eye.

"Where'd you learn to shoot like that, Franks?"

"My dad taught me, Sergeant, on a farm in Oklahoma."

"Wish I had more farm boys," he muttered, strolling down the line.

As the platoon formed up to march back to the barracks, Sergeant Kittle pulled me out of the ranks. "Private Franks here's a regular swinging dick with the M-14. He's gonna call cadence."

"Fo-ward march," I shouted, trying for the same mellow tone as Staff Sergeant Kittle. The platoon stepped out. "Left . . . right, ley-eft, right . . ."

"Sound off, Franks," Kittle said, marching behind me on the side of the column. "Give 'em something to march to."

"Walkin' through the jungle at the break of day," I sang.

The platoon chanted the reply.

"Great big alligator got in my way . . ." I called, proud to be leading troops, even a unit as small as a Basic Training platoon.

Our formation marched along the road, joined by other platoons returning from the firing ranges. I sang out every cadence song I knew. Then guys in the ranks called out theirs, as I kept up the "left, right, ley-eft, right" step.

For the first month of Basic, the new recruits in my barracks still spoke their native New York, Savannah, Tennessee, or Chicago Ghetto English. I'd come to realize that there was intelligent life east of the Mississippi, but it talked funny. Now we were learning to talk Army.

Sergeant Kittle beamed like a proud papa.

As we neared the water tower marking the boundary of the training brigade, I heard the first sweet bugle notes of Retreat over the loudspeakers, the ceremony marking the end of the duty day. "Platoon," I ordered without prompting from Kittle. "Halt. Pres-sent h'arms."

In unison, we saluted, stiff fingers just touching the edge of our helmets.

Across the parade ground, the color guard slowly lowered the flag on the tall pole. We held our salute until Retreat ended. I loved this ceremony. Like Reveille in the morning and Taps at night, Retreat gave shape to the day, a sense of purpose. Exactly what had been lacking in my shiftless life as a student in Austin. All around this sprawling post, troopers stood alone or in formation, saluting the colors: slick-sleeve privates like us, hard-shell noncommissioned officers (NCOs) like Sergeant Kittle, and commissioned officers— captains, majors, and colonels. And probably even the general commanding Fort Leonard Wood. *That's what soldiers do,* I realized as the bugle call faded. *And I'm becoming a soldier.*

B UT WE SURE HADN'T BECOME A BAND OF BROTHERS. A LOT OF the rednecks were wary of the black kids, and vice versa. But, we had to get along. When you sit on a row of commodes in the morning, kids of just about every color you can imagine lined up around you, a guy learns to cut his fellow troopers some slack.

At least *most* people learn that lesson. The cooks in the mess hall were another story. We were always rushed, going through the chow line with our stainless steel trays. Some of the soldiers serving chow were PFCs, who proudly wore their single yellow stripe of rank on the sleeves of their fatigues. One of them was a real pain in the ass, always harassing us to "move the fuck along."

One lunchtime, he decided to exert his authority over me as I waited for the hamburger bin on the steam table to be refilled. "Hey, asshole. You're holding up the line. This ain't your mama's kitchen."

I moved forward and piled mashed potatoes and gravy on my empty hamburger bun. As was my habit, I didn't say a word. I waited.

That evening I just happened to be near the mess hall when he came out. I walked up and hit him hard with my fist, square in the mouth, splitting his lip.

"There're probably some people in your life you can fuck with," I said as he rubbed the blood off his face. "But I'm not one of them. Don't ever say anything to me going through the chow line again."

Being a soldier, I had decided, didn't mean you had to be treed by pissants.

IN THE LAST WEEK OF BASIC, I RECEIVED ORDERS TO REPORT TO Fort Devens, Massachusetts, to be trained as a crypto-analyst—a code breaker—in the Army Security Agency (ASA), part of the Military Intelligence Branch. MI talent scouts had come to Fort Leonard Wood, searching for recruits who'd scored well on the aptitude tests. I might have been a terrible student in Austin, but I wasn't stupid. In fact, I'd managed to rack up some of the best test scores in my training brigade.

The sergeant from the ASA had been very persuasive. "I can't tell you too much about the job until we complete your security clearance," he'd said. "But it involves some of America's most sensitive intelligence."

Holy shit, I thought. James Bond, Agent 007. Martinis, shaken, not stirred. A shoulder holster under my dinner jacket. Maybe I'd have to seduce beautiful Russian spies.

This was a much better deal than chasing coeds and sneaking into drive-in movies.

AFTER GRADUATING FROM BASIC TRAINING—STANDING TALL with an Expert Rifleman badge on my uniform—and going home to Austin for Thanksgiving, I drove my 1963 red Ford Falcon convertible to New York, en route to Fort Devens, near Boston. Fred Webster, my buddy who'd also been selected for MI, shared the driving and expenses. Since we'd draw our December pay when we arrived, we decided to spend all our money in the city before heading up to Massachusetts, keeping back a few bucks for gas and hamburgers.

Spend we did. After paying for our hotel on East 38th Street in advance, we had about sixty bucks left. We went to every tourist spot in the city and each afternoon around five, we hit the bars. On our final day I laid down my last four dollars for two huge deli pastrami sandwiches at lunch, with extra kosher pickles for me, and four bottles of Schaefer beer. Fred had our cash reserve—a five and three ones—rolled up tight in the front pocket of his jeans.

At the United Nations, we stood in line for the afternoon tour of the General Assembly.

"Gotta find a toilet," Fred suddenly said. "Fast." Probably the spicy pastrami.

Ten minutes later he was back in the corridor, looking pale. "Had the runs bad."

On the corner of 42nd and First Avenue, Fred patted his jeans. "*Kee-rist,*" he said. "My money's gone. Must have dropped it in that toilet stall."

We ran back to the UN, but had no luck finding the missing cash.

Riding the elevator to the hotel lobby the next morning, we didn't know what the hell to do.

"We'll have to leave the car here and hitchhike," I said.

Fred stared down at our heavy duffle bags. "It's gonna be a long walk."

The black elevator operator looked us over. "You fellas get pickpocketed?"

"Lost our money, sir," I said.

The man was about my father's age, probably also a World War II vet. When he stopped the elevator at the lobby, he handed Fred a five-dollar bill. "I've walked in your shoes, boys," he said. "That'll get y'all some gas."

I remembered what my Uncle Bob had taught me when we fixed up those old houses in Midland. "Doesn't matter what color a person's skin is, Tommy Ray. It's their heart that counts."

As soon as we got paid, I mailed five dollars to that elevator operator who saved our bacon.

I SOON DISCOVERED THAT TRAINING TO BE A CRYPTO-ANALYST DID not involve martini glasses, shoulder holsters, or dinner jackets. There were no Baccarat tables at Fort Devens. And no beautiful Russian spies to seduce.

The ASA school worked around the clock to meet the worldwide demand for radio-intercept specialists and crypto-analysts. Besides the Cold War smoldering across Europe and northern Asia, there was a hot war boiling over in Vietnam. The Army was pushing students through the training on double twelve-hour shifts.

I was on nights. My class ate dinner in the mess hall, and then reported to school at 1800 hours. We had "lunch" at midnight, and more classes until 0600; after breakfast, we'd go to bed. The lopsided schedule took some getting used to, but I found the subject matter fascinating.

We learned that encrypted military radio traffic usually involved a key, a secret set of numbers or letters that both the sender and the receiver possessed, which transformed the meaningless blocks of digits into readable letters and words. Without the key, our instructors taught us, it was extremely difficult to break a code.

Sitting in class the first few days of the course, it seemed like we were facing an impossible challenge. But the owlish warrant officer teaching the Intro course assured us that we could break any code ever devised if we were patient and followed proper procedures.

Every language, he explained, had known "occurrence rates" for any given letter. The more specialized the words and phrases those letters composed—military commands and directions— the greater the chance of identifying words through the recurrence of letters.

I bent over my desk in the overheated classroom, frowning at the mimeographed lesson notes. Without the cipher key, how could we even identify letters?

"Mathematical probability," the instructor told us.

Coded text substituted numbers for letters. For example, 72463 62469 represented ten letters, maybe two words, maybe one, maybe one and a half. The purpose of cipher was to turn the comprehensible into gibberish.

Our mission as crypto-analysts was to determine what those letters might be in Russian, the language we used to learn our craft. Naturally, we could not produce an analysis using only a couple of five-number groups. But the beauty of the technique involved analyzing hundreds of these five-digit groups, searching for recurring patterns. We didn't have computers to make the task easier, just hand-levered Burroughs adding machines that could also be used to divide and multiply. And we all had a lot of sharp pencils.

One classroom exercise in February 1966 involved analyzing a cipher text to determine if 6 or 2 appeared more often than other numbers in a section of blocks. The instructor that night, a paunchy Irish-American master sergeant named Reilly, told us that these digits "might" represent a common Russian vowel or consonant such as и (*ee*) or я (*yah*), as in армия (*army*). After a lot of class discussion and frustrating attempts at analysis, we finally discovered the digit sequence 98462 did, in fact, spell that word.

But we had pages more of text to analyze. Hunching over the printed columns of number blocks in the problem message, I searched for other repetitions. Sure as hell, I discovered the sequence 79395 repeated in three places. And I now knew the digit 9 was a (*ah*) in this cipher.

". . . something, *ah*. Something, *ah* again," I muttered, chewing my pencil. Flipping open my Russian military vocabulary, the word батальон (*battalion*) suddenly stood out. So, the number 7 had to be б (*beh*), and 3 was т (*teh*).

The kid at the desk next to mine, a draftee named Feldman who'd majored in math at some eastern college, leaned over and helped. Together, we confirmed the analysis. And then Feldman jumped ahead, verifying the number-letter connections of л, ь, о, and н.

I carefully printed our answer and handed the worksheet to Sergeant Reilly.

"Outstanding, Franks! Way to go, Feldman. You men found the correct eight-letter word based on just the first five letters." He laughed. "I'd expect that from you, Feldman. But Private Franks, you sure you're from Texas?"

"Yes, Sergeant. Midland. I'm Texas proud."

"Well, you oughta be, boy."

BUT SITTING IN CLASS ALL NIGHT DIDN'T REALLY FEEL LIKE soldiering. I missed the rifle drill and marching in formation. So when I heard that the ASA Training Center and School Honor Guard had an opening, I volunteered.

Corporal Sam Long was the noncommissioned officer (NCO) in charge of the outfit, which had a reputation as one of the most squared-away ceremonial units on the East Coast. I'd stopped by the gym a couple of afternoons to watch men drill, so I knew I had to look sharp when I reported to Sam Long.

"You're tall," he said, coming out from behind the desk in his small office to shake my hand. His eyes slowly swept the spit shine on my low-quarter shoes, the crease in my pants, the knot in my tie. I'd had a haircut that morning, and shaved carefully less than an hour earlier. "That's good. Soldiers in an honor guard have to stand out at a parade or presenting the colors in a stadium. You done much marching?"

"I really liked close-order drill in Basic, Corporal." Sam Long had only two stripes on the sleeves of his tailored green uniform, but his quiet, confident manner generated respect—the key to success in an NCO. To junior enlisted soldiers like me, a noncommissioned officer was the most important figure in the chain of command. An NCO—whether corporal or sergeant—assigned work details and issued weekend passes.

"Well, Franks," he said, "we'll see what we can do with you."

THE SOLES OF OUR BOOTS CLAPPED SOFTLY ON THE HARDWOOD of the Boston Garden. Sam Long had instructed us to march "light" in this echoing old stadium. The Celtics fans were known as a rowdy but patriotic bunch; they sure belted out the National Anthem with enthusiasm when we presented to colors. But now it was halftime in an important late-season game, and the Celtics were down eleven points to the Knicks. Gripping the polished butt of my M-14, I sure hoped that the 18,000 blue-collar Celtics supporters were in the mood for our demonstration.

We split into two ranks of six and executed a precision crossing march-trough, with each member dropping his rifle, then snatching his counterpart's weapon as it hung in the air and snapping it up to High Port. A tossing rifle exchange followed. And then we repeated that exercise, twice, while marching slowly backwards, the two rows finally separated by almost half the court. To end the demonstration, we performed a fancy variation of the traditional Queen Anne Salute in a ripple maneuver of increasing speed, up one rank, down the other, our polished rifles spinning in the spotlight. The routine ended with the team down on one knee, heads bowed.

The crowd went nuts, cheering, clapping, stamping their feet.

I was proud to be a soldier.

THE HONOR GUARD BARRACKS WAS A SHOWPLACE, CLEAN AS A hospital, every surface gleaming. Both Corporal Long and our top kick, a tough old first sergeant named Scagliotti, made sure the building was always ready for a white glove inspection.

One drizzly Saturday morning that spring, a lieutenant we hardly ever saw came in the barracks while Sam was showing me how to re-assemble one of the new M-16 rifles, blindfolded.

"Hey, Corporal," the young officer said, tossing Sam a key ring, "get somebody to drive my car downtown and pick up that floor polish we ordered."

I finished with the weapon and removed the blindfold. Sam handed me the keys. "Got an errand for you, Franks."

As I drove the lieutenant's Ford back through the front gate with the big can of floor polish sitting on the passenger seat, the MP at the red brick guard post snapped off a crisp salute.

Stunned, I returned the salute. It wasn't until I was shifting gears up the hill to the barracks that I realized the MP had seen the blue-and-white officer's sticker on the windshield and assumed I was a lieutenant.

I enjoyed the feeling of having a buck sergeant MP salute me. During my first nine months in the Army, I'd had very little contact with officers, but I recognized that when you got bars pinned to your shoulders, you were entitled to respect.

"That's what I'm talking about," I said into the car mirror. "Respect."

I SUBMITTED MY APPLICATION TO OFFICER CANDIDATE SCHOOL IN the last weeks of crypto-analyst training. There were openings for qualified junior enlisted applicants at either Artillery or Infantry OCS. And I figured I might have to walk less in the Artillery.

Sam Long said that the final hurdle in the process would be an interview with First Sergeant Scagliotti. "Scag" had fought in Germany and Korea. He was single, lived alone in the cadre room on the top floor of the barracks, and was known to take a drink or two at the NCO club after duty hours.

Wearing my best-tailored uniform, I showed up five minutes early for the 0730 appointment that Tuesday in June. He kept me standing at his desk while he slowly read my thin personnel file, test scores, and class grades.

"Got a couple of questions, Private," he said, finally looking up from the papers.

For the next ten minutes, Scag grilled me on family background, my civilian education, and my opinion of the Army.

"Why do you want to be an officer, Franks?" he asked, snapping shut the file.

I'd been prepared for this question. "I think I can learn to lead troops, First Sergeant. So I want to find out if I'm officer material."

Scag frowned, turned away in his swivel chair, and shook his head in disgust. "Well, all right, Franks. It's okay by me if you want to go to OCS." He turned back to face me. "I'll tell you this much. You're making a big mistake. You'll never be an officer worth a damn. But if you stick with it, you might make a hell of a sergeant one day." Before I could answer, he spun the chair again, so I was facing his back. "Now get out of here."

"Thank you, First Sergeant," I muttered between clenched teeth.

Striding down the barracks stairs, I was truly pissed off. Who the *fuck* did that old man think he was? After all, I had two years of college. I was among the best students in my Crypto class. And the guys in the outfit looked up to me. Where did he get off saying I should limit my ambition to becoming a *sergeant*?

I stayed mad for weeks. My young man's pride had been bruised. Then, driving home to Austin on leave before reporting to OCS at Fort Sill, Oklahoma, I realized that First Sergeant Scagliotti had paid me a great compliment. He'd always been encouraging, seeing me help a new trooper in the barracks get his weapon or uniforms squared away. "You're a doer, Franks," he'd say, "not just a talker." In his mind, sergeants worked hands-on with the troops, and he thought I'd be good at it.

I promised myself to remember that if I ever did earn my commission as an officer.

I PARKED MY CAR ON THE HOT ASPHALT LOT AND LUGGED MY duffle bag under the steel arch topped with the sign reading, "Robinson Barracks, United States Army Artillery Officer Candidate School." It was Saturday, August 20, 1966, exactly one year after I'd enlisted. I figured arriving on a weekend would give me some quiet time to get settled in before the duty week began.

Bad figuring.

There was nothing quiet about Fort Sill, Oklahoma. Sprawling across the foothills of the Wichita Mountains, the post thumped and rumbled with howitzers and exploding shells around the clock, seven days a week.

And the duty week for new Artillery officer candidates did not include days off.

"PFC Franks reporting as ordered, Sir," I announced, saluting the first lieutenant behind the desk and handing over my paperwork. I was proud of the single stripe on the sleeves of my khaki shirt. At least I didn't have to say "Private Franks" anymore. My spit-shined shoes were like mirrors; my uniform was crisply starched.

The lieutenant hardly glanced at my orders. "Candidate Franks," he said scornfully. "You are no longer a PFC. You are another life form altogether. A Can-di-date. It is my duty to inform you that lower-class candidates are in fact a *very* low life form in this organization. Do you understand me, Candidate Franks?"

"Yes, Sir."

"Good. Because you will now demonstrate that understanding. You will hoist your duffle bag on your back, march out to that storm gutter, execute a left face, and low-crawl to your barracks, Building 3306."

"Yes, Sir." My first taste of OCS.

Grunting through the heat down in the pitted concrete gutter with a seventy-pound duffle on my back, I was grateful that Staff Sergeant Kittle had taken the time to teach his platoon how to low-crawl without ruining their elbows. The trick was to support your weight on your toes and the clenched muscles of your forearms, squirming along like a woolly caterpillar. The process wasn't really painful, but it sure pierced a young honor guard stud's ego. That, of course, was the purpose of the exercise.

T HE FIRST WEEKS OF THE SIX-MONTH ARTILLERY OCS COURSE combined all the physical hardships of Basic Training—Physical Training (PT) at 0545 hours, five-mile runs, "corrective" push-ups, and GI parties every day—with classroom challenges that made crypto school seem like first grade.

There were 120 candidates divided into six sections in my class. We lived in old World War II wooden barracks, with no air-conditioning, no fans. At least there were stalls for the toilets. We ran every morning, we cleaned the barracks, stood inspections, double-timed to classes, rushed through the chow line, gulped our food, and studied. Six days a week. After Saturday inspection, which was always conducted by a captain or major who peppered us with questions, we spent the rest of the weekend studying.

The ancient science of artillery, we learned, comprised a number of complex elements: every cannon in the Field Artillery inventory and its individual ballistics, projectile types, and fusing, as well as terrain characteristics and topography, battlefield surveying, explosive charges, metallurgy. We also drilled on the rigorous communication discipline of "fire missions," which involve ordering artillery shells to strike the enemy while avoiding friendly troops and civilians.

On the third afternoon of that hot, confusing first week, my section double-timed out to a firing range to observe a 105 mm howitzer battery in a training battalion. As we trotted up the road, we felt the pavement shake before we actually heard the smacking roar of the cannons.

The battery's six M-101 howitzer "tubes" stood in low, circular sandbagged pits, the guns' heavy barrels mounted on wheeled chassis, with V-shaped steel-beam "trails" spread to dampen the powerful recoil. We stuffed in our ear plugs and watched, fascinated, as the seven-man gun crews followed the precise orders that the lieutenant in command relayed over a field telephone from the fire direction center in a faded green tent surrounded by radio antennas.

"Battery adjust," he shouted. The crews stood by for a fire mission.

"Shell HE." The selected projectile would be high explosive.

"Lot X-ray Yankee." This was the exact type of HE shell to be fired.

"Charge Five." Five powder charges in the cylindrical brass canister.

"Fuse Quick." The shell would be fused to explode on impact.

"Center One Round." The gunners of the two middle howitzers threw open the shiny hinged breechblocks, and the loaders rammed home the designated, correctly charged and fused shells.

The command "Fire" was lost in a cracking blast as the cannoneers pulled their lanyards. Gouts of flame, bright even in the summer sunlight, shot from the muzzles. The bitter, piercing odor of cordite drifted into the bleachers where we sat.

Our ears ringing, we waited almost a minute while the 35-pound steel projectiles sailed through their curved trajectories and crashed down unseen on the West Range, 11,000 meters away.

"Candidates," our instructor proclaimed. "This is the Field Artillery, the King of Battle."

The tools of my new profession.

I SAT ON THE THREE-LEGGED CANVAS STOOL, MAP BOARD ON MY lap, binoculars hanging heavy from my neck. The other candidates in my section were lined up around me on the breezy gravel shelf of the observation post. It was November 4, the morning of our first live fire mission. We were on The Hill, a stony ridge of juniper and scrub oak that overlooked a rolling valley and the higher ground to the west. All of us were excited, most of us nervous. Five miles behind us a battery of 105 mm howitzers waited for the orders we would radio to the fire direction center.

Today we would each act as a Forward Observer, one of the most critical and demanding assignments in the Field Artillery. We had spent weeks in classrooms learning the theory underlying accurate and effective artillery fire. We understood the moving parts of the guns, the role of each crewmember, the energy of propellant charges, the muzzle velocity and weight of projectiles . . . and all the hundreds of other complex facts involved with firing big guns in combat.

Above all, we had been taught that accurate fire depended on crucial basic data. *If* we knew the exact location of the battery and had plotted it accurately on our firing charts, and *if* we had accurately plotted the target, then the firing battery would deliver the shell accurately. It would be our responsibility as Forward Observers to identify those target coordinates with precision.

The target Impact Area spread across the valley below. Car bodies painted white, yellow, and red had been dumped in random locations. A squat tower of limestone blocks splotched with blue-and-white stripes about 1,200 meters to the left was the only obvious landmark. But we had studied this terrain for days, both through calibrated artillery spotting glasses and on maps divided into 100,000-square meter grids. Each of us had memorized the elevation above sea level and the precise coordinates of every hilltop and knoll visible from this observation post.

We had stopped looking at the landscape like civilians. Now we instinctively saw the world around us in terms of six-digit coordinates on military maps or firing charts. Our visual perspectives automatically measured distance left (west) to right (east) and bottom (south) to top (north). Normal people saw rows of barracks, the commissary, or the softball diamond. We saw target coordinates.

I recognized this mental readjustment as a necessary and valuable adaptation to our situation. If all went well, we would graduate as Field Artillery second lieutenants in February 1967. And a few months later every one of us would be serving as a Forward Observer in Vietnam, calling real fire missions on real enemy targets. That was our reality. We struggled through each training day, constantly short of sleep, running from class to class, gulping our food in the mess hall, with no time to think of anything but the next gunnery test or barracks inspection. And, always, there was the sound of the cannons.

When I did have a moment to think about the future, I saw myself in Vietnam, in some dusty fire support base or out with the troops in a dark rice paddy. I ran, slept, ate, and studied in the hills of Oklahoma. But part of me was already in Vietnam.

First Lieutenant Rawson, our instructor, was a lanky guy who still had the deep leather tan he'd acquired from a year as a forward observer in Vietnam's Central Highlands. He had plotted and called in two demonstration fire missions that morning, working patiently through the procedure to make sure we all understood. He had wanted us to get used to the ripping snort that tore through the sky as a live 105 mm shell passed overhead to explode with a Fourth of July blast on a target 1000 meters down the valley.

"Okay," he said, striding along our row of stools, his battered spotting glasses gripped in his right hand, his compass in his left. "Candidate Franks, you have the next mission."

I felt a flash of excitement. *Showtime*. "Yes, Sir."

Lieutenant Rawson stood beside me, pointing down the valley. "Candidate, from the old blue tower . . ." He raised his binoculars, and I did the same. "Down from the skyline six mils . . ."

Our glasses had tiny etched calibration scales marked in "mils," the scale that artillerymen used to plot coordinates. Civilian compasses had 360 degrees. Ours were divided into 6400 mils, which provided far greater precision.

"Six mils down from the skyline, Sir," I repeated.

". . . Right two-five mils, there is a large yellow car body," he said.

I repeated his target description, remembering that "two-five" was the artilleryman's way of saying twenty-five.

". . . Further identified," he continued, "as being two mils to the left of the rectangular white rock. Enemy troops in the open."

Again, I reiterated his designation.

"Do you identify the target, Candidate Franks?"

My classmates listened and watched intently. I adjusted the focus wheel of my binoculars, studying the distant hillside shimmering against the etched mil scale. I had the target.

"Sir, Candidate Franks. Target identified."

"All right, Candidate. Plot your target coordinates and write out your fire mission order."

I dropped to my stool and snatched up the board with my map, divided into numbered and lettered grids. Using a clear plastic coordinate square, I located the target and stuck a red pushpin "dart" into my map. Then I double-checked my calculation and carefully printed the order on my commo pad.

Lieutenant Rawson silently studied my work, making sure I didn't make any disastrously gross errors. The howitzer shells I was about to order would pass overhead, and it was his responsibility to make sure I didn't call for a round that would strike our observation post.

He gave me the radio handset. "Candidate Franks, send your mission."

"Redleg one-eight," I said, making sure that I'd keyed the microphone button. "This is Redleg two-four. Fire mission, over."

"Send your mission, two-four, over." The voice from the fire direction center was calm.

I keyed the mike again. "XT 182 478." This was the grid square and the six-digit target coordinates I had plotted. "Enemy troops in the open."

The FDC confirmed my coordinates and the nature of the target. The battery would fire one adjusting round, using a high-explosive shell with a point-detonating fuse.

"I will adjust fire," I said, reading from my pad.

"Shot, over," the FDC reported.

My mouth went dry, and I had to swallow before confirming that my first live artillery round was on its way. "Shot, out," I repeated.

"Splash," the FDC now called. The round would explode in five seconds.

I stopped myself from scrunching down beneath my steel helmet as the incoming projectile ripped invisibly above the observation post. I had the target car body centered squarely in my glasses. The shell burst with a flash and a large gray smoke cloud 200 meters north and 100 meters west of the target, peppering the ground with hot shrapnel.

I felt Lieutenant Rawson poised behind me. "Right 100. Drop 400," I called.

The next shell burst south of the target.

"Add 200," I instructed the fire direction center.

"Shot . . ."

"Splash . . ."

This round hit the target. I could actually see the car body split as the shrapnel slammed into the metal.

"Fuse time," I ordered. "Fire for effect."

I watched with satisfaction as the shells exploded around the target like a wild fireworks finale. If that car body had been an enemy formation, they'd be "in a world of hurt," as Lieutenant Rawson put it.

I'd passed my first live fire test, and I felt pretty damn good about it. I think the whole section did.

But Lieutenant Rawson was stingy with praise. "Satisfactory, Candidate," he said, and then turned to the section. "That was the simplest possible fire mission. You have plenty of landmarks, daylight, excellent visibility, and perfect weather. And Candidate Franks here took his time." I sat uneasily on my stool.

"Imagine different conditions," Lieutenant Rawson continued. "Night. Monsoon rain so hard you can't see 100 meters. Triple canopy jungle. You're with an Infantry platoon that's just been ambushed. Enemy close on three sides. *Now* try plotting your target coordinates and ordering an accurate fire mission."

He let us consider that grim picture for a minute. Then he called the next candidate.

I WAS COMMISSIONED A SECOND LIEUTENANT OF FIELD ARTILLERY on February 14, 1967, Valentine's Day. My father wore a suit, my mother a new hat and white gloves. They were proud, and so was I.

Somehow, I'd not only made it through OCS with only one demerit—a failed weapons inspection—on my record, but my academic and professional skills scores had been in the top 10 percent. That made me a "distinguished military graduate," eligible for a Regular Army commission, the path to future career advancement. I decided against making a commitment to become a *lifer*—a twenty-year man. I'd be going to Vietnam for a year, that was certain. And when I came home—*when,* not if—I'd have only eighteen months left to serve. I planned to go back to college, get a degree, and land a good job. Maybe even find a nice girl and get married.

Meanwhile, I had to learn what being an officer was all about. And that took a little learning.

I was assigned temporarily as the assistant executive officer (AXO) of a 105 mm howitzer battery at Fort Sill, where I'd serve until shipping out for Vietnam. I had learned a lot about shooting cannons and adjusting fire. But I didn't know much about leading troops. For a year as an enlisted man, I had gotten used to obeying simple, precise orders. As an officer candidate, the orders I received were often shouted and backed up by corrective discipline, push-ups or even a forced march up and down Hill MB-4 carrying a full field pack. That was my leadership frame of reference.

One of my duties as AXO was to serve as mess officer. My first responsibility as a lieutenant was our mess hall. With my memories of the bullying cooks in the chow line at Fort Leonard Wood, I started off on the wrong foot with the young soldiers in Alpha Battery. Regulations said the concrete kitchen floor and the dining area linoleum had to be mopped and squeegeed dry no later than forty minutes after each meal. I threw major fits when this was not accomplished.

But the mess sergeant, a low-key black man named Evans, had his own methods. He patiently explained that there was a lot of food preparation for lunch immediately following breakfast. So it was a waste of time to clean the floors too early. I wasn't interested in excuses. But I wasn't making any progress shouting orders and piling extra duty on the already overworked cooks and helpers. They knew more about doing their jobs than I did.

My battery commander, an experienced captain named Ed Vernon, gave me some good advice. "Tom," he said, "the troops will work a lot better with *you* if you will work a little better with *them*."

I swallowed some of my ego. The next morning I asked Sergeant First Class Evans just to follow his "normal routine" while I observed. Naturally, he made the best use of his and his men's time. And all the mess hall floors were mopped and dried a good ten minutes before the doors opened for lunch.

"How do you think we can improve things around here, Sergeant?" I asked.

"Well, Sir," he said. "Some of the guys like music when they eat. But it's against regs for them to bring in their radios."

That was an easy one. I rigged up an extra radio from a day-room with loudspeakers. And now we had music at each meal. But the solution wasn't as simple as I'd thought. The black guys liked soul, the country boys Nashville, and the city guys rock 'n' roll. So I arranged a rotation that gave everybody a shot at their favorite music once a day.

This was a surreal period for me, almost like living in an airlock. One after another, my OCS classmates got their Vietnam orders and were gone. I knew it was only a matter of weeks or months before I would follow. So I took every chance I could to get out with the battery and sharpen my skills as a forward observer and fire direction officer.

I was sharing the rent on a small house in downtown Lawton, a mile from the main gate, with my OCS classmate Lieutenant Glenn Stewart. Raised in nearby Walters, Oklahoma, Glenn knew the area well. That was fine with me. I had sunk a lot of my paycheck into monthly payments on a new yellow Olds 442, one of the fastest cars out of Detroit. And most nights we'd troll the bars and drive-ins scouting for girls. Sometimes we were lucky, sometimes we weren't. There was an edge in the air. The war was getting hotter every day. Hair was longer, music louder. I wanted to cram in as much living as I could before heading to Southeast Asia.

One Friday night in March, Glenn and I cruised the downtown bars without success and then headed home at a reasonable hour. We had a battalion inspection in the morning, and I had to be at the mess hall before dawn.

"Hey," Glenn said as we pulled up to the house. "Whose car is that in the driveway?"

There was a tan station wagon parked in front of our little garage. And there were lights on in our living room.

Two really good-looking girls were perched on our old plaid couch, drinking bourbon and Coke, watching *The Avengers* on our TV.

"Suzi," Glenn said, "what are y'all up to?" He'd known Suzi Bassel since high school.

"We came by looking for a drink," she smiled. "The door was open, so we helped ourselves."

The other girl was tall and thin, with well-cut light brown hair, a nice sweater, and cool eyes. She was beautiful. We'd been searching for women all night and here they were in our living room waiting for us. Being a well-raised Christian boy, I glanced up to heaven. *Thank you, Jesus.*

Her name was Cathy Carley. She and Suzi were classmates at Cameron Junior College. Cathy, I immediately noticed, wore a fraternity pin on her sweater. *That's a challenge,* I thought.

"Well," I said after shaking hands. "I see you've already got a drink, so I guess we'll have to join you."

"Good luck," Cathy said, grinning with mischief. "We had to dig through that sink full of dirty dishes to find a couple of glasses to wash."

"Think you could find a couple more?" I asked.

She joined me in the narrow kitchen. "You guys will definitely not win the Good Housekeeping Seal of Approval."

She was only eighteen—"almost nineteen"—it turned out. But she had a quiet maturity about her, as well as a quick sense of humor.

I managed to get her phone number before they left. But Cathy cautioned me, "My dad is Dr. Otto Carley, the dentist. He's very strict; he doesn't let me date soldiers."

"I'm a lieutenant," I said with a straight face.

Dr. Carley allowed me to take Cathy out for a Coke at Wayne's Drive-in the next Friday. But there were ground rules. She had to be home by nine P.M. Our first date lasted exactly forty-five minutes. But he permitted me to take her out again the next week.

We talked a lot on the phone. Pretty soon Cathy's father and her mother, Gaynelle, were calling me "Tom" and inviting me to dinner. The story that Cathy and I agreed on was that young Tom Franks had "dropped out" of UT Austin to become an Army officer. At this stage, we didn't want to admit I'd flunked out and joined the Army as a private.

After that first Friday night in March, I stopped cruising the bars. Cathy returned the fraternity pin. I pushed the thought of Vietnam about as far away as I could. Spring passed, and I saw Cathy almost every night. Then summer came. We went water-skiing, swam, and spent every free moment together. I now knew what it meant to be in love.

IN AUGUST, I ATTENDED JUNGLE WARFARE SCHOOL IN PANAMA. When I got back in late September I was twenty pounds lighter, with round pink leech scars on my wrists and ankles and fungus between my toes. The first thing I did was go to the credit union and borrow five hundred dollars to buy a diamond engagement ring for Cathy, who was now a sophomore at Oklahoma State University in Stillwater. I drove my Olds north about a hundred miles an hour and reached the campus just after lunch on a Thursday. Cathy was on her way to class. But I convinced her to go for a ride instead. By the time I dropped her back at the sorority house to change for dinner, she was wearing that diamond.

MY ORDERS WERE SIMPLE: "REPORT TO 9TH INF DIV, RVN" NO later than 20 October 1967. I didn't know much about the 9th Infantry Division. I really didn't know much about the Republic of Vietnam, other than what I'd heard in barracks bull sessions and on the TV news. But I certainly knew I was joining a combat unit as a Forward Observer.

The Army authorized me to fly from my leave address in Austin, Texas, to Oakland, California, and report for a charter flight to Vietnam at Travis Air Force Base.

I drove Cathy down to meet my folks, and then back to Stillwater. We both cried saying goodbye. But we laughed that weekend, too. Returning to Austin, I realized I was a Texan who had seen almost nothing of the American West. I decided to cash in my plane ticket to Oakland and take a Greyhound through New Mexico, Arizona, and Nevada, then across the High Sierra from Reno.

The last week in Austin passed quickly. My mother starched and pressed all my khaki uniforms. She even ironed my underwear. I spent a few nights down at the DU house or drinking at Scholtz's Beer Garden with my buddies. We joked a lot and enjoyed our beer. But there was an underlying sadness.

My dad took off work that Tuesday morning so that he and my mother could drive me to the Greyhound station.

There wasn't much to say waiting for the bus. All three of us were choked up. Finally, the loudspeaker crackled, announcing the through-bus to Phoenix. Out on the ramp, I kissed my mother and hugged my dad.

"Got any advice?" I asked.

He was trying to smile, but there were tears on his deeply lined face. "Well," he finally said. "Make 'em a hand, Son."

Dad had grown up among farmers and oil field roughnecks, had worked hard his whole life in cotton fields, on drilling rigs, and in practically every kind of garage there was. In his world, a good "hand" was a man who earned his pay, who hauled his share, who did his duty.

I kissed my father's face. "I'll sure try, Dad."

SIX DAYS AND 11,000 MILES LATER, THE CHARTERED CONTINENTAL Airlines Boeing 707 descended through the night above the South China Sea toward Bien Hoa Air Base. I leaned against the cool, smeared window, trying to get a glimpse of the dark land below. There were tiny circles of light scattered among wide patches of empty black. Away to the left, the clouds were lit from below: the city glow of Saigon.

I was tired, and nursing a headache from the Wild Turkey I drank at Clark Field during our fuel stop in the Philippines. And I was more than a little nervous.

Then the captain came on the loudspeaker. "We'll be making our final approach in a couple of minutes," he announced. "So I'm going to ask you all to pull down your window shades. We don't want any light showing from the aircraft when we land."

As I tugged down the stiff plastic shade, I saw a chalky white parachute flare pop silently in the distance. A second later, a string of orange tracers looped down from the sky through the flare light and was swallowed by the dark. Some kind of gunship firing on the enemy, I thought.

Tommy Franks was going to war.

3

THE CRUCIBLE

Some veterans of the Vietnam War were foresighted enough to keep diaries of their experiences, allowing them to trace each detail of their tour of duty from a distance of decades.

Many others, I suspect, are like me. I couldn't sit down today with a calendar and a map of the Mekong Delta and produce a precise chronology of the months I spent in combat. I have only the dates on my award and service citations to stir my recollection, and a thin stack of letters I wrote to Cathy.

But I have my memories themselves. My time in Vietnam may have passed in a blur, but the images that I *have* retained stand out like islands in a swamp. I've joked that I shipped out to Vietnam as a rookie of twenty-two and came home twelve months later a fifty-year-old veteran. Some people laugh. But not the guys who served there.

RIDING THE OPEN TRUCK DOWN TO THE MEKONG DELTA THAT baking hot October Thursday was frightening. I was one of twelve officer replacements on the deuce-and-a-half's hard benches. We'd climbed aboard at Bearcat, the 9th Infantry Division's headquarters, fifty kilometers northeast of Saigon. The truck rolled past the huge American logistics base at Long Binh, over the New Port Bridge, and through the swarm of motorbikes, cyclo-pedicabs, and blue-and-white tin can Renault taxis of Saigon.

South of the city, we joined a convoy that was guarded head-and-tail by M113 armored personnel carriers—"tracks"—each mounting a .50 caliber machine gun. The rice paddies stretched to the flat horizon, ripening from green to gold. Muddy canals sliced the paddies like grid lines, and the occasional mounds of higher ground were thick with bamboo and scrub jungle. Along the roadside, peasants in black pajamas and conical hats either turned their backs on us or waved automatically, their faces blank. A water buffalo hauled a cart heaped with sugar cane toward us, while a three-wheel Lambretta scooter bus jammed with women and kids putted into our dust cloud.

The briefer at Bearcat had told us that these farmers were "basically neutral," siding neither with the government of the Republic of Vietnam nor the communist Vietcong and North Vietnamese Army. "They're just living along, trying to survive," the captain had explained. "We control the villages during the day. At night the VC and NVA take over."

Near the 3rd Brigade base camp at Tan An, we passed a burned-out track that villagers had stripped for scrap metal. Two little kids in torn T-shirts stood in the sparse shade of the wreck, holding up cans of Pabst Blue Ribbon beer and packs of Marlboros. *This is what war looks like,* I thought, wondering what had hit the track. Its aluminum armor could stop small arms fire and shrapnel, but it folded like cardboard when hit by the B-40 rocket propelled grenades (RPGs) the enemy used in ambushes. Perched up on the back of this deuce-and-a-half, we had no armor at all, except for our clumsy flak jackets.

The truck jolted along behind the lead track, keeping a convoy interval of twenty-five meters. I didn't know what was worse—the sun, the orange dust, or the choking diesel exhaust. I was hot, thirsty, and tired. And nervous. This was a lot different from the first day of Basic Training.

We turned off the laterite road onto a rutted track cutting between more paddies, finally stopping at a collection of droopy tents and plank huts capped with sheets of rusted metal. The camp perimeter was marked by a tall barbed wire fence, the tents and huts surrounded by shoulder-high stacks of faded green sandbags. Coils of concertina wire strung from engineer stakes formed the outer defense against infiltrators. Standing up in the truck bed, I saw that the base was really two compounds, one large, one small, separated by a hamlet of shabby wooden houses shaded by a few palms and banana trees. This was what troopers called a "ville," a satellite village beside a firebase that provided day labor and hooch girls who cleaned the barracks huts and washed uniforms. The whole setup looked like the slapdash oil field work sites in eastern Oklahoma I'd seen in my dad's pictures.

The 5th Battalion (Mechanized), 60th Infantry, was my new home. I'd been assigned as a Forward Observer with Bravo Battery, 2nd Battalion, 4th Artillery, which provided the 5-60's fire support with six 105 mm howitzers. Upon arrival at the base, I was greeted by a crimson sign at the barbed wire gate: "Welcome to Beautiful Downtown BINH PHUOC."

"Here you go, LT," the driver said as he handed down my gear. "Now you can tell the folks back home you 'been foooked.'"

I was getting over the jet lag, but I hadn't yet acclimatized to the sapping heat and humidity. I shouldered my M-16 and duffle bag and followed a skinny Spec-4 named Anderson along a wobbly boardwalk—duckboards, we called them—laid on clumps of dried mud.

"You take much incoming?" I asked him, passing between bunkers of stacked, dirt-filled 105 mm ammo crates, the roofs heavily sandbagged. It was obvious from the stagnant pools around the perimeter that you couldn't dig in very deep without hitting the soggy Delta water table.

"Nah, LT, nothing too heavy. Usually mortars, but the VC throw in some rockets now and then." I had a world of grunt shorthand to sort out: "rockets" were the 107 and 122 mm rockets the Vietcong were fond of firing into bases like Binh Phuoc. And "LT" was how soldiers addressed lieutenants in the boonies.

The Battery executive officer (XO) in the sandbagged orderly room was a first lieutenant. But he wasn't like anyone I'd known at Fort Sill. His eyes were crusted red, his face haggard, as if he hadn't had a full night's sleep in a long time. This was one old-looking man, though he had to be in his twenties like me. No, not *like me*, I thought. This guy had experienced things that I had not.

"Franks," he muttered, scratching his chin as he glanced at my orders. "Yeah, right. The new FO. Captain wants to put you with Bandido Charlie."

I frowned, not understanding.

"Charlie Company, 5th of the 60th. They call themselves 'Los Bandidos'; they've got the red kerchiefs and everything. The company's been down at Dong Tam, but they're headed back up here to the Battalion this afternoon."

I slid my stamped orders into the envelope. "Good outfit?"

The XO glanced at me skeptically. "Yeah, right," he repeated.

Up at Bearcat, I'd heard GIs call replacements "Ef-En-Gees": FNGs, or *fucking new guys*. In the XO's eyes, I was an FNG; what right had I earned to ask the quality of a combat unit? During the ten days I'd been in-country, being processed through the pipeline to Binh Phuoc, I'd noticed a cool formality toward replacements—not open hostility, just a certain sense of distance. There was none of the "Welcome aboard, let's grab a cup of coffee" you might expect joining a stateside unit. There was only one way I would earn the respect of these soldiers: by doing my job in combat.

Fair enough. I'll just have to make 'em a hand.

The field telephone buzzed, and the radio sitting on a crate burst with a static-garbled message.

"Alpha Company's got a suspected sniper in a hooch at, ah . . ." the commo man announced, turning to read the grid coordinates from the sector map mounted on the wall.

The XO nodded as he listened to the phone, then turned to the soldier, looking right past me. "What the fuck is a 'suspected' sniper? They're either in contact or they're not."

"Captain's in the Fire Direction Center," the soldier added.

"Good," the XO said. "He'll sort it out." Then he glanced back up at me as if I were an afterthought. "Anderson there will get you squared away with supply and the Bachelor Officer's Quarters. You can meet the Captain in the Fire Direction Center later."

I saluted, but the XO merely nodded. "Yeah, right."

As I left the orderly room with Anderson, the ground shook with the blast of a 105 howitzer.

"Spotting round, LT," Anderson said helpfully.

A Brigade staff major at Tan An had briefed us on the Rules of Engagement for the use of indirect artillery fire. Unless a unit was in direct contact with the enemy, an FO or an Infantry officer had to receive three separate clearances for fire support: one from his U.S. Army chain of command, one from the Army of the Republic of Vietnam (ARVN), and one from the "GVN," the appropriate Vietnamese government official, usually the district chief. But no clearance was needed if an officer prefaced the fire mission request with the words *"in contact,"* followed by his initials: "Whiskey Juliet," for example, for William Jones. No wonder the XO was pissed off over the report of a "suspected" sniper in a civilian hooch—it could take hours to get all the clearances the battery would need to fire that mission.

Following Anderson from the supply shed with my pile of bedding and a bag full of field gear, I felt the dried mud shake again as the six howitzers cut loose, firing for effect. Either the Battery commander had sorted out the confused fire mission request, or an "in contact" mission had been received.

Then and there, I resolved to try my damnedest to be decisive, to practice my profession to the best of my ability. Providing fire support in combat was no game. Enemy troops or Vietnamese civilians—or American soldiers—would live or die depending on how well I did my job.

At sunset, I was stretched out on my cot in the stifling barracks, wearing only GI shorts, my narrow cubicle marked off by a line of wall lockers. I was exhausted from what I thought had been a long, hard day. Just as my eyes were closing, though, the corrugated metal roof shook with a god-awful racket—the racket of machine guns, and the flat snap of a larger automatic weapon.

Jumping up, I grabbed my M-16 and pulled on my jungle boots without socks.

"What the fuck's happening?" I yelled to the lieutenant in the next cubicle.

He stepped around the end locker, a green towel around his waist, flip-flops on his feet, holding a nylon shaving kit. "Just the Mad Minute," he grinned. "You'll get used to it." Then he strolled off to take a shower.

I went to the barracks door, still holding my rifle. Another lieutenant came up the duckboards, looked at me strangely, then back toward the perimeter, where soldiers were firing M-60 and .50 caliber machine guns into the empty paddies to the south and west. A "duster" twin-barreled 40 mm automatic cannon mounted on a tank chassis pumped thick red tracers in the same direction.

The deeply tanned young officer paused on the step and explained the Mad Minute. Every day at sundown, the Battalion fired its crew-served automatic weapons toward the two sides of the perimeter that were not defended by the Battery's howitzers. On the sides that *were* defended by howitzers, there were beehive rounds—shells loaded with hundreds of razor-sharp steel flechettes—stacked, fused, and ready if needed.

The purpose of the Mad Minute was both to discourage infiltration from the undefended sides of the base and to make sure all the crew-served weapons were ready. "Any VC coming in at night from those quadrants," he said, "is instant hamburger."

The wiry lieutenant stuck out his hand. "Lee Alley," he said. "Recon Platoon."

"Thanks for the info," I shook his hand. "Tommy Von Franks, Royal Slobovian Hussars," I said, acknowledging my New Guy status. We were involved in a deadly serious business, but that didn't mean I had to take myself too seriously.

A few hours later, I woke up sweating as a howitzer slammed out a single round. Thirty seconds later, the ventilation panel at the end of the barracks glowed faintly. *Illumination round,* I realized: Some Infantry unit out on ambush patrol must have called for a flare. The air under my mosquito net was like soup. My gut rumbled; I wasn't used to the big white Aralen anti-malaria pills. "They'll make you shit through the eye of a needle," the medic at Bearcat had announced gleefully as he distributed the pills to the replacements. *Check.* I slid into my shower clogs, picked up my flashlight, and headed for the latrines.

Following Anderson around the base that afternoon, I'd seen shirtless soldiers working in clouds of black smoke, stirring sooty 55-gallon fuel drums cut in half. "Shit detail, LT," Anderson said. "Gotta burn the crap from the latrines with MO gas every day to keep the flies down. Usually the locals from the ville do it. Those guys must have fucked up to pull that duty."

Now, with my roll of toilet paper in one hand and a flashlight in the other, I two-stepped it to the first of the screened plank latrines. The stench was pretty bad. A lot of guys must have used it since they burned out the barrels. Before I sat down, I happened to shine my light down the hole. The meatloaf and dehydrated mashed potatoes I'd had for supper rose in my throat: The barrel below was a wriggling white heap of maggots.

My belly in a knot, I stumbled out of that latrine and ran to the next. This one had been burned. As I sat down, a howitzer fired another illumination round that popped about five kilometers—

"klicks"—to the west. In the dim light coming through the screen, I made out a message someone had scrawled on the door: "In this land of sun and fun, we never flush for number one."

This place is going to take some getting used to.

T HE COMPANY WAS SPREAD OUT, LINE-ABREAST BY PLATOONS. I slogged across the paddies of hip-high rice with the small command group in the center of the formation. Six hundred meters ahead, a mound of jungle and drooping palms rose from the flat landscape like a green loaf of bread. That was our objective. Before dawn, a UH-1 Huey chopper equipped with a nose-mounted "people sniffer" had detected heat and telltale carbon dioxide breath signatures, revealing humans concealed in that jungle. Intel suspected that about a hundred VC had dug into those trees, using the cover as a day sanctuary before moving on to lay ambushes along Highway 4 at night.

Our unit had been airlifted on what we called an "Eagle Flight"—a helicopter insertion—late that morning into a landing zone between the road and that patch of jungle cover. We'd moved along the paddy dikes in a single column about three klicks from the LZ, a long, hot walk. Then we spread into the standard sweep-and-clear formation. Working dismounted, without our tracks and their .50 caliber machine guns, the company had reverted to "straight leg" infantry.

But I had the power to call in artillery fire on the enemy—as long as I stayed cool and did my job. *Right—how am I supposed to keep cool?* The dry season had started; the sun was a pounding weight on my steel helmet.

In the week I'd been at Binh Phuoc, I'd absorbed a raft of useful information from my fellow officers and the "grunts"—the trooper term for infantrymen. Instead of lugging the regulation three cartons of C-rations in my rucksack, I only had one can of steak and potatoes, two cans of fruit, and a handful of coffee and sugar packets; I'd swapped the excess weight for two extra canteens of water. And instead of a bulky rucksack, I carried a small butt pack hooked to my web gear. I kept my poncho, but left behind its quilt-like liner. If we had to "RON"—Remain Overnight—in these paddies, staying warm wouldn't be a problem.

Watching the experienced guys in the line platoons, I'd learned to lengthen my M-16 rifle sling, which would allow me to carry the weapon muzzle-down across my back if I had to lift something with both hands. The grunts also taught me to load the twenty-round rifle magazines two shells short to prevent jamming. My dry socks were sealed in PX Saran Wrap, and thin C-ration four-packs of Winstons were tied in condoms.

I felt like a pretty boonie-smart trooper.

But I hadn't yet been under fire—at least not direct fire, the kind where the enemy's shooting at you face-to-face. We'd had two night mortar attacks at Binh Phuoc, which damaged some equipment but caused no serious casualties. The 82 mm rounds had whistled in after midnight, exploding across the base in a random pattern. I'd rushed to my temporary duty station in the Fire Direction Center, a pair of steel Conex shipping containers welded end-to-end and heaped with sandbags. Backing up the FDC officers with the "charts and darts"—sticking target-coordinate pins into the wide sector firing chart—I had helped plot the "counter fire" on the enemy mortar positions. Busy and watching the Battery officers "working" the firing solution, I didn't even flinch when shrapnel thudded into the sandbags and pinged off of the steel cover.

But that mortar fire had kept us awake most of two nights; short of sleep, I'd been dragging ass ever since.

Now I was physically tired, but hyper-alert. When we reached the cover of a chest-high dike running across our line of advance, the company commander radioed his platoon leaders to halt and to position their M-60 machine gunners.

"Let's put some fire on them, Franks," the captain said.

I had already obtained the required Army-ARVN-and-GVN clearances to order artillery fire on the clump of jungle ahead. Now I had to plot and order my first combat fire mission, calling down shells on a real enemy, not on a heap of painted car bodies strewn across the West Range at Fort Sill.

As I hauled myself up on the baked mud of the dike to get a better look at the target, I was aware that I'd be silhouetted against the yellow rice behind us. There were probably fifty Vietcong looking at me through the sights of their AK-47s and PK light machine guns, and I was definitely within killing range. And, like the grunts around me, I'd decided not to wear the heavy, sweltering flak jacket. I was breathing hard; my cracked lips were dry.

Screw it. This was why I'd joined the Army. I raised my binoculars and focused on the tree line, counting the etched mil lines right to left from the western edge of the mound, which was clearly visible on my plastic-covered map, then noting the two mils up from the horizontal that marked my initial aiming point. Just to be absolutely certain, I sat down on the dike and took an azimuth reading through the aperture of my M-2 compass.

I slid back down and leaned against the reverse slope of the dike, taking the PRC-25 handset from my Radio Telephone Operator, a freckled kid we called Whitey.

"Oscar Four, Five Zero. Fire mission, over," I called the Binh Phuoc FDC, using my best Fort Sill procedures.

"Go ahead, Nickel Nothin'," the young voice answered, translating my call sign—Five Zero—into grunt parlance.

"Entrenched enemy." I studied the map a final time. The Battery at Binh Phuoc was behind us. The shells would pass overhead toward the target coordinates. "Foxtrot Mike Four Three Five Six Two Four. One round. I will adjust fire."

"Roger," the voice said through the static.

"Shot, over," the same voice announced a moment later. The round was on its way.

"Splash, over," the FDC called next. I was back on the dike, watching the target through my binoculars. The round exploded in the trees fifty meters left and near the crest of the mound. "Right five zero."

The next shell blasted up a cloud of mud and shredded trees almost on the aiming point. "Fire for effect," I called, proud of my work.

A flurry of six-round salvos of high explosive, quick fused to explode on contact, smashed into the jungle. Kneeling on the dike top, I was absorbed in the damage we'd laid on the enemy.

My RTO, Whitey, tugged on my boot. "Not a good idea to stay up there like that, LT."

After four salvos, the low hillside was pocked with smoking craters. I called "end of mission."

"Nice shooting, Franks," the captain said.

The platoons moved cautiously forward, classic fire-and-maneuver, with the M-60s providing cover. I was soaked with sweat, holding my M-16 ready as we neared the tree line.

"Watch the fuck out for trip wires," a sergeant bellowed as the troops reached the smoldering edge of the jungle, firing their weapons from the hip.

I emptied a magazine into the splintered debris, then climbed over the rough edge of a shell crater, almost tripping on the shattered trunk of a nippa palm. The bitter stink of high explosive rose from the mud. But there were no dead enemy soldiers, no blood, no broken weapons or abandoned equipment in the crater. It was the same up and down the line, no sign of trenches, rifle pits, or bunkers: *Zilch, zero.*

I had just called in my first combat fire mission—and managed to destroy four hundred square meters of empty jungle.

The troopers lay around in the hot shade, sucking down water from their canteens, smoking, grab-assing, thankful not to have made contact.

I just sat there feeling kind of hollow, jangly from a long evening's worth of spent adrenaline. *Maybe next time we'd do some real damage.*

ANOTHER DAY, A NEW SWEEP, A DIFFERENT SECTOR. MORE INTEL on holed-up VC. After an Eagle Flight insertion, the company had humped klick after hot klick, through paddies irrigated for the second rice crop, past a hamlet full of silent women and kids but no young men, and down shadowy trails beside tall stands of bamboo that rattled in the afternoon breeze, making everyone nervous.

We filed across a log footbridge over a narrow canal, then split into a double column of two platoons each, entering separate trails through more high bamboo that rose to the south in a gradual slope. I was in the middle of the right column with the command group.

The VC ambush was perfectly placed and timed, hitting my column from the dense bamboo to our right, exploding a captured American Claymore mine and raking the trail with AK-47 fire. Bright green tracers slashed through the shade, cutting leaves and chipping wood.

Everybody was firing, M-16s on full automatic, M-60s pounding like jackhammers. I heard the *pook*-crack of M-79 grenade launchers. Propped on my elbows in the mud, I shot off two magazines toward the enemy tracers in the shadows.

"Man down," somebody shouted up ahead where the Claymore had blown. "Medic."

The troops reacted expertly, putting out a steady volume of fire. Through the noise and the thudding of my own heart, I heard the order. "Cover fire. Fall back by squads."

The command group was first, crawling twenty-five meters into the thicket to our left as the rifle squads at the ends of the column kept up the wall of fire. Away from the tangled trailside brush and "wait-a-minute" vines, there was space between the towering, leg-thick bamboo.

Whitey panted down beside me, lugging the PRC-25 radio clipped to his pack frame like an oversize green phone book. Now I heard the distinctive crack of AK fire from our left front. The VC had just sprung the leg of their L-shaped ambush.

I listened to the fire from our positions and to the First Platoon's small arms and grenade launchers to the lower left, trying to gain an acoustic image of the friendly and enemy positions. Coming into the bamboo grove, I had counted paces. In spite of the noise and my heaving chest, I grabbed Whitey's handset and called for fire support. I was dripping so much sweat onto the map cover that I needed to wipe the plastic clear. My coordinates had to be accurate; according to my estimate, the VC ambush position was only 150 meters to our east and south.

"Oscar Four, Nickel Nothin'. In contact. In close contact." I then gave the company commander's initials. "Ambush in bamboo, Hotel Lima Five Three Four Six Five Seven, over."

The Battery FDC at Binh Phuoc reacted immediately, with calm efficiency, putting down the first round left and long, then walking single shells toward us in twenty-five-meter increments. The leader of the 1st Platoon came up on the company frequency to announce that we had the easting range; the last spotting shell had exploded in the bamboo at the bottom leg of the ambush. Then the leader of 3rd Platoon at the southern end of our column called that the spotting round had been "range correct line"—on the target.

"Six rounds for effect," I called the FDC.

A young Infantry sergeant, who'd been crouching behind the trees nearby, jumped up and shouted. *"Friendly incoming!* Everybody down."

Helmet wedged down in the moldy layer of dead leaves, I acknowledged the "Shot" and "Splash" calls from the Battery. The mud shook beneath my chest. Incandescent shock waves flashed through the shadowy bamboo. Third and First Platoons reported that the barrage was on target. No more green tracers snapped through the bamboo.

Still panting, the map case shaking in my fingers, I felt a rush of satisfaction. We'd just smashed a textbook ambush.

Then the Battery called and told me, "You've got guns overhead." Lantern 03 and 04—two UH-1C Huey helicopter gunships—were orbiting the bamboo grove.

"Put some rockets around the 105 craters," I told the helo pilots. "I'll give you the coordinates."

"Don't need coordinates," Lantern 03 replied. "I can see the smoke clearly."

I rolled over on my back, staring up toward the sun through the bamboo. The cigarette tasted great; so did the tepid canteen water, despite the bitter Halazone pills I'd dropped into my canteens a few hours earlier to kill the canal water microbes. The whack-whomp-whack of the Huey rotors grew louder. Those gunships each carried 38 spin-stabilized rockets with antipersonnel warheads. In a minute, I knew, any VC who'd managed to survive the shelling would be dead.

The bamboo flashed and cracked—ten meters away. It was like a bolt of lightning and instant thunder from the sunny sky. Then came another blast, this one even closer. Then two more. Bamboo was splitting around us. Three more explosions a few meters to the left. The mud was dancing under my chest.

The gunships had identified the enemy positions . . . but they didn't know where *we* were. They were "walking" the rockets into the shell craters, but were doing it beginning on *our* positions. The guys around me were screaming at the treetops. "Knock off those rockets, you assholes!"

Through the blasts I managed to yell into the handset and stop the attack. My ears were ringing as I coughed up cordite fumes from the exploding rockets.

"Anybody hit?" a sergeant yelled. "Anybody down?"

It was a miracle: A salvo of twenty-some rockets had slashed across our position, but no one was wounded. As we formed up to pull back and join the other column, I was amazed to see that each rocket warhead, which contained several pounds of high explosive, had a blast-damage radius no larger than that of a hand grenade.

After a month in-country, I had placed my faith in the invincibility of American weapons. Now I had serious doubts about the killing power of these much smaller 2.75-inch rockets. I spoke to the captain, then grabbed Whitey's handset and called in more 105 rounds—HE and white phosphorous—on the VC coordinates.

With artillery still falling on the enemy, the platoons of our column rendezvoused at the edge of the bamboo. Two soldiers had been wounded by small arms, one in the hip, the other in his ankle. Trussed up in bloody green battle-dressing bandages, they hobbled along, helped by their buddies.

Then the other column emerged from the trees. Nobody was limping, but two soldiers carried the body of a dead trooper, tied in his poncho, swinging beneath a springy length of bamboo. The soldier at the far end of the pole was shorter than the one in front, his face red and puckered with exertion, wet with tears.

"Oh, the motherfuckers," he moaned. "The shitty bastards." Because of his height, he had to hold the machete-chopped end of the pole above his head. His hands were bleeding.

I slung my rifle across my back and lifted the pole from the soldier's hand.

"It's okay, LT," he pleaded as I shouldered the weight. "I can hack it. Andy was my buddy."

"I'll just give you a little break," I said. "Here, take my weapon off my back. That'll help."

Beside me, the youngster slung our two M-16s on his shoulders. He wiped his bleeding hands on the muddy legs of his jungle fatigues, but he couldn't stop crying.

The captain had called in a Medevac chopper for the two wounded and the dead man. We moved out into the paddies in a disciplined column toward the purple cloud of the smoke grenade marking the pickup zone. Nobody spoke. The troopers kept their weapons ready, scanning the tree lines, watching the edge of the dike for booby trap trip wires. Those boys had done their job today, pinning down that VC ambush until I could call in a fire mission and the Battery could respond as they did—with amazing accuracy. Tonight they'd shower off the stinking paddy ooze and sit outside their hooches in humid darkness, swatting mosquitoes as they fished beers out of their ice tubs, tapping the lids with their rusty church keys, drinking can after can, smoking, talking, maybe even managing to laugh.

Tomorrow these kids would be out humping patrols again. More would be wounded . . . more would be killed.

T HE BATTALION OFTEN CONDUCTED SWEEPS USING THE TRACKS, each company mounting ten APCs, churning up orange dust as the columns sped off in different directions to converge in hammer-and-anvil maneuvers. Sometimes we flushed out and destroyed a VC unit; usually we did not. On a long mission we'd RON in the boonies, the tracks drawn up in a defensive perimeter with their .50 cals and 106 mm recoilless rifles pointed toward the dark paddies and the darker tree lines.

Troops usually lugged their beer coolers in the APCs—which wasn't officially allowed, but was tolerated as long as the soldiers in the listening posts didn't drink more than a can or two before they left the perimeter for the outlying foxholes.

One night, I walked among the tracks, shooting the breeze with the platoon leaders and sitting on the back ramps with the grunts, talking football and cars.

In the dim glow of a red-lensed flashlight, I passed around pictures of my yellow Olds 442 like a proud daddy showing snapshots of his baby. "Hell of a car," I boasted.

These soldiers were my partners, my customers. Some of them had eleven months in-country; they knew one hell of a lot more about waging war than I did. I respected them. When I called in a fire mission, it was for one reason: to protect these troops by killing the enemy before he could kill those kids.

"That's shit-hot, LT," a soldier said, handing back the picture. "I'm gonna get me one of those back in the world."

Every trooper in Vietnam had a dream car, waiting to be driven off the dealer's lot after he'd completed his one-year tour and his DEROS—Date Eligible to Return from Overseas—finally came.

We all knew our DEROS. Mine was October 18, 1968, nearly ten months off. It was considered the worst possible luck to say the date out loud until you were really short—within thirty days of rotation home. The Army's inflexible twelve-month tour of duty, I was starting to realize, had as many bad points as good. Some officers rewarded good troops with base camp duty during that last month, but that luxury wasn't always available, and it was almost impossible for most line soldiers to concentrate on their jobs when they were short. With many companies undermanned, a short-timer might have to hump the paddies right up to his last day. I'd heard stories of troopers who'd been lifted from the boonies at dawn after an all-night firefight, then rushed through out-processing and put on a truck for Bien Hoa or Cam Ranh Bay and a charter jet back to the States that same afternoon.

In OCS, we'd been taught about "unit cohesion," the psychological glue that held an outfit together. That tie could be frayed by the stream of new men replacing the short-timers who'd survived to DEROS. But in good companies like Bandido Charlie or Lee Alley's Recon Platoon, pride made for a special cohesion—in spite of the turbulence.

I slept an hour or so that night, sprawled on the mud beside the high-sided command track, a poncho draped over my face and hands to keep the mosquitoes at bay. Just before sunrise—a favorite time for hit-and-run VC mortar attacks—I woke and made my breakfast.

On the inner corners of the APC's rear ramp, there were square recesses that we used as C-ration stoves. I mixed equal parts powdered coffee, cocoa, creamer, and two packets of sugar in an empty pound cake can, and filled it with canteen water. Then, reaching blindly into the track, I pinched off a piece of gummy C-4 explosive from a crate and dropped the chunk into the hole. I touched my Zippo to the C-4 and it caught fire, burning with an intense, odorless heat. In twenty seconds the drink was bubbling hot.

Sitting on the ramp, I savored the blend of coffee and chocolate, letting the sugar and caffeine burn through my fatigue. The eastern horizon melted quickly from a soft plum color to flat yellow, the sudden tropical sunrise that still took me by surprise.

When it was full daylight, the men in the listening-post rifle pits dumped the dirt from their sandbags, gathered up their Claymore mines and belts of M-60 ammo, and trudged back to the circle of tracks. They looked like oil patch roughnecks, stoop-shouldered, beat from a long night pushing pipe on a filthy drilling rig. It was an appropriate image: A good portion of the junior enlisted men in the battalion were from blue-collar homes. Many were white, the rest black or Hispanic. Most were draftees; others, like me, had enlisted out of patriotism and a sense of adventure. They weren't experts in English Comp or the Periodic Table of Elements.

But they kept their tools—their weapons—clean, and they used them well. They did not panic when tracers cracked past their faces in the bamboo thickets. They fired and maneuvered, just as their fathers had in the hedgerows of Normandy or the stinking jungles of Luzon.

They made the Army a hand.

Watching the troops in the humid morning sun, I felt a stab of love—as if these guys were all brothers or cousins I was meeting for the first time. We were a family out in this alien wilderness, bound by ties as close as blood.

A kid who'd been on a listening post shuffled by, clearly more exhausted than I was. In five minutes he'd be back on his track, as we went roaring and jolting out of here to deprive the VC mortars of an easy target. But now he stopped and yawned deeply.

"Geez, LT," he said. "That smells great. What you got there?"

"In Paris I think they call it your basic café au lait, but with chocolate."

"No shit. Don't have that in Kenosha. Taste good?"

"Take it." I handed him the can, turning the bent lid-handle so he didn't burn his fingers. "I've got a whole pot in the track."

Of course I didn't. But this soldier needed it more than I did.

"Far out. Thanks, LT."

The kid actually whistled as he strolled away sipping the sweet drink.

I WAS SHOULDER-DEEP IN STAGNANT CANAL WATER. THE MUD BANK shuddered as a mortar round hit the flooded paddy thirty meters behind me. We'd been pinned down since sunset; now, seven hours later, Charlie still wasn't ready to break contact.

The Company's insertion into the southwest edge of the Plain of Reeds that afternoon had been flawless. We had conducted a long sweep of paddies, villages, and stands of jungle, searching for the main force Vietcong battalion that Intel reported had recently set up in this sector.

We had found nothing. As usual, when our ARVN interpreter pressed the villagers for information, they swore on Buddha's head that they hadn't seen a thing.

Another dry hole, we thought, and headed west along this canal toward our pickup zone. Before we reached the PZ, though, the enemy cut loose with everything he had: AKs, light and heavy machine guns, 82 mm mortars, and at least two 75 mm recoilless rifles that blew huge holes out of the canal bank. By a miracle, no one had been badly wounded. But the only cover we had was the canal. And the enemy was determined to keep us here.

Back home, a lot of people believed the Vietcong were peasant guerrillas, forced to fight with a hodgepodge of old Japanese rifles and French carbines and whatever modern weapons they could capture or buy from the ARVN. Scanning the enemy units maneuvering in the last of the twilight, though, I'd seen well-disciplined squads in khaki shirts and shorts, wearing web gear and camouflaged boonie hats, laden down with ammo belts, lugging PK machine guns and mortars. And each VC heavy weapons squad had its own security element laying down AK-47 fire. These weren't part-time insurgents. They were first-rate light infantry.

A flare popped overhead and rocked gently beneath its parachute, casting weird shadows on the dark canal. Streams of 7.62 mm tracers poured down from a Spooky gunship, looping back and forth like neon fire hoses into the distant tree line. The Air Force guys must have seen the flash of that mortar tube.

Spooky was an AC-47, a converted 1940s troop carrier that could saturate a football field in seconds with six thousand machine gun rounds. I heard the crackling buzz of the old plane's three electrically driven miniguns, sharp against the drone of the engines. The flare burned out and the moonless night came back, darker than ever.

Suddenly I thought of that moment in the Continental charter flight approaching Bien Hoa, back when I'd arrived in-country. The tiny flare bursting in the distance, the stream of tracers swallowed by the black landscape: it was only ten weeks—and a thousand years—ago.

As soon as the gunship had banked away to the east, I reached up to the PRC-25 radio on the shelf that Whitey had hacked into the bank with his K-bar knife.

"Romeo Three," I called the Battery at Tan An. They were much closer than the guns at Ben Luc, so their fires would reach the target that much quicker. "VT and delay on those same coordinates. Urgent. Enemy moving in the open."

I hoped Spooky's miniguns had sent the VC mortar crews running for their bunkers in those trees. Maybe the airbursts would catch them. If not, the projectiles with delay fuses would penetrate the logs and mud before exploding.

While that fire mission came snorting in, I switched frequencies to the next closest artillery battery and called in another fire mission on the cluster of hooches to the left front where the enemy had shifted one of the 12.7mm heavy machine guns, no doubt digging it in. Each time one of our M-60 gunners snapped off a burst toward those low buildings, the 12.7 pounded the length of the canal bank, keeping us pinned in place for the mortars. We had to silence that gun.

As soon as the place was burning well and there was no incoming artillery fire to endanger Spooky, I called the gunship back in. "Put everything you've got on those burning hooches."

Spooky went to work.

The long night ground on, as a hundred young American soldiers took shelter in a stinking ditch.

As my dad always said, nothing much good ever happens after midnight. Amen and roger that.

At some point before dawn, Whitey tapped my shoulder. "LT, you might want to move down a little bit. I had to take a piss."

"No wonder the water just got so warm."

Flares lit the dark sky. Spooky droned overhead. The enemy fired, shifted weapons sites, and fired again. When I wasn't adjusting artillery and vectoring the gunship, I tried to estimate the amount of ordnance the Vietcong had expended since sunset. Thousands of light and heavy automatic weapons rounds; maybe a hundred mortar rounds. And those fucking recoilless rifles. We'd sure as hell been outgunned. If it hadn't been for Spooky and the artillery, we'd probably all be dead.

At first light, flights of Huey gunships took over from Spooky, raking the narrow, overgrown side canals leading deeper into the Plain of Reeds—the VC's escape routes.

In full daylight, after we went without taking enemy fire for thirty minutes, the Company crawled out of the mud and sat a few minutes in the warming sun. The guys on the M-60s took turns field stripping their guns and swabbing the working parts with oil—cleaning their weapons even before they got rid of the wriggling green-black leeches still clinging to their legs and crotches. Eventually Whitey and I set about helping each other, squirting bug juice and holding lit cigarettes on the leeches until the parasites dropped off, streaming with blood, and we ground them into the mud with our boot heels.

Over the flat western horizon, the hot, cloudless sky thumped and shuddered.

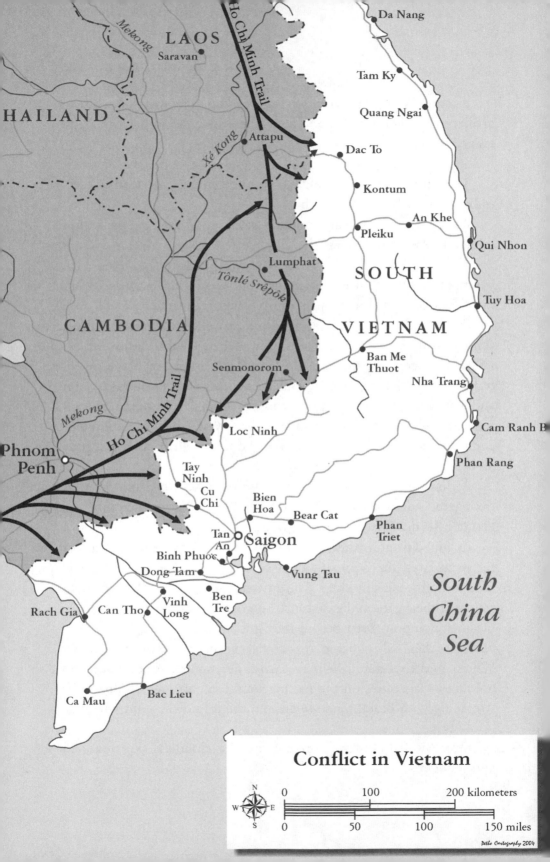

Da Nang

LAOS

Saravan

Ho Chi Minh Trail

Mekong

THAILAND

Xé Kong

Attapu

Tam Ky

Quang Ngai

Dac To

Kontum

An Khe

Pleiku

Qui Nhon

CAMBODIA

Lumphat

Tônlé Srêpôk

SOUTH

VIETNAM

Tuy Hoa

Senmonorom

Ban Me
Thuot

Nha Trang

Mekong

Ho Chi Minh Trail

Cam Ranh B

Loc Ninh

Phan Rang

Phnom
Penh

Tay
Ninh

Cu
Chi

Bien
Hoa

Bear Cat

Phan
Triet

Tan
An

Saigon

Binh Phuoc

Dong Tam

Vung Tau

South
China
Sea

Rach Gia

Can Tho

Vinh
Long

Ben
Tre

Ca Mau

Bac Lieu

Conflict in Vietnam

N
W E
S

0   100   200 kilometers

0   50   100   150 miles

DeLho Cartography 2004

Arc light, I thought. *Pound the sons of bitches.*

Flying too high to be seen, huge B-52s were laying down wide patterns of 750-pound bombs farther west in the Plain of Reeds. From the continuing rumble of explosions, the bombers were striking all the way to the Parrot's Beak and the Testicles, terrain features created by bends in the rivers that ran up toward Cambodia. An independent nation by a fluke of postcolonial history, Cambodia was also a major VC and NVA sanctuary. From that safe haven, North Vietnamese and Vietcong units like the one that had kept us pinned down all night could infiltrate the Delta, do their damage, then break into smaller units and slip back across the border, immune to pursuit by American ground forces. Then they would rest, regroup, and re-supply—and come back to hit our troops again and again.

I shouldered my weapon and followed the line of wet, exhausted troops down the slippery canal bank. The distant thud of the Arc Light continued to the west. *If I live long enough to get anywhere in this Army,* I thought, my brain soggy with fatigue, *I won't let the enemy operate from a refuge like that.*

Lieutenant Tommy Franks didn't know diddly about strategy, but I was learning about war at the soldier's level. Why would a commander ever be forced to see his soldiers killed week-in, month-out, and not be allowed to take the fight to the enemy? As they said in Midland, that was dumber than a box of rocks.

Back then, though, the last thing I was expecting was a lifetime of military command decisions. If I made it through this tour in one piece, I was marrying Cathy, getting out of the Army, and finishing college. In that order.

E VERY DAY AT SUNSET, THE BATTALION SENT AN AMBUSH PATROL outside the Binh Phuoc wire, often to sites too far to reach by foot before dark. Late one afternoon in December, I went down to a line of parked M-113s, where one of my platoon buddies was mounting up the nightly patrol. His two squads would ride out in tracks to a trail junction about ten klicks away.

"How 'bout letting me gun the second track tonight?" I said.

"Have at it, Tom."

Even though the M-113 offered no protection against large mines or RPGs, I loved to sit in the commander's hatch, my hands on the twin grips of the .50 caliber machine gun, as the thirteen tons of armor roared along the mud roads or across irrigation canals. It gave me a sense of invulnerability.

The track's aluminum deck was still hot from the sun as I hauled myself up, bent down the radio antenna, and tied on my personal flag. Many outfits had their own pennants, emblazoned with crossed sabers or pirates' skulls and crossbones. Some tracks flew the traditional Infantry guidon "Queen of Battle." Since the Artillery was the King of Battle, I'd given a tailor at Tan An ville a carton of Lucky Strikes to make me a black silk banner that said "Balls for the Queen" in white letters. High-explosive 105 mm projectiles weren't exactly cannon balls, but why sweat the details? I still had enough of the college boy in me to take my laughs where I could find them.

The platoon leader's track led the way, clanking along into the low eye of the sun. The GIs had opened the top hatch and perched themselves on ammo crates and sandbags, their upper bodies out in the open like mine. This wasn't just to catch the humid evening breeze. A mine buried in the road was much more dangerous to troopers inside a track than AK or machine-gun fire was to those sitting on sandbags with their upper bodies exposed.

After depositing the patrol, we sped back into the falling dusk, hitting almost thirty miles an hour on the solidly graveled stretches where the road ran along a berm above the paddies. But as we slowed for a muddy section of road, a patch of jungle snaked out from the left, probably an overgrown creek bed that flooded in the monsoon. As usual, I was hot, tired, and thirsty; my mind was on a cool shower and an ice-cold can of Blue Ribbon.

All of a sudden the .50 caliber on the platoon leader's track pounded out a long burst. "Contact, left front," his voice sounded loud in my radio earphones.

I saw the muzzle flashes just as a flurry of AK and machine gun rounds snapped by my head. Green tracers flew toward the track, several smacking the hull. Swinging my fifty-cal, I tripped the intercom switch and shouted to the driver. "Neutral-steer left." The driver spun the track to face the tree line head-on, presenting the enemy with our vehicles' most narrow and most heavily armored profile.

The machine gun's grips shuddered in my hands as I fired repeated bursts, walking the orange tracers into the tree line. Two months in-country, and this was probably my tenth firefight; my sense of fright had long since been replaced by focus and adrenaline.

Hot shell casings poured from the fifty's breech, pinging down between my feet. Three or four rounds to a burst, eight, nine bursts . . . fifteen. The last of the linked belt clattered out of the hundred-round ammo can. I unlatched the empty can, hefted another into place, and loaded a new belt. An AK still flashed low in the tree line. Five, six more bursts. Another AK, farther to the left. The fifty's heavy rounds were ripping up the trees.

Then something exploded in the hatch. It felt like a baseball bat slammed into my right leg just below the knee. Had the last round in the belt exploded in the half-open breech, cutting my leg with a shard of brass? Or had a VC ricocheted a bullet through the open hatch? *Shit*. Didn't matter. I was okay.

Beside me in the other track the gun on hatch ring was spinning to our rear. My buddy was engaging a VC crouching in the rice paddy *behind us* with his caliber 50.

"We're outta here, Tom," he radioed.

I loaded a third ammo can as the driver slammed into gear, and we roared up the road toward Binh Phuoc.

My leg was numb when we arrived. I pulled up the cuff of my fatigues, swabbed some iodine on my calf, and taped a square of gauze over the wound.

I flopped down in the damp wind of the pedestal fan in Bandido Charlie's "club"—a cubicle in one of the company hooches—and chugged the first icy beer in three gulps.

"How'd it go out there?" Lieutenant Charlie Taylor asked.

"A little contact," I said. "Assholes tried to sucker-punch us with a sniper. One more soul for Buddha. . . . By the way, you hear about this Aggie cadet from El Paso in a French whorehouse . . . ?"

"Hey, Tom. Look at the floor."

There was a puddle of blood as wide as a garbage can lid around my right boot.

THE MEDIC HAD ME ON THE INFIRMARY TABLE, SHINING A BRIGHT light on the leg as he squeezed a pressure compress. "Gotta probe that wound," he said, reaching back to a tray for a shiny steel poker. "This might smart a little."

Tap. Tap. He had the probe about four inches down in my calf muscle. Tap tap tap. The leg was no longer numb. There could have been a red-hot rod inside.

"Oh, *fuck*," I gasped.

"You got a chunk of something in there, LT. Piece of metal."

As the dust-off Huey flew southwest through the cool night toward the 3rd Surgical Hospital at Dong Tam, the morphine began to work. More bright lights. Medicine smells. Tired nurses. Some poor kid on a stretcher next to me, his head a ball of bloody green field dressings. My leg was swollen badly, but the morphine floated me away. I came out of surgery with invisible hammers pounding in my head and leg. Didn't want to puke in front of that good-looking nurse.

A surgeon with plastic GI glasses held up a twisted piece of steel with forceps. "Souvenir, Lieutenant. We had to cut pretty deep to get it. Damn lucky you didn't bleed out in your track. Still a risk of infection, so we're evacing you to the 3rd Field Hospital in Saigon."

More cool night air though an open Huey door. The pain came and went. The war did not. I started to shake.

I wasn't Balls-for-the-Queen invincible anymore.

The whirring overhead fans kept the ward cool, but played hell with the tinsel on the plastic Christmas tree. Breakfast had been early that morning. Orderlies changed the linen, and Vietnamese workers scrubbed down the floors and walls. Bob Hope's USO show swept through the hospital before lunch. My leg still had two drainage tubes, so I couldn't hobble out to a chair in the courtyard where the performance took place. Instead they rolled several beds down to the end of the corridor and opened the double doors so we could listen. The echoes were bad, and I couldn't understand the jokes. I fell asleep with the rock music pounding off the walls.

Some time later, I opened my eyes. Back in the ward. Someone was sitting on the side of the bed.

"Hi, Lieutenant." Her voice was soft. She was beautiful: long auburn hair on her bare shoulders, a little yellow-and-white sundress with a skirt that ended in the middle of her smooth, tan thighs. She leaned forward. I fought the temptation to scan her voluptuous body; I think I lost. "Merry Christmas," she said, then moved to the next bed. I was wide awake now.

That night, a Red Cross volunteer brought a tape recorder on wheels into the ward, so that we could all make a ten-minute tape for our families. I sent mine to Cathy. My leg was healing fine, I assured her. The Bob Hope show had been "fantastic." I missed her. And, oh, yes, a pretty movie star—her name was "Rachel Wells," I thought—had come to sit on my bed.

Thirty-seven years later, when Cathy and I met her in 2002 at the White House Correspondents' Dinner, Raquel Welch was still beautiful.

IN JANUARY 1968, WHEN I LEFT THE HOSPITAL, I WAS REASSIGNED AS an XO to Delta Battery 204 Artillery, an experimental unit that deployed lightweight M-102 Airborne 105 mm howitzers into the rice paddies, mounting the guns on large metal platforms kept level by four adjustable legs. Huge CH-54 Skycrane helicopters, looking like prehistoric insects, would lift the platforms out into flat, muddy terrain. And after the gun crews jacked down the legs to level the platforms, the choppers would return with the cannons and nets full of ammo crates.

Because my leg was still at risk of infection, I could not slog through the mud and leeches as a forward observer with the line companies. But I wasn't satisfied sitting on my ass back at the Battalion FDC in Tan An—where, in theory, I could keep my leg dry. So I jumped at the chance to get on the firing platforms with the guns. It was tough work: The dry-season sun turned the platforms into skillets. You could feel the heat through the cleated soles of your jungle boots.

When the enemy sprang the Tet Offensive in February 1968, the NVA and VC attacked every city, major town, and most of the fire bases in South Vietnam. Don't ask me where Delta Battery was on any particular day or night; we were lifted into one mess after another, sweating through the chain-gang labor of setting up and firing in support of besieged American and ARVN base camps. We slept when we could, which was not often, and broke our backs moving the Battery from one site to another, over and over again.

The VC didn't like us a bit. We put fire on the mangrove tangles and bamboo patches, where he'd holed up safely for years.

No sweat if my leg got wet and puffy, if the lymph glands in my crotch swelled up a little and I ran a fever. I was doing what seemed right: attacking the enemy with fast, accurate fire. The NVA and VC had launched their offensive to inflict maximum casualties on the Americans and ARVN, choosing to accelerate the grinding war of attrition, testing our firepower . . . and our willpower.

Back at Binh Phuoc, cannoneers worked in the gun pits shirtless, often without helmets, their flak jackets stacked nearby. Body armor was just too hot and awkward when you were manning the guns. But in Delta Battery, my new Battery commander, Captain Bill Bowen, insisted that the crews wear shirts, flak jackets, and helmets. Bill Bowen was a smart and dedicated officer, but he sure didn't understand troop psychology—or so I thought.

One day, after the captain flew off to survey the next firing site, the troops turned to me. "Hey, LT, we gotta keep all this shit on?"

"Go ahead and take it off."

When Captain Bowen returned an hour later, he told the soldiers to put their gear back on. Then he led me aside and tore a strip out of my ass for breaking procedure.

I was humiliated, frustrated. "Captain, you countermanded my order. You make me look like a fool in front of the troops."

He stared into my eyes. "Lieutenant Franks, when you learn to do your job, I won't have to do it for you. Being a good officer isn't running in a popularity contest."

I hated that ass-chewing. But I never forgot it. In fact, I followed his advice for the next thirty-five years.

That afternoon we were set up in the high reeds near the Bo Bo Canal, one of the main NVA infiltration roots from Cambodia. I sent word to all the platforms: henceforth, every swinging dick would wear his shirt, flak jacket, and steel pot. The troops greeted the news with sullen grousing; I knew they were pissed off, but they did as they were told.

After midnight, a Vietcong company waded silently toward the platforms, pushing boats loaded with RPGs. The fight was fast and particularly brutal. We'd made sure our M-60s were covering the perimeter, and that the guns could lay down Beehive rounds in a full circle. As red and green tracers slashed back and forth, the howitzer crews cranked down the tubes to zero elevation. Each gun fired Beehive independently, the flames glaring off the dark water as thousands of flechettes ripped up the paddies.

We killed a stack of VC in that frantic thirty minutes. And our own losses were light—a few troopers with minor wounds, but nothing requiring a dust off. All those sweaty helmets and flak jackets had stopped a lot of RPG fragments and AK ricochets. As we worked under the weight of the sun the next morning, I didn't hear a word of complaint.

A WEEK LATER, THE BATTERY MOVED TO A NEW FIREBASE FARTHER south. The first night we were in the new position, an enemy mortar round hit one of our ammo bunkers, and the enemy rushed that corner of the perimeter. The wire had been blown down, and smoke was rolling out of the smoldering heaps of sandbags. I pulled a few men from the gun crews and established a stopgap perimeter behind some trucks. With rifles and grenades, we held the line.

During the firefight, though, a 105 round cooked off in the rubble, and I got some fragments in my hands and arms. It wasn't a serious injury, but the Battalion ordered me back to Tan An on a light-duty assignment. My hands were bandaged, and I was still limping a bit, but I didn't like the idea of becoming a REMF (Rear Echelon Mother Fucker) while all my troops were fighting.

So I became an aerial observer—the flying version of an FO.

T HE O-1 BIRD DOG WAS A SINGLE-ENGINE CESSNA; THE PILOT SAT in front, the observer behind him. The high wing and wide windows provided an excellent view. And since the little plane cruised around 100 mph, the terrain below unfolded slowly, giving the observer plenty of time to scan. For the first few days I found it difficult to mark target coordinates from the air; I was used to the paddy-level perspective. But after a week or so, I got used to the job. Charlie took pot shots at us, but the old plane was built to take punishment. Droning along in the relatively cool air a couple thousand feet above the green-and-tan mosaic of paddies and scrub jungle, with canals and mangrove creeks twisting off into the haze, I regained my sense of don't-give-a-shit invulnerability.

And our pilots also displayed a certain contempt for danger. One guy—we called him the Lizard—flew like an old barnstormer. "Want to see the best way to lose altitude fast?" he called back on the intercom one morning in March.

"Sure. Why not?"

The brown line of the horizon flipped over as the plane turned upside down. Suddenly I was staring *up* at the paddies. My binoculars floated near my face for a second; I grabbed my map before it drifted out the open window. Now the nose was pointed straight down—and I seemed to weigh about three hundred pounds. "Oh, Jesus!" *This guy is nuts.*

We leveled off at around 200 feet, flying the opposite direction.

"That's what we call a 'Split-S,' " Lizard laughed.

Another day, Lizard's buddy Gator flew me on a long search pattern over the Plain of Reeds. We'd been up for five hours when we spotted a plume of cook-fire smoke from a mangrove swamp where no innocent civilian would be having a picnic. I got all the clearances and called in a fire mission from a 155 mm battery. The mangroves erupted in smoke and flame and I congratulated myself as we flew at a cool twelve-hundred-foot altitude. On the way back to Tan An, I used one of my empty canteens—marked "Pee" in grease pencil—for its designated purpose. Good thing I did.

"You been over the Tan An Bridge?" Gator asked.

"Only about twenty-five times," I said.

"Well," he shouted, looking back over his shoulder with a wicked grin. "Bet you never been *under* it."

He pulled a harsh Split-S, and suddenly our landing gear was about ten inches above the muddy river water. The low trestle bridge filled the windscreen. For a second, I considered popping open my door and jumping—without a parachute. Then the bottom of the bridge was directly overhead and we were out the other side, climbing above the hooches and sandbagged guard posts.

"That's good practice, Tom," he shouted. "Sometimes you want to get down below the canal banks if Charlie's shooting at you."

If I make it back to the airfield, I thought, *a beer's going to taste mighty good . . . followed by a few shots of Wild Turkey.*

The Lizard also taught me how to drop Mason jar bombs—an old Korean War trick. Out on the strip one morning, I watched him line up six one-pint Mason jars in the shade of the wing. He then plucked six oval M-26 fragmentation grenades from his helmet bag.

"You gotta make sure the bottom of the spoon's down inside the jar before you pull the pin," he said. I watched as he "loaded" the jars.

Grenades without their pins made me nervous. But, to my amazement, jamming a grenade into a Mason jar would hold the safety lever—the "spoon"—tight against the glass wall of the jar, keeping the four-second fuse from being activated until the jar smashed upon impact. With his first grenade jammed securely into a jar, he pulled the pin, clipped down the rubber-seal lid, and proceeded to assemble the remaining five jars.

Then he put the jars into the bag and handed it to me. "Treat 'em like eggs, Tom. Not a good idea to bang 'em around."

The grenades worked as advertised. As we were flying that afternoon, I heard a call on a 3rd Brigade frequency that an ARVN patrol had tracked some VC into a clump of banana trees. Lizard orbited the target at about a thousand feet, keeping the right wing tilted at a steep angle. I didn't need a Norden bombsight; I just dropped my jars through the sunlight, one after another, and watched them disappear into the green cover. Even from our altitude, we could see the grenades explode.

"Pretty far out, huh?" Lizard asked.

"You bet." This beat the hell out of wading with the leeches.

Just after sunset on another day, we were flying five hundred feet above a wide canal near Tan Tru. We were close to the coastal mangrove swamps, a zone Charlie used to smuggle munitions upriver, and sunset was the official curfew for boat traffic. We spotted a long black sampan slipping up the canal in the last of the twilight.

Lizard chopped the throttle, and we glided down quietly. My two jars landed close to the centerline of the sampan. There was a satisfying blast of secondary explosions as the grenades set off the ordnance concealed under a tarp.

"Owe you a beer," Lizard shouted.

"Damn right. I—" The plane jolted and yawed hard, as if we'd run over a tree trunk on a road. The plane was followed by wobbling tracers as Lizard dove. "Great job," I said. "He missed us."

"Not quite," Lizard yelled. "The sonofabitch shot our right wheel clean off."

I leaned out into the slipstream. Sure as hell, the right landing gear strut was cut halfway down as if by giant tin snips.

"Gonna be an interesting landing," Lizard commented.

I scrunched down on the flak jacket I always sat on, while Lizard radioed Tan An to get the crash trucks ready. As he banked south for a long, slow approach, I tugged my harness down so tight my arms went numb. The lights of the base rose as Lizard kept the plane nose-high, left wing down. Soon we were over the runway—fifteen feet, then ten. The left main gear and tail wheel touched the strip at the same second. I held my breath as Lizard nursed the stick and throttle, somehow keeping the right wing from jamming down to flip us until he'd bled off the speed. When the inevitable ground loop came, it was violent, but not catastrophic. This Bird Dog would live to hunt again.

That night in the Tan An club, I treated the pilots to shots and beers.

ONCE MY LEG HAD HEALED, I RETURNED TO BINH PHUOC AS THE 5th Battalion Artillery liaison officer, in charge of the four companies' FOs. Lieutenant Colonel Eric Antila had taken command of the Battalion. He was a quiet officer in his forties, a post–World War II Army draftee who'd later graduated from West Point. Since then, he'd earned a graduate degree in nuclear physics and was working on his Ph.D.

I had never met an intellect of Antila's caliber. But he also proved to be a brave and decisive combat leader.

"Franks," he greeted me that first morning at Battalion head-quarters on the far side of the Binh Phuoc ville. There was a leather-bound collection of poetry on his bookshelf, and a handful of small prints that I vaguely recognized as French impressionist paintings on the rough plank walls. "What do they call you, Tommy or Tom?"

"Usually Tom, Sir."

He smiled. "Okay, Tom. They say you know something about fire support." He leafed though the brown folder of my personnel file. "And your Artillery battalion commander, Bob Dirmeyer, calls you a 'young hero.' What do you think of that?"

"Well, Sir . . ." I began, my face growing hot under the six-month tan. "I just do my job."

"Tom, courage *is* our job. We are responsible to set the example for our soldiers. I hope to live up to the example that young officers like you and Lee Alley have set in 5-60."

In the nine months that Lee Alley had served in the Battalion, he had led troops through some of the heaviest fighting seen by any unit in Vietnam. Our previous Battalion commander, Lt. Colonel William Steele, had recommended Lee for the Medal of Honor after he saved wounded members of his Recon Platoon under intense fire and rallied the defenders of a firebase that hundreds of Viet Cong almost overran in November.

"Lee Alley is major league, Sir. I'm second-string farm club."

"They drink martinis on your farm club, Tom?"

"I tasted them a couple of times in college, Sir."

He smiled again. "Good. Because I do enjoy a Beefeater martini, and you and I are going to be spending a lot of time together."

That morning, in Eric Antila's office, I started one of the most important leadership schools I ever attended.

ON A WEDNESDAY AFTERNOON IN MARCH, I COMMANDED A track in the reaction force that Lee Alley led out of a new firebase south of Binh Phuoc on Highway 4. We got a call that a Battalion M-113 had been destroyed by a mine on the way to Cai Lay. The road was wide and fairly smooth, running along a berm above dry, weedy paddies. This was the heart of Indian Country, a sector where most of the men served full time in main force Vietcong units.

What we found could have been an image from Dante's *Inferno*— a book Eric Antila had recently convinced me to read, in an effort to "expand my mind."

The smoking crater was ten feet deep and at least as wide. Twisted pieces of the track stuck out of the hole, like the shreds of tin cans we'd blown up with cherry bombs out in the dry gullies around Midland. But a thirteen-ton armored personnel carrier was no stewed tomato can. This blast had been so powerful that the vehicle's big diesel engine and its prow were blown forty feet in opposite directions.

Climbing down to the rutted dirt, I couldn't believe I was looking at the remains of a track. Lee Alley dismounted and stood beside my driver and me. Lee's face was twisted with cold rage, his eyes narrow.

"That had to be at least 500 pounds of HE," he said, staring at the debris field. "The bastards probably planted an unexploded Air Force bomb and fused it with a blasting cap."

"Who was gunning it, Sir?" my driver asked.

"Lieutenant Bahr," Lee said softly.

First Lieutenant Dick Bahr was one of the more experienced platoon leaders in Charlie Company. As we stood at the edge of the crater, troops from the tracks behind us fanned out silently, beginning the search for the dead. For a moment I was rooted in place; then I forced myself to move, one boot in front of the other.

There had been five men on that track with Dick Bahr. One of them, the driver, had been thrown clear; he died with his body in one piece, curled on the dry mud about twenty feet away on the other side of the crater.

But the other soldiers had been blown into pieces. I advanced slowly with the troops along the edge of the berm, down into the green scum of the ditch water. A severed head bobbed on the surface, face down. The hair had been cut short, almost like a recruit in Basic.

"One of the new guys," a soldier whispered.

A naked arm from the elbow down was stuck on the muddy bank, already covered by flies. "Got a wedding ring," another soldier said. He reached down and cradled the arm in the bunched poncho he carried to collect body parts.

I climbed the bank and found part of a soldier's right leg, the foot still in the tightly laced jungle boot. Up on the berm beside the crater, the stench of high explosives, burnt flesh, and blood made me dizzy. I crossed the road like a zombie and helped the troops in the other ditch collect pieces of the dead men.

I have no idea how long we were out there. It might have been minutes. It felt like days. When it was over, we had three soggy ponchos laced up with green parachute cord through the grommets. Lumpy sacks of heavy meat.

As we lugged the ponchos to the ramp of Lee's track, a small crowd of Vietnamese civilians stood ten meters away, staring, their faces blank.

"Cocksuckers," a trooper swore, glaring at the peasants. "They had to see who planted that mine. We oughta take one of these bastards and zap him. That would make 'em talk."

I watched the farmers' faces. These people knew who planted that bomb. But had *they* planted it? Was it that old lady in the mismatched plastic sandals, her mouth stained red with betel juice? Or the guy with the twisted arm, who dug under the culvert so his buddies could slide in the long, heavy cylinder of the bomb? Maybe we were looking at a VC sapper squad, dressed up like peasants. If one of them pulled a grenade from under his long shirt, we'd be justified in killing them all.

No, these peasants were terrified. The VC controlled all these hamlets. I remembered a little village the other side of Dong Tam, where Army medics had vaccinated the kids against measles. One night the Vietcong came in and chopped off those children's arms—retribution for cooperating with the Imperialist enemy. The peasants on this road were not the enemy . . . they were the victims.

I turned away and closed my eyes, struggling not to choke on the stench and my own sour hatred. When I looked back, the peasants were walking away.

Six more months in this country.

AFTER WE'D DONE EVERYTHING WE COULD AT THE M-113 CRATER, Lt. Colonel Antila ordered us back to Binh Phuoc. The men were too stunned, too full of rage against anything or anybody Vietnamese to fight effectively. As the Graves Registration men removed the dead from Lee Alley's track, Antila walked along the line of tracks parked inside the base perimeter, calm, balanced, but obviously full of sorrow. He looked at all of us, then he looked at our tracks.

"These vehicles need maintenance," he said. "We just got in a shipment of new batteries and engine parts. That's your job for the next week. You'll be going back on ops, but not right away."

Some officers would have demanded an explanation for the disaster, or sought to shift the blame onto the dead themselves. But Eric Antila faced the tragedy with composure; he was concerned about his soldiers, not himself.

"You men did well," he said in the same soft tone as he walked along silently, hands clasped behind his back. "What happened today was not your fault. I am very sorry you lost your friends. The Chaplain's coming down from Tan An, and we'll have a memorial service tomorrow at 0800."

I studied Eric Antila's eyes. I knew he was gripped by anguish, but he never let it show. We were at war; he was commanding troops in combat. And his quiet resolve in meeting this catastrophe gave us all strength. In an hour he would grieve, but now he stood rock solid. *In war, it is necessary that commanders be able to delay their emotions until they can afford them.*

B ONDI BEACH WAS COOL AND SUNNY THAT THURSDAY MORNING in April, as I stood at the open window of the hotel bathroom, gazing down as water ran in the sink. I flushed the toilet, then flushed it again. *Fantastic.* A plastic ice tub filled with tall cans of Foster's beer stood on the wicker table beside the sink. Unlike the PX beer in Vietnam, these cans had the new pop-top tabs—a miracle, like hot and cold running water, like the fat steak I'd had for dinner the night before, my first evening of rest and recuperation (R&R).

I had slept on the Qantas Boeing all the way from Saigon's Tan Son Nhut Airport to Singapore. Then I had opened a handful of little bottles of airline bourbon and slept again, waking only when the jet's wheels screeched onto the runway at Sydney.

The wrinkled taxi driver announced he was a vet of Tobruk, where the Aussies had fought Romel's Afrika Korps, and asked if the Yanks were "thumping" the enemy in Vietnam. I assured him we were, which he said was "bloody bonzer"—I thought that must mean good.

The driver also declared that my hotel would be "swimming with beach Sheilas," girls from the nearby colleges spending one of the last warm autumn weekends in the sun. He was right.

A whole week in Australia. Seven nights and days. I was going to taste every minute. Hot showers. Ice cold Foster's. Steak three times a day. And those "Sheilas."

The week passed too quickly. Sitting in Sydney Airport, I was almost ready to climb on that jet and head back to the war. Australia, I'd decided, was the best country in the world. Perfect in every way. The beaches were clean and white. The food was incredible, and cheap. And I'd even learned to drink dry red wine with roast lamb. The American dollar was worth almost two-to-one against Aussie money. When I hit DEROS, I could take the money I'd saved, fly back down here, and just live for a couple of years. I'd enroll in the university and become a lawyer—a barrister, they called them.

That was my plan. But there was one catch: I had to break the news to Cathy. I wiped off the table and opened a piece of blue-and-red Airgram stationery.

"Dear Cathy," I wrote. "This is not easy, so I will get right to the point . . ." I was going to live in Australia, I told her; we would have to break the engagement. I was sorry, but things would all work out for the best.

I folded the letter, dropped it in the crimson pillar-box, and opened my last Foster's.

Of course, there was another catch in my perfect plan. I had to live through the rest of my tour in Vietnam.

"FIVE ZERO," THE VOICE SOUNDED IN MY RIGHT EARPHONE. "Rainbow Four. Say again your target coordinates."

The man speaking in my left earphone was Iron Horse Six, one of the Battalion's company commanders; his unit was in heavy contact down in the smoky string of houses, factories, and warehouses bunched along the south bank of the Kinh Doi Canal. With the May sun pouring through the little chopper's plastic bubble, even at 1,200 feet the cramped cockpit was an oven. Eric Antila and I had been riding in these H-23 Raven Command-and-Control helicopters for the first three days of this seemingly endless engagement. In the H-23, the pilot flew from the center of the narrow bench, the commander to his left, and the Artillery Liaison Officer to the right.

There wasn't sufficient radio capacity for me to communicate with both the infantry companies maneuvering below and the Artillery batteries who were providing their fire support. So in the two months I'd been flying as Antila's Battalion LNO, I'd developed my own Rube Goldberg communications system. I wired the right earphone in my green aircrew helmet to the PRC-25 radio gripped between my knees, which was tuned to the Artillery fire support channel. My left earphone was wired to the helicopter comm channel, which the Colonel used to talk to his company commanders and platoon leaders; my helmet mike was wired to the ground-unit "maneuver" frequency; and I used the PRC-25 handset to reach fire support. At first trying to work this jerry-rigged system was like being split down the middle, but I'd gotten used to it.

And a damn good thing, too. The battle, which had been raging along the Canal and through Saigon's southern districts, was the biggest engagement since February's Tet Offensive. In fact, at dawn that morning, before we climbed aboard the chopper, I'd heard someone on Armed Forces Radio calling the fight a "Second Tet." At least five NVA and Vietcong battalions had moved north through the rice paddies and assaulted a small ARVN Regional Force guard post at the long concrete Y span across the wide shipping canal—the "Y-Bridge."

Acting on intelligence, Lt. Colonel Antila had moved the Battalion and all its tracks north on the afternoon of May 6. Before daylight the next morning, the companies were engaged in street fighting with well-armed and well-trained enemy troops. The NVA and VC were determined to cross the bridge and fight their way four kilometers north into the heart of the capital.

That first morning, our battalion had engaged the superior enemy force alone on the south side of the Canal. But the 9th Division had fed more and more battalions into the fight, while all the LNOs and their commanders buzzed overhead, working fire support. In the Battalion's sector, I called in probably a hundred fire missions and air strikes, pounding the enemy among pastel-stucco cinderblock houses and factories. This had been a prosperous, pro-government district, built largely with American aid, a showcase of progress. I regretted destroying this neighborhood, but the enemy was using these buildings to fire RPGs, machine guns, and recoilless rifles down on our troops.

By the second day, I was directing the fires of as many as five artillery battalions. The Air Force was flying nonstop support from nearby Tan Son Nhut. And the combination of artillery fire and 500-pound bombs was devastating the enemy.

May 10 was day three. The previous night had been relatively quiet—just mortars and 107s every hour or so to keep us awake—but Charlie was back in force at dawn. By 1040 hours, the companies were maneuvering south along a main road, attempting to encircle the VC dug into the ruins of what had been an industrial complex.

I was running on canteens of coffee—and a total of roughly three hours' sleep in the past four nights and days.

"Five Zero," the battery FDC called again in my right earphone. "Did not copy target coordinates, over."

I shook myself awake and studied the plastic-covered mapboard on my lap. "Foxtrot Tango Four Six Five Eight Seven Four, over."

We were hovering right above the target—the safest place, because our incoming artillery shells would drop past our helicopter on an angle. Holding a hover exposed us to intermittent ground fire, but it couldn't be helped.

In any event, flying with Lt. Colonel Antila was always exciting. The man was fearless. Late the previous afternoon, we'd taken a machine gun round right in the bubble canopy. Antila just leaned over and shouted in the roar of the slipstream: "Tom, I don't know about *you*, but this makes *me* nervous."

"Shot, over," the battery called. A volley of shells was on its way to the targets immediately below us.

I closed my eyes for a second, images of my life rushing through my mind like a vivid, fragmented dream—driving down to Mexico with my fraternity brothers, the radio blaring Hank Williams. I was trying to tell one of my complicated Aggie jokes, but the music was too loud. . . .

"*Splash, over,*" the voice sounded.

Five seconds till impact. I closed my eyes again: Now I was working with my father, stripping down an old Evinrude outboard—or a tractor transmission, connected to a truck, that was somehow part of an electric generator. *She's a tough one, Tommy Ray. . . .*

I opened my eyes, squinting against the sun. The 155 mm shells exploded forty meters south and sixty meters east of the target. "Left five zero. Add five zero, over," I called.

As the battery acknowledged, my left earphone squawked with a frantic call from a forward observer with one of the companies.

"Heavy contact." They were taking RPG fire from a warehouse beside the highway.

I leaned close to my map and found the coordinates. Checking my clipboard, I identified the nearest battery, a 105 fire base ten klicks down the road. "In contact. Fire mission . . ." When I called the target coordinates, I added Eric Antila's authorizing initials, "Echo Alpha." Since the first day of the fight, he had told me to use his authorization without consulting him whenever one of the units was in contact. They had been in contact continuously, and I had used the initials Echo Alpha repeatedly.

Short of fuel, we landed in a field near the canal and staggered to another H-23. I had just enough time to take a leak and drink some more cold coffee.

By late afternoon the enemy attack had broken, and our tracks sped south down the highway firing at small groups of VC and NVA fleeing into the newly flooded second-crop rice paddies.

I WOKE UP WHEN THE HUEY FROM U.S. ARMY VIETNAM HEAD-quarters clattered in to land at the Battalion command post. The fighting had been over for four days. Eric Antila was up at Division with the other Battalion commanders, reporting on the engagement. A two-star general and two colonels climbed out of the helicopter and asked for the 5-60 Artillery LNO.

I buttoned my shirt and saluted. None of the senior officers shook my hand; nor did they smile, or exchange the usual pleasantries. One of the colonels was from the Inspector General's office; the other was a JAG lawyer. He presented a printed form and directed me to swear that my statement was voluntary, true, and complete.

What the fuck's all this about?

Half an hour later, as we drove from blasted house to shattered factory, I'd begun to figure it out.

"What hit this building?" the IG colonel asked, pointing at a ruined warehouse beside the canal.

"Five-hundred-pound high-drag bomb, Sir," I answered.

"And you ordered the air strike?"

"Yes, Sir."

The questions were all the same. We spent an hour driving through the area, reviewing targets on which I had ordered fire missions, or air strikes, or both. By the end of that hour I realized what was going on: These sour-faced senior REMFs were looking for someone to court-martial for employing excessive force in case there was trouble over the destruction of this district on the outskirts of Saigon.

And every time we stopped, either the General or one of the colonels would ask: "And you are *sure* that the unit you supported was in contact?"

It looked like I might be going to DEROS sooner than expected—wearing handcuffs.

We were examining a burned-out house near the command post when Lt. Colonel Antila's muddy jeep pulled up. He saluted the officers and walked along with us as we continued the inspection of the ruined buildings.

After he'd heard two of the team's formally phrased queries, Eric Antila stepped between the general and me. "Sir," he said quietly, looking the man right in the eye. "Those are excellent questions. But you're asking the wrong man. The duty log will reflect that every fire mission and air strike was cleared by Echo Alpha—Eric Antila. Lieutenant Franks simply relayed my orders."

The General squinted at Antila, then looked at me. "Lieutenant, you are dismissed," he finally said. Then he turned to the JAG lawyer, who swore in Lt. Colonel Antila.

Over the years, I have replayed that drama in my mind thousands of times. And I've learned more about Lt. Colonel Antila since that hot afternoon along the Kinh Doi Canal. He had been slated for retirement following this tour, a combat tour that he had specifically requested from his desk job as a nuclear weapons officer in Europe. He didn't have to risk his life in Vietnam. And he certainly didn't have to risk a court martial, a dishonorable discharge, and the loss of his pension to take care of an OCS lieutenant.

During my months in combat, I'd come to understand that a soldier owes loyalty to his unit and to his boss. A leader must be able to count on the complete support of his subordinates. As Eric Antila climbed into that jeep and assumed full responsibility for my actions during the Battle of the Y Bridge, however, I realized that loyalty not only flows up the chain of command: It flows *down* as well.

Eric Antila retired from the Army as a colonel, shortly after having bravely commanded one of the best battalions in Vietnam. I loved and respected him until his death in 2003. And all he taught me at the Y Bridge lives on to this day.

O N A SOUPY MONSOON NIGHT IN AUGUST 1968, I SAT AT A PLANK table in our makeshift club at Binh Phuoc, sipping bourbon and Blue Ribbon beer.

"My Cathy," I carefully printed on the notepaper. "In a drunken stupor, I write this thing. The last ordeal is beginning . . ."

I described my new assignment, flying as a scout in an OH-6 Light Observation Helicopter ("Loach"). I was replacing an officer who had been killed that day, and I was scared. Less than three months to DEROS, and my new assignment was one of the most dangerous jobs in Vietnam.

Since coming to my senses after the Y Bridge, I'd written Cathy whenever I'd had the chance. I wanted us to be engaged again. If I lived through this, I wanted to marry her. My Australian fantasy had been the pipe dream of a selfish young lieutenant trying to squeeze every last second of life out of his first week away from combat. But Cathy had cut me no slack. Could I blame her? Probably not.

I drank whiskey and beer and kept printing. "My Cathy, do what you will, but please pray for me. This is worse than anything I've ever done over here. . . . Please write to me when you can. I love you with all my being."

I licked the envelope—my tongue still sticky with booze—and then staggered back to my hooch to pack my gear for the morning chopper.

TIGER THREE-FIVE WAS THE RED BARON'S HELICOPTER, A stripped-down green Loach that we flew as the low element in a "Pink Team"—a three-aircraft package that included an OH-6 flying close to the ground, and two attack helicopters flying at higher altitudes. *Low* was the operative word. While two Huey or AH-1 Cobra gunships orbited overhead, the Baron would twirl his waxed red handlebar mustache and grin like a pirate.

"Let's go down and cut some grass, Tom."

Whipping along below treetop level at ninety knots was an interesting way to see Vietnam. The Baron's theory was that we were such a small, fast target that Charlie couldn't easily hit us—and when he tried we could usually spot his tracers, allowing the gunships to kill him or fix him in place while I called in artillery fire.

For six weeks of almost daily contact, the Baron's technique worked just fine. But we ran out of luck late one afternoon among the scrub jungle and bomb craters out near Cambodia. We'd been trolling along a tree line when something heavy slammed into the helicopter right behind our heads. Every red warning light on the Loach's panel flashed, and our earphones sounded with alarms. He hauled back on the cyclic, but we sank to the left.

"Tiger Four, this is the Baron," he called the guns overhead, his voice improbably calm. "Can't control the aircraft. We're going in."

We hit the top of a muddy rice-paddy dike at an angle and bounced once, the skids snapping off with a tearing screech. The little chopper came to rest upright, but listing to the left. I'd bruised my shoulder and cheek banging against the doorframe, but was otherwise unhurt. As I hit my quick-release harness with my right hand, I reached under the seat for my CAR-15 rifle. AK-47 rounds snapped into the mud around us.

"Get the fuck out," the Baron shouted.

I had my weapon, a bandoleer of ammo, and a helmet bag full of M-26 fragmentation grenades. Pounding toward a big bomb crater, I looked back to see the Baron limping behind me. He'd smashed his left leg on the control pedals when we'd hit.

As we dove into the crater, neither of us had a helmet. I'd left the radio in the wrecked chopper. I was winded from the sprint, my mouth felt like sandpaper, and the Baron winced with pain. When I peeked over the crater rim, I saw several VC in black pajamas and web gear running toward us from the trees about two hundred meters away.

Still panting, I flipped the CAR-15's selector switch to Automatic and let off a long burst. The VC dropped like sacks.

The gunships appeared out of the sunset, firing their mini-guns and launching four-rocket salvos.

As soon as they passed overhead, more VC fired from the trees behind us. The Baron was up now, shooting his CAR-15. I guarded the right front, and he covered the left rear. In five minutes, we burned up half our ammo. But still the VC maneuvered toward us, using the cover of the paddy dikes. With the sun so low, the gunships couldn't see the enemy in the long shadows. But every time we stuck our heads up, they'd fire. Then we'd fire. Then they'd fire again.

"How's your ammo holding out?" I asked the Baron.

"Three mags. You?"

I squeezed the green cotton bandoleer. "Two left."

Mosquitoes were rising in clouds now in the lulls between VC fire, a sure sign of nightfall. As the top of the crater snapped with enemy rounds, we hunkered down and prayed that the gunships above us would make another pass and get lucky. But without a radio we had no way to direct them toward the enemy, now less than thirty meters away.

"Frag time," I said, pulling the pin on a grenade.

"Roger that," the Baron answered.

A long time passed. I had less than one 20-round magazine left for the CAR-15, and four grenades.

I patted my .45 automatic. A lot of good that would do.

Lying back against the mud, I stared up at the sky. Three weeks to DEROS, and this was the end of the line. The VC crawling toward us through the dark had their own grenades. How soon before a couple dropped into our hole?

They'd take us prisoner if we ran out of ammo. I'd heard enough stories about what the VC did to helicopter crews they captured. I slipped my .45 out of the holster and chambered a round.

I will not die a prisoner.

This was the end of Tom Franks. No Cathy. No college degree. Sure as hell no happily ever after.

"Sonofabitch," I muttered.

Suddenly an OH-6 whined down to a hover beside the crater as the gunships crossed in front of and behind us, chopping up the dikes.

The Baron grabbed the hovering helicopter's right skid and hauled himself in. I scrambled into the left side. The dark paddies and the lighter mud of the bomb craters fell away.

As we climbed, the pilot headed due east, away from the enemy, away from the orange sunset over Cambodia.

PART II

PROFESSIONAL SOLDIER

If you know your enemy and know yourself, you need not fear the result of a hundred battles.

—SUN TZU

4

A NEW ARMY

I spent the next two weeks at home with my parents in Austin. Long, hot showers. My father's charcoaled steaks. My mother's cherry pie with ice cream. *Yes, Ma'am, I'd love another piece.*

I slept under clean sheets, the window open to the cool breeze. No mosquito net, no sandbags, no illumination rounds—no Mad Minute.

As the saying goes, I decompressed.

But the war had reached America—and so had the counterculture. I watched campus demonstrations on television almost every night. If a crowd of students wasn't chanting about legalizing marijuana, they were waving Vietcong flags.

The last VC flag I'd seen was in the ruins of an enemy bunker out in the Plain of Reeds, after I called in twenty-four rounds of 155 mm on the target.

I went down to the DU house only once. All the brothers I'd been close to had graduated, so I didn't have much in common with the guys I met. *Was I ever that young?* I wondered.

Raking leaves in my folks' yard one bright fall morning, I thought about the future. In less than a year, I'd be a civilian. I was feeling ready, at last, to get a degree, perhaps even go to law school. But it

wouldn't be easy sitting in class beside guys who'd used student defer-
ments to protest the war, while blue-collar kids who never made it to
college were out on listening posts or humping the paddies in the
Delta sun.

One evening after dinner, Mother helped me with my dress uniform as I prepared to report for duty at Fort Sill—my next duty assignment. She sewed the colorful 9th Infantry Division patch on the
shoulder of the right sleeve, designating that I'd served in combat
with the unit. My dad came into the kitchen and watched as I pinned
on the campaign ribbons and decorations.

"Those are oak leaf clusters." I tapped the little pins on the ribbons. "For second or third awards of the same medal."

In his deliberate way, he counted. "*Three* Purple Hearts."

"I was a big target." I'd actually been wounded several more
times; the Purple Hearts only signified the wounds for which I'd been
sent to the hospital.

"And all these medals with the 'V'?"

"V stands for valor, Dad. . . . Bronze Stars, Air Medals, Army
Commendation Medals. They sort of gave them out in Cracker Jack
boxes."

"I don't believe that, son." He ran his hand down the green serge
of my uniform. "We're so proud of you."

The television was playing in the living room. More protests.
Loud, chaotic.

"When we landed back at Travis, they advised us to wear civvies
on the plane ride home. People don't respect the uniform anymore,"
I said.

My father frowned. "*Some* don't. Most people do. You wear it—
and be proud."

"You bet."

I would wear that uniform to Fort Sill, where I'd train young
troopers to stay alive. And then my days as a soldier would be over.
At age twenty-three, it was time to put the war and the Army behind
me, to get on with my life.

But I had a problem. Fifteen days back in the States and I hadn't found the nerve to call Cathy. The last I'd heard from her was a cool note acknowledging the drunken idiocy of my letter on R&R in Sydney. She had sent the engagement ring back to her mother in Lawton for safekeeping, "until you can pick it up." End of engagement. End of story.

No—not the end of the story. The next morning, when my dad was at work and Mother was shopping with a neighbor, I picked up the phone.

The girl who answered at the sorority house promised that Cathy Carley would be right there. I started sweating, like waiting for the splash of an artillery spotting round close to our own position.

"This is Cathy."

Her voice was as I remembered, gentle but strong.

"It's me. Please don't hang up."

"Oh, Tom. I won't hang up. Are you all right?"

"I'm great. Even better now that I'm talking to you. Listen, I'm about to drive up to Oklahoma. Do you think maybe we could have a date?"

The line was silent. Finally, she spoke. "That would be fine, Tom."

CATHY AND I WERE MARRIED IN THE FORT SILL NEW POST CHAPEL on Saturday, March 22, 1969. Her wedding gown was beautiful. I bought a formal dress blue uniform, even though I'd need it for only a few more months since I had promised my new wife I was going to get out of the Army. We left the chapel arm-in-arm, beneath the traditional arch of sabres.

Our first house was a little renter in Lawton, much like the place Glenn Stewart and I had shared when I'd met Cathy. As she finished her student teaching at Lawton High School, I commanded a training battery in the Artillery School. We were both busy, but about as much in love as you can be. Each day, each night, the thought that I might live a long, happy, normal life became more and more real.

As April passed and Cathy began considering where she would teach after she finished her degree in June, I started to think about where I would go to college. Austin was a logical choice, but I had no interest in facing fellow students who might look upon a soldier recently returned from Vietnam with scorn, veiled or otherwise. Lawton and Fort Sill, on the other hand, were firmly pro-military; I'd be treated with deference and respect everywhere I wore my uniform. Maybe Cathy could teach in Lawton and I could finish my degree in Oklahoma. I might even become a rancher and raise cattle with Cathy's Uncle Don and her grandfather Jimmie Ellis—two men I thought of as the brother and granddad I'd never had.

The fact was, though, I loved the Army. *Maybe I can stay in and Cathy can teach . . .* , I thought. *No, I have to get out.* Once Vietnam ended and the Army shrank to its Cold War strength, there wouldn't be much future for an Artillery captain with a grand total of forty-five credit hours of Cs and Ds from the University of Texas. Without a degree, I'd have no career as an officer.

Then, late one afternoon in May, my battalion commander, Lt. Colonel Al Lamas, a former college football star, called me to his office. He'd been reading my ideas about better coordination between Infantry units and the Field Artillery units that supported them. I'd written the report drawing on my experience with Eric Antila and the 5-60, describing the separate-channel radio links I'd set up in the command-and-control helicopter to listen to the maneuvering ground units in one earphone and the Artillery fire bases in the other. And I'd described arming one of the Battalion's M-113 tracks with an electrically driven 7.62 mm minigun I'd picked up from a Navy Swiftboat detachment down at My Tho.

"These are innovative ideas, Tom," Lt. Colonel Lamas said.

"I like to tinker, Sir—to experiment. Guess I got that from my father."

He flipped through my personnel folder. "Your term of service expires in the fall. You plan to go back to school?"

"Yes, Sir, I'll do it right this time. I was just an immature kid when I started college."

"Well, you're mature now, Tom. The Army needs officers like you." He handed me a printed form.

"Degree Completion Program," I read.

"The Army will pay for you to finish college, Tom. And after you graduate, you're obligated to serve two years on active duty for every one that you've spent in school."

I scanned the sheet. This definitely was interesting. But the decision wasn't mine alone. "I'll talk to Cathy."

As I walked back to my office, the loudspeakers around the post were sounding Retreat. I stood at attention, saluting while the bugle sounded and the Colors were lowered on the parade ground. *This is who I am: I'm a soldier.*

O UR DAUGHTER, JACQUELINE, WAS BORN IN MAY 1971, AS I WAS finishing my degree in business administration at the University of Texas, Arlington.

In many ways, the little tasks of parenthood—cradling the baby in my arms, warming a bottle, rocking her back to sleep in the middle of the night—helped put my lingering memories of Vietnam into perspective. I was proud of my profession, but there was so much more to my life than weapons and tactics.

I spent a lot of time studying, squeezing three years of courses into twenty-two months. I was ready to learn, and with Cathy's help I had figured out how to study. The principles of accounting or business law were no sweat compared to spending a night up to my chest in canal water, calling in fire missions from three batteries while working targets with a Spooky gunship. When I graduated in December 1971, I'd racked up twenty-seven As, three Bs, and one lonely C, in marketing—a far different transcript from the one I'd received when I left Austin in 1965.

W ITH TWENTY-MONTH-OLD JACQY IN TOW, CATHY AND I arrived in Germany on a snowy morning in February 1973. A week later, I took command of Howitzer Battery, 1st Squadron, 2nd Armored Cavalry Regiment (ACR). The Battery was stationed at Hans Schemme *kaserne,* a massive old concrete Wermacht barracks in the heart of the Bavarian town of Bayreuth. Now this was something: I was a deployed commander and responsible for my own post. *Ain't this a great country.*

The Army's armored cavalry regiments preserve the traditions of the horse soldiers of the nineteenth century. Instead of battalions and companies, they are comprised of squadrons and troops—hybrid units that combine Armor, Infantry, and Artillery. My time with the 2nd ACR gave me an in-depth understanding of the Army's "maneuver" branches—experience that most Artillery officers never get.

During this tour, I devoted a lot of thought to tactics. In Vietnam I'd become fascinated by the dynamics of combat—moving troops and weapons in the most effective way to put maximum firepower on the enemy. I'd learned the value of mobility while serving in Delta Battery, lifting guns and firing platforms into traditional Viet Cong sanctuaries using helicopters. We'd had only six howitzers, but we'd been able to "take them to the enemy" and pursue him, rapidly shifting from one firing site to another. And, under the protection of those guns, the Infantry units we supported carried the fight into the overgrown canals and reed beds where Charlie thought he was safe.

That experience had given me a glimpse of how effective tactical flexibility could be. But that was one experiment, a small facet of a largely *static* war of attrition. Now, as America's ten-year engagement in Vietnam wound down, I was eager to learn more about *maneuver* warfare—to try my hand at making the system more dynamic.

There was another unusual feature of this new assignment: My Howitzer Battery was separated geographically from its parent organization, the 1st Squadron, which was located near Bindlach, "the Rock," six kilometers northeast of Bayreuth. Serving apart from the daily scrutiny and guidance of my bosses presented opportunities to experiment—opportunities to lead, opportunities to succeed or fail.

When I met the Squadron commander, Lt. Colonel Cal Hosmer, that winter morning in Bindlach, he made it clear that failure was a real possibility in 1973.

Glancing at my personnel file, he noted my time in college and the Artillery Advanced Course back at Fort Sill. "You've been away from soldiers for several years, Captain," Lt. Colonel Hosmer said. "I'm sure you've heard talk about problems in the Army. Well, we're part of that Army and we share those problems. There are bad soldiers in every one of our units. And yours is no exception."

By this point the last of the Vietnam-era draftees were completing their service, and the new all-volunteer Army had not yet taken hold. Like the rest of society, the Army was riddled with drugs. Morale wasn't good, and near-mutinous ill-discipline was rife in some outfits.

"There are rotten apples in your barrel, Captain," Hosmer concluded. "And you're going to have to get rid of them and shape that outfit up before it goes to hell."

"Yes, Sir."

Driving back down the mountain toward the Hansel and Gretel panorama of Bayreuth, I weighed the challenges ahead. The Battery was built around six M-109 155 mm self-propelled howitzers—big guns mounted on tracked chassis designed to maneuver with the Regiment's tanks and APCs.

Our area of operations was the Tri-Zonal Sector on the borders of West and East Germany and Czechoslovakia. The 2nd ACR was heavy in armor and artillery, and had several thousand infantrymen. But we were outgunned and outmanned by the Warsaw Pact arrayed on the other side of the Iron Curtain. Allied conventional forces would not prevail against the mass of Soviet tank armies, mechanized infantry, and artillery divisions.

So our defensive doctrine relied on a nuclear tripwire.

The Army had nuclear missiles and artillery down to the battery level, including in my command. There were "low yield" nuclear projectiles for each of the Battery's six guns, stored in a special weapons bunker near Bamberg, twenty miles west of my *kaserne*. During my first week in command, I visited that bunker with the three other officers in the Battery's Personnel Reliability Program, the fail-safe control system that guaranteed atomic weapons would be used only on the direct order of the President. The four of us formed two-man Red and Blue Teams, each carrying one half of the release cipher. If the day ever came when we had to go nuclear, a member of each team would combine ciphers with his counterpart to unlock the Permissive Action Links—large locks on the projectiles—which prevented loading them into the howitzers without presidential approval.

As part of my orientation, the warrant officer working that morning's shift had opened all six projectile cases for inspection. We stood in a circle in the floodlights staring down at the weapons. Had it not been for the markings and PAL on the conical projectiles, they could have been standard 155 mm high explosive rounds. But if the Cold War ever went hot and Soviet tanks rolled over the barbed-wire fences and minefields marking our sector of the border, the dark pines of the Böhmer Wald would have erupted with nuclear explosions. That was a prospect that could keep a twenty-seven-year-old captain awake nights—and it did.

In truth, though, we had concerns more immediate than the threat of an enemy invasion. I spent just as much time worrying about the nuclear weapons inspections to which we were subjected without warning. A cadre of tight-lipped, absolutely-no-bullshit officers from VII Corps, U.S. Army Europe, or the Defense Nuclear Agency would descend on the squadrons, the howitzer batteries, and the storage bunkers. If our state of training, our knowledge of procedures, our record keeping and projectile storage and maintenance did not meet incredibly rigorous standards, we would fail the inspection.

This was the military equivalent of bankruptcy. The Battery commander, the Squadron commander, and perhaps even the colonel commanding the Regiment would be relieved. Our next assignments would probably be as latrine orderlies at a National Guard training camp in northern Wisconsin.

Serving in Germany in the 1970s had its challenges.

Not the least of which was leading an inordinately high number of troops who did not want to be in the Army. Digging out the rotten apples that Lt. Colonel Hosmer had described would be my top priority.

There was no doubt that the Battery was in poor shape. When I'd driven past the guard at the *kaserne* gate that first morning, he was slouched inside the guard booth, rifle leaning against the wall, hands in his pockets. He'd removed a hand to toss off an insolent salute—his *left* hand.

Fortunately, the Army was blessed with a generation of hardworking career sergeants who had served multiple tours in Vietnam, had witnessed the erosion of discipline and morale, knew the ways of soldiers—and hadn't given up on their profession. My First Sergeant was one of these NCOs.

"Officers don't usually go upstairs alone, Sir," he said as we entered a wide corridor that morning. "And they always carry a sidearm. The troops call this Haight Ashbury. A soldier can knock on a couple of these doors and buy as much hash or methamphetamine as he can afford. And most of the dealers give credit until payday."

We continued past the closed doors. "The troopers who are against drugs don't want to be up here," the First Sergeant added.

I'd seen enough.

That afternoon I met with my officers and platoon sergeants. "Things are going to change in this Battery. I want a list of every confirmed or suspected doper and dealer on my desk tomorrow morning."

I needed a plan to combat this behavior. The Battery shared the *kaserne* with an Army Security Agency detachment, which had a robust collection of military intelligence eavesdropping equipment. This gave me an idea, and I took it to the JAG lawyer at Squadron headquarters. He chuckled when he heard it. "Have at it, Captain."

Late the next Friday night I sat at my desk, surrounded by two lieutenants, three sergeants, a squad of armed military policemen (MPs), and an agent from the Criminal Investigation Division (CID). An ASA technician was hunched over a console. The voices from the speaker were scratchy but comprehensible.

"Tony, you're an asshole. But just to end this hassle, I'll pay you two bucks for a nickel bag. And I'll take a hundred."

"It's three dollars a bag," a PFC named Tony said. "And I'm only selling two hundred at a time. I'm a businessman, not some punk on the street."

"You count the money. I count the product."

The tape ran smoothly across the reels of the recorder. In Barracks Room 314, a major deal for methamphetamine was in progress.

"Money is changing hands," the MP lieutenant said, standing up. "We can make an arrest, Sir."

The big MP corporal kicked open the door of Room 314 and the squad moved in. I followed close behind to observe the arrest and make sure the evidence was properly secured.

"You can't bust into a guy's room like that," Tony shouted as the MPs cuffed his wrists. "I know my rights."

The CID agent stood over the footlocker, photographing the heap of tiny cellophane bags of crystal meth and the stacks of fives and tens.

"We just got back from downtown," the buyer protested, claiming they'd been drinking at the Old Bailey, a local *Gasthaus*. "Swear to God. That shit was laying there when we came in." He turned to me with a face like a choirboy. "This ain't right, Captain. Somebody's using this room."

"Take the suspects away," I told the MPs.

Over the next several months, we bugged five more rooms and broke up four more dope deals, resulting in seven arrests that led to courts martial. One tough guy we busted with four bricks of hashish was so incensed, he took a swing at me. After I defended myself, the MPs arrested the trooper and took him to the dispensary.

During my time in Bayreuth, I drove an old Alfa Romeo sports car; maneuvering through the empty cobblestone streets early each morning was a great treat. One raw March dawn, I left the apartment where Cathy, Jacqy, and I lived and headed for the car. As I juggled my keys, I glanced down and saw that the cloth top of my

Alfa had been slashed into three ragged pieces. I looked around; a few other officers had convertibles parked in the lot, but none of the others had been touched. This wasn't vandalism. It was a message from the drug pushers to lay off.

The hell with them.

A week after the car's top was replaced, I came out in the morning to find it slashed again. This time they'd left a calling card—a note on a scrap of brown paper bag. "Next time it's your throat."

"We'll see," I said quietly.

My XO, Lieutenant Steve Hurst, got a tip that one of the most notorious dealers in the Battery—I'll call him Jones—had moved out of the barracks and was living with his German girlfriend down near the train station. We collected some MPs and a couple of German policemen, who obliged us with a search warrant, and then paid Jones a visit. It was almost 3:00 A.M., drizzling as usual.

Jones answered the door wearing only jockey shorts, brandishing a big Phillips screwdriver. "Get the fuck outta here."

Not a brilliant move, waving a weapon at a German cop. The stocky constable smashed the soldier's wrist with a lead-filled baton.

The CID investigator read Jones the charges in the Bindlach hospital as the doctors were putting a cast on his fractured arm.

Word spread fast: the days of peddling dope—and slashing car tops—in 1st Howitzer Battery were over.

But the dopers weren't the only problem. A number of the troopers just didn't give a damn about the Army anymore—if they ever had. Some had served in Vietnam before the United States pulled out the last combat units after the signing of the Paris Peace Accord. But most of the troublemakers had never heard a cap gun fired in anger. They were simply rotten apples, soured by the anti-military mood of the times, poisoning the morale of a much larger number of young men who were trying to do their jobs. The new Army, with volunteer enlistees filling the ranks, did not need these troublemakers.

We warned problem soldiers that they were risking "bad paper"— a General or Undesirable Discharge. Some of them shaped up.

Many others did not. For years, these troops had seen the Army's sense of purpose deteriorate, and its tradition of discipline along with it. In fact, the whole U.S. military—and especially the Army—had been wounded in the paddies and jungles of Vietnam. Like the nation it served, the Army had begun to doubt itself. We had fought a long, costly war to a stalemate, and then had withdrawn claiming "peace with honor." Pessimism and negativism extended from the Pentagon down to the infantry rifle squads and artillery gun crews serving out their time in Germany. And there was a vicious strain of criminals in uniform, like the dope dealers in my Battery, who were more than willing to exploit this bad situation.

I got rid of the bad apples in my unit. I couldn't change the whole Army, but I could reshape the small unit I commanded.

As the initial commotion subsided, I found I had more time to train the Battery to combat standards. I spent a lot of time with the Maintenance Platoon, making sure our self-propelled guns would stand up to the rigors of combat, and to the muddy hills of the Grafenwöhr training areas.

Our gun chiefs were Regular Army staff sergeants, eager to learn, and to do their jobs. Like those on the howitzer crews in Vietnam, they were steady guys with good hearts. They needed to be given responsibility and to be held accountable. Day by day, I encouraged them. We established high standards, and we met them. The outfit became fast and accurate.

But we had to do more than fire cannons quickly and strike targets precisely. We supported highly mobile armor and mechanized infantry units. And, even though our howitzers were self-propelled, we were slower and much less agile than the infantry and armor forces. And our problem was compounded by the fact that self-propelled howitzers weren't equipped with radios. We tried to follow the maneuver formations, signaling shifts in direction with old-fashioned flags. After all, everybody knew guns could never keep up with the speeding armor or Mech infantry. Why waste money by giving radios to artillerymen?

That made no sense to me. In the 5-60, the Infantry APCs as well as the mortar and recoilless rifle tracks shared communications, and it seemed to me they were a powerful team. When I suggested to the Army that howitzers should have radios, I got little encouragement.

So late one night, when I got home and found Cathy still awake, I handed her the Sears catalog. "What do you think?" I asked.

"A CB radio, Tom? They're almost forty dollars. Do we really need one?"

"Not *one,* Dear. Ten. One for each howitzer, one for me, and one apiece for the Fire Direction Center, the executive officer, and the first sergeant."

Cathy looked at me. Replacing the convertible tops had eaten into our savings. "We don't have the money," she said.

"We've got the credit union."

Three weeks later, on a road march to Grafenwöhr, the column halted when an infantry APC slid off a muddy turn. It was after sunset when the Squadron operations officer radioed that the route had been changed. I grabbed my handy new CB and called the gun chiefs. The Howitzer Battery took the prescribed detour—and arrived in Grafenwöhr *along with* rather than behind the squadron's tanks.

During the following weeks, we kept up with each movement of the maneuver forces. One night, when we pulled the guns into a defensive laager—a traditional armored circle-the-wagons position— Lt. Colonel Hosmer arrived by jeep. "Your old dinosaurs were pretty nimble out there today."

"You ain't seen nothing yet, Sir."

After we got back to the *kaserne,* I told the troops the beer call would be on me. I still had about thirty dollars of credit-union money in my wallet. The CB radios had made a major difference, and the troops were getting used to winning.

Morale may have been improving, but I still had a lot to learn about leadership. That summer, one of the Battery officers complained to me about a young trooper I'll call Garcia. He had been one of the Battery's best soldiers, but he'd gone to hell in a hurry.

"He's always late for morning formation," the lieutenant said. "His platoon sergeant has to ride him to shave and to wear a clean uniform. And last night, he cussed me out. I'm recommending a court martial, Sir."

The lieutenant handed me the paperwork and Garcia's personnel folder. There was something strange here: Garcia had re-enlisted six months earlier; he'd passed the GED for a high school diploma, and had been nominated for Soldier of the Quarter. "I'll talk to him," I said.

When Garcia shuffled into my office, it was obvious that he was not a happy soldier. He glared at me after a sloppy salute. "Wanted to see me?" No *Sir,* no *Captain.*

I wasn't about to play his game. "What the hell is wrong with you, Garcia? You used to be a sharp trooper. But your platoon leader is recommending we run your ass out of the Army. What's the story?"

Garcia studied my expression, his face clenched, flushing with anger. "You really want to know?"

"Let's hear it."

"Four months ago the Red Cross called that my grandma died. In East New York, Brooklyn." He started to cry. "She raised me and my little brother. I went to the chain of command and put in for emergency leave like I was supposed to. They said I couldn't be spared . . . that the *team* needed me. Request denied."

Garcia wiped his eyes, then stared at the floor.

"I was worried about my brother." He started sobbing again. "Well, they put him in a foster home. And then, last month, the Red Cross calls again. Some Brooklyn thug had screwed my brother and cut his throat. I wanted to go home to bury him, but again the lieutenant said the organization was more important. Request denied."

How could something like this have happened in a Battery of 180 soldiers, without my ever hearing about it?

When Garcia looked up, his face was hot with pain and hatred. "Captain, you can take this *organization*—the Battery, the Squadron, the U.S. Goddamn Army, the whole fucking country—and shove it up your ass."

There were tears on my own cheeks. I came out from behind the desk and put my arm around him. "What happened is my fault. I know it's too late now, but you've got your leave. Go home. Take as long as you need. When you get back, if you still want out of the Army, I'll make sure you get an Honorable Discharge."

The next morning, I assembled the officers and senior NCOs in the cramped Battery Ops Center.

"Soldiers have a lot of moving parts," I began. "They require regular maintenance. They are human beings, not machines. They will do amazing things if they know you care about them." I remembered the devotion of Lee Alley's men, the respect we all had for Lt. Colonel Antila.

I told them Garcia's story, without assigning blame to anyone but myself. "What I've learned is that being in charge doesn't automatically mean you know what's going on. That's going to change in this battery."

The Battery clerk brought in two stacks of personnel folders. I picked up a handful of individual records. "I'm not going home each night until I've read twenty of these. By the time this drill is over, I'll know every soldier's first name, hometown, and something about his family. I expect you to do the same."

The men at the table nodded.

"If a trooper comes to you with a problem, remember this: It's your problem, and it's *my* problem. We're not going to lose good soldiers because we don't give a rat's ass about them as people."

My commitment to the troops would mean less time with my family. Cathy was very understanding, but it was hard not seeing much of Jacqy. I went to work before she got up in the morning, and came home after she went to bed at night. Cathy always had a hot meal waiting, even when I didn't get back to the apartment until midnight. And the wives bonded in a special way to make up for the absence of their husbands. I've always respected Cathy for the way she cared for Army families.

IT WAS ONE OF THOSE MIDWINTER MORNINGS IN NÜRNBERG WHEN the fog freezes to the cobblestones. Dawn on Monday, January 20, 1975. Yawning, I walked across the courtyard of the huge old Merrell Barracks kaserne to Regimental headquarters. A cup of hot coffee was definitely in order.

Twelve hours earlier, Cathy and I had been in the Normandy Hotel in Paris, enjoying our first vacation in years.

"The Colonel wants you back here by 0700 tomorrow," LTC Charlie Zipp, the Regimental XO, had explained. "You're taking command of the 84th Armored Engineer Company."

We had driven rainy autoroutes and snowy autobahns all night on the way back to Bavaria. So much for our vacation. I was being assigned to yet another job in the 2nd ACR. I'd commanded the Howitzer Battery and served as the 1st Squadron Operations Officer (S-3) in Bindlach, and Colonel John Hudachek, the 2nd ACR commander, had brought me down to be his assistant S-3 in Nürnberg five months earlier. I was learning a whole lot about Armor and Infantry, about maneuver warfare. And Cathy and I were enjoying a staff job without the pressure of command. I could even get home most nights to see Jacqy before she went to bed. But that was about to end.

"I don't know much about the Engineers, Sir," I told Colonel Hudachek over a mug of coffee.

"You know how to lead troops, Tom," he said. "And that company sure as hell needs a leader." The 84th Armored Engineer Company was the Regiment's basket case. It was loaded with malcontents, most of them draftees finishing their service.

"They're about as close to a mob in uniform as I've seen," Colonel Hudachek said.

He had relieved the company commander and called me in to take his place. I took command at a breakfast ceremony in the company mess hall, and then walked into the orderly room. When I entered, the company clerk hardly glanced up from his *Penthouse*.

"Get me the platoon leaders and the First Sergeant," I ordered. "I'm your new commander."

There must have been something in my tone that got him motivated. "Yes, Sir." He dropped the magazine and grabbed the phone. "Right away, Sir."

What followed was a long, tiring day, spent talking individually with a parade of junior officers, platoon sergeants, and other senior NCOs. There were several potential leaders among them, but they were tentative and dispirited—uncertain of their authority. The Company had already been cut to about 70 percent strength through the Expeditious Discharge program—an administration elimination procedure—and courts martial.

"The ones we've got left just don't give a shit, Sir," the First Sergeant said, adding that many of the remaining troops had been restricted to the post as punishment for disciplinary infractions.

"We'll work on that, First Sergeant," I said.

It was late when I left the office. Instead of driving home, I decided to tour the Company's corner of the *kaserne*. My last stop was the notorious fourth floor.

The corridor's linoleum was filthy. There was obscene graffiti on the walls. I could smell hashish.

A tall, husky private in dirty fatigues walked toward me with a sour expression on his face.

"Fuck you," he said as he passed.

I could not believe what I'd heard. I spun around to see who he was talking to. There was nobody else in the hallway.

I suddenly pictured all those young troopers who had lost their lives serving, doing their duty in Vietnam. This malcontent punk did not deserve to wear the same uniform. I lost it.

"Hey, you," I said.

The soldier turned around to face me.

I grabbed his shoulders and slammed him against the wall, staring into his eyes. He stood there as if in shock as I walked away.

Colonel Hudachek was still in his office, wrapping up the day's paperwork, when I knocked on the door.

"Tom," he said. "How did the first day go?"

"I have to report that I just struck a soldier, Sir."

The Colonel nodded somberly. I sighed. Ten years in the Army, and it had come to this. Officers do not strike soldiers. I'd be lucky if the court martial resulted in an honorable discharge. In any event, my future in the military was over.

"What happened?"

I explained.

Colonel Hudachek frowned. "Captain. You cannot lay hands on a trooper."

"Yes, Sir."

He pointed. "Go stand in the corner."

I went to the corner of Colonel Hudachek's office and stared at him.

"You don't understand, Captain. *Stand in the corner. Face the wall.*"

I turned and faced the wall. Less than a minute passed.

"Go home, Tom. Get some sleep. I want you with your company early tomorrow. You've got a lot of work to do with those soldiers."

Standing in the corner—*exceptional punishment for exceptional times.* As I left the *kaserne,* I thought of Eric Antila among the ruined buildings along the Kinh Doi Canal. Loyalty still ran up—and down—the Army's chain of command.

T HE NEXT DAY, I SET ABOUT REBUILDING THIS ORPHAN UNIT.
    The troops standing in formation that morning were a sorry-looking bunch. Long hair; stained, dirty fatigues; unshined boots. Many hadn't bothered to shave—for several days, from the look of them. Staff Sergeant Kittle would have blown a gasket.

"First Sergeant," I asked as we walked the ranks. "You see anything abnormal?"

"Yes, Sir. They look like shit. But that's not *abnormal* for these guys."

I spotted a man in the front rank with a decent haircut, clean-shaven, spotless fatigues, and polished boots. I thought of Sam Long. When the honor guard looked especially sharp at a ceremony, he got Scag to write us a pass. I remembered Lee Alley sending his best soldiers to Saigon for long weekends.

"Looking good, trooper," I told the squared-away soldier. "Take the week off."

"Sir?" the kid asked.

"You've got a week's pass. Go skiing down in Garmish. Just sack out. Whatever you want."

The next day, there were three more soldiers with clean uniforms and polished boots. "You're looking like soldiers," I said. "Take a week off."

It wasn't exactly a silver bullet, but the approach had a slow, steady effect. I realized I was going to need both carrots and sticks—and the sticks would be just as important as the carrots. After four courts martial, the smell of hashish disappeared from the fourth floor of the *kaserne;* the number of troopers restricted to post dropped to zero.

But I knew getting these men to look and act like soldiers was only part of my task as a leader. They also had jobs to do. Engineers are the Army's heavy-lifters; an armored engineer company does its job under fire, salvaging damaged tanks, knocking down roadblocks, bulldozing enemy bunkers and trenches. One of the Company's basic tools was the Combat Engineer Vehicle (CEV), basically an M-60 tank with a wide, armored bulldozer blade in front, a retractable hydraulic boom crane, and a short-barreled 165 mm turret cannon for breaching obstacles. The Company had two of these vehicles—but neither of them had run in more than two years.

I spent a lot of time with the mechanics. And I went through the Company, finding soldiers who were good with their hands. We had a little competition: The first team to get a CEV fully operable would get a three-day pass. It was a virtual tie, I gave the whole company a long weekend. To reinforce the positive momentum, I worked with the Regimental headquarters and the German police to arrange a convoy for the Company right through downtown Nürnberg to the Feucht Training Area. The freshly painted CEVs led the column. The troops looked sharp. When German school kids on the sidewalks clapped and cheered, these American soldiers grinned with pride. We were back in business.

By December 1975 I was on my fourth assignment in the Regiment, once more as a captain holding down a major's job in the Operations shop—an artilleryman responsible for tank gunnery training. One snowy night, I took a few hours off and left a local training range to go home and change into dry fatigues and boots. Jacqy was in her pajamas, curled up under a quilt on the couch. I'd promised to be back early that day. Cathy had waited till Jacqy's bedtime, then had gone ahead and decorated the Christmas tree without me.

Juggling a ham sandwich and a mug of coffee, I pulled on my wet field jacket and headed for the apartment door. "I'll be back tomorrow early, promise."

Cathy peered out the blinds at the wet snow swirling down past the streetlights. "What a beautiful evening for a field exercise," she said, then kissed me goodnight.

"God help me," I said, mimicking George C. Scott as George Patton. "I do love it so."

It was a shared joke. But as I brushed the slush off the Jeep windshield, I recognized the underlying truth of those words. I *did* love being a soldier, helping to build a new Army out of the ashes of Vietnam.

It had been almost five years since I'd earned my bachelor's degree. On January 1, my official service obligation would be over. But the thought of being a civilian was uncomfortable.

"Let's wait and see what happens," I had suggested to Cathy when we'd talked about it earlier that week.

Cathy had agreed. "We'll just see what happens."

Those words would become yet another shared joke.

SIX AND A HALF YEARS LATER, MY BOOTS WERE DEEP IN THE springtime mud of another West German training range. I was a lieutenant colonel, commanding the 2nd Battalion, 78th Field Artillery, a self-propelled 155 mm howitzer unit of the 1st Armored Division. Our *kaserne* was in the Bavarian town of Bamberg, but we spent much of the year out on field exercises.

After leaving the 2nd ACR in 1976, I'd attended the Armed Forces Staff College—a graduate school for professional officers—and served in the Pentagon. My assignments in "the Building" had given me a real education in Army and Washington politics.

As a major serving in the office of the Army Inspector General as an "investigator," I'd learned that even senior officers weren't immune to moral turpitude and corruption. I'd investigated one general who'd get drunk every afternoon on Officers' Club gin, then order MPs to salute his dog. Another had a clever kickback scheme worked out with a corrupt defense contractor, and had hidden a fortune in offshore bank accounts. Then there was the general who chose secretaries based on their looks rather than their office skills. For a young major, this was interesting work: It was in this job that I learned to recognize that hopeless look in a guilty man's eyes when he realizes he's been caught.

After eighteen months as an inspector general, I'd worked for Army Chiefs of Staff General Bernie Rogers and General Shy Meyer, helping prepare them for congressional testimony. I'd discovered that some members of Congress, confronted with a choice between the nation's interests and those of their constituents—when it came to a pork-barrel weapons contract, for example, or beefing up a base back in the district—were all too eager to vote for the folks back home. Tommy Franks matured as a bureaucrat during those four years. *The idealism of youth was augmented by the pragmatism of politics.*

By the time I returned to West Germany in 1981, I was glad to get back to the troops. Commanding a battalion is one of the most demanding, but most rewarding, jobs in the Army. And I was fortunate to have the 2-78 for three years instead of the usual two. My 565 troops had proven to me that the all-volunteer Army was a success. Drug use in the ranks was no longer a problem; a service-wide program of random testing identified the dopers, who were quickly discharged. Open hostility between the races had disappeared, as black and Hispanic sergeants and officers took their rightful places in the service. In this critical area, the Army was leading the evolution of American society.

The troops recognized once again that wearing a military uniform was something they could take pride in. If they were led well, these soldiers would spend nights and weekends in the field on dangerous live-fire exercises, in any weather, eating cold C-rations and snatching sleep under dripping ponchos when they could, performing up to exacting standards.

Just as the quality of the troops had improved, our battlefield technology was now dramatically superior to the weapons and equipment I had mastered as a young officer. The Division's M-60 tanks had been "stabilized" to fire while rolling over rough terrain, and we were beginning to field night-vision sights. Within two years, several American armored divisions would be equipped with the new M-1 Abrams main battle tank, a quantum leap over anything in the Soviet inventory. Not only could the Abrams fire while jolting across broken ground; its thermal sight and computerized fire control could accurately track enemy armor day or night, in any weather, at long range.

Wire-guided TOW anti-tank missiles were now standard weapons, mounted on Jeeps, APCs, and helicopters. And the Artillery was about to introduce the revolutionary 155mm Copperhead projectile, which followed a laser beam to a target ten miles away.

Computers were showing up all over the Army. My battalion was equipped with the Field Artillery Digital Analog Computer (FADAC), a green fiberglass footlocker with a keyboard atop its case. With its blinking colored lights and beeping, it looked like one of the friendly robots in sci-fi movies; we called it "Freddy FADAC." The device revolutionized the way firing solutions were determined for the artillery: When the Fire Direction Center typed in target coordinates, the computer spat out the required tube elevations and azimuths for the guns. No more paper firing tables or charts and darts. I enjoyed showing off the system to my Armor and Infantry friends, who still thought of the Artillery as an old-fashioned branch.

With the hunger for tinkering and innovation I'd inherited from my father, I set out to put Freddy FADAC to the best possible use in maneuver warfare. My savvy Command Sergeant Major, Don Mann, and my new operations officer, Captain Michael Hayes, did some scrounging in motor pools all across Germany and found a spare maintenance truck. We stripped the boxy interior of its workbenches and tool chests, and built a mobile Tactical Operations Center (TOC) around the computer. Naturally we called the vehicle the TOC-A-TOY, after the chunky Tonka Toy moving vans so dear to the children in our housing area. With the TOC-A-TOY, the battalion could move much more quickly than had been possible just a year earlier.

More than ever, I was fascinated by the combination of speed and firepower. American military doctrine was evolving; in its latest incarnation, it was developing a rapid, nontraditional response to the prospect of a Soviet-led invasion of West Germany. In this "Air Land" battle, American forces would abandon fixed defensive positions and strike the enemy's flanks, and then, supported by attack helicopters and air power, penetrate to the rear and attack enemy command and control centers and supply lines.

Colonel Wayne Downing, my infantry brigade commander, had years of service in the Special Forces and Rangers; together we spent long hours discussing the battlefields of the future. He convinced me that small teams of highly skilled Special Operations Forces, inserted deep behind enemy lines, would play an important role.

Reading military journals late at night in my command track, I pictured those battlefields: seemingly chaotic, they would actually be tightly focused, and devastatingly effective.

I wanted a place in this new Army. The Division's senior officers thought highly of my battalion, but that was no guarantee I'd be promoted to full colonel and offered a chance at brigade command. The structure of fighting units was changing. Missiles and the new precision-guided munitions would soon augment cannon artillery. And there was a glut of majors and lieutenant colonels remaining from the Vietnam buildup. The "up-or-out" rule applied: Most lieutenant colonels would retire after serving twenty years.

Cathy and I had another of our familiar discussions about the future.

"We'll have to . . ." I began.

". . . wait and see," she said, finishing my thought.

Attending a Senior Service College was the key to advancement. Like many of my peers, I had my eye on the Army War College at Carlisle, Pennsylvania, near Gettysburg. A board had selected next year's attendees, but the list of those chosen was a closely guarded secret until the official roster was announced by the Pentagon. The spring of 1984 was a time of anticipation and uncertainty for the Franks family. Did we or didn't we have a future in the Army? ". . . wait and see."

Then one afternoon during a driving rainstorm, as the Battalion was training in Grafenwöhr, Major General Tom Healy, the Division commander, skidded up in his Jeep and came into the TOC-A-TOY for a briefing. I offered him coffee and some of Cathy's fudge-iced brownies, then described the training we were conducting.

General Healy seemed pleased. He grinned as he climbed back into his Jeep to leave. "Great brownies, Tom. Be sure Cathy brings the recipe to Carlisle."

I'd been selected for the War College. I smiled, even as I almost wept. It looked like the Franks family was about to make the Army a career.

And we would even become a real family again for a year.

This second tour in Germany had often kept me away from home, and once again Cathy managed our family life. Jacqy had started competitive swimming at age seven when we lived in Fairfax, Virginia, and had continued to excel in the sport with a local German swim team. She also became fluent in the language while attending a German girls' school for two years. I went to her swim meets and school activities when I could, but Cathy had done the heavy lifting for the past three years. Despite the fact that her father died during this time, she had given herself to Army families and had served as president of the Bamberg wives club. When we left the Battalion, she received an award from the VII Corps Commander for her service. I could not have been more proud.

IN JULY 1985, AFTER A YEAR AT THE WAR COLLEGE, I WAS ASSIGNED to Fort Hood, Texas, as the deputy operations officer of III Corps, which included most of the Army's heavy divisions based in the States. The corps commander, Lt. General Crosbie "Butch" Saint, had commanded the 1st Armored Division our last few months in Germany, and I had come to know him well. His selection of an Artillery officer for an important Ops assignment was a bit unusual. But I'd worked closely enough with the Armor and Infantry during the previous twelve years to have learned a great deal. And I was generally respected in the maneuver community as an artillery maverick who found ways to solve problems.

Within a few months of my arrival at Fort Hood, I set about designing a range to train artillerymen to hit moving targets. Traditionally, howitzers fired at enemy formations, trenches, bunkers, and parked armored vehicles. But an attacking enemy—whether it was the Soviet Army or one of its client armies in the Third World—couldn't be counted on to sit still, waiting for us to pound them with barrage fire. We needed to think about dynamic warfare.

Working with the engineers, I designed and built a snaking railroad through the sagebrush and juniper of Ft. Hood North Range, on which a radio-controlled locomotive would pull a train of target sleds representing tanks and APCs. Artillerymen from all over 3rd Corps trained on the range—observers calling in fire missions, the guns engaging the target sleds using smoke rounds. The technical aspects of the range were *interesting,* of course—but forcing artillerymen to think "out of the box" was truly *important.*

Next, we set out to improve tank gunnery training for our maneuver soldiers. For years, Armor crews had trained on long, narrow ranges built to accommodate the constricted field of vision of the sighting systems on our tanks. Moving and stationary targets were set in predictable positions. It was easy for tank gunners to "can" the Fort Hood ranges, consistently scoring very well in this less-than-realistic training.

Once we'd widened the Blackwell and Crittenberger Ranges and installed more moving and pop-up targets, tank crews were obliged to traverse their turrets continually, "searching" for randomly appearing silhouettes on both flanks, not just straight ahead. At first, the gunnery scores dropped in the face of these new challenges.

One morning, the commander of a tank battalion that had performed poorly on the new Blackwell Range came to me with his concerns. "Tom," he said, "this range is pretty goddamn tough. Maybe too tough."

"Well, Dave," I said, watching his tanks clanking back to the start lines through the Texas dust. "The last time I checked, *war* was pretty tough."

Soon enough our tank and Bradley crews became experts on the new, more challenging ranges. I was proud to watch as American soldiers, once again, rose to a new standard. The payoff of these new gunnery training techniques would be seen a few years later in the deserts of Kuwait and Iraq.

I WAS LEAVING FOR THE OFFICE ONE WEDNESDAY MORNING IN August 1986 when the phone rang.

"Tommy Ray?" Mother's voice was strained. "Your father fell down and he's in Midland Memorial Hospital. They think he's had a stroke."

Driving too fast on Texas state highways, Cathy, Jacqy, and I reached Midland by late afternoon. My parents had returned there in the 1970s; Dad had taken a job with B&B Vending Company, fixing and selling jukeboxes all around West Texas. It was the kind of work he did well. In fact, he'd bought the old jukebox from the Midland High Youth Center and refurbished it as a Christmas present for us. At age seventy-two, on medication for hypertension, he still worked his normal six days a week.

All of which only made it more of a shock to see him lying unconscious in the ICU. My father had always had a presence of calm strength. Now he seemed helpless.

The next day he was awake and coherent, but he drifted in and out of consciousness. He squeezed my hand. "When you and Cathy come home," he said weakly, "we'll go quail hunting. I'll get another dog, Tommy Ray. . . ."

"That'll be great, Dad."

He spoke with joy of the cruise that he and Mother had taken, a gift we had given them for their fiftieth wedding anniversary. Then he slept again.

Lucid once more, he looked at me intently. "I'm so proud of you. You've come a long way since that day in Austin when we put you on that Greyhound."

I really have worked hard to make 'em a hand, I thought.

When we finally left, the doctors told us he was resting comfortably. That evening, Cathy, Jacqy, and I went to a movie to relieve the stress. But the coming attractions were still playing when I was paged.

"Oh, Tommy Ray," my mother sobbed on the phone. "Your father just passed away."

As Cathy and I knelt in the hospital chapel, I smiled, remembering all the times I had called him for advice. "Dad, the Olds is running a little hot." *Change the fan belt and put in a new thermostat, son.* "The commode in the guest bathroom keeps dripping." *Get a pencil. Here's what you'll need to fix it.*

Once I'd called from the suburbs of northern Virginia when the garbage disposal had suddenly quit. "I guess I'll have to get a new one, Dad."

"Take a flashlight, Tommy Ray," he'd said in his patient way. "Get down on your knees and look at the bottom of the unit. If there's a red button sticking out, push it in. That's the reset button."

Of course, he'd been right. Again.

For years after my father's funeral on that hot summer morning in Midland, I found myself reaching for the phone—reaching out for his wisdom, his counsel. I still wish he were here to give it.

IN MAY 1987, I WAS PROMOTED TO COLONEL; TWO MONTHS LATER I became commander of the 1st Cavalry Division's Artillery (DIVARTY). This brigade-size unit included 155 mm and 8-inch self-propelled howitzers, and a battery of Multiple Launch Rocket Systems (MLRS). I stressed to my officers and senior sergeants that artillery was an integral part of the 1st Cavalry Division, every bit as lethal as the armored and mechanized infantry battalions we supported. The Division was rapidly evolving, thrashing out innovative combat doctrine based on the lightning speed and precision firepower of the new M-1 Abrams tank and M-2 Bradley infantry fighting vehicle. Artillery had to keep pace with these changes.

On Monday, February 22, 1988, I was working at my desk on new tactical maneuver concepts, listening to classical music on the radio as I struggled to transform theory into practical training procedures. A Bach violin sonata had just begun when the announcer interrupted with a brief news bulletin: An Army CH-47 helicopter had crashed near Chico in north Texas, killing an unknown number of soldiers.

I put down my pen. No matter how many years I'd worn the uniform, I was always struck by the sadness of young Americans dying in the service of their country . . . whether on a battlefield or in training.

But I had a lot of work to complete this morning, both at my desk and out on the firing ranges. I was again engrossed in maneuver concepts when my executive officer entered the office.

"Well, Colonel," he said. "We got them off okay."

I lowered my pen. "Got who off?"

"The rocket battery officers left on a Chinook for Fort Sill."

I was numb. How many Army CH-47 Chinook helicopters could there have been in the air near Chico—the direct flight path between Fort Hood and Fort Sill? That was *our* CH-47, carrying *our* MLRS battery officers to participate in a training exercise with another Corps artillery unit.

I was frozen in place. I had spent a lifetime planning for every battle contingency I could imagine—yet I'd not anticipated this simple peacetime catastrophe. Were there survivors? If so, how badly were they injured? What if they were all dead? Whom should I contact first—the chaplain? The psychologists at the post hospital? Or should I call Cathy first? She was my partner, my link to many of the soldiers' wives and families.

Slowly, my paralysis thawed. I had the XO call the Aviation Brigade to confirm the news bulletin on the accident. As he did, a local television channel gave a more thorough report. The helicopter had apparently suffered an in-flight fire, gone out of control, and exploded when it crashed. I hadn't felt such shock about casualties since that terrible day in March 1968, when the Vietcong mine had blown apart the Charlie Company track. It was hard to think. I was responsible for everything my unit did, or failed to do. I was responsible for my soldiers and for their families.

Over the next long hours, Cathy, the chaplain, and I visited the wives of five dead officers. I'd performed a number of difficult and unpleasant jobs in my Army career, but trying to comfort a trembling, grief-battered young widow with a crying toddler at her knee was the hardest thing I had ever done.

Late that night, I reviewed the crisis checklist the staff had drawn up. The medics were completing recovery of remains. The psychologists were in contact with the survivors. I had made my phone calls to the dead officers' parents. Now the steadying familiarity of Army procedures would continue.

Still, I couldn't get over the thought that I had failed as a leader. I owed my soldiers *and their families* better than I had given them. If somehow I could have anticipated. . . .

It wasn't normal to expect disaster; that was a given. But military command was not a normal profession. It was my *duty* to foresee. We lived with unusual risk every day, even in peacetime.

Every day. . . .

I laid a stack of blank three-by-five cards on my desk calendar. Then I brewed a pot of coffee.

On the first card, I printed, "23 Feb '88—The biggest challenges I may face today." Taking a sip of coffee, I listed five of the most important problems that *could* arise in the next twenty-four hours, as almost two thousand troopers practiced their dangerous profession. When I had finished, I flipped the card over and wrote: "Opportunities that may appear today."

Every morning since that Thursday in February 1988, I noted the "Challenges and Opportunities" that might occur on that day. More than five thousand cards later, I still do. The card itself isn't important; preparing myself for each day definitely is. Through complex operations in Afghanistan and Iraq, the process helped me to anticipate any number of problems . . . and solutions.

I GAVE UP COMMAND OF THE DIVISION ARTILLERY IN EARLY JUNE OF 1989. Jacqy graduated from Killeen High School the same day, and I counted the blessings of having been at Fort Hood the previous four years. Jacqy planned to attend Drury College in Springfield, Missouri, where she had received a swimming scholarship; I had been selected to become the 1st Cavalry Division Chief of Staff.

A few months later, I got the news that my name was on the brigadier general promotion list. As the Chief of Staff, I was up to my elbows in paperwork, completing an after-action report on desert war games out at the sprawling National Training Center in Fort Irwin, California. When I picked up the phone to call Cathy with the good news, I pictured First Sergeant Scagliotti in that barracks at Fort Devens. I never became a sergeant major, but maybe he'd be satisfied with the kind of officer I was turning out to be.

The next summer, I received orders to report for duty as the assistant commandant of the Artillery School at Fort Sill. That was a job where I could apply my theories on speed and firepower.

But those orders would soon change.

On Thursday, August 2, 1990, thousands of Iraqi troops and hundreds of armored vehicles rolled into Kuwait and occupied the small Arabian Gulf state after a brief, one-sided battle.

The new Division commander, Brigadier General John Tilelli, called me at home that night. "Tom, we'd better dust off our overseas deployment plans."

"Roger that, Sir."

The U.N. Security Council censured Iraq, and demanded that Saddam Hussein withdraw his occupation force from Kuwait immediately. But Saddam declared the formal annexation of Kuwait as Iraq's nineteenth province. More U.N. Security Council resolutions followed, but Iraq stood fast.

We were alerted to deploy to an unspecified location in "Southwest Asia." Everybody knew it was Saudi Arabia, because Air Force combat wings and the advanced party of the 82nd Airborne Division were already en route. We worked around the clock on the endless details of sending a heavy U.S. Army division to the other side of the world. When the 1st Cavalry deployed, I realized, it would take the field with a new breed of soldier and revolutionary weapons.

Army Chief of Staff General Carl Vuono visited the Division a few days later, and he and John Tilelli held a discussion behind closed doors. When they came out, I had a new job.

"Tom," John Tilelli said. "The Army's going to frock you to brigadier general."

In the face of the forthcoming battle in Iraq, my promotion to general officer was accelerated: though my official date of rank would be July 1991, I'd pin on a star immediately.

Then the other shoe dropped. Tilelli had requested—and General Vuono had agreed—that I become Assistant Division Commander for Operations and Maneuver, effective immediately. I would lead the Division's advance party to the desert.

Twenty-three years after Second Lieutenant Tommy Franks had boarded that Continental Airlines charter jet en route to Vietnam, I was to be a brigadier general—and going to war again.

5

FLAG RANK

I did not expect a merry Christmas.

Everybody in the Division Tactical Command Post was worn ragged. In the previous four months, the 17,000 men and women of the 1st Cavalry Division had worked long days and nights completing our deployment to Operation Desert Shield.

Leading the advanced party into Saudi Arabia, I'd met with the commander of the XVIII Airborne Corps, Lt. General Gary Luck, late on a hot, humid August night in the Arabian Gulf city of Dhahran. We would establish an assembly area where the division would stage thousands of troops and their equipment in the low dunes 160 kilometers west of the port of ad-Dammam. America's Cavalry Division was coming to town; we named the assembly area "Horse" (AA Horse), in honor of the division's history.

To our north, the 24th Infantry Division (Mechanized) and the 101st Airborne Division (Air Assault) had augmented the light infantry of the 82nd Airborne. During the first lonely weeks of August and September, those paratroopers had been positioned as a trip wire—the "speed bump"—in case Saddam Hussein decided to send his forces south into Saudi Arabia.

While we labored through the stifling heat, setting up brigade and battalion positions that stretched across an expanse of featureless desert, diplomats at the United Nations were trying to persuade the Iraqis to pull out of Kuwait to prevent a war. And the Security Council passed ten resolutions condemning the Iraqi aggression, which President George H. W. Bush had solemnly vowed would "not stand." But Saddam rebuffed the world community, stubbornly insisting that Kuwait was now its newest province. The United States and its NATO allies formed a historic coalition that now included forces from Iraq's Arab neighbors.

From the perspective of a soldier in the desert, war seemed inevitable. And preparing for war was the hardest work I had done since Vietnam.

With General John Tilelli receiving the troops at the port of ad-Dammam and me in the assembly area, we undertook the job of preparing soldiers for combat. That task was complicated because we would upgrade the Division's entire inventory of over 300 M1 Abrams tanks to the new M1A1. This tank had a longer range 120 mm gun, enhanced armor, and a nuclear-biological-chemical (NBC) protective system. We welcomed the NBC protection because the Iraqis had used nerve gas in their war with Iran and against Kurdish civilians in the North, and were suspected to possess biological agents. Intelligence at the time predicted Iraq would not hesitate to use these weapons of mass destruction (WMD) against Coalition forces.

The process of replacing the Division's armor was done as a "Total Package" fielding, which sounded like a straightforward logistics exercise. As I watched the endless convoys of Low Boy semitrailers loaded with the new M1A1s roll in from the port, I recognized the juggernaut of America's military-industrial power. But swapping one model of tank for another out in this baking wilderness, and then training the crews to use them while simultaneously creating a battle plan, was anything but simple.

While the crews were rigging out their new tanks, Brigadier General Joe Robles, the Assistant Division Commander for Support, had the engineers bulldoze and backhoe an armor qualification range from the dunes and gravel flats of eastern Saudi Arabia. John Tilelli insisted that the new "Pegasus Range" be dynamic, not a static, unchallenging firing line. Every Abrams tank and Bradley crew would qualify with their guns, both stopped and on the move, during November and early December. The scores were impressive. These young Americans were focused on going to war.

Waiting for diplomatic negotiations to run their course, we trained and honed tactics—twelve, fourteen hours a day, seven days a week. But diplomacy made little progress. At his headquarters in Riyadh, General Norman Schwarzkopf, the Commander in Chief of the U.S. Central Command, was developing a plan to liberate Kuwait. The Defense Department and the White House had approved his request to double the size of the Coalition forces to almost 550,000 American, British, French, and Arab troops—almost fourteen divisions of Allied combat power.

We'd all been so busy that Christmas surprised us. Certainly the troops in the Division command post didn't feel very festive. The GP medium tents and the tent-like extensions on our command tracks were hidden beneath tan camouflage netting, giving them the appearance of anthills back on the farm in Wynnewood. When the breeze blew from the burning latrine barrels, the place smelled a little like Binh Phuoc. No matter how many red-and-green garlands hung inside the tents, this corner of Saudi Arabia wasn't long on charm.

The troops tried to be cheerful, but it wasn't easy. The stark surroundings only added to the tense mood. Everyone recognized that we'd soon be in combat. And no one expected the fighting to be easy. The Iraqi army had deployed twenty-eight divisions to defend Kuwait, outnumbering Allied forces two to one. Their six elite Republican Guard divisions, equipped with Soviet-built T-72 tanks, were formidable, well-motivated combat units. And there was the prospect of confronting WMD.

Added to our general anxiety was old-fashioned homesickness. During the Cold War, most professional soldiers had managed to spend Christmas with their loved ones. And for many of the younger troops, this would be the first holiday when they didn't sit down at their parents' table for a turkey dinner. Mail was slow, and there weren't many chances to call home. But many of us had received care packages from our families, and had hoarded cookies and candy for a Christmas splurge.

To make the camp a bit more cheerful, I'd sent several resourceful scouts to search for a Christmas tree. On Christmas Eve we put the scraggly desert pine, cut from a local sheik's windbreak, in the big mess tent. With "God Rest Ye Merry Gentlemen" playing on a boom box, we broke out the goodies and decorated the tree with stars snipped from foil plates, strings of popcorn, and wads of colored commo wire. I contributed a couple of cases of Clausthaler nonalcoholic beer.

Sipping that poor substitute for the real thing, I remembered the times I'd been invited to Christmas parties in Army enlisted clubs. As always, I liked being with the troops, sharing family pictures, just kicking back and relaxing. Now, however, for the first time in uniform, I sensed a distance between the troops and me.

Then I realized: *I'm a general now.*

When I sat down at their tables, the eyes of the soldiers around me automatically went to the cloth stars on the lapels of my chocolate-chip desert uniform. Troops believed that generals were different, a separate class of being. Soldiers expected that, as a general, I'd have answers to all the important questions in their lives: What was Saddam Hussein's strategic plan? What were General Schwarzkopf's innermost thoughts? What mysterious factors determined the balance between hot chow and meals ready to eat (MRE)? What controlled the frequency of mail? And, for good measure, what type of grease really was best for the track bearings on the new M1A1s?

It would have been great if I could have answered those questions. The truth was, I could not. Being a general, I'd discovered, meant gathering as much information—always in short supply—as possible, then making decisions. And living with those decisions. It meant using judgment. And it meant not being able to spend as much time with the troops as I wanted to, and as I had in the past. I had a lot to learn.

Soon after General Tilelli had arrived in Dhahran and was busy offloading our equipment from the ships, a couple of American reporters showed up at AA Horse, unaccompanied by public affairs escorts. Naturally, they asked to see "the General." They knew how to flatter, and I was easily flattered. By the time they bounced off in their rented Toyota Land Cruiser, I had shared with them my wisdom about the optimum strategy for winning this war and the more brilliant aspects of my tactical acumen.

During my nightly situation report to General Tilelli, I noted with pride that I'd "had a good interview with those reporters."

For a moment, the secure telephone went silent. "What are you talking about?" Tilelli asked. He was not his normal friendly self.

I explained how interested the reporters had been in what I had to say. Another painful moment of silence on the channel.

"General Franks," he said formally, never a good sign. "Do not do things like that without talking to me first." He cleared his throat. My wire brushing was not yet over. "You have certain responsibilities. But overall command of this Division is not one of them. In the future, leave the reporters to me."

"Wilco, Sir." And I did comply.

As I shot the breeze with the troops in the mess tent on Christmas Eve, the mood improved a notch when a sergeant from the Signal detachment hooked up a microphone and bigger speakers to the boom box. This reinforced my conviction that sergeants really were the people that made the Army work. Now we could take turns leading off-key renditions of "Deck the Halls." Bowing to popular demand, I assaulted everyone's hearing with a verse of Wayne Newton's "Cowboy Christmas," figuring the pain of listening to me sing might offer a moment's distraction from worrying about Iraqi Sarin gas.

But when I started moving among the soldiers' tables—admiring pictures of Staff Sergeant Jones' little twins, or Warrant Officer Smith's son Jim in his Cub Scout uniform—the underlying mood of

lonely isolation descended over me again. One corporal flipped a button on his Seiko watch to check the time in Denver. "Linda and her
mom are probably decorating the tree, Sir," he said, handing me a
picture of a pretty, slender girl and her plump mother. For a moment,
no one at the table spoke. I pictured Jacqy and Cathy at my mother's
home in Midland. After a year and a half at Drury College, where she
was an Academic All-American, Jacqy had transferred to Oklahoma
State University. A tall, beautiful young woman, like her mother, she
was living in the same Tri-Delta sorority house Cathy had lived in
while I was in Vietnam. I had tried to be a good father, spending as
much time with her as possible. But being a good soldier, I had not
been the *best* father—the most thoughtful, the most involved, the
most *present*. In a few hours, Jacqy and Cathy would start opening
the gifts under the tree. How I wished I could be with them.

Outside the tent, the generator chugged. A gritty wind stole in
under the flaps. I joined a group of soldiers at the next table, and we
talked about the Dallas Cowboys' chances in the playoffs. A young
black Spec-4 named Jackson came over and sat down next to me, listening intently but not speaking. I had seen him around the command
post, driving a Humvee, standing perimeter guard. He was a sharp-
looking soldier, but he never seemed to smile, nor did he appear to
have any close friends. I had checked on Jackson's background, and
his company commander had explained that he was from a large,
poor family of sharecroppers somewhere in the Carolinas; he had enlisted at seventeen, and in all the time he'd been in the Division he
never seemed to receive any mail. Jackson did his job well, but to me
and his commander alike, he seemed very serious, almost too serious,
for his age. Now, as we sat together on Christmas Eve talking football, Jackson gazed at our family snapshots with interest—but he produced none of his own.

Eventually I moved to another table, where a Fire Support
major was belting out "I Saw Mommy Kissing Santa Claus." Jackson was right behind me, once again taking the chair next to mine.
He actually grinned when a master sergeant told an elaborate story
about a member of the *mutawwa'in,* the Saudi religious police, who

almost got run over up on the Tapline Road trying to stop a female American soldier driving a five-ton truck. Women were not allowed to drive in Saudi Arabia, or even to appear in public without a male relative. And outside their homes, women had to be covered from head to ankle in a dark cloak-like *abaya*. So the presence of thousands of American service women in desert uniform, many of them driving huge trucks—obviously unaccompanied by a male family member—was a constant source of irritation for the local religious police.

The story actually got a laugh out of Jackson. "That's great, Sergeant," he said.

I shifted tables. Jackson moved with me.

At the end of the party, we joined in singing "Silent Night." Specialist Jackson sang every verse in a strong, clear, and beautiful voice.

When the carol ended, Jackson put his arms around me. "Thank you so much, Sir. This is the best Christmas of my life."

I was out in the dark desert night before the soldiers could see the tears in my eyes. We'd been feeling sorry for ourselves, desperately missing our families, despite the Christmas tree and the cookies or perhaps because of them. And there was Jackson, enjoying the first real family Christmas he'd probably ever had. I had forgotten the simple truth I'd learned in Vietnam: Soldiers have two families, the one they're born into, and the other that includes all the men and women with whom they serve.

In a month, some of these kids would likely be dead.

Mindful of that young soldier named Garcia, who had fallen through the cracks in the 1st Squadron Howitzer Battery, I thought: This young man is fortunate to have the Army—and the Army is fortunate to have him.

THE AIR CAMPAIGN AGAINST IRAQ BEGAN AT 0400 ON JANUARY 17, 1991. Operation Desert Shield became Desert Storm. And around the clock for weeks, American, British, French, Italian, and Arab planes pounded the Iraqi army and Command and Control targets in and near Baghdad.

TURKEY

Murat

Maku

Tatvan

Baskale

Tabriz

azig

Dicle

Sanliurfa

Al Qamishli

Saqqez

Mosul

Arbil

IRAN

SYRIA

Ar Raqqah

Dayr az
Zawr

Tigris

Sulaymaniyah

Kirkuk

Bayji

Hamadan

Tikrit

Kermanshah

Haditah

Al Haqlaniyah

Khorramabad

Euphrates

Ar Rutbah

Ar Ramadi

Al Fallujah

Baghdad

Tigris

Al Küt

Karbalá

An Najaf

Al Amarah

Ahvaz

As Samáwah

Qurnah

An Násiríyah

Basrah

U.S. XVIII
Airborne Corps
3 Divisions & 1 ACR

Umm Qasr

RG

Sakakah

Rafha

4 Republican
Guard Divisions

RG

RG
RG

KUWAIT

Kuw

U.S. VII Corps
5 Divisions & 1 ACR

1st Cavalry
Division

Iraqi Army
Corps

Pe

Wadi al Bain

Arab-Islamic
Corps

Al Qaysumah

U.S. Marine Corps
2 Divisions

Al Mish'al

Iraq

Operation Desert Storm
February – March 1991

0   100   200 kilometers

0   50   100   150 miles

Petho Cartography 2004

SAUDI ARABIA

When the bombing began, the Division came under the operational control (OPCON) of General Frederick Franks (no relation) and his VII Corps. At a conference held beneath the emerald tile domes of King Khalid Military City, General Schwarzkopf briefed the Coalition's most senior leaders on the final Desert Storm plan. Rather than surging directly into the solid Iraqi defenses on Kuwait's borders, VII Corps' heavy divisions would conduct an audacious "left hook" maneuver toward the west and north. Then those divisions would wheel to the right and strike the enemy's exposed flank. Farther to the west, the lighter, faster units of the XVIII Airborne Corps would leapfrog north to seize Highway 8 on the Euphrates River, blocking the Iraqi line of retreat toward Baghdad. An amphibious task force feinting a landing in Kuwait would freeze the eastern Iraqi divisions along the coast, and the two Marine divisions just inland would push through the enemy minefields and bunkers and roll straight toward Kuwait City.

Surprise and speed were key elements of the plan.

So was deception. And deception was the responsibility of the 1st Cavalry Division. As the Army Forces Commander, Lt. General John Yeosock, and VII Corps Commander Frederick Franks briefed the Division's senior officers, we were told that our job was to convince the enemy that the main Allied attack would come up the historic invasion route into Iraq, the Wadi al Batin. The Wadi was a wide, dry riverbed that ran north from the Saudi plateau to the delta of the Tigris and Euphrates, forming the western border of Kuwait. Keeping the enemy's attention focused on the Wadi would divert him from the main Coalition thrust to the west.

Our mission was to engage the six Iraqi regular army divisions defending the Wadi in the south and fix the Tawalkana and Medina Republican Guards Divisions in their positions farther north. A successful deception would exploit the Iraqi military doctrine that had evolved during the war with Iran, under which Saddam's commanders deployed expendable infantry divisions—manned with draftees and reservists—on the front lines as cannon fodder to slow enemy attacks, while retaining the more disciplined, well-equipped Republican Guards farther to the rear as counter-attack forces. This was exactly how enemy forces were "stacked" when the air campaign began. And our job was to keep them that way.

Generals Yeosock and Franks gave us our mission. We devised the tactics.

Having studied the Iran-Iraq War, I recognized that massed long-range artillery had been a common feature on both sides of the battle lines. Iraqi commanders would expect the main Coalition assault to be preceded by an intense bombardment. Indeed, CENTCOM intelligence reported that concentrated American artillery fire would be the most important indicator to the Iraqis of the location and time of the Allied assault.

And, since the Wadi al Batin's escarpment walls offered natural flank protection, the choice of the valley as the invasion route north would seem plausible. But the Iraqis were neither stupid nor inexperienced; in fact, they had more commanders who had led troops in combat than we did. The Cavalry Division's job would be to convince these battle-hardened enemy commanders to hold their units in place, dug in against the relentless Coalition air campaign while they waited for the Coalition's main attack up the Wadi—an attack that would never come.

In late January, the Division moved north of the Tapline Road and took up positions west of the Wadi, where the borders of Saudi Arabia, Iraq, and Kuwait met. Our concept assumed that Iraqi aerial reconnaissance, which had been active along the border for months, had been blinded when Coalition fighters destroyed scores of enemy aircraft and sent the rest scurrying for dubious sanctuary in Iran. But we intended to let the Iraqis know there was a large and powerful American formation just below the border berm.

"We want to keep them guessing," I told Colonel Jim Gass, our DIVARTY commander, on the morning of February 7. He and his subordinate artillery battalion commanders stood beside me in front of a large tactical map in the Division command post. I tapped the sheet just north of the border. "Our first objective will be these observation towers. It's essential to blind the border guards and reconnaissance troops regarding our true strength and disposition."

The officers agreed. There was a line of forty-foot Iraqi observation towers about two kilometers north of the berm, marching off in both directions to the horizons like huge concrete fence posts. With this pool-table flat terrain, the towers allowed the Iraqis to see into our rear areas, even without the benefit of reconnaissance aircraft. And we'd discovered they used the towers to guide sappers—engineer demolitions experts—into our sector to plant mines. I'd been up on the berm with an intelligence team the previous afternoon, watching the Iraqi troops through binoculars. Each day they changed shifts in the towers every eight hours, beginning at dawn.

Today, we had a surprise for them. I outlined the plan, as the Artillery officers took careful notes.

That afternoon, just as the Iraqi observation teams prepared to rotate duty at several of the towers, a sand-brown Fire Support Team Vehicle (FIST-V) rolled up to the border berm. As I watched from my Humvee, the FIST-V, a modern variant of the old M-113 tracks, raised its squat T-shaped laser designator and illuminated the nearest tower with an invisible beam. At precisely 1358 Hours, the Fire Support Team verified their exact coordinates using a Global Positioning System (GPS) satellite receiver, and transmitted computerized target data to an M109 self-propelled 155 mm howitzer ten kilometers to the south. The gun fired a Copperhead high explosive projectile, which rode the laser beam precisely to the target.

Exploding like a firecracker, the tower disappeared in a cloud of smoke and pulverized concrete. By then, the FIST-V had already lased the next tower and within three minutes another Copperhead struck. As the survivors at the first tower ran for their truck, the area erupted with hundreds of exploding dual-purpose Improved conventional munitions (ICM) bomblets from another howitzer.

This attack was the first time American artillerymen had fired Copperheads and large volumes of ICM in combat—and the results were impressive. Three towers and their crews were destroyed in nine minutes. Now the enemy to our front was blind, and we would begin the main phase of our deception mission.

Over the next week, DIVARTY howitzers stole up to the berm day and night and engaged enemy positions and bunkers illuminated by lasers in FIST-Vs and OH-58 Kiowa helicopters. From the Persian Gulf beaches in the east to the border with Jordan in the west, these were the only Coalition guns firing. The enemy would have every reason to assume the Wadi al Batin would be our main axis of attack.

Just to make sure, though, we raised the deception ante. On the moonless night of February 13, I stood with Freddy Franks and John Tilelli on the cold sand near the Wadi al Batin. The desert around us suddenly erupted like a blast furnace. For ninety seconds, twenty-seven multiple launch rocket systems from the Division and VII Corps Artillery launched a massed salvo across the berm, into Iraqi positions straddling the Wadi. As the rockets blazed north, the sky was laced with hundreds of fiery pinwheel smoke clouds. Then the northern horizon shimmered, like heat lightning on the West Texas flatlands. Moments later, rippling blasts from thousands of ICM bomblets crackled through the dark. The trenches and sandbagged artillery pits of two Iraqi infantry divisions had just been saturated with fire.

But there was more work to do.

Near midnight on February 16, I stood beside Colonel Jim Gass's DIVARTY command track on the western lip of the Wadi. The darkness vanished as five battalions of 155 mm howitzers—ninety guns in all—and twenty-seven MLRS launchers fired a three-minute barrage that shook the ground beneath our boots. Once more, the northern horizon glowed and pulsed with overlapping explosions. A two-kilometer-wide sector thick with Iraqi ZSU-23mm antiaircraft artillery positions was pulverized by combined HE and ICM projectiles.

Between salvoes, we heard the distinctive rotor thwack of AH-64 Apache gunships. "Time for Act Two," Jim Gass shouted over the roar of the artillery. Twenty-four gunships from the 11th Aviation Brigade swept past, long dark shapes lit from below by the howitzer muzzle flashes. As they crossed the berm, the Apaches spread left and right into a wide attack formation. The last of the artillery projectiles struck as the choppers reached their targets, a series of radio towers and communications bunkers that connected the frontline Iraqi divisions with their corps headquarters deeper inside Iraq. Using infrared night sights, the Apaches launched laser-guided Hellfire missiles into the enemy towers and buildings, and engaged the Iraqi troops with their fast-firing 30 mm chain guns.

As the gunships hovered, an electronic intelligence (ELINT) plane orbiting nearby detected an enemy antiaircraft radar probing for the gunships. The plane transmitted target data to Gass's track. Twelve MLRS rockets burst above the radar site three minutes later, shredding the equipment and operators with what the Iraqis had come to call "steel rain."

With negotiations reaching a fever pitch, as the Iraqis tried desperately to avoid the impending Coalition ground assault, our artillery raids continued.

General Schwarzkopf alerted the coalition to be prepared to launch the ground attack by February 23 if the windy winter rain and blowing dust abated. We continued firing across the berm. Every night, psychological operations (PSYOP) units drove trucks fitted with gigantic loudspeakers slowly back and forth along the border, playing recordings of clanking tanks and Bradleys. And this ruse complemented another of our PSYOP efforts, which broadcast bogus radio transmissions mimicking several heavy divisions moving forward to their final preattack tactical assembly areas.

All this was followed on February 20 by our most ambitious deception maneuver: Operation Knight Strike. Any way we cut this deal, it would be impossible to execute a persuasive deception that didn't involve ground contact with the enemy. So, in Operation Knight Strike, Colonel Randy House, commander of the Division's 2nd "Blackjack"

Brigade, would sweep straight up the Wadi in a tank-heavy brigade wedge formation. The intention was to convince the Iraqis that this thrust was the spearhead of the main assault.

The operation jumped off at noon, with Bradleys of the 1st Squadron, 5th Cavalry, scouting ahead of rumbling M1A1 Abrams tanks. House would engage the Iraqi mechanized infantry and armor units we knew were dug in ten kilometers up the Wadi in a "movement to contact," a classic American offensive maneuver. We would accept the risk of encountering a much larger enemy force in order to accomplish our mission, but Randy House would not permit his brigade to become "decisively engaged." The operation would be a probe—not a commitment to stand toe to toe and slug it out.

To my mind, the critical distinction here was one I would encounter repeatedly in my military career: There is always a difference between a calculated operational risk, in which potential dangers and losses are carefully estimated and judged in advance, and a gamble, in which caution is thrown to the wind. An adaptive military unit can recover from risk, whereas a gamble can result in total loss. I knew the 2nd Brigade had enough firepower to defeat any front line Iraqi unit it would encounter in the Wadi, because I had studied the reconnaissance pictures and intelligence reports of the enemy positions. And I also had evaluated our battle damage assessments (BDA) from the four weeks of the air campaign. My time in Vietnam had taught me the value of soldiers' lives; we would take a risk in the Wadi deception, but we would not gamble with the lives of our troops.

I paced back and forth in the tactical command post, listening to the expected exchanges over the Brigade radio net as Randy House's armor moved north. For the first few kilometers they encountered no enemy contact, no land mines. Then the radio speaker burst with a series of rapid reports. Lt. Colonel Michael Parker, commander of the cavalry screening force, was in contact with a battalion of Iraqi mechanized infantry in low-slung BMP infantry fighting vehicles, supported by T-62 tanks. As the fight developed, Iraqi artillery fell among the maneuvering American vehicles.

House's armor reacted swiftly. The Abrams sped north and spread across the floor of the Wadi, in a maneuver the brigade had practiced day and night out at the National Training Center in the deserts of Fort Irwin, California.

What had been a thin wedge of lightly armored Bradleys quickly became a wall of M1A1 tanks firing high explosive antitank (HEAT) rounds into the enemy formation. The fight was fast, and one-sided. As the Iraqis fell back, they left behind the smoking hulks of BMPs and T-62 tanks, several with their turrets blown completely off.

"Proceeding to Phase Line Maryland," House reported, naming the next objective on his line of march.

"Roger," I replied. "Good work."

I lit my third cigar of the day, and fought the urge to climb into my Black Hawk and fly north to observe the battle firsthand. But this was Randy House's show, and he was doing a hell of a good job.

The tanks were back on the flanks of the Brigade wedge, with Parker's cavalry screen again scouting forward. House's troops had bloodied the enemy, and weathered their first experience of direct ground combat.

But then, as so often happens in war, the situation changed suddenly.

Amid the confusing babble of excited voices on the radio, I caught a garbled report of enemy 100 mm antitank guns in bunkers on the western slope of the Wadi. The Brigade net grew loud and frantic.

Randy was reporting that an artillery Fire Support Team had spotted the concealed Iraqi guns, but hadn't had time to order a fire mission before the Iraqis opened fire on three lightly armored tracks that had stopped to round up several surrendering Iraqi troops. The enemy shells had ripped through an M113 and two Bradleys. As an Abrams maneuvered to assist, it struck an antitank mine. The Iraqis had executed a well-planned ambush.

"General," Randy said. "We've got three KIA and nine WIA, some of them critical. I'm falling back to Phase Line Massachusetts."

I stared at the map. Three American soldiers had been killed and nine wounded. Randy sought to break contact, rather than expose additional thin-skinned Bradleys and M-113 tracks to hidden anti-tank guns. It was precisely what I would have wanted to do—but not the right course of action if we were to convince the Iraqis this was our main attack.

I took the microphone from my radio operator. "Blackjack Six, I want you to remain engaged, destroy those enemy positions, and retrieve the damaged vehicles."

There was a short pause. "Pegasus Eight, this is Blackjack Six, Wilco."

As Randy worked up in the Wadi, I alerted my Black Hawk crew that we were flying north. On the flight, I monitored the radio nets and heard House's FIST calling in missions and air strikes. As the 2nd Brigade's engineers were recovering the damaged vehicles, the Iraqi antitank guns, their crews and their bunkers, were being blown to bits by 155 mm artillery projectiles, 500-lb bombs, and hundreds of rounds from the 30 mm Gatling guns of circling Air Force A-10 Warthogs.

I greeted House at the brigade rally point on the berm. The medics were transferring the wounded to ambulance tracks. Three dead soldiers lay on stretchers, covered with ponchos beside another track. Randy was a brave man, in control. He was a good commander and I was proud of him.

I thought back to Eric Antila's reassuring words and calm manner after that terrible day in March 1968 when the VC blew up Dick Bahr's track near Cai Lay. I put my arm around Randy's shoulder. "You did well," I told him. "So did your soldiers. You got the job done."

The engineers were pulling back the damaged armor. "Everything that happened in the Wadi today was my responsibility, Colonel," I said formally. "Your mission was to move to contact, and you executed that mission to the letter." If there was going to be any negative reaction from higher headquarters, I wanted it on my head, not Randy's. As a young lieutenant in Vietnam, I had learned that loyalty flowed both up and down. And as a general I would honor that principle.

I inspected the battle damage on the wrecked vehicles, to make sure they hadn't been hit with friendly fire in the confusion of combat. With all the high-technology firepower deployed in this war zone, what we called "fratricide" was already proving to be a real danger. Two weeks earlier, one of the Air Force's high-speed anti-radiation (HARM) missiles, targeted on Iraqi air defenses, had mistakenly homed in on one of our ground-surveillance radars near the border berm, ripping the roof off the control van and wounding two soldiers. In the Wadi, however, the damage inflicted on the 2nd Brigade's vehicles had come from enemy fire.

As I returned to my helicopter, I stopped beside the stretchers of the dead soldiers, removed my helmet, and bowed my head. "Rest in peace," I murmured. These would not be the last soldiers we would lose in this war . . . and I knew it.

That dawn, I had printed on my daily three-by-five card under Challenges, "Casualties in the Wadi." Under Opportunities, I had written "Successful deception. The enemy remains fixed in place."

THE MAJOR COALITION GROUND ATTACK BEGAN BEFORE DAWN ON G-Day, February 24, 1991. Following the plan, the heavy divisions of VII Corps rolled across the flat desert into Iraq, moving north at high speed, well west of the Iraqi army formations stacked up in fixed defensive positions in the Wadi al Batin. To ensure that the enemy remained where he was, the Division sent Randy House's Blackjack Brigade back up the Wadi, preceded by massed barrages of 155 mm artillery and MLRS. The Brigade fought savagely, with armored task forces racing up both sides of the valley, destroying dug-in enemy armor to the left and right before withdrawing south of the berm to join the rest of the Division.

That night, as the eastern sky blackened from hundreds of burning Kuwaiti oil wells the Iraqis had set ablaze, we were in tactical positions south of the berm, being held as General Schwarzkopf's theater reserve. But when it became obvious the next afternoon that VII Corps had moved deep enough into Iraq to begin its wheeling turn to the east to strike the enemy's exposed flanks, Schwarzkopf issued new orders: "Send in the First Team, the 1st Cavalry Division. Destroy the Republican Guard. Let's go home."

We headed west and north through the breach in the Iraqi lines that the 1st Infantry Division had cut on G-Day. Driving ahead in brigade wedges at the fastest possible speed, we slashed through the disorganized remains of four Iraqi divisions, destroying their remnants and leaving behind thousands of confused prisoners of war for the MPs who followed us in the long support tail.

A gale-force *shamal* sandstorm blew out of the west. The sky turned brown, then a dark rusty orange. The wind howled, and it began to rain.

"Actually, Sir," one of the command post drivers explained as he wiped the smeared windshield of his Humvee. "It ain't raining so much as what you'd call *mudding*."

Visibility dropped to less than one hundred meters; our minimum flying ceiling was gone, and our helicopters were grounded. But the Division pressed on.

The thud of heavy guns sounded above the howling gale to the east. VII Corps' armor was smashing into the flanks of the Tawakalna and Medina Republican Guard Divisions, still oriented to the south, waiting for a main attack up the Wadi al Batin—an attack that never came. We raced north. Well-trained M1A1 and Bradley crews used thermal sights to pierce the sandstorm, targeting Iraqi armor with cannon fire and TOW missiles. In the largest tank battle since World War II, the Coalition was overwhelming the enemy.

By late afternoon on February 27, the wind dropped and the sky cleared. The 1st Cavalry's eight hundred tanks, Bradleys, and support vehicles had crossed 192 miles of desert in thirty-three hours, and were formed up on the right flank of the 3rd Armored Cavalry Regiment, which was positioned near the northern point of VII Corps.

Ahead of us, the Hammurabi and Adnan Republican Guard Divisions were scrambling away from the Wadi, hoping to escape up the Euphrates Valley on Highway 8. But the route was blocked by the 24th Infantry Division's northernmost brigade. And, with the arrival of the 1st Cav, we now had enough armor and artillery firepower to crush the enemy's best combat units.

Late that night, at General Tilelli's command post, the Division's senior officers met to discuss the next day's operations. We had orders to refuel, re-arm, and refit over the next twelve hours, and then to move forward to contact.

As we examined the grease-pencil symbols on John Tilelli's map, one of the staff officers scratched his jaw. "Well," he said. "Saddam is going to get his 'Mother of All Battles' after all."

Nobody laughed.

I had just lain down to rest my eyes—and was submerged in some kind of weird dream—when the duty officer shook me awake.

"Sir," he said with a big grin. "Flash message from Corps. Cease fire in the Theater effective tomorrow at 0800."

The war was over. Months of preparation. One hundred hours of combat.

I was proud of the Division, the troops, and the leaders. And I was thankful that John Tilelli had let me do my job. He had been a teacher and a friend. The 1st Cav had been fortunate to have him as a wartime commander, and I was fortunate to have him as a boss.

FLYING BACK TO FORT HOOD ON THE CHARTER JET IN MARCH, I reviewed the lessons I'd learned as a young general officer. Some thoughts concerned important tactical issues, others simply the realities of life in the field.

The months in the desert had reinforced my longstanding conviction that sergeants really were the backbone of the Army. The average trooper depends on NCOs for leadership by personal example. I thought of Sam Long and Scag, of Staff Sergeant Kittle—they had been examples of what a sergeant should be. If a noncommissioned officer is dedicated to his troops, the squad or section will have hard, realistic training, hot food when it's available, and the chance to take an occasional shower. If a sergeant is indifferent to the needs of his soldiers, their performance will suffer, and their lives might be wasted. A smart officer works hard to develop good NCOs.

Generals are not infallible. The Army doesn't issue wisdom when it pins on the stars. Leading soldiers as a general means more than creating tactics and giving orders. The officers commanding brigades and battalions, the company commanders and the platoon leaders—all of them know more about their unit strengths and weaknesses than the general who leads them. So a successful general must listen more than he talks. He must process amazing amounts of information and use it to make hard decisions. And he must "take the blame while giving the credit to others." The troops must understand that their generals care about them—that they will not gamble with their lives, but rather will guide them, with dedication, toward the success of their mission, and to victory.

Operation Desert Storm marked the debut of precision guided munitions (PGM)—the so-called "smart bombs" that have revolutionized modern warfare. But PGMs are clever, not actually smart: A Copperhead round will hit whatever target a laser illuminates, but human minds and hands must be there to lock the laser onto the target.

"God fights on the side with the best artillery," Napoleon said. And yet, going into Desert Storm, the Iraqi army had thousands of Soviet-built artillery pieces. They outgunned us by three to two. What doomed them was that they used those guns poorly. When their observation towers were destroyed and they lost their communications nets, they did not improvise and adapt. Under constant harassment from Coalition aircraft—and justifiably afraid of our counter-fire radar, which tracked incoming projectiles and targeted the enemy guns for immediate destruction—the Iraqis often chose to sit tight and hope for the best.

Our troops were a flexible, highly adaptable fighting force. Colonel Jim Gass transformed the 1st Cav's artillery into the

Division's third maneuver element, able to keep pace with the tanks and mechanized infantry. When our FIST-V tracks proved too slow for our needs, our Fire Support troops mounted laser designators on high-speed Bradleys. Innovation remained a hallmark of the American soldier.

It was in Desert Storm that I became convinced of the power of deception in warfare; it truly is a force multiplier. Through well-planned and deftly executed feints and ruses, the 1st Cavalry Division fixed in place enemy formations that vastly outnumbered us, sometimes by as much as six to one. We used every available tool to convince the Iraqis that the Division was the spearhead of a Coalition assault up the Wadi al Batin. And while the Iraqis waited, VII Corps maneuvered through the sandstorms in the empty desert to the west, and struck the Republican Guards in the flank like a sledgehammer.

The world's most enduring strategic thinker, Sun Tzu, advised warriors 2,500 years ago to "Make your way by unexpected routes and attack unguarded spots." That was exactly what Coalition forces accomplished during Desert Storm. The result was, without doubt, the most impressive example of coordinated, flexible maneuver since General George Patton's 3rd Army drove across Western Europe in World War II.

And the Desert Storm Coalition relied on speed as well. For almost two hundred years, the maxims of the Prussian strategist Carl von Clausewitz had dictated that mass—concentrated formations of troops and guns—was the key to victory. To achieve victory, Clausewitz advised, a military power must mass its forces at the enemy's "center of gravity." But the victory in Desert Storm proved that speed has a mass all its own. A fast-moving battalion of M1A1 tanks, in the right place at the right time, has more destructive mass than a division of Republican Guard T-72s at the wrong place, sitting in defensive positions. The Iraqis had fielded more men, more tanks, and more artillery pieces than the Coalition. What defeated them was the combination of superior technology, realistic training, and the fluid, flexible tactics of the Coalition forces.

But the campaign was not without problems. It was designed as an operation that coordinated the efforts of a multinational, multiservice force. U.S. Central Command had thousands of troops, airmen, and sailors divided into ground, air, and naval components, each with its own three-star commander. General Schwarzkopf was not only the Commander in Chief (CINC), but also the de facto combined force land component commander (CFLCC). The result was that Schwarzkopf's staff spent a great deal of time and energy planning and executing ground operations, while the air component commander, Air Force Lt. General Charles "Chuck" Horner, planned and conducted the air component. This tended to separate the operation into an air campaign and a ground campaign—a "deconflicted" strategy (leading off with weeks of air strikes, and avoiding the ground units' areas of operations) rather than truly joint warfare.

Reading the initial after-action reports, I devoted some serious thought to the complex challenges of joint command in modern warfare. And I realized that the challenges would only intensify in the years ahead. With the Cold War behind us, the American military was downsizing. In fact, several of the Divisions that had fought so well on the sands of Iraq in 1991 would roll up their flags and be disbanded, as part of the overall cut back in forces. Future senior commanders would be expected to do more with less. In years to come, it was clear that practical joint cooperation, rather than mere "deconfliction," would be essential to victory.

And future wars would be fought with weapons and other technologies that would have seemed like science fiction when I was a lieutenant in Vietnam.

WITH ITS MOAT AND NINETEENTH-CENTURY STONE BATTLEMENTS overlooking the waters of Hampton Roads, Fort Monroe, Virginia, seemed a strange setting for the Army's most innovative think tank when I got there in June 1992. But it was close enough to Washington for easy access to the Pentagon, while still far enough from the intrigues of the Beltway to allow the Louisiana Maneuvers (LAM) Task Force to ponder the Army of the twenty-first century in a relatively tranquil setting.

Army Chief of Staff General Gordon Sullivan, among the most innovative military leaders of the twentieth century, was creating a "Futures laboratory," and had chosen me as its director. He named the organization after a series of field exercises the Army held in rural Louisiana in the summer of 1940, when Chief of Staff General George C. Marshall—alarmed by Nazi Germany's stunning Blitzkrieg victory in France that spring—grabbed America's complacent peacetime Army by the scruff of its neck and shook it, searching for innovative tactics and energetic commanders to lead America in the looming global conflict. Out of that field exercise emerged leaders like George Patton—along with the principles of modern combined-arms warfare that led America to victory in World War II.

General Sullivan intended to use the end of the Cold War, as the Army withdrew formations from Europe, to shape and hone a leaner, but more flexible and lethal, fighting force.

When he selected me for the job, General Sullivan handed me a computer-generated briefing slide. "Keep this in mind," he said. His words could not have been more clear: "Smaller is not better. Better is better."

Future operational doctrine would no longer be three-dimensional, with victory going to the side that marshaled the largest fighting force with the greatest number of tanks, ships, and aircraft. Now there would be a fourth dimension: time. In the twenty-first century, operational success—what the military calls "effect"—would be found in both space and time: putting the most effective force, at the right place, at the right time. In this new way of thinking, the historical strategic imperatives of objective, mass, and economy of force would acquire new meaning. Suddenly, the timeworn banner "Revolution in Military Affairs," trotted out by strategic thinkers every few years to trumpet some small advance, was no longer mere hyperbole. It would become the new reality of war.

As General Sullivan outlined the Army's overall situation, though, it was undeniable that the fighting force of the future would be smaller than at any time since Vietnam. After the reunification of Germany in 1989, almost 300,000 soldiers and family members had been redeployed from Europe to the United States. The number of active duty Army divisions had fallen from eighteen to thirteen, and was scheduled to drop to ten. Overall, the Army had cut its ranks by 400,000 soldiers and civilian employees. And Congress and the Pentagon were slashing budgets, eager to cash in on the "peace dividend" that was due following the collapse of the Soviet Union.

The job of the LAM Task Force was to explore the potential of innovative technology, doctrine, procedures, and training to ensure that this leaner war-fighting force would also remain the world's most powerful. For years, I had tinkered with tactical innovation. Now, as a key player in this broad initiative to remake the Army, I was entering the big leagues.

My position as the brigadier general task force director was similar to that of a vice president in a large corporation. Its board of directors was comprised of the chief of staff and the Army's four-star generals. And, as in the corporate world, we had no shortage of consultants—a group of two-star generals with expertise in all facets of Army operations.

Our task from General Sullivan was to take a hard look at the most important things the Army did, the structure of our units, our training methods, and the procedures we used to develop and procure new weapons and equipment. We were physically located beside the headquarters of the Training and Doctrine Command (TRADOC), which was traditionally responsible for force structure, education, and training. And, in effect, TRADOC was the Task Force's most important customer.

The context for this wide-ranging reevaluation was the idea that America would no longer require a huge, expensive ground force based overseas. Instead the Army's war-fighting units would be stationed in the United States, and would be trained and equipped as a Power Projection force, able to deploy quickly anywhere in the world in time of crisis or conflict.

For decades, the Cold War Army's combat units had trained "on location," so to speak—in Western Europe or the Korean Peninsula, where they were most likely to see future combat. The war-fighting doctrine of the era, and the weapons systems it generated, produced the concept of the Air Land Battle, which depended on rapidly maneuvering large formations armed with high-technology weapons.

The Army never fought an Air Land Battle against the Soviet Union in Germany's Fulda Gap. But speeding north toward the Euphrates Valley on February 27, 1991, I had witnessed an Air Land Battle crushing the Iraqi Republican Guard. For better or worse, I would never again see the spectacle of five heavy divisions and two armored cavalry regiments with their thousands of tanks and fighting vehicles spread across hundreds of square miles of desert. Eighteen months after Operation Desert Storm, half of those Cold War units had been disbanded. When America went to war again, it would be with a smaller Army. Our job in the Task Force was to make sure that Army could still win wars.

Early in my work, it became obvious that future military operations would be much different from those I had seen in our long standoff against a monolithic, well-defined threat on the other side of the Iron Curtain.

The former Yugoslavia had imploded into a vicious civil war, and NATO was caught up in the widening Balkan conflict. There was the danger that American forces could become involved in the endless strife between Israel and the Palestinians. Brush-fire wars and rebellions were flaring across Africa. In Colombia, the government's endless struggle against left-wing guerrillas threatened to destabilize the region. And, though a tense truce prevailed on the Korean peninsula, it could shatter at any moment.

Despite Iraq's lopsided defeat in 1991, Saddam Hussein's regime was still a destabilizing threat to the region. Soon after the March ceasefire, Shiites in southern Iraq rebelled against the Baathist government that had repressed them for decades. And Kurdish tribes in the north followed suit. But as the Coalition forces withdrew, Saddam's military savagely crushed these revolts, massacring thousands and creating tens of thousands of refugees. The United States led a humanitarian assistance effort to rescue the Kurdish refugees starving in the northern mountains and the Shiites fleeing south to Kuwait and Saudi Arabia. Implementing a new set of U.N. Security Council resolutions, which required Saddam to stop the slaughter of his own people, the United States, Britain, and France imposed northern and southern no-fly zones in Iraq in 1991 and 1992.

Coalition forces had destroyed some stockpiles of chemical weapons before withdrawing from southern Iraq in April 1991. And, that summer, U.N. weapons inspectors attempted to supervise the destruction of Iraq's remaining caches of poison gas and biological weapons, as well as precursor chemicals and growth media. The destruction of long-range Iraqi missiles and the dismantling of Saddam's nuclear weapons production plants were also on the inspectors' agenda. But the regime stalled, equivocated, and actively resisted inspections each time the U.N. teams got too close to sensitive sites.

Controlled by U.N. sanctions and the no-fly zones, Saddam Hussein was temporarily contained—"in the box," in Pentagon jargon. A tense standoff had begun; it would last for years.

As I read each intelligence report on Iraq's dubious cooperation with the U.N. weapons inspectors, it was clear that Saddam's regime remained a threat.

But Iraq was only one crisis zone that had flared up since the collapse of the Soviet Union. And units of a downsized U.S. Army were committed to many of these trouble spots, performing such nontraditional operations as peacekeeping, peace enforcement, humanitarian assistance, and drug interdiction. Between 1990 and 1995, the

Army would conduct forty-seven major operational deployments—a 50 percent increase over the Cold War years.

The mission of the LAM Task Force was to understand the geostrategic context of the 1990s, and then to identify the force structure, weapons, and soldiers that the Army would need in the future to operate effectively in an increasingly dangerous and unpredictable world.

My work was fascinating, but arduous. If I'd expected a laid-back atmosphere of theoretical contemplation, with plenty of off-duty time for my family, General Sullivan and the board of four stars quickly set me straight. Being the Task Force director meant acting as meeting coordinator, travel facilitator, conference scheduler, academic and industry-expert recruiter, and confidant to the Chief.

Cathy and I bought a small sailboat, hoping to enjoy the creeks and inlets of Chesapeake Bay. But even with daylight saving time, I rarely got away from the office before dark. Cathy took advantage of her time by completing her master's degree in educational administration at George Washington University.

We did manage a long weekend in September 1992. Our daughter, Jacqy—the little girl who used to fall asleep on the couch in our apartment waiting for her daddy, Captain Franks, to come home from the kaserne—was marrying her own Army captain. Jacqy had met Patrick Matlock at Fort Hood in 1990 when he was a first lieutenant in the Cavalry's 3-32 Armor, one of the units that went on to fight so well during Desert Storm. Patrick was a sharp West Pointer, on a fast track for command. Their wedding was in the New Post Chapel at Fort Sill, Oklahoma, the same church where Cathy and I were married.

It was an emotional experience, watching Jacqy in her white gown, looking very much her mother's lovely daughter, on the arm of a young captain in Army dress blues, leaving that chapel under the arch of sabers. Somehow, twenty-three years had passed since the warm spring day when Cathy and I strode joyfully from the church, a beautiful young bride in white on the arm of a young captain.

My mother was there, brimming with happiness. At the reception, she looked at the Gulf War campaign ribbons on my uniform and asked her perennial question: "How much longer you got to do, Son?"

Mother never quite grasped that I was a professional soldier, that I wasn't "serving a set hitch"—as my father had during World War II.

I hugged her, feeling how light and frail she'd become since her cancer surgery in the 1980s. "Oh, Mother, it'll be a good while yet."

Less than a year after Jacqy's wedding, Cathy's mother, Gaynelle, called with the message we had been dreading. "Your mother's gone, Tom."

I'd thought I was prepared. But the news was still a cold shock. Mother's cancer had recurred. She'd moved to the suburbs of Dallas, where Gaynelle had cared for her like she was an older sister. Gaynelle had driven her to medical appointments and cooked for her in the small assisted-living apartment. And Gaynelle had been with Mother at the end. As we spoke, I recognized again that the bond of love extended past the ties of blood.

After the funeral, I returned to a desk stacked high with urgent tasks.

Around noon on a Saturday afternoon in May 1993, my long-suffering XO dropped a stack of electronic message printouts— precursors of today's ubiquitous e-mails—on my desk . . . just as I was about to leave to go sailing with Cathy.

"The Chief wants these worked by the 0730 conference call on Monday," he said.

I scanned the messages; they were mainly requests for information on the latest simulation technology that was available off-the-shelf in the civilian marketplace. One of my early recommendations had been to shortcut the laborious Cold War procurement process made notorious by the Pentagon's $640 toilet seat and $435 claw hammer. And, as they say, I'd been hoist upon my own petard. The board was scheduled to discuss the subject next week and I had to prepare General Sullivan for the meeting—a task that would take what was left of Saturday, and most of Sunday, to complete.

I reached for the phone to call Cathy. "Peace is hell," I muttered.

The work of the LAM Task Force was difficult, but we did make progress. We approached the task of creating a twenty-first century force by reviewing the six fundamental "domains," or building blocks, of the Army. Naturally, they bore a tongue-twisting acronym: DTLOMS, for Doctrine, Training, Leader Development, Organizations, Materiel, and Soldiers.

For almost fifty years, the Army's basic doctrine had focused on containment of the Soviet Union at the Iron Curtain by stationing heavy armor and mechanized infantry formations in Europe. And, because we couldn't match the Warsaw Pact in numbers of troops and tanks, our units—right down to individual howitzer batteries— had been armed with tactical nuclear weapons, as I had when I commanded the battery at Hans Schemme *kaserne* in the mid-1970s.

Now the cornerstone of our new doctrine would be rapid deployment of U.S.-based units virtually anywhere in the world. But it would be impossible to deploy thousands of tanks, infantry fighting vehicles, and all of their support base as quickly as might be necessary in a sudden crisis. The buildup for Operation Desert Storm had taken six months before all the units were in place for a ground war. It would be foolish to assume that the pace of future wars would be as slow.

The twenty-first century doctrine we developed at the Task Force involved prepositioning weapons and equipment at depots and onboard ships in the Mediterranean, the Middle East, the Indian Ocean, and Asia. In a crisis, troops would be airlifted in, joining up with their tanks, guns, trucks, ammunition—and their rations, field hospitals, and all the thousands of other bits and pieces a modern fighting force needs.

Training is as important to the Army as education is to civilian life, and at the Task Force we launched an intense, bottom-up study of Army training procedures. In the face of reduced "peacetime" budgets, we explored innovative ways to bring new troops up to combat readiness—techniques that would be both cheaper *and* more effective.

It soon became obvious that digitally assisted simulation was a critical technology that could supplement, if not totally replace, much of the complex and expensive live-fire training the Army had relied on since World War II. Drawing on civilian advances in virtual reality technology, the Army was soon buying simulators for most of its major weapon systems. The crews of Abrams tanks, Bradley fighting vehicles, and Apache gunships were now training in simulators that replicated the noise, jolting motion, and chaos of combat; the effect was so authentic that some Gulf War veterans reported the experience was almost too realistic.

Even the most convincing simulator, of course, could never totally replace the experience of boots-on-the-ground field exercises with actual weapons and equipment. But the Task Force did recommend dozens of computerized upgrades to the National Training Center at Fort Irwin, California, where the Army honed its desert warfare skills, and to the Joint Readiness Training Center at Fort Polk, Louisiana, where soldiers trained for dismounted operations and urban combat. Laser-simulated "fire" from tank guns and small arms taught soldiers to fight realistic, but bloodless battles, while video playbacks showed commanders how well their forces had maneuvered. We also promoted "man in the loop" feedback into simulation networks, which allowed separate branches of the combat arms located at different bases to war-game with their colleagues on a digital battlefield.

The accelerating revolution in simulation technology eventually reached beyond individual soldiers and combat units to their commanders and staffs. We now had the capability to simulate rapid deployment of large units, all the way up to corps level. In the past, the massive periodic exercise known as Return of Forces to Germany (REFORGER) had involved transporting thousands of troops across the Atlantic, an operation that cost tens of millions of dollars. Now the entire complex process—with all its inevitable problems and foulups—could be simulated by computer.

Within a year, high-tech breakthroughs began to snowball across the Army. As the Information Age matured in the civilian world, the

Private Franks, Basic Training, Fort Leonard Wood, Missouri, 1965. Staff Sergeant Kittle had his work cut out for him.

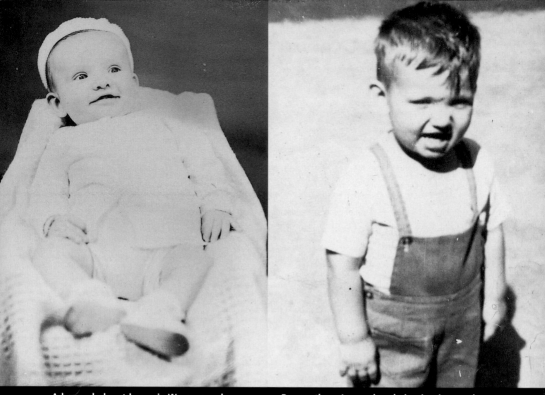

A happy baby at home in Wynnewood, Oklahoma, November 1945.

By age three I was already issuing instructions.

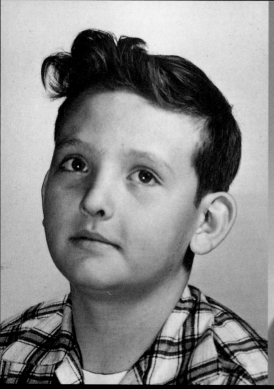

At age eight in Stratford, Oklahoma. My thoughts were on my horse and my new Daisy BB gun.

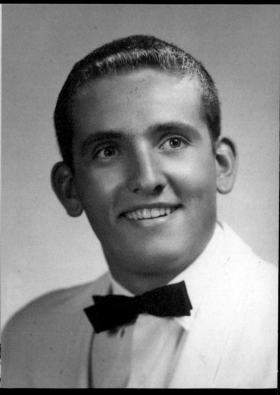

As a senior at Lee High School, with a white sports coat and a pink carnation.

As Second Lieutenant Franks, with my mother, February 14, 1967, the day I graduated from Officer Candidate School in Fort Sill, Oklahoma.

In beautiful downtown Binh Phuoc, Vietnam, holding a captured Vietcong flag, 1967.

With Vietnamese children in a Tan An orphanage, 1968. My mother and her friends "adopted" these kids and sent packages of clothing and school supplies to them.

On the rear deck of an M-113 armored personnel carrier—my home away from home—with 5-60th Infantry, South Vietnam, 1967.

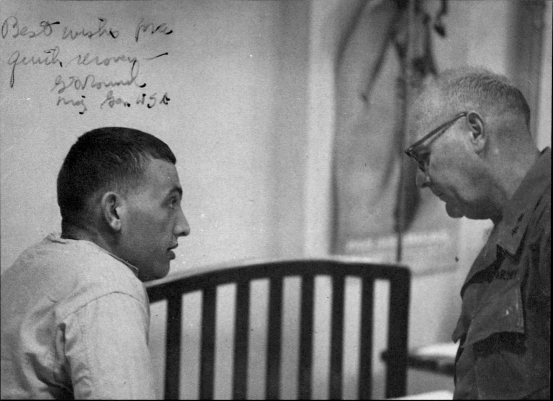

Best wishes for a
quick recovery —
[signature]
Maj Gen USA

Major General O'Connor, Commander 9th Infantry Division, visits me at 3rd Field Hospital in Saigon, December 1967, a few days before Raquel Welch's visit. I was recovering from an injury for which I received the Purple Heart.

I married Cathryn Jane Carley at New Post Chapel, Fort Sill, Oklahoma, March 22, 1969.

In Berlin at the height of the Cold War, with Captain John Paro, at the edge of the Iron Curtain, 1982.

As Commander 2-78 Field Artillery, Bamberg, Germany, with General Glen Otis, Commander U.S. Army Europe, and Colonel Wayne Downing, Commander 3rd Brigade, 1st Armored Division, 1983.

With General Norman Schwarzkopf at the end of Operation Desert Storm, March 1991.

On combined field maneuvers, Korea, 1996.

Promoted to General the day I took command of CENTCOM, with Cathy and General Hugh Shelton, MacDill Air Force Base, 2000.

With King Abdullah II of Jordan on a training exercise with Jordanian Special Forces near the Iraqi border, 2000.

On a motorcycle ride with King Abdullah II of Jordan, August 2001.

Meeting the Emir of Kuwait, Jabir Al-Ahmad Al-Jabir Al Sabah, 2001.

Discussions with Crown Prince Abdullah of Saudi Arabia (far right), 2001.

With President Islam Karimov, engaging regional leaders in support of Operation Enduring Freedom, Uzbekistan, 2001.

With President Imomali Rakhmonov of Tajikistan, more horse trading for basing and staging, 2001.

Discussion with President Pervez Musharraf of Pakistan, 2003.

Meeting with King Hamad ibn Isa II, Bahrain, 2003.

With President Hosni Mubarak of Egypt, January 2003.

Sheik Mohammed Bin Zayed, Military Chief of Staff of the United Arab Emirates, visits John Abizaid and me in my office at Camp As Sayliyah, 2003.

Drinking tea with Afghan opposition leaders; General Mohammed Mohaqeq, General Mohammed Attah, General Abdul Rashid Dostum, and me. Victory was the subject of our conversation. Mazar-e Sharif, Afghanistan, November 2001.

Talking tactics with Colonel John Mulholland, Commander 5th Special Forces Group (right), Bagram, Afghanistan, November 2001.

At the inauguration of President Hamid Karzai, December 22, 2001, Kabul, Afghanistan. In the background is a portrait of the assassinated Commander Ahmad Shah Massoud, the Lion of Panjshir.

concept of digital, three-dimensional "battlespace" became a reality. Plasma screens replaced paper maps in computerized command posts and higher-echelon headquarters. Bandwidth to receive and deliver data was becoming an asset as vital as ammunition and fuel.

With the growth of technology, the traditional Command and Control (C2) model rapidly evolved through C3—Command and Control and Communications—to C4, adding Computers as the fourth feature of the system. Eventually we added a fifth attribute—intelligence—to the system now known as C4I: Command, Control, Communications, Computers, and Intelligence.

Commanders were acquiring the ability to pierce the "fog and friction of war," that evocative metaphor frequently attributed to Clausewitz. For thousands of years, soldiers had longed for the power to see and understand what was happening on the field as the chaos of battle unfolded. Where is the enemy? Where are my own forces? Have we captured the objective or been pushed back? The revolution in sensor technology, coupled with flying observation platforms (many mounted on new Unmanned Aerial Vehicles), promised today's commanders the kind of Olympian perspective that Homer had given his gods.

With the power of remotely operated sensors mounted on UAVs, coupled with GPS satellite tracking and reliable, high-speed automated data links, soldiers would be able to see through smoke, clouds, and the darkest night, and understand the battlefield as never before. Our simulations now took place in digital Battlelabs that gave soldiers—from individual tank commanders to the four-star generals commanding theaters of war—an unprecedented degree of situational awareness.

The ability of GPS technology to pinpoint a vehicle's exact location was one of the high-tech breakthroughs exploited by the Task Force. And I was proud that we embraced this tool, regardless of its origins within private industry—proving that the Army was finally shaking its traditional "not invented here" narrow-mindedness. The Schneider Trucking Company had been the first firm to install GPS receivers with coded software, allowing dispatchers and managers to see instantly where any of their more than 400,000 trucks was at any time, anywhere in the nation. Each vehicle had a transponder that broadcast not only its position, but also its unit number and cargo. The military application of the technology was obvious, so one of our Task Force teams contacted the company; before long we had adapted the Schneider technology for military vehicles. Now armored, mechanized infantry, and logistics commanders could track their forces, day or night, in any weather, on any battlefield.

Another benefit of GPS technology was its role in preventing friendly fire incidents, which had plagued operations in the Gulf War. As this technology matured, we expedited the development of "Blue Force" tracking displays—plasma screens with digital sector templates, on which the positions of Blue (friendly) Forces were constantly updated. Though friendly fire would prove difficult to eliminate altogether, GPS would greatly reduce the risk of fratricide in years to come—another way that technology helped us not only attack the enemy, but also save lives on the battlefield.

To complement this system, the Task Force also exploited new digitized technology that transmitted images of tanks, fighting vehicles, and helicopter gunships from satellite and UAV sensors, linking it with GPS tracking to give us a more accurate picture of enemy force dispositions as well.

When the power of night-vision equipment, pinpoint laser sighting, and GPS tracking was coupled with the new generations of precision guided munitions (PGMs), the lethality of our weapons would expand exponentially. Among the hundreds of reports on pending technology I read as Task Force director, one of the most intriguing concerned the concept for a future Fire Direction/Close Air Support Controller, who would deploy with special operations forces (SOF) or small teams of infantry. This new breed of forward observer would locate enemy targets, and either illuminate them for laser-guided bombs or artillery projectiles, or transmit their exact GPS coordinates to aircraft overhead (with an accuracy within one meter).

The planes would then drop bombs that guided themselves precisely to those target coordinates, no matter what the weather or battlefield conditions. The new weapon was named the Joint Direct Attack Munition (JDAM).

"Now we're making real progress," I said as I finished the report.

I stared out the window at the sailboats on Hampton Roads, heeling to the northwest breeze. It was a scene of postcard tranquility—but in my mind I was looking through the Plexiglas bubble of an H-23 helicopter, at the smoke and flashes of howitzer shells and bombs exploding along the Kinh Doi Canal. I would have traded all those artillery battalions and fighter-bombers for about five JDAMs.

From my office inside the battlements of a stone fort built to withstand iron shot and black-powder shells, I had a window overlooking the waterway where the Monitor and the Merrimack revolutionized naval warfare in 1862. I also had a window into the way war would be fought in the battlespace of centuries to come. I could not conceive of the impact that this perspective would have on the next nine years of my life.

Ahead of me lay three more stars . . . and two more wars.

THE FROZEN MOUNTAINS OF CENTRAL KOREA LOOKED LIKE MINT ice cream through my night vision goggles. My Command and Control Black Hawk climbed to a hover, and the pilot flipped up his goggles to consult the tactical situation screen on his instrument panel.

"X-Ray North bearing 346 degrees True, Sir," he said.

It was late on a Thursday night in January 1997. Now a two-star general, I had been commander of the 2nd Infantry "Warrior" Division for almost two years—an exhilarating, demanding time that had felt a lot more like war than peace.

The 2nd Infantry Division was the largest, most lethal division in the Army, a "hybrid" outfit comprised of armor, mechanized infantry, air assault infantry, combat aviation, and artillery. We were also the major American war-fighting unit most closely deployed to a hostile force.

Twenty-six kilometers beyond our multipurpose training range, the Demilitarized Zone snaked across the mountainous peninsula, the border between prosperous, democratic South Korea and North Korea, the "Democratic People's Republic." The world's last surviving Stalinist dictatorship, North Korea was a diplomatically and economically isolated rogue nation, which flaunted its undeniable military power while appealing for international humanitarian aid to feed its starving population.

The contrast between the two Koreas was always dramatic on these clear winter nights, when the sub-zero Siberian air mass dominated Northeast Asia and visibility was perfect. Through the left windows of the Black Hawk, the urban glare of the Seoul megalopolis and the chains of industrial cities farther south bleached out the landscape's contours. Ahead through the cockpit windows, though, the lights faded and then stopped as if at a shoreline. Beyond the DMZ— an ironic appellation; it was in fact the most heavily militarized zone on the planet—North Korea was devoid of light, a black void. Millions of wretched, malnourished people waited out the freezing night in the unheated dormitories of collective farms and state factories that hadn't seen electric power for months, and couldn't even provide kerosene for lamps.

But North Korea's "Dear Leader," the ruthless and erratic dictator Kim Jong Il, boasted that his military of more than one million troops, airmen, and sailors was among the best equipped and best fed in the world.

I stared at the dark mountains just beyond the DMZ. There was plenty of electricity there, but it was cloaked inside a warren of concrete tunnels and fortified caves. The North Korean Army (NKA) had more than 8,000 long-range artillery systems—170 mm Koksan howitzers and heavy rocket launchers—hidden in those fortifications. Capable of firing 500,000 projectiles an hour, those weapons were close enough to devastate all of Seoul and its sprawling environs. To back up this firepower, the NKA fielded about 500 Scud medium-range ballistic missiles, many armed with chemical warheads. North Korea also had a robust biological weapons program, which produced anthrax and plague microbes. And Kim's regime hardly bothered to conceal its steady progress on nuclear weapons.

Although South Korea's army was well-equipped and ably commanded, it was America's 2nd Infantry Division and U.S. tactical fighter-bombers that formed the core deterrent to the NKA.

Intelligence on North Korean combat doctrine indicated that, if Kim decided to mount an attack on its neighbor to the south, it would come in the form of a massive artillery barrage, armored attacks south through valleys bisecting the DMZ, and commando raids carried out by the NKA's 120,000-man special forces. Tonight's field exercise was a test of our ability to counter this offensive threat.

The enemy had a numerical advantage in weapons and manpower. But we had superior technology and better-trained troops. Since taking command of the Division after nine months as the United Nations/Combined Forces Command's director of operations in Seoul, I had stressed training in flexible tactics and speed. And train we did—month in, month out. As one war game was wrapping up at a maneuver brigade headquarters at Camp Casey or Camp Hovey, another was beginning with the DIVARTY at Camp Stanley.

"We'll have less than one hour to respond effectively to an enemy attack," I had told my senior officers on taking command. "And the alert siren can sound any time. We must be prepared to fight tonight." Indeed, "Fight Tonight" was the Warrior Division's motto.

The key to victory would be to suppress the NKA artillery within minutes of their first salvo—rendering them unable to fire a second—and then to destroy their spearhead of T-62 tanks and infantry fighting vehicles before they could fan out onto the highways south of the DMZ. Protecting our key artillery and rocket systems long enough to reverse the momentum of an enemy first strike would be crucial.

In tonight's field exercise our new Paladin self-propelled howitzers and MLRS launchers would maneuver independently on the snowy mountainsides, taking cover in gorges and beneath bluffs, simulating firing and moving, high-speed "move and shoot" tactics that would protect our artillery while accurately striking the enemy's. Maneuver speed was essential for survival; accuracy was critical to victory.

And the essential element of accuracy was our capability to pinpoint enemy artillery systems within seconds after they fired their first projectiles. Counter-battery radar had been in the Army inventory since the 1940s, but our TPQ-37 Firefinder radars were the most sensitive such systems in the world. Their computers could instantly analyze the trajectory of incoming fire, and deliver the exact coordinates of enemy firing points to our counter-fire weapons within seconds. As the MLRS and longer range Army Tactical Missile Systems (ATACMS) batteries on alert fired their first retaliatory strikes, howitzer batteries would maneuver to hidden positions in the mountains, from which they would lay down a curtain of high explosive shells and ICM bomblets on the tunnel and cave entrances of the enemy.

Because the NKA's attack would likely combine artillery, armor, mechanized infantry, and special forces, our plans to defend South Korea had to include every element of the joint services and combined arms war-fighting team. Tonight, while the Paladins and MLRS tracks roared out of their bases into the surrounding hills, M1A1 Abrams tanks and Bradley fighting vehicles from the 1st "Iron" Brigade sped across frozen rice paddies to take up their own dominant positions on the high ground. Troop-carrying Black Hawk and Chinook helicopters from the Aviation Brigade supported the 1st Battalion 503rd Infantry (Air Assault) as they flew ahead to secure chokepoints in the passes overlooking the DMZ. And the Division's combined arms package was completed by AH-64 Apache gunships, being screened by smaller AH-58 Kiowa Warrior "armed scout" helicopters, hugging the rising terrain to interdict NKA tanks approaching into the battlespace.

As squadrons of Air Force F-16s fell into formation to the south, I removed my night-vision goggles and turned to the laptop computer mounted by my seat. The tactical situation was displayed there, in pulsing colored symbols. The picture was similar to what I'd seen in the war game we'd been rehearsing for days—similar, but not close enough. The artillery was taking too long to fire its simulated missions. I scanned the screen, and put my goggles back on to study the terrain below. I didn't like the spacing between the howitzers and the MLRS. The enemy's own counter-battery barrages could have done some real damage. Looking farther north, I saw that a company of Bradleys had missed its turn and was probably going to move into an Air Force target area—an impression confirmed by a quick check of my laptop's tactical display.

I understood the situation. The artillery and Bradley crews had been snug in their austere yet comfortable barracks, sacking out, watching a video, or waiting to use a barracks computer to send an e-mail home. When the alert siren sounded, they pulled their chemical protective suits over their winter uniforms, snatched up their flak jackets and helmets, and sprinted through the snow to their vehicles. Under these conditions, it wasn't easy to perform at the top of their game. But these were exactly the conditions the enemy would try to exploit—late night, bitter cold.

We weren't good enough. I punched the mike key on my secure command radio.

"Iron Six," I called the Brigade commander. "This is Warrior Six. Recall. Recall. Recall. Let's try it again."

"Wilco, Sir," Colonel Bill Marshall replied.

My pilot banked the Black Hawk to the east, and I watched the small shapes of the maneuvering vehicles turn on the snowy hillsides below and head back to their start lines. No doubt some of those troopers were bitching about that "bastard" that was keeping them up all night. So be it; soldiers always griped. But they also always did their jobs. I had never forgotten what Captain Bill Bowen had taught me out on those gun platforms in the Mekong Delta: Being a good officer wasn't the same thing as entering a popularity contest. This Division would live by an old adage: "The more you sweat in peace, the less you bleed in war."

My job was to make them sweat—because my responsibility was to be ready for a war everyone hoped would never come.

This wasn't easy for the troops. And it sure as hell wasn't easy for me. Cathy and I lived separately at this time, as did all of my commanders and key staff members who had their families in Korea with them. The families lived mostly in Seoul and we were billeted with our troops in the Division's tactical area of responsibility. Cathy had driven up from her house in Seoul, where she taught history at the American High School, to spend a long weekend with me in my quarters at Camp Red Cloud. The way this exercise was unfolding, there wouldn't be much time for a weekend.

That couldn't be helped. The troops weren't fighting a real war, but the training would be as close to actual combat as I could make it. And so it would be until the day I completed twenty-six months as the Division's commander, was promoted to three stars, and took command of the U.S. 3rd Army—"Patton's Own."

I WAS GLAD I HAD SAVED A CLEAN DESERT CAMOUFLAGE UNIFORM. AS always, Egypt's Western Desert was a dusty, flyblown place—not a pleasant spot to fight a war, as soldiers from the Pharaohs' armies to those of Field Marshal Bernard Montgomery had all discovered.

At least the war we had just fought in the Bright Star 99 exercise had been relatively bloodless. There'd been the usual injuries during training accidents, which was inevitable when 70,000 troops from eleven countries mixed it up for almost two months of realistic combat training. But we'd all survived.

It was November 1, 1999, and this was my second Bright Star since taking command of the 3rd Army in May 1997. Third Army—Army Forces, Central Command (ARCENT)—was the Army component of U.S. Central Command (CENTCOM). And I'd just gotten word that Marine General Anthony C. Zinni, CENTCOM's Commander in Chief, was bringing Defense Secretary Bill Cohen to see our new deployable, high-tech command center.

We were on the south end of Mubarak Military City. The base was named after Egyptian president Hosni Mubarak, one of several Arab leaders I'd met as I traveled the Command's area of responsibility, which stretched from the Horn of Africa through the Middle East to Pakistan. Over the past year, our area of responsibility had been expanded to include the Stans—the republics of former Soviet Central Asia—but I hadn't yet had a chance to visit exotic capitals like Tashkent, in Uzbekistan, or Dushanbe, which stood among ancient Mongol gardens beneath Tajikistan's snowy ridges.

And I probably wouldn't have that opportunity. My three-year tour of duty as ARCENT commander would end in spring 2000. Three-star generals were not promoted to four-stars unless they were assigned to a position requiring that rank. And there weren't that many four-star jobs in the U.S. military. Before I left for Egypt, Cathy and I had held another of our "We'll just have to wait and see . . ." discussions. There were, of course, fates much worse than retiring as a lieutenant general. And Cathy and I already had sketches of our planned retirement home in Texas.

If I had one resolution for my retirement, it was to spend more time with my granddaughter than I had been able to with Jacqy. Our first grandchild had been born in June 1997, when Jacqy and Patrick were stationed at Fort Knox, Kentucky. Anne Cathryn Matlock was named after her delighted and doting grandmother. I would have to wait until February 2000 for a similar honor, when Samuel Thomas Matlock would be born at Fort Leavenworth, Kansas.

But I would miss being a soldier. In Korea I had worked with a wonderful group of officers and NCOs to help build the 2nd Infantry Division into one of America's most modern, most capable military units. And I had been fortunate to serve under Lt. General Bill Crouch, my old boss from our 2nd ACR days in Germany, and both General Gary Luck and General John Tilelli, with whom I'd served during Operation Desert Shield/Desert Storm. In civilian life I expected to pursue a second career in the corporate world, and I hoped that my future colleagues would be as talented as those I'd leave behind in the Army.

And I would also miss command, with its responsibilities and unprecedented opportunities to lead troops and find innovative solutions to difficult problems. As I pulled on my clean uniform that November day in Egypt, I looked across the gravel walk at the squat, green windowless trailers of ARCENT's computerized command center. Since my days with the Louisiana Maneuvers Task Force, I had worked hard to incorporate Information Age technology into my assignments. We'd built a state-of-the-art headquarters at 3rd Army in Atlanta. But ARCENT's wars, if they came, would be thousands of miles away from Georgia, so I worked with military and civilian experts to construct a mobile headquarters that had almost as much bandwidth and interconnectivity as the permanent facility at Fort McPherson. These trailers, with their generators and support equipment, rolled easily on and off Air Force C-141 and C-5 transports; they could be up and operational in eight hours after landing anywhere in the area of responsibility.

And we needed that response flexibility. CENTCOM's AOR was becoming increasingly dangerous. Saddam Hussein had spent the 1990s defying both the terms of the ceasefire and a series of U.N. Security Council Resolutions.

By the fall of 1998, the Iraqis had thrown up so many barriers to the U.N. teams searching for weapons of mass destruction that chief inspector Richard Butler pulled his people out of the country. On December 15 of that year, a U.N. Security Council report condemned Saddam's government and military for refusing to allow the inspectors to examine WMD records and suspected production sites. The next day, President Bill Clinton authorized Secretary of Defense Cohen to attack the Iraqi regime. Tomahawk Land Attack Missiles (TLAMs) and U.S. and British warplanes pounded suspected Iraqi WMD sites and intelligence facilities for days during Operation Desert Fox. Since that operation ended, however, the Iraqis had attacked Coalition planes patrolling the northern and southern no-fly zones on virtually a daily basis. The situation in Iraq was a tinderbox.

And another, equally dangerous threat had spread across the region. The renegade Saudi millionaire Osama bin Laden, and his extremist Islamic terrorist group al Qaeda, had been mounting an increasingly bold series of attacks against American and Western interests. There was evidence that al Qaeda was active as early as 1993 in the bombing of New York's World Trade Center; that attack had been followed by an ambitious, but thwarted, plot to hijack and destroy airliners flying between America and the Far East. Then, on August 7, 1998, bin Laden's al Qaeda conducted its most audacious assault to date, simultaneously attacking the U.S. embassies in Dar es Salaam, Tanzania, and Nairobi, Kenya, using massive truck bombs that killed more than two hundred innocent people.

President Clinton had responded by launching TLAMs against a suspected al Qaeda chemical weapons laboratory in the Sudan and several terrorist training camps in Afghanistan, which had become bin Laden's main sanctuary and base of operations. Controlled by the ruthless, almost medieval Taliban Islamic extremists, Afghanistan had become a "terrorist sponsored state." By 1999, I was convinced beyond a doubt that before long the United States would be fighting terrorism on the ground somewhere in CENTCOM's area of responsibility.

At the moment, however, my personal responsibility was to give my boss and Secretary Cohen a tour of ARCENT's deployable headquarters.

Bill Cohen had a well-earned reputation as a thoughtful, decisive Secretary of Defense. When the staff lit up the plasma screens and ran the tapes of the Bright Star exercise, showing how the friendly Coalition "Greenland" had defeated the aggressors of "Orangeland," Cohen asked all the right questions. He seemed especially impressed that we had assembled the system using commercially available hardware. Our staff officers and sergeants were on their toes. They answered all the secretary's questions, and he left with a smile on his face. I was proud of the command post—and of the young men and women who had made it such a success.

The next morning, Tony Zinni dropped by as we were packing up for the flight back to Atlanta. Tony was in great spirits, which I attributed to the success of Bright Star. I couldn't help but return his smile. He was one of the friendliest senior officers I'd encountered in thirty-five years in the military—and also one of the smartest. A muscular fireplug of a guy in his mid-fifties, Tony was raised in blue-collar Philadelphia by his Italian immigrant parents; his face looked like that of a tough, broken-nosed Roman Emperor from a third-century coin.

He and I had overlapped in Vietnam in 1967, but at opposite ends of the country. While I'd been an Artillery lieutenant down in the Mekong Delta, Tony had served up in I Corps as an infantry adviser to the South Vietnamese Marines. He'd learned to speak the language fluently, eat their food—including puppy steamed in banana leaves—and had immersed himself in Vietnam's complex and ancient civilization. As he advanced in rank, Tony had retained his intellectual curiosity and affinity for foreign cultures, and the trait had served him well as CENTCOM's Commander in Chief.

"Tom," he said casually. "Where are you off to next?"

"Christmas with the troops," I said, "probably in Saudi, Kuwait, Bahrain, and Qatar."

"When you return to the States, call me," he said casually. Then he added, "I've recommended to Secretary Cohen that you be my successor in CENTCOM when I retire next summer."

I stared at Tony but had no voice to answer. CENTCOM Commander-in-Chief. Jesus—that was probably the most critical assignment in the U.S. military.

"No guarantees, Tom, but I think Cohen likes the idea. We'll know more after the first of the year."

Standing there, I remembered Lt. Colonel Al Lamas, who had convinced me to stay in the Army in 1969; Colonel John Hudachek, who had declined to court-martial me for shoving that mutinous trooper in Germany; and, above all, Eric Antila, who had given me faith in the profession of arms that hot May morning beside the Kinh Doi Canal. Because of them, I was still a soldier. And now, thanks to all of them, thanks to Tony Zinni—and, no doubt, thanks to fate—I might just assume one of the highest responsibilities the military had to offer.

Tony and I shook hands. He walked away as I tapped the digits of our home telephone number into my Iridium satellite phone. "Cathy, honey . . . how would you like to move to Tampa?"

PART III

COMMANDER IN CHIEF

Everything is very simple in war, but the simplest thing is difficult. These difficulties accumulate and produce a friction, which no man can imagine exactly who has not seen war.

—CARL VON CLAUSEWITZ, *On War*

6

A DANGEROUS NEIGHBORHOOD

I looked up from the classified messages on my lap as the young Air Force driver rolled down her window and punched the day's entry code into the cypherpad. The black steel gate slid open, and we turned into the palm-shaded parking circle at CENTCOM headquarters.

In the three years I'd spent commanding ARCENT, I had come to CENTCOM in Tampa many times. But this Monday morning was different. Tony Zinni had asked me down to discuss the Command's future. In less than a month, I would go through my Senate confirmation hearing to become his successor as commander in chief, U.S. Central Command (CINCCENT).

From the outside, the building could have been just another high-tech Sun Belt corporation. But the two MPs at the lobby checkpoint, wearing tan-and-brown camouflage uniforms and armed with 9 mm Beretta pistols, were obviously not civilians.

As we exchanged salutes, their "Good morning, Sir," was friendly. Although they clearly recognized me, the guards dutifully scrutinized my Defense Department ID before entering my name in the log. This headquarters housed some of the most sensitive intelligence and communications technology in the world.

One of Tony's aides, a young Navy lieutenant, escorted me up to the second floor. Passing members of all four services on the stairs, I had a clear reminder of what lay ahead: For the first time, I would be leading a unified command.

Like the other regional combatant commands, CENTCOM had been a creation of the Goldwater-Nichols Department of Defense Reorganization Act of 1986. These commands had no permanent forces of their own, but instead drew on the Army, Air Force, Navy, Marine Corps, and Special Operations Command to fulfill their missions. In military circles it was said that CINCs wore "purple suits," blending the traditional colors of the Army, Navy, Air Force, and Marine Corps.

I examined a hardwood plaque that had been mounted in the corridor since my last visit, depicting CENTCOM's area of responsibility. This Command covered the most diverse, strategically vital—and unstable—region of the planet.

CENTCOM was responsible for maintaining stability in a region that spanned twenty-five countries, from Kenya and the Horn of Africa, north through the deserts of Sudan, Egypt and Jordan, continuing across the Red Sea and Arabian Gulf, through Iraq, Iran, and Afghanistan and the former Soviet Stans, right up to the Chinese border. Pakistan occupied the region's far right flank.

The area was home to more than five hundred million people in eighteen ethnic groups and countless tribes. They practiced all of the world's great religions, and spoke seven major languages and hundreds of dialects. Approximately two-thirds of this population was under twenty-five years of age, underemployed, and restless. Demographers call it a "significant youth cohort"—military planners and diplomats call it big damn trouble down the road. These dissatisfied young people, we knew, represented millions of potential terrorist recruits.

The region's economies were just as diverse, and potentially just as volatile: The Neolithic realm of Eritrean nomads on the Horn of Africa wasn't far from the oil-rich Gulf emirates; in Central Asia, the stagnant leftover Perestroika of the former Soviet republics came head-to-head with overheated twenty-first century capitalism.

CENTCOM's area of responsibility included the historical land and sea crossroads linking Europe, Asia, and Africa—and held 65 percent of the world's known petroleum reserves.

When I arrived, Tony was on the phone with Secretary Cohen; I waited in a small alcove outside the CINC's office that the staff called the Trophy Room. The room was furnished with Central Asian carpets, an inlaid ivory-and-brass Arab table, and glass-fronted cases of weapons. Most of the pistols, assault rifles, and machine guns were battlefield trophies—many from Operation Desert Storm—but a number were ceremonial arms presented by foreign leaders to Tony or his predecessors. Here was where the CINC greeted visiting foreign dignitaries: no Spartan military office, the chamber sent a clear message that the commander appreciated the culture of the region for which he was responsible.

After finishing his call, Tony greeted me warmly, grabbing my hand with his strong fingers and grinning broadly. In his spacious office, he pointed to the map of the area of responsibility on an easel beside the sofa. "Your new home, Tom. A dangerous neighborhood."

As Tony spoke, I scanned the map and reflected on the history etched within its borders. War had smoldered in the Sudan and the Horn of Africa for decades. In 1993, in the dusty alleys of Mogadishu, Somalia, the U.S. military had suffered one of its most grave defeats, a bloody debacle that left the Clinton administration gun-shy about committing American ground forces in the region and gave us the reputation of a paper tiger.

Although Libya and Israel were technically in our area of "interest," not "responsibility," they could not be ignored. Libya was an oil-rich outcast nation controlled by the mercurial Muammar Qaddafi.

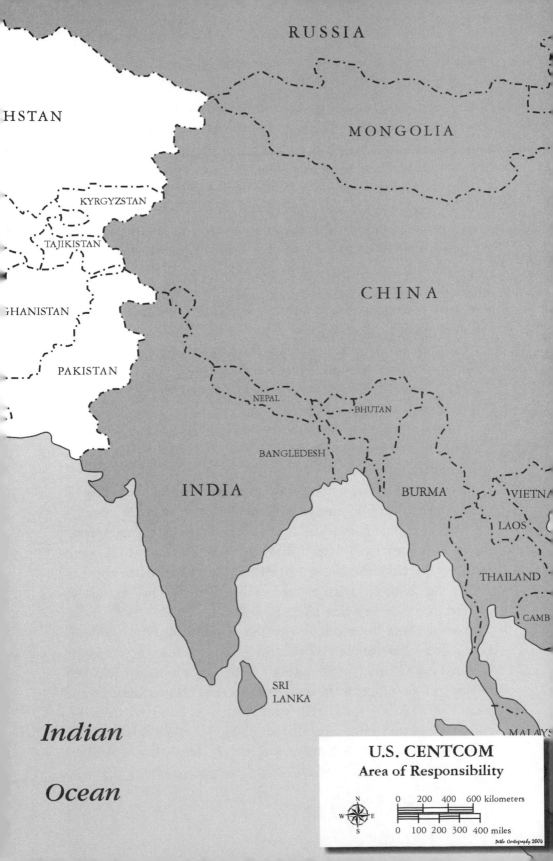

And the unending Israeli-Arab conflict dominated the geostrategic reality of the Middle East. The region's strongest military power, Israel defended its right to exist with a deterrent arsenal of nuclear weapons. But so far it had been incapable of making peace with the Palestinians.

Iraq, of course, remained a flashpoint. Almost ten years after the Gulf War ceasefire, Coalition aircrews were fired upon almost daily as they enforced the no-fly zones.

Iran had become an enigma. For more than two decades the country had been a theocracy, ruled by Shiite clerics who despised the West in general and America in particular. New, ostensibly moderate leaders were emerging, but Iran was still sponsoring terrorism and developing weapons of mass destruction.

Pakistan already possessed nuclear weapons, and was gripped in a tense standoff with its nuclear neighbor, India.

And remote, landlocked Afghanistan, under the Taliban, was al Qaeda's principal stronghold.

"Sure you want this job, Tom?" Tony joked as he finished his briefing.

"I've been volunteering for hard jobs all my life, Sir."

It was in this meeting that I learned how critical the policy of "engagement"—establishing a personal rapport with the region's government and military leaders—would be to my new assignment.

"Tom," Tony said, "you'll drink a lot of tea in this job—and vodka up in the Stans. But it's worth the heartburn when you can pick up the phone in Tampa and speak directly with a prime minister or a crown prince on a first-name basis."

Author Dana Priest once described Tony Zinni as "a modern-day proconsul, descendant of the warrior statesman who ruled the Roman Empire's outlying territory." That was the man I watched that day in his office: a statesman who knew and understood the leaders of this highly charged region and was eager to share his insights about them. Some, including Egyptian President Hosni Mubarak and Jordan's King Abdullah, I'd met. But I had no firsthand knowledge of the Central Asian leadership. And so I listened closely, for almost an hour, as Tony described the political and military elite of the former Soviet Union's orphan republics.

Then, in his forthright way, he laid out his view of the most serious threats and challenges we would face over the next several years.

"The region will not become stable until there's a permanent, equitable peace settlement between Israel and the Palestinians."

The odds of that happening on my watch are not good, I thought, *unless the United States of America takes a serious hand in brokering the agreement.*

Tony turned his attention to Iraq. We discussed Saddam's massacre of an estimated 300,000 Shiites, and the status of the no-fly zones as well as the regime's success at smuggling oil. Tony's view was that our national policy of containment was working. I agreed that we were "containing" whatever was happening inside Iraq within its borders. The problem in my mind was that we didn't know enough about what that was.

After the U.N. weapons experts had been forced out in 1998, they had announced that Saddam may have produced and hidden thousands of liters of weaponized anthrax and botulinum toxin, more than enough to kill every human on Earth.

I glanced at the map. "What about Afghanistan?"

"A failed state. The Taliban has set the clock back to the Dark Ages. Afghanistan is al Qaeda's sanctuary. We destroyed some of the training camps in 1998, but terrorist recruits from all over the Muslim world keep flocking in."

"What else should I start worrying about?"

"I wish I could tell you." Tony spread his hands in resignation. "You'll find out our intelligence picture for the region is pretty sad. That's another reason engagement is so important. We need friends out there who can give us the true picture. I'd like to know a lot more about what's happening in Iraq, and with Osama bin Laden and AQ [al Qaeda]. But the fact is I do not."

Tony shook his head. "Tom, don't be surprised if the CENT-COM you command is not the same as the one that I've commanded," he said. "The only certainty in this region is uncertainty."

As I rode back to the airfield to catch my plane for Atlanta, Tony's words weighed heavily on my mind. *The only certainty in this region is uncertainty.*

THE WEEKS AFTER I ASSUMED COMMAND ON JULY 7, 2000, WERE predictably hectic. From the perspective of the commander's well-appointed office in Tampa, CENTCOM proved to be a larger and more intricate organization than I had imagined. My command diary for that period evokes the sheer volume and complexity of material that I had to process.

One evening as I sat at my desk thinking, organizing files, and looking through old papers, I came across a poem I'd written as a young, ambitious captain in 1971:

GRANT ME:

- One opportunity to influence the course of history.
- The foresight to anticipate that opportunity.
- The conviction to plan for it.
- The fortitude to implement the plan.
- The intensity of action to make it work.
- The flexibility to change it when it won't.
- The loyalty to self to admit defeat.
- The humility owed to victory.
- The tenacity to continue.

I smiled as I read the words, written almost thirty years before, and remembered the adage "Be careful what you wish for." Time would tell.

Immediately after the change of command in July, I met with CENTCOM's component commanders: Lt. General P. T. Mikolashek, my successor at ARCENT; Vice Admiral Willie Moore, the commander of the Naval Component; the Air Force Component commander, Lt. General Chuck Wald; Lt. General Frank Libutti, USMC, commander of MARCENT; and the Special Operations commander, Rear Admiral Bert Calland, an experienced SEAL. They were able leaders, all men I'd served with over the years. Once we had been peers; now I would be their boss, "the Old Man." But they would remain friends.

That day, we worked through a long agenda that included terrorism, WMD proliferation, Iraq's no-fly zones, maritime interdiction, and the thorny details of treaty arrangements with most of the countries in the area of responsibiity.

One of the problems I had inherited had to do with our naval forces. The Pentagon was considering reducing the full-time aircraft carrier battle group presence in the northern Arabian Gulf to part-time, only three-quarters of any given year. But Willie Moore and I agreed that we must have a carrier on hand twelve months of every year to support Operation Southern Watch (OSW) in Iraq's southern no-fly zone. I knew I'd have to do some lobbying on my next visit to the Pentagon.

Early on July 10, I met with my J-3 Operations Director, Air Force Major General Sandy Sandstrom, and my J-2 Intelligence Director, Army Brigadier General Keith Alexander, to discuss response options (ROs) for Iraqi provocations. At the time, if the Iraqis fired on a Coalition aircraft, the typical response was to attack the pieces of the air defense system involved in the incident—a gun, a missile launcher, a transmitter, or a radar.

"It seems to me," I told Sandy and Keith, "that we'll get much greater leverage if we respond asymmetrically." In other words, rather than attacking one ZSU-23 mm cannon or an SA-6 missile launcher, it would probably be to our advantage to destroy the command and control architecture in that sector.

"That might make the Iraqis think twice before firing at our kids in the cockpits," I said.

And from that day forward, CENTCOM pressed the Washington bureaucracy for more "kinetic" (our military's term for the use of lethal fire), more unpredictable, more asymmetrical responses to Iraqi violations in the no-fly zones. Bill Cohen and Hugh Shelton supported this new approach and our pilots began to degrade Iraq's air defense capabilities. But we knew we would not eliminate the threat to our aircrews until we destroyed the command and control and radar facilities clustered in and around Baghdad. Tony Zinni had done that with Desert Fox in 1998, but those defenses had been re-built almost immediately. The more I thought about it, the more con-vinced I became: We needed a new policy on Iraq.

No matter which party won the November elections, I knew, there was going to be new leadership in the White House in January. And so, beginning on July 17, I asked my staff to prepare policy op-tions on Iraq—which we would provide a new administration imme-diately following the elections.

"It seems to me that we have three possible courses of action," I suggested. The first would be to maintain the status quo by continu-ing our monitoring of the no-fly zones, and our Maritime Interdic-tion of oil smuggling in defiance of UN sanctions. "That's your basic containment," I said.

Another option would be intentional escalation, using asymmet-rical and unpredictable responses to Iraqi provocations in the no-fly zones or at sea.

And, of course, there was a third option: simply to back off, and let the situation with Iraq develop.

"We don't know which direction a new administration may take us," I told my staff. "But now is the time to start developing options."

Four days later I met with Army Colonel Gary Harrell, whom I had just hired as CENTCOM's director of joint security after he was recommended by my longtime friend General Pete Schoomaker, the then-commander of U.S. Special Operations Command (SOCOM). Gary was on the promotion list to brigadier general and had years of experience in the elite Special Mission Units (SMUs) of the Joint

Special Operations Command (JSOC). Since the mid-1990s, when the terrorist threat against Americans in the region had begun to rise, the position had been filled by a Military Police officer. But I wanted a Special Operator in the job, someone who thought like a shooter and could check the vulnerability of our installations from the perspective of a bad guy on the outside looking in.

This proved to be a good decision. Gary understood terrorism from his time as an SMU commander in Mogadishu, Somalia, in 1993 during the brutal combat made famous in the book and film *Black Hawk Down*. And he developed force protection procedures for CENTCOM subordinate commanders and troops, which over the next three years would save hundreds of American lives.

Almost every day I spoke by telephone with foreign civilian and military leaders in the region, absorbing their concerns and learning the way they thought.

Then, on July 22, I began my first trip as CINCCENT to the area of responsibility.

THE HIGH-ALTITUDE SUNLIGHT POURING INTO THE FLIGHT DECK was harsh as I walked forward through the dull fluorescent glow of the jet's fuselage. The CENTCOM Commander in Chief's Air Force EC-135 Command and Control plane—a modified 1962 Boeing 707—had no windows in the cabin.

Through the cockpit windows, I squinted at the bright Sunday over the Aegean. I greeted the crew with a joke I'd been milking since my ARCENT days: "Are we there yet?"

" 'Morning, General," said the pilot, Air Force Major Bill Nichols, glancing at the digital clock on the instrument panel. "Actually, afternoon. It's 1405 in Greece. There was about an hour of night back over the Atlantic."

We'd taken off from MacDill Air Force Base around 8:00 P.M. on a humid, cloudy Saturday evening. Eleven hours and 98 degrees of longitude later, we were cruising through a bright Mediterranean summer afternoon toward Souda Bay on the coast of Crete. This would be our rest stop on a trip that would take us to Kenya, the Arabian Gulf, and Egypt. A relaxed introductory meeting with Kenya's President Daniel Arap Moi would be followed by more substantive talks with Kenyan and Arab civilian and military leaders. As Tony Zinni had suggested, I was about to increase my tea intake.

I slid into the empty seat opposite the navigator and leaned over to scan his radarscope. From the vantage point of 33,000 feet, the Greek islands were a swarm of green blips to the north and east, with the long bulk of Crete to the south.

The copilot dipped the right wing to turn. Through the windscreen I saw the island's mountains rising brown and massive ahead. Cathy came up to the flight deck and rested her hand on my shoulder. I pointed down between the jutting engines at the blue Aegean.

"Your basic wine dark sea," I said, thinking of the *Odyssey*.

"You're a beer man, Tom," she deadpanned.

I grinned and squeezed her hand. My new position had so far proven to be a parade of long days, and short nights, but one benefit was being able to bring Cathy on these official trips. It was important that my counterparts see her as a poised, educated American woman, my partner, and a model to others in a region where women were slowly emerging into public life. And it was important to me to have her at my side.

A faint shimmer came over the southern horizon; it was Egypt and the Suez entrance to the Red Sea. We banked again, beginning our approach to the U.S. Navy base at Souda Bay. My ears popped; the plane's pressure hull had accumulated a lot of hours since 1962. I might have even heard this same jet at Binh Phuoc in 1967, growling unseen above the monsoon clouds. But since then the aircraft had been steadily upgraded—same wings, same fuselage, but a communications suite with a bandwidth that rivaled that of Air Force One. The plane's secure satellite links allowed me to speak or exchange classified e-mail with my Tampa headquarters, with the Pentagon and the White House, and with virtually every American and Allied military command in the world. The aircraft could also be refueled in flight, allowing us to fly for days if necessary, provided the flight crew got adequate sleep in the onboard bunks.

I looked out the left cockpit windows toward the tan islands to the north. One of them was Delos, the birthplace of Apollo, the cultural and commercial center of the world for centuries. The planet was much smaller then, horizons were close.

By July 2000, of course, the limit of horizons had vanished. In the intelligence compartment of this aircraft, I could study satellite imagery of almost any patch of terrain or sea on the planet. That was a resource the Roman proconsul Scaurus—who crisscrossed the Middle East in the first century B.C.—could never have imagined, despite all the legions he commanded.

Like Scaurus, in the coming months I would be called upon to practice both statecraft and diplomacy. During nights on training ranges in Germany, in tents in the Saudi desert, and in a string of hotel rooms and BOQs, I had read about both war and peace: the accumulated wisdom of Sun Tzu and Clausewitz, Bertram Russell and Gandhi. And what had gradually come clear in my mind was that war involved a continuum of interaction between nations, factions, and tribes. Across the breadth of this continuum, I perceived five distinct states of interaction—states I categorized as the Five Cs.

At one end of the spectrum was *Conflict,* in which the armed forces of two nations or more engaged in combat. That usually arose from a *Crisis,* a state of angry tension between opponents. *Coexistence* was one step removed: Potentially hostile countries or tribes overcame their antagonisms to live side-by-side. *Collaboration* was an endeavor in which parties worked toward their mutual benefit. Finally, active *Cooperation* was the most positive relationship: open borders, joint commercial and governmental enterprises, harmony and progress.

I was born in 1945, near the end of the greatest conflict in history. In my lifetime, the major combatants of World War II had moved from one end of the continuum to the other—from conflict to cooperation.

At virtually every point in the region lying below that hazy Mediterranean horizon, nations were gripped in conflict or crisis—or, at best, co-existence. My responsibility would be to help move these states as far along the Five C continuum as possible—from conflict to crisis to co-existence and beyond. I didn't know my prospects for success. But I was determined to try.

"IT IS AN HONOR TO MEET YOU, YOUR HIGHNESS," I SAID. Crown Prince Abdullah's handshake was firm, his eyes bright. "How are you, General? How is the President?"

Outside the tall windows of the Saudi Arabian summer palace in Jeddah, the Red Sea was shimmering in the heat. But this reception room was chilled by air-conditioning ducts hidden behind alabaster screens. From a gold-and-silver pot, a servant filled the Sevres cup before me with tea.

It was the tenth day of my trip, the fourth country I had visited. In Kenya I had learned of that nation's recent history of drought and natural disaster; in Kuwait, Bahrain, and Qatar, I'd reviewed with the Arab leaders the growing menace of terrorism, the threats posed by Iraq and Iran, and the status of military cooperation.

Abdullah, my gracious host in Saudi Arabia, was the nation's de facto ruler. Regent to his half-brother, King Fahd, who had been crippled by a stroke in 1996, the Crown Prince was among the world's richest men. He was also a savvy politician who carefully balanced his positions as the protector of Islam's holiest sites and custodian of one of the world's largest reserves of oil. The industrialized world needed Saudi oil; Saudi Arabia grudgingly needed the military shield of the West. Unlike that of the Gulf states, whose friendship with the United States was based on mutual respect, Saudi Arabia's relationship with America was complex and highly charged.

The presence of U.S. military forces in the Kingdom, though a small fraction of its strength during the Gulf War, was a constant irritant to the Saudi population. Saudi Arabia was the home of fiercely xenophobic Wahhabism, one of the most fundamentalist sects of Islam. In November 1995, terrorists had exploded a car bomb at the Saudi National Guard headquarters in Riyadh, killing five American advisers. Seven months later, on June 25, 1996, a huge truck bomb destroyed the American barracks at the Khobar Towers in Dhahran. Nineteen service members were killed and hundreds were wounded. In the wake of these events, official Saudi resistance to our military presence increased.

We were entering a phase that my subordinate commanders called "death by a thousand cuts." Although most American military personnel in Saudi Arabia had been transferred to remote locations like Prince Sultan Air Base in the empty desert south of Riyadh, cultural friction remained a way of life in Saudi Arabia. One issue concerned the Saudis' insistence that American servicewomen wear the *abaya*—a full-length black robe—while off base. I was not happy with this edict. The thought that in the morning a woman could risk her life in a combat mission against Iraqi air defenses in the no-fly zone, and in the afternoon have to shroud herself in an *abaya* if she appeared in public, struck me as one of the thousand cuts—small but meaningful wounds to the respect between our two nations.

And there were more difficult problems in our relationship. Many Saudis viewed America as Israel's sponsor and irrational ally, equally culpable in the repression of the Palestinians. Some wealthy members of the Saudi royal family funded Islamic schools (*madrasas*) worldwide, many of which preached virulent anti-Semitism and hatred for the West. And a few of these same influential Saudis backed the Taliban in Afghanistan, even though they harbored Osama bin Laden, who had pledged to destabilize the Saudi throne.

After we exchanged formal greetings, the Crown Prince spoke his mind about Israel's tightening grip on Jerusalem, which he considered a threat to Muslim access to al Aqsa Mosque, the third most sacred site in Islam.

"The news that America might finally open its embassy in Jerusalem is very disturbing," he added. "That would be official recognition of complete Israeli occupation of the Holy City."

I'd been briefed on this subject, but was still new at diplomacy, not yet used to speaking obliquely. "Sir, the position of the United States is to support peace between Israel and the Palestinians. The President is working hard to see negotiations resumed."

"America could have many friends in the Muslim world," Abdullah said. "But Israel divides us. Unless there is peace, terrorism will spread around the globe."

"Your Highness," I said, "terrorism is spreading like a cancer. We can *all* work harder to stop it, America and the Kingdom of Saudi Arabia . . ."

He spread his hands in acceptance, and then smiled. "We ask God for reason and logic. And I am sure we will work side by side to stop the spread of terrorism."

"Sir, you have my commitment to be your friend and your partner." Breaking protocol, I held out my hand, Midland style.

Crown Prince Abdullah shook it. "We have heard a lot about you, General."

"I hope some of it good."

"A lot of it good." He rose. The audience was ending. "We have high expectations."

That night on the plane, I thought back on my favorite jobs in the military—commanding a brigade, a division, a field army. Straightforward soldier's work. My world was becoming a lot more complex.

WASHINGTON'S SUMMER HUMIDITY DIDN'T SEEM BAD AFTER THE steam bath of the Arabian Gulf and Red Sea. I spent part of Thursday morning of August 10 at the State Department, briefing Secretary Madeleine Albright on my trip. A good listener, she asked thoughtful and probing questions—though she knew she was in the final months of her cabinet tenure, whatever the presidential election might bring.

At the Pentagon, I called on the Service Chiefs, hoping to build a foundation of reciprocal trust and support. Tony Zinni had cautioned me that the Chiefs of Staff of the Army and Air Force, the Chief of Naval Operations, and the Commandant of the Marines Corps were often suspicious—and no doubt a little jealous—of the regional CINCs, the "Combatant Commanders." Most four-star officers wanted to command forces in wartime, but the Goldwater-Nichols Act relegated the Service Chiefs to a support and advisory role. The services provided the troops, the materiel, the ships and planes, and they were "resourced" to do their jobs by Title X of the U.S. Code.

In other words, the regional combatant commands depended on the "Title X Community"—the separate armed service branches—for troops and weapons, and all the traditional "bullets and beans" needed for military operations. And the Title X Service Chiefs could be inflexible bean counters.

But it was the CINCs who fought the wars. My chain of command ran directly to the Secretary of Defense and the President. I knew it, and the Service Chiefs knew it.

I had spent thirty-five years trying to work around the problem of service parochialism; now, as a CINC, I saw how that kind of narrow thinking had affected even the highest levels of military planning. As I worked out force requirements for CENTCOM, it became obvious that each of the services was focused on winning wars—alone. They were funded as independent entities, and had no real inclination to fight *together* as part of a joint team. During my time in Korea, we had worked hard on "jointness," but our operations were far from perfect. If we were to get it right in CENT-COM, I would need to spend a lot of time with the Joint Staff and the Service Chiefs. We needed to train together, to think together, to plan together.

In my short time in this command, I already knew that America's relationships with the nations in the region were critically important. We needed friends and allies wherever we conducted military operations, and especially within CENTCOM's area of responsibility. We had to build confidence and trust—the kind of trust that could only be maintained through personal diplomacy and by helping these countries resolve their chronic problems.

Air Force C-17 transports flying field hospitals, tents, blankets, and food into an earthquake-shattered country would win more hearts and minds than a thousand hours of propaganda broadcasts. And one of my challenges would be convincing the Service Chiefs that this was important work.

Walking the Pentagon E-Ring, I stopped and made a note to tell my staff when I returned to Tampa: "The Services need to think about their true relevance to the world in which we live."

Famine and drought in East Africa, the AIDS pandemic on that unfortunate continent, the stagnant economies across so much of our area of resposibility, as well as the environmental degradation spreading through the region—every one of these problems was as grave a potential threat to America's national security as hostile military forces. The Service Chiefs would need to start thinking along these nontraditional lines.

But I also had to keep the Chiefs happy, because they provided my command's troops, planes, and ships. And the individual services were responsible for funding the combatant commands. The Air Force provided CENTCOM's funding; the Army financed European Command, while the Navy controlled Pacific Command's budget. *Hell of a way to do business,* I thought. But I was a new CINC. I would soon become wise in the ways of the Title X world.

My call on the chairman of the Joint Chiefs of Staff, Army General Hugh Shelton, was pleasant and informative. I'd known Hugh since my days in ARCENT, when he had been CINC of U.S. Special Operations Command. Tall and craggy, with a Carolina twang to his voice, Hugh had served two combat tours in Vietnam—as a Green Beret and a paratroop company commander—before rising steadily in command responsibility. People sometimes mistook Hugh's soft-spoken southern manner for lack of intellect. Big mistake. Hugh Shelton understood the military and Beltway politics as well as any Washington insider, uniformed or civilian.

When I mentioned that my staff had scheduled an afternoon office call with Richard Clarke, the counterterrorism specialist on the National Security Council, Hugh frowned.

"Tom," he said. "Secretary Cohen prefers that the CINCs coordinate their contacts with senior civilian officials through his office. That's especially true with Dick Clarke."

I listened. Washington at the CINC level was new territory.

"Clarke's been over at the NSC so long that he thinks he owns counterterrorism—and knows more about the subject than anybody in government," Hugh added. "He likes to talk, drops a lot of names, and thinks highly of himself. But in many ways he's not very practical. Be careful in dealing with him."

I thanked Hugh for the heads-up.

Clarke's secretary had told my staff that he would see me in his "White House office." But the Pentagon driver took me to the Old Executive Office Building, a separate facility connected to the West Wing. *A small point,* I thought, as I climbed the marble stairs to Clarke's office.

"General Franks," he said, rising from his desk to shake my hand. Then he ducked back to close an orange-bordered Top Secret/Sensitive folder on his desk.

Security conscious, I thought. A good trait for a counterterrorism specialist.

Clarke spoke quickly and intensely, as if he possessed urgent information that was critical to my mission. With his wiry, close-cropped gray hair, probing dark eyes, and serious manner, he reminded me of an actor cast as a high government official dealing with a grave crisis.

The subject was al Qaeda and the Taliban. Clarke began a review of the available intelligence, which was recent but predictably imprecise. He described the success of the 1998 TLAM strikes into Afghanistan, but had nothing to say about the strike against the suspected chemical weapons plant in the Sudan. *Interesting,* I thought. There had been a flap about that strike, with a number of news stories suggesting that it had been based on faulty intelligence and that the Sudan facility had had nothing to do with chemical weapons. I wondered if Clarke thought it also had been a success.

We then discussed the United Arab Emirates, a federation of seven small, immensely wealthy Gulf oil states that (along with Saudi Arabia and Pakistan) had extended diplomatic recognition and financial aid to the Taliban.

Clarke told me about his close personal ties with the royal family in Abu Dhabi. He described a direct connection between UAE and the Taliban, and told me that this conduit had proven very helpful to him in working the "bin Laden problem."

I listened without commenting.

I asked about intelligence reporting on al Qaeda. "Dick, for CENTCOM to build realistic operational plans, we need usable intelligence," I told him. "TLAMs will hit the exact coordinates that are programmed into their guidance systems. But reports about the cave where Osama bin Laden was thought to have slept last week don't produce a target. Eventually we may figure out a trend, but in order to strike him we need real-time information."

Clarke smiled knowingly and described "technologies" that he thought would help with the problem.

I understood at once he was referring to the Predator UAV, a reconnaissance drone that could loiter over hostile territory for hours transmitting high-quality real-time video, day or night. The CIA was working to arm the Predator with a Hellfire missile system. A potentially powerful tool, I thought, even as I reminded myself of an old military adage—"It is dangerous to confuse desire with capability." I wondered if Dick Clarke had ever heard the expression.

I was interested in destroying the al Qaeda threat. But my visit with Clarke had not moved me any closer to that objective. I left his office hoping that my emphasis on practical solutions to real problems would spur him to home in on some real targeting opportunities. But I suspected that Dick was better at identifying a problem than at finding a workable solution.

O N A THURSDAY MORNING IN LATE SEPTEMBER 2000, I GATHERED the senior CENTCOM staff directors in my Tampa office to review the Command's operational posture toward al Qaeda.

My deputy commander, Marine Lt. General Michael "Rifle" De-Long, sat in the easy chair to my right, while Army Brigadier General Keith Alexander and Air Force Major General Sandy Sandstrom occupied the leather sofa. Several specialists from the Sensitive Compartmented Intelligence Facility (SCIF) had set up folding chairs. A collection of stained old mugs and space age insulated cups crowded the coffee table.

"Have we *ever* had any HUMINT [human intelligence] worth a rat's ass out of Afghanistan?" I asked Keith Alexander.

"Sir," he said. "I wish I could tell you that we have. But the truth is we have *not*. We have had periodic reports from locals who sometimes work with the Agency, but never anything close to real-time."

Tom Eckert, my special adviser (SPAD), a senior CIA officer and my direct link to Agency Director George Tenet, rose to speak. "Most Agency assets in Afghanistan are with the Northern Alliance." He went to the tactical map. "Up here, near the borders of Uzbekistan and Tajikistan. Al Qaeda is predominantly in the south, with the Taliban in the Pashtun region around Kandahar and Jalalabad."

"As you know, Sir," Keith Alexander continued, "the NA's more of a shotgun-wedding than an alliance. They're really a collection of Panjshiris, Tajik and Uzbek tribal militias that General Ahmed Shah Massoud keeps together through his charisma."

My staff nodded their agreement.

"CIA has people with them providing some funds and materiel," Tom Eckert added. "In return, the Alliance fights the Taliban. But

Keith's right. The problem is that our leverage is in the north. We are much less influential with the Pashtuns in the south. Many of their leaders are in Pakistan, and there is no cohesive opposition in southern Afghanistan. We're hurting for HUMINT down there."

"Got it," I said.

Collecting human intelligence had been a problem since the post-Vietnam purges of our intelligence services. In the late 1970s, the CIA and the National Security Agency had begun to focus on "technical" intelligence—imagery from aircraft and satellites—and on electronic communications intercepts. We could read the license plate of a car from space, but know nothing useful about the people inside that car. We could eavesdrop on a cell phone conversation in Tehran, but have no idea who was speaking.

Ever since I'd been an OCS candidate at Fort Sill, I had recognized the importance of precise targeting. Like all the combatant commands, CENTCOM had contingency plans. Air strikes using TLAMs and manned bombers against al Qaeda targets in Afghanistan were among our plans. Our problem was targeting—real-time targeting.

Sandy Sandstrom's Operations shop had drawn up a series of al Qaeda target-set options, based on imagery and electronic intelligence. These involved known or probable training camps and what we optimistically called "guest" facilities—some houses and offices where the Intel community believed Osama and his lieutenants occasionally conducted business. Tracing al Qaeda through communications intercepts was no longer easy. Once, Osama bin Laden had used a satellite phone for everything from positioning his forces to chatting with his mother in Saudi Arabia. But Osama had abandoned the practice after press leaks revealed that the August 1998 TLAM strikes after the East Africa embassy bombings had targeted the last known location of this phone. Al Qaeda now used a collection of old Soviet commo gear, some civilian single-sideband short wave sets, a bunch of Motorola CB-type radios, encrypted e-mail routed through anonymous Third World Internet cafes—and, no doubt, old-fashioned runners carrying notes.

Given the quality of our intelligence, I wasn't convinced that we could ever destroy al Qaeda in Afghanistan using only cruise missiles and air strikes. But I had directed Sandy's Ops people to work closely with Vice Admiral Willie Moore, our Naval Component commander, to improve the response times of our "TLAM shooters," just in case.

If we were ever to launch an effective attack against al Qaeda, I knew it would require ground operations. We would have to go in, get the intelligence, and act on it. But any SOF raid would have to be robust enough to defeat the heavily armed, battle-hardened circle of security forces that surrounded Osama bin Laden and his lieutenants. And this kind of operation would require Special Mission Units—international overflights, staging clearances, and precise enough intelligence to tell us where to "aim" our insertions. More important, such an operation would require a serious policy decision. I believed we could handle the staging and overflight requirements, but national approval to launch a high-risk SOF operation into Afghanistan—in the absence of solid, actionable intelligence—was not likely in the post-Mogadishu era.

Despite these obstacles, we would work on the problem. I knew that Pakistan—specifically the Pakistani Inter-Services Intelligence Directorate (ISID)—had excellent connections with the Taliban. My next step would be to visit Islamabad and meet with Pakistan's President Pervez Musharraf. His military needed help; so did we. Maybe we could make a deal.

I also told the staff that we needed to build stronger ties to the FBI, the CIA, and the State Department. Whatever their problems, those agencies had good people, many with a broad understanding of the region, and we needed to take advantage of every asset in America's arsenal. "I don't know about you guys," I said, as the meeting broke up, "but I need all the help I can get."

The lack of timely, useful intelligence on al Qaeda extended beyond our limited knowledge of their sanctuary in Afghanistan. We knew that al Qaeda was forming cells, not only all across the Muslim world, but in Europe and even North America. And building that kind of clandestine infrastructure costs money. Both the United States and our allies in Europe had legislation in place to freeze known terrorist assets and stop the flow of bank transfers between known terrorist-related organizations. But given the inability of world financial institutions to block the flood of narco-dollars, I wasn't too hopeful. We would have to lean harder on the Saudis and on other states that permitted millions of dollars in charitable donations to be transferred easily into al Qaeda accounts. But these states did not yet feel the same urgency we felt in the United States.

I added the terrorist funding issue to my list of topics to discuss over teacups out in the area of responsibility—a list that was growing longer as I prepared to fly back to the region on October 12, 2000. A new Palestinian uprising, known as the 2nd Intifada, was literally exploding on the West Bank and in the Gaza Strip. Israeli Defense Force (IDF) soldiers were fighting Palestinians armed with Kalashnikovs in the streets of the occupied territories—and Israeli civilians were dying in the blasts of suicide bombs.

On Wednesday, October 11, the day before my departure, I spoke with George Tenet, Director of Central Intelligence, over the STU-III, a Top Secret–encrypted, point-to-point telephone that served as my voice link to Washington. Since my first stop in the AOR would be Pakistan, I wanted to discuss with him my approach to President Musharraf.

"George," I said, "as a practical matter, Pakistan will continue an 'accommodation' with the Taliban until we're able to offer a better alternative. Musharraf is between a rock and a hard place—India and the Pressler Amendment."

In 1985, Congress had adopted an amendment to the Foreign Assistance Act, introduced by Senator Larry Pressler, that banned most economic aid and military assistance to Pakistan unless the U.S. President annually certified that Pakistan was not working on and did not possess nuclear weapons. The act became a moot point in May 1998, when Pakistan announced that it had exploded five nuclear weapons as a deterrent to India's large nuclear arsenal.

"Musharraf's a soldier," I told George. "So are most of the key players in his government. You have to see their world from the military perspective."

"I'm listening, Tom."

"Afghanistan offers the Pakistanis what we call 'strategic depth.' That's battlespace to maneuver and support Pakistani combat forces in the event of another war with India."

"That's what my people tell me also," George said.

The problem with Pakistan's acceptance of the Taliban, of course, was that by extension Musharraf's government was also tacitly accepting the safe harbor Afghanistan was providing for al Qaeda.

"George, I'd like to find a practical way for Musharraf to exert his influence on the Taliban to squeeze bin Laden."

"We're working on it hard, Tom."

"If you agree, I'll coordinate with your station chief in Islamabad."

"I agree. We'll do it together."

As a bargaining chip in Islamabad, I planned to suggest that the United States might help Pakistan—within the constraints of Pressler—to modernize her conventional forces, thus reducing her reliance on nuclear arms.

Since I got to bed very late that night, I filled out my daily Challenges and Opportunities card for the next morning before falling asleep. On the Challenges side, almost as an afterthought, I wrote: "Remember Force Protection."

M y PHONE RANG AT 5:14 A.M.

"Damn," I said, rolling out of bed. "Good news never comes before six A.M."

"General," Vice Admiral Willie Moore said. The Naval Component Commander was calling from Manama, Bahrain. "Very bad news. There's been an explosion aboard our destroyer, USS *Cole,* in Aden harbor, Yemen."

Aden was at the southern tip of the Arabian Peninsula, near the mouth of the Red Sea. It had been a commercial port since the time of Alexander the Great.

"What's the current situation, Willie?"

"Comm with the ship is bad," he reported. "But we know there's been loss of life. A Marine Fast Response Team is en route from the Gulf, and medical teams are flying in from Bahrain and Europe." A serious explosion aboard a warship would involve burn victims; time was crucial. There were also some allies in the area who were willing to help. "French military and naval forces have responded from Djibouti," Moore told me. "They may be there already." The French kept a robust naval, ground, and air force contingent in their former colony across the Bab el Mendeb strait from Yemen. Although our relations with their government were not always cordial, the French military were solid citizens, especially in an emergency like this.

"Any ideas on the cause, Willie?"

"Too soon to know for sure. We suspect terrorism."

"Thanks. Please keep me posted. I'll inform Washington."

The sun was rising as I reached my office. Rifle DeLong was already there with a thin stack of messages about the *Cole*.

"Stand up the Crisis Action Team, Rifle," I said, taking the reports.

"Already done, Sir. They're buckling up the last of their Comms right now."

I could not ask for a better deputy commander than Rifle DeLong, a warfighting leader and one of the most skilled managers I'd met in uniform. Like so many of our generation, he had gone from boy to man in the mud of Vietnam; I trusted his judgment and valued his counsel.

One of the situation briefs Rifle had assembled was a fact sheet on Yemen. It was one of the more interesting countries in a decidedly exotic AOR. In fact, Yemen had been a unified nation for only about ten years, having emerged from one of the most vicious civil conflicts of the Cold War period. After gaining independence from the British protectorate, the highly tribal and fiercely Islamic North Yemen had fought a civil war with leftist, secular South Yemen, a former British colony centered on the port of Aden. Nasser's Egypt aided the south;

the conservative Arab states pumped arms and volunteers into the north. During the mid-1960s, the struggle was marked by massacres and the use of chemical weapons; it wasn't until 1990 that a single, ostensibly unified republic emerged, with its capital in Sanaa in the tribal north. Though the strife never fully ended, there were signs of hope: Recently the Yemenis had begun channeling international aid into the resurrection of Aden as a commercial port and the United States had begun to refuel warships in Aden Harbor.

A brief status report indicated that the *Cole* had made a scheduled refueling stop in Aden on the morning of October 12. This was not a formal port visit, in which military-to-military formalities were exchanged. Rather, the *Cole* had tied up to a floating refueling "dolphin," a pontoon well separated from the old stone docks and breakwater to take on fuel before proceeding to the northern Arabian Gulf.

As the morning progressed, bits of hard information streamed in. I called Hugh Shelton, advising him that the Marine Fast Response Team, a C-130 Medevac aircraft, and French military medical teams were arriving in Aden. "We still don't know the cause of the explosion," I told him.

Hugh and I discussed the Threat Condition (Threat Con) status in Aden at the time the *Cole* arrived. "It was Bravo," I explained. "No indicators of increased threat."

Threat Cons ascended in order of severity, from Alpha—no perceived terrorist threat—through Delta, which indicated an imminent risk of attack. Threat Con Bravo was the prevailing condition in most of the ports of the AOR; the *Cole*'s captain would have had no reason to suspect attack when he moored his vessel to the fuel dolphin.

Although by late morning there was no official confirmation that terrorists had attacked the ship, the news media was reporting that the *Cole* had been struck by a terrorist bomb. "Willie Moore reports that he can't rule out a terrorist attack," I told Shelton and the Vice Chairman, Air Force General Dick Myers, in a quick series of calls. "But the investigation is just getting under way. Willie will give us the facts without hyperbole."

"The media is getting hungry up here," Hugh commented. "They always do at times like this."

I glanced at the television in the corner of my office. CNN was running nonstop coverage, recycling file tape on generic warships and earlier terrorist attacks, including the American embassy bombings in East Africa.

"The CNN factor, Rifle," I commented to Mike DeLong. Ever since the Gulf War, and the proliferation of cable and satellite news networks, the competition for "scoop" reporting had become rabid. Any unusual event with good "visual" potential became a headline. Accurate or not, that headline became reality in the public perception. Military commanders might not have liked this trend, but we had to live with it.

In the early afternoon, I spoke to Admiral Vern Clark, Chief of Naval Operations at the Pentagon, where he was preparing for the press conference.

"We should not describe more than we know, Vern," I said. "Let's avoid speculation and present only the facts we are sure of."

"Tom," he said, "you don't understand Washington. You've seen the reporting. The media will eat us alive unless we give them something."

"The situation still isn't clear, Vern," I said. "I recommend we stick to the facts. Remember the old adage, 'The first reports from the scouts are always wrong.'"

Brigadier General Gary Harrell, my security director, was conducting a vulnerability assessment of facilities in Saudi Arabia. I needed him on the ground in Yemen. "Get down there, Gary," I said. "I want tight security around that ship. Treat it like a crime scene, because that's exactly what it is."

The State Department was preparing to send out a Foreign Emergency Support Team (FEST), which would probably include FBI investigators. "Work with the FEST on the ground, Gary. Keep your eyes open and stay on top of things. This is going to get worse before it gets better."

I finished the conversation with Gary as the first casualty report came in: five sailors confirmed dead, and a number missing. The French had evacuated the most critically wounded to Djibouti, saving their lives through quick, skillful intervention. We owed them one for that.

Just before 3:00 P.M., I called Hugh Shelton again. "I'm about to leave for the AOR. First stop, Oman. I've scrubbed the rest of the trip schedule. But I'll be in the region and get to Yemen within two or three days. The last thing they need right now is a four-star getting in the way, but it's important that the CINC move to the sound of the guns—the troops need it, and I need it."

"We've got a pressure cooker up here with the media, Tom."

"Short-term pain, long-term gain, Hugh."

From this point on, there would be two separate information streams: one a politically sensitive series of Washington press conferences, the other a professional investigation and presentation of the facts as they emerged.

"Hugh," I said, "I recommend you suggest to the SecDef that there should be a thorough external investigation—something like the Wayne Downing investigation of the Khobar Towers bombing in Saudi Arabia. We have to avoid any perception of a cover-up."

Before leaving for the airfield, I had the staff start assembling all statements on the incident from the political leadership, including Senator John Warner, Chairman of the Senate Armed Services Committee. I had already been up to the Hill three times testifying on routine budget and operational matters, and I suspected Congress would hold hearings on this incident. I also directed Rifle DeLong to put together a clear, factual information paper on the process that was used to select Aden as a refueling port and the specifics of why the *Cole* had stopped there.

Once the media started chasing its tail on this, all kinds of political knives would be sharpened. Unfortunately, finding scapegoats following tragedies was part of our national character. So it was essential that we present the unvarnished truth in a clear, concise package—accurately describing both the terrorist threat level in Aden at the time of the attack, and the operational reasons for the refueling stop, within the confines of a twenty-second sound bite.

I boarded the old gray jet for the flight to Muscat, Oman, on the eastern corner of the Arabian Peninsula. En route, I reviewed the file of background reading and situation reports laid out for me by my traveling staff—among them reports from Willie Moore at NAV-CENT; from Gary Harrell, who had just reached Aden; from Rifle DeLong back in Tampa; and from Hugh Shelton in the Pentagon.

It was painfully obvious: Terrorists had struck the *Cole*. A Burke class guided missile destroyer as large as many World War II cruisers, the ship had entered Aden Port guided by a local pilot. Small boats had helped the *Cole*'s crew secure their mooring lines to the fueling dolphin. Given Threat Con Bravo, the captain had posted armed sentries on deck; the *Cole*'s Phalanx, a set of multibarreled 20 mm automatic cannon systems, was standing by against air attack. The refueling itself was uneventful. But as the crew prepared to leave the dolphin, a long, flat-bottomed boat with the appearance of a typical garbage scow moved slowly across the harbor.

The two young Arab men standing at its helm waved as the boat approached the *Cole*'s portside. When the scow reached the *Cole*'s midships, the men detonated a large bomb they had hidden beneath a tarp. The explosion had the force of a cruise missile, blasting a wide hole in the destroyer's hull, devastating several interior decks. The flaming shockwave gutted the center of the ship, knocking out electrical power, destroying water lines needed for firefighting. The ship began to flood.

The latest casualty report carried an update: Twelve known dead, at least five missing in the flooded compartments. Scores wounded, many critically burned.

I turned off the light above my seat and tried to nap before landing in Oman. But sleep did not come. This attack bore the fingerprints of al Qaeda. They had been quiet for months, but it was obvious that a great deal of planning had gone into this operation. How would the

White House respond? Rifle DeLong was updating the status of our TLAM launchers in the "shoot basket" of the northern Arabian Sea. But I knew the al Qaeda sites we had targeted in Afghanistan would be deserted if Osama bin Laden was, in fact, behind this attack. In any event, it would take time for the facts to emerge. There was a national election in less than a month. I was not sure how America would respond. But I expected that CENTCOM would be put through the political wringer—and I would be right in the middle.

I spent three days on the ground in Oman, remaining in constant contact with Rifle DeLong, Willie Moore, Hugh Shelton, and Gary Harrell, who was keeping me updated from Aden. The Yemeni government was in denial, trying to launch its own investigation, but culturally unable to keep pace with the demands of the American civilian and military investigators arriving by the planeload.

The Omanis grieved at our loss, but showed signs of concern that this latest terrorist attack might lessen our resolve and commitment to the region. I assured the Minister of Defense that America remained determined to be a positive force in the area, and that our position would not be shaken. And I carried the same message to the desert hunting camp of Oman's Sultan Qaboos bin Sa'id al-Said.

An archetypal Arab monarch, Qaboos was a man of culture, with a graying beard, a silk saffron turban, robes of finely spun wool. His condolences were sincere. "General, your nation has suffered a great loss. The Arab world is in mourning," he said in flawless English. "How can we help you?"

"Your friendship is a great help, Your Highness."

"That you will always have, General Franks."

I stared at his dark, intelligent eyes. There was no guile there, no secret agenda. Sultan Qaboos would become a friend—a trusted ally during the trying times that lay ahead.

I STOOD ON THE HEAT-BUCKLED DECK OF THE COLE, GAZING DOWN at the hole in the ship's side. The Captain, Commander Kirk Lippold, explained the nature of the damage, the compartments where the sailors had died, the current condition of the wounded. The crew had worked through this sapping heat for seventy-two hours, keeping their ship afloat. They were all exhausted, many still suffering from shock. The harbor was dazzling and bright; a stiff, humid breeze snapped the large American flag flying at the bridge. The stench of soot, burned flesh, and bunker oil was overpowering. As I walked through the ship, there was little I could do or say to relieve the pain I saw on the faces of the crew. I thought back to my days in Vietnam, and my eyes welled with tears—tears of respect, admiration, and remorse. And a renewed taste of the rage I had felt so long ago.

That afternoon I sat in the southern palace of Yemeni President Ali Abdullah Saleh. He was shaken, uncertain of what tone to set. American Ambassador Barbara Bodine had suggested that I remain quiet and listen to what Saleh would say. This was my introduction to Saleh, so I decided to begin the meeting as the ambassador suggested. If he was sincere, I would be cooperative.

As Saleh began to speak, I could see that he was concerned that the *Cole*'s crew was being adequately housed. Were they actually staying onboard the damaged ship, in what had to be miserable conditions? I knew that this concern for the comfort of guests was no mere façade for Westerners; it was deeply ingrained in the Arab culture. I assured the President that the crew was being well cared for and that the captain was doing a good job. We were proud of him, his officers, and the crew.

"Mr. President," I added, "Secretary Cohen has asked me to thank you for all that you have done for us. It is a good start."

The President seemed to relax. "We have always had good relations with your country, with Schwarzkopf and with Zinni. I am only sorry that the friendship between you and me has begun under these circumstances."

Saleh seemed to pose the point as a question rather than a statement, so I took pains to reassure him. "Sir, America's friendship with

Yemen is firm and will not be easily shaken. We will work together. We must share information. Our people have made a good start investigating this tragedy, but it is only a start. Our relationship will grow because it is in the best interest of both our countries."

President Saleh briefly consulted officials seated beside him at the huge inlaid silver-and-brass table. "There are many confusing statements, accusations in your press. It troubles us. We are doing our best to help."

"Our press troubles us, also, Sir," I said, looking into his eyes.

He promised to aid the investigation, noting that he had formed a special committee. I knew the Yemenis would learn the truth; we had to make sure they shared it with us.

"Mr. President, it is very important that your committee provides all the evidence it discovers to our investigators," I said.

President Saleh stood and handed me two videotapes and a plastic folder containing the identity cards of several Arabs. "These are TV tapes from our cameras at the port," he said. "They may be helpful. And the identity cards belong to men we are sure were involved in this terrible attack."

I took the evidence, noting the time so I could record it for "chain of custody" purposes. The FBI is notoriously precise in documenting "who had what evidence, when" during its investigations. Saleh was working to gain my trust—and he had made a good beginning.

TEN DAYS LATER I SAT IN THE GLARE OF THE TELEVISION LIGHTS IN the hearing room of the Senate Armed Services Committee. Beside me at the witness table were Walter Slocombe, Undersecretary of Defense for Policy, and Edward Walker, Assistant Secretary of State for Near Eastern Affairs.

The committee chairman, Senator John Warner, a Virginia Republican, had set a reasonable tone for this public hearing, giving us the opportunity to explain to the nation why the *Cole* had been in Yemen, and why the Pentagon and CENTCOM had not foreseen the risk the ship faced. We would cover this ground again in closed session, during which we could discuss the full classified record. But as I knew from my days as ARCENT commander and my brief tenure as CENTCOM CINC, public congressional hearings had more to do with politics than with exposing facts.

The facts, which I covered in my opening remarks, were relatively straightforward. CENTCOM kept a robust naval presence in the region, including at least one aircraft carrier battle group in the northern Arabian Gulf and a number of other combatant and support ships based out of Bahrain. These vessels reached the area on long transits from American East and West Coast ports. A guided missile destroyer like the *Cole* cruised around 25 knots, and used a lot of fuel. Naval operational procedure called for warships to reach their operating areas with at least 51 percent of their fuel capacity filled. And therefore it was routine for certain types of ships arriving at the southern end of the Red Sea en route to the Arabian Gulf to stop in Yemen to fill their fuel tanks.

Before 1999 our ships had fueled in Djibouti, but that had proved problematic: The fueling pier was decrepit, unsafe, and the harbor was crowded with ships waiting to take on fuel. And once alongside that dock in Djibouti, the pump rates were so slow and the fuel so frequently contaminated with water that a warship could waste up to a week trying to refuel.

When the new fuel dolphin had become available in Aden in 1999, NAVCENT did a security review and determined the port was suitable for brief stops for fuel (BSF). There were thirteen such BSFs in 1999, and fourteen in 2000 before the attack on the *Cole*. All prior fueling stops had passed without incident, and there had been no intelligence indicating a heightened security threat in Yemen when the *Cole* entered Aden Port.

So much for the facts.

As the senators posed their questions, it became clear that some of them had their own interpretation of events. The committee

Minority Leader, the influential Michigan Democrat Carl Levin, hammered away at us, pressuring us to admit that the *Cole*'s visit had been part of an ill-advised policy of engagement with Yemen that involved extending a lucrative naval fueling contract in a port that was a known terrorist haven. Walt Slocombe, Ed Walker, and I stuck to the facts, while the Republicans and Democrats on the dais debated with us and each other. The debate involved far more statements of opinion than questions. Senator Levin seemed determined that I admit that our system of determining threat conditions was flawed. The *Cole* was attacked; ipso facto, Threat Condition Bravo had been set in error.

In response I described the decision-making process, and backed the judgment of my naval commander, Vice Admiral Willie Moore. In the past year, CENTCOM ships had conducted 186 port stops in eight different harbors all over the region—all at Threat Con Bravo. There was no intelligence that the risk was higher in Aden Harbor on October 12.

Late in the hearing, I experienced one of those CNN moments so dear to television producers. A sensational front-page article in that morning's *Washington Times* had been taken as fact by several committee staffers. In a leaked "top-secret intelligence report," Bill Gertz reported, the National Security Agency had warned that "On the day the destroyer USS *Cole* was bombed" terrorists were planning an attack in the region. Why had the *Cole* docked in Aden to take on fuel? Gertz's article noted that the warning was not received aboard the *Cole* until after the ship had been attacked. The wording of the article implied that the military had sat on vital intelligence, thus dooming the *Cole*'s sailors. The story's sub-headline, "Tardy Transmission at Fault," clearly implied that the intelligence community and the military had dropped the ball.

Senator Jeff Sessions, an Alabama Republican, demanded to know whether we—"people in authority who ought to know these answers"—had "any sense of embarrassment" about this.

As I explained the truth—that the NSA warning had *not* related to CENTCOM's region—the panel seemed less interested in an explanation than in the television footage showing the righteous indignation of several members. Amazed at the scene, I couldn't help envisioning the horde of press aides who would soon be editing and sending this footage back home to the Senators' constituents.

As we left the Senate office building to prepare for a House Armed Services Committee hearing that afternoon, I turned to Walt Slocombe. "Do I look shiny?" I asked.

"Not especially. Why?"

"Well, I thought I might—because we've just been wire-brushed for about three hours."

While the country counted hanging chads and the courts in Florida and Washington deliberated, I returned to the AOR, enlisting potential friends and allies in our ongoing efforts to curb terrorism, ease humanitarian crises, and facilitate the sharing of intelligence. The *Cole* investigation was completed a few months later, leaving no scapegoats, but a strong whiff of politics, in its wake.

O N JANUARY 9, 2001, IN THE WANING DAYS OF THE CLINTON administration, Dick Clarke called me from the NSC to discuss the government's pursuit of Osama bin Laden and al Qaeda. He talked for a while without advancing any meaningful options. George Tenet had already briefed me on Agency activities in Afghanistan and Central Asia, but I listened to Clarke patiently, because he said that the incoming administration was going to retain him in his counterterrorism position in the NSC.

As we spoke on the STU-III, Clarke shared sensitive information regarding the Predator Plus program. He told me the operation was moving ahead well and might soon reap results. He also said our HUMINT performance was improving, but did not elaborate.

"Great," I said. "We're standing by for target coordinates."

I never received a single operational recommendation, or a single page of actionable intelligence, from Richard Clarke.

GENERAL HEADQUARTERS IN RAWALPINDI WAS COOL AND SHADY, an old stone fort of the British Raj. President Pervez Musharraf received me in his wood-paneled office on January 19, 2001, wearing a paratrooper smock and sharply pressed khaki twill trousers.

This was a soldier-to-soldier exchange, and Musharraf fell naturally into the idiom of military acronym and jargon. He announced that he would brief me on the "macro situation" and then break the discussion down to detail. I listened, as if to a general officer well accustomed to summarizing complex information—which of course is what Musharraf had been, before leading an Army coup against Pakistan's corrupt civilian government in 1999.

After commanding units in combat during two wars with India, Musharraf had taught at Pakistan's senior military schools. He was an astute strategist, and our meeting became a kind of wide-ranging lecture on his country and its military posture.

Pakistan, he insisted, was firmly in favor of peace in the region, opposed to terrorism, and against extremism in any form, including religious zealotry—"both Hindu and Islamic," he assured me.

"We never intended to begin an arms race," he said, referring to Pakistan's growing nuclear arsenal. "Our weapons are meant to maintain peace with honor and to preserve our dignity. They are a deterrent, not a first-strike capability."

As if following my thoughts, Musharraf added that the only reason Pakistan had invested so much wealth and energy into developing ballistic missiles was that their air force had been crippled by America's arms embargo.

I nodded, indicating my understanding.

He then focused on Afghanistan. "We have no choice but to work with the Taliban," he said. "I can assure you that we dislike their extremism, but they brought stability to Afghanistan and ended the bloodshed after the Soviets left. We must have stability, on at least one border."

There was a large, beautifully engraved map of the Subcontinent on the wall. As he spoke, I studied the topography. Soldiers prefer to defend from the high ground, but much of Pakistan was located in the arid plains of the Indus Valley. In the event of an Indian invasion, the Pakistani military would take up positions to protect Islamabad. They would indeed require lines of communication into Afghanistan. This was the "strategic depth" that George Tenet and I had discussed.

"I understand your situation," I said.

"You know, General," Musharraf said. "The Taliban is isolated. We have some influence with them, but we don't control them. I will do my best to help, but we need help from the international community."

The help he had in mind, of course, was U.S. economic and military aid. I was not here to grant concessions. But I would carry this message back to Washington.

"Pakistan would like to help with the problem of Osama bin Laden and al Qaeda," he said, stating his case directly. "If we can increase our influence with the Taliban, it is possible they would agree to expel him to some neutral state for either exile or to be put on trial."

"I am here to listen, General Musharraf," I said.

Musharraf continued his briefing, but the crucial information had already been exchanged. If we helped him with Pakistan's needs, he would help us with the Taliban and al Qaeda.

As we spoke, it struck me that it was appropriate we both wore uniforms. For years, American officials and diplomatic envoys in business suits had hectored soldier-politicians such as Pervez Musharraf about human rights and representative government. Of course I believed in these issues with equal conviction, but at this point in history we needed to establish priorities. Stopping al Qaeda was such a priority, and Musharraf was willing to help.

The President walked me out to the embassy car, and we stood in the shade of tall eucalyptus trees.

"You must come back soon so we can play golf," Musharraf said.

"That would be a pleasure, Sir."

Pervez Musharraf would be both friend and ally in the days ahead.

WITH THE OTHER UNIFIED COMMAND CINCs, I MET THE NEW Secretary of Defense, Donald Rumsfeld, on February 7, 2001. Wearing a well-cut dark suit, button-down shirt, and a red power tie, the Secretary was cordial as he showed us around his E-Ring office.

"It's a little bare in here, gentlemen," he said, studying us through his rimless glasses. "We're still getting unpacked."

There was an original Remington bronze, and several boxes leaning against one wall. The Secretary saw me glancing toward a tall, hardwood reading desk. I'd seen pictures of these stand-up desks, and remembered that John Kennedy had used one.

"I've always found that you think best on your feet. I try to walk as much as I can every day," he said, and grinned. "I guess I've come to the right building for that."

We listened closely. Rumsfeld was known as an unorthodox, innovative thinker. "Outside the box" was the phrase many used to describe his mind, in both praise and denigration. So far this handshake meeting was following that pattern: the Secretary had prepared no discussion agenda.

Like my colleagues, I'd been diligent, staying up late to prep on important topics in advance of this first meeting. I was prepared to discuss the no-fly zones in Iraq; the terrorist threat in the region; the new deployable command post I was having built for CENTCOM.

But Donald Rumsfeld seemed averse to talking business at this first encounter. He did control the conversation, however. Despite his soft-spoken manner, Rumsfeld imparted authority. I left the meeting with the impression that I had just spent time with a person who had been more interested in learning about us—America's uniformed military leaders—than in having us learn anything about him. Sitting in the bus with the other CINCs and Service Chiefs on the way to the White House, I thought: *Rumsfeld knows what he wants. The rest of us will know soon enough.*

We were headed to meet President George W. Bush and the remainder of the national security team. As we entered the Cabinet Room, I was aware of the history that had unfolded here: Within these paneled walls Abraham Lincoln, Teddy Roosevelt, Woodrow Wilson, FDR, and JFK had made decisions about world peace and global conflict. And I was stunned by the friendliness of the staff. I had never been invited to the Clinton White House, but colleagues had described a palpable coolness toward military officers. If their reports were accurate, this would be a very different White House.

President George W. Bush looked younger than I had expected. There was a bounce to his step as he came around the table and shook hands with each of us.

"We've got to get a picture of this, General," he said with a smile. "How often do two boys from Midland, Texas, make it this far?"

"Mr. President," I said, "there were days when I thought I'd never make it to second lieutenant."

As we sat down, we were joined by Vice President Cheney, National Security Adviser Dr. Condoleezza Rice, and Andrew Card, the President's Chief of Staff. After Secretary Rumsfeld made some introductory remarks, each commander proceeded to describe his responsibilities.

As I gave my ten-minute brief on CENTCOM and the AOR, the Cabinet Room was absolutely silent. The President was focused, listened intently, and asked about troop levels and the leadership personalities in the region.

Later that evening, our wives joined us for a reception and dinner in the White House's Blue Room. As Cathy and I chatted with old friends and spoke with Condi Rice and Vice President Dick Cheney,

President Bush walked up and said, "Four stars. Wow! Midland boy has done well."

I grinned, looked around the room, and said, "Mr. President, *two* boys from Midland seem to have done well."

When we were about to be seated for dinner, President Bush tapped a glass and said, "Bow with me, please." As he said grace, I was struck by both the eloquence and the simplicity of the prayer. And I was reminded of the Pledge of Allegiance—*One Nation, under God*. There was a certain comfort in hearing the president of the United States pray to a "Heavenly Father." I was pleased on that night to have a man of faith in the White House.

And throughout the critical years of American history that followed, my opinion never changed.

ON MARCH 7, 2001, I HAD MY FIRST EXTENDED DISCUSSION WITH Donald Rumsfeld in the conference room of his Pentagon office. The SecDef managed to stay seated for several hours, although he did stroll over to the coffee bar on a few occasions to refill his cup with decaf. Deputy Defense Secretary Paul D. Wolfowitz and Rumsfeld's tall, imposing intellectual alter ego, Special Assistant Steve Cambone, also attended the session.

"I'm going over to the House Armed Services Committee again tomorrow, Mr. Secretary," I told him. "I've been in the job eight months and this will be my eighth hearing."

Rumsfeld winced, and turned to Cambone. "Steve, keep a log of congressional testimony senior DoD civilians and military are called on to give." Then he turned back to me. "How was your last trip to the region?"

During my career I'd known a number of senior civilians in the Defense Department. Many of them had tried to out-acronym the people in uniform, but this man was different. I think I might have heard him use the term "AOR" twice, but he always seemed more comfortable with civilian vernacular. This didn't mean he was not focused on his military responsibilities. Quite the contrary: I would come to learn that he viewed his role as that of an advocate for—and a challenger of—the armed services. Don Rumsfeld was no mere "like-thinking affiliate," as several secretaries have been described, but rather a leader who wanted to use his own ideas to bring about change.

At this early time in his tenure, he was already beginning to discuss *transformation*—changing the military to "meet the needs of the twenty-first century." *This guy intends to change things,* I thought as we spoke. I was certain that the days ahead would mark the beginning of any number of studies that would make the Service Chiefs cringe—how to split the resource pie, how to adjust the "end-strengths" of their branches, how to make America's armed forces more "joint"—and the list went on. *Good for him.*

Some Secretaries of Defense saw themselves as five-stars positioned slightly above a constellation of four-star flag officers. Rumsfeld wasn't so much elevated above us as he was in an orbit all his own. Generals and admirals learn to think in vertical and horizontal patterns. Rumsfeld's mind worked on the oblique—cross-cutting the traditional. I had heard the rumblings of discontent from a few colleagues, who accused him of being "out in left field" when it came to the practicalities of national defense. Maybe so, but my earliest sessions with him convinced me that he would be good for the military. Popularity is never as important as respect.

In response to Rumsfeld's question, I described my most recent meetings in Bahrain, Qatar, and the UAE. The Secretary asked about the reaction I'd encountered in those countries to our recent attacks on several targets in Iraq. These strikes had included a rather vigorous Response Option, launched in the wake of a series of SA-2 missile launches at our planes. I carefully explained the Response Option procedure (avoiding the acronym) and said that our Arab allies had been ambivalent about the results, but generally appreciated the fact that we would use force when we thought it necessary.

"How are the Saudis?" Rumsfeld asked.

I explained the "death of a thousand cuts" problems we were facing, and the fact that the British military mission in Saudi Arabia was also having trouble.

"The Saudis are difficult," I said. "On one hand, they want a close relationship with us. On the other, the Royals don't want to create problems for themselves with their subjects, who would like to see us leave."

Then I devoted ten minutes to a careful description of Iraq's escalating reaction to our air patrols in both Operation Southern Watch and Operation Northern Watch, and told the Secretary that we'd need to modify our approach—either the number of patrols, or the air tracks they fly—to reduce the risk to our aircrews.

Rumsfeld was quiet for a moment, and then looked directly at me with his dispassionate blue gaze. "It seems to me we are just boring holes in the sky, General." He continued, "We need concrete goals. The current policy is open-ended. I want to recommend goals, objectives, approaches that make sense. Think out of the box. I don't care how we've always done it. Containment has not changed the regime's behavior. We still see Saddam shooting at our aircrews. You have a lot of work to do, General."

Rumsfeld smiled; I was about to reply when he continued, shifting focus as he spoke. "The sanctions against Iraq are collapsing," he said flatly. "The Arabs make vague promises of help, but deliver nothing. The Gulf War coalition is down to the British and us. And that can't last forever."

He was being open, and so would I. "The Israel-Palestine situation affects everything out there, Sir. The Intifada is all over media in the region every day. Until we solve that issue, the Arabs are not going to take risk to help us solve the Saddam problem."

The discussion continued for two more hours, free-ranging and unpredictable.

As I returned to my hotel room across from the Pentagon, I tried to transcribe the pages of notes I had taken. The meeting had been exhausting, but exhilarating. I hadn't had such a mental workout since those long sessions around the LAM Task Force conference table at Fort Monroe. I could understand why some generals disliked and distrusted Secretary Donald Rumsfeld; you didn't want to walk into his office with a neat stack of briefing charts that followed a train of logic from A to B, because Rumsfeld would redirect the briefing after the first chart. He not only thought outside the box—he didn't recognize that the box existed.

THE SECRETARY HAD DIRECTED ME TO THINK YEARS INTO THE future, but I still had the daily, weekly, and monthly responsibilities of running a large and active command. I traveled the AOR. I tweaked our Response Options in the no-fly zones of Iraq. And I spent hours with my new J-3 Operations Director, Air Force Major General Gene Renuart, and the new J-2 Intelligence Director, Army Brigadier General Jeff Kimmons, building target "sets"—categories of installations—on suspected al Qaeda and Taliban facilities in Afghanistan.

I suspected that our policy toward al Qaeda was soon to change. There was nothing dramatic in the signals I got, but I sensed frustration in the Pentagon and the intelligence community with the pinprick, standoff retaliations we'd employed in the past. The new Administration would settle on a robust approach, of that I was sure. It would take time to line up the requisite policy positions, diplomatic initiatives, and military power, but it would come.

In April, I got a visit at MacDill from Eric Antila, who had long since retired from the Army as a colonel. He looked old and tired—probably ill. We spent two hours "smoking and joking" on easy chairs in my office, talking about the days and nights we'd spent in Vietnam and about what we had learned.

"I was lucky, Tom," he said. "I had good, brave young soldiers, willing to be led. An officer can ask for nothing more."

How true, I thought. "We were lucky to have you, too, Sir."

On his way out, I took this fine old soldier through the Trophy Room. He was interested in the weapons—and in chatting with every trooper he passed by. "I'm so proud of you, General. You were the best lieutenant I ever knew. You cared about the troops, and I've always remembered that."

I looked at the floor with tears in my eyes. "Colonel, you cared about this lieutenant. And that's why I'm here today."

Eric Antila smiled wisely as he walked away. I never saw him again; he died a few months later. But his memory—with its reminder of the value of loyalty to subordinates—would stay with me during one of the most demanding times of my life.

Through the spring of 2001 and into the summer, protecting our deployed troops from terrorists remained an ever-present concern. I spent long days and weekends with our air, ground, and naval component commanders, working to ensure that there would be no repeats of Khobar Towers and the *Cole*.

The summer found our intelligence people working with the CIA and the Defense Intelligence Agency, collecting and analyzing persistent but unspecific indications of planned terrorist activity in the Middle East. This was "all source" information—a blend of human intelligence and technical intelligence. I ordered the component commanders to have their people keep a lower profile. On several occasions, I increased our force protection posture—the Threat Con—but never as a result of a specific threat. Something was brewing, but the best minds at the CIA and the National Security Agency could not pin down the threats with any degree of certainty. Where would we see a terrorist act . . . and when?

As I read the increasingly alarming reports of potential attacks on Western facilities in the region, a thought formed. Al Qaeda had used cars, trucks, and boats as suicide bombs. What about small planes loaded with high explosives? I sent a note—first to our embassy in Riyadh, then to other embassies across the AOR—asking the ambassadors to pass on my concerns to their hosts. "We should work to tune the host nations in the region in to this type of threat," I said.

IN THE FIRST WEEK OF SEPTEMBER, I WORKED WITH GEORGE TENET and an Assistant Secretary of State, Christiana Rocca, to arrange a meeting with General Mahmoud Ahmed, the head of the Pakistani Inter-Services Intelligence Directorate, during a scheduled visit to Washington. I was eager to look deeper into the links between Pakistan and the Taliban, and to assess the possibility that Pakistan might help us get to Osama bin Laden and al Qaeda by increasing cooperation with our agencies. The meeting was set for September 10, 2001.

ON FRIDAY, SEPTEMBER 7, I SPOKE TO THE CENTCOM intelligence staff in the MacDill base theater about the roles and responsibilities of the Command as I envisioned them.

At the end of the presentation, a young sergeant raised her hand and asked, "General, what keeps you awake at night?"

A helluva question. I thought a minute, then answered. "A terrorist attack against the World Trade Center in New York—that's what keeps me awake at night."

The men and women in the audience listened intently.

"If international terrorists were to strike a major blow against America," I added, "I fear the specter of the nation's military operating as combatants within our borders for the first time since the 1860s."

I spoke about the excesses of Reconstruction after the Civil War, which had resulted in the enactment of Posse Comitatus, the law that prevents military forces from serving as policemen inside the United States. Would that stricture survive a full-blown terrorist attack?

"So, the thing that keeps me awake at night, Sergeant," I emphasized, "is the possible use of our armed forces against American citizens. We do our job well, but we're trained to fight foreign enemies. We're not police officers, sheriffs, or the FBI. If we were ever required to act in that capacity during a major emergency like an attack on the World Trade Center, the effect on America could be devastating. Martial law would not sit well in a free and open society."

7

A NEW KIND OF WAR

The narrow road from the air base into Hania circled Souda Bay, descending through olive groves and terraced vineyards. We entered a village of whitewashed houses with orange tile roofs.

I stretched my legs in my seat. Beside me in the Navy sedan, Cathy was dozing; jet lag was an occupational hazard. We'd be in Pakistan tomorrow, but for now I was looking forward to enjoying this rest stop in the Aegean sun, treating the flight crew to a seafood dinner, and storing up some sleep.

I had used most of the ten-hour flight from Andrews Air Force Base in Washington to Greece to plow through the paperwork my executive officer, Navy Captain Van Mauney, had culled since leaving Tampa the previous day.

There had been one disturbing intelligence report. General Ahmad Shah Massoud, leader of the Afghan Northern Alliance anti-Taliban opposition, was dead—fatally wounded at his headquarters near the border with Uzbekistan when two Arab assassins posing as journalists exploded a suicide bomb hidden in their video camera. This had the signature of an al Qaeda operation. I wasn't surprised. Osama bin Laden and Taliban leader Mullah Omar had a lot to gain by weakening the Northern Alliance.

I only wished that the news of the assassination had reached me in Washington before my meeting on September 10 with General Mahmoud Ahmed of the Pakistani Inter-Services Intelligence Directorate. Our conversation had been that of one professional officer to another—a "frank and open" discussion, as the diplomats say. Polite, in other words, but bare-knuckled. Pakistan needed parts for their American-made F-16 fighter-bombers, C-130 transports, and P-3 naval reconnaissance planes. We needed solid intelligence on al Qaeda and Osama bin Laden—information we could use to build targets. With Secretary Rumsfeld's blessing, and DCI George Tenet's encouragement, I had informed General Mahmoud that cooperation was a two-way street. He got the message, and promised to brief President Musharraf on the content of our meeting.

Now, having landed in Crete, Cathy and I unpacked overnight bags in our suite at the Kydon Hotel, overlooking the medieval Venetian port, and then headed to the market across the street to buy the "fixings"—as they say in Midland—for an afternoon snack.

Fish vendors chanted their catches under the echoing concrete dome as we strolled into the shop of our friend Spiros Marsellos. He grinned broadly as he recognized us.

"Kalo'ste," he proclaimed. "Welcome back to Crete."

Spiros knew what we'd come for: the best collection of olives in Greece. Dipping into big plastic barrels, he offered us samples of glistening purple-black Kalamata olives, and the larger green Volos variety. We left his shop with a plastic sack heavy with quarter-liter containers. Next we bought a wedge of German Ementhaler cheese and a dark crusty loaf of local *mavro* peasant bread. What we didn't eat for lunch we'd share with the crew on the next day's flight.

I had a shower, shared the picnic with Cathy, and stretched out for a nap. It wasn't hard to fall asleep.

THE POUNDING ON THE HOTEL-ROOM DOOR BROUGHT ME WIDE awake in less than a second. Sitting up, I instinctively checked my watch. Just after 4:00 P.M. Something was wrong; our wake-up wasn't scheduled until five.

"General Franks . . ." It was Van Mauney.

I opened the door.

"Sir," he said, his face pale. "You'd better check the TV. An airplane just crashed into one of the towers of the World Trade Center in New York."

I pulled on my clothes as Cathy found the remote and turned on the television. "Osama bin Laden," I said, striding out the door. "I'm going to the COMM room."

Our communications center down the hall had several civilian phone lines and a large television tuned to CNN International. The room was filled with my staff. We watched silently as the channel flashed videotape replays of the burning skyscraper. The commentary was understandably chaotic, and often contradictory; it was difficult to distinguish live images from tape. But then the wide screen snapped into a telephoto shot of a second jet slamming into the southern tower.

As I watched the flames and roiling black smoke, a colorful graphic appeared on the bottom of the screen: "America Under Attack."

"Osama bin Laden," I said. *Son of a bitch!*

My fists clenched, but then the habits of a combat soldier returned. I was filled with cold rage, but externally calm. Now I understood the reason for Massoud's assassination. Having anticipated American retaliation in Afghanistan, bin Laden had taken preemptive action to cripple the Northern Alliance.

Slowly, I accepted the new reality: this terrorist, who had already killed hundreds of American diplomats, service members, and innocent foreign civilians, had just executed his most successful attack against my country, right on American soil. An unexpected insight flashed across my mind: *Bin Laden is no coward. He's a deadly adversary, a worthy, bold commander of dedicated and capable forces.*

The phone line to CENTCOM headquarters in Tampa rang. It was Rifle DeLong. We could talk on this nonsecure line while my communications people scrambled to set up an encrypted link.

"General," Mike said, "a SITREP. Washington reports that the aircraft were both hijacked, one from Logan Airport in Boston."

"I understand, Rifle," I said. "Stand up our Crisis Action Team (CAT) if you haven't done so already. Establish contact with the Joint Staff CAT in the Pentagon. Contact our embassies and the senior U.S. military officers in each of the AOR countries . . . ."

After my years as a commander—and fourteen months as CINC—these initial orders were almost automatic. But I was fighting complex emotions and ricocheting thoughts. A highly organized enemy had delivered a fierce attack on America. New York was the cultural, economic, and financial heart of our nation. And a chunk of the city was burning.

By now President George Bush was on the screen speaking from a school in Florida, where he had been showcasing his education policy. The nation, he said, had suffered an "apparent terrorist attack."

As Rifle and I spoke, CNN broadcast the collapse of the southern tower of the World Trade Center. I was hypnotized by the mushroom of smoke, debris, and dust. "All those people," I said softly.

"Another item, Sir," announced Rifle, the unflappable Marine. "We just got word that a Predator flying in the OSW zone has been shot down by the Iraqis."

"Roger," I acknowledged, slipping that fact into its proper mental slot. "Prepare a kinetic response option." No matter what was happening in New York, Saddam Hussein and his military had to understand that they would not be permitted to take advantage of the situation.

I then got a message from Major General Sy Johnson, who commanded our military liaison mission in Saudi Arabia. General Ali bin Muhayya, Chief of the Saudi Arabia General Staff, had just cancelled a visit I had scheduled with him next week during my return leg from Pakistan. Another mental note: Osama bin Laden was a Saudi. The Royal Family's attitude toward their homegrown terrorists had vacillated for years between toleration and extermination. Now they were openly apprehensive about publicly associating with the American military.

I called Mike DeLong again with another order. "Rifle, contact the U.S. Special Operations Command and the 6th Air Mobility Wing at MacDill immediately. Have them go to Force Protection Level Delta." If multiple terrorist cells were operating on this Tuesday, CENTCOM headquarters and MacDill Air Force Base would be obvious targets, and I wanted our people and facilities protected.

A few minutes later, Rifle telephoned again. "A third aircraft, Sir. It just struck the Pentagon. A wide-body full of fuel, like the other ones. It's on the west side, and there's lots of damage."

How many more? I thought.

Even as Rifle spoke, CNN displayed the familiar gray façade of the Pentagon boiling with dark smoke and orange flame.

"The National Military Command Center in the Pentagon is still manned," Rifle announced. "But communications are difficult."

"Roger," I acknowledged, my thoughts jumping ahead.

This much I knew already: America would respond militarily. That response would be aimed at al Qaeda. And it would be launched in Afghanistan. CENTCOM's commander and senior officers would have no time to grieve. This was not just another terrorist outrage: These attacks were an obvious act of war. And the first battles of that war would be fought in my area of responsibility.

"Rifle, find out as soon as possible the status of our TLAM shooters. How many missiles will be available to be launched into Afghanistan in twenty-four hours? How many in forty-eight hours?"

"Aye, aye, Sir," Mike said. "Incidentally, the FAA has closed all U.S. airspace, grounded every flight. And Secretary Rumsfeld has ordered Threat Con Delta for all deployed military forces."

I acknowledged the information. Delta was ordered only when attack was imminent—or had already occurred.

The television coverage continued in an uninterrupted nightmare. A section of the Pentagon roof collapsed. Moments later came jittery telephoto shots of smoke rising from a green pasture southeast of Pittsburgh, where a fourth hijacked airliner, United Airlines Flight 93, had slammed into the earth, killing all on board.

I could no longer work on this phone. I needed secure satellite voice and data links. My communicators said it would take about an hour to lead the fiber-optic cables from the hotel roof, where they had set up the satellite antennas, down the outside of the building to the Comm room.

"Son of a bitch," I said. "I'll work on the roof."

I sat hunched in a plastic chair on the gritty concrete roof of the Kydon Hotel speaking over an encrypted satellite link to the CENT-COM staff in Florida. Referring to notes, I directed Gene Renuart to begin strike targeting for Afghanistan. We had struggled—with incomplete intelligence—to identify al Qaeda training camps, barracks, command-and-control facilities, communications centers, and support complexes. And we had built target sets for key Taliban installations, air defense sites, and early warning radars. The time had come when that effort would pay off.

Next, I directed the staff to coordinate with Vice Admiral Willie Moore to ensure that our ships in the region canceled all port calls and immediately put to sea. The image of the USS *Cole* smoldering in Aden harbor still haunted me.

With the afternoon sun cooling and the shadows stretching down from the nearby hills, I crossed the immediate-action tasks off my list one by one. As I worked beside the satellite antennas, Van Mauney and my aide, Marine Lt. Colonel Jeff Haynes, sat nearby, managing the telephones, receiving and delivering information and orders. After the initial shock of the television images, everyone had assumed an attitude of cool, dedicated professionalism. I dictated immediate instructions to every senior American military representative in the region to acknowledge receipt of the order to move to Threat Con Delta. Al Qaeda might still be planning to strike more American targets—especially isolated military units—and I didn't want our commanders caught off guard in the event they hadn't yet received the order from the Pentagon.

As dusk fell on the roof, I heard a strange sound, more like an electronic chime than anything animate. It was the sunset call of the owls of Athena, the tiny birds with huge eyes whose image first appeared on Greek coins 2500 years ago. Those little owls had sent their haunting call across Aegean hills during centuries of peace and war. Now they announced the arrival of nightfall, on the first day of a war that might well last for decades.

I sat back in the creaking plastic chair and eased my shoulders. The calf muscle of my right leg was twitching and stiffening up, a reminder of a hot December night in Binh Phuoc some thirty-four years earlier.

"Rifle," I told my deputy, "I'm planning to head back to Tampa as soon as I can."

"U.S. airspace is closed, Sir," he answered.

My aircraft crew confirmed this. It would be impossible to file a flight plan. I considered continuing the trip to meet President Musharraf in Pakistan. If ever there was a time for some arm-twisting, it was now. Musharraf had spoken of international help in dealing with the Taliban when we'd met in January. Well, there would be plenty of American help forthcoming if he joined us in this fight. And with his corner of the world now in the crosshairs of the American military, he would have to declare what side he was on pretty damn fast.

But I also wanted to get back to Tampa. So I told Rifle to let Hugh Shelton know that I would wait six hours before deciding which direction to fly.

Next, I had a conference call with Rifle and Gene Renuart. "Okay," I said. "Here's what we've got. Only al Qaeda and Osama bin Laden have the capability to launch an operation of this magnitude. Gene, I want you and Jeff Kimmons to concentrate on fine-tuning the target sets in Afghanistan." I thought a moment. "What's the latest casualty estimate?"

"The media is talking anywhere from six to ten thousand dead in New York alone," Rifle DeLong answered, keeping emotion from his voice. "They're revising it down, but it's going to be bad."

"Several hundred missing at the Pentagon, Sir," Gene added. "Somewhere around eighty confirmed dead so far."

"Let's build the target sets based on five assumptions," I said. "First, the attack on America was delivered by al Qaeda operating out of Afghanistan. Second, the people who planned and ordered the strike are located in Afghanistan. Third, there *will* be a national decision to strike. Fourth, the reason for our action will be legally undisputed, which means we will build a coalition of cooperative nations. And fifth, we will receive either acquiescence or cooperation from all the regional leaders to hit Afghanistan."

"Roger that, Sir," Gene added.

"Okay," I said. "Let's get to work."

Van Mauney brought me the classified status report on Tomahawk missiles I'd requested earlier. We would have 80 TLAMs in the shoot baskets in the Arabian Sea within twenty-four hours, and up to 200 within forty-eight hours. As I read the report, submerged Los Angeles–class attack submarines and Burke Class destroyers were speeding toward the Straits of Hormuz at flank speed.

It was dark now. The breeze had stopped completely. Athena's owls peeped and chirped, and I worked through the final items on my immediate action list.

Those practical steps had helped me keep my thoughts in line. But it had not been easy. My mind was bouncing back and forth at high speed. What was our exact troop strength in the region? Their readiness status? How many operational groups *could* al Qaeda put in the field? Had I done enough to protect our forces? Had any of my friends been killed in the Pentagon?

I had no doubt that we were going to war. And it would be a war like none ever fought. There would be a national decision to put troops on the ground, and America now deployed military technology that hadn't even been imagined when I'd been with the 1st Cavalry troops in Desert Storm, just a decade before. The wish lists of the Louisiana Maneuvers Task Force were now operational hardware. Weapons would not be a problem. But was I up to the challenge of being the senior combatant commander in this new kind of war?

Sitting back in the hard plastic chair on the hotel roof, I reflected on that talk I'd given to the CENTCOM intelligence staff the previous Friday. America was in deep shock, reeling from the images of airliners smashing into buildings and those proud towers collapsing like flaming tinsel. Would my fellow citizens now be persuaded to abandon their hard-won individual freedoms to earn a bit more security in a clearly insecure world?

As I stood up, another thought struck me. *Today is like Pearl Harbor.* The world was one way before today, and will never be that way again. *We stand at a crease in history.*

L ATER THAT EVENING, WITH EXHAUSTION SETTING IN AND nothing left to do but wait for clearance to fly, Cathy and I took the aircrew to dinner; the members of our traveling staff stayed behind, chained to their phones and computers. We walked through the quiet waterfront to the lamp-lit, sandstone-block courtyard of the Mylos Taverna. As we filed to our corner table, the normally effusive chatter of the Greek patrons dropped to a whisper. I scanned the nearby tables; faces everywhere were drawn with sadness. Yiannis, our usually smiling waiter, approached silently and shook my hand as if at a funeral.

"Everyone is so sorry, General," the man said.

W ELL AFTER MIDNIGHT, RIFLE DELONG REPORTED ON THE situation in the Pentagon. "Secretary Rumsfeld stayed in the building and helped evacuate some of the casualties," he said.

"The crisis plan calls for DepSecDef to be moved to an alternate command facility, Site R, along with key members of the national leadership. I believe they're in place now." *Rumsfeld still at the Pentagon, Paul Wolfowitz at Site R,* I thought.

I closed my eyes and nodded. Moving to Site R was part of America's plan to respond to impending nuclear attack. *What the hell have we come to?*

As the night passed, Rifle updated me on the readiness of our forces, the locations of our aircraft carrier battle groups, and the "Global Power" timelines for missions by B-2 Stealth bombers flying from Whiteman Air Force Base in Missouri.

I had received an intelligence alert that as many as thirty additional terrorist strikes were possible worldwide. But there had been no more attacks . . . so far. Maybe this was because we'd buttoned up, sealing our vulnerabilities by going to Threat Con Delta.

By now, CNN was running tape of President Bush flying back to Andrews and landing in Marine One on the White House lawn. The immediate crisis was over: The President was back in the Oval Office, the Secretary of Defense was in the wounded Pentagon. America was putting on her "game face." I was proud of my country.

THE NEXT MORNING, THE FLIGHT CREW RECEIVED GREEK AIR traffic control permission to take off from Crete and head west. We didn't have clearance to enter U.S. airspace, but I was confident it would come.

Ninety minutes later, as we crossed the Western Mediterranean, I spoke by secure phone to Hugh Shelton.

"Tom," he said. "Everybody in Washington, from the President on down, is leaning forward on this."

"We're looking at *serious* operations against al Qaeda and Afghanistan?" I asked.

"Count on it, Tom."

By the time we were over Spain, the Pentagon had cleared Spar 06 all the way to Tampa. I worked steadily at my desk, wargaming with my onboard staff and the senior leadership at CENTCOM. I was interrupted by several phone calls. The first was from His Majesty King Abdullah of Jordan, a close ally and a personal friend. "You can depend on Jordan to stand by America," he said.

"That means a lot right now, Sir."

Another call was from Sheik Salman bin Hamid al Khalifa, the Crown Prince of Bahrain and commander of his nation's military. "Bahrain is with you," he said. Our engagement efforts over the previous fourteen months were obviously paying off. These Gulf States would stand by America in the period ahead.

I was still running on coffee and adrenaline, but I knew I'd need some sleep soon. As I sat back stretching in my seat, Cathy entered the compartment, returning from the galley with a Diet Coke. While there she'd spoken to one of the communications NCOs; almost in passing, he mentioned that we had the sky to ourselves. "All the radio frequencies are silent. There's no traffic over the Atlantic."

The cumulative shock of the past sixteen hours had suddenly struck Cathy hard, turning that brief comment into the stark image of a world viciously swept clear of peaceful commerce. She, too, had felt the crease in history.

W E LANDED AT MACDILL JUST AFTER 1500 HOURS ON Wednesday, September 12. I'd had a total of four hours of sleep in the past thirty, but there were many long days—and nights—ahead.

As we left the plane, I spoke to Jeff Haynes. "Please make sure the enlisted aides get that bed into my office. I'm going to be bunking at the headquarters for a while."

Cathy watched silently as I spoke. Our marriage had lasted through almost thirty-three years and two wars. This would be our third. She knew my work habits well and never complained.

We hugged. "Make sure to eat and get some sleep when you can," she said.

"You bet, Dear." I tried to sound convincing. She knew better.

I was still in sport clothes from the plane trip. On the short drive to CENTCOM headquarters, though, I noticed Air Force security police wearing desert camouflage uniforms, Kevlar vests, and helmets—and armed with M-4 automatic carbines and handguns.

A squad of airmen near the largest hangar piled green sandbags in a chest-high horseshoe checkpoint. As we passed, I saw that their black M-60 machine gun was loaded with a belt of ammunition. Sandbags and machine guns, a hint of mildew in the humid breeze: The uniforms and helmets were different, but the weapons were the same. This could have been a flight line in Vietnam during the Tet Offensive.

This time, though, the war had been brought to American soil.

FOR THE CENTCOM STAFF AND ME, THE TEN DAYS AND NIGHTS between Tuesday, September 11, and Friday, September 21, 2001, were a time of intense focus—and fatigue, and caffeine overload. Some days seemed never to end; some nights passed in a fast-forward blur. In a way this was like combat, but without the noise, the sense of imminent danger, or that strange after-contact elation.

But I do have very vivid recollections of the time.

At headquarters that first afternoon, I changed into DCUs and met first with Rifle DeLong and my Chief of Staff, Army Colonel Michael Hayes. Michael was a solid professional, a man I'd known since 1981 in Germany. I couldn't ask for better people beside me than Rifle and Michael Hayes . . . and I knew it.

Scanning a stack of classified documents that had been laid out on my desk in order of urgency, I noted that the Crisis Action Team had been going around the clock since the crisis began. "The whole staff is going to be working long hours," I said. "I want to make sure people don't burn out. This isn't just another passing crisis. We're in this for the long haul."

Michael made a quick note. "Yes, Sir. Understood."

"Will you want to see the directors this afternoon?" Rifle asked.

"Give me ten minutes," I said, looking at the messages on my blotter.

As they left, I looked at the easel to the right of my desk, a tactical map of Afghanistan. The map of Iraq, where CENTCOM was engaging Saddam Hussein's air defenses in the no-fly zones, occupied another easel on the left side of the desk.

Taking a swig of hot coffee, I picked up the Red Switch telephone behind my desk; with its Top Secret encryption and point-to-point programming capability, it would be an important link to the Pentagon and the White House in the coming weeks. I touched a single button on the phone, and Hugh Shelton answered immediately.

"The President is determined to act, Tom," Hugh said. "And Secretary Rumsfeld wants military options for Afghanistan."

"When does he want them?"

"People in the White House and the Building are moving ahead at full bore. How soon can you provide a full range of operational concepts?"

A full range. *No more token retaliation. No more million-dollar TLAMs into empty tents. No more pinpricks.*

I paused before answering. All the unified combatant commands were required to "build" and maintain complex plans to meet a wide variety of contingencies. U.S. Pacific Command for example, had several detailed OPLANs on the shelf to respond to aggression from North Korea. Scores of analogous plans existed in Southern Command and European Command.

And in CENTCOM we had more than a dozen contingency blueprints, laying out precise plans for hostage situations, evacuating embassies, opening the Strait of Hormuz, and intervening should the Iraqis cross certain "Red Lines." We had al Qaeda and Taliban target sets in Afghanistan and plans to strike those targets with TLAMs and manned bombers.

But CENTCOM had *not* developed a plan for conventional ground operations in Afghanistan. Nor had diplomatic arrangements for basing, staging, overflight and access been made with Afghanistan's neighbors. There simply had been no stomach in Washington for sustained face-to-face combat in this remote, primitive, landlocked country halfway around the world—*no stomach since at least 1993.*

From Hugh Shelton's tone, it was clear that this was about to change. America's military was going to war in a country where twenty-some years earlier the Soviet Union had invested 620,000 men over the course of eleven years, at a cost of more than 15,000 killed and almost 55,000 wounded.

I knew Don Rumsfeld would want a far different type of operation. In the previous eight months, I had learned a great deal about Rumsfeld's mind. *He might just be a good Secretary of War.* There were so many problems inherent in waging war in remote, landlocked, mountainous Afghanistan that any workable plan would have to transcend conventional thinking. Rumsfeld had little time for what he saw as stale solutions to challenging new problems. He liked to brainstorm. And he responded well to imaginative concepts. For years I had worked on innovation and building tactical flexibility. Now it was time to see if those efforts would pay off.

It helped to know that the President was determined to act. America was through with half measures and pinpricks; we were at war.

"Hugh, we will have conceptual options by tomorrow. My assumption is that America will do *nothing* unless we intend to do *something.* You will not receive from me a wrist-slap plan that launches jets and missiles and hopes for a good outcome."

"Understand and agree, Tom."

"It'll take a week to ten days for a complete proposed course of action," I continued. "In the meantime, we should begin ship, aircraft, and troop staging to set conditions to, One: destroy al Qaeda in

Afghanistan; and Two: remove the Taliban regime. And those should be the key mission tasks."

"Concur," Hugh said. "Time is critical."

We were both thinking about the intelligence warnings of potential new terrorist attacks. It might be a matter of striking back before we were hit again. Time was indeed crucial.

I replaced the red phone in its cradle and thought for a moment, about the new kind of threat America was facing, and new kind of war we were about to wage.

Commanders and scholars have always spoken of the *art* of waging war. Yet any war involves confronting certain basic hard, cold facts—the *science* of war. Gaining the fullest possible understanding of the enemy's strengths, capabilities, and intentions. Giving adequate consideration to the terrain on which combat will take place. Evaluating transportation requirements, and the support of forces in adequate numbers—in this case halfway around the world. Choosing the correct mix of units to fulfill the mission—the aspect of military planning known as "correlation of forces," which entails comparing friendly and enemy weapons and capabilities. All these elements lend themselves to modeling, to the strict judgments of empirical analysis.

All this *science* would have to be explained to Don Rumsfeld, the National Security team, and ultimately to George W. Bush. And then we would discuss the *art* of war—the value of maneuver speed, mass of force, economy of effort, risk, timing, endstate . . . and exit strategy.

The plan I would present would include both art and science. We *would not* repeat the mistakes of the Soviets. We *would* destroy the al Qaeda network in Afghanistan. And we *would* remove the Taliban from power. As my dad would have said, "Lots of work to do . . . and not long to do it."

LATE ON THE AFTERNOON OF SEPTEMBER 12, CENTCOM's SENIOR staff, including the heads of the directorates, filed into my office. There was none of the usual premeeting banter.

As I looked into their faces, I was grateful for the quality of the team that sat with me that September afternoon.

DeLong was a brilliant, complete officer, tempered in combat as a young man flying Marine helicopters during heavy fighting in Vietnam; later he assisted in the chaotic evacuation of Saigon. Like most of my senior officers, he had commanded warfighting units. "Rifle" was a well-earned nickname.

Gene Renuart, J-3 Director for Operations, had earned his commission through Officer Training School and later commanded a squadron of A-10 Warthog ground-attack jets in the Gulf War. In the 1990s he became the commanding general of Joint Task Force Southwest Asia, which patrolled the Southern No-Fly Zone in Iraq. The assignment gave him valuable experience—not only with airpower but also with multinational coalitions, which would be an asset in the months ahead.

My J-4 Director for Logistics was Army Major General Denny Jackson. If we launched a sustained effort in the remote regions of Southwest Asia, the challenge of supplying tens of thousands of tons of materiel, jet fuel, munitions, food, tents, field hospitals, generators—and also meeting the Humanitarian Assistance (HA) needs of millions of refugees—would be his responsibility. Denny was an imaginative, nimble logistician, a fan of private-sector innovations. In fact, he'd already borrowed techniques from Amazon.com's CEO Jeff Bezos to build a cutting-edge, computerized distribution system for our forces deployed in the region.

The J-2 Director for Intelligence, Army Brigadier General Jeff Kimmons, was an expert in strategic and battlefield reconnaissance. He had a Special Operations background, which I knew would prove invaluable in the weeks ahead. And he was among the military's most experienced hands-on operators of Unmanned Aerial Vehicles (UAVs), including the Predator and the new Air Force long-range jet, the Global Hawk. Jeff was skilled at managing human intelligence sources, which helped explain his frustration with the nonspecific and dated intelligence reports we had received on al Qaeda.

Our J-5 Director for Political-Military Affairs was Navy Rear Admiral Jay "Rabbit" Campbell, a savvy professional whose negotiating skills would prove critical in working with the State Department and our regional ambassadors in arranging required basing, staging, and overflight in the countries bordering Afghanistan.

My new senior CIA officer, Pat Hailey, was one of several reliable intelligence links CENTCOM had developed to other U.S. government agencies, allies, and international organizations. During the chaos surrounding a catastrophe, a certain amount of wheel-spinning and flailing inevitably occurs. And in this crisis, the dust was literally still settling. In such a situation, the organization with extensive connections, both vertically and horizontally, could exert unusual leverage. Pat Hailey had those connections, and I intended to use them.

My link to the State Department was my Political Adviser or POLAD, Ambassador Marty Cheshes. A seasoned Foreign Service officer with experience in East Africa and the Middle East, Marty sat squarely with me in the leadership circle. I knew I'd be drawing heavily on him as we prepared to go to war. Although I had made eleven trips to the region and had visited with many key leaders, we still had a lot of work ahead to establish working alliances with the countries surrounding landlocked Afghanistan.

"I've just been on the phone with General Shelton," I told my team. "President Bush has ordered the Secretary to prepare a robust response to yesterday's attacks." The faces surrounding me were somber, but focused and determined.

I had commanded Army units from howitzer battery up through field-army; now I was commanding a massive multiservice organization. I'd also worked for enough thoughtful and effective leaders to learn that it's essential in the early stages of a crisis for the person in charge to make his vision clear. If you know what the boss wants, you work more efficiently.

"Obviously, America *will* retaliate," I said, and then paused to let that message take hold. "The question is *how* and *when*. I told Hugh Shelton that it's better to do nothing if we don't intend to respond forcefully. The United States has suffered the worst attack since World War II. We're way beyond the point of token reprisal. I'm confident that this President intends to fight terrorism in a serious way. I expect to destroy al Qaeda in Afghanistan, and remove the Taliban from power. They coexist ideologically and physically."

I went to the map. "So I'm assuming that CENTCOM will be required to conduct major combat operations in Afghanistan, staging and basing in Central and Southwest Asia. The Secretary wants to know how we intend to conduct the operation. We have a complicated plan to build. But we don't have a lot of time. I told Hugh Shelton I'd deliver a complete recommendation in a week to ten days."

As the meeting ended, I was confident that these good men all understood the task we faced. They also knew the meaning of hard work—and how much it would be needed in the days and nights ahead.

"You're all professionals," I said. "I'm glad each of you is on this team."

IT WAS LATE NIGHT, MAYBE EARLY MORNING. I'D GRABBED A NAP earlier and eaten a cold Whopper from Burger King. Now I was on my second pot of coffee.

When several of the directors returned to my office to continue our discussion, they looked as tired as I felt. I directed their gaze toward the map of Afghanistan, swinging an unlit cigar in an oval to indicate the borders.

"No doubt about it, guys—this son of a bitch is definitely landlocked. We can't make use of the Marines' amphibious capabilities. Whatever the final shape of the operation, it'll depend on airlift. Can we count on overflight rights for the duration? And where do we stage? Where do we base?" I pointed toward Iran on Afghanistan's western border. "The mullahs aren't about to let us in. In the north, maybe we can strike a deal with President Karimov in Uzbekistan. Maybe even with the Turkmenbashi." Saparmurad Niyazov, the President of Turkmenistan, was known as the Turkmenbashi, "the father of all Turkmen." Niyazov was a mercurial, sometimes brutal despot, but he recognized and respected power.

"Uzbekistan, of course, will be vital to the operation. The Northern Alliance is right up on their border. But President Karimov is sitting on the fence. We need bases on his territory, especially here—Karshi-Khanabad. But we've got to convince him we'll stay the course once we go in."

During two meetings in the previous year with President Islam Karimov, I had learned several important things: He was worried about the increasingly savage Islamic Movement of Uzbekistan (IMU), a homegrown terrorist group that fought alongside al Qaeda and the Taliban against the Northern Alliance. And he feared Russian intervention should war flare up in the region. He and I had discussed the possible use of the old Soviet air base at Karshi-Khanabad—K-2, as it was known—but only in general terms. Of course, that was before 9/11; now, with the stakes having gone up, so had K-2's value, and Karimov knew it. But the Uzbekistani President was mindful of America's failed efforts in Somalia. And he wasn't convinced that the United States was serious about its commitment to Central Asia.

"I think we can work out our issues with Tajikistan and Kyrgyzstan," I added. "Pakistan is another matter. President Musharraf likes and respects us, but he's got a heavy-duty Islamic extremist population to deal with. And I can't see conducting operations inside Afghanistan without basing, staging, and overflight support from the Paks."

Gene Renuart nodded. "Overshoot rights, too, Boss. Anyway you cut the plan, we're going to use a lot of TLAMs. We'll have to have Pakistani permission, or at least acquiescence, because all those birds will be flying across a couple hundred miles of their territory inbound to the targets."

Another call came in from the Chairman, and our floating meeting broke again.

LATER, AFTER A SHOWER AND A CHANGE INTO A FRESH UNIFORM, I went down the hall to see Marty Cheshes. As we chatted, he jotted notes on a yellow pad. One road to solving our basing and staging problems, I knew, would run through Colin Powell at State. When Powell called, presidents and prime ministers picked up the phone.

Another path of negotiation would run from me, directly to the heads of state, ministers of defense, and military leaders I knew best.

"I've got calls and e-mails in to all the appropriate bureaus at State," Marty said. "The Secretary has already let people know this is a priority issue."

OUTSIDE MY OFFICE, IT WAS ANOTHER BRIGHT, HOT FLORIDA morning. Inside it was cool, the blinds drawn against the glare. Was it Thursday or Friday? I'd lost track. The key directors were back.

"To summarize," I told them, "the long poles of this operation will be *access* and *sustainment*. Any operation we conduct in Afghanistan will be dependent on airlift . . . thousands of tons a day."

Denny Jackson, my logistician, nodded pleasantly; he didn't seem troubled by the challenge.

"And we're also facing a potential humanitarian disaster that we must prevent from the onset of the operation. A large segment of the more than 26 million Afghans depends on nongovernmental organizations for their daily bread, not to mention blankets, fuel for the winter, and seeds for the spring planting. But NGOs don't usually stick around during combat." I looked toward Denny. "We're probably going to have to figure out a way to supply several million internally displaced people with their basic needs by air until the military situation stabilizes."

I stood up, stretched my stiff leg. "Terrain," I said. "Look at this place. You've got summits in the Hindu Kush over twenty thousand feet, ridges in these long east-west ranges topping out above twelve thousand, and most of the passes are anywhere from nine to eleven thousand feet. What's that going to do to helicopter operations?"

Pat Hailey spoke up. "General, the people we have with the Northern Alliance report that flying helicopters in Afghanistan is nasty. And it'll be snowing in the mountains and high valleys in a few weeks, which will complicate matters."

"All right," I said. "What kind of operation are we proposing? The President is going to want to go in there and clean house. What military options do we present him?"

Rifle DeLong answered. "Jeff and Gene have a list of good candidates for a solid TLAM strike. If the President wants to start kinetics immediately, we've got the targets."

I read the list. We would use TLAMs to take down the enemy's Integrated Air Defense System (IADS) to pave the way for conventional air strikes. The Taliban's IADS was not robust, but they did have early warning radars and Soviet-built surface-to-air missile sites. And the TLAM missions would demoralize the enemy and degrade his combat capability, so al Qaeda training camps and Taliban barracks where significant numbers of troops were billeted were also valuable targets.

But the strikes we launched would have to be extremely accurate. Inadvertent civilian casualties—collateral damage, or CD—would be a major concern.

"When the kinetics start," I said, "we don't want to see a lot of dead non-combatants on CNN."

"Or on al-Jazeera," Rifle added.

"Roger that," I said. Al-Jazeera, the Arabic language satellite channel based in Qatar, had helped transform al Qaeda and bin Laden into heroes on the Arab-Muslim "street."

One of my weapons of choice in the initial strike would be the Block III Tomahawk land attack missile (TLAM), which could deliver a thousand-pound high explosive warhead on targets 1,500 miles away, with precision that would have been considered science fiction a decade earlier. The range and accuracy of the Block III would allow us to kill the enemy, and destroy his installations and equipment, without endangering large numbers of civilians. The missile's guidance relied on computerized inertial navigation, terrain-following radar, and GPS satellite signals. When the Navy's TLAM shooters assured me they could launch a half-ton warhead through a low, fast, evasive track, threading the needle of gorges and mountain passes, and then through a three-by-four foot window more than a thousand miles over the horizon, day or night, I knew it wasn't bravado: It was the confidence that comes with twenty-first century engineering.

The United States had used Tomahawks in the Balkans, in Iraq, and in response to terrorist attacks. The weapon was impressively destructive, and equally effective in limiting civilian casualties.

"The Navy confirms that we have two hundred TLAMs in the shoot basket as of 0200 Zulu today," Gene Renuart added.

"Yes—one option is a major league TLAM strike," I said. "And a second is TLAMs initially, leading into—or simultaneous with—Global Power sorties."

Our B-2 Stealth bomber capability was known as Global Power, because the huge bat-winged stealth aircraft could literally span the planet. Taking off from Whiteman Air Force Base in Missouri's Ozark foothills, with multiple aerial refuelings the B-2 flew bombing missions anywhere in the world; their roundtrips sometimes lasted over forty hours. And the B-2s were invisible to radar. When they arrived at night over a target, they dropped precision joint direct attack munitions (JDAMs), GPS-guided one- or two-thousand pound bombs that invariably struck within a few feet of their programmed aiming point.

One advantage of Global Power was flexibility: The weapon systems officer aboard the aircraft could load precise target coordinates into the JDAMs using real time intelligence all the way to the target. For example, if a UAV transmitted images of enemy missile launchers being moved to escape incoming TLAMs, new target locations could be passed to the B-2s en route, and JDAMs could be programmed up to the last few minutes to strike the missile launchers.

A second option, then, would involve a massive TLAM launch, followed up with Global Power support. But Afghanistan was a huge, mountainous country, riddled with caves and strewn with camouflaged bunker complexes. There were thousands of rat holes, and only a finite number of JDAMs. And after the attacks of 9/11, it wasn't likely that Mullah Omar or Osama bin Laden would be lounging around their headquarters, waiting for the bombs to land.

"One of those two options will be good prep for boots on the ground," I told the directors. "But I want more than the usual-suspect options, the predictable mix of missiles and air strikes. The question is *whose* boots, and how many pairs." I turned to Pat Hailey. "What can the Agency do for us? What's the current status of the Northern Alliance and the other anti-Taliban forces?"

Ever thoughtful, Pat paused a moment. "As you know, we've had people with the Northern Alliance for years. Their reporting indicates that opposition troops have the potential to take on the Taliban and their al Qaeda allies . . . *if* the Alliance can pull itself together after Massoud's assassination, and receives significant materiel support." Pat ticked off items on his fingers: "Winter uniforms, arms and ammunition, radios, food, medicine, blankets . . . hay and oats for their horses, saddles, and probably a few helicopters."

"They're also going to need close air support," Gene Renuart, the veteran ground attack pilot, commented.

"That means SOF teams with Air Force combat air controllers," Rifle added.

"Okay," I added. "We have a third option: SOF."

Special Operations Forces, drawn from the CIA's Special Activities Division (the Agency's "Ground Force"), the Army's Green Berets, and the Navy's SEALs were trained to augment and lead guerrilla forces against conventional enemies. And among the critical new capabilities of the SOF were the highly skilled Air Force combat air controllers. These were tough NCOs who used satellite radios, GPS, and laser target designators to pinpoint enemy formations, fortifications, and vehicles for strike aircraft or heavy bombers dropping JDAMs. Years earlier, I had seen similar, but far less capable teams, working with Air Force Field Auxiliary units. Now, like many of our more technological innovations, the teams were "war-winners."

And we would call on the special mission operators from JSOC at Fort Bragg to hunt down and eliminate terrorist leaders and "exploit" (search and analyze) suspected WMD sites.

Beefed up by Special Operations Forces and supported by American air power, we knew that the Northern Alliance and other tribal militias could destroy the numerically superior Taliban and al Qaeda. But the Northern Alliance fielded a total of only about 20,000 troops, armed and equipped between "poor" and "fair" on a scale of military effectiveness. The Taliban and al Qaeda had at least twice that many fighters, along with more tanks and APCs, more artillery, and more automatic weapons. This was not what strategists call a "favorable balance of forces."

"And the Northern Alliance is in disarray," Pat Hailey cautioned. "Since the assassination of Massoud, we have to start from scratch. We had a lot invested in Massoud—literally."

And Osama bin Laden had destroyed that investment, I realized. He was indeed a cunning, imaginative enemy.

"All right," I told the staff. "We've discussed three options. Here's a fourth. Run the first three simultaneously, as the lead-in for the deployment of conventional American ground combat forces. First we see what the Northern Alliance, with our help, can do. Then we use larger formations if we have to."

The men seated around the office listened intently. My proposal involved sending battalions and brigades of American soldiers and Marines into one of the most inhospitable countries in the world, to wage war against a zealous and intractable enemy. Many of al Qaeda and the Taliban's troops had been fighting in that harsh terrain for years. A large number had served as *mujahhedin* in the long, bloody struggle that eventually ousted the Soviet Army. The implicit lesson of Afghanistan's recent history was not to put large numbers of American troops on the ground to accomplish the mission—unless absolutely necessary.

Two things were certain: Each of the four options presented staging, basing, and overflight challenges, as well as complex terrain and weather issues. And each would require a detailed intelligence evaluation of the skill and determination of the enemy.

For years I'd studied the strategy and tactics of past wars. As my staff and I reviewed our options in September 2001, I could not think of a historical parallel for the military campaign under consideration. The operation represented a revolution in warfighting. We would introduce the most advanced military technology in the world—TLAMs, JDAMs, Stealth bombers, laser target designators, and satellite communications—onto one of the world's most primitive battlefields. The Northern Alliance, with its tribal affiliates, a few broken-down Russian tanks and rickety transport helicopters, and thousands of horses, would move heavy weapons and munitions on the backs of donkeys and camels in a synchronized ballet, taking advantage of all that firepower and techno-sophistication. The Taliban and al Qaeda forces had twice as many troops as the Northern Alliance, and they were far better equipped. But I was confident that the balance of power was about to change.

I glanced at the digital clock behind my desk. It was almost noon. "Okay, brothers," I told the staff. "Get your asses out of here and go to work. We've got serious time constraints. Oh, yeah, by the way, I don't want that to affect the quality of your product."

I grinned, then rose and returned to my desk. The staff filed out. For a few minutes I was alone with the faint hum of the air conditioning. Then Jeff Haynes entered with a fresh stack of messages. I poured another mug of black coffee and started reading.

AFTER A FEW DAYS, I REALIZED I NEEDED TO GET OUT OF THE office, to move around the building and talk to people. I didn't intend to micromanage the planners, but I needed a firsthand sense of the progress they were making and the problems they faced.

One area of intense activity was the Sensitive Compartmented Intelligence Facility (SCIF), a maze of large and small windowless rooms behind a cipher-locked steel door, which opened in turn onto a checkpoint manned around the clock by an armed security guard. In the fluorescent lighting of the SCIF, the only way to tell night from day—or the day of the week, for that matter—was to look at one of the wall clocks, which blinked out the time in Tampa, Iraq, Pakistan, and Afghanistan. I'm sure I'm not the only one who's ever cocked an eyebrow upon learning that Afghanistan was thirty minutes out of sync with the rest of the world—thirty minutes and two thousand years.

During those early weeks of war planning, I conferred several times a day with Donald Rumsfeld and his deputy, Paul Wolfowitz, by secure telephone or video telephone conference (VTC). One advantage of the VTC was that we could consult and share intelligence imagery and sensitive planning graphics on a real-time basis.

One morning in the small J-2 conference room in the SCIF I was on a VTC, briefing the Secretary on high-value targets. Usually, these briefings were the occasion for a string of questions on the Secretary's part. This time, however, Rumsfeld listened without interrupting, his face set in concentration.

"All right, General," he said when I'd completed the brief. "Good progress. Keep it up." From Don Rumsfeld, that was high praise indeed. The video screen clicked to black as the connection was cut. His growing confidence was gratifying: Though our detailed briefings would continue, the Secretary wasn't breathing over my shoulder.

In this first week after 9/11, the country was outraged and impatient. People wanted America to strike back hard, and they didn't want to wait. On the Internet, the anecdotal evidence was already emerging. Among the images I saw in those first couple of weeks was a digitally doctored photograph of a squadron of B-52 Stratofortresses bearing the logos of American and United Airlines on their tails, dropping long strings of bombs over snowy desert mountains.

The photo caption matched the national mood: "United & American Airlines Announce New, Non-Stop Service to Afghanistan."

"HERE'S THE MOONLIGHT DATA, GENERAL," JEFF KIMMONS said, handing me a printout.

Gene Renuart and I had been looking at moon illumination from the end of September through October. Inserting Special Operations Forces by helicopter was best accomplished on dark, moonless nights. The Taliban and al Qaeda had hundreds of former Soviet Army anti-aircraft guns; their 23mm ZSUs, mounted on a pickup or towed behind an old Zil truck, were an especially effective weapon. The last thing we wanted was for one of our troop-laden helicopters, straining at high altitudes to cross passes, to be silhouetted against the moon.

There was a full moon coming up on Tuesday, October 2. It would wane into a last quarter crescent by October 10. But on the nights of Saturday and Sunday, October 6 and 7, that waning crescent moon wouldn't rise over northern Afghanistan until three hours after sunset.

"We might have a good window here, Jeff," I said.

THE WAR ROOM IN THE SCIF WAS CROWDED WITH OFFICERS AND a handful of civilian staff. With its wide oak table and rows of outlying chairs, the facility could have been a conference room anywhere in corporate America, except for the sign above the projector screen: "Top Secret-Code Word." This morning—yet again—the subject at hand was progress on basing rights. Rear Admiral Jay Campbell was at the podium, using a laser pointer on the projection of the Afghanistan Theater map.

"Within a week," Campbell said, "the Pakistanis will probably be on board with these CSAR bases." The ruby dot of his laser pointer flicked across southwestern desert airbases near Dalbandin and Quetta, at which our Combat Search and Rescue units would be staged. Those units would protect the aircrews flying missions over southern Afghanistan. Should aviators be forced to eject anywhere south and east of a line from Kabul to Kandahar, CSAR would launch from those bases to bring them out.

Access to Dalbandin and Quetta: that was progress. The personal relationship I had with President Musharraf, which had paved the way for direct appeals from the White House and Colin Powell, was paying off.

"But we're still working on the Stans," Campbell said. The former Soviet republics north of Afghanistan had not yet signed on. This was, after all, Central Asia; in thousands of years of history there, a simple trade had never happened overnight. The negotiations were taking time; then again, America had lots of carrots and just as many sticks, and I was confident that—eventually—we would prevail.

Eventually, however, was a problem. We were hoping for quick agreement on basing rights in Uzbekistan and Tajikistan, but that was by no means a done deal, and Musharraf still might balk at allowing us to base large numbers of special operations forces in his territory, especially in remote areas near Afghanistan where Muslim fundamentalism and support for the Taliban ran deepest. We needed to stage SOF, particularly the elite SMU troopers of the Joint Special Operations Command, close enough to strike al Qaeda in their mountain redoubt in southeast Afghanistan. And we needed to stage them soon.

As I studied the map on the projector screen, a plan took shape. Afghanistan might be landlocked, but many Taliban and al Qaeda installations lay within range of a ship-borne helicopter force flying from the Northern Arabian Sea. The MH-53 Pave Lows and MH-60 Direct Action Penetrators of the 160th Special Operations Aviation Regiment needed a relatively large base, with room for the big choppers as well as adequate maintenance and ordnance facilities. The Navy's helicopter carriers, on which the Marine Expeditionary Units deployed, were not big enough for the force I envisioned. I needed a steel lily pad—a Forward Operating Base (FOB)—just off the coast of Pakistan, and I needed it soon.

In the mid-1990s, the Navy had developed the capacity to transform fleet aircraft carriers into floating Special Operations bases. The USS *America* had carried more than 2,000 special operators and their helicopters during military operations in Haiti in 1994. If we could not secure bases in Pakistan, we would need a carrier to serve as the floating base for our SOF mission in the south. That would take time.

In my office, I reached for the Red Switch and called Admiral Vernon Clark, the Chief of Naval Operations. "Vern, we're going to need an aircraft carrier for unusual duty . . ."

Two weeks later, having sailed halfway around the world at flank speed, the USS *Kitty Hawk* would arrive in the northern Arabian Sea, just south of the Strait of Hormuz. We would have a "lily pad" in place.

"MICHAEL," I SAID, AS COLONEL HAYES ENTERED MY office. "I've got a job for you."

"Don't like the sound of *that,* Sir," he said, grinning.

"State thinks that we may well have a few friends in this operation," I explained. "I'm betting that we're actually going to see a large coalition form. That means allied reps liaising with this headquarters, here at MacDill." I waved my hand toward the windows. "We're going to have to put them someplace."

". . . office space, housing, vehicles, and parking," Michael offered.

"You just got yourself a task, Colonel Hayes."

When Michael began that September afternoon, neither of us realized that within three months our "Coalition Village," near the MacDill flight line, would eventually consist of sixty-eight single- and double-wide trailers, housing the offices of fifty-two nations in what President Bush had designated the Global War on Terrorism. The work Michael Hayes did built the coalition—literally. Without his ability to organize a plan and navigate an incredible maze of local and international finance, CENTCOM could not have functioned as it did.

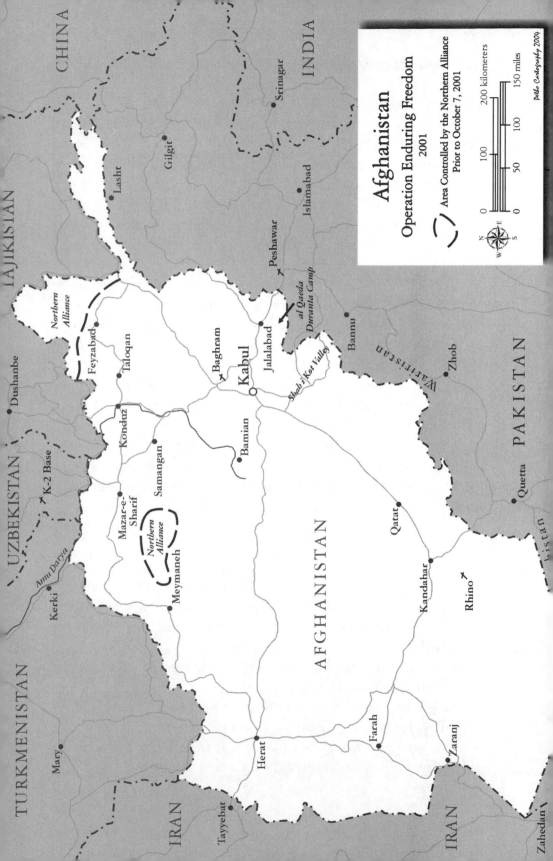

"B Y THE WAY, GENERAL," RUMSFELD HAD SAID AT THE END of one of our video conferences in late September, "don't forget about Iraq."

"I won't, Mr. Secretary," I'd said. "We've got aircrews flying in harm's way over Iraq every day."

Rumsfeld and I both realized that we were still flying Northern and Southern Watch as we had since 1992—and our pilots were being shot at during almost every mission. Every morning when I listed Challenges on my three-by-five card, I led off with "Shootdown, OSW/ONW." Even while I was absorbed in Afghanistan, Iraq never left my mind. At some point I knew that America would change or abandon its containment strategy, which had not succeeded in ensuring Saddam Hussein's compliance with U.N. sanctions. Planning for that day, I thought, was the only wise course of action.

And my concern was only heightened by the terrorist anthrax mailings of that fall—which, for me, immediately called to mind Iraq's weapons of mass destruction program. As late as January 1999—after the U.N. inspectors were thrown out of Iraq—the United Nations was reporting that Saddam could be in possession of thousands of liters of weaponized anthrax. It was a thought that didn't help me sleep at night.

O N THE MORNING OF THURSDAY, SEPTEMBER 20, 2001, GENE Renuart and I boarded *Spar 06* again and flew to Washington. We carried ten copies of a Top Secret brief outlining the concept for military operations to destroy al Qaeda and the Taliban in Afghanistan.

At 1:00 P.M. the next day, I would present these concepts to the President in the White House.

An Air Force flight attendant brought a pot of black coffee. One of these days, I was going to ease back on the caffeine, but not today. Once we were wheels-up, Gene and I spread the briefing charts on the table in front of us and reviewed the operational concept.

We had divided the campaign into four phases, the first of which was already under way. Phase I, SET CONDITIONS AND BUILD FORCES TO PROVIDE THE NATIONAL COMMAND AUTHORITY CREDIBLE MILITARY OPTIONS, involved laying the groundwork for the operation, and included the completion of basing and staging agreements with Afghanistan's neighbors. On this front, the White House, the Pentagon, the State Department, CIA, and CENTCOM were making progress. I was confident that the Stans would soon be in place. President Bush had announced that the nations of the world would either be with us or against us in the war on terrorism, and the Central Asian leaders seemed to be reading that message loud and clear. They had plenty to gain by joining the coalition, and a lot to lose if they did not. Horse-trading was under way all across the region. Basing and staging were going to cost us money, but the agreements reached would be worth the dollars spent.

Another of the tasks in Phase I involved inserting advance teams of CIA officers—wielding satellite phones and sacks of hundred dollar bills—into Afghanistan to begin bolstering the fractured Northern Alliance and other "tribals" in the anti-Taliban opposition. Here, too, we were making strides. Already Agency officers had made contact with the principal warlords. Generals Mohammed Fahim Khan—the Tajik successor to the murdered Ahmad Shah Massoud—and Abdul Rashid Dostum, the Uzbek militia leader based farther west, were counting their initial support money, and preparing to accept CIA paramilitary operators from the Agency's Special Activities Division.

Dostum's longtime friends—and rivals—Mohammed Attah and Mohammed Mohahqeq, a Shia Muslim Hazara, were standing by to receive their Agency liaison officers as well. These officers would lay the groundwork for our Special Forces Teams, which would follow almost immediately. Known as "A-Teams" for years, these twelve-man units now went under the acronym ODA—Operational Detachment Alpha, some of the toughest and best-trained soldiers in the American military.

And the CIA was preparing to move large quantities of former Soviet Army weapons and ammunition—the standard ordnance of all
Afghan combatants—from stockpiles in Europe. At first this materiel
would be air-dropped by C-130s; later, once we'd nailed down our
basing in the Stans, it would be airlifted to our new allies by MH-47
Chinook helicopters of the 160th Special Operations Aviation Regiment. In the meantime, CIA pilots flying Soviet-era Mi-17 helicopters
were carrying radios, aerial navigation beacons, and supplies into
northern Afghanistan.

Completing the arrangements for active military participation
from coalition allies—especially high-skill European, Canadian,
and Australian Special Operations Forces—was another element of
Phase I. I was very encouraged by the role these allies were performing. Our NATO partners and Australia were taking practical
steps to bring troops to the fight at the exact times and places where
we wanted them.

A final task in Phase I was preparing for the inevitable Humanitarian Assistance crisis we knew we would see as civilians were displaced
by combat. The Air Force was cranking up to airdrop thousands of
tons of Humanitarian Daily Rations, the civilian version of military
MREs. The barley and lentil stew we brought might not have been
haute cuisine, but I was confident that it would not be turned down by
the hungry refugees we assisted.

Phase II, CONDUCT INITIAL COMBAT OPERATIONS AND CONTINUE
TO SET CONDITIONS FOR FOLLOW-ON OPERATIONS, would begin as
Phase I preparations were completed. The Afghanistan campaign
would be a unique page in military history, and flexibility was a key
ingredient of the plan. Gene Renuart, Jeff Kimmons, and their staffs
had worked hard on the targets for this phase of operations. Tomahawk missiles, tactical aircraft, B-2 Stealth bombers, and B-52s
would take out Taliban and al Qaeda Command and Control targets,
early warning radars, and major air defense systems—principally
Soviet-built SA-3 missiles.

Special Forces Teams would infiltrate into Afghanistan as the air
campaign unfolded, and begin to provide air support to the Northern

Alliance and other opposition forces. The Japan-based aircraft carrier *Kitty Hawk* would set up shop as a floating SOF Forward Operating Base in international waters off the coast of Pakistan.

Once the antiaircraft threat was reduced, jets from carriers in the Arabian Sea would overfly Pakistan's western deserts and attack targets across Afghanistan. And B-2s from the United States, as well as B-52s from the British island of Diego Garcia in the Indian Ocean, would deliver their heavy loads of ordnance during the longest air sorties ever flown. The B-52s would employ JDAMs, giving each plane the capacity to drop twenty-five tons of precision-guided munitions on a single sortie.

As air operations unfolded and SOF teams were deployed, the Northern Alliance and their associated tribals, resupplied and equipped compliments of the CIA, would go on the offensive. We would leverage technology and the courage of the Afghans themselves to liberate their country.

This campaign was not going to be a matter of lobbing missiles into mud huts. We were going to war—boots-on-the ground war.

Phase III, CONDUCT DECISIVE COMBAT OPERATIONS IN AFGHANISTAN, CONTINUE TO BUILD COALITION, AND CONDUCT OPERATIONS AOR WIDE, would flow seamlessly from Phase II. Once our indigenous allies, augmented by about 200 SOF, had routed the enemy, we would bring in Coalition troops—including American soldiers and Marines—to seek out and eliminate pockets of resistance. I estimated we would need no more than ten to twelve thousand American ground troops to complete this phase.

Secretary Rumsfeld and I agreed that the U.S. force should remain small. We wanted to avoid a cumbersome Soviet-style occupation by armored divisions. It hadn't worked for the Soviets, and it wouldn't work for us. Flexibility and rapid reaction—airborne and helicopter-borne night assault by small, lethal, and unpredictable units coupled with unprecedented precision—would be the hallmarks of America's first war in the twenty-first century.

Phase IV was the final stage: ESTABLISH CAPABILITY OF COALITION PARTNERS TO PREVENT THE RE-EMERGENCE OF TERRORISM AND PROVIDE

SUPPORT FOR HUMANITARIAN ASSISTANCE EFFORTS. This phase would develop over a three-to-five-year period. I was certain that surviving Taliban and al Qaeda units would resort to guerrilla combat once their large formations had been destroyed. So stabilizing and rebuilding Afghanistan, a country that had known nothing but war and privation for thousands of years, would require both counterinsurgency and civil affairs military forces. In this regard, I was pleased that our allies had already pledged their support. It would be a strong coalition, not simply the United States, that would help a liberated Afghanistan to rejoin the family of nations.

I felt the familiar popping in my ears as the plane's old pressure hull responded to our descent. Gathering my notes, I looked forward to discussing the presentation with the Secretary of Defense and to the White House meeting.

A T THE PENTAGON THAT AFTERNOON, THINGS GOT BUSY FAST. First I had to return calls to partners in the growing coalition and potential allies in the AOR. Then Gene and I would fine-tune the target sets with the Defense Intelligence Agency and CIA. We had to move right along because I had a meeting scheduled with the SecDef.

I spoke with General Jean-Pierre Kelche, chief of staff of the French Armed Forces. France, he said, was "vigorously" pursuing contributions to the developing campaign, including an aircraft carrier, airlift, tactical fighter-bombers, and Special Operations Forces. Good news there.

A huddle with Joint Staff planners helped firm up the Humanitarian Assistance aspect of the operation. Air Force C-17s making the long haul from Ramstein Air Base in Germany would fly over Turkmenistan and Uzbekistan to drop hundreds of thousands of humanitarian rations in Afghanistan. The HA operation would begin the same day as the air campaign; the launching of simultaneous kinetic and humanitarian efforts in this fashion was without precedent, but it was the only responsible way to mount this campaign. Any potential risk from our military action would be offset by the benefits we were bringing to the Afghan people.

And there was more good news: Sultan Qaboos of Oman gave his permission for AC-130 Spectre gunships and a SOF support team to operate out of the Masira Island air base in the northern Arabian Sea, well within range of Afghanistan.

Air Force Lt. General Chuck Wald, our air component commander, called from Saudi Arabia. He wanted to augment the Combined Air Operation Center (CAOC) by about one hundred personnel for the coming campaign, but he suspected that the Saudis would not approve the request if he went to them formally. Another cut among the thousand. "Go ahead and fly them in, Chuck," I said. "Once they're on the ground, we'll request forgiveness. That's easier than asking permission."

Next I called Wendy Chamberlin, the American Ambassador to Pakistan. A recent arrival in the post, she was already making headway with the leadership. President Musharraf, she reported, had granted permission for Coalition aircraft to overfly Pakistan. Implicit in this was the TLAM "overshoot" authorization that Gene Renuart had mentioned. Musharraf had also agreed to a detailed list of seventy-four basing and staging activities to be conducted in Pakistan, from Combat Search and Rescue, to refueling and operating communications relay sites, to establishing a medical evacuation point near the Afghan border. In return, Musharraf requested that the campaign plan not involve the Indian government or the Indian military, especially in any way that would put Indian forces in Pakistani air or sea space. He also asked that the Coalition not "advertise" Indian political involvement, which would inflame sensitivities in Pakistan.

The requests were reasonable, and well worth the effort in exchange for a secure southern flank in Afghanistan. I asked Wendy to extend my personal thanks to President Musharraf, and to tell him that I would try to minimize the visibility of Indian involvement. "And we're working to get relief from the Pressler Amendment," I told her, and asked her to pass the message along. "I know Pakistan needs military spares and I'll try to help."

"Musharraf will be pleased, General."

"We are also working on Humanitarian Assistance and financial aid to help Pakistan handle any influx of refugees," I said. Wendy replied that Musharraf had expressed confidence in his ability to handle incoming refugees, but that they would accept any financial aid gratefully. "General, President Musharraf also asked for you to visit him as soon as possible."

"Wendy, please tell him I'll do that as soon as I can. Tell him to polish up his golf game."

"We're on a roll, Sir," Gene said.

But the roll wouldn't last long. Just after lunch, a few minutes before my scheduled meeting with the Secretary of Defense, I checked in with Hugh Shelton.

"Tom, the Chiefs have requested that you and your J-3 brief them in the Tank . . . along with the Secretary. It's SOP before taking a plan across the river to the White House."

"Damn it!" I said.

Judging from Hugh's expression, he wasn't too pleased either. I was prepared to present a concept to the Secretary, not a formal OPLAN to the Service Chiefs. Hugh Shelton needed to keep the Chiefs onboard, and I knew it. But my intuition told me that briefing them in front of the Secretary would be "a bridge too far." The Chiefs were likely to "posture," and the Secretary was likely to become frustrated. I suggested to Hugh that we brief twice, once for Secretary Rumsfeld, and later for the Service Chiefs.

"No time, Tom. This will be a good chance for all the key players to get to know each other better. We can make it work."

"Okay, Hugh, we'll give it a shot."

As Gene and I walked along the E-Ring to the Tank, I forced myself to relax. Maybe this would be a painless bureaucratic exercise.

It may have been an exercise, but it was not painless.

The Tank was an ornate place, its hardwood table gleaming, the furniture several pay grades higher than was found in the offices of most Pentagon staff officers. With its gold drapes framing the decorative wood-paneled false windows, the Tank was officially known as the Gold Room.

When we arrived, Secretary Rumsfeld was standing at the head of the table, speed-reading his way through a stack of documents.

Deputy Secretary of Defense Paul Wolfowitz and the Chiefs were seated around the table—Admiral Vern Clark, Chief of Naval Operations; Army Chief of Staff, General Eric Shinseki; Air Force Chief of Staff, General Mike Ryan; and his successor, General John Jumper. The Commandant of the Marine Corps, General Jim Jones, sat beside Hugh Shelton and Dick Myers, the Vice Chairman. I took my seat, while Gene Renuart stood by the podium, and my aide, Lt. Colonel Jeff Haynes, distributed the briefing sheets.

We'll sure as hell get back every *one of those briefing papers before we leave,* I thought. The Pentagon was notorious for leaks. Secretary Rumsfeld cautioned everyone in the room that this concept was as highly classified as you could get—that it was "Sensitive" and "Compartmented." But I'd briefed here before; something told me we had a fifty-fifty chance of opening the *New York Times* tomorrow morning and reading the minutes of this meeting.

It soon became clear, however, that security would be only one problem in the Tank this afternoon.

Once the Chiefs had scanned the stacked pages, and Gene Renuart had begun to explain Phase I of the campaign concept, Hugh Shelton asked for "opinions" from the Chiefs. He could not have recognized the trouble that simple question would create.

One after another the Chiefs offered their views of the concept. The Army argued the efficacy of Land Power, and described the difficulties of sustaining Army forces. The Marine view suggested "From the Sea" as the most effective approach to war-fighting—even in a landlocked country. Airpower was offered by the Air Force Chief as the most powerful of the contributing arms. None of which, of course, meshed totally with CENTCOM's operational concept—or my view of joint warfare.

We endured half an hour of this aimless dialogue, a waste of time that neither the Secretary nor I could spare. The briefing had been intended to provide information on a campaign that CENTCOM had carefully and laboriously developed, with the inputs of our Army, Navy, Marine, Air Force, and Special Operations Component Commanders—three-star generals nominated by these same Service Chiefs. I had no tolerance for this parochial bullshit. And Rumsfeld was becoming visibly annoyed. I could see in his expression that this was not what he expected.

The Chiefs must have noticed, too; at length, they began directing their glances—and their caveats—toward me. "Don't take this wrong, Tom . . . Just to play the devil's advocate . . ." And so it went.

Gene Renuart plowed ahead, his bald pate growing red.

"That's not particularly helpful, General," Rumsfeld finally said, staring coldly at the offending Chief.

Still, they persisted. Rumsfeld looked pointedly at his watch.

I'd had enough. "Look," I said, standing to sweep up the briefing charts before me on the polished tabletop. "We have a lot of work to do. Mr. Secretary, I'll put this concept together tonight and have it to you tomorrow morning."

The room was silent.

"We're finished for today," Rumsfeld said.

B EFORE I MET WITH THE SecDef THE NEXT MORNING, MARINE Corps Commandant General Jim Jones asked to speak to me in his office. When I arrived, I found Jim and the CNO, Admiral Vern Clark, sitting beside Jones's desk.

"Tom," Clark said. "We really do support you."

"Nothing we said yesterday was meant as criticism, Tom," Jones added.

"Great," I began. "I do want your input."

They relaxed.

"But I want your advice as the Joint Chiefs of Staff, *not* as individual Service Chiefs scrabbling for the biggest piece of pie in this operation." I didn't give them time to respond. "Look. You guys each have a three-star who commands a service component for me, and represents the service expertise we need to put together a joint plan. It's best to let those guys know your ideas. And then trust them to work for all of us to build a cohesive approach, rather than a patch-work of service interests."

Clark and Jones understood my reasoning. I wanted to nail this problem here and now. "If you don't trust those three-stars to repre-sent you and assist me in joint war-fighting," I told them, "you should replace them."

They nodded again. But I wasn't finished.

"Yesterday in the Tank, you guys came across like a mob of Title Ten motherfuckers, not like the Joint Chiefs of Staff. Thanks for hearing me out," I said, then turned and left.

I knew they'd gotten my message: No operation that is totally satisfying to any *one* service is truly a *joint* operation.

"GENERAL FRANKS," DONALD RUMSFELD SAID TEN MINUTES later in his office. "Would you please explain what *that* was all about yesterday?"

I had cooled down, but I still resented the bureaucratic shark at-tack in the Tank. "Mr. Secretary," I began, keeping my voice even. "I know you appreciate that unity of command is an essential military principle."

Rumsfeld fixed me in his thoughtful blue gaze.

"We've developed this campaign concept on your orders, Mr. Secretary. You informed me that the President wanted a thorough op-eration to destroy al Qaeda in Afghanistan and remove the Taliban from power."

"That's correct, General."

I thought for a moment before continuing. I was the senior com-mander at the start of a war. I had to solidify the lines of authority. "I work for you and for the President, not for the Service Chiefs. They were fighting for turf yesterday. If this continues, our troops—and the country—will suffer. We should not allow narrow-minded four-stars to advance their share of the budget at the expense of the mission."

I remained silent. And so did the Secretary. A moment passed.

"Mr. Secretary," I said. "I have to know before we take this briefing to the White House that unity of command prevails. I will follow every lawful order that you and the President give me. But I must have command authority to execute those orders."

Rumsfeld thought before replying. "You have that authority, General. You are the commander."

"Thank you, Mr. Secretary."

Donald Rumsfeld and I now knew each other a little better.

I N THE EARLY AFTERNOON, I JOINED HUGH SHELTON, DICK MYERS, and Major General Dell Dailey, the Commander of JSOC, for the drive to the White House. Secretary Rumsfeld followed us a few minutes later in a Lincoln Navigator.

President Bush received us in a comfortable study in the second-floor living quarters. Vice President Dick Cheney arrived as we did. I noticed at once that neither Secretary of State Colin Powell nor National Security Adviser Condoleezza Rice was present. Rumsfeld had stressed the need for secrecy, and the group in this parlor was the smallest "compartment" possible.

It was a hot day, and the President noted that we looked warm in our Class A uniforms. "Maybe these folks would like a Coke," the President said to a White House waiter. He brought a tray with ice, several bottles of Diet Coke, and crystal glasses with the Presidential seal and then left, closing the door.

The President appeared relaxed and thoughtful as he poured each of us a Coke.

"Tommy," he said, lighting a cigar. "Come over here and sit," he said, pointing to a chair beside him.

"Well, Don," the President said to Rumsfeld. "What's Tommy got for us today?"

"The General has prepared an operational concept for Afghanistan, Mr. President." The Secretary looked at me and nodded. "Go ahead, General."

I distributed the briefing charts. "Mr. President, the operation will be executed in four phases," I began. "Phase I is already under way . . ."

President Bush was reading ahead; almost immediately he began asking questions. "How's progress on securing host nation support? We getting the bases we need?"

I explained that President Musharraf had approved virtually every one of our requests concerning overflight, basing, and staging.

"That's good," the President said.

I added that Sultan Qaboos had granted permission for us to stage AC-130 gunships and SOF forces on Masira Island. And I was about to explain the importance of that location when the President spoke: "That puts how much of Afghanistan within the range of our aircraft?"

President Bush, I knew, had flown fighters himself. He understood the strengths and limitations of airpower.

"We will have plenty of operational range, Mr. President," I said. "Plus we will establish aerial refueling tracks inside Afghanistan once the fight begins."

As I moved from page to page in the briefing, the President read closely, puffing his cigar in concentration. On virtually every page, he asked a pertinent question. The briefing had been scheduled for two hours, a significant block of time considering the President's commitments during this period of crisis. I realized we were going to run long, but felt I had to answer his questions as completely as possible.

After about the sixth exchange, Don Rumsfeld pointedly checked his watch. "You'll have to move on, General."

The President glanced up from a page showing Taliban early warning radar locations. "We're okay, Don. This is important information."

"Go ahead, General. Just move along as quickly as you can," Rumsfeld said.

I moved from one briefing chart to the next. The President asked his questions, and Secretary Rumsfeld listened attentively, joining the conversation on a number of occasions to stress key points.

Flipping back to the target sets, the President looked up. "We are going into Afghanistan to destroy the Taliban and al Qaeda. This is not retaliation. We are at war against terrorism, not the Afghan people."

In my thirty-six-year career, I had seen examples of confident leadership. But this was one of the most direct and decisive statements of policy I had ever heard.

Next Major General Dell Dailey presented a summary of the Special Mission Unit targets in Afghanistan. We had been focusing on a suspicious Soviet-era fertilizer plant near Mazar-e Sharif. The factory was surrounded by guard posts, and there were checkpoints on the roads leading in and out. Persistent intelligence reports showed al Qaeda members traveling to and from the plant. If the terrorists were working on chemical or biological weapons, that was a logical site.

As Dell Dailey finished his briefing, Secretary Rumsfeld spoke. "Mr. President, this campaign is going to be unprecedented. A lot of traditional lines will be blurred. I recommend that operational control of the CIA be given to the Department of Defense."

Rumsfeld and I had discussed this. It was essential that I, as the commander, have control over all the forces in the theater, and I knew the Secretary wanted to give me that authority. After yesterday's debacle in the Tank, it was obvious that we'd need a "single belly button" to push when the shooting started.

Vice President Dick Cheney answered Rumsfeld. "Before this operation begins, we will review all the command relationships."

That was good enough for me.

"Anything else, Tommy?" the President asked.

"I believe it is essential that we begin the Humanitarian Assistance operation simultaneously with the kinetics, Sir. We want the Afghan people to know that we are not attacking them, but that our war is with al Qaeda and the Taliban."

The President smiled. "That's what I'd expect from a boy from Midland."

We laughed.

"Seriously," the President said. "That's exactly what we want to do."

At the end of the briefing, the President stacked his charts and studied the campaign summary for a moment. "When can you execute this plan, Tommy?"

"We'll have the air forces in position in five days, Sir. All of our CSAR will not yet be staged, but we can plan around that by using TLAMs and B-2 bombers in the north. I'll need forty-eight hours advance warning before we initiate kinetics."

"Okay," the President said. "But what's your *ideal* timing, Tommy?"

Everyone in the room, including Donald Rumsfeld, listened intently. I knew the political pressure the President was under to demonstrate American resolve through military action against al Qaeda. Ground Zero in New York, and a big wedge of the Pentagon across the Potomac, were in ruins. But he was willing to give me the time I needed.

"Mr. President," I said, "in about two weeks, we'll have the required support from the nations in the region. I believe that will give Colin Powell and the State Department the time necessary to finalize CSAR and SOF staging in Uzbekistan."

The President considered this. "I understand . . . two weeks."

"Sir," I said. "We could begin the air operation sooner. But over the long haul, that would not be the best plan. We want air and SOF operations to be as near-simultaneous as we can get them."

"I understand," the President said. "A large air operation would make a statement." Again he paused to think. "On the other hand, I'm willing to wait. When we do this, we'll do it right. My message to the American people is to be patient."

As we rose to leave, the President spoke again. "Absolute secrecy is the key here."

There was a round of "Yes, Mr. President" and "Understand, Sir."

Dell Dailey, the ultimate special operator, said nothing.

"General," the President said to him. "Tell your people not to talk."

Dell looked calmly into the President's face. "Sir, my people never talk."

D RIVING BACK TO THE PENTAGON, I REMEMBERED A POEM I HAD written during another national crisis, November 1979, when extremists took hostage the staff of the American Embassy in Tehran, and the nation's tenacity had been tested. I had carried a wrinkled copy in my wallet since that time. As the sedan crossed the Memorial Bridge toward Virginia, I read the poem again.

RESOLVE

Will squandered in an earlier time,
Was recast—

Tempered liquid hot
In a bath of Irresolute Times,
Conscience misplaced,
The metal would be tightly bound,
Slick and pulsing sweat—

Measure it, weigh it, stand in
Awe—test it not.

8

HISTORIC VICTORY

The small J-2 Conference Room in the SCIF was chilly from the air-conditioning needed to cool the banks of electronics. It was 0900 on Sunday, October 7, 2001, less than one month since 9/11. The war would begin in three and a half hours.

I'd been at headquarters since before midnight, reviewing our final checks of targeting intelligence, the weather, and the status of the B-2s, which were already fifteen hours into their flight from Missouri. Toward dawn I began my calls, notifying our most important contacts in the region that hostilities were imminent. George Tenet was alerting CIA stations worldwide to the pending onset of kinetics.

At 0820, my last call was to King Abdullah of Jordan: "It will begin soon, Sir."

"May God be with your forces, General," the King said. "You fight a righteous battle."

The Threat Con in the AOR had just gone to Delta. The Department of Defense weather satellite showed a clear evening over Afghanistan, with some blowing dust in the western desert near the Iranian border. Visibility was excellent in both Kabul and Kandahar. My long checklist was almost complete.

As I watched, the dark projector screen blinked into the image of Air Force Lt. General Chuck Wald at the Combined Air Operations Center at Prince Sultan Air Base in Saudi Arabia. CENTCOM's other component commanders were waiting on the loop in Bahrain, Kuwait, and on Masira Island off Oman. Secretary Rumsfeld and the new Chairman of the Joint Chiefs of Staff, Dick Myers, were observing from the Pentagon Operations Center, but would not participate directly. Dick had become the chairman only a week earlier, but as the former Vice Chairman was fully up to speed.

The red light appeared on the camera I was facing. "Good morning from Tampa," I said. "Good afternoon, good evening, as the case applies." I glanced at my notes. "We have a force of forty thousand men and women involved in this operation. There are three hundred and ninety-three aircraft and thirty-two ships. A total of thirty-one nations are involved. You have all received the Rules of Engagement. Command and Control is in place. I have the Execute Order from the Secretary. I'm going to go around the horn and ask you to confirm your state of readiness. Chuck, you're up first."

"General, good afternoon," Air Component Commander Chuck Wald said. "I have the Execute Order. CSAR is in place. The B-2s are en route to their targets. Command and Control is green. No show-stoppers, Sir."

"Any questions, Chuck?"

"None, Sir."

The comm officer at the panel to my left did his magic and Vice Admiral Willie Moore, Naval Component Commander, appeared at his headquarters in Manama, Bahrain. "General," he said with a grin, "I hoped you would say I'm getting better looking. I have my Execute Order. Command and Control is full up. We have no issues. We are at go. . . ." I smiled at Willie's joke, but admired his professionalism even more.

The round robin moved to Major General Dell Dailey, commanding Task Force Sword. Dell's Special Mission Unit operators were prepared to deploy to the *Kitty Hawk* when the carrier neared

Oman on Wednesday. These elite troops would be on station in the northern Arabian Sea within seven days completing final rehearsals for their operations.

"No issues," Dell said.

Finally, Director of Central Intelligence George Tenet came on the loop from Langley. "No issues, General."

I faced the camera. "All right. I'm satisfied. Kinetics begin at 1230 hours East Coast time, 1630 Zulu, 2100 hours Afghanistan time. Any questions?" There were none. "Good. My final point is this: Use adult common sense. This is the beginning of tomorrow's history. I want you to focus on two things: Accomplish the mission, and protect the force."

As soon as I arrived back in my office, I took a call on the STU-III from General Dick Myers and Secretary Rumsfeld.

"Great job," Dick said. "We're here to support you."

"General," Donald Rumsfeld added. "The President said to extend to you his respect and best wishes. We're going to finish what began on September 11."

"God bless you, Mr. Secretary," I said. The Secretary of Defense was about to become a Secretary of War. "God bless America."

The words of my country's unofficial motto resonated, and I sensed their profound meaning. There had been a rebirth of patriotism in America since the 9/11 terrorist attacks. Teachers reported that even young children were asking questions, trying hard to understand the words of the Pledge of Allegiance: "one nation . . . indivisible. . . ." A few days after 9/11, I'd been riding on Tampa's Bayshore Boulevard when I saw a group of people on a corner, waving flags. Since then, the "Bayshore Patriots" had met on that corner each Friday.

My troops were going to war for a united country.

B ACK IN MY OFFICE AS I WAITED FOR THE FIRST STRIKE REPORTS, I received a series of calls from my four-star colleagues, including several of the Service Chiefs with whom I had quarreled in the Tank. Their basic message was the same: "We're here to help you."

Willie Moore called from Bahrain. "The first TLAMs were launched at 1419 Zulu, General. There will be a forty-minute pulse with Time-on-Target as scheduled, 1630 Zulu." I called Dick Myers to report that the Tomahawks had been launched successfully.

Jeff Haynes turned on the wide-screen television in the corner of the office. "The President's speaking, Sir."

I'd almost forgotten. "On my orders," President Bush announced to the world, "the United States military has begun strikes against al Qaeda training camps and military installations of the Taliban regime in Afghanistan."

He spoke directly to the members of the Armed Services, assuring them they had his "full confidence."

Secretary Rumsfeld called. He and Dick Myers were about to face the media in the Pentagon press center. "Anything new I should know about?" he asked.

"The operation is proceeding normally, Mr. Secretary."

"Fine, General. Be available, and be friendly."

Rumsfeld was in good spirits, rightfully proud and confident. He'd convinced the Saudis to allow us to conduct the air war from the CAOC at Prince Sultan Air Base. And he had won over Uzbek President Islam Karimov. At their press conference in the presidential palace in Tashkent two days earlier, Karimov and Rumsfeld had announced that Uzbekistan would allow overflight of Coalition Humanitarian Assistance transports and open its airbases for "cargo planes" and search-and-rescue helicopters.

What went unmentioned in their press conference was the Uzbek President's agreement to allow the staging of Special Operations forces at Uzbek bases. President Karimov had committed his support for the coalition effort, but he needed protection from internal criticism. So even as Karimov was making his joint public announcement with Rumsfeld about his country's willingness to facilitate humanitarian support, Colonel John Mulholland's Special Forces teams were well hidden in Uzbekistan, setting up Task Force Dagger at the K-2 air base, preparing for insertion into the camps of the Northern Alliance's commanders. The boots of American soldiers would soon be on Afghan ground.

For years, America had tried to fight terrorism over-the-horizon, with cruise missiles. That approach represented one point on the continuum of conflict. Troops actually "in contact" with the enemy was another, far different point. The Taliban and al Qaeda would soon learn how well American soldiers fought.

At least I *hoped* it would be soon: Donald Rumsfeld had been aptly described as being "genetically impatient."

After speaking with Rumsfeld, I went to the Joint Operations Center (JOC) in the SCIF, the broad-bandwidth heart of an Information Age headquarters. The thirty-two members of the dayshift were at their computers, crammed in elbow to elbow. The floor snaked with bundles of multicolored fiber-optic cable. On the far wall were four wide plasma screens. One displayed real-time overhead reconnaissance video of targets in Afghanistan. Another was a detailed tactical computer chart, pulsing with the digital blocks identifying the American and British surface ship and submarine TLAM shooters in the northern Arabian Sea, as well as the inbound missiles, Air Force heavy and tactical bombers, and Navy F/A-18 Hornet and F-14 Bobcat fighter-bombers off the aircraft carriers *Enterprise* and *Carl Vinson*.

"We have munitions on the ground, Sir," Gene Renuart reported as I took my seat.

The Comm people could switch from CNN's U.S. channels to CNN International, the BBC, Sky TV, and other English-language satellite stations, giving me strategic "situational awareness": seeing the breaking news just as foreign leaders and average people around the world viewed it.

The scene was incredible. Ten years earlier, in my LAM Task Force office above the stone battlements of Fort Monroe, I had dreamed of such an Olympian view of the battlefield. Now I watched in real time as Predator UAVs transmitted night-vision video of TLAMs and JDAMs silently blasting air defense radar sites and C2 buildings around Kabul and Kandahar. One of the display screens split into four segments. We were now observing video links from individual strike aircraft as their laser-guided GBU-12 500-pound bombs smashed into al Qaeda's Tarnak Farms and Duranta training camps. Judging from the pickups and military trucks parked near the buildings, not all the terrorists had abandoned the camps.

Individual compounds around Jalalabad, as well as the cave complexes of Tora Bora, were taking a pounding from the B-52s. I thought back to the moonscape of bomb craters the B-52s had plowed up out near the Cambodian border so many years before. Then I pictured the unforgettable images of the World Trade Center towers collapsing. *Crush the bastards,* I thought.

An hour later, however, a Predator orbiting near Kandahar revealed the unpleasant news that three Taliban and al Qaeda targets had *not* been hit: a helicopter pad from which the Taliban flew their few airworthy Mi-8s; an airstrip long enough to handle twin-engine Soviet-era AN-26 turboprops; and a bunker complex. The J-2 and the CIA had identified these as potential "leadership" targets; two of them were potential escape routes, while the bunker was a possible hideout for terrorists who should now be dead. These targets had been on the strike list, which every relevant intelligence agency had vetted. But none of the three had been struck . . . and I wanted to know why.

Furious, I called Gene Renuart and Rifle DeLong aside. Keeping my voice even, I made my point. "Pass this on to Chuck Wald in the CAOC. 'In the future pay attention to *my* priorities—priorities based on the needs of the joint team, not the desire of a single service.'" We had worked our collective asses off to make this strike a success. But at least three potential home-run balls had crossed the plate without a swing. I did not want a repeat performance of this problem.

"I'm on it, Sir," Gene said, with no excuses or apologies—exactly what I would expect from an officer of his caliber.

Overall, however, the first wave of attacks was extremely effective. All but one of the Taliban's air defense fire-control radars were destroyed, along with every missile launcher that had been identified in prestrike reconnaissance. Our TLAMs also hit the early warning radars protecting the borders. Afghanistan's Integrated Air Defense System, never robust yet still threatening, had been crippled.

Fighter-bombers were now "loitering" in prearranged holding patterns, waiting for the UAVs to locate emerging targets. Aerial refueling tankers were able to fly tracks within Afghan airspace, allowing the strike aircraft to gas up without returning to the carriers or the bases in the Middle East. The heavy bombers would continue to strike al Qaeda targets around the clock.

We had crippled the enemy's air defenses, but they still had the power to threaten our helicopters with hundreds of ZSU-23 mm automatic cannons and shoulder-fired antiaircraft missiles—man portable air defense systems (MANPADS). Most of the Taliban and al Qaeda MANPADS were the old, short-range Soviet-built SA-7s, which could be "spoofed" by dispensing flares that confused the heat-seeking warheads. But you couldn't spoof a string of 23 mm rounds fired down from a cave overlooking a high pass in the Hindu Kush.

Despite this threat, I knew John Mulholland's Special Forces were cranking up for insertion into northern Afghanistan. The sooner we had the teams' combat air controllers designating Taliban and al Qaeda targets for the bombers, the quicker Northern Alliance troops could climb out of their World War I–style trenches and advance on the enemy. The campaign hinged on linking Special Forces, Northern Alliance units, and air power. We needed to move quickly. It was already fall in the mountains of Afghanistan, and winter was coming fast.

The plan involved considerable risk. But it was not a reckless gamble.

It's a military axiom that no plan survives initial contact with the enemy. We had made contact; now we needed to exploit our advantage, as the President had said, "without pause."

I was back in my office when Jeff Haynes came in. "General, they need you in the SCIF. Predator's got a target."

I went directly to Room 235 in the SCIF—the Fusion Cell, our video link to Predator UAVs flying over Afghanistan. The connection ran from CENTCOM to a van parked near the CIA headquarters building in Langley, Virginia, and then by satellite to the UAVs. From that van the Predators' "pilots" flew the drone aircraft—and what they saw through the video link, I was watching in the Fusion Cell.

It was a bright fall afternoon in Tampa, but late on a clear, star-lit night near Kandahar. The UAV was in a slow, banking orbit, watching a convoy of three vehicles and a motorcycle as it sped out of a mud-walled compound toward the city. The lead vehicle was a Toyota Land Cruiser, the second a dusty white dual-cab pickup, trailed by another pickup with armed men crammed into the open cargo bed.

"The convoy profile fits Taliban leadership, Sir," Brigadier General Jeff Kimmons told me as I sat down before the video screen.

I felt a familiar rush of adrenalin, similar to what I'd known flying as an aerial observer on the pink teams so many years before. This time I wasn't strapped into an OH-6 down at the paddy level, but watching through the Predator's infrared video eye over a satellite downlink. And this wasn't just another routine reconnaissance mission flown by a harmless drone. This Predator was armed with two Hellfire laser-guided missiles.

The armed Predator was a sensitive CIA covert action program that had been operating for several months from a secret base in Central Asia, hunting Osama bin Laden and his al Qaeda associates in Afghanistan. This was the operation I had discussed with Richard Clarke. The weapon had been great in theory, but lacking in practicality—until tonight.

As Donald Rumsfeld had arranged with George Tenet, CENTCOM had operational control over CIA activities in the the-ater of war, including the armed Predator. But my lines of authority in the Agency had not yet been fully tested.

The grainy image shimmered, then clicked into sharper focus.

"Can we get a tighter close-up?" I asked the drone operator at Langley.

"I'll try, Sir," the young voice answered.

For several minutes the pilot maneuvered the Predator, keeping it west of the convoy, several thousand feet above the potholed black-top road.

A duty officer from the CIA Operations Directorate was in the van at Langley. "General," the officer said. "This target has all the characteristics of a leadership convoy. You have armed lead and trail vehicles. And the pickup in the middle is a dual cab. That could be Mullah Omar's personal vehicle."

I watched the small convoy moving steadily southwest toward the city lights of Kandahar. If we could hit it now, in this open desert, there would be no risk of collateral damage. If the convoy stopped, we'd have a .9 probability of kill—only a 10 percent risk of missing the target. But if we fired at moving vehicles, the kill probability was only .3 probability—a 70 percent risk of failure.

CENTCOM's senior Judge Advocate General (JAG), Navy Captain Shelly Young, stood by my chair. She was the lawyer who would keep me square with the Rules of Engagement and the Law of Land Warfare, should I decide to shoot. And Shelly was not your typical *on one hand—on the other hand* attorney.

Shelly studied the convoy. "Valid target," she said.

"Gene," I told Operations Director Renuart, "check with the CAOC to see if we can build a kill box for the F-14s or F-18s to strike the convoy a few miles closer to Kandahar." The "kill box" was the imaginary 200-by-400 meter rectangle into which bombs were to be delivered. I visualized the moving-target range I'd built at Fort Hood years earlier. Destroying that convoy would require precise timing and delivery of ordnance by aircraft flying at 20,000 feet. A very tough time-distance calculation, but a much higher probability of kill than I'd have using the Predator's Hellfire against moving vehicles.

Ten minutes passed. Then another ten. The CAOC couldn't build a kill box quickly enough. We had missed a chance.

I watched the plasma screen. Led by the motorcycle, the convoy sped through the empty streets of Kandahar, past housing compounds of mud-block walls surrounding open courtyards. The vehicles stopped near the city's center, a district of two- and three-story buildings interspersed with more walled compounds. The Predator orbited, unseen at a safe altitude, its video eye locked onto the vehicles. A digital clock at the corner of the screen read 1505 Hours Eastern Time. It was 0435 in Kandahar, two hours until dawn.

"Give me an exact fuel status on the UAV," I ordered the operator.

"Sir, we're good for two hours, ten minutes before Bingo fuel and RTB." Bingo fuel was the minimum needed to return to base safely.

"Hold station," I ordered.

Several people from the convoy ran into a compound on the right side of a street. "How long to orient the Predator and take a Hellfire shot?" I asked.

"Valid target for Hellfire," Shelly added as we waited for the answer.

"Lining up for a shot," the operator at Langley said. "About five minutes until launch."

The men who had run into the compound returned to their vehicles, carrying several large containers.

"MANPADS," I muttered, spotting the shoulder-fired missile cases. "What's the status of the Hellfire?" I asked Langley.

"Lining up now. . . ."

Too late. The vehicles sped out of town, away from Kandahar's lights.

"Goddamn it." Still no shot.

No matter. If we could keep the Predator flying, this convoy would stop again. Fifteen minutes passed; twenty-five; forty. The vehicles were headed away from the city at high speed. Then, suddenly, they stopped—in the courtyard of a mosque, a large, domed building surrounded by mud huts and several two- and three-story structures, upscale homes by Afghan standards.

"Line-up the Predator to launch a Hellfire," I said. "Take out the dual-cab."

"No issues . . . valid target," Shelly Young said.

Vehicle doors opened; the occupants jumped out and moved rapidly toward the mosque. "Quickly, quickly," I instructed Langley.

People emerged from the mosque and greeted the men leaving the vehicles. After shaking hands, the men from inside placed their hands on their hearts—a clear sign of deference. "This is a leadership target," I said as the entire group entered the building. As I watched I remembered my final conversation with President Bush. We had discussed unintended damage to civilians—"collatoral damage"—and the President had reminded me that the enemy was al Qaeda and the Taliban, not the Afghan people. "And this is not about religion," he'd said. "If you see bin Laden go into a mosque, wait until he comes out to kill him." *Wait till they come out,* I thought.

"How much station time left on the Predator?"

"Less than an hour, Sir," the operator said.

"Can you take out one of the sedans parked near the wall? Maybe that will persuade the people to leave the mosque and give us a shot at the principals."

About five minutes later, a dark sedan disintegrated in a fireball. The men who'd been guarding the vehicles ran in every direction. None of them looked up. They had no idea what had hit them.

As two Navy F/A-18 Hornets circled above Kandahar, armed with laser-guided GBU-12 500-pound bombs, I watched intently as the people on the ground ran from the mosque and scurried into the remaining vehicles. As well-armed security guards dashed to catch up, the cars and trucks sped away and raced along the gravel road to the northeast. They stopped about half a mile away, in front of a large, multistory house behind a fortress-like wall.

"Have the jets identify the compound and get ready to drop," I ordered the CAOC in Saudi Arabia. "I'm going to clear this with the Secretary as a high collateral damage target."

Shelly Young concurred.

The Fusion Cell was getting crowded. Jeff Kimmons was in the corner, talking to CIA; according to their analysis, the leadership principals and guards were in the buildings inside the compound.

I walked down the hall to my office, got on the STU III, and explained the situation to Secretary Rumsfeld.

"I'll call the President immediately, General, and call you back. If the targets come out of the house before I get back to you, kill them." Within five minutes, President Bush had approved the target for immediate strike.

As I rushed into the Fusion Cell, a CIA officer at Langley was on the secure speaker phone with Kimmons. "Don't shoot," he told Jeff. "We think this building is a mosque."

I clenched my fists and swore silently. There was no dome, no minaret like the other structure. "It doesn't look like a mosque to me," I said.

"You're still good, Sir," Shelly Young advised.

"Some of the people have left the building, but some are still inside," Jeff Kimmons said.

"Have the pilots execute the drop," I ordered Chuck Wald in the CAOC, seven thousand miles away.

As the Predator banked away to avoid the incoming bombers, the compound disappeared in a cloud of dust and smoke. Sixty seconds later, we received the pilot reports: the target had been completely destroyed.

Within an hour, Dick Myers called on the STU-III. "Tom," he said, "John Jumper has been watching the Predator scene at Air Force Ops here in the Pentagon and he tells me that the principals had left the house before the bombs went in. He knows this is your business, says he's just trying to be helpful."

A Title X cook stirs the broth. What the hell was happening to the chain of command?

General Gary Luck—my old boss from Desert Storm and Korea, now retired and a Senior Mentor with Joint Forces Command—had come to Tampa to advise me and absorb the Lessons Learned from this new kind of war. He had been standing silently in the corner of the Fusion Cell when Myers delivered the message from Jumper, watching and listening. When I looked up he shook his head, sharing my frustration.

In combat, there had to be one line of authority. But in this goat rope there had been CENTCOM, the Pentagon, the White House, the CIA . . . and the gratuitous advice of a Service Chief. I expected that someone in Washington would leak some version of this story to the press within a week. I would not be disappointed.

After thanking the Secretary for his quick reaction and the President's, I called Dick Myers.

"Dick, we're gonna have to unscrew the Service contributions to this fight. I respect what Johnny Jumper's folks think they saw on the downlinks of a CIA Predator. And we'll work our way through the frustration and friction of this joint, interagency equation. But we'll need not only unity of command, but also unity of effort. I'll provide the command, you work on the Service Chiefs to get the unity of effort."

"I hear you, Tom." Dick was clearly frustrated, too.

"We need Jumper to focus on the Air Force contribution," I said. "Hit the directed targets, with the right munitions, on the directed timelines. I'll work the Agency Predator, target selection, and execution. And the Secretary and I will sort out timings and authorities. I'd appreciate it if you would remove the fucking Predator downlink from the Building. My name is not Westmoreland, and I'm not going to go along with Washington giving tactics and targets to our kids in the cockpits and on the ground in Afghanistan."

Dick continued to listen patiently. "I agree, and I'll help. This is your fight, Tom."

I then met with Gene Renuart and Jeff Kimmons. "Not a bad beginning, guys. The fight is on, and I'm proud of your professionalism."

They waited, knowing I had more on my mind.

"Having said that," I continued, "I want you to have an immediate huddle with the Air Component folks and the CIA. Lots of lessons to be learned here. Deconflict the Predator airspace issue, determine realistic strike timelines for both the armed drone and our jets, and identify any 'personality' issues that I need to resolve. We're going to fight a joint fight . . . and we're going to start right now."

In other words, the air, land, naval, and special ops components were going to act as a true team.

Later, the CENTCOM staff would refer to the period between that Sunday evening in Tampa and October 18 as "the Ten Days from Hell." Clausewitz's fog and friction were descending on the Command.

THROUGHOUT THOSE EARLY DAYS, THE SLOW PACE OF OUR operations was a source of constant frustration.

Our problem did not stem from a single, easily resolved source. There were predicaments inside dilemmas. As a result, we were unable to insert Colonel John Mulholland's Special Forces teams into northern Afghanistan as quickly as either Secretary Rumsfeld or I wanted—an understatement of historical proportions.

Rumsfeld's chronic impatience had never been so obvious. At this point in the operation I had two scheduled phone calls a day with the Secretary, one at 0745, the second at 1630. And there were many unscheduled discussions, some long, some short, to the point, and what you might call *blunt*.

For ten days, the first words the Secretary spoke in virtually every conversation concerned the Special Forces. "When is something going to happen, General?" "I do not see any movement, General Franks." "What is the situation with those teams, General?" The variations were few, and subtle: "Can you predict *when* something is going to happen?" "Where *are* the teams, General?"

Rumsfeld was never personally abusive. But he was not what you would call "user-friendly." His questions continued—relentlessly.

The answer was that we were all working on it. But moving the Special Forces teams, with their vital combat air controllers, out of K-2 on the Uzbek plains, across the valley of the Amu Darya River—the Oxus of Alexander the Great—and into the Afghan highlands to link up with the Northern Alliance, proved a formidable challenge.

The tactical situation in the north was complex. Taliban forces, supported by groups of al Qaeda troops, occupied the major towns and cities near the borders of Turkmenistan, Uzbekistan, and Tajikistan. And they controlled the roads with a couple hundred former Soviet tanks and APCs, and dozens of ZSU-23-4s, a particularly nasty tracked anti-aircraft weapon that was also a powerful anti-infantry tool.

The Northern Alliance's best-defended enclave was in Afghanistan's far northeastern corner—the former bastion of General Ahmad Shah Massoud, now commanded by Mohammed Fahim Khan. Abdul Rashid Dostum, an ethnic Uzbek, commanded the next strongest NA formation. His forces and those of his erstwhile rival and sometimes ally, Mohammed Attah, held a string of strategic ridges and valleys south of the crossroads town of Mazar-e Sharif.

None of these "warlords" was a choirboy when it came to human rights, but they were saints compared to the Taliban. And they had experienced troops. They hated the Taliban and the *araban* (their derisive term for al Qaeda, which included large numbers of Chechens and Pakistanis), and they were more than eager to work with us.

Our plan hinged on combining these tough, highly motivated opposition fighters with the Coalition's massive air power. To do so, however, we had to have a Special Forces team—Operational Detachments Alpha (ODA)—with each of the local Northern Alliance commanders.

And that was where we were stuck. An advance CIA team, code name Jawbreaker, was with Fahim, but other Agency officers had yet to link up with Dostum, Attah, and their subordinates. Although we were establishing communications with the disparate Northern Alliance leaders, we'd yet to place any Agency officers physically with them to pave the way for our Special Forces.

John Mulholland's Task Force Dagger was growing, ready to move at K2. We needed links with the NA and transportation to insert the teams. The CIA had access to a few semi-airworthy Mi-17s, which they were using to support the Northern Alliance. And, because the

Taliban used similar helicopters, these aircraft were less likely to draw ground fire than the MH-60 Pave Hawks and the MH-47s of the 160th SOAR. I had wanted Mulholland's Green Berets to be inserted on the Mi-17s, but the arrangement was not working.

As Mulholland reported, the old choppers never showed up on schedule. And when they did arrive, they usually limped in with hydraulic trouble or engine problems that kept them grounded.

And then there was the terrible weather. Our first attempted team insertions—one each to Fahim and Dostum—were turned back by zero-visibility dust storms. Subsequent flights encountered rain that turned into blinding snow as the old helicopters tried to crest the high passes. Soon it was obvious that the old Soviet equipment would not be reliable enough to meet our required timelines.

But the K-2 air base was not yet ready to support the helicopters of the 160th SOAR that were standing by to be airlifted in from Germany. Mulholland and his Green Berets, assisted by hardworking Air Force base operations crews, were struggling to transform K-2 into a Forward Operating Base, but as each day passed the probability of bad weather along the mountainous infiltration routes increased.

And that wasn't the only challenge. The Agency advance officers faced the same or worse conditions operating out of Dushanbe, Tajikistan. After initial contact with Northern Alliance commanders, the CIA teams were often unable to return for days. And, struggling to master their new satellite phones, the NA leaders went through batteries more quickly than they could be resupplied so we would frequently lose contact with them for prolonged periods.

Finally, six days into the operation, on a conference call linking me with John Mulholland, Gary Harrell, and Bert Calland, the report we'd been waiting for came in: Task Force Dagger would have MH-60 Pave Hawks and MH-47s up and flying within twenty-four hours.

"That's great news," I told the team.

But on the next day John Mulholland reported that bad weather had struck again, almost causing the first Coalition casualties of the campaign. An MH-60 carrying a team en route to Dostum had had its rotors ice up in a freezing mist above twelve thousand feet. The aircraft had "mushed in," landing hard, and had been destroyed and abandoned; the Green Berets and the crew had slogged down through the snow to a lower altitude, where they were picked up by a CSAR chopper. And another Pave Hawk had been hit by ground fire straining up a steep valley toward a pass; it had limped back to K-2.

"We'll stay with it, Sir," Mulholland reported. "But it's tough going here."

That afternoon, I answered another barrage of questions from Donald Rumsfeld. "What's the status of the teams, General?" he began.

I explained the difficulties, but made the mistake of slipping into aviation terminology, cluttering my report with terms like "altitude density," which affected lift capability in mountain helicopter operations.

"Do we have the right equipment out there, General?" Rumsfeld demanded.

"We do, Mr. Secretary, but this is going to take a while."

Rumsfeld was not pleased. The Coalition had been bombing Afghanistan for over a week. International journalists who had swarmed in from Pakistan were transmitting video of American planes bombing mountainsides. Networks were running and rerunning tape of Taliban armored vehicles moving in daylight with apparent impunity. The BBC had broadcast a long, pessimistic report on the Northern Alliance being "penned up" behind their trench lines. Rumsfeld wanted results. He wanted to report tangible achievements—something beyond the airdrops of humanitarian daily rations.

And even these humanitarian flights from Ramstein were beginning to cause problems. Oxfam International got wide media play by reporting that hungry villagers in the bleak northern mountains were chasing the bright yellow plastic ration packs into mine fields. Although there was no evidence that this had actually happened, the perception tainted the remarkable humanitarian effort.

But there was more bad news. Since August, the Taliban had been detaining eight Western volunteer workers from the German organization Shelter Now. And they were threatening to try them for espionage and deliver their harsh brand of Islamic justice. Dell Dailey's operators aboard the *Kitty Hawk* were planning a rescue operation together with Agency field officers, but the media was spinning the drama to imply that the United States was powerless to help these innocent pawns.

I was concerned, but in the video conferences I had with the White House I noticed no anxiety from President George Bush as I described our difficulties in infiltrating the Special Forces. "Stick to the plan, Tommy," the President said. "We will be patient. This will take as long as it takes."

The next afternoon, before my scheduled call with Rumsfeld, John Mulholland reported that a combination of rotten weather and ground fire had turned back yet another infiltration flight.

The Secretary was somber. "General Franks, this isn't working. I want you to build options that *will* work."

Finally, I decided to get away from the unblinking fluorescent glare and ceaseless buzz of hot electronics in the JOC and the Fusion Cell.

"Open a bottle of wine," I told Cathy. "I'll be home in fifteen minutes."

After dinner, I was too agitated to relax. I went to my study and used the secure phone to request an unscheduled conference call with Rumsfeld and Dick Myers. I was exhausted—tired of having to explain every operational problem to the Secretary. I knew we would get our Special Forces on the ground soon, and that the situation would change once we did. But I did not think the Secretary believed this.

"Mr. Secretary," I said, "from your comments earlier today, it appears that you no longer have confidence in me. . . ."

"General . . ." Rumsfeld began.

"No, Sir. Please hear me out. It is essential for the mission that you have confidence in the commander. If you have lost confidence . . . you should select another commander."

The line was silent.

"General Franks," Donald Rumsfeld finally said. "You have my complete confidence. This operation will succeed."

"I concur, Tom," Dick Myers added. "You're doing a great job under difficult circumstances and we will support you in every way we can."

"Thank you, Mr. Secretary. Thanks, Dick. One thing you can do is remind the Service Chiefs about the chain of command. They're still working hard on their individual service *cottage industries,* and it's not helping."

"I'll take care of it," Dick Myers said. And I believe to this day that he did everything in his power to keep the Chiefs in their designated lanes.

During my regular call with the Secretary the next morning, Rumsfeld did not lead off with an impatient question about the teams. Instead, he asked me to comment on the use of precision-guided, 5000-pound "deep penetrator" bombs in the White Mountains. I explained the effectiveness of this operation: though on television the global audience may have seen these as random explosions on blank hillsides, they were actually precision strikes that were killing al Qaeda and destroying their sanctuaries.

"Interesting," Rumsfeld said. "I like learning these details."

"You ask, Mr. Secretary, and I answer."

THE TEN DAYS FROM HELL ENDED ON FRIDAY, OCTOBER 19.
Near midnight, Afghan time—early afternoon in Tampa—John Mulholland inserted the first Special Forces A-Team into General Dostum's mud-brick village headquarters south of Mazar-e Sharif. The 160th SOAR MH-47s that had been trying for several nights to lift the team—ODA 595—through the mountains had finally succeeded. We now had a twelve-man highly skilled Green Beret team—call sign TIGER 02—with Dostum's militia. Good weather was forecast in the coming seventy-two hours, and Mulholland reported that two more A-Teams would be inserted, one each with Mohammed Fahim and Mohammed Attah. As more CIA elements linked up with other warlords, additional A-Teams would be inserted with other Northern Alliance units.

"Things are moving, Sir," Mulholland reported.

I was pleased. But we were still working on the "dress code" these teams would take into combat. It is part of the Special Forces' culture to adopt the appearance of the indigenous troops with whom they serve. The teams would be fighting alongside Tajik, Uzbek, and Hazara tribesmen, fierce mountain warriors who wore distinctive clothing. And, until we were able to provide the Northern Alliance with European-style battledress, their fighters made do with their homespun. John Mulholland correctly wanted his men to blend in, which meant "going native." That made good tactical sense as well. The enemy had trained snipers who would easily spot Americans in Desert Camouflage Uniform. But there were legal concerns in Washington.

It was a vexing problem. American soldiers fighting out of uniform might not be treated as prisoners of war if captured, but rather be executed as spies. On the other hand, any captured Green Beret would likely be executed regardless of what he wore. The final compromise required our men to wear at least "one prominent item" of regulation uniform—a DCU shirt, jacket, or trousers would suffice.

This was shaping up to be a strange war.

As soon as I heard from Mulholland, I called Dick Myers. "Tell the Secretary that we've got Special Forces troopers on the ground and more are on the way."

"That's good news, Tom. The Secretary will be pleased."

Twenty minutes later I was back at the commander's console in the Joint Operations Center, watching digital aircraft ID blocks move across the image of Afghanistan on the plasma screen. In the far north, the symbol for TIGER 02, transmitted by secure satellite uplink, appeared at the center of the shaded oval representing Dostum's area of operations.

It was 1429 hours in Tampa, almost 0100 on October 20 in Afghanistan. Four Air Force MC-130 transports from the 1st Special Operations Wing were moving in trail formation, crossing into Afghanistan from the Baluchistan panhandle of Pakistan. They carried two hundred men from the 75th Ranger Regiment, who would parachute onto the high desert plateau within minutes. Overhead, an AC-130 Spectre gunship was circling the Rangers' objective: a long paved airstrip, code name Rhino.

Sheik Mohammed Bin Zayed, Military Chief of Staff of the United Arab Emirates, had told me about the desert airstrip, located on a dry lake bed. A passionate falconer, he'd had the facility built to serve a well-equipped hunting camp. "If you can use the airfield," he told me, "you may not have to put so much pressure on Musharraf for basing. It will be better for him if you can keep your troop strength in Pakistan small."

Provided with the airstrip's exact coordinates, we had planned an operation with our Special Operators. The goal of the Rangers would be to secure the field as a lodgment for U.S. Marines, our first conventional force in Afghanistan.

Northeast of the Rangers, a string of MH-47s from the *Kitty Hawk* were nearing Kandahar, supported by a second AC-130 Spectre. These helicopters carried Task Force Gecko, elite operators from Major General Dell Dailey's Special Mission Units. Their objective was the central Kandahar compound of the Taliban leader Mullah Mohammed Omar.

We had intentionally chosen not to bomb that target, hoping it would serve as a magnet for Omar and his deputies. And we anticipated that the maze of rooms and sheds inside the compound walls might contain a trove of intelligence: tactical maps, radio frequencies, satellite telephone numbers, lists of overseas agents, perhaps even the locations of secret refuges in Afghanistan where Taliban or al Qaeda leaders might be hiding. The Gecko operators had orders to take the site by force, to kill or capture any enemy found there, and to exploit the target for intelligence.

Like the Ranger airdrop at Rhino, the SMU mission in Kandahar was a moderate-to-high-risk operation. But I had confidence that the Rangers and the SMU operators could handle themselves deep in enemy territory. This two-part operation also had a strategic purpose:

Attacking the Taliban's heartland would demonstrate that we could strike anywhere, at any time of our choosing. And this would serve to fix the Taliban's limited forces in the south. If we threatened his stronghold in Kandahar, Mullah Omar would not send his reserves north to reinforce the Taliban and al Qaeda units garrisoned along the Uzbek and Tajik borders.

Indeed, it was in the northern mountains, not the southwestern desert, where we would focus our main effort. As I worked with Dell Dailey on his plan, I remembered the 1st Cavalry Division's successful deception in the Wadi al Batin. That feint had worked perfectly; I expected the same in this case.

"Be kinetic," I'd told Dell. "Kill or capture, and use the Spectres to demonstrate overwhelming force."

Dell Dailey called from his op center. "Missions on target in nine minutes."

I watched the symbols moving toward the objectives. "Any activity on the ground, Dell?"

"Negative, Sir. No issues, no drama." Dell's voice was calm, as if he were describing a training exercise.

Now we waited. I stood up and shook a kink out of my right leg. The freshest reconnaissance imagery revealed that the Taliban had installed a security force at Objective Rhino. The Spectre was going to prep the targets with machine-gun and automatic cannon fire, destroying any crew-served weapons with the onboard 105 mm cannon. At no time during the long war against the Soviet occupation had Afghans witnessed such a devastating weapon. I was glad we had these gunships in theater, and that two of them were over these objectives tonight.

At 1451 hours, he called again. "Task Force Rhino and Task Force Gecko on their objectives."

We also had a Predator up, observing the Gecko mission. Although I'd seen the rehearsal at Fort Benning, the sheer speed of the insertion was unbelievable. The big tandem-rotor helicopters swept in from two directions, so low that the pilots flying on night-vision goggles had to pop up to clear the compound walls. As the dust billowed, the operators pounded off the tailgates and moved toward their objectives, firing on the run.

While I watched, smoke from the compound and dust clouds from the helicopters' rotors obscured the Predator video. We waited until 1535 hours, when Dell called again. "Gecko and Rhino secure. Resistance at both objectives. Enemy KIA. Friendly WIA. Continuing the mission." The Taliban had attempted to defend the sites, as we had expected; several of our men had been wounded, some of the enemy killed. The Rangers secured their objectives at Rhino, took several prisoners, and called in two MC-130s to extract the Task Force.

In Kandahar, Task Force Gecko finished its work and departed on the waiting helicopters. One of the MH-47s struck the edge of a compound wall lifting out of the landing zone. The helicopter's big two-wheel right landing gear was ripped away, but the aircraft was otherwise undamaged.

I was about to return to my office to call Dick Myers when Dell called with an update—and the news was bad. An MH-60 Penetrator standing by with the Quick Reaction Force at an isolated airstrip inside Pakistan had crashed in a "dust-out," rolling over, severely damaging the helicopter, and killing two Rangers.

It was a sad loss. True to the Rangers' creed, these young soldiers had led the way.

A S PART OF THE OVERALL INFORMATION PLAN, TORIE CLARK'S Public Affairs office at the Pentagon released dramatic night-vision video of the Ranger airdrop at Rhino, the phosphorescent green sky blossoming with parachutes in a scene evocative of those grainy World War II newsreels of the Normandy invasion. That was exactly the message we wanted to register with the Taliban: *You are exposed. Lethal Coalition forces can drop from the night sky at any time, at any place. You can expect us back.*

Our plan received support from an unlikely source: a national magazine. In an article on the missions at Gecko and Rhino, one of its star reporters presented a badly distorted version of the operations.

One of the most glaring mistakes was a description of the Kandahar mission, which, the reporter claimed, "was initiated by sixteen AC-130 gunships."

Sixteen gunships, I thought. *Excellent.* We knew from communications intercepts that the Taliban and al Qaeda were terrified of the AC-130s. Now, thanks to this article, they would believe that CENTCOM could put sixteen of these weapons on a single target. That was fiction, not fact. We had a total of nine Spectre gunships in the AOR and usually could operate three or four over Afghanistan on any given night. But the erroneous reporting furthered the operation. I wondered if the unnamed "senior officer" who fed the reporter this information had done so intentionally, or had simply been one of those ill-informed, disgruntled leakers finishing a dead-end career in some Pentagon cubicle.

I would never know. But as the Taliban concentrated its reserves to protect Kandahar and the south, John Mulholland continued to insert his teams into the north.

E VERY WAR PRODUCES MEMORABLE IMAGES: THE MARINE FLAG-raising on Iwo Jima's Mount Suribachi, frost-bitten troops retreating over the snowy ridges of Korea, Medevac dust-offs in Vietnam.

The first visual icon of Operation Enduring Freedom showed Special Forces soldiers on horseback, charging across a barren slope with their Northern Alliance partners. Dressed in a motley blend of camouflage uniforms and checkered ethnic scarves, the Americans wore beards and mushroom-shaped *pakol* hats.

Studying the news magazine photographs, though, I recognized details the casual observer might have missed: green fiberglass cases carrying satellite radios, GPS equipment, and laser target-designators lashed to the soldiers' saddles. It was as if warriors from the future had been transported to an earlier century. And that image captured this most unusual war: resourceful young troops carrying the world's most advanced military technology onto a battlefield where horse cavalry still prevailed. I was thankful for American technology—and I was awed by the performance of these young men.

As I left for a brief trip to the AOR to consult with our critical allies, the Green Berets and our combat aviators forged a partnership that would break the back of the Taliban and al Qaeda.

After meeting with Crown Prince Abdullah and other senior members of the royal family in Riyadh, Saudi Arabia, I flew into Muscat, Oman, to reconnect with Sultan Qaboos "Your Majesty," I told the Sultan, "Crown Prince Abdullah supports our operations against the Taliban and al Qaeda. And, as you know, General Wald, who commands our Air Component, is based in the Kingdom."

Sultan Qaboos nodded.

"I recently visited his Royal Highness and raised the issue of continuing the war through Ramadan."

"And what was his opinion, General?" Sultan Qaboos asked.

Joining me in the meeting was Britain's Prince Andrew, the Duke of York, wearing his Royal Navy uniform. Prince Andrew was visiting Oman to observe British forces on a previously scheduled training exercise. Like the Sultan, he listened intently. His nation was our firmest ally in this war. If the sensitivities of the Muslim world forced us to pause for a lunar month when Ramadan began on November 17, we risked a potentially crippling loss of momentum. By late December, the mountains of Afghanistan would be impassable with snow.

On the other hand, we needed the support of Muslim nations like Saudi Arabia and Oman—and for many of their citizens Ramadan was sacred. President Bush and Secretary Rumsfeld had instructed me to sound out my contacts on this crucial point.

"These leaders hope we can defeat the Taliban and al Qaeda before the start of Ramadan." I shook my head. "But they understand that this may not be possible. I now ask your opinion, Sir."

"General," the Sultan said. "Permit me a question. People are asking if the United States will finish the job this time." He was referring to the token strikes we had launched against the Iraqi regime and Osama bin Laden in 1998.

"America is a different country since 9/11, Sir. I am a different man. We will finish the job."

Sultan Qaboos was pleased. "Good. As for the Holy Month of Ramadan, I don't think it will make any difference. Muslims sometimes go to war during Ramadan." He stood and shook my hand. "You must continue the battle, General Franks. This Ramadan is for war."

I DID NOT PLAY GOLF IN ISLAMABAD, DESPITE MY EARLIER PROMISE to President Musharraf, when I returned to meet with him again after my trip to Oman.

The Northern Alliance was being revitalized through its partnership with our Special Forces teams. All across the combat zones in the Panjshir and Amu Darya Valleys, Taliban forces and their al Qaeda supporters had been struck by the bombs our special operators had "lazed" onto their targets. Linking combat air controllers to flights of fighter-bombers and B-52s orbiting high above the battlefield had proven even more lethal than military theorists could have imagined.

The enemy seemed incapable of understanding the nature of our precision weapons. Hundreds of Taliban and al Qaeda had been killed in the initial engagements. And Northern Alliance units, supplied with weapons, munitions, winter uniforms, food, medicines—as well as oats for their horses—were ready to take the offensive.

When I summarized the tactical picture for Musharraf, he predicted that the Taliban regime "must soon collapse—hopefully before Ramadan."

"I hope so, Mr. President," I said. "The Afghan people have suffered under the Taliban and al Qaeda long enough."

"Do you know where Osama bin Laden is?" he asked.

"No, Sir. Do you?"

Musharraf smiled. "We think he is still in Afghanistan, in the east—Tora Bora. My intelligence officers would know if he had crossed into Pakistan."

"We're going after him," I emphasized. "We won't stop until we get him."

"And when you do have him," Musharraf said, "will you put him on trial?"

"General Musharraf, I'm a military man. We will take him dead or alive. If alive, I'm sure he will be tried as the murderer he is."

FLYING ACROSS AFGHANISTAN, TOWARD TAJIKISTAN, I HAD AN unusual conversation with Donald Rumsfeld. The Secretary, too, was airborne, headed to Tashkent for more negotiations with President Karimov. "Are you sure those Special Forces teams have senior enough officers in command?" he asked. "It seems to me the Northern Alliance generals won't really listen to young captains and majors."

"Mr. Secretary, in a few weeks the warlords will think of those captains and majors as their sons. Our youngsters are very good at what they do."

"You are the commander," he said. "But keep an eye on it."

Months later, Assistant Secretary of Defense Torie Clark told me, "You and Don Rumsfeld complement each other. You make him a better Secretary, and he makes you a better General."

I think she was right.

MOHAMMED FAHIM KHAN SAT OPPOSITE ME AT A FOLDING TABLE in the echoing belly of the C-17 transport. He wore a cashmere *pakol*, and his beard was neatly trimmed. But Fahim still looked like a Mafia enforcer.

It was late on the last Tuesday in October, a cold night in Dushanbe, Tajikistan. The huge aircraft stood alone on a ramp at the far end of the civilian airport. Fahim and a man introduced as his

"Minister of Finance" had arrived in a dusty Mercedes sedan. A veteran CIA Operations Directorate officer I'll call Hank, who had accompanied me on this trip, sat to my right. To my left, Colonel John Mulholland, a husky soldier who made me look small, rested the worn elbows of his DCUs on the tabletop. He was beyond tired.

We drank strong Air Force coffee, not tea. But this was a tea-drinking negotiation if there ever was one.

As the leader of the Northern Alliance—he had assumed command after Massoud's assassination—Fahim had come to the meeting to bargain. He led the largest, best-equipped opposition force in Afghanistan. And he had witnessed the effective combination of our Special Forces and a seemingly inexhaustible supply of precision-guided weapons.

"If I can help you and you can help me," he said through the Agency interpreter, "we both win. My people have fought terrorism for years, with special intensity since the Taliban took power. With both our efforts combined, there will be positive results."

"You ain't seen nothing yet," I said, hoping the interpreter, who spoke with a British inflection, would capture the idiom.

Apparently he did, because Fahim replied with an adage of his own. "We respect all and trust all."

"Will you trust me with your life?" I asked.

"We are soldiers and have no choice. Our lives are in the hands of God."

He speaks well. But will he press the fight when things get tough? There was a reason he had brought his "finance minister."

I spread John Mulholland's tactical map on the table. "What are your intentions, General?"

With a gold mechanical pencil he made a series of neat symbols on the map. First, he drew a line of advance south from the Panshir Valley to the Shamali Plains north of Kabul. Then he circled several northern towns, where the Taliban and its al Qaeda allies had grouped: Taloqan, Konduz, and Mazar-e Sharif. "These are our immediate objectives. Your Air Force should concentrate its bombing to allow our forces to take these cities. Then I will move south to

Bagram." He outlined the jet plane symbol on the sheet that represented the former Soviet air force base north of Kabul.

His plan made good tactical sense. If Fahim did in fact have the loyalty of all the Northern Alliance commanders, he was poised to destroy enemy concentrations across the north and open a vital land bridge to Uzbekistan. With that route clear, we could support opposition forces via a passable highway system that ran through Central Asia all the way to Europe. Vital humanitarian support could flow to the beleaguered Afghans. And, at the end of the day, it would be the Afghans who would determine the success of our operations. If they were provided for, Phase IV (Reconstruction) would be accelerated immeasurably.

Fahim discussed the details of his tactical plan. Taloqan, he said, was a vital early objective because it would give his fighters an airfield.

"And Kabul?" I asked.

Fahim studied me with his deep-set eyes. "We will not enter Kabul until you give permission."

It was the politically correct answer. Was he sincere? That was the crucial issue. In Pakistan, I had met with several Pashtun opposition leaders from southern Afghanistan. The most impressive was Hamid Karzai, who was sophisticated and multilingual, a man equally at home among tribal chiefs, diplomats, and soldiers. Karzai had broken with the Taliban soon after their Muslim extremist regime began its repression. The CIA station in Islamabad—virtually our Afghanistan embassy in exile—supported Karzai as a future national leader who could unite the disparate ethnic factions.

And I too was impressed. We needed to build a Pashtun opposition force to fight the Taliban. I believed Karzai was just the right Pashtun leader to build that force. If enemy resistance suddenly collapsed and the Northern Alliance composed of Tajiks, Uzbeks, and Hazaras swept into the vacuum of Kabul, Afghanistan might face another civil war that pitted the northern factions against the majority Pashtuns. It was obvious from Fahim's answer that he understood and respected the problem. I wondered about his view of Hamid Karzai.

It was time to discuss the price of rugs.

"What more do you need from us?" I asked. Glancing over, I saw John Mulholland studying Fahim's face. Our Special Forces teams were already making better progress with Dostum south of Mazar-e Sharif than with Fahim's larger units in the northeast.

"General Dostum needs weapons and ammunition more than we do," Fahim said, an unexpected admission. "He can capture Mazar-e Sharif quickly if you support him."

"But what do *you* need?" I pressed.

Fahim conferred with his finance minister. "What kind of additional logistical . . . and financial support can you provide?" He looked across at Hank, avoiding my eyes.

Hank laid out a computer printout listing ammunition, communications gear, and medical supplies. "I need an airfield big enough for C-130s."

Fahim smiled politely. "Your C-130 is a famous airplane. Those with guns have destroyed the spirit of the Taliban and the Arabs."

"And if you had your supplies . . ." Hank asked.

"If I take Taloqan and its airport—" Fahim began, then turned to his money man and whispered before continuing, "—I will need three million U.S. dollars a month."

"You need three million dollars to launch your offensive and secure Mazar-e Sharif?" I asked.

Hank and I had prepared for this. He was good cop, I was bad. We waited.

"Oh, no. For the entire operation," Fahim added, "I will need seven million dollars a month."

I stood up and glared at the interpreter. "This is bullshit. Translate *that*."

I walked down the front steps of the transport, took a leak, and smoked a cigarette on the tarmac. This was the performance we had rehearsed. In the brightly lit tunnel of the cargo bay, Hank was lecturing Fahim. "General Franks is very angry."

I reentered the plane and sat down at the table. Hank nodded, and then spoke to Fahim. "It's agreed. Five million for the entire north. You will take Mazar-e Sharif before Ramadan, and stop outside Kabul until you receive permission to enter the capital."

"Yes," Fahim said.

As Fahim and his finance minister left the plane, I could picture duffle bags filled with millions of dollars being loaded into his Mercedes. I hoped the car had good springs; that many stacks of hundreds would make a heavy load.

I didn't know whether we had traded a horse or bought a carpet. But I was certain that General Mohammed Fahim Khan and the units of the Northern Alliance were going to war with us. As my father would have said, "This car needs a little work, Tommy Ray. But she's gonna be a good one in a month or two."

D URING MY LIFE, I HAD KNOWN THE "PRIMORDIAL VIOLENCE" OF war that Clausewitz had described. In Vietnam, my frame of reference had been narrow, one grid-square at a time. As a one-star general in Desert Storm, my viewpoint had been much broader, but still limited to tactical problems. Now I led a joint Coalition and had a wider vision. I trusted my subordinates. I would observe their actions, but not try to control their individual engagements, even though I had the ability to do so from CENTCOM's high-technology headquarters. I'd witnessed politicians and generals choosing targets in Vietnam; it hadn't worked then, and it wouldn't work now. CENTCOM "pushed strategy up," rather than waiting for Washington to "push tactics down."

Don Rumsfeld was a hard taskmaster—but he never tried to control the tactics of our war-fight. The same could not be said for others in the DoD bureaucracy. While Dick Myers and Pete Pace, the Vice Chairman, were quick to provide support, and slow to critique, a number of officers on the Joint Staff were on their own tactical wavelength, and it was these officers who were the focus of my strategic "push."

For me, the course of the war in Afghanistan in the first weeks of November 2001 unfolded in a blur of long video-lit days and nights—decisions made and objectives realized. (I will leave the job of recapturing every detail to the military historians.) What was important was that those fights produced victories, and the victories were historic.

Good to his word, Mohammed Fahim Khan delivered the vital towns of the north. Taloqan, Konduz, and Herat fell in rapid succession, all within a week. Tiger 02, the Special Forces team supporting General Abdul Rashid Dostum—led by a young captain, a seasoned master sergeant, and a lanky sergeant first class, whose *noms de guerre* were Mark, Paul, and Mike—fought one of the most tactically skillful and courageous small-unit actions in American military history. Facing determined enemy resistance, terrible weather, and mounting casualties among their indigenous troops, these Green Berets used maneuver and air power to destroy an army the Soviets had failed to dislodge with more than a half million men. Dostum's forces routed the Taliban and al Qaeda, and captured Mazar-e Sharif on the afternoon of November 9, 2001.

The Taliban and their *araban* auxiliaries were defeated in the north.

Other Tiger Teams operating in the south used Coalition air power to pound the enemy into submission. Hamid Karzai, who could affect the persona of a well-manicured scholar, was up to his chin in fierce combat north of Kandahar. When his forces were almost overrun by five hundred Taliban advancing up a steep valley in a convoy of pickup trucks, Karzai trusted his American Special Forces advisers, led by a brave young soldier named Captain Jason Amerine, and held his ground. Amerine's team called in repeated air strikes, some impacting within two hundred meters of Karzai's fighting positions near the provincial capital of Tarin Kot. That engagement destroyed the last of the Taliban's operational reserves; the fall of Kandahar followed quickly.

I WATCHED THE PLASMA SCREENS OF THE JOC AS DELL DAILEY'S operators choppered in to rescue the Shelter Now hostages and fly

them to Pakistan and as Marine Expeditionary Unit 15 reoccupied
Objective Rhino. As Winston Churchill said decades earlier, this was
the "beginning of the end."

O N THE MORNING OF NOVEMBER 27, 2001, I RECEIVED AN
unexpected call from Secretary Rumsfeld. At the time I was
working with Gene Renuart and the operations staff on air support
for Afghan units pushing into the Spin Mountains around Tora Bora.

"General Franks, the President wants us to look at options for
Iraq. What is the status of your planning?"

Throughout the operation in Afghanistan, the situation in Iraq
had remained an issue—it was always within my peripheral vision.
The pattern of attacks on our aircraft patrolling the no-fly zones had
triggered Response Options at varying levels. It was a low-grade war,
but a war just the same. Every morning, as I jotted my daily notes on
a fresh index card, I listed "Air crew shootdown in Iraq" as a likely
challenge.

"Mr. Secretary," I said, "we have a plan, of course. OPLAN
1003."

"What's your opinion of it, General?"

"Desert Storm II. It's out of date, under revision because conditions have changed. We have different force levels in the region than
we had when the plan was written. And we obviously have learned
some valuable lessons about precision weapons and Special Operations from our experience in Afghanistan."

"Okay, Tom," Rumsfeld said. "Please dust it off and get back to
me next week."

Son of a bitch, I thought. *No rest for the weary . . .*

"Gene," I said. "Grab Jeff Kimmons and come see me. New
work to be done."

O N THE MORNING OF DECEMBER 22, 2001, CATHY AND I SAT
side by side on the nylon sling seats of an MH-47. Outside the

Plexiglas windows, the arid winter hills of eastern Afghanistan unfolded. We were fifteen minutes south of Bagram Air Base, now the headquarters of the Coalition. The smoggy, half-ruined sprawl of Kabul lay ahead in a bowl-shaped valley.

"It looks like Los Angeles after an earthquake," I shouted over the rotor thump. The city had been battered by the years of war.

Cathy looked at me and smiled.

Gary Harrell sat opposite in the cargo bay, snoring. Like most veteran Special Operators, he could sleep in the middle of a hurricane.

I was tired, but not sleepy. For the past three days we had been crisscrossing the AOR, staging out of Oman aboard a C-17. Wayne Newton's USO troupe had traveled with us to the Marine base at Rhino, to Kandahar, and on to Pakistan, bringing Christmas cheer to the troops. And this morning, Cathy and I were attending ceremonies marking the installation of Hamid Karzai's interim government, which had been selected at a U.N.-sponsored conference in Bonn, Germany, three weeks earlier.

I knew there was still hard fighting ahead in Afghanistan. But the main resistance had been shattered. The remnants of the Taliban and al Qaeda were hiding in the snowy mountains of the southeast, subjected to relentless bombing. And twenty-five million Afghans had been liberated, in less than three months of military operations.

The helicopter landed in a rubble-strewn lot near the American Embassy. Marines in Humvees escorted our black Chevy SUVs to the government hall.

There were crowds of camera-toting reporters, jostling for position. Bearded Northern Alliance soldiers in ragged fatigues gaped at the Western dignitaries arriving in their shiny vehicles. An Afghan official in a suit and tie bowed, then led us to the entrance. "Welcome, if you please," he said, flashing gold teeth.

We passed through a metal detector guarded on each side by unsmiling Northern Alliance soldiers toting Kalashnikovs.

As we mounted the staircase toward the main hall, Cathy said, "Don't you have a gun, Tom?"

I patted the holster at the small of my back. "You bet."

Gary Harrell leaned over and winked at us. "I'm packing three handguns and two knives," he said.

"Well," Cathy replied, "that must be a *ceremonial* metal detector."

A throng from the pages of Kipling filled the echoing room, a rainbow of turbans, robes, and sashes. We took our assigned seats in the front row. Around us were representatives of over twenty Coalition partners, British, French, Germans, and other NATO allies.

Mohammed Fahim Khan dipped his head in respect. Hamid Karzai smiled warmly and shook our hands.

Banners hung on the walls, emblazoned with Persian script and English. "Death to Terrorism." "May Allah Bestow Peace and Prosperity on the World." Behind the dais hung a huge portrait of Ahmad Shah Massoud, "the Lion of Panjshir," now the nation's martyr.

A boy in a blue robe led a blind, white-bearded mullah to the podium. The old man smiled, felt for the microphone, and then began to chant Koranic verses. Everyone stood for the national anthem of the new Afghanistan, a rousing march. We had no interpreter for the speeches that followed, but it was easy to understand the mood of triumph.

After the second speaker concluded his animated remarks, he suddenly raised his right fist. "Massoud!" he called, as if in prayer himself. "Mas*soud*!"

Around us, hundreds of people raised their fists. "Massoud!" they shouted in reply. "*Massoud!*"

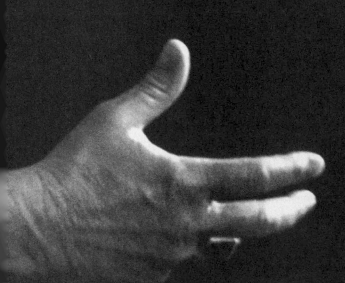

PART IV

A REVOLUTION IN WARFARE

Battles are won by slaughter and maneuver.
The greater the general, the more he contributes in
maneuver, the less he demands in slaughter.

—WINSTON CHURCHILL

9

COMMANDER'S CONCEPT

As we filed out of the ceremonial hall among the Afghan and foreign dignitaries, I spotted our convoy of SUVs through the bullet-starred lobby windows. We were scheduled to attend a reception at the Presidential Palace, fly back to Bagram Air Base on the Special Ops helicopters, and leave Afghanistan aboard a C-17 transport.

A beat-up Russian Lada police car, followed by a Marine Humvee mounting an M-60 machine gun, led our motorcade. From our Chevy Suburban we had a good view of the teeming streets, which looked like a blend of newsreels from bombed-out Berlin and a 1950s travelogue of the "Exotic East." Kabul had suffered years of shelling during the wars of the past two decades. Now, the blocks of roofless buildings had become home to thousands of returning refugees. I saw families piling up scavenged bricks to form cubicles inside the ruins. The predominant color—a dusty brown—was dotted by the bright blue of the ubiquitous UN plastic shelter tarps. I also spotted white USAID flour sacks emblazoned with American flags, and stacks of the yellow

Humanitarian Daily Rations our C-17s had dropped by the pallet-load for weeks.

All along the wide avenue, vendors sold kebabs from smoking grills, as well as pots and pans and sweaters, scarves, and caps in gaudy yellows and reds. Many women still hid beneath blue *burqas,* but we also saw women in Western dress, and even a few teenage girls in jeans. Only weeks earlier, that would have cost them a public flogging from the enforcers of the Ministry of Vice and Virtue.

"Look, Tom," Cathy said, pointing across the street.

A group of little schoolgirls, wearing black-and-white uniforms, stood with their teacher waving Afghan and American flags at the long motorcade of dignitaries en route to the Palace. The Taliban had not allowed girls to attend school.

Gary Harrell rolled down his window. "Listen," he said.

A young entrepreneur in a baseball cap stood at his packing-crate kiosk peddling music cassettes. From the speakers of his boom box, a woman singer was belting out a soulful Pashtun love song, accompanied by *tabla* drums and double-reed flutes.

The Taliban had banned music as blasphemy. Now, they and their al Qaeda allies were on the run, dead, or sitting in prison camps—and music had returned to the streets of Kabul.

"Sounds like freedom to me," I said.

Life in Afghanistan was returning to normal—moving slowly and painfully, but steadily, toward the future, and away from the medieval darkness of the past. We had launched Operation Enduring Freedom, I reminded myself, on October 7. Today, only seventy-six days later, most of the nation had been liberated. The remnants of the Taliban had retreated into the trackless high country north of Kandahar, or had joined al Qaeda survivors taking refuge in the mountains of the southeast. And Afghan troops under Commander Hazrat Ali—supported by American, European, and Australian SOF—were closing on the enemy in the Tora Bora region.

In my last phone conversation with President Musharraf, I learned that the Pakistani Army's 11th Corps was sealing its side of the border and had rounded up hundreds of fleeing Taliban and al Qaeda who had struggled over the snowy passes from Afghanistan. Many were disillusioned young Pakistani volunteers, whose madrasa teachers had convinced them to fight in Afghanistan to protect Islam. These battle-weary jihadists had never counted on waging their holy war against Special Mission Units and Spectre gunships.

"We have about seventy Arab prisoners," Musharraf had told me. "They're al Qaeda, mostly Saudis and Yemenis. I will turn them over to you."

And he confirmed our earlier agreement about incursions by Coalition forces over the ill-defined border into Pakistan when "in hot pursuit" of Taliban and al Qaeda. "Your troops are very disciplined," he commented. "I know they will be discreet."

We left it that way. I passed word to Bert Calland and Dell Dailey, and to the British and Australian SAS: Our friends in Islamabad wanted the terrorists dead or captured just as much as we did.

And we were pounding the Taliban and al Qaeda from the air, day and night, with laser-guided GBUs and JDAMs, and with the AC-130 Spectres. We had solved the technical problems of establishing real-time video and data links between the Predators flying recon and the AC-130s. What the CIA and Air Force Predator operators were watching on their plasma screens in the Langley parking lot and the CAOC in Saudi Arabia, the targeting officers were also watching onboard the gunships patrolling north of Kandahar and above the Spin Mountains. When the UAVs spotted the enemy, the AC-130s would arrive in a matter of minutes.

Combat operations had gone remarkably well. But I knew the war was not over. Hazrat Ali reported that a large group of Arabs had taken refuge in the redoubt of caves and tunnels southwest of the Khyber Pass. And Ali's Afghan troops had encountered fierce resistance from heavily armed fighters dug into concentric defensive rings.

Tora Bora would be a "gunfight," and it would happen soon—before any al Qaeda leaders who might be holed up there could escape.

Before leaving CENTCOM headquarters, I'd discussed with Gene Renuart and our Ground Component Commander, Lt. General P. T. Mikolashek, the Coalition force structure we would use to stabilize the country.

Secretary Rumsfeld and I agreed that we should not flood the country with large formations of conventional troops. "We don't want to repeat the Soviets' mistakes," I told the Secretary. "There's nothing to be gained by blundering around those mountains and gorges with armor battalions chasing a lightly armed enemy." This was the time to confirm our strategy. "I plan to keep the force small. We'll tailor it to meet the mission, not try to build a mission around the force."

Our footprint had to be small, for both military and geopolitical reasons. I envisioned a total of about 10,000 American soldiers, airmen, special operators, and helicopter air assault crews, along with robust in-country close air support. The three brigades from the 10th Mountain and 101st Airborne (Air Assault) Divisions, as well as the Marine Expeditionary Units now at Camp Rhino and Kandahar, seemed about right. Mikolashek had the task and was working it.

Now, as I arrived at the Presidential Palace, I saw the scars that years of war and anarchy had left on the echoing reception room. The polished floor, once graced with wide carpets, now showed only dark rectangles; the carpets had been stolen or damaged in the fighting that had plagued Afghanistan for so many years. Brightly uniformed Palace waiters graciously offered tea and sweet sherbet drinks in chipped and mismatched cups and glasses.

But the atmosphere was festive, triumphant. This was the first time most of these victorious Afghans had met socially in years. Many of them had been enemies—and sometimes allies—in the decade of strife between the Soviet withdrawal in 1989 and the solidification of Taliban power in the late 1990s. Now they were members of a victorious and unprecedented multiethnic alliance that had both liberated twenty-five million people and unified the country.

This reception was the equivalent of a winning team's post–Super Bowl celebration. Most of the commanders spoke Dari, the Afghan Persian lingua franca. As I made the rounds of the ballroom, though, I passed a couple of age-worn fighters—one in a tan pakol, the other in a saffron turban—making do in pidgin Russian, their only common language. The men bowed, shook my hand, and then swept their palms to their hearts as a sign of respect.

Had I been a proconsul, I would have worn a purple-trimmed toga and a laurel wreath. But I preferred to appear in the DCUs and tan boots of an American soldier. It was a reminder that the force I had commanded—together with these Afghan brothers-in-arms—had liberated, not conquered, their nation.

The circle of well-wishers around Hamid Karzai respectfully opened as Cathy and I approached.

"Sir," I said, offering my hand. "This is a great day for Afghanistan."

He smiled and dipped his head in respect to Cathy. "General Franks," he said, addressing me in fluent English, "this is a great day for the entire world. America gave us the tools to defeat tyranny."

We left Karzai to the lines of fellow citizens waiting to offer their congratulations and allegiance.

General Mohammed Fahim Khan strode across the room, arms spread, grinning broadly, and gave me a rib-cracking hug. Fahim was wearing a pinstriped suit; as Afghanistan's presumptive minister of defense, he'd soon be engaged in the political as well as the military future of his country.

Skipping the normal pleasantries, Fahim stared at me intently; he spoke slowly and deliberately, so that the interpreter caught every word.

"General Franks," he told me, "I am Panjshiri. I will be accused in the days ahead of having desires to become the president of Afghanistan." He waited for the translation to finish. "Some will think I want the Northern Alliance to remain the most powerful force in the country."

I nodded; he wasn't wrong about that.

"General," he continued in the same tone, "you should not believe this. I am and I will remain loyal to the Pashtun, Hamid Karzai, because I believe the future of Afghanistan is all that matters. At this point in history, Hamid Karzai is the man to assure our future."

"General Fahim Khan," I said, addressing him formally. "I agree with your view of history."

He allowed a slight smile to cross his face, then reached out and gripped my hand. "Do you remember when we met in Dushanbe, Tajikistan?"

I nodded again.

"I did not know you," he continued. "And you did not know me. But, General, now we know each other. You must admit that what I told you I would do, I have done."

"Sir," I replied, "you and your comrades have accomplished more than I could have ever expected."

Now he smiled. "General Franks, you asked me at that meeting if I would trust you with my life. Now, General, after what we have done, I hope that you would trust me with your life."

"I trust you completely," I answered.

Cathy and I circulated among the guests, drinking the obligatory tea and juice while chatting with the other commanders. At one point, General Dostum approached me, gripped my hand hard, and smiled. "Good afternoon, General. I'm honored to see you here." He released my hand, came to attention, and inclined his head. "You are a great leader and I am at your service. Who do you want me to fight now?"

He was serious. The Afghans had been at war for most of their lives. *Bringing stability to this country,* I thought, *will be no quick and easy process.*

"Sometimes, General," I said, "a soldier must wage peace, not war." Dostum paused, as if he had just been exposed to a new concept. Then he smiled.

When it was time to leave, I looked around for the restrooms. "Gotta find the boys' room."

"And the girls' room," Cathy added.

When my interpreter asked a senior servant about the nearest facilities, though, he drew a puzzled stare. An older man with a trimmed gray beard and a sapphire turban was summoned, but he too seemed confused. *Where do these people go to take a leak?* I wondered.

Finally, we were led down a corridor to a small, dark room. As I stepped through the door and groped for a light, the stench rose around me. The Presidential Palace was the epitome of luxury in Kabul, but in this part of the building there was no electricity. And, as the pool of sewage on the floor made clear, no operable plumbing. Fortunately I was wearing my boots; Cathy had chosen sensible walking shoes, and the penlight she'd stashed in her purse was a welcome accessory.

As we left the building, walking down the cracked marble stairs toward the waiting vehicles, I pictured the refugee families squatting in their ruins, no electricity, running water, or sanitation. Cathy and I exchanged a glance.

"Room for improvement, Tom," she said.

"It's going to be a *long* time before these people have the basic necessities for a decent life," I said. "We've only made a beginning in this country,"

When we climbed into the SUV, Gary Harrell was sitting in the right front seat, listening to a small tactical radio. He acknowledged the message, then turned back to face me, frowning.

"Sir," he said, "little change of plans. We'll be driving back to Bagram in the trucks."

I could tell something had happened. "Let's have it, Gary."

"General, the second helo pilot reported a corkscrew off the port-side of our bird on the flight down. I've laid on road security with the Afghans all the way back to Bagram. We'll be safer on the road."

We'd been fired upon. A "corkscrew" was soldier's jargon for a shoulder-fired missile, probably an SA-7. The term described the spiral smoke trail as the rocket sought its target. Although the Special Ops helicopters had electronic equipment to divert heat-seeking missiles, there was no sense pushing our luck. Negotiating forty-five kilometers of road, recently swept of mines, would be safer than flying.

Cathy understood the conversation, but she was steadfast and calm as always.

"Got it, Gary," I said. "Let's go."

"Right, Sir."

I reached over and tapped his sleeve. "Just remember, I'll be really pissed off if you get us killed. And so will Cathy." I winked at her.

"No worry, General," Gary said.

On the ride up the valley to Bagram, we passed scores of wrecked tanks, trucks, and buses that had struck mines at some point in Afghanistan's violent history. As we drove, I looked into the eyes of the Afghans we passed. They were tired eyes, but filled with hope. I was glad we'd taken this beat-up road; it gave us a chance to see a few of the twenty-five million people who now had a chance for a better life.

O N THURSDAY, DECEMBER 27, WE'D BEEN AIRBORNE FOR ABOUT an hour, homeward bound after an overnight in Sicily, when I got down to work in the plane's small conference room. Cathy was resting, trying to catch up on lost sleep from the hectic leapfrog schedule around the AOR. In the past five days, we had visited Oman, Afghanistan, Pakistan, seven Coalition bases, and five U.S. Navy ships, spending Christmas with the sailors on two carriers in the northern Arabian Sea. We'd been on C-17s, C-130s, three kinds of helicopters, and a twin-turboprop Carrier Onboard Delivery plane (COD), which had given Cathy the thrill of her first flight-deck tail-hook landing and catapult-launch takeoff.

Despite the pace of the trip, I was glad that Cathy and I had been able to spend Christmas together because I knew I wouldn't have much time at home in the coming weeks. With stability operations in Afghanistan moving ahead well, I would have to turn my attention to the task Secretary Rumsfeld had given me during the Thanksgiving holidays: bringing our Iraq planning up to date.

"Your homework, General," said Van Mauney, laying a stack of orange-bordered Top Secret file folders on the table before me.

The folders contained the latest "iteration" in the painstaking revision process that began in late November. In the four weeks since then, I had briefed Donald Rumsfeld several times, in person and via video teleconference. Hundreds of hours of work had gone into the effort. But as I opened the top folder, I knew we were just beginning a long, deliberate process.

We did not yet have a plan for decisive military operations against the Baathist regime of Saddam Hussein. If the President ever chose to conduct such an operation, the final OPLAN would be hundreds of pages long, with thousands of pages of specialized appendices covering everything from basing and staging to emergency landing fields, to the frequencies of enemy air defense radars, to the number of MREs to be shipped to the forces.

What the SecDef had requested on November 27 was not a new plan. He'd asked me to give him a "Commander's Concept"—the philosophical underpinnings of what might eventually become a plan. It was that concept, which had taken three weeks to complete, that filled the folders.

The existing plan, OPLAN 1003, had last been updated after Desert Fox in 1998, but it was based on Desert Storm–era thinking. It was troop-heavy, involving a long buildup and a series of air strikes before boots hit the ground. It didn't account for our current troop dispositions, advances in Precision-Guided Munitions, or breakthroughs in command-and-control technology—not to mention the lessons we were learning in Afghanistan.

On the afternoon of December 4, 2001, seven days after that conversation, Gene Renuart and I met in the J-2 conference room in the SCIF and presented the first iteration of my Commander's Concept to Rumsfeld and JCS Chairman Dick Myers in the Pentagon via secure VTC.

Before the camera focus shifted to Rumsfeld and Myers, I saw that JCS Vice Chairman General Pete Pace and Under Secretary of Defense for Policy Douglas J. Feith were also attending the session. I certainly had no problem with Pete Pace sitting in. He was one of the brightest, most energetic officers I knew.

But Doug Feith was another matter. No one could deny Feith's academic achievements; he had a *magna cum laude* bachelor's from Harvard and another *magna* from Georgetown Law School. But Feith was a theorist whose ideas were often impractical; among some uniformed officers in the Building, he had a reputation for confusing abstract memoranda with results in the field. My dealings with him had left me ambivalent: I liked him personally, but I wasn't convinced that the Secretary was always well-served by his advice. Feith was a master of the off-the-wall question that rarely had relevance to operational problems. It was obvious that Don Rumsfeld trusted him, and I wanted to use the products of his intellect. But I had little time—or inclination—to answer Feith's "mind teasers." So I generally ignored his contributions, and focused on what the Secretary had to say. And Rumsfeld never allowed Feith to interfere in my business. I was always thankful for that.

I turned to the charts and expanded on the major points.

"Mr. Secretary," I said, pointing to the first page: ASSUMPTIONS. "If we initiate military operations in Iraq, I am assuming the principal objective will be to remove the regime of Saddam Hussein."

I had not asked Donald Rumsfeld's permission to propose this assumption. That's not how military strategists operate. My duty was to recommend the most effective and decisive employment of our armed forces in solving a particular problem. The civilian leadership—the Secretary of Defense and the President of the United States—would determine whether my strategic assumptions were appropriate.

I waited a moment, watching Rumsfeld consider my words.

"General," he said after a pause. "That is my assumption, too. The President will ultimately make that decision."

"And, Mr. Secretary," I continued, "my second assumption is that if we conduct military operations, the objective will be to leave Iraq without the military capacity to threaten its neighbors with either conventional forces or weapons of mass destruction."

Rumsfeld nodded. "I agree. If—and I emphasize *if*—this operation occurs, we will leave Iraq a unified nation with the ability to defend itself."

"Sir," I said, "you already know what I think of OPLAN 1003. But it is the plan we have today. It details force structure, logistics, and all the other requirements for a major operation. It's too big, too slow, and out-of-date. But if Saddam miscalculates, as he's prone to do, and shoots down one of our aircraft, launches missiles into Kuwait or Israel, or decides to attack the Kurds, we need to have some practical and immediate response prepared."

Rumsfeld weighed this logic. "Cruise missiles and air strikes?"

"It's what we have on the books right now, Mr. Secretary," I continued. "It's stale, conventional, predictable. Worst of all, it is premised on continuing the policy of containment. My Commander's Concept has a different set of objectives."

I flipped a page and pointed to ENDSTATE, and to two red-highlighted starbursts: REGIME CHANGE and WMD REMOVAL.

Rumsfeld and Myers studied the page. "General," Rumsfeld said, "let's get back to the existing plan. After initial air strikes, the ground-force buildup takes an inordinate amount of time."

"We can do better. I wanted to show you *what we have* before proposing *where we go*."

"Proceed, General," Rumsfeld said with a smile.

Donald Rumsfeld usually liked his briefings swift and concise. This one moved more slowly; he obviously wanted to lay a solid foundation for whatever circumstances might develop in the coming months. The intelligence community had been speculating about a possible connection between Saddam's regime and known terrorists, including al Qaeda. The evidence was not airtight, but it was certain that several terrorist camps of the Ansar al Islam group were up and running in northern Iraq.

These camps were examples of the terrorist "harbors" that President Bush had vowed to crush. One known terrorist, a Jordanian-born Palestinian named Abu Musab Zarqawi who had joined al Qaeda in Afghanistan—where he specialized in developing chemical and biological weapons—was now confirmed to operate from one of the camps in Iraq. Badly wounded fighting Coalition forces in Afghanistan, Zarqawi had received medical treatment in Baghdad before setting up with Ansar al Islam. And evidence suggested that he had been joined there by other al Qaeda leaders, who had been ushered through Baghdad and given safe passage into northern Iraq by Iraqi security forces.

What was especially troubling about this intelligence were reports that Zarqawi and his al Qaeda colleagues were using the camps to train other terrorists for WMD attacks in France, Britain, Chechnya, and the former Soviet Republic of Georgia. (In January 2003, when British police broke up a terrorist cell in Manchester that Zarqawi had helped train, they discovered traces of ricin, the deadly biological toxin, in the terrorists' flat; reports indicated that they were plotting to use it to poison the food supply on military bases across Britain.)

If the evidence were confirmed that the Iraqi regime was in fact linked to al Qaeda, there would be an insatiable appetite in Washington for immediate action. Our Special Operators had discovered proof in Afghanistan that the terrorists were trying to acquire a chemical and biological capability. And the U.N. inspectors' January 1999 report stated that Iraq could have ample supplies of such weapons.

Saddam Hussein, a dictator bent on repressing Shia Muslims, and Osama bin Laden, one of the world's foremost Islamic extremists—if these two were indeed collaborating, it was proof that war made strange bedfellows. Yet I knew that money transcended both ideology and faith, and bin Laden had plenty of money. Any power that could provide al Qaeda with nerve agents or anthrax was a major strategic concern, and Saddam was very likely in a position to make such elements available for the right price.

It would have been foolish not to consider our options for eliminating that threat.

As I concluded my summary of the existing 1003 plan, I noted that we'd trimmed planned force levels from 500,000 troops to around 400,000. But even that was still way too large, I told the Secretary. "This is not 1990. The Iraqi military today is not the one we faced in 1991. And our own forces are much different. We see that in Afghanistan. We need to refine our assumptions."

I told the Secretary that I wanted to develop new options for Iraq, and he agreed. From that point on it was clear: Don Rumsfeld was eager to be part of the solution.

My briefings to Rumsfeld—and to the President—would be based on a simple philosophy: Never assume that the boss knows all there is to know about an issue when he sits down at the table. Give him every piece of information you think he needs, even if it's laborious. Rumsfeld's famous impatience sometimes made this tough. But it was better that he understood every aspect of an issue before he reached a decision, even if it meant breaking the problem at hand down into the most fundamental terms. I have known officers who go through their careers trying to sound smart by making simple issues seem complex. My preference has always been to make the complex simple enough to be understood. War is a complex business, but it is composed of straightforward elements. And only if we all understood those elements were we likely to reach the same—and the right—conclusions.

If one reason to brief the boss was to educate him, the other was to stimulate him. When Donald Rumsfeld requested that we consider a new strategic approach to Iraq, I set out to educate him on the fundamentals—and to stimulate him to support my conclusions. Sometimes I succeeded. Other times I did not. But the process of "iterations" we began during that early December meeting would stimulate us both.

"If we intend to remove Saddam's regime," I said, turning to the next chart, "we will have to consider a range of operational requirements—basing, staging, overflight, deployment, logistics, sustainment, command and control, and intelligence. In Afghanistan, these requirements presented one set of problems. For Iraq, the basic problems remain, but the scale will be larger."

I lifted the OPTIONS page.

"What strategic options do we have? OPTION ONE." I flipped the sheet. "I call this the ROBUST OPTION," I explained.

"Were every country in the region to join us and offer complete support, including basing, staging, overflight, financial assistance, and maybe even troops," I continued, "this would indeed be the optimal situation."

I gestured to the map to illustrate my point. "This way, we could operate without restriction from Turkey in the north, Jordan and Saudi Arabia in the west and south, from Kuwait, and from air and naval bases in all the Gulf states. In addition, we could draw on support from Egypt and stage forces in Central Asia—as well as in Hungary, Romania, and Bulgaria, where we are continuing to upgrade former Warsaw Pact bases."

I presented a diagram showing hypothetical ground, Special Forces, and air operations launched from the north, west, and south, and from carriers in the Mediterranean, the Red Sea, and the Arabian Gulf. "This option has the advantage of allowing us to conduct simultaneous or near-simultaneous operations, Mr. Secretary. Simultaneous operations, not separate air and ground campaigns, represent optimum mass."

I turned to the next chart. "The second possibility is the REDUCED OPTION," I said. "This option is premised on operating from fewer countries, with reduced basing, staging, and overflight. It would mean a less simultaneous introduction of forces, and a more sequential attack of the target sets. It is a more conventional approach—air first, and then ground."

The next chart was UNILATERAL OPTION. "Here we assume minimum staging, basing, and overflight—our only operating bases would be in Kuwait and on carriers in the Gulf. This operation would be absolutely sequential. We would have to introduce our ground forces gradually, because there is simply not enough infrastructure in Kuwait to stage large formations at the same time. This is not an option we would want to execute."

That marked the end of the briefing. "Mr. Secretary, I know you are not *fulfilled* by what I've given you today. But it is a beginning, and I wanted to make sure we were on the same page on strategic assumptions and support options."

"Well, General, you have a lot of work ahead of you," he said, stacking the pages. "Today is Tuesday. Let's get together again next Wednesday, December 12. I want to hear more details at that time."

The screen went blank. Gene had been taking notes in his oversized journal; the staff called it the "Black Book of Death," because the workload it represented was enough to kill even the hardiest group of staff officers.

"Hey, Boss," Gene said. "Things are looking up. The Secretary just gave us eight whole days. Last time it was only a week."

"Piece of cake, J-3," I said.

The staff was already working seven sixteen-plus-hour days a week. But I knew that producing this next iteration of the Commander's Concept wouldn't be too demanding—because I already had a model in mind.

For the next several days I spent my time brainstorming; when I wasn't in my office with Gene, I was with our senior Operations staff or with Jeff Kimmons, and the Intel crew in the SCIF. During the hectic twenty-six days we'd just spent planning Afghanistan, I had developed a planning technique that focused on "Lines of Operation"—the tasks any given mission would call for—and "Slices," the various aspects of the country that would be affected by the lines of operation.

As I thought about a potential operation in Iraq, a number of obvious lines of operation presented themselves. One was KINETICS: OPERATIONAL FIRES—the firing of TLAMs and air strikes from manned bombers, as well as close air support from fighter-bombers and AC-130 Spectres, and eventually Marine and Army helicopter gunships. Another line was OPERATIONAL MANEUVER—conventional ground forces. Another was SPECIAL FORCES. And there were other important lines, both political and diplomatic: HUMANITARIAN ASSISTANCE, INFORMATION OPERATIONS, DECEPTION.

The diplomatic line would involve work by the State Department, the CIA, my personal contacts in the region, and the heavy hitters—President Bush, Vice President Cheney, and Secretaries Rumsfeld and Powell.

I knew that Iraq would differ in complexity from Afghanistan by several orders of magnitude. Our objectives in Afghanistan had been to remove the Taliban and destroy al Qaeda's base of operations, and to accomplish this we had focused our lines on a limited number of targets. Destroying enemy ground formations had been one of our most important tasks, and many of our lines of operation had supported this task.

Iraq represented a vastly more difficult challenge. Although diminished since the Gulf War, Iraq's military still fielded a force roughly ten times larger than the Taliban and al Qaeda combined. And, unlike the enemy in Afghanistan, Iraq's forces were equipped with an impressive array of armor, artillery, and air defense systems.

Afghanistan under the Taliban had been a brutal theocracy. Saddam's Iraq was a twenty-first century totalitarian police state, with highly centralized leadership that survived and wielded power through a well-developed internal intelligence and security apparatus that spread outward from Saddam Hussein, his two sons, Uday and Qusay, and their circle of fellow al-Bu Nasir tribesmen from the region of Tikrit.

The organizations that kept Saddam in power included the Iraqi Intelligence Service—the dreaded *Mukhabarat*—and the Special Security Organization, the *Al Amn al-Khas*. The Special Republican Guard provided physical security for regime leadership. And the core of Iraq's military power resided in the combat formations of the Republican Guard. These organizations were analogous to Hitler's Gestapo, SS security forces, and his Waffen SS armor and mechanized infantry divisions—with a good measure of Soviet KGB internal security thrown in.

Saddam ruled through brutal repression and fear. He had also developed a huge and loyal following by lavishly rewarding the most faithful members of his regime and their families. Once the UN oil embargo had begun after the Gulf War, Saddam had siphoned off billions of dollars of Oil for Food Program revenues to continue this system of rewards, building huge palace complexes while continuing to invest in covert and illegal weapons programs.

Unlike Afghanistan, which Donald Rumsfeld once disparaged as having a "handful of radar stations, a few tanks, and lots of pickup trucks full of zealots," Iraq contained hundreds of strategically significant targets. As we fleshed out our concept during that week in mid-December 2001, I began to create a conceptual diagram of how, should the President order it, CENTCOM would apply the necessary lines of operation to attack or influence what Clausewitz had described more than one hundred years before as the enemy's "centers of gravity"—the slices.

I envisioned the slices as a series of pillars, a kind of Stonehenge that supported the weight of the Baathists and Saddam Hussein. Early one morning, I took a pad and began to draw the columns that represented the foundations of Iraqi power. I then added columns to represent the essential elements of the Iraqi nation and people. A military campaign would affect not only Saddam and his followers, but also Iraq's civilian population, its economic infrastructure—including oil and water resources—and its natural environment.

In Afghanistan, our military objectives had been relatively straightforward—to remove the Taliban regime, destroy al Qaeda and its operating and training bases, and prevent resurgence of the terrorist support structure—and we had accomplished our mission. The Taliban no longer existed, as either a government or a cohesive military force. Al Qaeda had lost hundreds of its best-trained and experienced leaders and fighters; its operating and training bases were rubble, and its soldiers were on the run.

But to achieve even those simple objectives in Afghanistan, the lines of operation had been complex and rigorous. The Diplomatic line had required negotiations and backroom bargaining to secure the staging, basing, and overflight we needed to employ military force effectively in the landlocked country. The Special Operations line had included not only insertion and support, but also sustaining the Northern Alliance and other opposition groups, often by helicopter lift or airdrop. The Operational Fires line had required unprecedented coordination of air and naval assets. The Humanitarian Assistance line had involved the United Nations and scores of nongovernmental organizations. And building the "Coalition of the Willing" into a practical and efficient force had involved an extraordinarily intense inter-agency effort in Washington and around the world.

The lines of operation for Iraq would be even more complex. Our policy goal would be to remove Saddam Hussein from power—hopefully by diplomacy, but by military force if necessary. To do so, we would have to influence the pressure points that kept him in power. Only if the regime were threatened would Saddam comply with the U.N. Security Council resolutions, which he had flouted at every turn for more than a decade.

In theory, diplomatic and economic pressure under an umbrella of military threat might cause Saddam to disarm. By this logic, war was merely one of several options. The State Department was optimistic that the United Nations might resume the type of effective inspections that had unearthed huge stockpiles of Iraqi weapons of mass destruction in the 1990s.

Many on Capitol Hill—and in the Pentagon—hoped that exiles under the leadership of Ahmad Chalabi and the Iraqi National Congress might ride a groundswell of popular discontent to bring down Saddam. And there was the possibility of intensifying international financial pressure to force changes in Iraq.

Indeed, the Lines of Operation I listed on my legal pad involved much more than troops, tanks, and planes:

- OPERATIONAL FIRES
- SOF OPERATIONS
- OPERATIONAL MANEUVER
- INFORMATION OPS
- UNCONVENTIONAL WARFARE/SUPPORT OPPOSITION GROUPS
- POLITICAL-MILITARY
- CIVIL-MILITARY OPERATIONS

Next, I began to list what I envisioned as the "Slices" we would need to effect in order to accomplish the goal of removing the regime. After several hours, I settled on nine Slices—the columns that kept Saddam in power:

- LEADERSHIP
- INTERNAL SECURITY/REGIME INTELLIGENCE
- WMD INFRASTRUCTURE/R&D
- REPUBLICAN GUARD/SPECIAL REPUBLICAN GUARD FORCES
- SELECTED REGULAR ARMY FORCES
- TERRITORY (SOUTH, NORTH, WEST)
- INFRASTRUCTURE
- CIVILIAN POPULATION
- COMMERCIAL AND DIPLOMATIC LEVERAGE

I then created a matrix, matching the Lines as rows with the Slices as columns.

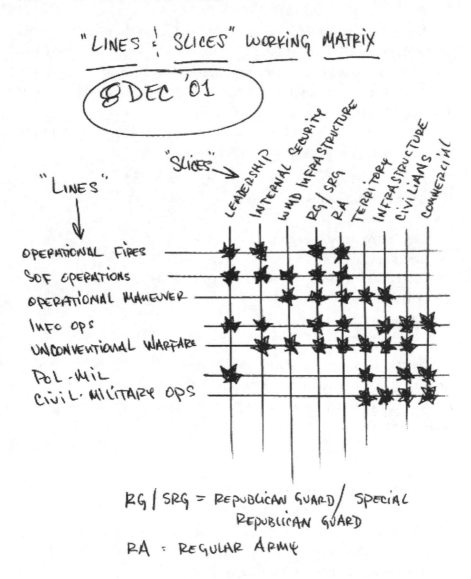

"LINES & SLICES" WORKING MATRIX

8 DEC '01

"Slices" →

"LINES" ↓

| | LEADERSHIP | INTERNAL SECURITY | WMD INFRASTRUCTURE | RG/SRG | RA | TERRITORY | INFRASTRUCTURE | CIVILIANS | COMMERCIAL |

OPERATIONAL FIRES
SOF OPERATIONS
OPERATIONAL MANEUVER
INFO OPS
UNCONVENTIONAL WARFARE
POL-MIL
CIVIL-MILITARY OPS

RG/SRG = REPUBLICAN GUARD/ SPECIAL
REPUBLICAN GUARD

RA = REGULAR ARMY

The starbursts at the intersections of Lines and Slices represented points of focus we would use to develop the specifics of a detailed plan. For example, the starburst at the intersection of "Operational Fires" and "Leadership" meant we would attack leadership targets using bombs and missiles. Simply stated, the starbursts helped the Component Commanders and staff match specific military tools to specific targets, resulting in better synergy among traditionally independent arms and services.

Before proceeding further, I called in my resident strategic wizard, Gene Renuart.

"General," he said, leaning over my desk and tilting the pad to read my tightly packed printing. "This is interesting."

"Should I continue this drill? Does it lead anywhere?"

"If you don't, I will," Gene said.

I made a show of grabbing back the pad. "Go back to your Doomsday Book," I said with a grin, hefting the pad as if it weighed twenty pounds. "This is what you call your basic *grand strategy.*"

By the night of Tuesday, December 11, we were ready for a walk-through of the next afternoon's VTC with Donald Rumsfeld. Because the iterative evolution of the Commander's Concept was a sensitive and highly classified process, I'd limited staff participation to a handful of senior officers. And Gene had personally supervised a trooper in the Operations shop as he produced the graphics.

I knew there would be adjustments to the Lines and Slices—additions, consolidations, and swap-outs—as we worked through future iterations. As I examined the work my staff had produced under extreme time constraints, though, I believed we had a template that could produce a decisive victory—should the President decide that the time had come to remove Saddam Hussein and his regime from power.

"Is it too much razzle-dazzle for the SecDef, General?" Gene asked.

"No," I said. "I think he'll like it. This is important, complex information, without extra decorations pinned on just to impress the audience. It's written in English, and you've avoided using acronyms." Donald Rumsfeld has about a five-second span of interest in briefing graphics that use baroque ornamentation to state the obvious. "You don't show the SecDef a chart that explains that a circle is round," I said. "But he'll be interested in this."

And interested he was. Our VTC the following afternoon, scheduled for forty-five minutes, ran twice as long.

"General Franks," Rumsfeld asked when I'd completed the briefing, "what's next?"

Aware that we might move from the conceptual to the practical at any time, I chose my words carefully. "Mr. Secretary," I said, "we want to begin now to improve our force posture in the region."

"The President has not made a decision to go to war, and we can take no action that commits the nation to do so," Rumsfeld said.

That was understood. But if there were even a chance of attacking Saddam in the foreseeable future, there were steps we could take to strengthen our presence in the region, without showing our hand. "Mr. Secretary, we can triple the size of the conventional ground force in Kuwait as a hedge against miscalculation by Saddam, while we continue ops in Afghanistan. We can increase the number of aircraft carrier battle groups in the region from one to three, cycling them in and out, but always having three within short steaming distance should events require a larger air capability. We can begin infrastructure improvements in the region. And we can begin to discuss contingency requirements with some of our allies—without committing America to war."

Dick Myers was taking notes as I spoke; I realized that my recommendations this afternoon could become policy tomorrow. *Be careful what you wish for,* I reminded myself; *you just might get it.*

"How visible will these activities be?" Rumsfeld asked.

"Mr. Secretary, the troop increases in Kuwait will be seen as training exercises, and we can time the carrier cruises to draw minimum attention. I don't envision any CNN moments, but there is no guarantee."

Intel had reported that Saddam and his military advisers accepted what they saw on CNN as holy writ, assuming that the cable channel would report all critical developments. To the Iraqis, the open Western media may have been less politically useful than the Arab press and the al-Jazeera network—but it was more reliable.

"I'm thinking in terms of spikes, Mr. Secretary—spurts of activity followed by periods of inactivity. We want the Iraqis to become accustomed to military expansion, and then *apparent* contraction."

I moved my open hand up and down. "I see this as a sine wave—peaks and valleys. If nothing happens for a few weeks after a spike, they'll get used to us adjusting our force levels. Do you remember the boy who cried wolf? We're staging a lot of our Afghanistan operations out of the Gulf. Nobody would notice if we doubled the number of B-1 and B-52 bombers on Diego Garcia or in Oman."

I gestured again, as if pushing a weight.

"We can also expand our materiel base," I added. "I'd like to move the weapons and equipment we've got pre-positioned in Qatar up to Kuwait. If we use Army intra-theater ships to do this, we can transport tanks, Bradleys, and artillery for an entire brigade without raising any eyebrows."

"Interesting," the Secretary murmured. "How much is all this going to cost, General Franks?"

With Rumsfeld, money was always an issue. "A lot," I said. "I'll get back to you with the number."

Of course, I'd already begun thinking about the money. I would need to establish a Special Operations Joint Task Force in either Qatar or Kuwait as soon as possible, and I also hoped to ship CENTCOM's new deployable command post to Qatar when it was completed and all the information systems had been tested. The Command had been steadily enlarging its operational footprint in Qatar for three years. We had completed about 70 percent of the troop infrastructure at the Army's prepositioned storage site Camp As Sayliyah near Doha, with barracks, mess halls, and even a gym and swimming pool. So Qatar could absorb a build-up. If we were going to increase our military presence to a credible level, we'd also need a Marine Expeditionary Brigade stationed offshore on ships. And more strike aircraft would require more aerial refueling tankers and an enhanced CSAR capability. . . . The list, as they say, went on and on.

"How long will all this take?" Rumsfeld asked. We'd begun this spin-up two weeks earlier as a conceptual exercise; now the Secretary wanted to know what the timeline looked like.

I did some quick calculation. "Mr. Secretary, if we do this using spikes, we'll wind up with about a hundred thousand troops, two hundred tanks, one hundred attack helicopters, and two hundred and fifty strike aircraft in about six months. This would become a standing force in theater. We could train it, exercise it, kick up clouds of dust in the desert. CNN might get breathless for a day or two. But that would not provoke Saddam into an ill-considered reaction."

Rumsfeld listened thoughtfully.

"It would be a hedge against uncertainty, Sir," I continued. "All or some of the force might be needed in Somalia, the Sudan, or Afghanistan. With a force of that size, you can quickly add ground forces, grow the air component to several Air Expeditionary Wings, and send in additional carrier battle groups when they're needed."

With Dick Myers still taking notes, I continued. "With a heavy Army division and increased command and control, and adding the necessary bits and pieces . . . over time, we'll have around four hundred attack aircraft, two hundred and sixty attack helicopters, five hundred and fifty tanks, and two hundred and thirty thousand troops in the region."

"All those troops wouldn't fit into Kuwait," Rumsfeld said.

"Not today, Mr. Secretary. Neither would the land-based aircraft. And we wouldn't want all the planes there. Kuwait's too close to Iraqi missiles and WMD. So we're going to need enhanced basing up and down the Gulf."

"General," Rumsfeld said, smiling, "this is a good beginning, but I need more detail before I take it to the President. I don't know what he will decide to do, but you need to work more quickly than the military usually works."

I glanced at Gene again. We were iterating this exercise in one-week bites; it was hard to imagine moving any faster. I explained that I was leaving in a week to attend Hamid Karzai's inauguration in Kabul. "Sir, I'd like some time to refine our assumptions and analyze the elements we've identified as necessary to execute this concept. I recommend we begin the inter-agency work that will be necessary with State and the intelligence community."

"Let's talk next week," Rumsfeld had said. "I want this to be worked by a very small group. There are still too many leakers, and this must not be leaked. Thanks, everyone." The screen went black.

On the morning of Wednesday, December 19, I spoke briefly to Secretary Rumsfeld just before a scheduled VTC in which I would give President Bush a situation report on Afghanistan.

"We've killed a lot of Taliban and al Qaeda, Mr. Secretary," I told him. "The terrorists are literally heading for the hills, toward their traditional refuges in the Spin Mountains. And we've received intelligence reporting that hundreds of Islamic Movement of Uzbekistan terrorists were killed during the Northern Alliance November offensives."

"President Karimov will be pleased, General," Rumsfeld said. "Are you making progress on Iraq?"

I wanted to be well prepared for the next iteration, and I knew Gene and Jeff Kimmons could use the time I'd be spending in the AOR to work on the matrix. "I'll have something to show you when I get back on December 27, Mr. Secretary."

"The President will want to see the concept soon, General," Rumsfeld said.

W E HAD ARRIVED IN MUSCAT, OMAN, LATE ON DECEMBER 20. I'd had the stack of folders lying before me faxed to Spar 06, so I could review the latest iteration over the next few days as we visited the troops in Afghanistan and attended Karzai's inauguration.

Gene and the small group of planners had done good work; the four proposed campaign phases were now fleshed out in a manner similar to the Afghanistan concept I'd taken to the White House on September 21. We had a long way to go before this concept would become a plan, but by the time of our return flight I was confident that the concept was ready for the President's consideration.

We landed at MacDill late on the afternoon of December 27. I'd had about twenty minutes to clear my desk when Pete Pace called to tell me that the SecDef wanted a secure VTC to review the concept.

When we finished the last of the twenty-six briefing charts, Rumsfeld smiled. "Good job, General," Rumsfeld said. I waited for the other shoe. "The President will want to see this soon—maybe tomorrow. He's in Crawford for the holidays."

I figured Rumsfeld would want us to set up a secure VTC from MacDill. But I also knew the President liked to look me in the eye when we discussed important matters. "Do you want us to schedule a VTC?" I asked.

"He may want you to come to Crawford," Rumsfeld said. "I'll let you know."

That evening, I was grilling steak when Rumsfeld called on the Red Switch secure phone.

"The President does want you to do the briefing out in Crawford tomorrow," he said. "He'll meet you at the ranch at 8:30 A.M."

"Got it, Mr. Secretary. I'll meet you there."

"I won't be there, General. But I'll be up on the secure VTC."

It would be very unusual for a combatant commander to meet the President without the Secretary of Defense present. But I knew the Secretary was going to his own western retreat near Taos, New Mexico, for the holidays, so I took the opportunity to tease him a little. "Well, Mr. Secretary," I said. "I ain't going unless you go."

"He didn't ask me," Rumsfeld said. "He asked you. Dress casually, General. And you may have to speak to the press."

"Okay, Sir," I said. "But I'm pretty pissed. I'm not sure I can function without you as my security blanket."

We both laughed. "You'll do fine," Rumsfeld said.

THE AIR FORCE G-5 GULFSTREAM LANDED IN WACO AT 0800. I HAD conked out after take-off, making up for some lost longitude-dislocation sleep—Flight Surgeon jargon for jet lag—while Gene Renuart reviewed the briefing notes. Marine One, the President's helicopter, was waiting beside Air Force One to take us on the short flight to Crawford. I enjoyed the sight of the rolling central Texas plains. After touching down on the helipad of the Prairie Chapel Ranch, we got into SUVs for the ride to the cluster of gray doublewides that comprise the office complex of the Western White House. A covey of quail flew out of a brush thicket as we drove. It felt like home.

When we arrived, George Bush stepped out of one of the prefabs, wearing jeans, a plaid shirt, and boots. It was a cold morning; I was glad I'd worn my black fleece jacket over my thin DCUs. "Tommy," the President said, shaking my hand warmly. "Thanks for coming. Know you've been on the road." He greeted Gene Renuart. "General, great to see you again. You folks taking good care of Tommy?"

"He takes care of us, Mr. President," Gene said.

President Bush and I entered the SCIF in the second doublewide. He took a seat at the head of the small oak table, facing a wide plasma VTC screen at the end of the room. I sat to his right. The first order of business was my situation report on Afghanistan. The President touched a button on the black console, and the screen opened into separate rectangles for the members of the National Security Council elsewhere in the country.

Colin Powell, Condi Rice, George Tenet, and Andy Card were in the familiar wood-paneled White House Situation Room. Vice President Dick Cheney, dressed in a sport coat and turtleneck, was at his vacation home in Wyoming. And Donald Rumsfeld appeared from what looked to be a study in his Taos ranch house, his white shirt open at the collar.

"What's the agenda, Don?" the President asked.

"Mr. President, General Franks is just back from Afghanistan and would like to bring us up to date on the situation there."

George Bush turned to me and smiled. "Tommy, what's this I hear about you dodging missiles over Kabul?"

Oops. Someone had been telling stories out of school. "Nothing serious, Mr. President. Been shot at before."

"Tommy," President Bush said, wagging his finger. "I don't want you to go getting yourself killed. That's the last thing we need. Got work for you, important work."

"I understand, Mr. President," I said, smiling. *My first ass-chewing from the President of the United States.*

"How are things going in Afghanistan, Tommy?" the President continued.

"Hamid Karzai sends his respects, Sir. His inauguration was a sight to behold. Two months ago, Afghanistan was a terrorist-sponsored state. Today, twenty-six million Afghans have hope for a future."

"He's a good man," George Bush said. But the levity disappeared from his eyes a moment later, replaced by sharp focus. "What's the intelligence on Osama bin Laden?"

"Unconfirmed reports have it that Osama has been seen in the White Mountains, Sir. The Tora Bora area. Rugged country, almost inaccessible in mid-winter. We will keep pressure on him if he's there, and President Musharraf has his troops sealing their side of the border."

After I had worked through the items on my report summary, we took a break while the NSC and Pentagon deputies departed, leaving behind only the principals to continue the VTC. I went out in the brisk morning air to stretch my stiff leg, then re-entered the SCIF with Gene Renuart to deliver the initial Commander's Concept on Iraq.

"Everybody have their briefing charts?" Rumsfeld asked, holding up the stack of multicolored pages that had been transmitted by classified fax. By this time, he knew the brief as well as I did. "Good. General Franks, go ahead."

"Mr. President," I began, "our current plan for Iraq is called Operations Plan 1003, which was last updated in 1998. As I've told Secretary Rumsfeld, it is basically Desert Storm II."

After summarizing the plan's major elements, I outlined the current strength of Iraq's military and its state of combat readiness. "At the start of the air campaign in 1991," I said, pointing to a column of figures on the slide, "the Iraqis had over a million men in uniform. Today they have around three hundred and fifty thousand. They had sixty-eight divisions then, today twenty-three. Almost six thousand tanks in 1991, today an estimated twenty-six hundred and sixty." I proceeded down the column: 1780 APCs compared to 4800 in 1991. Their artillery had decreased from 4000 rocket launchers and guns to about 2700—smaller, but still a dangerous threat to an attacking force.

"General Franks," Vice President Cheney asked, "you've described an Iraqi force around half the size it was when the Gulf War began. Does that mean it is only half as effective?"

Since 9/11, I'd attended four presidential briefings and more than twenty secure VTCs with the President and the National Security Council. Dick Cheney never asked more than one or two questions at each briefing, but they consistently cut to the core of the issue at hand. And he always sought information that would further President Bush's understanding of an important point. Cheney had been Secretary of Defense in the Gulf War, and I knew Bush had great respect for him.

"Sir," I answered, "smaller does not necessarily mean weaker. The Republican Guard, for example, has dropped from ten divisions to six. But those units are well manned and well armed—what we call combat ready. Four of them are heavy divisions, with upgraded T-72 tanks. Iraqi military doctrine would probably position them as a defense-in-depth force around Baghdad."

When I'd completed my summary, it was the President's turn to ask the questions. "What do you think of the plan, Tommy?"

"Mr. President, it's outdated. It calls for troop levels of at least four hundred thousand, which would require a very visible six-month force build-up. That would definitely eliminate operational surprise."

"I understand," the President said.

"Sir," I continued, "not only is the Iraqi military smaller than it was in 1991, advances in our precision weapons and command and control make our forces much more capable than they were then, even though we have reduced overall military end strength since the end of the Cold War."

Facing the NSC members on the plasma screen, I continued my briefing. "The President and Secretary Rumsfeld have asked CENTCOM to develop a Commander's Concept—new options to meet contingencies in Iraq."

I turned to a chart labeled OVERARCHING CONCEPT. "Please note that Regime Change and WMD Removal are the working assumptions of this concept."

There was a murmur of assent around the loop.

My lines-and-slices chart had become a major part of the presentation. "This matrix demonstrates the synergy among the lines of operation," I said. "For example, if we have multiple, highly skilled Special Operations Forces identifying targets for Precision Guided Munitions, we will need fewer conventional ground forces. That's an important lesson learned from Afghanistan."

Again, the VTC participants nodded.

"Further," I continued, "successful diplomatic negotiations that secure us basing and staging in neighboring countries will allow more simultaneous air and ground operations. I see this campaign in four dimensions, with time—unprecedented speed of operation—being a major factor."

President Bush's questions continued throughout the briefing. "What are your targets on the Regular Iraqi Army?" he asked when I'd completed the presentation. "We wouldn't want to cause unnecessary casualties among Iraqis that Saddam Hussein has drafted against their will."

"Sir," I replied, "this is only a concept at this point. We have identified potential target *sets,* not point targets."

"Tommy," Colin Powell asked, "what kind of deployment timelines do you have in mind?"

I scanned the faces on the screen. Colin had focused on one of the most important elements of the briefing—no surprise, coming from the former JCS chairman. "Just as in Afghanistan," I responded, "we've divided this concept into four phases."

As Gene arrayed the four sheets, I named them:

"Phase I—Preparation. Phase II—Shape the Battlespace. Phase III—Decisive Operations. Phase IV—Post-Hostility Operations."

Condi Rice fixed on the strategic element of the concept. "General Franks," she asked, "the timelines are all hypothetical, aren't they? I see the phases begin with N-DAY, which is indicated as 'POTUS Decision.'" She was right: The conceptual timeline moved along a continuum starting with N DAY, the moment when President Bush would authorize the military build-up in the region, and we would alert troops and prepare their transport from American bases to the region. From there, the continuum ran to C-DAY, when the flow of forces would begin; to A-DAY, the beginning of air operations; from there to G-DAY, when ground operations would be initiated; to the end of major combat operations and the launch of Phase IV—reconstruction.

On the chart we'd prepared, the length of the arrows connecting these benchmarks suggested their anticipated duration. But each arrow was tagged X-DAYS to emphasize that the actual time had not yet been determined. As yet, there were simply too many variables— size of force? simultaneous or sequential operations?—to propose timing with any degree of certainty.

I then discussed each phase's endstate, the goals to be completed before moving on to the next step. In Phase I, the endstate included establishing an "air bridge" to transport forces into the region and securing "regional and international support for operations." At this point, the concept anticipated separate air operations in Phase II to shape the battlespace before ground operations could begin. I had ideas about how this traditional approach could be truncated, or even combined into a simultaneous joint air-ground operation, but I did not yet want to discuss these possibilities with the principals. We were still talking about a concept, not a plan; I had work to do with Don Rumsfeld before we could get into that level of detail.

The endstate of Phase III specified two very clear goals: "regime forces defeated or capitulated," and "regime leaders dead, apprehended, or marginalized."

It was understood that the final phase, Phase IV—post hostility operations—would last the longest: years, not months. So Gene Renuart's graphics people had split that phase's wide arrow into segments, and marked its duration UNKNOWN rather than X-DAYS. The endstate of Phase IV included the establishment of a representative form of government in a country capable of defending its territorial borders and maintaining internal security, without any weapons of mass destruction.

I was aware that Phase IV might well prove more challenging than major combat operations. This phase would draw heavily on our Information, Political-Military and Civil-Military lines of operation—including a massive Humanitarian Assistance effort—as well as extensive site "exploitation" (investigation and analysis) by WMD and intelligence experts. Also critical would be the support we hoped to secure from the international community, and from nongovernmental organizations (NGOs).

And we knew that maintaining internal security would be another challenge. Saddam Hussein's Baathists had been in power for three decades. They wouldn't relinquish that power without a fight—even after we'd destroyed the Iraqi military.

Reaching the end of the briefing, I outlined the three options I'd first presented to Rumsfeld a few weeks earlier—the ROBUST, REDUCED, and UNILATERAL OPTIONS—and the implication of each.

"Even in the Unilateral Option," I explained, "the Brits and Australians would be with us. We would begin ground operations with as few as one hundred thousand troops, and continue to build our force levels as long as necessary to ensure success. The key will be to continue to flow forces until we are sure we have the correct troop-to-task ratio."

I pointed to the X DAYS timeline. "We want simultaneous ground operations from Kuwait, Jordan, and Turkey if we can get them. I'm confident from conversations with the Kuwaitis and King Abdullah that we can base and stage forces in Kuwait and Jordan, but I am much less confident of the Turks."

From there, the conversation turned to how we could begin to "adjust"—that is, degrade—Iraqi air defenses by responding "vigorously" to Iraqi violations in the no-fly zones. I also summarized my agreement with Secretary Rumsfeld to begin improving CENTCOM's infrastructure in the Gulf, increasing ramp space at air bases, shipping prepositioned equipment from Qatar to Kuwait, and completing our deployable command post.

"Mr. President," I said, "after 9/11, you asked the world, 'Are you with us or against us?' If we are going to disarm Saddam Hussein, we're going to have to ask the same question of the region's leaders." It was a point Secretary Rumsfeld and I had discussed before the briefing. "I have personal contacts with many of these leaders, and Secretaries Rumsfeld and Powell have close relationships with others. Diplomacy will be an essential line of operations."

Secretary Powell was listening closely, but he made no comment. It was obvious to me that the State Department would have a major role to play in the weeks and months ahead. I couldn't read Colin's silence—whether it was concern about the prospect of war with the Iraqis, or concern about his department's chances of lining up the coalition and gaining the support of the international community.

The ROBUST, REDUCED, and UNILATERAL options, I noted, were based on the degree of cooperation we would receive from each of the countries in the region. Moving forward to get that support would require a presidential decision. Once we had regional cooperation, we could begin building forces and infrastructure in a measured way— spikes and valleys of activity, the type of ambiguity we would need to preserve operational surprise in the event of war in Iraq.

I next handed the President the two pages of assumptions I had prepared, along with a list of items that would require presidential decisions.

Primary among my assumptions was that Iraq possessed and would use weapons of mass destruction, so our forces would likely be fighting in a toxic environment. Intelligence operations would attempt to confirm the extent and locations of Iraq's WMD programs and the regime's doctrine for the use of WMD, but without a robust human intelligence infrastructure—which we did not have—I was not confident we would be able to preempt WMD use.

There were opposition groups inside Iraq that would likely support military operations to remove Saddam. They could be cultivated through covert operations that the President could order.

"Mr. President," I continued, "as in Afghanistan, it's beyond the purview of the military to conduct international negotiations to establish a broad-based provisional government that the people would accept once the regime is removed. But the State Department did a great job with a similar challenge in Afghanistan. The Bonn Conference was a huge success story, and I believe comparable work will be required for Iraq." At this point, I could tell from Don Rumsfeld's body language that he thought I was discussing topics outside my lane. He was uncomfortable, but he said nothing, and I carried on.

As in the Gulf War, I said, we assumed that Iraq would attack Israel with missiles in order to gain sympathy in the Arab world. This time, however, Israel could retaliate, dangerously widening the conflict. If the President authorized it, we would reduce or eliminate this threat by augmenting Israeli defenses with Patriot missiles, and through well-planned use of special operations forces to deny missile "firing baskets" in western Iraq—the potential launching sites for a variety of missiles that we either knew or suspected the Iraqis possessed.

The President seemed pleased with the thoroughness of the briefing. "Tommy," he said after I'd concluded, "heck of a job." He stacked his briefing charts. "Don," he told Rumsfeld, "Keep working on this concept. It's headed in the right direction."

"We'll keep at it, Mr. President," Rumsfeld said. "But we're not recommending war or war timing—just prudent preparatory steps."

The President nodded, then turned to the Director of Central Intelligence. "George," he said to DCI Tenet, "your people have done a great job in Afghanistan. What do you have in Iraq?"

"Iraq's a different situation, Sir," Tenet said. "Our human intelligence capability is thin, and we've got a lot of bridges to rebuild with the opposition groups. They were badly burned in the failed uprisings after Desert Storm, and we've got a credibility problem." He praised our new concept for Iraq, and said that the Agency would support CENTCOM in every possible way.

Then Condi Rice faced the camera. "General Franks, you mentioned the strength of the Republican Guards. What happens if Saddam defends Baghdad with those forces?"

Good question. "We'll do a lot of thinking about the Baghdad problem in the days ahead—about Tikrit, too," I replied. "There are ways to defeat concentrated enemy formations around built-up areas without going gun barrel to gun barrel. I don't have the answer yet . . . but I will get it." Gene Renuart, an air strategist par excellence, nodded from the other side of the small oak table.

Vice President Cheney asked his second question. "Tommy, if there are scuds with chemical or biological warheads landing in our rear areas, how will our allies react? Are our troops properly trained and equipped?"

I made a note. "Mr. Vice President," I said, "WMD, if Saddam uses it, will be the greatest problem we face. I understand your question, but our work is too immature at this point to give you a good answer."

Before the VTC ended, President Bush addressed us all. "We should remain optimistic that diplomacy and international pressure will succeed in disarming the regime."

The faces on the screens nodded in agreement.

"But if this approach isn't successful, we have to have other options. That's why I asked Secretary Rumsfeld and Tommy to work on this concept. The worst thing that could happen to America would be a combination of WMD and terrorism. There have been no U.N. inspectors in Iraq since 1998. We don't know what kind of weapons they've developed, and we don't know Saddam's intentions . . . but we do know he used WMD before, on the Iranians and on his own people."

The President paused.

"Protecting the security of the United States is my responsibility," he continued. "We cannot allow weapons of mass destruction to fall into the hands of terrorists." He shook his head. "*I* will not allow that to happen."

The President's statement expressed a fundamental premise in the Global War on Terrorism—and what he said made perfect sense to me. America had been attacked less than one hundred days earlier. We had defeated the enemy in one theater. But the country could not now withdraw into a defensive crouch and wait to be attacked again—this time, quite possibly, by weapons much more destructive than hijacked airliners.

Outside in the bright, cold morning I turned to say goodbye to the President.

"Come on, Tommy," he said, grinning. "Hop in the truck. We're going to go talk to the press."

S POT, THE PRESIDENT'S ENGLISH SPRINGER SPANIEL, WAS IN THE pickup's front seat when we climbed in, wagging her bobbed tail. She gave my cheek a lick, then rested her chin on George Bush's shoulder as he drove.

"You're a good girl," the President said to his dog, and then turned to me with a grin. "In Washington, some of the reporters call her Spot," he added. "More dignified, I guess. But down here she's Spotty. I don't know who loves this place more, me or Spotty."

The frost was burning off the grass as the sun rose higher. I understood why the President and Laura Bush enjoyed escaping the hectic pace of Washington for the ranch.

We pulled up to the renovated homestead known as the Governor's House, the ranch's guest quarters. There was a microphone stand about fifty yards further down the gravel road where the traveling White House media waited with their cameras, shuffling in the December chill.

Spotty bounded out of the truck cab with us and trotted toward the rostrum. I stood to the left as the President greeted the media; as Spotty leaned against my leg, I bent down to pet her head.

"As you can see," the President said, resting his arms comfortably on the rostrum, "I've invited a guest to the ranch. Tommy Franks is no stranger to Texas." He mentioned my Midland background—and Laura's—and then turned to the matter at hand. "Tommy has just come back from the Afghan theater." He mentioned that we'd had a teleconference with the national security team, and that I'd given an update on Afghanistan.

We had talked about more than Afghanistan on the VTC, of course. But our discussion of contingency options for Iraq was sensitive, compartmented Top Secret information. Such conversations were somehow going to have to remain secret in leak-prone Washington for months to come, if our linked diplomatic and military strategy were to stand a chance of success.

The President asked me to "say a few words."

I noted that Cathy and I had spent the holidays with "a great bunch of young people"—soldiers, sailors, airmen, and Marines—in Afghanistan and the front-line states of Southwest Asia. We had also had the chance to attend the inauguration of Hamid Karzai and his interim government. "For the first time in decades," I added, more than twenty-six million people would have a chance for democratic representation.

A reporter asked President Bush if Osama bin Laden had "eluded the manhunt" in the mountains of Afghanistan. The President replied forcefully and clearly, underscoring the success of our operation in his usual relaxed, confident manner. "This is a guy who, three months ago, was in control of a country. Now he's maybe in control of a cave. He's on the run."

The questions turned to our long-range military plan in Afghanistan. When would we withdraw? "I imagine us being there for quite a long period of time," the President said. "But my timetable is going to be set by Tommy Franks." He added that he'd given me "a well-defined mission . . . and when Tommy says, 'Mission complete, Mr. President,' that's when we start moving troops out."

I fielded a few more questions on operations in Afghanistan, and the President spoke at length about defusing military tensions between India and Pakistan. He made a point of praising President Musharraf as "very helpful" in the war against the Taliban and al Qaeda and the hunt for bin Laden. Before wrapping up the press conference, the President made a point of telling the press, "I hope 2002 is a year of peace, but I'm also realistic."

Then he announced that he was "giving Tommy a tour of my ranch." We walked back to the Governor's House, where the President signed the Armed Services Appropriations Bill for fiscal year 2002 that was spread out on the kitchen counter. He gave me one of the pens he'd used, and then sat down at the kitchen table to tape his weekly radio broadcast.

As he finished the broadcast, Bush grabbed two Diet Cokes from the refrigerator and said, "Let's go for a ride, Tommy." Spotty must have recognized the word *ride;* she dashed ahead of us to the pickup.

The President's chainsaw and tools clanked in the back of the truck as we jolted off the gravel road onto a rougher lane toward a stony creek bed. "Lots of nice oaks and elms down here, Tommy," he said, pointing to the trees along the banks. "But the underbrush was stunting them so I'm clearing out the thickets. I like that kind of work."

There was a wide pile of branches and tangled briars on the side of a handsome stand of hardwoods. Across a stream, I saw a rain-washed ash heap, the remnants of a brush pile the President had cleared and burned over the Thanksgiving holidays.

As we finished the drive, Laura Bush met us at the house, a striking, single-story limestone block crescent that hugged a gentle rise beside a ten-acre fishing pond. Gene, Van Mauney, and Jeff Haynes climbed down from the Secret Service SUV that had been trailing the President's F-250 pickup.

"Come in," Laura said. "I'll show you around."

Laura Bush led us on a tour of the rooms. The plumbing included an eco-friendly ground-filter system that recycled sink and shower water to irrigate the lawn and garden. "Can get real dry out here in the summer, Tommy," the President explained. "Water's too precious to waste."

The ranch house was both heated and cooled by innovative geothermal wells—a system the President explained enthusiastically. It was a fascinating window into George Bush's personality: An hour earlier, he had been absorbed by the sweeping issues of peace and war. Now he was engrossed in the efficiency of a heat-exchange process that exploited the temperature differences between surface air and the constant sixty-two degrees at the bottom of the well shafts.

"You all are staying for lunch, I hope, Tommy," he said.

I checked my watch. Rumsfeld wanted to see another iteration of the Commander's Concept in ten days. If we left now, I could schedule a session with the senior planning staff this afternoon. In the next round, I wanted to be able to offer the SecDef and the President practical options, not just hypothetical choices. And that would take work.

"Sorry, Sir," I said. "We've got lots to do today back at Tampa."

As *Marine One* lifted off the helipad, I thought about what lay ahead. It was not certain that America would go to war in Iraq. But it *was* certain that we would "set conditions" in the region, and improve the military infrastructure that would allow us to launch a decisive campaign, should the President order us to do so.

The steps Secretary Rumsfeld and I had reviewed, and then presented to President Bush, would allow us to lay sufficient foundation for any future contingencies, without crossing the threshold and committing the country to war. Rumsfeld was adamant that we draw a line in our preparations that would not force the President's hand. This was the way Rumsfeld operated. We both followed the President's orders. George Bush had approved a series of initial steps that would build a military capability that could disarm Iraq and remove Saddam Hussein from power. But he had not ordered us to war.

I sat back in the comfortable seat of *Marine One*, listening to the familiar rotor thump and feeling the distinctive wobbly shudder of helicopter flight. That always reminded me of war: the Hueys and

Loaches of Vietnam, the Black Hawks of Desert Storm, the MH-47s over the bomb-scarred valleys of Afghanistan.

Would I fly into Iraq aboard a helicopter in the coming year? I had no way of knowing. But I knew the months ahead would be busy—completing decisive combat operations in Afghanistan, even as we prepared for a much larger campaign that might await us in Iraq sometime in the future.

Make 'em a hand, I thought, as the helicopter touched down in Waco and we boarded the jet that would take us back to Tampa.

I WORKED LATE THAT FRIDAY, WIDENING THE CIRCLE OF SENIOR STAFF involved with the PHASE I tasks. We met twice on Saturday, but I eased up Sunday afternoon. Most of these officers had taken only a few hours away from headquarters for Christmas, and at this rate, we wouldn't have much of a New Year's. So I sent them home with the admonition that I didn't want to see them "until next year."

I knew Rifle DeLong, Gene Renuart, and Jeff Kimmons would sneak back to their offices. And I intended to fine-tune the options we were developing to be ready for the next iteration with Secretary Rumsfeld. I hadn't had a day off since 9/11, and I didn't intend to take one until I was satisfied that we had credible Iraq options for the President.

I had been Commander in Chief of CENTCOM for almost eighteen months. A CINC's tour of duty was normally two years, so I had about six months left to do this job right. And I intended to use every minute.

Cathy and I had engaged in one of our "wait and see" talks during the last AOR trip. When this assignment ended, I wasn't interested in any Title X job Don Rumsfeld might offer. I was a warfighter. My military career would end next summer.

But on Monday morning, December 31, the SecDef called. "I've just spoken to the President. We'd like you to stay on at CENTCOM for another year. What do you think?"

"Thanks, Mr. Secretary. I'd like to discuss it with Cathy. I'll get back to you in a couple days."

"Tom," she told me that evening, "I've always backed whatever you want to do."

The Pentagon switchboard connected me to Rumsfeld at his Taos retreat. "We'd be honored to serve another year, Mr. Secretary."

Putting down the phone, I realized that my command appearance with the President at Crawford had been my "oral exams" for this third year in command of CENTCOM.

If America went to war in Iraq, it would likely be on my watch.

O N MONDAY, JANUARY 7, 2002, CENTCOM's INNER PLANNING circle met in the larger SCIF conference room. For internal working purposes, the Commander's Concept would be the foundation for a new plan—OPLAN 1003V, the adaptation of 1003 we'd refined through three iterations with the SecDef.

The main topic of discussion was what I termed the GENERATED START CONCEPT—a blueprint for "generating" the necessary ground, air, and naval presence in the region that would enable us, at the orders of the President, to commence decisive military operations to meet the Endstate objective of REGIME CHANGE. We needed a force-deployment framework, and the generated start was a first step toward identifying that structure.

As the planning proceeded over the coming months, we would identify the specifics for flowing the force—though these specifics were always dependent on whether we intended to execute a ROBUST, REDUCED, or UNILATERAL OPTION. Would we be able to posture troops in Turkey, Jordan, Saudi Arabia, Kuwait, and the Gulf States? Would our NATO allies allow us to base and stage? Exactly how many key air targets were available? The variables seemed endless.

So did the stream of questions from the Pentagon. The OSD staff and the Secretary were making us jump through hoops. What response would CENTCOM consider appropriate if the Iraqis launched

WMD attacks as we were deploying forces, or in the early stages of PHASE II, or as we closed on Baghdad? What were the specifics on the basing, airport and seaport enhancements we would need in the region? How would our timelines be affected if we had SOF and HUMINT assets inside Iraq to identify targets, as we'd had after October 20, 2001, in Afghanistan? The list of questions seemed endless. After leaving the headquarters late most nights, my directors met each morning at 0400 to prepare for my morning call with the SecDef.

Since the start of Operation Enduring Freedom, we'd become accustomed to the demands of Secretary Rumsfeld. But now even my industrious planners found that the daily barrage of tasks and questions was beginning to border on harassment. These officers, whom Gene called the "fifty-pound brains," were the most important people on the staff. Colonel Mike Fitzgerald and Colonel Dave Halverson, the lead planners, were the most selfless, hardest-working colonels I had ever known. So if they were feeling harassed, I had better address the problem head on.

I called all the "brains" together in the SCIF one afternoon in January. A good part of their discontent stemmed from the extra stress involved in compartmentalizing the planning to help prevent leaks, which would derail the process. Only a small group of senior CENTCOM officers knew significant aspects of the evolving concept, and only four of us had the full picture. Our people were isolated from each other, running on a treadmill in a vacuum. Not good for a tightly knit team.

"Okay," I said, standing in the front of the room. "Here's the deal, guys. I know OSD—Rumsfeld, Wolfowitz, and Feith—are demanding a lot. But they are not the enemy. Don't start thinking *good guys—bad guys*. We're all on the same side."

They could see I was serious.

"I'll worry about OSD, all of them—including Doug Feith, who's getting a reputation around here as the dumbest fucking guy on the planet," I continued. "Your job is to make *me* feel warm and fuzzy. Look, we're all professionals. Let's earn our pay."

We might be grousing among ourselves about the workload, but we would not be disloyal to the boss.

The iterations continued. As Yogi might have put it, the long days and nights were like post-9/11 déjà vu all over again. And—painful though it was—the process brought progress.

SECRETARY RUMSFELD WANTED TO KNOW OUR CONTINGENCY PLANS in case Saddam Hussein provoked us through a blatant casus belli—attacking the Kurds or, more likely, shooting down a Coalition aircraft in the no-fly zones.

This made me rethink all of our standing Response Options, including the Badger Plan, our designated response if enemy air defenses shot down one of our planes. And the rethinking resulted in three levels of response: Red, White, and Blue. Red, the least kinetic, would consist of an immediate TLAM strike on important Iraqi air defense targets. White included expanded TLAM and air strikes over forty-eight hours. And Blue would call for air operations followed by ground operations, to establish an enclave inside Iraq that would be expanded by rapidly deploying follow-on forces.

Some of the planners began calling this the "Running Start" option, and I adopted the term in my discussions with the Secretary.

During one of our conference calls, I told Rumsfeld, "Mr. Secretary, there are only two ways to go to war. Either the enemy starts it on his schedule—or we start it on ours. Since we do not have a decision to go to war on our timeline, we need options in case Saddam starts one on his timeline. I like the idea of a 'running start' as an option. We continue to build forces and infrastructure in the region to support diplomacy. And if the President makes a decision to attack, we will begin with what we have in place and follow on—for as long as necessary, with as much force as necessary."

"I understand," Rumsfeld said, "but we need a realistic consideration of timing. What are the various timelines? How long do you project each phase to last?"

"Working it," I said.

"Good," he said. "Let's make it February 1."

Christ, I thought as we hung up. *That's next week.*

I turned to Gene and Rifle DeLong. "Hope you lads have plenty of coffee in your offices, 'cause we've got some long nights coming up, and I ain't sharing mine."

I WAS WORKING THROUGH A SET OF ESTIMATES ON THE EVENING OF Tuesday, January 29, when Jeff Haynes came into my office. "General," he said, walking to the television set, "you wanted me to remind you about the State of the Union."

"Thanks, Marine," I said, making a final note as he tuned in CNN. I would switch back and forth between CBS and Fox after the speech to see what kind of spin the networks were applying to the President's words.

As he spoke, George Bush looked confident and determined.

"We last met in an hour of shock and suffering," the President said. "In four short months, our nation has comforted the victims, begun to rebuild New York and the Pentagon, rallied a great coalition, captured, arrested, and rid the world of thousands of terrorists, destroyed Afghanistan's terrorist training camps, saved a people from starvation, and freed a country from brutal oppression."

The applause was loud from both sides of the aisle.

Four short months, I thought—the longest 120 days and nights of my life.

"And terrorist leaders who urged followers to sacrifice their lives are running for their own," Bush added to more applause.

He nodded to the House chamber's upper gallery, introducing Afghanistan's interim leader, Chairman Hamid Karzai, to another standing ovation.

As his address continued, the President turned to the subject of weapons of mass destruction and rogue states—issues that occupied my thoughts every day. He spoke of North Korea and Iran, two regimes he described as sponsors of terrorism that sought WMD.

Then Bush turned to Iraq—and I watched the unofficial beginning of the President's diplomatic effort to disarm Saddam Hussein.

"Iraq continues to flaunt its hostility toward America and to support terror," he said. "The Iraqi regime has plotted to develop anthrax, and nerve gas, and nuclear weapons for over a decade. This is a regime that has already used poison gas to murder thousands of its own citizens—leaving the bodies of mothers huddled over their dead children." The House chamber was absolutely still. "This is a regime that agreed to international inspections—then kicked out the inspectors. This is a regime that has something to hide from the civilized world."

The President paused, and then spoke slowly, emphasizing his words. "States like these, and their terrorist allies, constitute an axis of evil, arming to threaten the peace of the world. By seeking weapons of mass destruction, these regimes pose a grave and growing danger."

Having suffered one devastating terrorist attack, he stressed, the United States must be prepared to act to prevent others. "America will do what is necessary to ensure our nation's security," he continued. "We'll be deliberate, yet time is not on our side. I will not wait on events, while dangers gather. I will not stand by, as peril draws closer and closer. The United States of America will not permit the world's most dangerous regimes to threaten us with the world's most destructive weapons."

Both sides stood to deliver a ringing ovation.

"Our war on terror is well begun, but it is only begun. This campaign may not be finished on our watch—yet it must be and it will be waged on our watch."

I thought back to a discussion I'd had with Tony Zinni more than two years before. *Iraq is a problem that's not going to go away anytime soon.*

The President's words rang in my ears: a war that will be *waged on our watch*. I had just extended my watch at Central Command for a third year. It sounded as though the Iraqi problem would soon be met—head-on.

THE FEBRUARY 1 BRIEFING TO SECRETARY RUMSFELD WAS GOING well. We'd modified the Generated Start Concept so that operations from the start of Phase I to the end of Phase III were now projected to last only about four months.

"Here's our current timeline," I said, turning to the next chart. "Given the work already under way in the region, we will complete pre-positioning of equipment and the upgrades to airports, seaports, and other military infrastructure in a few months.

"As Phase I is completed, we could flow steadily for the next sixty days, while continuing spikes of activity to lend credence to our deception. During the sixty days we would increase kinetic strikes in the no-fly zones to weaken Iraq's integrated air defenses. And, if we can develop a northern front in Turkey, with other conventional units staging out of Kuwait, and SOF staging in Jordan and Saudi Arabia, we will see a ground force troop level of approximately 160,000."

I turned to the next chart. "If the President decides to attack, A-Day would begin Phase II—an air-centric phase of about three weeks, depending on the time of year and the weather. We would use mostly precision munitions, but the seasonal *shamal* sandstorms would affect our laser target-designating systems and reconnaissance flights."

The following chart was PHASE III: DECISIVE COMBAT OPERATIONS.

"We would begin G-Day when the ground forces attack. It could last up to one hundred and thirty-five days," I continued, "again depending on the time of year and the defensive tactics used by the Iraqis."

Then I turned to reveal the next chart: PHASE IV: POST-HOSTILITY OPERATIONS. "As stability operations proceed, force levels would continue to grow—perhaps to as many as two hundred and fifty thousand troops, or until we are sure we've met our endstate objectives."

"And all of this is predicated on Phase I preparations having been completed?" Rumsfeld asked.

"Yes, Sir. If Saddam Hussein triggers a war today—before Phase I is finished—we could start ground operations about forty-five days after the beginning of air operations. At that point we'd have in place

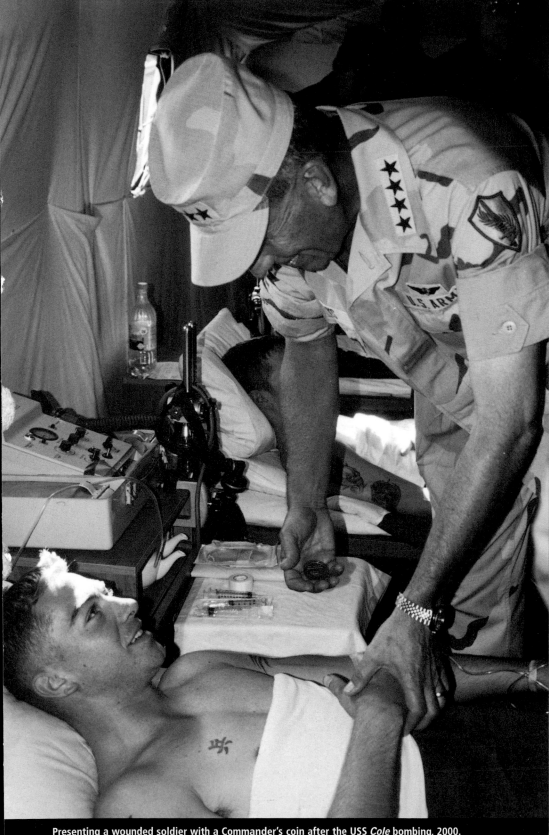

Presenting a wounded soldier with a Commander's coin after the USS *Cole* bombing, 2000.

A meeting in the "Trophy Room" at CENTCOM headquarters on MacDill Air Force Base during the planning of Operation Enduring Freedom, September 2001. (Left to right) Captain Van Mauney, Marine Lieutenant General Rifle DeLong, myself, and my Political Advisor, Ambassador Martin L. Cheshes.

Dancing with Cathy during a surprise Neal McCoy appearance a few days before leaving for the AOR.

A wonderful composite of our family and dear friends at a CENTCOM event. Front row: Cathy, Jacqy, Sam; second row: Pauline Franks Bourjes, Lieutenant General Dan McNeill and wife, Maureen; third row: Rita and Dr. James Carley, Joan Carley; fourth row: Kat and Wayne Newton, Kathy DeLong; fifth row: Tara Carley Maher, Killian Carley Maher.

With Secretary of Defense Donald Rumsfeld. Our working relationship evolved into a fruitful collaboration—and valued friendship.

Cathy with battle-weary Special Forces troops at the USO Show, Kandahar, Afghanistan, December 2001.

Briefing the Coalition's Senior National Representatives on Operation Enduring Freedom, CENTCOM Main Conference, MacDill Air Force Base, 2001.

With President George W. Bush at Prairie Chapel Ranch, Crawford, Texas, December 28, 2001.

News conference in the Coalition Media Center at Camp As Sayliyah, in Doha, Qatar, Sunday, March 30, 2003.

Meeting the press at the Pentagon.

Receiving the President's order to execute Operation Iraqi Freedom by video teleconference. (Left to right) Group Captain Geoff Brown of the Australian Air Component, myself, Lieutenant General Buzz Moseley, and Air Vice Marshal Glenn Torpy of the Royal Air Force, Prince Sultan Air Base, Saudi Arabia, March 19, 2003.

On the ground in Iraq: Marines braving the *shalam* sandstorm of March 2003.

Tanks of the V Corps, 3rd Infantry Division, on the road to Baghdad, March 2003.

A tyrant and his regime in flames: downtown Baghdad, April 2003.

Arriving in Baghdad with Lieutenant General David McKiernan (left) and Chief Warrant Officer Four Steve Holcomb, April 16, 2003.

The "Band of Brothers": Major General Dell Dailey, Vice Admiral Tim Keating, Lieutenant General Buzz Moseley, myself, Lieutenant General Earl Hailston, Brigadier General Gary Harrell, and Lieutenant General David McKiernan at Saddam Hussein's palace, Baghdad, April 16, 2003.

Our ad hoc press briefing in the palace of Saddam.

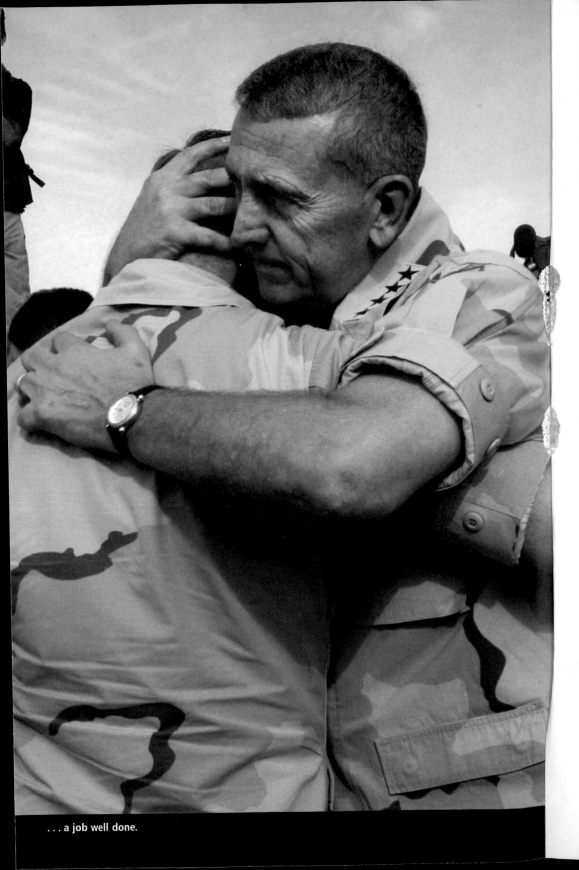

. . . a job well done.

a force of about one hundred and five thousand troops: a reinforced heavy Army division, an armored cavalry regiment, a Marine Expeditionary Force, and most of our air assets. We could launch, and the remainder of the forces would flow in behind them. I don't like such a sequential approach, Mr. Secretary. But it's feasible."

Even as I moved through my charts, though, my mind was turning over another, more private discussion I planned to have with Don Rumsfeld in the next hour. Ever since the 1st Cavalry Division's successful feint operation during Desert Storm, I had believed that a well-conceived and well-executed operational deception would work on the Iraqi military and its regime leaders. Their intelligence was focused almost entirely on internal security—repressing the Kurds and Shiites and preempting coup attempts—and not on warfighting.

And I had an ace in the hole so sensitive that I would only discuss it with Secretary Rumsfeld face-to-face. Several Arab heads of state, with whom I had close relationships, had provided valuable information based on their own personal contacts with Saddam Hussein. And I knew these leaders were invaluable conduits through which we could pass information—and disinformation—*to* the Iraqi regime.

Wrapping up the briefing, I moved on to one of the final charts: RUNNING START. "This is another timing alternative we're examining," I explained. "If we are far enough along with our preparations in the region, we could conceivably compress the air campaign to the point that air and ground operations—preceded by extensive Special Forces work—would be virtually simultaneous. And we could launch the operations while follow-on forces were still deploying."

This was a revolutionary concept, way outside the box of conventional doctrine. But I had been a maverick all my life. When existing doctrine didn't get the job done, I would try to find another way to do it—whether it meant rigging a Rube Goldberg radio network on the H-23 Raven helicopter in Vietnam, putting CB radios in howitzers in the 2nd ACR, building the TOC-A-TOY mobile Fire Direction Center in the 2-78 Artillery, or teaching artillerymen to hit moving targets at Fort Hood. It also meant that I was frequently on the outside of the Army's conservative mainstream.

Desert Storm had reinforced my conviction that maneuver speed and tactical surprise were the greatest force multipliers in war. In southern Iraq, American and British forces had slammed into the weak flanks of the Iraqi Republican Guard, maneuvering through a blinding sandstorm to surprise the enemy. Fast-moving battalion wedges had engaged and defeated dug-in Iraqi brigades. It was not only technology that overwhelmed the Republican Guard on battlefields such as 73 Easting and Medina Ridge, but the effect of speed. At many of our initial points of contact, the Iraqis outnumbered our attacking forces. Just as in physics, though, the effects of mass increased with velocity.

I knew our military forces would break the will of the Iraqi army, and we would do it with unprecedented speed. The size of our attack force was less important than the speed and flexibility of its maneuver. The Running Start would involve risk, but it would not be a gamble.

And we would do everything possible to minimize the risk. It would be essential to control Iraq's western deserts, because that's where Saddam Hussein would want to set up missile launchers. The UN's weapons inspectors, and our intelligence community, estimated that Iraq either had secretly retained Scud Theater Ballistic Missiles (TBM), or had modified shorter-range systems such as the Ababil-100 to operate at ranges greater than the 150 kilometers permitted under Security Council resolutions.

"If the Iraqis manage to strike Tel Aviv or Riyadh with chemical or biological warheads, it would be a serious strategic dislocator," I stressed. "Similar to what we saw in 1991, but potentially much worse." If Israel were to retaliate, in other words, the war could be transformed into a religious conflict in the eyes of the Arab world. The resolve of our Saudi allies would probably crumble, and we would be evicted from our low-profile but vital Combined Air Operations Center at Prince Sultan Air Base and SOF and CSAR bases elsewhere in the Kingdom.

But I was confident that we could wrest control of Iraq's western desert using Special Ops forces linked to strike aircraft employing

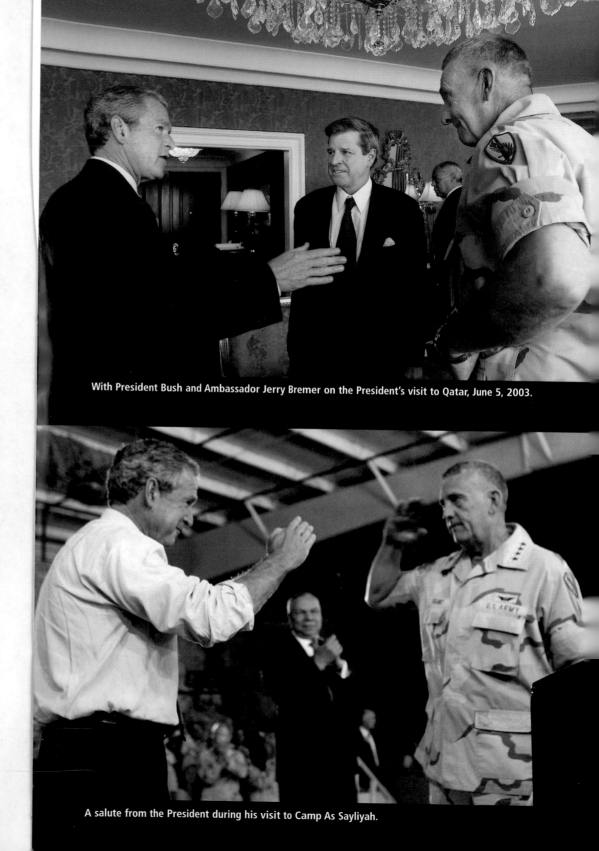

With President Bush and Ambassador Jerry Bremer on the President's visit to Qatar, June 5, 2003.

A salute from the President during his visit to Camp As Sayliyah.

PGMs, just as we had in Afghanistan. "By the time we have a ground force in place in Kuwait and Turkey," I told Rumsfeld, "we will have enough Special Operators staged in Jordan and Saudi Arabia to move in and control the western 25 percent of Iraq."

"Remember, there's a fine balance between thorough preparation and triggering a war," Rumsfeld reminded me. "And the President has not decided to go to war."

"I understand, Mr. Secretary."

I BRIEFED THE PRESIDENT AND THE NATIONAL SECURITY COUNCIL on the afternoon of Thursday, February 7, in the White House Situation Room. Just as I had during the December VTC from Texas, I reported on the situation in Afghanistan, summarizing our plans for offensive operations to destroy the remaining al Qaeda redoubt in the mountains south of Kabul.

"The snow will be gone from the mountain passes soon," I said. "And we will go in from several directions on the ground while simultaneously inserting air assault forces into the objective."

I pointed out the key aspects of the maneuver scheme on a tactical map. "We'll use elements of the 10th Mountain and 101st Airborne Divisions, Coalition SOF—including Germans and Australians—and our Afghan allies. I'll keep Secretary Rumsfeld posted as the operation unfolds."

"Is he in there, Tommy?" President Bush asked. Everyone knew who *he* was: bin Laden.

"The intel people think there's a possibility," I said. "President Musharraf does not believe he's in Pakistan. The truth is, Mr. President, I am not sure. He's not on the radio, and I've seen no credible reporting on bin Laden's whereabouts." I made a *zero* sign with my thumb and forefinger.

"This is tough, inaccessible country," I continued. "The Mujahedin hid from the Soviets in these mountains for years. That's why our Afghan allies are essential. They know every cave and tunnel."

"Any other Afghanistan questions for Tommy?" the President asked. There were none.

I turned to Iraq.

Presenting the TIMINGS chart, I announced that we'd reduced the projected maximum duration of Phases I through III to 225 days—including a three-month "generation of forces" in the region, a six-week combined air and SOF phase (during which we would seize and protect Iraq's southern oil fields from sabotage), and up to ninety days of decisive combat operations.

Ideally, of course, Phase III—DECISIVE COMBAT OPERATIONS—wouldn't require three full months of conventional warfare, with American tanks slugging it out with the Republican Guard. We planned to take control of Iraq's airspace from the start. And if the handful of airworthy combat planes the Iraqis could still fly challenged Coalition fighters, they'd survive about a day. If they stayed in their concrete revetments, we'd destroy them with PGMs. Enemy ground formations would have to contend with the combined destructive mass of our rapidly maneuvering armor, artillery, and mechanized infantry—all of which employed their own lethal mix of long-range precision munitions—as well as our heavy bombers and strike aircraft.

But if the Iraqis were to site their tanks and artillery in villages and city neighborhoods, near mosques, schools, and hospitals—as we knew they weren't above doing—we would take measures to avoid civilian casualties. It was a tactical problem, one we would address using the same combination of Information Age reconnaissance and target designation that we had perfected in the mountains and deserts of Afghanistan, but it would take time. We could locate and destroy individual armored vehicles and artillery pieces without unacceptably high collateral damage, just as we had used Predators to identify targets for bombers dropping GBUs and JDAMS in cities like Kandahar and Jalalabad.

And it seemed likely that our troops would be fighting on a battlefield contaminated with chemical or biological agents. That would obviously slow things down—especially if coalition forces were obliged to wear masks, gloves and MOPP protective suits in the oppressive summer heat. That, of course, was the worst case: Phase III *could* take up to ninety days.

Our plans to counter resistance from irregular forces went beyond the scope of this briefing. But my CENTCOM planners were considering that problem as well. Our intelligence indicated that formations such as the *Al Amn al-Khas* Special Security Organization and the Special Republican Guard had received training in unconventional warfare. These were Saddam's tribal loyalists, privileged Sunni Baathist fanatics with blood on their hands, who could expect little mercy from the Shiites and Kurds they had massacred for years. Some, we knew, would rather die than surrender. And, by flowing forces with the right skills to meet and crush armed resistance, even after Phase III was completed, we intended to accommodate them in that regard.

I knew we would win the fight, but we did not want to devastate Iraq in the process. We wouldn't repeat the performance of Soviet Marshals Zhukov and Konev, encircling Berlin and pounding the rubble into increasingly smaller pieces to destroy the defenders. Nor, for that matter, would the Coalition repeat the performance of Lieutenant Tommy Franks along the Kinh Doi Canal, calling in scores of fire missions and air strikes to push the enemy out of the buildings on the outskirts of Saigon.

The campaign I envisioned would in fact be a "revolution in warfare," to use a shopworn term that had been bandied about by both professional and amateur strategists since the Wermacht launched the Blitzkrieg in 1939. We would employ the remarkable innovations that forward-looking thinkers—including those I'd worked with in the Louisiana Maneuvers Task Force—had envisioned years earlier. We would conduct fast and flexible maneuver, coupled with precise, lethal firepower.

"The combat readiness of the Iraqi military fluctuates throughout the year," I explained, "depending on the stage of their training cycle." I displayed these timing considerations with the same type of red-yellow-and-green "traffic light" charts I had used in my briefings on Afghanistan. A red light indicated the most dangerous period—*Stop, don't advance.* Yellow meant *Proceed with caution.* And green signaled the optimal conditions: *Proceed with confidence.*

Saddam's army usually conducted large-unit training from early May to late September. During those months, we could assume that formations such as the Republican Guard and the better regular army divisions would be fully staffed and well-equipped with weapons and munitions. And their command and control would also be at their most efficient during those summer months. For us, that was a red-light scenario.

In October and November, the larger Iraqi units would begin standing down, but their combat readiness would still be elevated. *Yellow light.*

From December through February, though, the Iraqi military traditionally conducted company-level and individual training. Its tanks were moved to firing ranges, when they weren't undergoing maintenance. Soldiers were attending classes at training centers far from their home bases. *Green light.*

Weather was also a factor. Since our troops would likely be fighting in MOPP suits to protect against chemical and biological weapons, the mid-summer daytime desert heat, which could reach 130 degrees Fahrenheit, constituted a yellow light. And the sandstorms of early spring were another obstacle to avoid if at all possible.

"Therefore, Mr. President," I said, "optimum operational timing would be from December to mid-March."

I had briefed the NSC at this level of detail because I wanted to impress on them the complexity of our decision process from a purely military perspective. During a VTC a week earlier, Secretary Rumsfeld had lobbed one of his rhetorical grenades, wondering if we would conceivably be able to begin a campaign in April 2002—in less than three months—if required. But our deployment would take three months, which would put us into May. And I really did not want to start the ground operation after April 1 of whatever year we might have to fight.

I hoped that this briefing would squelch speculation that a decisive operation in Iraq would be a simple matter requiring relatively few troops. Some staffers in the Pentagon had suggested that one heavy division with massive air support could kick open a door, through which exiled Iraqi opposition groups would march triumphantly to liberate their country. This line of thinking was absurd, and I wanted to terminate it as quickly as possible.

None of these "strategists" had ever sent troops against Iraq's T-72s. I had. And if the President ordered me to go to war, I wanted to do it at a time and in a manner that gave our troopers the best chance of accomplishing their mission fast, with the fewest possible casualties.

On another chart, I explained two shaded areas. The lower half of the chart indicated Phase I military preparations, including equipment upgrades for Army, Air Force, and Marine units that would deploy first, as well as the estimated completion dates for ongoing expansions and improvements of port and base infrastructure in the region. The upper half of the chart showed possible timing for the diplomatic efforts that would be undertaken as another part of Phase I. It would be key to link our deployments and operational actions to strategic events such as United Nations meetings, international visits, and holiday periods. This would be relatively easy—and very important.

"I've got trips scheduled to meet with senior leaders in the region," I explained, "and I can lay some groundwork. But Secretary Powell and Secretary Rumsfeld will have to orchestrate the diplomatic heavy lifting."

Both Secretaries nodded, and the President smiled.

"Mr. President," Andy Card added, "we'll have congressional elections in November. And that should also be considered in discussions of timing."

"That is no consideration at all," George Bush snapped. "If we go to war, it will be because the security of America requires it. Timing will have nothing to do with congressional elections or polls." I knew the President respected Card, but he was sending a message to his National Security team: his priorities were clear.

Like the rest of the NSC, Secretaries Powell and Rumsfeld watched this sharp exchange in silence. I sensed the tension between Donald Rumsfeld and Colin Powell. That came as no surprise to anyone who knew them both: these were two brilliant, dedicated public servants, two strong-willed personalities with egos to match their cabinet rank. Tireless workers with different strategic visions, they were "gifted," as the Op Ed writers often described them, with equal but totally different bases of experience.

Colin Powell saw America as the first among equals in a family of free nations. I think he saw America's mission in the world as creating international networks to ease tensions in the Middle East and Southwest Asia, fight HIV/AIDS and poverty, promote human rights, curb narcotics trafficking, lower trade barriers, and, of course, combat global terrorism. But he also put great stock in international organizations like the United Nations and NATO, and partnerships such as those that had forged the Oslo Agreement to resolve the intractable Arab-Israeli conflict.

Secretary of Defense Donald Rumsfeld had also thought through a spectrum of international security priorities before 9/11. Since then, however, winning the global war on terrorism and transforming the Defense Department had rightly become his principal focus. When President Bush announced to the nations of the world that they were either with us or against us in this struggle, Donald Rumsfeld agreed without reservation. Like a New Frontier cold warrior, Rumsfeld was willing to "pay any price, bear any burden," to "support any friend, oppose any foe," to assure America's survival.

Rumsfeld believed in *realpolitik*. He would fly halfway around the world for a sit-down meeting with Uzbek President Islam Karimov—whose human rights record was tarnished at best—in order to secure the vital K-2 airbase for American operations in Afghanistan. He'd probably have shaken hands with the devil if that had furthered our goals in the war on terrorism.

The rift that eventually grew between the State and Defense Departments over our Iraq policy has been portrayed as stemming from personal animosity between the two cabinet secretaries. That is too simplistic. These two men did see the world differently, but in my view it was the convergence and overlap of their responsibilities—coupled with the personalities of their subordinates—that was the true cause of friction in everyday relations between State and Defense.

The State Department, which is responsible for international relations and diplomacy, posts ambassadors to the United Nations and most of the sovereign nations on the planet. On a given day, Colin Powell uses this network to advance U.S. policies that range from human rights to commercial interests. Similarly, the Defense Department has senior military officers in virtually every country—working with the ambassadors on security and military matters. It's as if each department were an octopus, its tentacles reaching around the world. In many cases, military decisions and objectives affect an ambassador's ability to do his job; likewise, the priorities of our ambassadors regularly affect the work being done by the military.

Each of these departments, too, is a huge bureaucracy. Each comes complete with hundreds of personalities, many of them contending for power, and angling to ensure that any given decision goes their way. Over the past year I'd seen considerable friction develop between the departments. In many cases State viewed Defense as a bunch of hawks—advocating military action without regard for regional or international consequences. And Defense viewed State as a bunch of bureaucrats, fond of having meetings and writing papers, but slow to act on important issues. The truth was probably to be found between the poles, but one thing was for sure: There was insufficient trust between the departments.

And that lack of trust was compounded by Deputy Secretary of Defense Paul Wolfowitz; Deputy Secretary of State Rich Armitage; Doug Feith, the Undersecretary of Defense for Policy; and their senior staff members. Make no mistake, these men served their country passionately. Donald Rumsfeld and Colin Powell were loyal to these helpers; the views they developed and the points they presented throughout the planning of the war would make that very clear. But in many cases these advisers' deep and inflexible commitment to their own ideas was disruptive and divisive, as they sought to influence their bosses—and ultimately George W. Bush—with respect to Iraq policy. On far too many occasions the Washington bureaucracy fought like cats in a sack. I believe that better listening, more intellectual flexibility, and more willingness to learn and compromise would have better served their superiors, the Commander-in-Chief, and our country.

On the final briefing chart, I described the positioning of an "optimum force" on Iraq's borders. By that I meant a mix of troops, planes, and ships that would both add weight to our diplomatic pressure, and serve as the core of a decisive campaign. My proposed deployment pattern, I stressed, could accomplish this goal without provoking Saddam into an ill-advised reaction.

Playing devil's advocate, Rumsfeld joined the discussion. Would CENTCOM have to wait until December to initiate decisive operations?

I knew the SecDef wanted me to emphasize for the NSC the most favorable timing for a possible major operation. "Mr. Secretary," I said, "we can deploy and execute at any time the President orders us to do so."

"Could we go earlier, if necessary?" President Bush asked, always mindful of the potential nexus of WMD and terrorism.

"We could, Mr. President," I answered. "But it would be ugly. A longer, sequential operation with higher casualties on both sides. And probably with considerably more destruction of Iraqi infrastructure than if we conduct the kind of operation I have described."

"Mr. President," Rumsfeld said, speaking with that crisp precision he reserved for important statements, "General Franks is working on a more simultaneous operation that just might *fracture* Iraqi resistance in a significantly shorter period than ninety days of major ground combat."

I chose not to elaborate. In the past week, I had broached with Rumsfeld the idea of a decisive "five-front" operation, which would combine simultaneous assaults from Kuwait and Turkey, with SOF quickly occupying the "Scud baskets" of the western desert; a combined information and PSYOP "front," designed to erode the resolve of the Iraqi military; and an operational fires front targeting Baghdad and its Republican Guard defenses.

"We're in the early, thinking stage on this," Rumsfeld added.

George Bush nodded and ended the briefing: "Great job, Tommy. Keep it up. We will do what we have to do to protect America."

THE AIR-CONDITIONING IN THE JOC WAS ROARING; ALL THE consoles were manned, and the massed electronics were pumping out a lot of heat.

I sat at the commander's station in the room's dim glow, watching the air and ground picture in Afghanistan on the plasma screens. It was before dawn in Tampa on Thursday, March 7, 2002. For five days, coalition forces had been locked in combat on the high ridges and in the gorges of Paktia and Khost Provinces. Five months to the day after the war began, Operation Anaconda marked the first major engagement for our conventional forces in Afghanistan. The operation combined light infantry from the 10th Mountain and the 101st Airborne Divisions, American Special Forces and British, Australian, German, Danish, Canadian, and French SOF, as well as Pashtun and Panjshiri Afghan troops.

As the name implied, the mission of Anaconda was to encircle and squeeze into extinction an al Qaeda and Taliban force whose strength was estimated to be as many as two thousand well-armed Arabs, Afghans, Chechens, Uzbeks, and Pakistanis. The enemy were survivors who'd escaped the Coalition offensive that had liberated most of Afghanistan in November and December. Many of these terrorists had been pushed south out of Tora Bora into the steep Shah-i-Kot Valley; surrounded by towering snowy ridges, the area bristled with trenches, bunkers, and mortar pits, as well as caves and tunnels that had been used by fighters like them for years.

Unlike the terrorists who had been killed or captured—or had managed to slip through Pakistani and Coalition blocking forces on the Afghan-Pakistani border—the hard-core al Qaeda and Taliban in the Shah-i-Kot region appeared determined to make a stand.

ARCENT commander Lt. General P. T. Mikolashek, and 10th Mountain Division commander Major General Franklin "Buster" Hagenback had proposed clearing Shah-i-Kot, and I had agreed. The operation would be decisive: a focused and lethal unified effort. "Think *joint*," I told them. "Think inter-service reliance."

I had been pushing the importance of joint warfare on this team since a late February commanders' briefing, just before Anaconda was scheduled to begin. The secure VTC link connected CENTCOM with the air operations center in Saudi Arabia, Mikolashek's forward headquarters in Kuwait, and a host of other participants: Buster Hagenbeck; Brigadier General Gary Harrell; Colonel John Mulholland, who commanded the Special Forces in-country; and Major General Dell Dailey, whose Special Mission Units had the task of capturing or killing al Qaeda leadership.

I listened as Mikolashek and the commanders in Afghanistan presented an excellent plan that made good use of conventional light infantry, Afghan forces, Special Forces, and Coalition Special Mission Units. Air Force Lt. General Buzz Moseley, CENTCOM's Air Component Commander, contributed a thorough air plan, including Predator UAV reconnaissance, fighter-bombers, and A-10 close air-support aircraft.

Very impressive, I thought as I reviewed the plan. *But not exactly right.* These were very credible plans, but they weren't completely coordinated. I was reminded of Desert Storm—a patchwork of "deconflicted" service operations, not a true joint effort.

"Love it," I said. "But I need you guys to meet each other in a personal way. Lots of moving parts here. Put 'em together like a watch."

I was looking at some uncomfortable general officers on those VTC screens. But Mother Nature was on our side. At the outset of the conference, Buster Hagenbeck had mentioned that bad weather might delay the planned February 27 start date by several days. This was one time I was thankful for bad weather. These commanders—my friends—and their staffs used those extra days to great advantage, knitting the ground and air missions tightly together into a new, revised plan—a truly joint operation.

And it was a good thing, because our forces ran into tough enemy resistance during the first three days of the operation. Early on March 2, Special Forces teams led a convoy of about four hundred newly organized Pashtun fighters into the Shah-i-Kot Valley, the first phase of the hammer-and-anvil operation. Their mission was to attack along the western ridge and force the enemy into kill zones where several companies of 10th Mountain troops and SOF would be blocking positions on the south and east sides of the Valley.

As so often happens in war, the carefully balanced details of the plan didn't survive first contact with the enemy. As I've always said, in any war plan the enemy gets a vote. And that morning al Qaeda cast their vote with mortars, volleys of RPGs, and heavy machine gun fire—all from concealed, fortified positions. To further complicate the operation, the Afghan troops entering from the north were misidentified as enemy troops, and attacked by friendly air support.

As this occurred, the 10th Mountain light infantry and SOF teams began their insertions into positions in the snowy passes that could serve as escape roots into Pakistan. The enemy fiercely defended the landing zones along the pine-forested ridges. MH-47 Chinooks were battered with RPGs and machine-gun fire. Navy SEALs, Green Berets, Rangers, and 10th Mountain troopers were taking casualties. Anaconda was turning into a hell of a fight.

Apache gunships of the 101st Airborne engaged the enemy at close range on the steep mountainside, killing scores, but suffering casualties among the aviators and damage to the helicopters. My logistician, Denny Jackson, organized the airlift of additional gunships, while Marines from Kandahar joined the fight with Super Cobras to provide gunship support to the deploying light infantry. And a virtual conveyor belt of fixed-wing aircraft pounded the al Qaeda positions.

The enemy fought with fierce determination. It became clear on day three that al Qaeda intended to win this battle—or die in place. They were eager to engage Coalition forces at close quarters rather than suffering precision bombing from unseen planes, as they had in previous weeks around Jalalabad and Kandahar.

As I watched the battle from the JOC, the air picture showed a steady stream of fighter-bombers working the shrinking circle of enemy resistance at the head of the valley and in the caves on the eastern and western slopes. A-10 Warthogs were striking al Qaeda mortar pits and bunkers, rotating back and forth from Bagram Air Base. B-52s from Diego Garcia circled high above, dropping strings of JDAMs on fortified enemy positions. And attack helicopters were hitting al Qaeda bunkers with 30 mm chain guns and rockets.

Al Qaeda had made their stand in what they had considered an invulnerable redoubt. When Soviet air assault troops had tried to capture this area in the 1980s, they had suffered hundreds killed and wounded. And they had not defeated the enemy.

Anaconda would produce a different result. This time, it was al Qaeda and the Taliban who suffered the heavy losses. The Coalition was overrunning this last bastion, sealing caves and tunnels—and the enemy inside—with powerful demolition charges, destroying huge caches of ordnance. Our young infantrymen, combat aviators, and SOF troops were killing hundreds of the enemy's best-armed, most highly motivated fighters, many of whom were battle-hardened veterans of the fighting in Chechnya and the Balkans. They would not survive to fight again.

As I made my way out of the windowless SCIF, I realized we were winning a decisive battle. Before Anaconda ended, the last of the enemy's cohesive, well-armed forces in Afghanistan would be destroyed.

Over the coming weeks, there were dramatic press accounts of the battle. Many of them cited our troops' courage, skill, and stamina—but others described "breakdowns" and blunders that were supposedly responsible for Coalition casualties. We had eight troopers Killed in Action, and eighty-two wounded, out of 2027 troops engaged during the two-week operation. It was impossible to count enemy losses accurately—many were blown to bits, others sealed in caves by rockslides our forces triggered with explosive charges—but the final intelligence estimate was that hundreds of enemy soldiers were killed.

More important, the last al Qaeda sanctuary in Afghanistan had been destroyed. And it would never be rebuilt.

I cried after that battle—having postponed my emotions until I could afford them—as I had seen Eric Artila do so many years before. I thought of the wives, kids, moms, and dads who were mourning the loss of their loved ones, and I mourned with them. But I also celebrated the lives of these young heroes.

When I was in Bagram twelve days later, pinning Purple Hearts on brave young 10th Mountain and 101st Airborne troopers, I called Operation Anaconda "an unqualified and absolute success." The press reacted negatively. How, they asked, could any battle be a success when Americans had been killed and wounded?

As I left Bagram and flew above the scarred brown hills of Afghanistan, I thought about the reporters' questions, and about the cost of war. When weapons were fired, people died—on both sides. I remembered the first time I read about Operation Husky, the July 1943 Allied invasion of Sicily. Hundreds of American and British paratroopers and glider-borne troops had been killed when friendly naval forces off the coast mistakenly fired on the gliders and their transports. As the tow planes released the gliders short of their drop zones, they had crashed into the Mediterranean. Our losses had not stopped us in 1943. We had been engaged in a war of national survival—and America had persevered.

I could only hope that one day this new generation of reporters would come to understand the nature of war: the realities of combat, the ugly face of battle. Because once again America was engaged in a struggle for survival.

10

THE PLAN

RAMSTEIN, GERMANY
MARCH 21, 2002

The screen went dark, the lights of the conference room came up, and I stood at the head of the table. It was late afternoon on Thursday, March 21, 2002, the end of a long day working Iraq options with CENTCOM's component commanders at NATO's Warrior Prep Center across the autobahn from Ramstein Air Base. Outside, the hillsides of the Saarland were budding into spring green. But the sterile, windowless conference room could have been on the equator or at the South Pole.

This was the first time my ground, air, naval, and Special Ops commanders had sat down with my staff directors and me to discuss the shape and scope of a possible military operation to remove the regime of Saddam Hussein.

Gene Renuart and Jeff Kimmons had done a masterful job outlining the current iteration of the Commander's Concept. Seven lines of operation, nine slices representing Iraqi centers of gravity.

I had summarized my discussions with the President and the NSC in Crawford and at the White House: If the President ordered CENTCOM to war, the operation would not be a reprise of Desert Storm. We would go into Iraq fast and hard, not slow and heavy, launching as simultaneously as possible from as many countries as American carrot-and-stick negotiators could deliver.

"The President hopes war will not be necessary," I said. "The NSC believes bilateral and international diplomacy might work." I shook my head. These officers had to understand the true nature of our responsibility. "The civilian leadership will negotiate, at the UN and with heads of state and ministers around the world. For them, military planning is a prudent step. It's our job to do that planning."

I let them absorb my words.

"Guys," I said, "there's a burglar in the house." They all understood the Special Ops expression: You didn't roll over and go back to sleep when there was an intruder downstairs with a gun. This was an urgent mission, one that would require their complete focus. "We need rock-solid planning—joint planning for joint execution."

I looked around the conference table. We were wearing "Euro-casual" civvies for security reasons, but each of us had a small nametag on his sport coat or sweater. "I see *Army, Navy, Air Force,* and *Marine Corps* on your name tags," I said. "But the tags I want to see will read *JOINT*—all the Services acting together as one.

"Up in Paktia Province the other day, soldiers, Navy SEALs, Air Force crews, Marine Cobra pilots, and Bert Calland and Dell Dailey's special operators were fighting, dying, and killing al Qaeda. There were no ground campaigns, air campaigns, or SOF campaigns. There was one integrated plan, and our people fought as a joint force."

That drew a look of satisfaction from the component commanders.

"If we have to fight in Iraq," I told them, "we'll do it as a joint team. We will not take orders from the Service Chiefs in Washington. I will take my orders from the Secretary of Defense . . . and you will take your orders from me. No time for Service parochialism."

I held up my hand. "One last point. What we discussed today goes no further than the people in this room. This command does not leak. We are military professionals, not a bunch of self-serving assholes."

I could see that my message had registered.

"Okay," I said. "Let's go get a beer and eat some schnitzel."

The session had gone well, I thought. The commanders recognized the tough job that lay ahead. And I believed they understood my feelings about joint warfighting . . . and leaks.

But one morning in early May back in Tampa, my Public Affairs director, Rear Admiral Craig Quigley, brought me a copy of a *Los Angeles Times* story by William Arkin that was loaded with leaked details about the Ramstein conference and our Iraq planning. According to Arkin's unnamed Pentagon sources, the planning was "simplistic and myopic." Arkin also criticized the iterative planning process (which had "emerged in February," he wrote), citing "senior Defense Department officials, civilians who are not tied to any individual service." The anonymous Pentagon sources had accused CENTCOM of gross incompetence, strategic ineptitude, and ignoring the "successful elements" of Desert Storm, the Kosovo air campaign, and operations in Afghanistan. The story contained Top Secret compartmented information, including options for simultaneous land and air operations from several directions.

"This would be funny," I told Craig Quigley, "if it weren't for all the references to 'Top Secret, Polo Step'." *Polo Step* was the sensitive planning compartment's code name.

It was obvious that someone who had been with me in Ramstein had reported the content of our meeting to an unnamed member or members of the Pentagon community, and that person had leaked his guts out, sniping at the planning options we'd been developing— options that apparently didn't comport with his views. "[T]he emerging Iraq plan was never officially brought into 'the tank,' " the article read, "for discussion among the heads of all the services." *Unmitigated bullshit*, I thought. On March 29, we had briefed the Service Chiefs—in the Tank. We'd seen the normal amount of service-parochial kibitzing, but Dick Myers had kept the Chiefs on a tighter rein, and it had been a productive session.

I wouldn't let my anger over this interfere with my job, of course. But I *would* let the SecDef know what I thought of these Pentagon leakers, who were jeopardizing America's sons and daughters.

"Mr. Secretary," I told Rumsfeld the next afternoon, "if I sound angry, it's because I am." I reminded him of just how much compartmented material had appeared in the Arkin story. "I'd like everyone in OSD and the JCS who knows the details of our planning process to be polygraphed—and prosecuted if they're discovered to have leaked Top Secret information."

Rumsfeld let me cool off. "It's unbelievable," he said.

"Mr. Secretary, Washington, D.C. is the only vessel on this planet that leaks from the top."

"I'll work on it, General."

Over the next few days Rumsfeld held "Come to Jesus" meetings with the Chiefs and the OSD staff, and I discussed my disappointment with the leak with the CENTCOM staff and my components. The leaks slowed down, and though a few "trickles" continued, they were never as damaging as the information that some self-serving bastard had fed to a reporter.

THE WHITE HOUSE SITUATION ROOM WAS PLEASANTLY COOL AFTER the sweltering August heat of downtown Washington. Colin Powell and George Tenet had just arrived; they'd both been caught in rush-hour traffic. All our shirt collars were damp with sweat.

"The Brits still classify Washington as a tropical hardship post," someone quipped as Powell took his place beside the President.

Gene Renuart and I had come to the White House on this first Monday in August to brief the President and the NSC on the latest version of what had become OPLAN 1003V—no longer a concept, now a full-blown plan. We would summarize the progress we'd made since our meeting at Camp David in May, when I had described a series of military options to remove Saddam Hussein from power.

At that May meeting, in one of the most eloquent presentations I'd ever heard, Colin Powell had made a case that the world today was far different from what it had been in 1990–1991—when the coalition to remove Saddam from Kuwait had been formed. It would not be easy to build a large coalition, he argued, to line up a consensus in the UN for military operations. Colin's presentation was not negative, not positive—simply a statement of reality as he saw it. As I listened, I was impressed by the balance of what I was hearing. The Secretary of State was issuing a caution—*this won't be easy*. But there was no arguing, no hand-wringing. At several points during the discussion the President and Vice President Cheney had nodded their heads in agreement. "I don't know whether or not we can get all the international support we need," Powell said. "But we will try." I agreed that the UN would be difficult, but I had been thinking hard about our coalition needs myself—and in my view the nations in the CENTCOM region would provide all the required—if not all the desired—support.

Between mid-May and late July, I had made three trips to the AOR, concentrating on infrastructure improvements and the buildup of our forces. I'd met with leaders in Qatar, Oman, the UAE, Bahrain, and Jordan. And, as always, I visited our troops in Afghanistan.

Lieutenant General Dan McNeill, Commander of XVIII Airborne Corps, had taken command of Task Force 180, our Coalition force, establishing his headquarters at Bagram Air Base. I had served with Dan in Korea during the 1990s; he was a seasoned veteran, and I was pleased to have him on the team.

President Bush had stressed his concern that we maintain momentum in Afghanistan—even if we executed the 1003V plan for Iraq. I agreed. "Mr. President," I told him, "we will stay focused on Afghanistan, because strategically our operations there will be the 'flank' of Iraq." Having discussed this with Secretary Rumsfeld, we agreed that our U.S. force level would remain about 9,500 troops unless there was a reason for change, at which point we would discuss it. Dan McNeill was exactly the man we needed on the ground, to keep the pressure on Osama bin Laden and the remnants of al Qaeda. As we moved toward war with Iraq, Dan joined the team, became a member of CENTCOM, and attended every planning session and briefing. After I introduced him to President Musharraf and Hamid Karzai, he established irreplaceable relationships with them and other regional leaders. Because of his efforts, our misison in Afghanistan never suffered.

Now, as the President and the NSC members listened, I announced the progress I had made.

"Mr. President," I said, "if a decision is made to execute a military operation in Iraq, we will not have to go it alone. We have tentative agreements for access, overflight, basing, and staging across the Gulf."

The room was quiet. I had discussed with regional heads of state and their defense ministers the upgrading of bases we used routinely for training and to stage forces for operations in Afghanistan. And, privately, I had informed them that we were improving infrastructure and posturing forces in case it became necessary to disarm Iraq by force. Kuwait had always been onboard; it was our anchor. Now we had the commitment of King Abdullah of Jordan and the Gulf state leaders to permit staging, basing, and overflight—for naval forces, strike and reconnaissance aircraft, refueling tankers, and SOF—at a number of strategic sites close to Iraq.

The Emir of Qatar, Sheik Hamad ibn Khalifa al Thani, had granted permission to base fighter aircraft at al Udeid, and to move our deployable command post to Camp As Sayliyah as soon as it was completed by our contractors in Florida.

I'd reminded the Emir that, at out first meeting after I'd become the CENTCOM commander, I had asked what I could do for him.

"Send me ten thousand American soldiers," he'd replied with a smile.

On my most recent trip to Qatar, I fulfilled his request. "I may be two years late," I told him, "but you will have your American troops."

Colin Powell listened closely as I praised the American ambassadors in the region for their help in achieving the results I was describing. He smiled and credited his diplomats for all they'd accomplished.
"Good folks," he said.

"Mr. President," I said, "as I've informed Secretary Rumsfeld,
each regional leader understands that we are conducting contingency
planning, that you have not made a decision to go to war."

Rumsfeld nodded.

"With overlapping aircraft carrier 'evolutions,'" I told the President, "as well as increased 'training' deployments of 3rd Infantry Division battalions to Kuwait, and the increased number of aircraft we
have in Operation Southern Watch, we are close to having a force
that could execute Red, White, or Blue Options, should it become
necessary."

Since 9/11, the NSC had absorbed a lot of detailed military information. But they were in for a lot more.

"The 3rd ID," I continued, "is a mechanized infantry unit with
organic armor and artillery and years of desert experience rotating
its brigades through Kuwait. It does not seem to alarm the Iraqis
that Division units are arriving on Kuwaiti training ranges with additional MLRS launchers and attack helicopters. Their intelligence
is simply not sophisticated enough to pick up on such incremental
changes."

"Understand completely," the President said.

"We've flown over four thousand sorties over Iraq since January,"
I said, consulting my notes. "And Iraqi air defenses have targeted our
aircraft or violated the no-fly zones fifty-two times. That's double the
rate of last year."

"Would it make sense to reduce our risk by cutting back on the
number of sorties?" Condi Rice asked.

"Condi," I answered, "at some point it might make sense to cut
back, but not yet. We want to continue to use response options to degrade the Iraqi Integrated Air Defense System. If it ever comes to
war, we'll want their IADS as weak as possible."

The next charts showed the peaks and valleys of our force flow. "In a month," I said, "we will have the lead elements of a Running Start force in place."

"But these steps are not taking us beyond a point of no return?" Donald Rumsfeld asked.

"No, Mr. Secretary."

The next chart was headed REVISED TIMING. "With current base and infrastructure enhancements," I said, "the anticipated duration of the first three phases of the overall operation has been revised to a 45-90-90 timeline."

In other words, we could begin operations by deploying forces while launching an air and SOF campaign to shape the battlespace— all of which would take about forty-five days. During that time, we would target Iraq's suspected WMD sites, Republican Guards formations, and command and control facilities, and prevent their use of Theater Ballistic Missiles. Ground forces would begin to arrive and move through their staging areas—in Kuwait and possibly in Turkey—into Iraq; their initial combat operations would carry on for the next ninety days. And our "decisive offensive operations" would then be conducted for a maximum of three months, to "complete regime destruction." Obviously this 45-90-90 would be followed by a much longer Phase IV. "I don't know how long," I added.

"We call it the Running Start because the units reaching the theater would not wait for follow-on forces to arrive, but rather would proceed directly toward their objectives."

"General Franks," Dick Cheney asked, "would the major objectives of the Running Start remain unchanged?"

The answer was yes. "Both the strategic objective of regime change, and our operational objectives of securing the oil fields and water infrastructure, while preventing Saddam's use of long-range missiles—and WMD—are unchanged."

My next chart was entitled HYBRID CONCEPT, a combination of the GENERATED and RUNNING START options. Like the other concepts we had considered, Hybrid had four phases. The initial deployment in Phase I would be greatly accelerated by a massive air-lift, using the Civilian Reserve Air Fleet (CRAF) to augment our military transport capabilities. Tens of thousands of troops would be moved to the war zone within a week. And less than two weeks later they would be matched up with their equipment, which would be shipped by sea. This buildup of forces would be protected by a combat air umbrella of eight hundred strike planes from carriers and land bases around the Gulf. In Phase II, we would launch air and Special Operations Forces into Iraq for about two weeks to destroy key target sets and set conditions for deploying heavy units. Then the heavy units would launch their operations in Phase III, which could last up to ninety days, and would complete the destruction of the Iraqi military.

"The Hybrid is a bit sequential," I explained, "and we favor simultaneous ops from as many directions as possible. But the value of the concept is that it gives the President the option to wait for a buildup of forces . . . or to attack earlier if he chooses.

"If we use the Civilian Reserve Air Fleet, Mr. President," I added, "it certainly will be a quintessential CNN moment. But it will not commit the country to war. We will have tipped our hand, but we will not yet have started shooting."

President Bush considered this a moment. "Good," he said. "We're not going to war unless we have to."

"A rapid force deployment," I continued, "enhances our military capability on Iraq's borders, and also assists in placing diplomatic pressure on Saddam's regime."

The NSC members were poring over the HYBRID CONCEPT chart, and I wanted to make sure they understood the flexibility of the model. "This is not etched in stone," I explained to the President. "There are lots of possible variations. But the basic idea is that—once we have the required infrastructure in place—we can expand our troop level very rapidly, move into kinetic operations at any point of your choosing, and push follow-on forces behind the lead units."

President Bush nodded again.

I turned to the STRATEGIC RISKS chart. "As we've discussed, Saddam Hussein could try to desynchronize our attack by launching missiles at his neighbors. Kuwait, Saudi Arabia, Jordan, and Israel could be targets, with Israel being the most dangerous to us from a strategic perspective."

To counter this threat, I explained, deploying Patriot PAC-3 missiles to the region would be a prudent step. This upgraded variant of the Patriot offered significant protection from Scuds and other Theater Ballistic Missiles, and could augment the new Arrow 2 anti-TBM missile the Israelis were fielding. "If we deploy the PAC-3 now, Mr. President, we can mitigate, if not eliminate, the problem."

The President was listening closely. "Tommy, how are you doing with the Baghdad problem?"

"Fortress Baghdad" was an ongoing concern among the civilian leadership; I had been huddling with my senior staff on the matter for weeks. Overhead imagery and electronic intelligence confirmed that the Republican Guard divisions and Special Republican Guard units positioned in and around Baghdad would be vulnerable to air attack with Precision Guided Munitions. We were working on what I called an "Inside-Out" approach: Instead of attacking from the outside of the defensive cordon around the capital, we would destroy the enemy inside the cordon by relentless air attack, working from the center outward. The more concentrated the Republican Guard positions were, the more vulnerable they became. And attacking in and around Baghdad had the added benefit of making the city "inhospitable" to forces looking for a place to hide. As Eric Antila had told me thirty years before, "Rats never swim *toward* a sinking ship."

But the concept needed more work, so I gave the President a cautious answer. "I'm optimistic that we will have a practical solution to the problem soon, Mr. President. And I'll bring it to Secretary Rumsfeld as soon as we have something solid."

Like the "Challenges" I posed to myself on my daily three-by-five cards, this room offered me no shortage of brain-teasing questions:

"What if the Iraqis block their oil pipelines to Jordan, Syria, and Turkey?"

"Is a northern front from Turkey a real possibility?"

"What happens if Saddam uses WMD on our troops?"

"Might he blow up Iraq's water infrastructure?"

All good questions, and we discussed each in turn. None of them would be fully answered in this session, but now that so many issues were on the table, the principals would contemplate and suggest possible solutions in the months ahead. This was a thoughtful collection of players: I sensed more teamwork among them all than our national media would ever admit.

As the discussion slowed, I introduced a collection of difficult problems under a single heading: CATASTROPHIC SUCCESS.

If Iraqi resistance did "fracture" quickly, as I thought possible—or if a military coup toppled Saddam's regime at the onset of the campaign, or early uprisings developed among the Shiites and the Kurds—what would we do?

"We would continue the operation," Donald Rumsfeld said, "to restore and maintain order until the Iraqis can govern themselves."

To a person, the NSC concurred.

I briefed the room on targeting, starting as usual with the basics. Using imagery of important regime buildings in central Baghdad—including Baath Party headquarters and the command center of the *Mukhabarat* Special Security Organization—I explained how destroying these structures would blind and paralyze Saddam's inner leadership circle.

"We know where they are," I said, "and we know who works there." Killing regime leaders and destroying their command and control apparatus would be a priority. This would not be like searching for Mullah Omar in a warren of mud-brick or cinderblock compounds in Kandahar. TLAMs, JDAMs, and the whole alphabet soup of available Precision Guided Munitions would be our weapons of choice. These targets lay close to upscale apartment buildings and private homes; many belonged to regime leaders and sympathizers. But Iraq's apolitical, educated elite—the physicians, engineers, and managers who would be needed to rebuild their country—also lived in these neighborhoods.

"CENTCOM's targeteers are working hard on the problem," I assured the NSC. "The target sets on the Regime Leadership slice are a tough nut. But we're going to crack it."

My final chart was potentially the most important: PHASE IV STABILITY OPERATIONS.

"The Generated and Running Starts," I explained, "and the Hybrid Concept all project Phase III ending with a maximum of two hundred and fifty thousand troops in Iraq. We will have to stand up a new Iraqi army, and create a constabulary that includes a representative tribal, religious, and ethnic mix. It will take time.

"And well-designed and well-funded reconstruction projects that put large numbers of Iraqis to work and quickly meet community needs—and expectations—will be the keys to our success in Phase IV."

"We will want to get Iraqis in charge of Iraq as soon as possible," Don Rumsfeld said. On hearing his words, heads nodded around the table.

"At some point," I said, "we can begin drawing down our force. We'll want to retain a core strength of at least fifty thousand men, and our troop reductions should parallel deployment of representative, professional Iraqi security forces. Our exit strategy will be tied to effective governance by Iraqis, not to a timeline."

I saw further nods around the table. And then Condi Rice tapped her watch; we were out of time.

President Bush thanked me warmly as the meeting concluded. "See you soon," he said.

Colin Powell was friendly as we shook hands on leaving the room. But it was obvious that something was on his mind.

I DIDN'T HAVE TO WAIT LONG TO FIND OUT WHAT IT WAS. ON Thursday, September 5, the day before I was scheduled to fly to Washington for another NSC briefing on Iraq—to be followed by weekend discussions at Camp David—Colin called me in Tampa.

"Tom, I'm sorry to interrupt you because I know how busy you are," he said, a gentleman as always. "But I want you to hear this from me up front."

Colin had concerns. He was from a generation of generals who believed that overwhelming military force was found in troop strength—sheer numbers of soldiers and tanks on the ground. As Chairman of the Joint Chiefs of Staff during Desert Storm, General Colin Powell had seen the number of coalition ground forces rise to more than five hundred thousand. Indeed, this principle of overwhelming force was often referred to as the "Powell Doctrine."

I had a lot of respect for Colin Powell—even as I'd come to believe that the days of half-million-strong mobilizations were over.

"I'm going to critique your plan up at Camp David," he said. "I've got problems with force size and support of that force, given such long lines of communication."

All right, I thought. *He's honest enough to put his cards on the table.* We had basic differences in strategic thinking; fair enough. At least he was giving me a warning, rather than blindsiding me in front of the NSC and the President. "Thank you, Mr. Secretary," I said. "I'll do my best to answer your concerns."

I sat a moment at my desk. Colin Powell was the free world's leading diplomat. But he no longer wore Army green. He'd earned his right to an opinion, but had relinquished responsibility for the conduct of military operations when he retired as the Chairman of the Joint Chiefs of Staff in 1993.

I picked up the Red Switch and spoke to Don Rumsfeld. "I appreciate his call," I said. "But I wanted to tell him that the military has changed since he left it."

Rumsfeld chuckled. "You could say that, Tom. But just be calm and professional. Answer his comments, point by point. If Colin has doubts, I want him to get them on the table in front of the President and the NSC. Otherwise, we'll look like we're steamrolling."

I BRIEFED THE NSC—MINUS PRESIDENT BUSH—IN THE SITUATION Room in the White House on the morning of September 6, describing what I would discuss with the President the next day at Camp David.

After the meeting, Rumsfeld came over. "We'll be riding up to Camp David with Vice President Cheney in his helicopter. I'll give you a lift to the helipad at the Observatory."

The Vice President's residence is on the grounds of the Naval Observatory on upper Massachusetts Avenue. At the helipad we boarded Marine Two for the flight to Camp David. It was a pleasant flight, west-northwest out of the District, over the thick traffic of the Beltway and into Maryland's Appalachian foothills.

The drill for overnight guests at Camp David was interesting. White House staff took our bags, and we were each assigned a golf cart with a small laminated map mounted on the dash, indicating the route to our cabins. Camp David is a rolling, thickly wooded area, with narrow, curving blacktop lanes—not the best-marked routes in the world. Since my days as an Artillery officer candidate at Fort Sill, I'd taken pride in accurate map reading. But I'll be damned if I didn't get lost trying to follow the line diagram of the route from the helipad to my cabin.

"Don't tell the President," I joked to the efficient young Secret Service woman who eventually guided me to the cabin.

At the Saturday morning discussion, Colin Powell did raise his concerns. Soft-spoken and polite, ever the diplomat, he questioned the friendly-to-enemy force ratios, and made the point rather forcefully that the Coalition would have "extremely long" supply lines. "These are issues we should consider," he said.

Thanking him for his thoughts, I used a detailed map to introduce the concept of five simultaneous operational fronts. "We are moving into a new strategic and operational paradigm here, Mr. Secretary," I said.

As Powell listened intently, I continued. "By applying military mass simultaneously at key points, rather than trying to push a

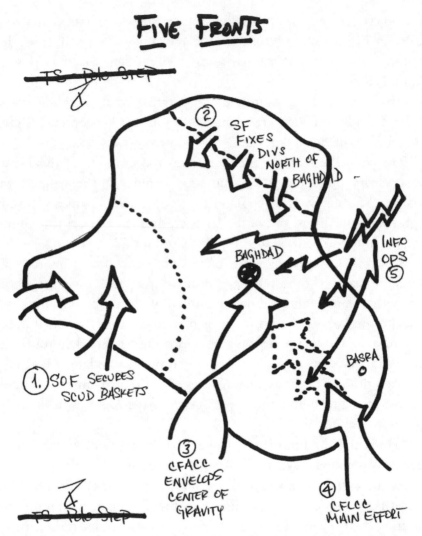

An early sketch of the five-front concept that became the basis for Operation Iraqi Freedom.

broad, slow conventional advance, we throw the enemy off balance. We saw this in Afghanistan—fast, rapid maneuver. This creates momentum. We put our forces deep into the enemy's territory, moving so quickly that the Iraqis will not have time to react. When they finally do move, they become targets for the air component and precision artillery fires. Speed and momentum are the keys."

Colin Powell didn't debate the brief I gave, and he didn't ask any more operational questions. I don't know whether I satisfied his concerns, but it was important that he forced the detailed discussion in front of the national security team, including the President.

Don Rumsfeld looked around the pine-paneled room as the session wrapped up, and thanked me for the presentation. "I want all of you to be comfortable with this plan," he said.

As I left Camp David, I felt good about the work we had done.

GENE RENUART AND I RETURNED TO MacDILL LATE ON Tuesday, September 10.

The day before, we'd briefed Dick Myers and the Service Chiefs in the Tank. All in all it was a good session—probably because Dick was working hard to build consensus, and also because Don Rumsfeld had let it be known he expected the Joint Chiefs to be *joint*. Although the Chiefs still found it hard to think beyond the boundaries of their individual services—especially when it came to procuring weapon systems and maintaining their authorized "end-strengths"—repeated reminders from Rumsfeld and Dick Myers were slowly forcing them to build the "transformational" national defense that Donald Rumsfeld envisioned.

One positive outcome of my trips to the Tank that summer was that the services were dredging through their budgets to produce the funding needed to upgrade basing and infrastructure in the region. To four-stars jealously guarding their appropriations, this was about as pleasant an exercise as multiple root canals. As a result, though, CENTCOM got new ramp space at airbases in Oman, Qatar, and Kuwait. We increased the number of Army forces in the region. The SOF got upgraded helicopters. And the Navy increased the tempo of aircraft carrier and TLAM shooters in and out of the Gulf and Northern Arabian Sea.

Since our planning called for the majority of Coalition ground forces to stage through Kuwait, the tiny nation was suddenly set to become one of the largest American bases in the world. Seaports, fuel pipelines, additional water capacity—a major consideration in the virtually rainless Gulf—and basic camp construction were all under way.

On my latest visit to Riyadh, I'd confirmed that the Saudis weren't willing to host another Desert Storm coalition. But neither would they create a diplomatic crisis by ordering the Coalition military units already working in the Kingdom to leave. This meant that we could continue operating the Combined Air Operations Center at Prince Sultan Air Base—and, unknown to the media, conducting Combat Search and Rescue and Special Operations recon work out of a small airbase north of the Tapline Road, near the border of Iraq's western desert. If we could keep those two important sites operating, and continue flying refueling tankers and recon planes out of Prince Sultan Air Base, Saudi Arabia would make an important contribution to freeing Iraq—without jeopardizing its position in the larger Muslim world.

With most of the staff work completed on both the "generated" and "running start" options, the 1003V Hybrid plan became the focus of our attention. It was becoming more detailed each day, as CENTCOM's targeteers refined intelligence and reached new estimates on the Iraqi order of battle. It was no surprise that the six Republican Guard divisions had received the largest allocations of fuel, ammunition, and spare parts. Although our HUMINT on the units was sketchy, technical intelligence revealed them to be the most powerful, best-equipped divisions in the Iraqi military, with combat-readiness levels of more than 90 percent. As they moved from field training to garrison duty, the Republican Guard seemed likely to hold the main defensive line on the outskirts of Baghdad.

"You know," I told Jeff Kimmons as we reviewed the latest satellite images of the Al Nida Republican Guard Armored Division moving back to its laagers and maintenance bases south of Baghdad, "the guys in that outfit have never been exposed to precision targeting."

"They're not going to enjoy their first exposure," Jeff said.

In fact, the upgrades we'd made to our ground-based indirect fire systems since Desert Storm had transformed our medium- to long-range artillery into all-weather standoff weapons that would be a great complement to the air component's guided munitions.

The best thing the Republican Guard could do for us, I realized, was to dig in around Baghdad and form a static, Soviet-style "ring of steel" defense. Once kinetics began, they wouldn't have time to evade our precision firepower by dispersing. And if they did manage to spread out, they would lose their cohesiveness and the effect of their own massed firepower. Their T-72s had been upgraded with thermal sights, and these tanks fired a variety of Russian wire-guided missiles. But we were at least one generation ahead of them in precision ordnance, and a quantum leap beyond them in combined arms maneuver tactics and joint operations. In fact, the Iraqi military had virtually no joint characteristics; their air force was small and obsolete, and their helicopter gunships would amount to nothing more than targets to our F-16s and F/A-18s.

Weapons of mass destruction remained the enemy's hole card. We could defend our troops, but we would never preempt regime use of WMD, because intelligence on the threat was not actionable: We knew the Iraqis had WMD, but we didn't know where it was being hidden. If ever we needed human intelligence, it was now. I knew George Tenet would do his best with the assets he had, but there was no time to undo decades of damage to America's espionage capabilities. Sun Tzu was as right today as he had been 2,500 years ago: *Spies are useful everywhere.*

As we studied the emerging picture of the enemy, the 1003V Hybrid plan was evolving into a practical war plan that would soon be ready if the President ordered us to fight. Each team contributing to the OPLAN knew it by a different name, to minimize the risk of leaks. In Europe, for example, the Army V Corps team hammering out the tactical and logistical challenges of launching a main effort attack from the Kuwaiti border to Baghdad, called their exercise "Imminent Victory."

The V Corps wargamers' work helped us estimate vital time-and-distance factors, the meat and potatoes of tactical planners. How fast and how far could an armor brigade advance along the paved road network of the Euphrates Valley, or through the open desert farther west, given varying levels of enemy resistance? Equally important, how fast and how far could specific Iraqi army formations move, under constant air attack, to counter our advance? In the fall of 2002, these were theoretical questions. But I had to assume that these computer war games would become tank tracks in the dusty soil of Iraq sometime in the future—perhaps the near future.

A picture was forming in my mind: Army, Marine Corps, and British armor battalions moving north at maximum speed, converging on the Iraqi regime's centers of gravity: Basra in the south, Baghdad in the country's center. As my father used to say when he approached the problem of clearing land, "You kill the roots, Tommy Ray, and the tree will fall."

At an earlier CENTCOM huddle with my subordinate commanders, I had reminded them of a basic tactical principle: speed kills . . . the enemy.

General George Patton—one of America's most innovative field commanders—had recognized the importance of maneuver speed during his dramatic breakthrough and offensive across central France in 1944. He had used the same principle to turn the U.S. 3rd Army north, 90 degrees off its axis of advance, into the flank of the German juggernaut in the Battle of the Bulge. Patton understood that the ultimate objective of any campaign is the enemy's center of gravity. Indeed, the only time Patton's army bogged down was when it laid siege to the heavily fortified German garrison at Metz. World War II gave us a colorful tanker's adage for this principle of maneuver: "Haul ass and bypass."

O NE YEAR AND ONE DAY AFTER THE 9/11 ATTACKS ON AMERICA, I joined the rest of the world in tuning my television to the image of the U.N. General Assembly Hall. The hall was filled to capacity, with some delegates wearing their distinctive national dress: flowing robes, turbans, a variety of Islamic headgear. Almost to a person, however, it was a somber audience that had gathered to hear President Bush's address.

In starkly eloquent words, the President recalled the terrorist attacks of 9/11. Yet despite our successful military campaign in Afghanistan, he said, the world was still "challenged today by outlaw groups and regimes that accept no law of morality and no limit to their violent ambitions."

The President quickly turned his focus on Iraq. He reviewed Saddam Hussein's defiance of the series of U.N. resolutions that dated back to the Gulf War ceasefire—resolutions that required Iraq to account for and destroy its weapons of mass destruction, stop human rights abuses against its citizens, and accept internationally recognized rule of law.

Then he cited a report from the U.N. Commission on Human Rights that found that Iraq had subjected "tens of thousands of political opponents and ordinary citizens" to arbitrary imprisonment and summary execution. He also cited U.N. Security Council resolutions that demanded Iraq renounce terrorism, but which Saddam Hussein had consistently defied, plotting the assassination of regional leaders and harboring al Qaeda terrorists known to have escaped from Afghanistan.

As to weapons of mass destruction, the President said that Iraq had expelled UN inspectors—but not before they had discovered grim evidence of the regime's ongoing WMD program.

"From 1991 to 1995," President Bush told the General Assembly, "the Iraqi regime said it had no biological weapons." But he noted that after the defection of a senior Iraqi weapons official, this was exposed as a lie. Saddam's regime then "admitted to producing tens of thousands of liters of anthrax and other deadly biological agents for use with Scud warheads, aerial bombs, and aircraft spray tanks."

George Bush paused for emphasis.

"U.N. inspectors believe Iraq has produced two to four times the amount of biological agents it declared," the President stressed, "and has failed to account for more than three metric tons of material that could be used to produce biological weapons."

Bush continued to catalog Iraqi defiance of Security Council resolutions, including the expulsion of UN inspectors in 1998. In a series of hard-hitting, staccato paragraphs—each leading with the phrase "If the Iraqi regime wishes peace . . ."—Bush called on Saddam Hussein and his government to comply with all Security Council resolutions and cease its illicit trade in oil, which diverted funds from the people in defiance of U.N.-mandated sanctions.

"The President ended by saying, 'Events can turn in one of two ways.' If the international community failed to act, the Iraqi people would continue to 'live in brutal submission,' and Saddam's regime would continue to threaten stability in the Middle East."

But if the international community met its responsibilities, he concluded, "the people of Iraq can shake off their captivity," and one day "join a democratic Afghanistan and a democratic Palestine, inspiring reforms throughout the Muslim world." He evoked a transformed Middle East, where honest government and respect for women and the "great Islamic tradition of learning can triumph."

Speaking slowly and deliberately, President Bush called upon the international community to act. "We cannot stand by and do nothing while dangers gather. We must stand up for our security, and for the permanent rights and the hopes of mankind. By heritage and by choice, the United States of America will make that stand. And, delegates to the United Nations, you have the power to make that stand, as well."

The applause was unenthusiastic, and many delegates sat motionless. I clicked off the TV before the network could chime in with their views on what the President had said. In my opinion, it didn't matter how the General Assembly or the media reacted to George Bush's speech. He was throwing down the gauntlet, putting the world on notice that the United States would "stand up for our security."

I found the President's emphasis on Iraq's human rights abuses, and the dangers of its weapons of mass destruction potential, equally persuasive. With the exception of North Korea, no other contemporary state had systematically brutalized its citizens with such ferocity.

The atrocities of Saddam Hussein's execution squads put them in the same category as the Hutu militias in Rwanda and Cambodia's Khmer Rouge.

And the United Nations inspectors' warning that Iraq had failed to account for thousands of liters of weaponized anthrax, and tons of precursor chemicals, was especially alarming. When I'd taken command of CENTCOM, the CIA had briefed me on Iraq's biological weapons, which they described as potentially the most dangerous facet of Saddam's WMD program. Anthrax spores were easy to conceal and transport. A small seed culture of spores could be transformed into a powerful bio arsenal, using only a few hundred kilograms of growth medium.

Two years earlier, George Tenet had testified before Congress that al Qaeda was actively seeking to acquire chemical weapons. The warning hadn't aroused much media interest until Coalition forces in Afghanistan found an al Qaeda videotape that showed a group of dogs being gassed in a closed room. As the first puff of pale white vapor reached the chained animals they went into spasms, collapsed with their legs twitching violently, and died within seconds. A few months later we found that experimental gas chamber at the al Qaeda Duranta Camp near Jalalabad.

And while many al Qaeda leaders had been killed, others had sought sanctuary in Iraq. The question was: *Had terrorism and WMD already joined? If not, how long could it be before they did?*

I didn't know the answer. But I was concerned with the question—which I didn't think our patchwork intelligence architecture could answer without putting troops on the ground.

WHILE I WAS TRAVELING IN THE AOR IN SEPTEMBER, THE NSC released its National Security Strategy statement, which expressed the administration's new doctrine of preemption. The President had first articulated this concept at his West Point graduation speech in June. Now a mature policy, the doctrine stated that the

United States, as a sovereign nation, had the right to employ the anticipatory use of force to preempt a threat to its security.

The media immediately speculated that war with Iraq was inevitable—even imminent.

I knew better. But I also realized, as I read the NSC statement in the windowless cabin of Spar 06, that President Bush had virtually cleared the decks for action, putting the world on notice that America would act decisively in its own defense.

If we'd had such a strategy in place years earlier, I realized, we might have been given the authority to remove the Taliban from power, and destroy al Qaeda in Afghanistan, *before* the terrorist attacks of 9/11.

IN LATE SEPTEMBER I RETURNED TO THE GULF. ONE OF MY FIRST stops WAS Qatar, where I met with Sheik Hamad, the Emir, in an elegant seafront Emiri Diwan palace. The conversation focused almost exclusively on Iraq.

"Saddam can never be trusted," the Emir said. He adjusted his white *kefiya* and stroked his mustache. "General Franks, you have the opportunity to save the Iraqi people."

"Sir," I answered. "President Bush has not yet chosen the course of war. But if he does, we will be ready."

THEN I CALLED ON LEADERS IN JORDAN, YEMEN, PAKISTAN, AND Turkey. And I visited coalition troops in Afghanistan, where Dan McNeill updated me on his operations along Pakistan's border. Pervez Musharraf was cooperating and our troops were keeping pressure on al Qaeda. We had seen no reporting on Osama bin Laden, but I was convinced that the coalition was pushing as hard as possible to locate him.

I met with King Abdullah II at Amman's Baraka Palace. He smiled, reaching across the inlaid rosewood table to shake my hand.

"Did you bring any Texas barbeque with you?" he teased. "You always promise, but you never deliver. You spoiled me in Tampa. I love that barbeque."

Once more, I was impressed by the King's openness and honesty. Since the death of his father, King Hussein, Abdullah had worked to improve Jordan's pro-Western position, despite a majority Palestinian population and the unending rancor of the Intifada. Jordan remained balanced between the menace of Iraq and the explosive Arab-Israeli conflict. Now I was going to ask him to support a Coalition that might be required to disarm Iraq and depose Saddam's regime.

As we met, a joint Anglo-American resolution calling on Iraq to accept rigorous, unrestricted weapons inspections from the United Nations Monitoring, Verification and Inspection Commission (UNMOVIC) was under heated discussion in the Security Council. George Bush and Prime Minister Tony Blair were demanding a resolution with teeth, one that would subject Iraq to "serious consequences" if it did not comply.

On November 8, 2002, the U.N. Security Council finally adopted Resolution 1441, which recognized "the threat Iraq's non-compliance with Council resolutions and proliferation of weapons of mass destruction and long-range missiles poses to international peace and security." This resolution repeated the "serious consequences" Iraq would face if it did not cooperate fully with UN weapons inspectors, who would begin arriving in Baghdad later that month.

Bush had already won overwhelming Senate authorization to employ force against Iraq if it continued to defy the international community. And on this day in Amman, I was betting that force would be required.

"General," the king said, "I must protect my nation's interests. But I assure you those interests coincide with America's. You can count on Jordan."

"Your Majesty," I answered, "we will not forget Jordan's friendship."

That day I knew I was in the presence of a friend—and that, if we went to war in Iraq, there would be a western front.

THE PRESIDENTIAL RESIDENCE IN SANAA WAS LESS SUMPTUOUS than Abdullah's Baraka Palace. But President Ali Abdullah Saleh was just as welcoming. After the attack on the *Cole,* and especially since 9/11, Saleh had shifted Yemen's foreign policy away from radical Arab states toward the West. But he had kept open his lines of communication with Libya and Syria . . . and with Saddam Hussein.

Saleh had rugged Bedouin features and a clipped mustache, but he wore Bond Street suits. He could have been a CEO or a successful banker—which, I suppose, did describe some of his duties. During my last visit to Sanaa, he had told me: "I speak frequently to Saddam. He always asks about General Franks."

"I hope that you tell him I am a great soldier and that he should trust me," I said with a smile.

The president opened his hands, an Arab gesture of agreement. "Of course, General. What else would I tell President Saddam?"

I sipped at my aromatic Yemeni coffee, waiting for him to continue.

"You know, General Franks," he said, "you had better be careful if you intend to attack Iraq. Saddam has very powerful forces."

Our complex game was under way. I knew that Saleh and Saddam had once been close, so my host was dutifully conveying the Iraqi dictator's message. But I also believed Saleh was anxious to improve relations with the West. He would act as a conduit to Saddam.

"I realize that, Mr. President," I said. "His forces are very powerful. But his intelligence services are not very good. So, if it comes to war, maybe I'll attack from the west."

He nodded, but did not speak.

"And maybe I will also attack from Turkey," I added. "Both the Jordanians and the Turks are our friends, you know."

He smiled and sipped his own coffee. We waited in silence.

After a moment, President Saleh spoke. "Do you have any message you would like me to pass to Saddam?"

I'd already floated my most important message, but it couldn't hurt to punctuate it with an expression of resolve. "Please tell him that you know me very well, and that I am a serious man. Saddam should cooperate with the United Nations immediately if he truly loves his country."

As Spar 06 lifted off over the stony ochre hills of Yemen, I knew that President Saleh was probably chatting with Saddam on a Soviet-era secure telephone. Ali Abdullah Saleh was a friend . . . of sorts. I knew he would faithfully convey to Saddam, his old comrade, the information I had offered.

If we were going to have the advantage of operational surprise—which would be critical if we went to war—deception would be key.

And Ali Saleh would be one valuable tool in creating that deception.

M Y MEETING IN ANKARA, TURKEY, WITH GENERAL HILMI Özkök, Commander of the Turkish Armed Forces, was interesting, if less productive than those with my contacts elsewhere in the region.

The General was a thoroughly professional officer—fluent in English, with years of experience in NATO. He was part of a new Turkish military that had relinquished its traditional role of political intervention through coups. Today he was receiving a pair of American four-stars in high-stakes negotiations. As always in Turkey, though, the atmosphere was subdued, indirect.

My colleague at the meeting was NATO's top uniformed officer, Air Force General Joe Ralston, the Supreme Allied Commander in Europe. Technically, I was on Joe's turf—Turkey was part of European Command—but he was there for more than protocol reasons. I wanted access to Northern Iraq to stage the 4th Infantry

Division, the mirror image of the 3rd ID that would spearhead ground attack operations from the south. Joe was there to help me make the deal.

I took the lead in arguing the case for Turkish cooperation. General Özkök listened patiently.

He pursed his lips in discomfort when I finished. "General Franks, General Ralston," he said formally. "Your points are very well taken. Saddam Hussein is a threat to the stability of this region. But we must wait until after next week's election to approach my new government."

I got the feeling that the General, a secular man who enjoyed a glass of wine, was not an avid fan of the Islamist administration that was almost certain to take over in mid-November. But these were new days in Turkey. If the country's bid to join the European Union stood any chance of succeeding, he knew that the military must refrain from politics.

Secretary Rumsfeld had authorized Joe and me to sweeten the deal by alluding to possible economic aid that the country badly needed. But the General was in no position to move the question. "I cannot promise the new government will agree, even though your arguments are persuasive."

I sympathized with the General. Whatever his new government decided, I was optimistic that Turkey would continue to grant the Coalition basing for U-2 reconnaissance flights over Iraq, as well as combat aircraft operations out of Incirlik Air Base. And I remained hopeful that Turkey would also allow Coalition SOF to stage from its territory, provided their operations were not made public, even if we were not permitted to stage a large conventional force there. This arrangement would be similar to the one we had made with President Karimov in Uzbekistan during operations in Afghanistan.

As we prepared to leave the General's office, he thanked us for coming. "Let us hope war can be avoided," he said.

"Of course, Sir," I answered. "Nobody hates war like a soldier."

O N FRIDAY, NOVEMBER 22, I WAS PREPARING FOR ANOTHER TRIP. This one would take me from the Horn of Africa to Kyrgyzstan, across 160 degrees of longitude and ten time zones. I was looking forward to the trip because I would spend Thanksgiving with the troops in Afghanistan. But I had one reservation: In recent months, Donald Rumsfeld had been decidedly cranky each time I was away on an extended trip to the AOR.

"Tom," Dick Myers told me, "if he thinks you're out eating goats' eyeballs in some sheik's tent, he starts asking, 'Where's Franks? I want to talk to General Franks.'"

"Dick," I joked. "There's a new invention called a telephone."

"Well, Tom," he'd advised, "just stay in touch. You make him feel good—and he likes to know where you are and what you're doing."

"You bet, Dick," I'd said. "Thanks for the heads-up."

Before I left for Bahrain, I briefed the Secretary on our force request and timing considerations for the Hybrid 1003V plan. Military units are comprised of both people and equipment. And time was required to prepare both of these elements. Since World War I, the convention of the "warning order" or "alert order" had become institutionalized. CENTCOM did not alert troops. We presented formal requests to the Secretary, and Rumsfeld, through the Chairman, would identify units and task the Services and other CINCs to provide the forces.

I transmitted CENTCOM's official request for deployment of the "Pre–N-Day" force—the troops the President would commit to the region long before any decision to go to war. This initial deployment would occur as a series of training exercises and force enhancements, due to increased Iraqi opposition in the no-fly zones.

Even though it was only the first phase of a much larger deployment, the request was impressive—a total of 128,000 soldiers, sailors, airmen and Marines. They would be in the Gulf by February 15, 2003.

I also requested at this time that the Pre–N-Day force be augmented, beginning on N-Day, by Special Mission Units and additional Navy and Air Force personnel, to bring the force total to over 200,000 before G-Day. And, because our Hybrid plan drew on both the Generated and Running Starts, I asked that the Pentagon also alert the 101st Airborne Division (Air Assault), as well as follow-on support units and additional SOF, to be prepared for deployment no later than March 20, 2003.

This would raise the total force to 210,000 troops in what would become the Iraq Theater of Operations.

"Are you satisfied with this force structure, Tom?" Rumsfeld asked. He'd begun calling me Tom when Cathy and I started going out to dinner with the Rumsfelds in January 2002. Cathy always called me Tom, and before long Don Rumsfeld did, too.

Rumsfeld liked to eat at Washington's restaurants—on the early side, not fashionably late. For one thing, he was an early riser like me. For another, dining before the trendy crowd filled Sushi Ko or the Palm also kept the tourists at bay.

The Secretary and I did have different tastes in food, however. One night, at the Old Ebbitt Grill near the White House, I ordered calves' liver with bacon and onions—a childhood staple from my Oklahoma and Texas days, because liver was always cheap.

"This is great, Mr. Secretary," I'd said. "You really ought to try some."

"No thanks," he said, finishing his second dozen Blue Point oysters. "I'll stick with these."

That night I'd reached for the check, but he took it from the waiter. "Come on, Sir," I said. "Let me buy a meal for a change."

Rumsfeld shook his head. "Wouldn't be right," he said, handing over his credit card. "Subordinates shouldn't have to pay." He grinned. "Besides, I have more money than you do."

Those nights out with Don and Joyce Rumsfeld had cemented a bond of trust and friendship that was to grow between us.

By day, of course, we were all business. I glanced again at the Top Secret deployment request before handing it to the SecDef. "Mr. Secretary," I said, "we wanted a credible standing force, one that would give weight to our diplomacy. This is the best that Gene Renuart's Fifty-Pound Brains can produce. I think they did a damn good job. I'd go to war with this force structure."

"You may have to, Tom."

W E LEFT FOR THE AOR TWO HOURS LATER, AND ON THIS TRIP I got to know my new Director of Strategic Communications. Jim Wilkinson was a bright and personable young Texan, a Naval Reserve officer on loan from the White House, where he'd been handling public affairs for President Bush. I'd asked Donald Rumsfeld and his public relations assistant, Torie Clark, for a skilled PR man as the buildup for a possible major operation in Iraq progressed.

"I don't deal well with the media," I'd told the Secretary. "That's more Norm Schwarzkopf's style. I need someone press-savvy to help me navigate the rapids." The Secretary had smiled . . . and two weeks later I had Jim Wilkinson.

Jim looked a little like Tom Sawyer, without the fishing pole. But he proved to be one of the most astute press handlers I could have hoped for. He arrived in Tampa spring-loaded with a brilliant media relations plan that he'd worked out with Torie Clark.

She and Rumsfeld had hatched something innovative for print and electronic media coverage of the operation, should we go to war. When I heard the term "embedded media," it sounded dangerous. Assigning newspaper and magazine writers and broadcast correspondents to combat units could present problems: transportation, support, and liability. And there were concerns about operational security, in this age of satellite phones and Internet video cameras.

But when Torie and Jim briefed me on the details of the program, I saw it as a winner. One of the reasons the press coverage in Afghanistan had been so error-ridden and mediocre—and often antimilitary in its bias—was that the journalists had been kept away from combat operations. Instead, they had to depend on leakers for their stories—the kinds of leakers responsible for those famous *sixteen* AC-130 gunships prepping Objective Gecko.

If the media were actually living and marching with the troops, on the other hand, they would experience war from the perspective of the soldier or Marine. "At least they'll get their facts straight," I said. "Besides, the American people deserve to see the professionalism of their sons and daughters in uniform."

One aspect of the embedding program that won over commanders was the weeklong course in Joint Military Contingency Training for Media that the Pentagon was conducting at the Marine Corps base in Quantico, Virginia. It was billed as a boot camp that would teach reporters how to stay alive in combat—and how not to become a burden to the units to which they were assigned. The training itself became a media event, with Marine gunny sergeants and Army NCOs in DCUs and Kevlar helmets sweating squad-size groups of journalists up through the briars of Cardiac Hill. There were mock gas attacks with smoke grenades, and ambushes with "aggressors" firing deafening bursts of blank cartridges from M-60 machine guns.

"L.L. Bean is doing big business," Jim Wilkinson told me. "You've got newsies sitting around Nathan's on M Street comparing the merits of cleated boot soles and cargo pocket trousers."

When the program was announced, some Army battalion and brigade commanders complained about the prospect of "babysitting" a bunch of reporters. But when the word spread that the Marine Corps—probably the most PR-wise branch of the military—was seeking "embeds," the Army joined in the competition for the best print and broadcast reporters.

And as the process unfolded, it became clear that the traditional distrust and animosity between the military and the media was breaking down. I heard reports that journalists who had moved to Camp Pendleton, Fort Stewart, and Fort Bragg were already talking fondly of "my outfit." This same spirit was spreading on the ships and air bases where reporters were embedded. There was a certain Ernie Pyle spirit developing—reporters bonding with the soldiers and Marines, the troops teaching "their" journalists how to heat an MRE pouch on the engine block of a Humvee and the best way to treat blisters. I pictured the contemporary equivalent of Staff Sgt. Kittle or Corporal Sam Long showing grads of Columbia Journalism School the essential items to carry in a butt pack.

By late November, Torie advised me, there could be as many as six hundred embeds accredited to the Command. "If we conduct this operation, General," she said, "it'll be the best-covered war in history."

On the plane ride out to the AOR, I told Jim Wilkinson with mock gruffness that riding herd on this gaggle of reporters would be his responsibility. "I don't give a rat's ass what you do with 'em," I said, "just keep them out of my hair."

Jim was no more impressed by star-quality journalists than he was by four-star generals. That was one of the reasons I liked him— besides the fact that he was a Texan who enjoyed the occasional cold beer. But he predicted we'd all get along just fine. "You're going to learn to love the media, General," he told me. I never did, but I did come to trust Jim Wilkinson.

THE JOINT OPERATIONS CENTER AT CENTCOM'S DEPLOYABLE Command Post in Qatar was in a doublewide trailer, about as long as the permanent facility back at Tampa, but a lot narrower. This JOC also had a more industrial feel, with air-conditioning ducts and fiber-optic cable bundles exposed overhead. Like the JOC at MacDill, this operations center—a sealed rectangular "shelter" within the echoing expanse of a huge green warehouse at Camp as Sayliyah—was softly lit and strangely quiet, even though it housed a hive of eighty-four officers and senior NCOs working their computer consoles and phone networks.

"Let's run the Romeo Tango Four-Six switch check one more time with feeling," a lanky colonel from J-6 Communications Director Brigadier General Dennis Moran's shop announced. A last check to validate the most intricate global military communication system in history.

Moran had dark circles under his sunken eyes; like the rest of us, he was running on caffeine and adrenaline. On display nearby was a greeting card somebody had adapted to the mission at hand: crossing out the word "Christmas," the joker had penciled in a new message: "MERRY MOTHER OF ALL WARGAMES."

Exercise Internal Look 03 was one of the most elaborate simulations any combatant command had ever conducted. And it had proven a very valuable, if exhausting, rehearsal of the Hybrid 1003V OPLAN.

The exercise was a "rock drill," a term with its origins in the Civil War, when officers placed stones on the ground to represent friendly and enemy positions. Instead of chunks of rock, we used computerized simulation vignettes to test our plan for practicality. For four days and nights we simulated the first stages of Phase III—battalions and brigades of the 3rd ID and 1 MEF crossing the digital berm of the Iraqi border, as electronic TLAMs and strike packages from the USS *Nimitz* and *Kitty Hawk* pounded regime leadership target sets in and around a digital Baghdad.

The wargame unfolding on the wide plasma screens gave us detailed "Blue Force" tracking—a God's-eye view that revealed the progress of our units against combinations and permutations of preprogrammed enemy resistance. This was the Information Age's contribution to the science of war. The CENTCOM staff's cumulative decades of experience provided the art of war.

I was as tired as everyone else, but pleased with the exercise. The simulations allowed my component commanders and me to fight a vividly realistic, but bloodless, campaign. As expected, problems had emerged: communications bandwidth problems, misinterpreted orders, timing-and-distance issues, seams between elements of the joint force. And the list went on.

The old saw from Fort Monroe, "Peace is hell," had never been more appropriate. So was the adage "Train hard, Fight easy." We were knocking the rough edges off a very complex plan. And getting some scraped knuckles in the process.

But the exercise was delivering the goods. In military jargon, this intricate simulation was "validating" the strategic assumptions we'd constructed in the Hybrid 1003V plan.

It was a complex plan. Our ground offensive would proceed along two main avenues of advance from the south, each route having several axes. Army forces, led by the 3rd Infantry Division, would attack up lines of march west of the Euphrates River in a long arc that curved from lines of departure in Kuwait to reach Baghdad. The 1st Marine Expeditionary Force—divided into reinforced Regimental combat teams—would follow the road network along the Tigris River, farther east. The Army and Marines would link up to destroy any surviving Republican Guard units south of the capital. The 4th Infantry Division would advance south from staging areas in Turkey, provided we could persuade the Turks to lend us their territory for a few months. A division-plus-size British ground force would pivot northeast out of Kuwait and isolate Basra, forming a protective cordon around the southern oil fields. And U.S., Brit, and Australian Special Operations Forces would control Iraq's western desert, preventing the regime freedom of action to launch long-range missiles toward Jordan and Israel.

On paper it looked like an attack against a numerically superior enemy with a relatively small offensive force. Was I tempting fate by defying the war college maxim that an attacking force should have a 3-to-1 numerical advantage over an entrenched defender? "Not a bit of it," as my Brit friends would say. On the twenty-first-century battlefield, strength would derive from the mass of effective firepower, not simply the number of boots or tank tracks on the ground.

Our ground forces, supported by overwhelming air power, would move so fast and deep into the Iraqi rear that time-and-distance factors would preclude the enemy's defensive maneuver. And this slow-reacting enemy would be fixed in place by the combined effect of artillery, air support, and attack helicopters.

Without question, our lines of communication would be long and exposed in places, stretching more than three hundred miles from the border of Kuwait to the outskirts of Baghdad. But the object was to destroy the Iraqi military's will to fight. A larger, slower, methodical, attrition-based attack model could defeat the enemy in detail, and our lines of communication could be better protected with such a force. But the time it would take to stage and launch such a juggernaut would leave Saddam too many strategic options: He could use the time to destroy Iraq's water or oil infrastructure, launch missiles against his neighbors, or use WMD against our troops—and his track record suggested he wouldn't think twice about any of those options.

No, maneuver speed would be our most important asset. If high-balling armor units could sustain that speed for days and nights on end, they would own the initiative, and our momentum would overwhelm Iraq's ability to react—tactically and strategically. We would not apply overwhelming force. Rather, we would apply the overwhelming "mass of effect" of a smaller force. Speed would represent a mass all its own.

In one of the Porta Potties outside the main Command Post in Qatar, someone had scrawled on the green plastic wall, "Franks is a speed freak." I took a ballpoint and wrote, "You bet," and then affixed my John Hancock: "Tommy R. Franks, General, USA, Commanding."

The results of our wargaming convinced me that we could actually combine several phases of the campaign into a single, simultaneous effort, which would take much less time than the one hundred and eighty days I had envisioned. The result came to be known as "5-11-16-125": *five days* to position the final airbridge after the President made a decision to launch the operation, *eleven days* to flow the final pieces of the "start force," *sixteen days* of combined air and special operations attacks against key targets, and a total of *125 days* to complete the destruction of Iraqi forces and the removal of the regime.

This was a true revolution in warfare.

I took great satisfaction in the jointness of the team I saw developing in CENTCOM. We had men and women in the As Sayliyah JOC, at Camp Doha in Kuwait, at the CAOC in Saudi Arabia, on the ships in the Gulf, at the Special Ops FOBs, and back in Tampa, and they all functioned as a unified team. An Army major could relay a request for close air support from a Marine captain on the ground to a flight of Air Force F-16 fighter-bombers. A senior Air Force NCO at U.S. Space Command in Colorado could serve a Special Forces A-Team's requirement for reconnaissance satellite coverage. Navy ships could launch TLAMs on targets identified by a CIA Ground Branch operator.

"I like it," I told the gang in JOC. "From where I'm sitting, you guys are beginning to look like genuine joint interagency warfighters."

BACK FROM THE AOR, I BOUNCED AMONG CENTCOM HEADquarters in Tampa, the Pentagon, the White House, and Camp David. Now that the Hybrid concept had become OPLAN 1003V, it was all a matter of fine-tuning. Week after week, we wrestled the "what ifs"—considering contingencies as diverse as the loss of Turkey, the loss of Special Ops FOBs in Jordan, the loss of bases in Saudi Arabia, Fortress Baghdad, and Iraqi use of WMD.

As the military commander, part of my job was to project confidence. And that was not difficult, because I *was* confident.

But many in Washington were anxious. The U.N. inspectors, who had returned to Iraq in late November, were encountering a mixture of cooperation and blatant interference. When the Iraqis produced an ostensibly "full and final" WMD declaration as thick as ten Manhattan phone books, Iraqi Deputy Prime Minister Tariq Aziz claimed that it proved his country had no weapons of mass destruction—despite the fact that the document was basically a collection of papers judged false back in the 1990s by the same U.N. inspectors to whom Iraq presented the declaration. For Saddam Hussein's regime, time was running out.

None of us wanted to precipitate a war if diplomacy might still work. But we did want to build a military force in the region to add muscle to that diplomacy. And this involved a certain risk. So far, no one in Washington had leaked the specifics of our planning. Editorial and op-ed pages were debating the merits of preemptive military action, but there wasn't much vocal opposition to our approach in either Congress or the media. And, as the window for diplomacy was closing, hundreds of reporters and correspondents were either already embedded with Coalition military units or awaiting assignment.

Our force level was mounting in the theater. By mid-January, it seemed probable that the President would commit the nation to war—sooner rather than later.

I MET WITH KING ABDULLAH II OF JORDAN IN HIS HOME IN AMMAN on the afternoon of Thursday, January 23, 2003. "General," he said, "from reliable intelligence sources, I believe the Iraqis are hiding chemical and biological weapons."

The Jordanians did have *reliable* intelligence sources in Iraq. I trusted them, and I trusted the king's judgment. And I wasn't surprised at what his sources had reported. I'd spent days and nights over the previous twelve years worrying about Saddam's WMD program, and the effect that such weapons could have on our troops—or on my country. I thanked the king, left his home, drove to the hotel, and straight to the Comm room to pass the information I'd been given to Secretary Rumsfeld.

Four days later, on Monday, January 27, I was flying from Pakistan to refuel at Crete when my trip coordinator, Air Force Lt. Colonel Manny Chaves, tapped me on the shoulder. "Thirty-five knot crosswinds at Souda Bay, General," he reported. "Looks like we're going to have to head to Cairo."

"Damn it," I said. My unannounced arrival in Egypt would cause a spin-up at the embassy and probably in President Hosni

Mubarak's office. "Not a hard decision, Manny. Either crash into a Greek mountainside or head to Cairo."

Hosni Mubarak was friendly as always. But he was clearly concerned with our military buildup and the tension in Iraq.

He leaned close and spoke to me in accented but readily comprehensible English. "General Franks," he said, choosing his words carefully, as Abdullah had done. "You must be very, very careful. We have spoken with Saddam Hussein. He is a madman. He has WMD—biologicals, actually—and he will use them on your troops."

An hour later, in the Embassy communications room, I passed this message to Don Rumsfeld.

THROUGHOUT OUR PLANNING OF 1003V, WE DISCUSSED PHASE IV—"the Day After." A postwar Iraq might be modeled on post–World War II Japan or Germany. We considered the pros and cons of senior U.S. Army and Marine Corps officers and British military commanders working with Iraqi tribal sheiks all across the country. And we studied the feasibility of an interim government in Iraq formed with international support, along the lines of Hamid Karzai's administration in Afghanistan.

As in Afghanistan, I knew that humanitarian assistance and reconstruction—linked to security—would become top priorities as soon as major combat operations ended. And our planning assumption was that we would guide the Iraqi interim government in building a military and a paramilitary security force drawn from the better units of the defeated regular army. These units would serve side-by-side with Coalition forces to restore order and prevent clashes among the religious and ethnic factions, just as the Northern Alliance and anti-Taliban Pashtun oppositions groups were forming a new Afghan National Army.

Reconstruction—including a host of New Deal–style public works projects—would be required to employ large numbers of Iraqis to jump-start momentum to build a "new Iraq." With a disciplined,

Arabic-speaking security force cooperating with the Coalition military, the stage would be set for reconstruction nationwide. Heads of households would have jobs, living wages to feed their families, and the chance to send their children to school, rather than putting them to work as child labor. Iraqis would have a stake in the future of a free Iraq.

There was no question: Phase IV would be a crucial period. Having won the war, we would have to secure the peace. And securing the peace would not be easy in a country that had been raped and massacred for more than three decades under Saddam Hussein. There were deep divisions among Sunnis and Shias, Kurds and Arabs, haves and have-nots; the region's traditional tribal rivalries would be hard to overcome. It would take time—perhaps years. And the costs would be high, certainly in money and conceivably in lives.

There was no doubt about the actions that would be required. Coalition military leaders across Iraq would provide civil affairs expertise, governance assistance, security, and Humanitarian Assistance to millions of Iraqis. Our conventional forces and Special Forces teams had the capability and expertise to accomplish these tasks, and Gene Renuart's fifty-pound brains had done a masterful job in identifying and providing the resources to Coalition units to do the job.

Given our key policy goal of establishing a representative government in Iraq, though, it would be necessary to establish civilian control across the country as soon as possible. The questions were: How long would it be necessary to maintain military rule in Iraq? How quickly could the Iraqis take over? What form should a "Provisional Authority" take? These were tough questions, and there was no easy recipe for the answers.

On one hand, larger Coalition military forces and martial law might be required to stay in country for years, in order to preserve security. On the other, the Iraqis might claim their country as their own: they might welcome the liberation and organize themselves swiftly to control Iraq without Coalition help.

These problems commanded hours and days of discussion and debate among CENTCOM planners and Washington officials. If a true consensus leader—a kind of Iraqi Hamid Karzai—could be located, then a representative government might be possible in the short term. Majority and minority factions would be represented, and Iraq would become a model for the Arab-Muslim world. But where to find that consensus leader?

Many in Washington considered Ahmad Chalabi a likely choice. Chalabi had risen to prominence after Congress passed, and President Bill Clinton signed, the Iraq Liberation Act of 1998. This legislation declared that it would be the "policy of the United States to seek to remove the Saddam Hussein regime from power in Iraq and to replace it with a democratic government." The Act directed the President to designate one or more suitable Iraqi opposition organizations to receive assistance. Chalabi's umbrella Iraqi National Congress, led mainly by anti-Saddam exiles, was designated such a group.

But Chalabi had his fervent detractors, in both the State Department and the CIA. They cited his trail of questionable financial dealings over a span of years in the Middle East, and doubted that he had maintained the close contacts inside Iraq that he claimed—especially because he had not lived in the country for over thirty years. In many ways, Chalabi suffered the fate of other exile-émigré leaders, from White Russians in 1920s Paris to the Gaullist Free French in England during World War II: No matter how sincerely he may have desired to liberate his homeland, he was badly out of touch with what it would take to do so. I met Chalabi only once, and while I was impressed by his sincerity, I was disappointed by his obvious view of his own importance, and his stated opinion that he could "easily" rally Iraq around himself. He might be a good man, but I knew enough about the difficulties Iraq faced to see him as naïve.

And many leaders in the region were uniformly set against Chalabi as an outsider, a "Gucci" leader who would never be able to unite the ethnic and religious factions. In Washington, the battle lines were drawn. With no Iraqi Karzai in evidence, the debate between the State and Defense Departments continued. Meanwhile, America drew closer to war. Iraq's new leadership would have to be identified on the fly, even as the military liberation was under way. Perhaps an Iraqi general would step forward, or a figure from the educated elite.

However it played out, of course, a Provisional Authority would be required. As I read the newspaper stories—and watched the TV news channels wring their hands over the prospect that I would serve as the so-called "MacArthur of Iraq"—I weighed the obvious pluses and minuses of such an occupation:

- Improved security . . . under control of a *perceived occupying bully*
- Improved near-term efficiency . . . giving rise to *longer-term dependency*
- Improved ability to dispense reconstruction funding . . . with *reduced ability to obtain such funding from the U.S. Congress or the international community*

I could see no elegant solution to this very complex problem. Civilian control of government has long been an American value. How to move Iraq forward using this distinctly American model was problematic. One thing was certain, however: Phase IV would require civilian leadership. In addition to boots on the ground, we would need *wingtips* on the ground—hundreds, perhaps thousands, of civilians from America and the international community, from governmental advisers to eager investors.

Key to all of this, of course, would be security. But security would not be possible in Iraq without immediate reconstruction and civic action.

Then, on a warm Florida afternoon, Don Rumsfeld called. "Tom," he said, "do you know Jay Garner?"

"Yes, Mr. Secretary," I told Rumsfeld. "I love him. Great Army general." I repeated one of my favorite stories about Lt. General Jay

Garner: When he retired, a reporter asked him whether he would change anything about his life if he had it to live again. "Sure, I'd change a lot of things," Jay answered. "But I'd marry the same woman, and I'd join the United States Army."

"Good," Rumsfeld said. "I like him too. How would he do as our senior man in charge of Iraqi occupation and reconstruction?"

"He'd be great," I said. Garner had been very effective in preventing a humanitarian disaster among northern Iraq's Kurds after Desert Storm in 1991. "Huge job," I told Rumsfeld. "But Jay could do it if you trust him . . . and if he could get the right support from every agency of the U.S. government. That's going to include levels of funding unheard of since World War II."

"He'll be your subordinate," Rumsfeld said, "but he'll be my man in Iraq."

"That will work, but we'll have to fight the problem of every bureaucrat inside the Beltway fucking with him if he's perceived as a Washington guy rather than a Tommy Franks guy."

"You are the commander," the Secretary said. "He will work for you."

Over the weeks ahead, Jay Garner and I would meet; he would build a team of specialists and experts from across the U.S. government, deploy the team to Kuwait, establish links with our commanders on the ground, and prepare to enter Iraq on the heels of our attacking troops.

Jay and his team spent countless hours with the CENTCOM staff and the key planners on the Joint Staff and in OSD, hammering out processes and procedures that would place U.S. Army civil affairs specialists in every province in Iraq. Secured by Coalition forces, these teams would work with Iraqis to build local governance in each major population center. And local Iraqis would represent every ethnic, tribal, and religious interest in the country in establishing national leadership. Jay and his headquarters would set up operations in Baghdad, co-located with our on-scene Coalition commander and would organize the required ministries—Oil, Defense, Constabulary,

Treasury, and so on—to provide "provisional authority" during transition to a new Iraqi government.

But the challenge was daunting, and it was clear that certain practical steps would be required as soon as Saddam's regime was removed:

- Securing massive funding for the immediate needs of the Iraqi people
- Hiring tens of thousands of Iraqi ex-soldiers, all of whom needed money to care for their families
- Identifying political leadership that would be trusted by Iraqis, and capable of assisting and ultimately replacing an occupying military force
- Implementing a de-Baathification policy that wasn't so cumbersome that it essentially disenfranchised Iraq's educated middle class
- Adjusting American expectations that the process would be fast and painless

The military coalition would liberate Iraq, set conditions for civilian authority to stand-up a provisional government supported by Coalition stability forces, and provide security until Iraq could field her own security forces—a common-sense approach to a complex problem.

Naming Jay Garner was a good first step, but it was only a first step. Washington would be responsible for providing the policy—and, I hoped, sufficient resources—to win the hearts and minds of the Iraqi people: jobs, power grids, water infrastructure, schools, hospitals, and the promise of prosperity. Iraq's oil wealth would be shared by people who had experienced only abuse, sacrifice, and penury for more than thirty years.

The plan depended on two equal imperatives—*security* and *civil action*. Only if we achieved both could Iraq be transformed into an example of the power of representative government.

I WAS GLAD THAT WE HAD FINALLY REACHED THE STAGE IN THE iterations where a *plan*—not just a Commander's Concept—was emerging. For one thing, we were finally able to move beyond the hypothetical environment we'd been working in for months, and start deploying ships, planes, and troops.

For another, I had already spent longer than I liked skirting the issue of a "war plan" in my dealings with the press.

At one press conference in Tampa on May 21, 2002, a reporter had asked me about the force level necessary for a successful invasion of Iraq. "My boss has not yet asked me to put together a plan to do that," I had answered, and it was the truth. In May 2002, we were offering the President options, not a plan.

I couldn't request the Army to cut deployment orders and move equipment based on a concept. A plan was a different instrument altogether. A concept was theory. A plan was something we could execute.

In May 2002, we were still discussing theory; I had no executable document in my headquarters. Now we had finalized 1003V. We had a plan.

O N MONDAY, FEBRUARY 3, 2003, I RECEIVED A LONG-AWAITED Defense Department Inspector General report that had been pending since October 2002. It stemmed from a complaint that a disgruntled officer serving on my staff had filed in October 2002.

At the center of his allegations was my wife, Cathy. Specifically, the officer complained that I had allowed subordinates on official duty time to provide personal services to Cathy; that I had violated military regulations by allowing Cathy to fly on government aircraft; and, most seriously, that I had breached Department of Defense security regulations by giving her unauthorized access to classified information.

I believed the charges were absurd. But I also recognized their dangerous potential to upset the command at a time of pressing activity in both Afghanistan and the Arabian Gulf. As soon as the allegations had surfaced, I'd called Donald Rumsfeld.

"Mr. Secretary, I don't believe there's anything to this, but I think every charge should be investigated thoroughly. If I have made any mistakes, I'll own up to them. It's important that the investigation be open and complete."

"We'll get the IG working on it. But I don't want you sidetracked," Rumsfeld had said.

"Let the chips fall where they will. I've got important work to do," I'd said.

That had been in October, and since then the bureaucratic wheels had ground slowly. I knew from my own experience as a young major investigating general officer conduct that this level of investigation should have moved more quickly. But I had no control over the process.

The report, when it did come, was very thorough. The IG found no substance to the allegation that my staff had provided personal services to Cathy, and as to her accompanying me on trips to the AOR, the report noted no wrongdoing.

The most serious allegation was that I had allowed her to see Top Secret documents aboard the aircraft. This was in fact not true, but I could not prove that I hadn't discussed such documents with my staff while she was present in the aircraft conference room. When the matter had been raised in 2002, Cathy had signed an "Inadvertent Disclosure Agreement" that prevented her from divulging any information she might have overheard. Coupled with the fact that she had had a Secret security clearance for more than two years, this satisfied me—and Donald Rumsfeld.

On my first trip to Washington after the IG report was released, I had discussed the matter with the Secretary.

"The more power and authority a person has, the more careful he must be," he'd said. "Remember, perceptions count."

"Got it, Sir," I had said.

And with that, I proceeded to do my job.

O N WEDNESDAY, FEBRUARY 5, 2003, COLIN POWELL MADE HIS long-awaited presentation on the threat of Iraqi weapons of mass destruction to the United Nations Security Council. He had prepared for this event by studying agent reports, overhead imagery, communications intercepts, and other technical "collection" that the Central Intelligence Agency had compiled for his review. Powell had also pored over the voluminous reports of the U.N. weapons inspectors themselves, who had determined that Iraq had not accounted for massive quantities of biological weapons and precursor compounds for nerve gas such as Sarin and VX.

As the world watched, Colin Powell, with Director of Central Intelligence George Tenet seated behind him, made the case to the Security Council that, at best, Saddam Hussein's regime had willfully deceived United Nations weapons inspectors since 1991—and were still doing so.

The Secretary of State used recordings of communications intercepts in which Iraqi military and security organization officers discussed hiding "forbidden ammo" from inspectors. He showed reconnaissance satellite images of suspicious industrial sites and suspected mobile bio-weapon laboratories.

He cited the links between Saddam Hussein's government and an aligned al Qaeda terrorist-group Ansar al-Islam, led by Abu Musab al-Zarqawi.

"Ambition and hatred are enough to bring Iraq and al Qaeda together," he emphasized.

Since Saddam Hussein "is determined to keep his weapons of mass destruction . . . and make more," Colin asked, "Should we take the risk that he will not someday use these weapons at a time and a place of his choosing, at a time when the world is in a much weaker position to respond? The United States will not and cannot run that risk to the American people."

Some of the Security Council members endorsed his findings. France, Germany, and Russia did not.

As the Secretary spoke, I thought: *This is a powerful presentation; there is no way we can leave the fate of our children and grandchildren to chance. To do so would be a mistake—of grave proportions.*

JOHN ABIZAID WAS A BRILLIANT LEADER WITH A STRONG RECORD of combat leadership. He knew the region well and spoke Arabic. With him as my Forward Deputy in Qatar, and Rifle DeLong managing CENTCOM Main as my Rear Deputy in Tampa, I was able to move around the region, maintaining contact with key leaders, while shuttling to Washington regularly to confer with Donald Rumsfeld and the President.

On Wednesday, March 5, I had my last prewar meeting on Iraq with the President and the National Security team in the White House. Coalition ground, naval, air, and Special Operations forces in the region were growing rapidly, and now totaled more than two hundred thousand troops. An additional sixty thousand American and British combat and support units were en route to the Gulf.

By the third week of March, our total strength in all components—including our Gulf State Coalition allies in Kuwait—would number 292,000. Of these, there would be approximately 170,000 soldiers and Marines assigned to the Combined Forces Land Component Command (CFLCC).

"Mr. President," I reported, "all key infrastructure improvements have been completed, and the required force is now in place in the theater."

George Bush was focused—very serious. "Where are we with Turkey?"

It was one of our few remaining major concerns: The new Turkish government had, in fact, denied permission to pass the 4th Infantry Division through their territory into Iraq. But we had been given approval to overfly Turkey from aircraft carriers in the Mediterranean, and negotiations based on a multibillion-dollar aid package were still ongoing.

"The 4th Infantry, with all their equipment loaded on thirty-seven ships, is in the eastern Med, Sir," I explained. "If the Turks change their minds, we will offload and be on Iraq's northern border within ten days. If not, we will transit the Suez and offload the Division in Kuwait—probably after commencement of hostilities."

Bringing in those combat troops would raise our Land Component strength by 15,000 soldiers. But the President, Rumsfeld, and I had discussed another equally important function of the 4th ID: to serve as a cornerstone of our deception plan. While the Division remained poised in the Mediterranean to fix enemy units in the north, we were passing information to the Iraqi regime through clandestine conduits that we had a secret arrangement with the Turks, who, at the last moment, would open their ports to the Division. And reconnaissance indicated that almost thirteen Iraqi divisions remained north of Baghdad: Saddam, it appeared, might be taking the bait.

Next, I explained the time phasing of combat operations. The latest aerial satellite imagery revealed a thin speed bump of Iraqi regular army forces between the Kuwaiti border and the cities south of Baghdad, where Saddam's defense was structured in depth with the Republican Guard. This enemy force positioning was exactly as our intelligence planners had predicted: if our deception worked, we would be ready to initiate near-simultaneous air, ground, and SOF operations on the President's order.

"Mr. President," I concluded, "I would like forty-eight hours' warning if you decide to execute this operation. That will give me time to get the Special Operators into western Iraq to close the Scud baskets."

Rumsfeld, Cheney, Powell, and the President discussed giving Saddam Hussein one final ultimatum. Either he would leave Iraq voluntarily—together with his sons Uday and Qusay, who were their dictator father's surrogates—or the Coalition would enter and remove them from power.

"Forty-eight hours," President Bush repeated. "Two days. All right, Tommy, you'll have the warning if it comes to that."

I DIDN'T HAVE TIME TO PASS THROUGH TAMPA BEFORE HEADING BACK to CENTCOM Forward in Qatar. But I did speak to Cathy, Jacqy, and the grandkids on the phone.

"I'll talk to you in a day or so, dear," I told Cathy as the Pentagon sedan rolled up to Spar 06 on the ramp at Andrews.

My fingers went to the wedding ring Cathy had given me so long ago, and I felt a tear cross my face. I pulled a small Bible and a wrinkled American flag from my uniform pocket. The flag was one Jacqy had given me as I'd deployed to Desert Shield in 1990. After that war I'd returned it to her as a souvenir; now she'd sent it to me again for luck. And the Bible was a gift from Cathy's grandfather, Jimmie Ellis, whom I had loved as the grandparent I'd never had, until his death in 1994.

I opened the Bible to my favorite scripture, Ephesians 6: 11–17. "Put on the whole armor of God . . . stand your ground . . . putting on the sturdy belt of truth . . . and the breastplate of God's righteousness . . . use faith as your shield . . . and take the sword of the spirit, which is the word of God." How many times had I turned to this page? And how many more times, in the days ahead, would I call on my faith as a source of strength?

I SAT ALONE IN MY OFFICE IN THE PREFAB HEADQUARTERS NEAR THE JOC in the warehouse in Camp As Sayliyah, watching as George Bush addressed the nation and the world. It was before dawn on Tuesday, March 18, 2003, in Qatar, and primetime Monday night in the States.

The President traced the Iraqi regime's "history of reckless aggression." And then he issued the ultimatum we had discussed two weeks earlier in the White House.

"Saddam Hussein and his sons must leave Iraq within forty-eight hours," Bush said. "Their refusal to do so will result in military conflict, commenced at a time of our choosing."

The clock was running. I was about to command troops in battle once more. But this time I would not ride in an APC through the jungle in Vietnam, or in a Humvee across the gravel beds of the Wadi al Batin. I would watch the battle on wide plasma screens, far from the rattle of the guns, the blast of shells, the screams of the wounded.

I would be physically safe—but I would share the fatigue, the elation, and the fears of my troops.

OUR FINAL PREWAR VIDEO TELECONFERENCE WAS ENDING ON THE afternoon of Wednesday, March 19, 2003.

"Mr. President," I said, facing George Bush through the secure VTC link, "this force is ready. D-Day, H-Hour is 2100 hours tonight Iraqi time, 1800 hours Greenwich Mean, 1300 hours East Coast time."

President Bush nodded to the members of the National Security Council seated with him in Washington, then turned toward me.

"All right. For the sake of peace in the world and security for our country and the rest of the free world . . ." He paused; his advisers listened intently. ". . . And for the freedom of the Iraqi people, as of this moment I will give Secretary Rumsfeld the order necessary to execute Operation Iraqi Freedom.

"Tommy," the President added, his voice firm, "may God bless the troops."

"Mr. President," I answered, "may God bless America."

I saluted, and the Commander in Chief returned the salute.

11

OPERATION IRAQI FREEDOM

The new Air Force C-40, a modified Boeing 737, was a lot more efficient and comfortable than the old 1962 Spar 06 that had carried me back and forth across the planet since July 2000. The C-40 didn't have the inflight refueling capability of the old jet, but the communications suite was state of the art. And the new plane had windows— a welcome creature comfort in a time of long nights and little sleep.

We climbed steeply away from Prince Sultan Air Base to our cruising altitude of 31,000 feet. And from my seat on the portside, the desert of the Arabian Peninsula below looked brown and empty. In an hour I'd be back in the CENTCOM Command Center inside Building 217, an echoing warehouse at Camp As Sayliyah, Qatar.

My aide, Marine Major Chris Goedeke—"Grinch" to all of us who worked with him—appeared, carrying some messages back from the forward Comm center. He stooped to look out the window. "Great day to go flying, Sir."

Grinch was a decorated aviator with Marine Corps pilot's wings on his DCUs. He'd flown A-6 Intruders in Desert Storm, and I knew he'd rather be suiting up for a combat mission this afternoon. I understood how he felt: A part of me wanted to be up on the berm in Kuwait, checking rounds in the magazines of my M-16. But both of us had different work to do.

We finally had a name for our plan: The Hybrid 1003V OPLAN had officially been dubbed Operation Iraqi Freedom. It was the President's decision, and I liked it. The goal of this campaign was not conquest, not oil, but freedom for twenty-six million Iraqis—and, for the world, freedom from the threat of weapons of mass destruction falling into the hands of terrorists.

The Coalition that had been assembled to win this war numbered about 290,000 soldiers, sailors, airmen, Marines, Coast Guardsmen, and Special Operators from America, the United Kingdom, Australia, and Europe. In all, the force included men and women from twenty-three nations, with our Arab Gulf allies providing essential staging areas, air bases, and ports, as well as maritime security and crucial force protection for our long logistic "tail."

As we leveled off, the borders of Saudi Arabia, Jordan, and Iraq stretched northwest to the horizon. Several thousand Special Forces soldiers and Special Mission troopers—many of them veterans of combat in Afghanistan—were joined by British and Australian Special Air Service operators at bases in Jordan and northern Saudi Arabia, prepared to attack into western Iraq. Operation Iraqi Freedom would represent the largest combat formation of special operators in history.

Their first mission, which would begin in less than four hours, was to destroy the enemy's visual observation posts (VISOBS) along Iraq's western borders. Special operators would laser-designate the large stone structures and smaller steel towers. And AH-6 Little Birds (modern versions of the Loaches the Red Baron and I had flown in Vietnam), MH-60 Defensive Armed Penetrators (DAPs), and Air Force fighter-bombers would take them out with Hellfire missiles and 500-pound bombs.

These strikes would perform a critical role in the days to come: blinding the enemy. With the Iraqis' surveillance powers eliminated, hundreds of Special Operations teams in helicopters and all-terrain vehicles would swarm across the borders in the night, seizing control of potential missile-launching sites—the famous "Scud baskets"—and a series of airstrips in Iraq's western desert. I wanted the first shots of this war to be fired in the west. Even though Iraqi intelligence was mediocre at best, Baghdad would certainly learn within hours that our forces were probing their border with Jordan.

"I want a ripple effect," I'd told Gary Harrell and Dell Dailey during our last meeting a few days earlier. "We'll take out the nine towers facing Jordan first, and eliminate the twenty-four along the western Saudi border several hours later."

As Dell's SMU troopers hit the first VISOBS and crossed the border, Gary's Coalition SOF units would infiltrate western Iraq. At the same time, other Special Forces and CIA operators would penetrate southern Iraq from Kuwait to link up with "friends" in the Shia-controlled southern marshes. Their objectives would be to secure river crossing sites and crucial dams on Iraq's key reservoirs, to prevent sabotage that could flood wide sections of the river valleys.

I gazed to the north now, toward Kuwait. Tomorrow night, artillery and Apache gunships from Lt. General David McKiernan's Combined Forces Land Component Command (CFLCC) would destroy the observation towers on the Kuwaiti border just north of the soldiers of the 3rd Infantry Division, Marines of the 1 MEF, and infantrymen and tankers of the British 1st Armoured Division—almost 170,000 troops in all—who were poised in their pre-assault positions, ready to breach the berm into southeastern Iraq.

The SOF activity in the west was not only the beginning of the first kinetic phase of Operation Iraqi Freedom; it was also part of an intricate deception plan. A rigidly compartmented strategic effort had been in progress for months, feeding disinformation to the regime of Saddam Hussein. Because of the sensitivity of the deception, only a few of us in the U.S. government were aware of it.

At the center of it all was a man we called "April Fool," an American military officer who had been approached by an operative of the Iraqi *Mukhabarat* foreign intelligence directorate who was working undercover as a diplomat. The Iraqi, whom we referred to as "the Colonel," had recruited April as a double agent. Unknown to the *Mukhabarat,* the officer had contacted his chain of command within hours of the Iraqi's initial overture.

Jeff Kimmons, my J-2 Intelligence Director, had met me in the SCIF at MacDill two days later. "We may have a chance to influence Iraqi behavior," Jeff said. "We don't know how high this Iraqi goes, but we'll have April Fool work with him, and we'll see where it takes us."

"This could be huge, Jeff," I said. "Stay plugged in with the folks handling April and keep me posted."

Shortly thereafter, April Fool began a series of clandestine meetings with the Colonel, delivering to him copies of outdated maps and actual annexes from the old 1003 Plan—all marked Top Secret/Polo Step.

And for each tranche of documents, the Colonel had paid several thousand dollars. At the end of each clandestine meeting, the American had announced he could provide even more sensitive parts of CENTCOM's war plan.

Over several weeks in late 2002 and early 2003, April Fool sold the Iraqis detailed operational information—all of it convincingly authentic, most of it produced in CENTCOM's deception cell.

The storyline we sold them went as follows: The Coalition was planning to build up only a portion of its ground force in Kuwait, while preparing a major airborne assault into northern Iraq from above Tikrit to the oil fields around the city of Kirkuk. Helicopter-borne Air Assault forces would then reinforce the paratroopers. Then, once several airstrips were secured, C-17 transports would deliver tanks and Bradleys to join them. This small armored force would then be reinforced by the 4th Infantry Division, which the Turkish government would permit—at the last possible minute—to pass through Turkey and steamroll its way south to Baghdad.

The purpose of April Fool's work was to create doubt among Iraq's leadership as to where, when, and with what size force the

Coalition would launch its attack. If the deception succeeded, Saddam would keep the better part of thirteen enemy divisions north of Baghdad to defend against the 4th Infantry until it was too late to use them to counter the main Coalition attack coming out of Kuwait.

April Fool's relationship with the colonel culminated in the delivery of a detailed schematic of the 82nd Airborne Division's drop zones near Tikrit and Kirkuk—less than two weeks before the start of Operation Iraqi Freedom.

I didn't know on March 19 whether the deception had been successful. But I knew what our reconnaissance imagery told us: Despite our sizable buildup of forces in Kuwait to the south, Saddam's Republican Guard and regular army divisions had not moved significantly from their northerly position—no doubt waiting for an assault that would never come.

As WE ADJUSTED THE WINDOW SHADE AGAINST THE SUN, GRINCH and I pored over the latest attack timeline Gene Renuart had just transmitted to the plane via encrypted fax. Across the top of the page ran a bar tracing the first four days of the operation: D-DAY, D+1, D+2, D+3. Each day began at 2400 hours (midnight) Iraqi time. And H-Hour, D-Day, the commencement of hostilities, was 2100 hours tonight, March 19.

I studied this latest revision closely, because it represented a shift from the timeline I had sent to Secretary Rumsfeld earlier in the week. The objectives for March 19 still included destruction of the VISOBS in western Iraq and the insertion of the special operators. On D+1—tomorrow, March 20—the aerial reconnaissance of roads and minefields and ground reconnaissance of the assault routes into southern Iraq would begin on schedule at 2000 hours. Two hours later special operators, including Polish commandos, would seize the offshore gas and oil platforms (GOPLATS) and the main oil tanker-loading terminal at Al Faw on the Iraq-Iran border at the head of the Arabian Gulf. All of this was unchanged.

But on the original timeline, the main Coalition ground attack—G-Day—had been scheduled to begin at 0600 hours, Friday, March 21, D+2. On this final revision, that assault was advanced eight and a half hours, to 2130 hours on March 20, D+1. Instead of crossing the cuts in the border berm as dawn was breaking, followed immediately by the large maneuver formations, Marine and Army ground reconnaissance units would attack the night before.

I had adjusted the timing because of some intelligence I had received twelve hours earlier—intelligence that was too important to ignore. As I was preparing to leave the headquarters that morning to fly to Saudi Arabia to visit Buzz Moseley and our Air Component, Jeff Kimmons walked into the War Room with several of his analysts.

"Got some interesting material here, General," Jeff reported.

We had been watching the southern Iraqi oil fields carefully for weeks to identify any attempt by the regime to destroy the Rumilyah complex. In the reconnaissance and satellite imagery Jeff had shown me this morning, the normal small flares burning at vent stacks designed to relieve excess gas pressure had been replaced by obvious wellhead fires. Six wells had been torched.

"General," Jeff said, "these aren't maintenance burns. Some of the flames are shooting up three hundred feet. We have no confirmation yet of a more widespread problem, but you've seen the reports from some of our Shia tribal contacts: Railroad cars filled with demolitions have been moving into Rumilyah."

There were 454 active wellheads in that stretch of desert, and another 609 wells capped in reserve. This field represented the future of the Iraqi people. Its destruction would undercut the country's recovery from decades of the Baathist dictatorship's abuse.

I had never forgotten the nightmare image of Kuwait's oil fields in flames on the desert horizon in 1991, set ablaze by retreating Iraqi saboteurs. Intelligence reports indicated that the Iraqis would likely not initiate "substantial" sabotage until they were certain war had begun. And the certain signal the Iraqis expected was the start of a Desert Storm–type air campaign—the so-called "Shock and Awe" air operations that the media promised would "surely precede any ground campaign."

"If this is worst case, Jeff," I'd said, "and they're wiring the field for destruction, how long do we have to save the wells?"

"Possibly forty-eight hours, General. This is a very large area, but if the Iraqis are serious, they can do a great deal of damage once they start."

Two days. Securing the Rumilyah Oil Fields was the first objective of Lt. General Jim Conway's 1 MEF. Could the Marines execute early? Saving Iraq's petroleum—and the water infrastructure that supported the country's agriculture—from die-hard Baathist sabotage were major operational goals of the campaign.

I called an immediate phone conference with Jeff, his analysts, and Dave McKiernan. I'd been preaching the Gospel of Flexibility for months. Now we would see if my sermons had produced any converts.

"David, I know you've seen the reconnaissance shots of Rumilyah," I'd said. "Kimmons' best guess is that we're running out of time. Is it possible to get Jim Conway's Marines into the fields a day earlier than planned?"

"We'll work it, Sir," McKiernan said. "If it can be done, the Marines can do it."

McKiernan was a veteran Armor officer. As a lieutenant colonel during Desert Storm, he'd run VII Corps' Tactical Command Post, which had coordinated the operations of six American and British divisions. He was smart, tireless, fearless, and resilient—a friend and the ideal officer to command the Coalition's land forces.

"Thanks for being as good as you are," I'd told him as I hung up the phone.

This is going to be a hell of a day, I thought, heading for the new Spar 06, on my way to Saudi Arabia to confer with Buzz Moseley before my VTC with the President later that afternoon.

"Buzz," I said when he met me at the plane, "that bald spot on top of your head is even larger than when I saw you last week."

Moseley grinned.

We reviewed the operational timeline for Buzz's Combined Forces Air Component Command (CFACC), which included three land-based Air Force Expeditionary Wings and five Naval Air Wings on carriers in the Gulf and Mediterranean. He was set to execute A-Day at 2100 on March 21. And, as I'd anticipated, there were too many interdependent factors involved in the air operations side of this campaign—suppressing enemy defenses and allotting CSAR aircraft and refueling tankers—to shift the start of A-Day at this point.

When I told him I'd asked Dave McKiernan to look at moving the Marines into the oil fields early, Buzz thought a moment. "Boss," he said, "we can accelerate our timing if you want us to. It'll be a bitch, but we *can* do it. If you're asking my professional opinion, though, I think we should stay with our planned timing for the major air operation. Better that we give David's guys more close support than they've ever dreamed of when they attack, but hold off on the strategic air power target sets until the scheduled A-Day."

I looked at Buzz. *This is the best airman alive,* I thought. *He's my friend. I'd trust him with my life. If he says we can execute G-Day before A-Day and still achieve our objectives, we'll do it.*

"Okay, Buzz. We're going to try to go early with the ground ops."

"Roger that, General. We can help make it happen."

So the initiation of air operations would begin as originally scheduled: 2100 hours on March 21. If Dave McKiernan and Jim Conway could manage it, though, our ground forces would get a jump on the schedule—and reach the Rumilyah oil field in time to save it. This sealed a decision that had been a long time coming: We would initiate G-Day almost twenty-four hours before A-Day.

During months of planning, the length of air operations in preparation for the ground attack had steadily decreased. Two months earlier, we had projected sixteen days and nights of air and SOF operations to "shape the battlespace" before the first Coalition armor crossed the berm. Now our Abrams tanks and Bradleys would already be deep inside Iraq when Buzz Moseley's airmen delivered a possible knockout blow to the regime in Baghdad on the night of Friday, March 21.

I knew the armchair strategists, and what the staff had started calling the "TV generals"—retired officers working for the networks—might find fault with my decision. But I also knew it was correct. Communications intercepts had revealed that the Iraqis would not destroy the oil fields any sooner than necessary, because they were earning about fifty million dollars a day from those wells through the U.N.'s oil-for-food program. But I was also certain that Saddam *would* order the sabotage when air operations against regime leadership targets made it obvious that war had begun.

So it was imperative that we capture those wells if we could. But saving the Rumilyah field would be only one of the advantages of executing G-Day before A-Day. By operating in a manner that the Iraqis would never anticipate, we would achieve operational surprise—despite the fact that we had deployed almost 290,000 Land, Air, and Naval Component personnel to the area.

When I told Don Rumsfeld we were considering moving up the timing of G-Day, he accepted the change immediately. "You're the commander, Tom," he'd said. "You have to make the call."

I knew the Secretary trusted me. But I'd also taken some other measures to keep the rest of the Pentagon calm. On March 17, two days before D-Day, I had faxed a "letter of concern" to Rumsfeld's deputy, Paul Wolfowitz. Although I couched the message in polite terms, its intent was blunt: Keep Washington focused on policy and strategy. *Leave me the hell alone to run the war.*

Operation Enduring Freedom in Afghanistan had been nitpicked by the Service Chiefs and the Joint Staff, and I did not intend to see a recurrence of such divisiveness in Iraq. Paul Wolfowitz was a friend, and I knew he would spread the word around the E-Ring that Tommy Franks wasn't about to be treed by Chihuahuas while he was trying to orchestrate what had shaped up to be the most complex and fully integrated joint-service military operation in history.

My memo to Wolfowitz put the Pentagon on notice. "The presence of the Service Chiefs at my daily Secure VTCs with the Secretary is not helpful. They do not have sufficient Joint background or understanding," I wrote, "to be operationally useful."

"I understand the capabilities of the force," the message said, "and I will use it to the best advantage." And I issued a warning about leaking our plan to the media: "Leaks of classified information and the views of pundits to 'spur' me to do more, better, faster will not motivate me."

My point was simple: While we at CENTCOM were executing the war plan, Washington should focus on "policy-level issues." And there were plenty of them to focus on, as I outlined:

I am concerned about:

- The practical mechanics of a reward program for information on WMD and hidden regime leaders.
- A functional plan and policy to pay Iraqi military units so they can be immediately co-opted and put to work for the Coalition on reconstruction. [I wanted to see those defeated enemy troops kept in coherent units, commanded by their own officers, and paid in a combination of humanitarian assistance food and cash.]
- Finalizing the "Black List" of suspected regime war criminals and determining what their legal status will be.

In my view, these were among the strategic tasks Washington needed to address.

My concern was prompted in part by America's recent warfighting history. During the Vietnam War, Defense Secretary Robert McNamara and his Whiz Kids had repeatedly picked individual bombing targets and approved battalion-size maneuvers. That was not going to happen in Iraq. I knew the President and Don Rumsfeld would back me up, so I felt free to pass the message along to the bureaucracy beneath them: *You pay attention to the day* after and *I'll pay attention to the day* of.

I was blessed with the best component commanders and the best combatant staff any four-star had ever taken to war. And I was confident that the campaign that was about to begin was going to defeat the enemy with historic speed. Washington needed to get ready for the occupation and reconstruction—because combat operations just might be over sooner than anyone could imagine. At NSC briefings, Rumsfeld and I referred to that possibility as "catastrophic success."

In the closing of my memo, I had reminded Wolfowitz of the moral compass that would guide me in the days ahead: "I carry an American Flag and a Bible in my pocket, and I wear a wedding band on my left hand. I understand the mission and the strategic context within which it will be accomplished. I will become tentative only when directed to do so."

A S SOON AS THE PRESIDENT ISSUED THE EXECUTE ORDER, I'D called Dave McKiernan. "General," David told me, "I've talked to Jim Conway. His Marines are moving to the line of departure now. They will attack into the oil fields beginning with ground recon tomorrow night, on the new timeline you requested."

After months of staff work, the planning was over.

W E WERE STILL AT CRUISING ALTITUDE; THE SHIMMER OF THE Arabian Gulf was creeping across the eastern horizon. Staring at the vast desert below, I thought of Iraq's great twin rivers, the Tigris and Euphrates, emptying through the marshy delta some archaeologists believed was the site of the Bible's Garden of Eden.

And I thought of the long curving valley between the two rivers—Mesopotamia, the cradle of civilization, the site of the most ancient traces of agriculture that marked the dawn of the Neolithic Revolution. Thirteen thousand years ago, hunter-gatherers lived in this valley, learning to cultivate rye. Agriculture had led to humanity's first permanent settlements, which over the millennia had become the sophisticated city-states of the Fertile Crescent. Here was a place where empires had risen and fallen throughout human history.

Soon the brigades of the 3rd Infantry and 101st Airborne Divisions would seize their first tactical objectives, near the ruins of ancient Ur and Babylon. This land, where war chariots and bronze weaponry were created thousands of years ago, was about to experience another extraordinary clash of arms. . . . And so, I realized, would I.

As Spar 06 began its approach, I thought of a similar scene I'd witnessed more than thirty years earlier: that old Continental charter jet full of GIs inbound for Bien Hoa, descending through the night above the South China Sea toward the deeper darkness of Vietnam.

Iraqi Freedom represented my fourth journey into war. I carried with me the memory of every moment that had gone before: Stepping off that bus on a hot August afternoon at Fort Leonard Wood, Missouri. Easing my feet into those boots after Staff Sergeant Kittle had shown me the old soldier's trick of stretching the leather. Corporal Sam Long teaching me to field strip and reassemble weapons in that overheated barracks at Fort Devens. I hoped the troopers saddling up for war tonight had their own Staff Sergeant Kittles and Corporal Sam Longs. I hoped they had commanders like Lt. Colonel Eric Antila.

I knew we had done everything we could to prepare for this operation. I had selected and helped season the hardest working, most talented wartime command I had ever seen. CENTCOM's component commanders and flag officers were versatile, resilient, and dedicated to the mission and to their people.

The plan we were launching was complex but flexible. And when contact with the enemy inevitably altered its details—as it had in every military campaign plan in history—our troops and their leaders would adapt.

Our young people would do their jobs with courage, skill, and honor. Privates would step forward to lead when their sergeants fell wounded or dead. Lieutenants would take the place of fallen captains. Medics would rush into enemy fire to save their comrades. I had seen such heroism in the rice paddies and jungles of Vietnam, and again on the bloody gravel of the Wadi al Batin. It was our heritage, a tradition that found its roots at the Chosin Reservoir in the frozen hills of Korea, the black sand of Iwo Jima, the shell-splintered stumps of the Argonne Forest . . . all the way back to the icy cobblestones of Trenton, where Washington's ragged Continentals had beaten the best professional soldiers of the British Empire.

Beginning tonight, American, British, Australian, Polish, Czech, Italian, and Spanish troopers would all do their duty. And we would prevail.

This Coalition would disarm Saddam Hussein's regime and free Iraq. We would take every precaution to minimize death and suffering. We would be guided by the words of Winston Churchill: "Battles are won by slaughter and maneuver. The greater the general, the more he contributes in maneuver, the less he demands in slaughter." We would put our faith in maneuver.

The landing gear came thumping down. The concrete expanse of Al Udeid Air Base rose to meet us, and with it the challenge of Iraqi Freedom.

A T ABOUT 1800 HOURS, THREE HOURS BEFORE THE SPECIAL OPS kickoff, I walked back into the Forward Headquarters. The building's interior had the look of a high-technology factory surrounded by a refugee camp. One of twenty-six identical green warehouses in the mile-long rectangular compound, it was as broad and high as a Home Depot. Instead of lumber, plumbing fixtures, and hardware, though, the floor was covered with scores of "shelters" of different sizes. Some, like the Joint Operations Center (JOC), resembled windowless doublewide mobile homes. Others, the size of camper trailers, contained the offices of component liaison officers and planning specialists.

The domains of Gene Renuart and Jeff Kimmons were featureless, aluminum-walled boxes, filled with computer consoles and plasma screens, each marked with bright placards reading "No Entry" in English and Arabic. And the CENTCOM Forward SCIF, guarded by armed sentries around-the-clock and entered through a single vault door, was a brown aluminum structure that took up most of the building's western end.

My office was a single-wide prefab in the northeastern quadrant of the warehouse, sitting beside an identical space occupied by Lt. General John Abizaid, my forward deputy, and connected by a series of offices housing my XO, Captain Van Mauney; Grinch Goedeke; Command Sergeant Major Dwight Brown; and a joint administrative support staff. The Command Conference Room, with racks of video teleconference stations and matching STU-III communications, was in an adjacent shelter. My small war room, equipped with plasma screens and secure communications, stood nearby. Another office complex, with cots, showers, and a kitchenette, was located at the far end of the building, but it got little use; I preferred being closer to the action—the JOC, the Intelligence Fusion Cell, and the SCIF.

Among the sprawl of prefabs were rows of desert-tan lightweight fabric tents, all beneath a warehouse roof that was crisscrossed with girders, ventilation conduits and wiring. The tents were state-of-the-art, exterior framed, air-conditioned spaces; they reminded me of outdoor show displays at a state fair back in the Southwest. Some six hundred officers, sergeants, Navy petty officers, civilian contractors, electronics technicians, admin specialists, and support staff worked twelve-to-sixteen-hour shifts around the clock. Most of them slept in the other warehouses spread across the compound—when they found a moment to sleep.

The headquarters—Building #217—was the technological nerve center of Operation Iraqi Freedom; at times it seemed to be wired as intricately as the human brain. Along the sides of every aisle ran tubular protective conduits for the hundreds of miles of power and fiber-optic cables connecting the shelters. The entire complex was cooled to 85 degrees Fahrenheit by an industrial air-conditioning plant outside the building, and each prefab and tent inside the warehouse had its own individual air-conditioning system, connected to smaller plants by long flexible ducts.

With its mega-channel, encrypted satellite voice and data links, and its multiple Secure Video Teleconference facilities, Building #217 used bandwidth equivalent to that of a large U.S. city. I could reach Secretary Rumsfeld, JCS Chairman Dick Myers, Rifle DeLong—or the President—within seconds by secure voice or video link. And a Red Switch voice console connected me to the Service Chiefs and my component commanders at the touch of a button. We communicated by both voice and video at scheduled times twenty-four hours a day.

The crown jewels of this "network-centric" headquarters were the Blue Force and Red Force Tracking systems. Every important shelter in the headquarters was equipped with plasma-screen displays, on which the staff tracked the positions of friendly—"Blue"—Coalition formations, all the way down to a tank company or individual aircraft. Virtually every vehicle and every aircraft carried a GPS transponder that transmitted coded data on their coordinates, direction, and speed via satellite to each Component headquarters, to CENTCOM Main in Tampa, to the Pentagon, and to our headquarters in Qatar.

On the Blue Force screens, friendly force locations appeared as small, bright blue boxes. The ground force element of this system, Force XXI Battle Command, Brigade and Below (FBCB2), was an outgrowth of work done in the mid-1990s by the Louisiana Maneuvers Task Force. On the large-scale displays, the units massed in their pre-assault assembly areas looked like a solid blue smear. By clicking on increasingly more focused data boxes on the screen, however, I could zoom in on smaller and smaller units, from corps, to division, to brigade, all the way down to a single Armored Cavalry scout troop in Bradleys.

On the Red Force screens, similar red boxes represented enemy formations. We had no GPS transponders on Iraq's planes, of course, or on the tanks of an armored brigade in the Medina Republican Guard Division. But we had other means of determining enemy locations and order of battle. Our reconnaissance capability covered a wide band of the electromagnetic spectrum. And visual imagery from UAVs and medium and high-altitude reconnaissance aircraft—presented in both live video and digital photography—was augmented by satellite coverage. Sensors on these platforms provided not only daylight photography, but also an infrared-detecting capability that could identify the heat radiating from vehicle engines . . . or a man's body. Synthetic aperture radar scanning from aircraft and satellites could detect the shape of armored vehicles, trucks, or artillery pieces. And JSTARS reconnaissance aircraft could pinpoint moving vehicles in any weather or light condition.

A wide variety of electronic sensors also swept up enemy radio and radar transmissions, cell- and satellite-phone conversations, landline communications and data transmissions—even the Iraqis' military e-mail system.

And, in recent months, a Human Intelligence network had been built inside Iraq—not a robust network, but a patchwork of CIA operators designed to help fill in the blanks in our intelligence picture.

This mass of imagery, electronic data, and agent reports—"All Source Intelligence"—was combined and analyzed in Jeff Kimmons' J-2 Fusion Cell near the JOC. It was here that the small digital Red Force boxes were loaded into our enemy database. This enemy "picture" was the best any commander had ever had in wartime—but there was a certain amount of time required for analysis and tracking. If an artillery battalion in the Iraqi 51st Division near Basra moved a few kilometers overnight, for example, dispersing among the walled compounds typical of the region, it would take the J-2 shop several hours to identify its new location and reposition the unit's red icon in the database. When I looked at the checkerboard of Red Force tracking, I knew I was seeing enemy information that was historically accurate, but not up to the minute.

It was technically possible to see combination-view displays that superimposed the relative positions of red and blue icons on the same screen. But I preferred to watch the situation on side-by-side screens, remembering that friendly information was accurate in real time, while enemy information was dated. As I reminded myself over and over, a commander should never permit himself to "know more than he knows."

The Blue and Red Force Tracking provided an accurate, evolving, near-real-time picture of operational-level force disposition: how far our companies, battalions, and brigades had advanced toward their objectives—day or night, in any weather. And this unprecedented level of awareness gave our team the confidence to exercise a new degree of flexibility. When I made the judgment that the Iraqi military was in no position to react to our early attack into the oil fields, it was not bravado. With Gene Renuart and Jeff Kimmons working together with me to measure the time-and-distance capabilities of the major enemy formations nearest to the Kuwait border, it was a matter of simple calculation: Our Marine forces, with their superior mobility and firepower, could reach the oil fields before the enemy units in southern Iraq had any chance of intercepting them.

AFTER SIGNING THE REVISED FRAGMENTARY ORDER, CENTCOM (FRAGO) 09–009, directing the early start of G-Day, I scanned the latest batch of PSYOP leaflets that Gene Renuart's people had produced. One of our main concerns was that the Iraqis might try to preempt our attack by launching WMD strikes against our massing troops, and I wanted our PSYOP effort to dissuade the Iraqis from exercising the WMD options I believed they had. Renuart and his team had taken on the task of creating these leaflets, which combined sophisticated images with clear and concise Arabic text. And, for the past twenty-four hours, Coalition planes flying Operation Southern Watch tracks in the no-fly zone had been dumping hundreds of thousands of them on Iraqi positions.

The message of the leaflets was powerful and direct. One showed a battlefield montage, in which heavily armed Coalition troops protected by gas masks and MOPP suits attacked unprotected Iraqi soldiers, choking and falling through a haze of poison gas that had been dispensed by their own military. The leaflet also featured an actual photograph of a dead Kurdish mother clutching her dead infant—victims of the nerve gas Saddam had used against his own citizens in 1988. The red Arabic text on the front read: "Nobody benefits from the use of weapons of mass destruction." The back of the leaflet carried a warning: "Any unit that chooses to use weapons of mass destruction will face swift and severe retribution by Coalition forces. Unit commanders will be held accountable if weapons of mass destruction are used."

The PSYOP shop had also produced a series of leaflets aimed at preventing sabotage of Iraq's oil fields. The front of a typical leaflet showed a well-maintained and obviously productive oil field with adjacent refinery and pumping station. The back displayed a similar facility, with flames engulfing charred and melted equipment. "Attention Iraqi Military and Security Forces!" it read. "Do not destroy Iraqi oil fields. If the Oil Industry is destroyed, your livelihood will be RUINED!"

"What's your opinion, Sir?" Gene Renuart asked.

I flipped through the last of the leaflets. "Let's keep dropping these—the more the better. For one thing, if these messages persuade even a few Iraqis to think twice, they'll be worth the trouble. For another, every time an Iraqi soldier picks up one of the leaflets, he gets a reminder: The enemy's air defenses cannot prevent us from flying anywhere we choose. And where there are leaflets today, there just might be bombs tomorrow."

A S I WAITED FOR THE BEGINNING OF HOSTILITIES, I DECIDED TO grab a quick meal in the mess hall. Whenever possible, I tried to have dinner with the troops—and tonight, Dwight Brown told me, they were serving chicken-fried steak with cream gravy and cornbread.

Brown shared my taste for down-home food and country music, which was one reason he'd been with me since my time in 3rd Army. Another reason was that he was the best senior enlisted man I'd ever served with.

But then every trooper I ate with that night, sharing home-style cooking and swapping corny jokes, was exceptional.

THE DINNER WAS GOOD, BUT THE JOKING DIDN'T LAST LONG. I was back in the War Room at 2045 hours, fifteen minutes before the first VISOB takedowns were scheduled to begin.

As soon as the Predator infrared video showed the first group of towers falling silently in a cloud of sparks from a Hellfire hit, I switched off the display and returned to a pressing problem that had begun twenty-four hours earlier.

Sitting at this same table on Tuesday night, Jeff Kimmons and Gene Renuart had handed me an Intel report and two digital prints of overhead imagery. "Interesting HUMINT out of Baghdad, Sir," Jeff said. "CIA sources report they *might* have a handle on a meeting of Saddam Hussein and his sons over the next day or so."

"How solid is it?"

"The sources are rated reliable, General. But we don't yet know where this 'possible meeting' will take place."

The report came from two trusted agents in a new network the Agency had built in Baghdad. If we did get the location of such a meeting, we would definitely go after these "high-value targets." This could be a true decapitation strike. Killing Saddam Hussein and his two sons would cripple the regime.

Saddam's sons were his heirs apparent; they also held powerful military positions. Qusay Hussein, the older son, was the commander of the Special Republican Guard, the Special Security Organization, and the Republican Guard combat formations. And the younger son, Uday, was a feared and psychopathic tyrant in his own right, who commanded the Fedayeen Saddam—irregular forces that numbered approximately 40,000.

The CIA's tip was interesting, but we couldn't do anything without a location.

"They're working it," Gene Renuart told me. The strong suspicion was that the meeting would be taking place in a complex in the southern part of the city called Dora Farms, a riverside property belonging to Saddam Hussein's wife, Sajida.

I examined the satellite photo of the walled complex: a luxury villa, garages, several nondescript outbuildings. "The problem," I said, "is that the President's ultimatum giving Saddam and his sons forty-eight hours to leave Iraq won't expire until 0400, day after tomorrow. The President gave Saddam forty-eight hours, and I know George W. Bush well enough to know he won't take a shot until that expires. Get the Navy shooters into their TLAM launch baskets, and have the targeteers work up firing solutions for that target and the other possible locations. But don't expect permission to shoot until the ultimatum period is over."

When I wrote the next day's three-by-five card before turning in that night, on the Opportunities side I printed two words: "Regime Decapitation."

That was Tuesday evening.

Tonight was Wednesday, D-Day. With the evolving intelligence on Dora Farms still too imprecise to act on, I turned back to the ongoing Special Ops.

Gene and John Abizaid joined me in the War Room shortly after 2130 hours to monitor the action. Together we watched the Blue Force Tracker and the Predator feeds as the gunships of the 160th Special Operations Aviation Regiment destroyed the VISOBS, one after another. Thinking back to those observation towers disintegrating in the blast of laser-directed 155 mm projectiles near the Wadi al

Batin thirteen years before, I was certain that the Iraqis manning our targets tonight had been hit so quickly that many of the outposts hadn't even had time to radio for help.

But I was equally sure that some of the VISOBS *had* reported—and that before long Saddam Hussein would know he had a problem on the Jordanian border.

"Teams on the move," Dell Dailey confirmed from his base in Saudi Arabia.

"Infiltration under way," Gary Harrell reported from his command post across the compound in Qatar.

I had chalked up maybe four hours of uninterrupted sleep in the past forty-eight. Short of a major emergency, there was no reason for me to stay in the War Room for the duration of the night's activity. We were on plan, and I didn't intend to interfere with the work of the two best special operators I knew.

"Good luck tonight," I told Gary and Dell.

"I'm going to bed," I told Gene. "Try to get some sleep yourself."

Back in my room, I stretched out in front of an old movie, *She Wore a Yellow Ribbon*. I must have seen it five times at the picture shows in Midland. John Wayne as a broken-down old horse soldier; weary as I was, I could relate to that. I was asleep before the Cavalry troop saddled up and left the fort.

The ring of the Red Switch next to my bed woke me like a shot.

It was Dick Myers. "Tom," he said, "I'm in the White House with the President, Secretary Rumsfeld, and George Tenet. Are you aware of the emerging target at Dora Farms?"

I was fully awake, bone tired but alert.

"We started working it last night," I said.

"Can you strike it tonight?" Dick continued.

I juggled the phone as I pulled on my boots.

"The TLAMs are spinning, Dick," I said. "I'll have to get with Gene Renuart and Tim Keating, our Naval Component commander, on launch windows and time of flight, but I see no problem. By the way, how solid is the intel?"

"George Tenet thinks it's good, Tom."

"I'll get back to you as quick as I can."

J EFF, GENE, AND TIM KEATING COMPLETED THE WEAPONEERING IN less than an hour—a TLAM package of twenty-four missiles targeted on the Dora Farms complex, and sixteen more on regime command and control sites inside the city. These additional targets were valuable in two ways: We were planning to strike them on A-Day anyway—and spreading the strikes around a little tonight might provide some cover to the agents who had pinpointed Dora Farms for us.

As I reviewed the aim points, Dick Myers called again from the White House.

"Tom, we've got some refined targeting information. One of the sources says the site includes a strongpoint, a rebarred-concrete bunker. TLAMs won't do the job against this target. Can we put an air breather on it?"

"No fucking way," I said.

We both understood that the F-117 Stealth fighter-bomber was the only aircraft in the theater that was capable of bombing a target that close to Baghdad before we destroyed the city's air defenses. F-117s were virtually invisible to radar, and they were invisible to ground observers while flying at night at high altitude. In daylight, though, they became relatively slow, defenseless targets. According to the weather and light data, the sun would rise over Baghdad at 0609 hours Iraqi time this morning. But first twilight—when aircraft became visible from the ground—would be half an hour earlier. That meant that if we used the F-117s, they would have to be well away from Baghdad's Missile Engagement Zone by 0530 hours at the latest.

This sure as hell was a short timeline—not the easiest operational problem I'd ever tackled.

"I'll work it with Buzz," I told Dick. Buzz Moseley responded in typical fashion: "We're on it, Boss."

One of the key considerations was whether to create a "corridor" through the Iraqi air defenses from Kuwait all the way to the target by striking enemy antiaircraft guns, surface-to-air missiles, and radars before the F-117s flew the mission. That would provide an added degree of protection. But opening the corridor would alert the enemy that there was a strike inbound. And, over almost twelve years of Operation Southern Watch, the Iraqis had learned our operational patterns just as we had learned theirs. This was not a simple business.

And there were other considerations. SOF insertions were already in progress. We had blacked-out MH-53 Pave Low and MH-60 DAP helicopters flying low and fast to avoid ground fire. Even though we knew their planned ingress-egress routes, Special Ops pilots survived by being unpredictable. The last thing we needed was to have a Pave Low knocked out of the sky by a bomb one of our own F-16s had dropped to open a corridor for an inbound F-117.

I started a round of calls to Gary Harrell and Dell Dailey to give them a heads-up that there might be unexpected air activity.

"Not to worry," Gary said in his laconic way.

Dell saw no problem either. "But I've got an aircraft loss to report, Sir," he added.

One of our helicopters had suffered a brownout in the dust while dropping Special Mission troopers and Agency field officers near the crucial Euphrates River town of An Nasiriyah. The main rotor had hit the ground at an angle, and the big helicopter rolled on its side. The passengers and crew were shaken up, but not badly injured. They put up a defense perimeter, removed classified equipment from the chopper, and got on with the mission. These troopers were needed to survey the two main highway bridges across the river, and to "hang out in the weeds"—to act as combat air controllers in case the enemy attempted to reinforce or destroy the bridges. Both the 3rd ID and the 1 MEF would need intact spans to cross the Euphrates on their way to Baghdad.

"We'll use an F-16 to destroy the damaged helicopter," Dell said. "Continuing the mission."

Losing an aircraft was not good. But in war the enemy also gets a vote. And Murphy's law prevails: *Anything that can go wrong will go wrong.* "Good work, guys," I told Gary and Dell. "Drive on."

In the middle of these calls, Buzz reached me again. "This is what we've got, General," he explained. "We have the F-117 Nighthawks, the EGBU 2,000-pound bunker busters, and the pilots in Qatar at Al Udeid. Now all I've got to do is get them married together, get a mission planned, and fly them to Baghdad . . . before the sun comes up."

"Right, Buzz," I said smiling. My thoughts were spinning, almost as fast as they had on 9/11 on the roof of the Kydon Hotel. "What are the probabilities of mission success with a single aircraft?"

Buzz didn't hesitate. "A single plane gives us a probability of .5."

Again I thought before speaking. Normally I was a glass-half-full optimist, but tonight there could be no risk of failure. "What does it take to get one hundred percent—two planes?"

"Probability of success goes to 1.0, General."

"Two planes—do it, Buzz," I said.

"Roger, Boss, two Nighthawks on the way."

Gene introduced the next complication. "Striking the leadership target is probably going to trigger a strong reaction, even if we do kill the sons of bitches."

I knew exactly what he meant. For the past two days we had been receiving increasingly urgent Intelligence reporting that Republican Guard units in Baghdad had moved south to the city of Al Kut—and that they had been issued mustard gas and an unknown nerve agent. Other reports were noting that Ababil-100 Theater Ballistic Missile launchers were moving around unpredictably. Chemical weapons and TBMs—not a good combination. If the Republican Guard cadres who guarded Iraq's WMD had been issued their munitions and were en route to link up with the missile shooters, we were looking at a strong possibility of gas attacks into our crowded staging areas in Kuwait. I placed our forces there on a high state of alert. The planned decapitation strike on Dora Farms might be the triggering event.

"Jeff," I told my J-2, "let's refine the additional TLAM targets. If we're going to hit Dora Farms, we'll also want to do some serious damage to their intel and security forces."

I was on the Red Switch again when Grinch came through the door. "Sir, the Chairman's been trying to get you from the White House."

Damn, I thought. For a moment I wished I had those two headsets I'd rigged up thirty-five years earlier in that little helicopter over the Kinh Doi Canal south of Saigon.

"I'm here, Dick. We're making chicken salad out of chicken shit."

"Don't get pissed off at me, Tom," he began.

"I'd never get pissed at you, Dick. You're my brother."

"I've been speaking directly to your Air Component Commander," he said. "Tried to reach you first, but you were stuck on the phone, and we've got a hell of a time crunch here."

"No big deal, Dick." My fax to Wolfowitz had done what I wanted, chasing the folks in the E-Ring and inside OSD out from underfoot. But Dick Myers was no interloper; he was my solid anchor in the Building. I'd never cut him out of the loop. "How's Buzz doing?"

"He's trying to make the mission happen, Tom. Looks good so far."

"Yep, two 117s, and we're going to add a few targets to the TLAM list as well. May as well hit 'em with a right hook and a left jab."

"Roger, Tom. But I need your drop-dead, no-shit decision time. We want to hit those targets, but the President doesn't want to lose two good pilots for nothing."

"Time on target must be no later than 0530 Iraq time, Dick, with takeoff from Al Udeid no later than 0330. They'll have a two-hour trip inbound with one air refueling. I need the President's decision by 0315, so the jets can start engines and taxi." I looked at the pulsing digits of the clock on the wall: 0227. "We've got less than an hour for Go-No-Go, Dick."

"Understand, Tom. We'll get back to you."

Dick Myers understood, of course. He had flown scores of combat missions over North Vietnam as a young pilot. He knew the realities of war. I was glad the President and the Secretary of Defense had him there in the Oval Office.

Buzz reported back at 0259. "Two aircraft armed with the selected weapons. Pilots briefed. They're sitting in the aircraft. Nobody's thrilled with the timing, but you know these Stealth guys. They'd fly into the Gates of Hell to hit a good target."

I fought the temptation to ask the names of those F-117 pilots. Even with a strike success probability of 1.0, their planes ran the risk of being spotted during egress after sunrise. There was a good chance that one of these young warriors wouldn't come home.

The digits on the wall clock clicked to 0312 hours. I sighed and looked at Gene. "It's getting late, J-3."

I could picture the scene in the Oval Office: the President surrounded by his advisers, weighing the pros and cons. George Bush had flown fighters. He understood the mechanics of mission planning and execution. And he knew how to make a decision.

The Red Switch rang. It was Dick Myers. "The mission is a go, Tom. Please execute."

"Got it." I called Buzz Moseley. "Launch the mission, Buzz," I said. "Good luck to all."

Both aircraft launched successfully at 0338 hours.

Now we would coordinate the final TLAM launch sequence. Time passed in the unblinking fluorescent glare of the War Room. One of the aspects of a Stealth mission was that the aircraft did not transmit Blue Force Tracker data. The only mission status we received with the aircraft inbound to the target was the confirmation that they had refueled at their tankers.

Tim Keating reported from Bahrain that the surface vessels and submarines in the North Arabian Gulf had launched their salvos of

TLAMs on schedule, beginning at 0439 hours. The missiles would strike their targets within minutes of the Stealths' bunker-buster EGUB-27s.

The plasma screens continued to display special operator insertions in the west and south, and on the oil platforms just offshore from the Al Faw peninsula.

"The Poles have secured their GOPLAT objective," Gene reported. "No friendly casualties, light enemy resistance."

That was good news. Sabotage of the offshore oil-loading manifolds and production platforms would have crippled Iraq's petroleum industry, and caused an environmental catastrophe that would have dwarfed the Exxon Valdez oil spill in Alaska.

With the Stealth mission still under way, though, it was hard to absorb good news.

I didn't have time to twist my knuckles, however; within a few minutes Don Rumsfeld was on the line. The President was considering doing a press conference as soon as the Dora Farms strike went down. "Put on your speechwriter's cap, Tom," he said. "We need your input. What's your opinion?"

"Baghdad's full of foreign reporters, Mr. Secretary," I said. "There'll be bombs and TLAMs impacting just to the south along the river and some missile strikes in the city itself. We're looking at a real CNN moment."

"So you recommend that the President make an address?" Rumsfeld was thoughtful, choosing his words with care. "A presidential statement would not interfere with your operations?"

The Iraqis wouldn't need CNN to tell them that kinetics had begun. "Sir," I told Rumsfeld. "I recommend that the President do the address."

"Okay, Tom," Rumsfeld said. "Put on your wordsmith hat."

We proceeded to walk through the phraseology of the President's remarks. "We don't want to jeopardize your operational security in any way," Rumsfeld stressed.

As I listened to proposed phrasing of the draft speech, I tried to balance the security of the troops against the impact the President's words would have on the international audience. We did not want President Bush to speak in a way that sounded good to America and our allies, but inadvertently compromised our plan.

The secure fax on the side table whirred, printing out a semi-final draft of the wording we'd selected.

"My fellow citizens, at this hour, American and Coalition forces are in the early stages of military operations to disarm Iraq, to free its people and to defend the world from grave danger."

That introduction seemed about right. The reference to "early stages" was particularly important. "We don't want to let the enemy think this is another pinprick TLAM strike that got lucky," I told Rumsfeld. "But we also don't want the Iraqis to start gearing up for G-Day right this minute."

"These are in the opening stages of what will be a broad and concerted campaign," the statement said a few lines later. "That's good, Mr. Secretary," I told Rumsfeld. "It implies there will be a long air operation. But the enemy's got a surprise coming."

I read the rest of the text. It was solid. "I concur with the wording, Sir."

At 0541 hours, I was switching among satellite TV channels. Right on schedule, a correspondent on the balcony of the Palestine Hotel in Baghdad reported "heavy explosions" south of the city, and in the western suburbs. Predictably, the Iraqi air defenses ripped apart the dawn sky with tracers and antiaircraft missiles.

It was daylight in Iraq. And we hadn't yet heard from the Stealth pilots.

WHEN THE STRIKE REPORT DID COME, IT CAPTURED SOME OF the drama of the attack. The two F-117s—call signs *Ram 01* and *Ram 02*—had approached Dora Farms from either side of a descending oval flight path, one from the east, the other from the west. The sun was almost above the horizon. A cloud deck had shielded them from ground observation, but also obscured the target complex.

At the last moment, the pilots had found a break in the clouds that gave them six seconds to identify the targets visually and drop their bombs. But the aiming points were so close, and the new GPS-guided weapons—which had never before been used in combat—were so accurate that the bombs clustered as they fell and almost collided.

The weapons were fused to penetrate deep before exploding to "bust" the fortified shelter beneath the luxurious buildings on the Tigris River, where Saddam and his sons were thought to be meeting.

Climbing back through the clouds, the pilots had seen their weapons explode, and then witnessed the spectacle of the incoming TLAMs strike across the compound in a progression of fiery blasts.

Both aircraft returned safely to Al Udeid, well after daylight.

"We're working BDA and Agency reports now, General," Jeff Kimmons told me on the phone as I got out of the shower.

With all our advances in technology—Battle Damage Assessment (BDA)—was still a recurrent problem. Short of eyewitness reports from a target site, we had to rely on imagery. If a Predator UAV spotted a platoon of six Iraqi tanks half-hidden in a palm grove, for example, it could identify the target for an air strike. After the smoke cleared, the Predator or satellite imagery might reveal that two or three tanks were obviously destroyed. Communications intercepts might reflect that there is no radio traffic from any of the tanks. And with no movement from those that were *not* obviously struck, it would be easy to conclude that all six were out of action. But how could we know for sure? Should Jeff Kimmons and Gene Renuart's targeteers cross that entire Iraqi armor platoon off their list, or should Buzz Moseley's pilots return to strike the ones we weren't sure of?

It was a problem that would plague us, I knew, in the days and nights ahead.

From the Dora Farms BDA, we knew little. Saddam was either dead or alive, wounded or healthy. We would find out eventually, and in the meantime there would be many other "emerging" targets to strike. On a battlefield, intelligence reporting on such targets is sometimes accurate, sometimes not. But we would never want to miss a chance to decapitate the regime and end the war early.

Don't fret about things you can't control, I thought. Morning was breaking on Thursday, March 20, and we had a war to fight.

B EFORE THE OPERATION BEGAN, I HAD WORKED HARD WITH THE staff and component commanders to make sure we would have constant access to each other once the hectic pace of the warfight kicked in. We needed a communications "rhythm" that would guarantee mutual consultation without needless interference, either up or down the chain of command. I would be the commander, issuing guidance and prodding where necessary, but I was not going to command the troopers down in the "weeds," like some Hollywood notion of a senior commander moving stick-pins around on a detailed operational map. Wars don't work that way today; I'm not sure they ever did.

With the unprecedented situational awareness to which we had access, it would be tempting for me to try to maneuver small formations. But I would resist that temptation. A military organization like this Coalition is too large and complex for one man to direct at the tactical level. I would command the warfight, but I would do so *through* my subordinates. There would be times when I'd give orders to those subordinates, and I expected them to obey those orders. But I would not tell Major General Buford "Buff" Blount, commander of the 3rd Infantry Division, or Lt. General Jim Conway, the 1 MEF commander, where and how I wanted one of their platoons or companies to conduct an attack. I didn't *need* to—that was their job, and they knew how to do it.

I would, however, be kept well informed on the tactical situation, so that I could make operational decisions.

And, I had to "feed the beast" in Washington, keeping Don Rumsfeld, Dick Myers, and the President fully and accurately informed as to the progress—and problems—of the campaign. This would be doubly important because of the media embedded with our forces. The reporters filing their stories from the maneuver units would not have access to the Blue Force Tracker. For many, their perspective would be limited to a single company or battalion's Area of Operations. What might appear to be a major crisis to one of them would often be a minor glitch for the overall Coalition force.

But I knew the gang inside the Beltway would be channel surfing from the get-go in this campaign, trying to pierce the fog and friction via Fox and CNN—not to mention Al-Jazeera.

So, in order to command Coalition forces effectively while meeting my responsibilities to civilian authorities—seven thousand miles and eight time zones away from the action—I established a battle rhythm of scheduled VTCs, updates, intelligence reviews, and literally hundreds of other daily coordination activities, which occupied the staff's time and mine from D-Day to the end of the campaign.

In the preceding week, I had also begun a disciplined personal schedule that gave shape and focus to my day. After waking at 0400, I called the JOC on the hotline for an update. Then I hit the treadmill for half an hour, watching American and international television. After having a shower and eating two or three soft-boiled eggs, I would take my Ford Expedition to Building 217, with a Neal McCoy CD playing on the stereo.

THE DORA FARMS STRIKE HAD DISRUPTED THIS PATTERN. BUT BY 0720 hours on Thursday, March 20, D+1, the first full day of Operation Iraqi Freedom, I was back on schedule. My workday began with reading cables and messages from OSD, Dick Myers, embassies in the region, Rifle DeLong back at CENTCOM Main, and the component commanders. It took me a good hour to work through the stack.

At 0800, as I finished the papers, my staff principals filed into my office—a windowless shelter like the rest, set up with a secure VTC capability and four plasma screens on one wall. I had a desk at one end of a T-shaped conference table with five chairs on each side. John Abizaid sat at the far end, facing me; our Chief of Staff, Army General Steve Whitcomb, sat to his left, and the directors lined both sides of the table.

After a quick review of Coalition ground, air, and naval operations from Gene Renuart, I turned to Jeff Kimmons. "J-2, what do you have for us?"

"Here's what we've got so far on the regime leadership strike," he said. "Reports are coming in in dribs and drabs. The preliminary BDA summary and imagery show smashed buildings, fire damage, the burnt-out gaggle of SUVs, the type of vehicles associated with Saddam Hussein and his sons' bodyguards," Jeff said. "And an agent reports that Saddam was pulled from the wreckage, badly injured, maybe still alive. His face was covered with an oxygen mask as the stretcher was hoisted into an ambulance."

"Let's not nibble this to death," I said. "That strike is over. We'll find out what happened eventually. You know my feelings about the first reports from scouts . . ."

"They're always wrong," John Abizaid said. They'd heard my sermon on this before.

Of course, as we learned later, Saddam and his sons had survived the Dora Farms strike. But it had been worth the effort: Never again would they feel secure among their most-trusted advisers. Who had betrayed their presence at that location? Either there were spies close to them, or the Coalition's reconnaissance system was sophisticated enough to track their movements. Had we zeroed in on their encrypted cell phones? Were our satellites tracking their vehicles' unique heat signatures from space? Bottom line, we were keeping them guessing.

The courageous pilots of Ram 01 and Ram 02—along with Buzz Moseley's targeteers, who executed the strike on highly perishable real-time intelligence—had shown Saddam, Uday, and Qusay Hussein there was no safe place to hide. Drive a vehicle, talk on the phone, send an e-mail, write a note . . . *whatever you do, the Coalition is watching.*

A T 0900, WE MOVED TO THE CONFERENCE ROOM FOR A VTC with the component commanders at their headquarters in the AOR, and with supporting headquarters all over the world. Even though it was after midnight on the East Coast, CENTCOM's "night general" in Tampa, the night shifts at the Joint Staff in the Pentagon, Transportation Command, the CIA ops center, and the European Command in Germany—which didn't have a serious time-zone disconnect—were all on the loop.

Each principal staff officer described key ongoing activities in his area of responsibility: Denny Jackson on logistics, Rear Admiral Jim "Rookie" Robb on planning, and Jim Wilkinson on public affairs. Brigadier General Vince Brooks, our operations "briefer," took notes, which we used to format the presentation he would give later at the media center. A brilliant young officer, Vince would become the voice of Operation Iraqi Freedom. I had known him for years—he had worked for me in Korea and 3rd Army—and he would be superb in this role as well. On this, the first day of the operation, he listened intently as the component commanders provided their updates.

Gary Harrell, who had the most boots on the ground at this point, delivered a succinct report. Teams of operators had been inserted into numerous sites across the western desert. They'd cut—"interdicted" in military parlance—the main highway connecting Iraq to Jordan, and they controlled the western 25 percent of Iraq. The SOF task force in the north had linked up with Kurdish Peshmerga guerrillas and were deployed along the Green Line separating the Kurdish Autonomous Zone from the rest of Iraq—helping fix the enemy divisions in the north.

The Iraqis were blinded, stumbling . . . and we had been at war only about twelve hours. Dave McKiernan would kick off G-Day tonight, with A-Day going tomorrow.

"Okay," I said. "You're all doing great work. Let's execute the plan like we've wargamed it. Do the mission—and *protect the force.*"

A S THE FIRST MORNING OF THE WAR PROGRESSED, I REVIEWED final attack plans with Dave McKiernan and the Land Component staff in another VTC.

The V Corps commander, Lt. General William "Scott" Wallace, and Jim Conway gave precise, complete briefings: Their units' troop strengths and equipment and supply inventories were good. Their formations were in pre-assault assembly areas near the border berm. Once artillery, MLRS, and helicopter gunships had destroyed the remaining Iraqi VISOBS, combat engineers would bulldoze lanes through the high walls of sand and gravel.

Then our tankers and mechanized infantry troopers would move forward, using large, collapsible steel bridge units to span the deep antitank ditches on the Iraqi side of the border. In the next twenty-four hours, thousands of tracked and wheeled vehicles would advance north through those breaches in the berm and over the bridge spans.

Their commanders combined decades of rigorous training and leadership experience. Most had served in combat during Desert Storm or in the Balkans. They had maneuvered units through training exercises in Kuwait and endless Cold War field maneuvers in Germany and the mountains of Korea. They knew their routes of advance, phase lines, and objectives—but they also knew from firsthand experience that Murphy's law was always in effect, ready to cause problems.

"You all know my thoughts on battle tempo," I told them. "Remember—speed and momentum." I'd never seen a situation where speed was going to be more critical. Saddam Hussein's arsenal of ballistic missiles, shorter-range rockets, and artillery was impressive, and our intelligence told us that some of them were likely armed with chemical or biological warheads. All-source intelligence indicated that Republican Guard and SSO troops arrayed around Baghdad were holding WMD, and we could expect them to use those weapons as we closed the noose on the capital—unless we got there before the Iraqis were ready. Our speed of advance would not only kill the enemy, it would save Coalition lives.

This was an important operational principle: By striking hard and fast, our units would disrupt the Iraqis' ability to react effectively. An Iraqi armor brigade commander might learn that the Bradleys of our cavalry scouts had penetrated his outer defensive perimeter. But by the time he could maneuver *his* tanks and artillery to counterattack, we would have our own tanks attacking in battalion wedges through his operational area, destroying every Iraqi tank and gun in their way. And overhead, attack helicopters and strike aircraft would kill any vehicle that moved.

"The key is speed, guys," I reminded them. "We are going to *win* this fight—and we'll do it by getting inside the enemy's decision cycle. Remember: *Speed kills . . . the enemy.*"

T HE FIRST MORNING OF THE WAR PASSED QUICKLY IN THE VAST, teeming hive of Building 217. Working around me were teams devoted to every imaginable discipline and specialty involved in modern warfighting: intelligence, communications, weather, Public Affairs, Political-Military, Planning, Logistics (with all their sub-specialists), Transportation, Civil Affairs, Humanitarian Assistance, PSYOP—"about a thousand of your closest friends," Grinch joked.

Around midday, a symbol flashed on the computer map across from my desk. A Patriot battery of the Army's 32nd Air and Missile Defense Command had just fired a missile to engage an incoming Iraqi TBM. With the click of a mouse, I was able to zoom in on the battery, which was near the 101st Airborne Division's Tactical Assembly Area in northwestern Kuwait—a featureless dustbowl near the border berm. In the blink of a few pixels on the screen, the

Patriot missile successfully destroyed the enemy warhead high in the atmosphere.

The digital clock said 1224 hours. *It didn't take the Iraqis long to retaliate for last night,* I thought.

My phone rang. "You on that TBM engagement in Kuwait, General?" Jeff Kimmons asked. "That was an Ababil-100 from a launch basket south of Basra."

A PAC-3 Patriot launched from one of twenty-seven batteries stationed in Kuwait, Bahrain, Qatar, Saudi Arabia, and Jordan had destroyed it. The Patriot was extremely effective against Theater Ballistic Missiles. And we had launchers positioned to guard Coalition bases and troop concentrations from incoming missiles throughout much of the theater. I had no idea if the Ababil-100's warhead was conventional or WMD, and given the destruction of the enemy weapon at transonic speed, we might never know. The point was that a warhead streaking down directly toward an assembly area crowded with four thousand soldiers and a hundred Black Hawk, Chinook, and Apache helicopters had been neutralized.

The preliminary engagement report, which we received a few minutes later, confirmed what had happened. The U.S. Navy Aegis destroyer in the northern Gulf, USS *Higgins,* detected the TBM two seconds after launch. After it flashed a warning to the Air Defense operations center at Camp Doha, Kuwait, the radars of Battery D, 5th Battalion, 52nd ADA had tracked the missile as it streaked out of the atmosphere. Our computers worked a firing solution within fourteen seconds, and two Patriots were fired, destroying the warhead high above the desert floor.

"One to nothing," I told Jeff. "We can expect more."

I called Buzz Moseley. "Can you do some missile hunting?'

"I've got F-16s up right now, Boss. We'll find them."

That afternoon the Iraqis fired four more missiles at our forces in Kuwait. Our Patriots destroyed two; the other two fell in the empty desert or the Gulf and were not engaged.

At 1435 hours, Buzz reported that his fighter-bombers had located and destroyed two of the Ababil-100 mobile launchers.

"Good work, Buzz," I said. "You're not using up all your CBUs, are you?" Cluster Bomb Units, which released hundreds of small, lethal bomblets, were the weapons of choice against mobile missile launchers.

"It only took two, General. We've got plenty."

On that morning's three-by-five card, I had led the list of Challenges with "WMD Threat," as I had for the previous week—and would continue to do for the days and weeks ahead.

As I had hoped, Don Rumsfeld and Dick Myers were the only two faces visible when the picture clicked open for our scheduled VTC. It was 1500 hours—0700 in the Pentagon.

"Mr. Secretary," I reported, "We are on-plan. Our Special Operations Forces are in control of their initial objectives in the western desert."

Using a digital map, I pointed out the positions of the Joint Special Operations Task Force-West (JSOTF-W) teams, which had already established Forward Operating Bases (FOBs) at five sites inside Iraq. "General Harrell's troops have surrounded the H2 Airfield and the highway town of Ar Rutbah," I said, and proceeded to describe the events of the previous eighteen hours. "Dave McKiernan's troops and Marines are set to move into the southern oil fields tonight. And, of course," I added, "we have air supremacy in the battlespace."

"What are your plans for the 4th Infantry, Tom?" Rumsfeld asked.

"I want to keep the ships in the Med a while longer, Sir," I said. "The docks in Kuwait are still crowded. It will take only six days for the 4th ID's sea convoy to get to Kuwait once they receive the movement order, and it makes no sense for them to sit at anchor in the harbor. The division is serving a better purpose as a feint force."

"That's your call, Tom," Don Rumsfeld said.

"Dick," I asked General Myers, "can you keep TRANSCOM and the Navy from blowing gaskets over this? We're already getting some rumbles of discontent. They want those ships offloaded and moving."

Myers agreed to run interference. "Everyone in Washington is behind you, Tom," Rumsfeld said at the end of the VTC.

The Ten Days from Hell seemed a lifetime ago. Whatever happened in this operation, I knew there would be no "I don't see any movement, General Franks" calls from the Secretary, as there had been during those early days in Afghanistan. There was no Blue Force Tracker in Don Rumsfeld's office, but there was a television. And as he watched it, the movement of Coalition troops would be impossible to miss.

B EFORE TURNING IN ON THURSDAY NIGHT, I ORDERED THE RELEASE of a statement to our forces about to enter combat. In drafting the message, I'd tried to put myself in the boots of a Marine rifleman, a trooper jolting along in a Bradley, a sailor working on the dark, hazardous flightdeck of the USS *Nimitz,* or an airman in the cockpit of an A-10 rolling in through streams of tracers to strike an enemy tank column.

"Men and women of Operation Iraqi Freedom," the message began:

> The President of the United States—our Commander in Chief—in agreement with the leadership of our coalition partners has ordered the initiation of combat operations. Our objectives are clear. We will disarm Iraq and remove the regime that has refused to disarm peacefully. We will liberate the Iraqi people from a dictator who uses torture, murder, hunger, and terror as tools of oppression. We will bring food, medicines, and other humanitarian assistance to Iraqis in need. We will take care to protect innocent civilians and the infrastructure that supports them, and we will help the Iraqi people start anew to build a future of their own with a government of their choice.
>
> You have my highest personal confidence and the confidence of your Commander in Chief. You are now in harm's way. Our task will not be easy, but we are fighting for a just cause and the outcome is not in doubt. I am proud of you—all that you have done and all you will achieve in the days ahead.
>
> We will all do our duty. May God bless each of you, this coalition, and the United States of America.

TURKEY

Murat

Maku

azig

Tatvan

Baskale

Tabriz

Dicle

Sanliurfa

Al Qamishli

Saqqez

IRAN

Ar Raqqah

173d AB
BDE

Bashur
Air Base

SYRIA

Dayr az
Zawr

Mosul

Arbil

SOF Sulaymaniyah

Kirkuk

Hamadan

Bayji

NORTHERN
OIL FIELDS

Tigris

Kermanshah

Tikrīt

Haditah

Al Haqlaniyah

Khorramabad

H1

Euphrates

Al Fallujah

Baghdad

VISOBS

H2

Ar Rutbah

Ar Ramadi

SOF

H3

Karbalā

Tigris

Al Küt

SOF

22

An Najaf

7

6

1 MEF

Al Amarah

Ahvaz

V Corps

8

RUMAILAH
OIL FIELDS

VISOBS

1

Qurnah

As Samāwah

An Nāsirīyah

Basrah

29

8

Umm Qasr

U.K.

Sakakah

1 MEF
& U.K.

Rafha

VISOBS

Kuw

KUWAIT

Per
G

Coalition Forces
Staging Bases

Al Qaysumah

SAUDI ARABIA

Al Mish'ab

Iraq

Operation Iraqi Freedom
March - May 2003

N
W E
S

0   100   200 kilometers

0   50   100   150 miles

Petho Cartography 2004

O634 HOURS IRAQ TIME, FRIDAY, MARCH 21, D+2. I SAT IN THE War Room, watching the rectangular Blue Force icons on the plasma screens advance north from the solid black line marking the Kuwaiti border with Iraq.

After sunset the night before, the engineers had breached the berm, cut the fence obstacles, and laid their portable bridges across the antitank ditches. Recon units in Bradleys and Marine LAVs were already twenty kilometers inside Iraq.

G-Day had begun.

"One MEF Force Recon units and Buff Blount's Cav scouts crossed their lines of departure beginning at 2100 last night," David McKiernan reported on the conference call from Camp Doha, Kuwait. "The Marines and V Corps' troopers were right behind them and are moving out fast, General."

John Abizaid, Gene Renuart, and I studied the blinking blue symbols. The Red Force Tracker indicated that the Iraqi 51st Mechanized Division, a regular army force equipped with T-55 and T-62 tanks, its ranks filled with both Sunni and Shiite conscripts, was deployed through the Rumilyah Oil Fields. But the latest imagery showed only two additional wellheads on fire—no major sabotage yet.

And with the VISOBS along the Kuwait-Iraq border destroyed, the Iraqis would not be able to estimate the size or composition of the Coalition force racing north. The early launch had delivered at least some degree of operational surprise.

To exploit that surprise, a robust Electronic Warfare operation was under way, jamming many—but not all—Iraqi military radio channels, while leaving some links up so that we could eavesdrop. And our planes and long-range artillery were striking key enemy communication nodes, radio repeater stations, tactical switchboards, and regional headquarters of selected regular army units.

"We've got only a small force minding the store up in the oil fields," McKiernan continued. "But Jim Conway's Marines are hauling ass. With any luck, they will get Rumilyah intact."

The lead Marine units would sweep into the Rumilyah fields within hours.

With first light on G-Day, Brigade Combat Teams (BCTs) of the 3rd Infantry Division and Marine Regimental Combat Teams (RCTs) had begun the main assault north toward Baghdad. These were fast-moving, self-contained formations that combined armor, mechanized infantry, and artillery—an average of 5,000 troops each. They would advance along separate routes, but would link up when necessary to mass firepower against concentrated enemy defenses.

The 3rd Infantry Division's Second BCT, a tank-heavy armored formation, followed the Bradleys of the 3rd Squadron, 7th Cavalry Regiment (3-7 Cav). Their first objective was Tallil Air Base. And from there the troops would speed north to An Nasiriyah, to seize the highway bridge across the Euphrates and hold it for the Marines.

One Marine RCT was poised to seize the southern oil fields; another was moving up to take over the bridge from the 3rd ID. From there the Marines would seize other bridges across the Euphrates and the Saddam Canal.

These bridges would become the 1 MEF's doorway into the heart of Mesopotamia, where armies had clashed throughout the millennia. The Marine RCTs would advance up Highways 1 and 7 through Shiite farm towns, staying west of the six Iraqi regular army divisions dug into a "staircase" of defensive positions just north of Basra. Ultimately, the 1 MEF would cross the Tigris and advance north along Highway 6 to the eastern side of Baghdad.

The success of the Marine operation would depend in large part on fixing those six divisions in place. If the enemy hunkered down, they would be pounded by Coalition air, day and night. If they broke out of their bunkers and trench lines, Buzz Moseley's air component and the Marines' air-ground team would destroy them in the open.

While the Marines and the Army's V Corps moved toward Baghdad, the British 1st Armoured Division would hook sharply to the northeast to isolate Basra, Iraq's second-largest city. Intel estimated that the vast majority of Basra's population of almost one million Shiites would remain neutral, neither helping nor hindering, while the Brits dealt with the Baathist leadership of the garrison.

"So far, enemy resistance has been sporadic and relatively light," McKiernan reported. "The lead Army formations have encountered some poorly organized enemy armor units and dismounted troops. Some of them will fight. Some have surrendered. And a lot seem to have abandoned their positions and just melted away. We do not anticipate any major fights for the next few hours."

Buzz Moseley was on the loop as well. "Are you giving those troopers and Marines plenty of air support, Buzz?" I asked.

"We sure are, General," he said. "We've flown over two hundred sorties in the first two hours, and the tempo is picking up. It is going to be a busy day. And the strategic set hasn't even begun yet."

"The airmen have been doing great work for us, General," McKiernan added. David McKiernan was one of the straightest, most serious-minded officers I'd met in my thirty-eight years as a soldier. I knew he would tell me if the air support wasn't up to Buzz Moseley's high standards.

Close Air Support would be key to the operation. Ever since the planning for Anaconda the year before in Afghanistan, I had sermonized to the component commanders about the importance of linking ground and air operations into one seamless whole. If a soldier or Marine needed fires on a target, he had to be able to call on support from strike aircraft, helicopter gunships, or artillery with equal ease.

And if a Predator or Global Hawk located Iraqi armor, that data had to flow simultaneously to the Land and Air Components, so that *all* our firepower—both air and ground—could be brought to bear.

"All right," I said, wrapping up the call. "Things *will* get more hectic. I want you guys eating with the same fork. *Fight jointly.*"

"Understand, Boss," Buzz said.

"Yes, Sir," David said.

I thought it would be good to loosen David up a little at the beginning of the campaign. But I knew it wouldn't be easy to get him to laugh at one of my lame jokes.

"Hey, Buzz," I said. "Reach into that fancy phone you've got with all the buttons and shake your twin brother David's hand."

"Hi, David," Buzz said.

"Nice to meet you, Buzz," David replied. I could almost hear him smile.

A N HOUR LATER, DENNY JACKSON, MY CHIEF "LOGGIE," forwarded me a new set of status updates from the support command in Kuwait. There was a new concern emerging: Congestion at the main commercial port of Shuaibah, at the container-ship terminal at Shuwaikh, and at the Naval Base docks in Kuwait City. Denny's people were working magic, getting cargoes off the ships and into the lines of communication—the road networks through Kuwait and into Iraq. But there was a limit to what they could do. During Operation Desert Storm, the Coalition had enjoyed the use of four big commercial ports on Saudi Arabia's Gulf and Red Sea coasts. In Operation Iraqi Freedom, we did not have those facilities.

Denny Jackson, working with TRANSCOM, Coalition port support units, and the Kuwaiti government, had done an amazing job, getting a ground force of 170,000 troops up and running, supplied with vehicles, weapons, ammunition, fuel, food, water—and hundreds of thousands of tons of other supplies—in less than three months. And they'd done it in "spikes," to maintain the overall operational deception.

Now the 101st Airborne Division was offloading the last of their gear and getting stood up for combat in their assembly areas. Meanwhile, the 2nd ACR, a formation almost the size of a World War II armored division, was en route from the States. With that unit and the 4th ID due to offload in the weeks ahead, there were going to be more backups on the docks. So capturing and de-mining the Iraqi ports of Umm Qasr was a priority for the British forces and the 1 MEF.

Even with all of this going on, some officers in the Pentagon—and the TV generals—were complaining that the Coalition didn't have *enough* troops on the ground to start the war. These "strategists" obviously wanted a rerun of Desert Storm—560,000 troops and a separate, protracted air campaign before launching a ground operation with multiple heavy divisions on a broad front. *That Desert Storm force wasn't exactly perfect in protecting Kuwait's oil fields*, I thought.

Building up a Desert Storm–size force in Kuwait would have taken months of effort—very visible effort—and would have sacrificed the crucial element of operational surprise we now enjoyed. If we had tried jamming twelve or thirteen divisions, cheek-by-jowl, across the narrow border of northern Kuwait, we could never have deceived the enemy into thinking that the main effort would come from the north or west.

And, if operational surprise *had* been sacrificed, I suspected that the Iraqis would have repositioned their Republican Guard and regular army units, making for an attrition slugfest that would cost thousands of lives.

And there was another factor: A densely concentrated Coalition force in northern Kuwait would have offered a tempting target for Iraqi artillery and missiles—armed with either conventional or WMD projectiles. We had avoided that problem by passing the combat units through the Kuwait staging camps one after another. The 101st Airborne, for example, was mounting up for combat in the camps that the 3rd ID had just vacated; when the 4th Infantry Division eventually arrived in Kuwait, it would use the same facilities.

And support was another issue. Today, our ground troops operate "leaner and meaner" than in past wars. Even so, the more combat troops we committed into Iraq, the larger the support force it would take to provide them fuel, food, ammunition, medical care, etc.

Kuwait was essentially our only staging area . . . and only so many troops would fit in Kuwait.

Terrain was another important consideration. The pattern of rivers, canals, marshes, and lakes in southern and central Iraq restricted the approach routes from Kuwait to Baghdad. There were several classic choke points—narrow lanes of passable terrain—that advancing forces would have to negotiate en route to the capital. The narrow Karbala Gap, between that city in the Euphrates Valley and the barrier of Lake Razzaza to the west, was one such feature. And in the 1 MEF's axis of advance to the east, there were similar natural barriers, particularly where Highway 7 crossed the Tigris River to join Highway 6 at al Kut.

Sheer numbers—troops, tanks, infantry fighting vehicles, and artillery—would not change the immutable dictates of that terrain. There were only a limited number of routes to Baghdad, and Baghdad was where the Coalition was headed.

The capital was the center of gravity of the Baathist regime; as long as his troops still controlled the city, Saddam Hussein would never relinquish power. Therefore, Coalition forces had to advance on Baghdad so rapidly—bypassing and fixing enemy formations in place—that the capital would be cut off before Iraqi divisions could fall back and turn the sprawling city into a "fortress," as many feared it might become. This mission would not be accomplished by massed armor or mechanized infantry divisions, lined up for miles waiting to thread the needle of the Karbala Gap or cross the Tigris on pontoon bridges.

As I had briefed the President and the NSC, "Coalition strength during decisive combat will derive from the mass of effective firepower, not simply the number of boots or tank tracks on the ground."

Operation Desert Storm had introduced the public to the idea of "smart weapons," in the form of those amazing videos of laser-guided bombs smashing bridges and ministry buildings. But only a fraction of the aerial weapons dropped in Desert Storm were precision guided munitions. In this campaign, almost 70 percent of the bombs we dropped would be PGMs—many of them the JDAMs that had decimated the Taliban and al Qaeda in the mountains and caves of Afghanistan.

Our technology advantage gave us every tool we needed to take advantage of operational surprise. A Marine reconnaissance platoon roaring along the canal banks in eight-wheeled Light Armored Vehicles (LAVs) could laser-designate a battalion of T-72s and call down a storm of GBU-12 bombs. An SOF trooper hidden in a farmer's house could transmit the coordinates of a concealed Iraqi artillery battery, and moments later witness a barrage of MLRS rockets burst above the enemy. A 3rd ID sergeant in a Bradley controlled more firepower than a Desert Storm armored battalion. And Predator UAVs cruising deep in the enemy's rear could transmit GPS aim points for precision JDAM strikes.

These were the force multipliers that made possible this truly joint war.

I knew that no amount of talk could convince the strategic kibitzers that the force we'd be moving into Iraq was adequate to accomplish the mission. The speed, flexibility, courage, and joint-force strength of the young warriors facing the enemy tonight would be all the argument I needed.

After midnight, I wrote out my next day's Challenges and Opportunities card. The lead challenge, once again, read: "WMD Threat."

With the major Iraqi formations apparently fixed in place—not yet reacting to our attack—the lead opportunity read:

"Exploit operational advantage."

12

A CAMPAIGN UNLIKE
ANY OTHER

The first three weeks of the operation were a time of intense concentration, constant evaluation and decision, stress, fatigue, frustration, and eventual exhilaration. We all worked with little sleep, drank too much coffee, and were carried along by regular spikes of adrenaline.

Throughout the course of Operation Iraqi Freedom, Van Mauney kept a detailed log that chronicled each of the hundreds of meetings I attended and the thousands of conversations I had with staff, component commanders, the Pentagon, and the White House. His notes became part of CENTCOM's massive classified history, which also includes the message traffic that passed through the Command's Forward and Main headquarters. When my own memories have proven unclear or incomplete, this invaluable contemporaneous record has filled in the gaps.

In some ways, those long and very busy days and nights recalled the weeks immediately following 9/11, as we planned and executed Operation Enduring Freedom. But the complex responsibilities of commanding the Operation Iraqi Freedom Coalition surpassed anything I had experienced as a military officer.

Once we committed the force to war, the challenges and decision-points never stopped.

GENE RENUART SAT BESIDE ME IN THE WAR ROOM. IT WAS 2115 hours on March 21. John Abizaid was in his chair at the far end of the table. The secure speakerphone was open to Buzz Moseley in the CAOC.

A-Day had begun—what the media called "Shock and Awe."

On one plasma screen, the Air Picture displayed hundreds of multicolored icons streaming across the digital map toward Baghdad—strike aircraft and their supporting tankers, electronic warfare jammers, and the Special Ops Combat Search and Rescue forces.

"Showtime, Buzz," I said.

"It'll be a good show, too, Boss," Buzz replied.

TLAMs launched from American and British surface ships and submarines in the Arabian Gulf, and Conventional Air Launched Cruise Missiles (CALCMs) fired from B-52 bombers approaching from bases in Great Britain and the Indian Ocean, would be the first munitions to strike the targets in central Baghdad.

Gene had a list of the individual aim points on his laptop computer, which was online with the CAOC and the J-2 Fusion Cell.

"It's starting, General," he said, nodding to the symbols on the screen.

I used the TV remote to flip from CNN to Fox to Al-Jazeera.

As the icons blinked on Gene's computer, a CNN camera scanned the district of concentrated regime leadership buildings and presidential palaces on the sharp bend of the Tigris opposite the Palestine Hotel.

The CNN picture erupted with huge fireballs, smoky orange blasts that spread glowing shockwaves and were mirrored in the flat black surface of the river. A series of explosions marched through the government compounds as the cruise missiles struck their targets.

I surfed through the channels, listening to the excited commentary of the correspondents.

". . . incredible. The blasts are shaking the hotel walls . . ."

". . . different type of explosion now . . . bigger, louder . . ."

". . . Al-Jazeera is reporting that 'all Baghdad is on fire,'" one British reporter breathlessly announced.

John Abizaid, who spoke near-fluent Arabic, was watching the Al-Jazeera coverage. "They're saying that 'Flames engulf the entire capital,'" he reported.

"Motherfuckers," Jim Wilkinson swore—a strong comment from a good East Texas Christian boy.

Gene Renuart shook his head. "That's bullshit, General," he said, pointing to the screen. "The *lights* are still on. We've hit our aim points precisely. That's what's burning."

As we watched the cruise missiles strike their targets with incredible accuracy, the broad boulevards and avenues of Baghdad remained bright with mile after mile of streetlights. The Ministry of Defense and the selected buildings of the Abbasid Palace complex disappeared in fireballs—but the windows in apartment buildings nearby remained lit. On the streets along the river, traffic signals flashed green, yellow, and red, as they would on any other day.

I had decided to leave Iraq's electrical power grid untouched after discussions with Secretary Rumsfeld and the President. The decision made sense, operationally and strategically. "If we have to go to war, Tommy," the President had told me in February, "we're not going to destroy Iraq. We're going to liberate the country from Saddam Hussein's regime."

So in building our target sets we excluded power plants, transformer stations, and electrical pylons and lines. This would allow some Iraqi military units to function more efficiently, but the importance of preserving the national infrastructure outweighed any momentary tactical disadvantage. Every Republican Guard or Special Security Organization command post—and the key "nodes" in the Integrated Air Defense System—had its own electrical generators, so bombing the power grid would not affect them. But cutting power across Iraq *would* have an impact on more than one hundred hospitals, especially in the Kurdish north and Shiite south, where the regime had been stingy supplying backup generators to nonmilitary institutions.

One outcome of this decision was the spectacle we saw tonight on the television screens: The sight of traffic lights blinking and streetlights shining along a broad, empty avenue, as the multistory Republican Guard headquarters building collapsed into a heap of smoking rubble.

"International Baath Party Headquarters . . ." Renuart said, "just about . . . *now.*" A massive glass-and-concrete high-rise on the western embankment burst apart under four consecutive explosions.

". . . and the New Presidential Palace." Another cascading wave of fireballs, their glare reflected in the Tigris.

"This *is* shock," a television reporter ad-libbed dramatically. "And the sheer power of this bombardment *is* awesome."

The sky above Baghdad was once again a network of bright, looping antiaircraft tracers and the occasional smoke trail of an SA-2 or SA-6 missile.

Those surface-to-air missiles might have made the regime leaders feel good, but they would pose little threat to our strike aircraft converging on Baghdad from four directions. The Iraqis were firing their SAMs unguided—"ballistically"—because if they activated one of their fire-direction radars, Wild Weasel jets skirting the city's Missile Engagement Zone (MEZ) would launch supersonic HARM missiles that would home in on the site, destroying it and its crew.

After forty-six minutes of cruise missile attacks that saw over 300 TLAMs and CALCMs strike Baghdad and targets in the environs, the first wave of aircraft arrived overhead. The bombing was led by the F-117s from Al Udeid and B-2 Stealth bombers that had flown from Whiteman Air Force Base in Missouri. Invisible to radar, the aircraft operated well above the Iraqi antiaircraft tracers, long before the waning moon had risen over the mountains of Iran to the east.

More regime facilities exploded along the curving Tigris as the JDAMs from the Stealth planes found their targets. "There goes *Mukhabarat* headquarters," Gene said. "The Iraqi Intelligence Service just lost its command and control."

I watched the Air Picture as air suppression support packages of F-15s cleared the Baghdad MEZ. They were temporarily pulling back, leaving the sky to the F-117s and B-2s. These planes did not transmit even encrypted identification data, so we had no way of charting their progress other than the TV coverage of explosions on precisely selected targets—emergency command posts of Iraqi military intelligence, the luxury villas of senior Baathist leaders, and a checkerboard of communications stations on which the Iraqi air defense system depended to integrate its fires. After tonight, Iraq's IADS would be reduced to a few antiaircraft guns fired through "iron sights."

Gene scrolled down several computer screens and checked the digital clock on the War Room wall. "Special targets coming up, General."

Unknown to either the Iraqis or the international television correspondents on their hotel balconies, our Stealth aircraft were dropping GPS-guided bombs on specific "high-value" point targets. Many of these bombs were fused to explode a few milliseconds after penetrating the structure to reduce blast damage to surrounding civilian structures. The guidance on these munitions was so accurate that such a bomb, dropped from twenty-six thousand feet, had a "circular error probable" (CEP) of less than two meters—about six feet.

The targets of these bombs were the offices and homes of senior Baath leaders and officers of the Special Security Organization and the Special Republican Guard. Communications intercepts and our meager HUMINT resources had indicated that these leaders were likely to wait out heavy Coalition air attacks in their homes, which were largely spread throughout the affluent Mansour neighborhood. It was uncertain whether this intelligence was accurate. But the destruction of these targets by weapons falling from the black night sky would make these key leaders nervous—and the more nervous they became, the less effective they'd be at controlling the Iraqi military.

Our airmen did everything possible to limit civilian casualties. In many cases, we bombed regime and military buildings at night when we knew they would not be occupied. On some occasions we actually dropped leaflets warning people to avoid certain buildings. This had a dual benefit: It greatly reduced casualties, while disrupting the regime's initial attempt to take a "business as usual" attitude toward our air operations. Using precise targeting and extremely cautious delivery techniques, coupled with the most conservative "weaponeering" (munition selection), allowed us to eliminate the regime's command and control apparatus without causing unnecessary civilian casualties. Again, the fear factor spreading among these Baathist thugs who were responsible for the massacre of so many thousands of innocent people would be just as important as the actual targets we destroyed.

The Air Picture changed once more. Now the icons were streaming toward two ridges and a steep valley in far northeastern Iraq, right on the border of Iran. These were the camps of the Ansar al-Islam terrorists, where al Qaeda leader Abu Musab Zarqawi had trained disciples in the use of chemical and biological weapons. But this strike was more than just another TLAM bashing. Soon Special Forces and SMU operators, leading Kurdish Peshmerga fighters, would be storming the camps, collecting evidence, taking prisoners, and killing all those who resisted.

DURING OPERATION ENDURING FREEDOM, I HAD TOLD DON Rumsfeld that I didn't intend to spend a lot of time in front of the TV cameras touting Coalition victories and narrating smart-bomb videos. That went double for Operation Iraqi Freedom. The early days of the operation would offer unprecedented opportunities to brag about the Coalition's high-tech arsenal. But I knew the Arab-Muslim world well enough by now to recognize that such grandstanding would be seen as bullying throughout the region—by the Arab media and on the Arab street.

And I believed that Phase IV, the reconstruction phase, would last months if not years longer than the destruction of large, cohesive enemy formations. I wanted to be responsive to the media—but I intended to pace myself for the long haul.

I did give in to Jim Wilkinson's arm-twisting on March 22, when I agreed to speak to eleven hundred assembled reporters in the Press Center at Camp As Sayliyah.

Stepping out onto the futuristic briefing stage, I was accompanied by several of my fellow officers from the Coalition's British, Australian, and European contingent. And I opened by noting that our prayers "go out to the families of those who have already made the ultimate sacrifice."

After restating the Coalition's goals in Operation Iraqi Freedom—ending the dictatorship of Saddam Hussein and disarming his cruel regime—I described the nature of the fighting.

"This will be a campaign unlike any other in history," I said, "a campaign characterized by shock, by surprise, by flexibility, by the employment of precise munitions on a scale never before seen, and by the application of overwhelming force . . .

"Our plan introduces these forces across the breadth and depth of Iraq, in some cases simultaneously and in some cases sequentially."

I explained the sequence of combat operations, running from D-Day to G-Day to A-Day and added that we would continue to strike emerging targets while closely linking ground and air operations.

During the question-and-answer period that followed, a reporter from a Washington, D.C., radio station asked me "what was the greatest surprise" I had encountered to date.

"Actually," I said, "when I got up this morning and looked at my computer and realized that my wife had sent me a 'happy anniversary' note . . . and I had forgotten to send her one."

That got a laugh—even from the scowling representatives of Al-Jazeera, sitting in a block with their Arab colleagues. Of course I had actually arranged to have flowers delivered to Cathy at our home in Tampa. But I had learned over the years that sometimes it's useful to operate behind a self-deprecating façade.

"CAN YOU GET ME A TIGHTER VIEW ON THAT PICTURE?" JEFF Kimmons asked the Air Force Predator operator in the CAOC in Saudi Arabia.

It was 0710 hours on Sunday, March 23.

John Abizaid, several staff directors, and I were watching video from a UAV flying six thousand feet above As Samawah, a city on the Euphrates River about one hundred kilometers west of An Nasiriyah.

"This is pretty wild, General," Jeff Kimmons said.

"Looks like *Black Hawk Down,*" Gene added.

The Predator feed showed five dusty white Toyota pickup trucks, each mounting a heavy machine gun—crammed with men in civilian clothes armed with Kalashnikovs and RPGs—speeding south through rutted alleys toward the highway that looped around the southern outskirts of As Samawah. A motorcycle with a sidecar carrying what looked like a 75 mm recoilless rifle bounced out of a walled compound and joined the attack force.

Ahead on the highway, a long column of Abrams tanks and Bradleys from the 1st Brigade Combat Team of the 3rd ID was moving steadily west, each tracked vehicle at a proper interval to provide its gunners the maximum arc of protective fire to the sides. How many times had I traveled in an artillery liaison track in similar convoys, my *Balls for the Queen* pendant fluttering in the humid breeze?

The pickups continued to weave through the alleys, closing in on our armored column

Scott Wallace, the V Corps Commander, was working to seize key highway bridges on the Euphrates—which were almost all near cities—while trying to isolate and bypass urban areas on the race northwest to Baghdad. At As Samawah and An Nasiriyah, however, this had proven difficult.

In both these small cities, Coalition forces in tanks, armored personnel carriers, and helicopter gunships had crushed initial resistance from regular army units. Some of the Iraqi soldiers had fought, others had surrendered, and many had run away. But now a different enemy, one we had not expected to fight this far south, had emerged from the smoke of the battlefield.

Overnight, Jeff's J-2 directorate had done a fast but thorough analysis of the threat, which had appeared the previous day at An Nasiriyah and the approaches to Basra. The Intel shop's work summarized what we had learned about the irregular forces operating in the Shiite homeland of the south. Known collectively as the Fedayeen, these unconventional fighters included the Saddam Fedayeen—"Saddam's Martyrs," a group of ill-trained but fanatical regime loyalists; *Al Quds,* local Baath militia commanded by party leaders and national Baath Party militia members; and the volunteers known as the "Lions of Saddam," a group of Sunni boys eighteen and younger who had received rudimentary military training.

"What's their total strength, Jeff?" I asked.

"Well, General," he said, "like you often say, 'That's an excellent question. I wish I had an excellent answer.' We're working the numbers."

He handed around copies of the latest estimates. In our final operational planning we had anticipated there might be up to forty thousand of these Fedayeen-type irregulars recruited to conduct urban warfare in Baghdad. But at no point had I thought these forces would be moved into the south to fight as guerrillas.

Our lack of reliable HUMINT had given us a nasty surprise: We'd had no warning that Saddam had dispatched these paramilitary forces from Baghdad. Our analysts had seen reconnaissance images of pickup trucks, their cargo bays covered by tarps, and civilian buses loaded with passengers moving south, but this had raised no concern. The traffic was taken to be normal commerce.

The first indications we had of the presence of irregulars in these southern towns came from the Special Operators we'd inserted into the cities, beginning on D-Day.

And the previous evening a group of surrendering Shiite conscripts had revealed that the Fedayeen's weapons of choice were armed pickup trucks—like those barreling toward our convoy right now. They called them "technicals," using the English word the Somali warlords had used in the early 1990s to describe their improvised gun trucks that dominated the streets of Mogadishu.

There was a significant difference between the conflict in Somalia and Operation Iraqi Freedom, however. Technicals could hurt a convoy of "soft-skinned" Humvees and trucks. But an open pickup mounting a 12.7 mm machine gun was about as effective as a horsefly when it attacked an M-1 tank or a Bradley.

"We are now estimating from two to four thousand Fedayeen in An Nasiriyah and As Samawah," Jeff said. "The numbers increase as you head north. There are probably up to forty thousand of these paramilitary fighters in the towns along Highway 8, including An Najaf."

"Son of a bitch," I said, scanning Jeff's report. "The enemy does get a vote."

"Scott Wallace confirms that the irregulars are ineffective against the armor, Sir," Gene said. "But they're going to be a problem for the truck convoys along our Lines of Communication." David McKiernan and Scott Wallace had made provisions for road security, using light infantry from the 82nd Airborne Division to protect our trucks. But it would take a while to get those troops in place.

We watched the Predator display as the pickups neared Highway 8 at the city's edge. "Those guys are in for a surprise, General," Gene said.

As the first technicals broke free of the adobe houses facing the highway, the Abrams and Bradleys swung their turrets to target them. We couldn't hear the blast of gunfire, but we saw the first pickup stagger and wobble under the impact of .50 caliber machine gun rounds. Dead fighters flipped over the sides of the truck, but the man at the technical's machine gun continued to fire. A survivor beside him in the cargo bay launched an RPG, but the back-blast from the rocket tube set on fire a wounded man slumped near the tailgate. The RPG warhead did not fly far enough to arm itself before it bounced harmlessly off the thick armor of one of the Abrams tanks.

When a Bradley opened fire with its 25 mm chain gun, the technical and its crew disappeared in a cloud of smoking chunks.

Still the enemy attacked. Halfway down the column, another technical managed to slam into a Bradley. Five enemy fighters scrambled onto the Bradley's hull and fired their assault rifles at the armored-glass observation blocks in the buttoned-down hatches. The trooper commanding the Bradley swung his turret, knocking off two of the enemy with the barrel of the chain gun. Then the Bradley spun hard right, and the tank behind it swept the hull with 7.62 mm rounds fired from its remotely operated external machine gun—its "coax."

Despite the one-sided slaughter the technicals kept coming, speeding toward the armored column across the dried mud of the roadside. Two of the three remaining pickups were destroyed before they reached the highway. The last one collided with an Abrams; the surviving Fedayeen jumping onto the tank. But again other armored vehicles killed the enemy with machine-gun fire. The bodies of the Fedayeen fell onto the road—and into the path of the long line of advancing armor.

The ambush was over in less than ten minutes. The tanks and Bradleys of the 1st BCT had hardly broken stride.

FOR THE NEXT INTENSE TWENTY-FOUR HOURS, JEFF KIMMON'S reconnaissance specialists and Gene Renuart's Operations team tracked the Fedayeen, using overhead imagery from UAVs and manned aircraft. Our ground forces and attack helicopters were engaging the irregulars and driving them back into the cities.

A pattern soon emerged: The Fedayeen would attack our convoys, and then the surviving enemy would gather in the cities inside walled compounds, usually surrounding modern, two-story buildings. Satellite pictures of Basra, As Samawah, and An Nasiriyah revealed that these compounds were either local Baath Party headquarters or offices of the *Mukhabarat* intelligence service.

Gene and Jeff brought me the images and the reports of the analysts in the Fusion Cell. "They're puddling at these sites," Jeff Kimmons said, studying a recon image of As Samawah.

"Every time, Sir," Gene said.

"Get with Buzz Moseley," I said. "Pass his people the GPS coordinates of these targets. PGMs only. Hit them when the puddles are biggest."

And Buzz Moseley's airmen did kill the Fedayeen—day and night. The enemy never learned. In the coming days, as the British 1st Armoured Division, the 1 MEF regiments, and the brigades of the 3rd ID entered city after city, they would find Baath Party and Mukhabarat offices reduced to heaps of concrete, littered with the burnt-out skeletons of technicals.

B UT THE FEDAYEEN CONTINUED TO FIGHT SAVAGELY, CHARGING out of the shelter of the towns along the rivers, firing wildly at our armored columns. Soldiers and Marines cut them down with cannon, machine guns, rifles, even pistols. And helicopter gunships often destroyed the technicals before they reached Coalition forces moving up their routes of advance.

The enemy's tactics became even more unorthodox and brutal. Some would advance with white flags flying, as if they were regular Iraqi troops surrendering. When they would get close to the Coalition forces, the white flags fell and the paramilitaries opened fire. Their attacks failed, and enemy dead lay strewn along the roads.

The Fedayeen also resorted to herding women and children ahead of their advancing technicals as human shields. Even though our forces were near exhaustion from long days of combat, they made every effort to select their targets as precisely as possible, using thermal sights to zero in on the stronger heat signature of the technicals. Still, some of these civilians were killed and wounded, cruelly victimized by their own countrymen.

It took several days for Coalition land and air forces to adapt to all of the Fedayeen's tactics. But we did adapt.

Slowly, the intensity of the attacks abated. As it did, I reflected on the fanaticism of these fighters—and on their lack of effective leadership. Despite the casualties they caused among our forces and the human shields—and the temporary disruption of our supply routes—I recognized that it was better to engage and kill this zealous enemy along the southern highways than to fight forty thousand of them in the streets of Baghdad.

We guarded the tactics of our approach to the Fedayeen as an operational secret. Jim Wilkinson and Vince Brooks didn't brief the press.

And the embedded reporters covering the war had no Blue Force Tracker to help them grasp the broad success of our troops. They were unable to watch the Coalition's steady progress, with units racing ahead to their objectives and across phase lines days ahead of the plan's schedule.

"Jeez, General," Jim Wilkinson complained one day, "the public is going to think we're powerless to counter these Fedayeen attacks. Can't we show them some video of the JDAMs smashing the Baath headquarters in a couple of those towns?"

"We *could* do that, Jim," I replied, "but we're not going to." He looked like a kid who wasn't getting the new bike he'd been promised for Christmas.

Jim Wilkinson was probably the best public affairs director I'd ever seen, adept at keeping the media informed without jeopardizing operational security. I knew how frustrating his job was becoming: We were winning the war, but he could say hardly anything about it.

"I'll tell you why that's a bad idea," I continued. "First, we don't want to tip our hand on our tactics." Jim nodded, accepting the logic.

"And second," I said, "those first couple of days, you and Vince showed some video of PGMs hitting aim points, and it was exactly the right thing to do. But Al-Jazeera and Al Arabia TV would eat us alive on the Arab street if we did that every day—if we fed the media a steady diet of GBUs and JDAMs blowing away tanks and killing Iraqis. The enemy knows we're kicking his ass. In a week or so, the whole world will know it."

"Got it, General." Jim Wilkinson was trying hard to be patient.

AFTER GRABBING A BOWL OF CHILI AT MY DESK, I HAD JUST STARTED the Commander's brief for the scheduled postlunch VTC with Secretary Rumsfeld when the Red Switch telephone rang. It was David McKiernan.

"What's up, Brother?" I asked.

"I have a tactical situation to report, Sir," he said.

"Go ahead."

"General," he continued, "we had several KIA and at least twelve MIA troops from a V Corps support unit that was ambushed this morning in An Nasiriyah."

Killed in Action and Missing in Action. Bad news.

I stared at the map. An Nasiriyah—ever since the Marines arrived on D+3, they had run into a meat grinder of Fedayeen ambushes as the RCT tried to consolidate its bridgeheads. I checked the Blue Force Tracker. What was an *Army* unit doing there?

"Got it, David," I said. "What are the details?"

"Still incomplete, Sir," he said. "Here's what's certain. This was the 507th, a Patriot battalion maintenance company running a truck convoy along the Main Supply Route. Sometime around 0700, the lead Humvee missed a GPS waypoint. The trucks and Humvees drove right into An Nasiriyah. They got ambushed inside the city."

"How bad, David?"

"The Marines at one of the bridges rescued some survivors. Those troopers said they lost most of their people, KIA or captured. We're estimating at least ten KIA, twelve MIA.

"The survivors describe mixed Fedayeen and some regulars. They even ran into a tank hidden in what looked like a schoolyard."

I shook my head. Yet another report of Iraqis placing weapons in schools and mosques.

"Thanks, David," I said. "Call me when you have more details."

"Get me Dell Dailey and the Agency," I told Van Mauney. "We've got some kids captured up at An Nasiriyah, and hostage rescue is a task for JSOC and the CIA."

Agency assets were thin in southern Iraq, but we did have several mixed teams of SOF and Agency Ground Force officers in the area. "Spread the word," I said. "We want those troopers back as soon as possible."

This was a bad turn of events, and I knew the media would be all over it. "Stick around," I told Jim Wilkinson. "We're going to have to work up some media talking points."

I HAD NO IDEA HOW QUICK OR HOW NEGATIVE THE MEDIA COVERAGE of the ambush and its aftermath would be.

When Jim Wilkinson came to my office later that afternoon, it looked like his grin was gone forever. "Al-Jazeera has just broadcast video of our soldiers from the ambush, Sir," he said. Jim punched a few buttons on my TV remote, and one of the screens opened on the internal Press Center circuit.

I rubbed my eyes and leaned forward to watch.

"It's not pretty, General," Jim said.

That was an understatement. The fuzzy videotape showed a row of dead soldiers in bloodstained DCUs, lying on the concrete floor of a nondescript room. The camera panned across their faces. They looked young. Several had ugly wounds to the torso or limbs, what appeared to be the result of close-range rifle fire or shrapnel. Two had obviously been shot in the head.

"Damn," I muttered. The networks in the States would be running this footage—some of those families would see their kids dead before the Army had time to notify them.

The image jumped to another room with dusty whitewashed walls. I saw the corner of a desk. Probably a military or Baathist militia office. Six soldiers, one of them a young black woman who identified herself as "Shoshana," sat against the wall. Several spoke only their first names when the Arab reporter thrust the microphone in their faces. One gave his full name—"Peter C. Miller"—and said he was from Kansas.

Smart kid, I thought. At least his family would know he was alive. And giving his name to the reporter might afford him some measure of protection; at that point, at least, it could be proven that he was still alive and healthy.

As soon as I finished with Jim I would call Dick Myers and speak to the Secretary. Other than planning a rescue operation with Dell Dailey, I wouldn't have much to report. Some tired young maintenance troops, in combat for the first time, had taken a wrong turn and entered a Fedayeen hornet's nest.

"Thanks, Jim," I said.

The call to Rumsfeld was short and straightforward, with no recrimination.

"We're getting JSOC spun up, Mr. Secretary," I reported. "If we can pinpoint the location, we'll go in there and get those kids back."

"What can we do to help from this end?"

"Not a thing, Mr. Secretary. You did it all when you placed JSOC and the CIA operators under our control. We have what we need."

"We'll be standing by to help, Tom," Rumsfeld said.

I TOLD VAN MAUNEY TO SET UP IN THE WAR ROOM FOR A BRIEFING on the major operation pending that night—a deep attack that the Apache gunships of the 11th Attack Helicopter Regiment would conduct, flying from a Forward Air Refueling Point (FARP) in the open desert south of An Najaf.

The 11th AHR's mission was to destroy the artillery and armor of the Medina Republican Guard Division north of the narrow Karbala Gap. These Medina Division units were the strongest Iraqi blocking force between the advancing V Corps and Baghdad.

I had reviewed the plans for this attack several times. Army doctrine that had evolved from the AirLand Battle concepts of the 1980s called for Apaches, armed with Hellfire missiles and a 30 mm automatic cannon, to strike deep into enemy territory to destroy armored formations and their supporting artillery.

Tonight's mission was a classic deep strike.

The principal staff directors joined John Abizaid and me in the War Room to hear the CFLCC staff review the details of the mission, just as they had during our train-ups and rehearsals in January.

The operation was rated a moderate risk, but it had the potential of a high payoff if the gunships could cripple the Medina Division in one fast, hard-hitting blow.

Deep Strike doctrine depended on thorough Suppression of Enemy Air Defenses (SEAD), another tactic that had matured out of AirLand Battle planning. Dave McKiernan and Scott Wallace had worked hard to identify fixed and mobile air defense missiles and antiaircraft sites along the 11th AHR's infiltration routes. The Apaches would fly fast and low to minimize their exposure to Iraqi ground fire.

Scott Wallace was satisfied with the plan; so was David McKiernan. The SEAD package appeared robust: Corps Artillery would fire thirty-two Army Tactical Missile System (ATACMS) long-range missiles—each armed with 950 bomblets—that would saturate the identified antiaircraft sites. And Buzz Moseley had several flights of jets standing by to pound emerging enemy air defenses.

"Any issues we need to know about, David?" I asked.

"Corps is working final problems with fuel," David said. "They say they'll be good to go."

"Good luck, all of you," I said. "We'll go over the strike results early tomorrow."

I handed the classified mission profile book to Grinch to lock up, then stood and stretched. My accumulated sleep debt was finally catching up with my caffeine load. "I need about three uninterrupted hours of sleep," I told Van Mauney. "More if there isn't another spin-up."

Just as I was checking the latest message traffic before turning in, though, Gene Renuart was called away from the War Room. He returned a few minutes later.

"General, we're getting an update on the weather from the CAOC."

More bad news? I wondered as the Comm operator set up a VTC with the Meteorological Cell in the weather center at Prince Sultan Air Base.

"Here's the overall picture, Sir," the Air Force major said. What followed was ten minutes of the most ominous weather forecasting I had ever sat through.

A large depression was deepening above the Balkans. The low pressure system, a tight, minihurricane-like storm, was projected to dip south into the Eastern Mediterranean—and stall. Then a strong cold front would cut across the region like a giant scythe, bringing gale winds from the west southwest, thunderstorms . . . and blowing dust.

Looking at the weather map, I recognized what we were facing: This had all the earmarks of a classic *shamal* sandstorm. When I closed my eyes, I saw that wall of brown dust that had swept over southern Iraq and Kuwait during Operation Desert Storm.

"Two questions, Major," I said. "No—make that three. When will it hit? How bad will it get? How long will it last?"

The officer looked at his computer console. "We'll see the wind increase around 1800 Local tomorrow, Sir. It will be peaking out with fifty-knot gusts by late tomorrow night. The dust load will be major. Our models call for zero-zero conditions."

Zero visibility, I thought. *Zero ceiling.*

"And how long will this storm last?"

"Current models call for seventy-two hours of marginal conditions, Sir."

The young man had a troubled, *don't shoot the messenger* look.

"Thanks, son," I said.

Down the table someone muttered, "The mother of all sand-storms."

Nobody laughed.

T HE HEADQUARTERS PHONE BESIDE MY BED JOLTED ME OUT OF sleep. It was just past 0320 hours. For one disorienting moment, I couldn't remember where I was.

"Bad news on the 11th AHR's deep strike, Sir," Gene said.

"I'll be right over."

Bad news was an understatement.

"It's kind of a *coulda, woulda, shoulda* deal, General," Gene reported.

Murphy had been out throwing his wrenches again tonight.

The 11th AHR had been late reaching its refueling point near the 3rd ID's forward positions. And there hadn't been enough fuel, so some gunships had to be eliminated from the attack in order to apportion the available fuel. When the Apaches arrived, they found their staging area was ankle-deep in talcum-fine dust, which of course became a blinding pall as scores of rotor blades beat the air. Refueling conditions were difficult, to say the least.

And as the mile-long line of helicopters, maintenance trucks, and fuel tankers stood in the dust cloud, a bunch of Iraqi *civilians*—some undoubtedly Fedayeen—passed through the area, appearing through the haze to gawk, and disappearing just as quickly. These intruders had witnessed thirty-six Apache gunships, loaded with missiles, fueling for a mission. There was only one direction they would fly—north toward the enemy formations above the Karbala Gap.

And there was more. On the Regiment's leapfrog movement from Kuwait, some essential communications gear was inadvertently left behind. Without the missing gear, the 11th AHR intelligence officer could not connect to the Corps Intel shop. After frantic calls via satellite radio, Colonel Bill Wolf, the regimental commander, managed to reschedule the SEAD fires at the last moment to better coordinate with the delayed launch time. But instead of leaving for the objective before midnight, the Apaches did not begin lifting off until 0115 hours.

The rescheduled SEAD fire with the Army tactical missiles went off on schedule. But due to poor communications, the patrolling fighter-bombers never received the change of schedule and returned to their bases before the gunships had actually departed for the attack.

And when the long columns of fast, low-flying Apaches crossed the Euphrates, they encountered another nasty surprise. Training for the mission, the aviators had planned dogleg routes to avoid the villages and towns on their tactical maps. But what had not appeared on these maps was the evenly distributed network of farmhouses and large farming compounds—all of them brightly lit.

The aviators had not been prepared for the intensity of this ground lighting, which had two negative consequences. First, the bright lights of the mud-walled compounds, which spread uninterrupted all the way northeast to the bright city glow of Baghdad, maxed out the pilots' night-vision goggles, rendering them useless. And, just as serious, the lighting illuminated the long, dark shapes of the Apaches from below as they sped north, only a hundred feet above the ground.

Almost as soon as the advancing gunships entered this farm country, entire blocks of lights blinked out for several seconds, then snapped on again—a signal to the hundreds, perhaps thousands, of Iraqi soldiers and Fedayeen hiding among the adobe sheds and date groves. Shortly thereafter, the aviators met a virtually solid wall of small-arms fire, sheets of yellow, red, and white tracers. The enemy was firing everything they had, from bolt-action hunting rifles to AK-47s to machine guns and automatic cannons. One after another, the Apaches were hit. Several crewmen were wounded.

Some of the aircraft were forced to abort, but others pressed ahead along the fifty-nautical-mile route to the dug-in positions of the Medina Republican Guard Division. The Apaches sailed through repeated small arms and automatic weapons ambushes. Some crews were lucky, initially receiving only a few bullet holes from small arms. As the gunships continued on their course, though, the battle damage accumulated.

The Apache is a tough, well-armored aircraft, but it wasn't designed for this kind of punishment. On the secure radio channels, pilots were calling out warnings, reporting "heavy fire," indicating the damage their aircraft had sustained.

In the end, only one of the Regiment's Apache units reached its objective, a long oasis where thirty T-72 Republican Guard tanks were dug in. But the ground fire there was so intense that the gunships had to withdraw before firing a single missile.

Thirty Apaches had launched from the refueling point. Twenty-nine made it back with some degree of battle damage. But one of the Apaches had its hydraulics shot out and made a hard landing in enemy territory. Its two crewmen, Chief Warrant Officers Ron Young and David Williams, were taken prisoner.

Not a single tank or artillery piece of the Medina Division was damaged in the attack.

"All right," I said, "got it. Talk to me tomorrow about the new tactics we intend to employ to be able to use Apaches in this environment."

It's a blessing we didn't lose the whole battalion, I thought.

Clearly, we had some work ahead of us if we were going to adapt to the enemy's tactics. The Apache was still one of the greatest killers on the battlefield; I was proud of the aircrews, and I still had confidence in their leaders. Our job now was to think through the problem. Before this war was won, we would need those gunships.

Almost automatically I looked over at the Blue Force Tracker screen. The 3rd ID was moving past An Najaf, maneuvering along Highway 9 toward the Karbala Gap. The red rectangles of the Medina Division's brigades were still stacked like bricks across the highways leading to Baghdad. And the Marines were in a fight in An Nasiriyah, forced to clear the warren of narrow streets of Fedayeen block by block.

I thought about the past twenty-four hours. The Fedayeen. Those maintenance troops killed, wounded, and captured. Now this disaster with the Apaches. And I couldn't forget the weather forecast. Within twenty-four hours, we would have no helicopters and no Predators in the air.

The enemy, and his friend Murphy, weren't the only ones who got a vote. Mother Nature was lining up to take her turn.

I needed a hot shower and more coffee. There was a long day ahead, and probably a longer one after that. But before I left the War Room I took a final long look at our forces' situation. Coalition troops were still pouring into Iraq, snaking up the long lines of advance spearheaded by the soldiers and Marines. We were in for a difficult period, but I had no doubt of the outcome.

We would win this fight.

WITH THE AIR-CONDITIONING SYSTEM ROARING IN THE conference room, the Comm sergeant had to turn up the audio on the VTC. I could taste the dust on the rim of my coffee cup. It was afternoon on March 25 in Qatar, early morning in Washington.

President Bush sat at the head of the table in the White House Situation Room, surrounded by the members of the NSC. He looked rested. Vice President Cheney was quiet, thoughtful. Don Rumsfeld and Dick Myers appeared tired. George Tenet was relaxed, chewing on an unlit cigar.

". . . the oil fields are secure, Mr. President," I continued, working through my agenda. "The firefighters from Boots and Coots are extinguishing the wellhead fires."

"Those are good Texas boys, Tommy," President Bush added.

"You bet, Sir," I said. "There were only nine fires; our special operators and Marines defused the demolition charges before there was further damage. Navy SEALs and the Polish commandos captured the offshore platforms and the big manifold. They had been wired for demolition, too."

"Mr. President," Don Rumsfeld added, "the Coalition's action not only saved Iraq's southern oil fields, it prevented what was potentially the gravest ecological disaster in modern times. If they'd blown that manifold on the Al Faw Peninsula, the cleanup of the Gulf would have taken years."

"The Brits have Basra isolated and are taking on the Fedayeen," I added. "In the air we continue to use PGMs on Republican Guard formations to good effect. V Corps and 1 MEF are refueling, resupplying, and pushing scouts forward to continue the advance. David McKiernan's got a brigade of the 82nd securing our lines of communication in the west. The 101st will air assault north in stages as soon as weather permits."

"Tommy," President Bush said, "everybody here is proud of you and the troops. The country is behind you. If you need anything at all, get on the phone and call Don Rumsfeld."

"Don't tell him that, Sir," Rumsfeld joked.

The President's manner changed. "It looks like we've reached the end of the string with Turkey," he said. "Nothing we can do will persuade them to let our troops transit their territory."

"Mr. President, I'd like to keep the 4th ID up there another twenty-four hours. Our deception is holding. We've got eleven Iraqi divisions fixed in the north. I want to keep them there until Buzz Moseley's airmen can reduce their effectiveness."

"All right, Tommy," the President said. "That's your call. You will start moving them tomorrow?"

"Yes, Sir. And they'll begin offloading in Kuwait in about nine days. The docks should be clear by then."

Don Rumsfeld said something I couldn't hear, and the President nodded. "Have your plans changed for the 173rd Airborne?" the President asked.

The plan called for approximately one thousand paratroopers of the 173rd Airborne Brigade, stationed in Italy, to jump onto the Bashur Airfield in northeast Iraq, an area under the control of the Kurdish Peshmerga militia and our Special Forces. These airborne troops had been scheduled to provide security for the 4th ID advancing out of Turkey.

Now I intended to use them to establish an air bridge at Bashur, where we could land armored vehicles and beef up the SOF presence in the north. That would meet two goals. The airborne assault would further the April Fool deception that we planned a second front in the north. And by strengthening the Special Operations team in that area, we could replicate the type of operations we had performed so effectively with the Northern Alliance in Afghanistan.

"Yes, Mr. President. The 173rd will still parachute into Bashur. But now we'll use them to beef up the SOF to put more pressure on the northern Iraqi units."

"Okay, Tommy," the President said when I finished my summary.

"Naval Special Operations and British Marines are within a day or two of opening the port at Umm Qasr," I added. "We'll be unloading Humanitarian Assistance supplies soon."

George Bush leaned forward, gazing into the camera. "How are the troops, Tommy? What's their morale?"

"Sir, the embedded media provide a pretty good indication. The troops are tired, but focused. They haven't lost their resolve. They're dealing well with casualties—fighting with the effectiveness you would expect, Mr. President."

Bush sat back. "Tommy, I want to thank you, your command, and all the troops for this great effort. Keep up the good work."

THE BIG SANDSTORM WAS EVEN WORSE THAN PREDICTED. REDDISH brown dust formed a high dome in the western desert and rolled over southern Iraq . . . and over 170,000 Coalition troops. Visibility dropped to ten meters or less. Helicopters were grounded, their rotors lashed down against the gritty wind as the fine yet abrasive dust worked its way into vulnerable electronics bays. Predators remained tethered to their steel launch pads. Convoys crept along, the weary drivers steering blindly toward GPS waypoints. Rain pounded down through the red dust, turning the air to mud, making visibility even worse.

Our maneuver units first slowed to cope with this challenge, then stopped altogether. The Fedayeen continued to attack, careening out of the blowing dust in their technicals. But the soldiers' Bradleys and the Marines' LAVs had thermal sights that pierced the wall of orange sand. As the Fedayeen attacked, their vehicle engines and the hot barrels of their machine guns glowed brightly. Some Fedayeen broke through and inflicted casualties. Most died in the swirling dust, as surely as their comrades had died in the glaring sunlight in the days before.

Our long logistics convoys crawled ahead, eventually linking up with the armor and infantry units that were managing to creep forward during lulls in the sandstorm.

And, as the troopers inched on, scouts and SOF recon teams infiltrated more and more Iraqi positions, identifying the precise GPS coordinates of enemy armor and artillery. Self-propelled Paladin howitzers fired night and day, as if their crews were not aware that the worst *shamal* in recent history was blowing. Each gun operated independently, using its own onboard GPS navigation system and computer to calculate aim points miles distant from their firing positions.

When I read the reports of these fire missions, I thought back to the CB radios we'd bought for the crews of the old Howitzer Battery in Bayreuth. *Times have changed.*

As the sandstorm rose in intensity, and movement on the battlefield virtually stopped, Gene Renuart came to see me before our morning staff huddle.

"I've been talking to Buzz Moseley, General," he said. "We . . ."

"Don't tell me, Gene." I held up my hand. "There's going to be an Air Force coup. My palace is surrounded."

"Not yet, Boss," Gene said. "We've actually been discussing how to take advantage of this shitty weather."

Gene called for Jeff Kimmons, and the two of them spread a stack of reconnaissance pictures out on the conference table.

"We can use the sandstorm to destroy the RG formations," Gene said, pointing to the orange blocks of the Medina and Hammurabi Republican Guard Divisions spread out south of Baghdad.

"They started to maneuver a little when 3rd ID's scouts pushed north of Najaf," Jeff explained. "Then the sandstorm blew up, and they decided not to move because we seemed to be bogged down."

"Where'd they get *that* idea?" I asked.

Gene pointed to the TV on the wall—some retired officer holding forth. "We are seeing what the military calls a 'pause.' The Coalition has stopped to rearm and refit. They've sort of run out of steam . . ."

"The enemy formations haven't moved for sixteen hours," Jeff said. "They're hunkered down. The old *see no evil, hear no evil* . . ."

"Get Buzz," I interrupted. What Gene and Jeff were suggesting was a tactic that just might win this war, at a time that many were characterizing as our "darkest hour."

"Great minds think alike, General," Buzz Moseley said. "We're all over it."

By 2000 hours, B-52s, B-1s, and a whole range of Air Force, Marine, and Navy fighter-bombers would be flying above the dense ochre dome of the sandstorm, delivering precision-guided bombs through the zero-visibility, zero-ceiling weather.

I was confident that we were looking at the end of organized Iraqi resistance.

I SAT ALONE IN MY OFFICE WATCHING THE AIR PICTURE. STRIKE aircraft of all sizes were moving over a wide curved kill zone that stretched from Al Kut in the Tigris Valley in the east to the Karbala Gap in the west. The sand continued to blow. The Republican Guard units were hunkered down, and they were destroyed in place, tank by BMP fighting vehicle by artillery piece. The bombardment that lasted from the night of March 25 through the morning of March 27 was one of the fiercest, and most effective, in the history of warfare.

But no one in the international press understood what was happening. All the embedded reporters were with the ground units, except for some that were with ships. There were no correspondents flying in the cockpits of our strike planes or sitting in the targeting cells in the CAOC.

"I'm taking a beating out there," said Jim Wilkinson, pointing toward the Press Center at the far end of Camp As Sayliyah. "I've got to tell those reporters something. They're filing stories that we've lost the war."

"Good," I said. "We couldn't ask for a better deception."

"Damn, General," Jim said. "We should tell them *something*."

"Tell them we're riding out the weather by focusing on air-delivered weapons," I said. "That'll give them something to think about. The enemy already knows what we're doing."

L ATER THAT NIGHT, WITH THE SANDSTORM STILL RAGING, JIM came back to my office. His face was set in an angry scowl.

"General," he said, "you're always telling us not to get treed by pissants, but what am I supposed to do about these motherfucking TV generals?"

"Free press, Jim," I said. "The Fourth Estate and all that. The embeds are doing good work, getting the troops' story out to the people. Some of the retired gentlemen on TV are just enjoying their fifteen minutes of fame. It'll be interesting to see if the networks have them back on to eat crow in a week or two."

Jim plopped down in front of my desk and handed me a stack of Nexis and Google downloads of TV military specialists' commentary. "Check out this dude," he said, indicating a passage he'd highlighted.

A pundit's name was listed, followed by "Lt. Colonel, retired . . . senior war planner." I was beginning to see where Jim's frustration was coming from.

"Not just a war planner, General," he said. "A *senior* war planner."

I scanned the rest of the excerpts, shook my head, chuckled, and leaned back in my chair. I knew a number of these "experts"—many were much better TV analysts than they had been military officers. The negative commentary was predictable: The Coalition offensive was "bogged down," "stalled," "stymied" in the face of stiffening resistance and mounting casualties. Gene Renuart was so angry, he'd stopped watching television.

I glanced at the Blue Force Tracker, then brought up the latest Operations summary on my computer. Despite the *shamal,* the 3-7 Cav and the lead brigade of the 3rd ID had swept through enemy territory faster than any armored force in history—more rapidly than Rommel's Afrika Korps or George Patton's 3rd Army. They had attacked 251 miles in six days—two-thirds of the way to Baghdad—fighting through almost constant Fedayeen ambushes. The 3rd ID was now setting up for the push through the Karbala Gap to the capital, Saddam's center of gravity.

Coalition casualties—each one a tragedy to the soldier, Marine, or airman's loved ones—were far lower than anticipated. Enemy losses, especially among the suicidal Fedayeen, had been staggering. And, of course, Buzz Moseley's Air Component was pounding the enemy around the clock.

But more than a few television pundits were ready to declare the campaign lost, the plan irreparably flawed. And one particular retired four-star was driving the bandwagon, with others clambering to get on board.

"Interesting phenomenon here, Jim," I said. "You've got retired four-stars holding forth on platoon- and company-level tactics, while your retired majors and lieutenant colonels are waxing eloquent on Coalition strategy."

"You're right, General," Jim said, gathering up his printouts. "Meanwhile, though, I've got eleven hundred frantic reporters out in the Press Center. They think they've tasted blood, and they want in on the kill."

"Historical perspective, Jim," I said. "Lincoln's wife, Mary, called the Civil War correspondents the 'vampire press' for their attacks on the President. Those same reporters sang Lincoln's praises after Appomattox."

"You ain't as handsome as Abe Lincoln, Boss," Jim said, grinning at last. "But your ears are just as big."

I tossed a paper clip at him. "Get the hell out of here. Go spill some of that East Texas hayseed blood in the Press Center."

IT WAS 0921 HOURS, MARCH 27. THE MORNING VTC WITH THE component commanders had started at 0900. David McKiernan was moving through the Battle Update Assessment for the previous twenty-four hours. The *shamal* was blowing itself out, and our troops were advancing much faster. David completed his summary of 3rd ID movements.

"The 2nd BCT was in heavy contact with mounted and dismounted Fedayeen near An Najaf . . ."

Suddenly, the audio feed from Camp Doha, Kuwait, was overwhelmed by the deep wail of a Giant Voice missile alarm, echoing through David's headquarters.

David reached down calmly and pulled his black M-40 protective mask out of the pouch strapped to his hip. "Everybody put their masks on," he called above the rising banshee pitch of the siren.

"TBM alarm," John Abizaid said.

"One more incoming," Gene Renuart added.

Iraqi mobile Ababil-100 and Al Samoud Theater Ballistic Missile launchers north of Basra had been striking Kuwait for a week. Each time the Patriot radars detected an incoming missile the siren sounded, and the troops pulled on their protective gear against poison or bio weapons.

"Sorry, Sir," David said toward the VTC camera, looking like some kind of space monster from an old Buck Rogers serial. "Can you still hear—"

His muffled voice was lost in a cracking boom that shook the walls of CFLCC headquarters.

"Patriot launch," Jeff Kimmons said.

Another boom. "*Two* Patriots," I said. "They must have acquired the inbound missile."

There was a Patriot anti-TBM battery right across the road from David's headquarters. They wouldn't have fired two missiles unless they had a solid radar lock on an enemy warhead.

We waited. There was some confusion at Camp Doha, but most of the staff visible on the screen continued working at their computer consoles, wearing their Kevlar helmets and masks.

ARCENT had been using that headquarters for several years. The Iraqis didn't have the best military intelligence, but they could have plotted the coordinates of that building. And their new TBMs— upgraded with black-market technology—were certainly capable of hitting a point target as large as the CFLCC headquarters.

Then another explosion; the Patriots had intercepted the Iraqi missile.

Even if that warhead hadn't contained poison gas, the effect of several hundred kilos of high explosive would have wiped out McKiernan and his staff.

When the VTC ended, I spoke to Buzz Moseley. "Have you got anything on that latest TBM launch?"

"The radar guys in Air Defense Command had the launch coordinates within two minutes of intercept," he said. "Same launch basket, an Al-Samoud north of Basra. We've got jets on it."

Ten minutes later I got a call from Moseley.

"Hey, Boss," he said. "We just got the strike report from the pilots. Scratch one Al-Samoud launcher."

Buzz was rightfully proud of his airmen. And with luck the message was spreading among the Iraqi missile crews: *You launch, you die.*

"MURPHY RIDES AGAIN, GENERAL," JIM WILKINSON SAID. It was just after dawn on Friday, March 28. I was alone in my office, reading through the cables and messages. Jim knew I tried to keep early mornings to myself, so I knew he must have something important.

He handed me a printout of a *New York Times* story by reporter Jim Dwyer, who was embedded with the 101st Airborne.

"A Gulf Commander Sees a Longer Road," the headline read.

Jim shook his head. "A couple of reporters ambushed Scott Wallace when he popped in to visit General Petreaus at the 101st command post."

I scanned the story. Scott Wallace seemed to have been his usual honest and direct self. But the article had a decidedly negative spin.

Jim had highlighted the relevant passages. I read the two sections slowly, to make sure I didn't miss anything.

"The enemy we're fighting is a bit different than the one we wargamed against, because of these paramilitary forces," General Wallace said. "We knew they were here, but we did not know how they would fight. . . .

"I've got to give my best military judgment, given the weather, the long lines of communication, and given that we have to pull up our long line of logistics," General Wallace said. "We've got to take this pause. We're still fighting the enemy every night. We're doing things to keep him operating at a higher tempo than the one we're operating at."

I read the story again. Scott's quotes reflected basically accurate information from the perspective of a corps commander, but the article was distinctly pessimistic.

"Not a helpful story, Jim," I said.

"A friggin' disaster, General," he said. "The takeaway is that we're bogged down and didn't plan this operation worth a damn."

"Neither of those statements is true, Jim. You know that."

"Sir, *I* know that. You know that. The whole Coalition, including General Wallace, knows that." He waved his hands in frustration. "But perception is reality in the media. My phone has been ringing off the hook for the last hour. Everybody wants to interview you about Wallace's comments."

I remembered the ill-advised interview I'd given those two prowling reporters who'd found me at Assembly Area Horse in 1990 in the early days of Desert Shield.

"Stick to operational truth," I told Jim. "I'll get with David McKiernan on this."

When I talked to McKiernan, he assured me that he'd spoken with Scott Wallace and that Wallace would "watch his own lane" carefully in the future.

"That's good enough for me," I said. "Scott is a hell of a commander. Tell him I love him and I trust him."

T WENTY MINUTES LATER, JIM WAS BACK IN MY OFFICE.
"What now?" I said.

Jim grabbed the TV remote and clicked into the Press Center circuit. Another Al-Jazeera tape was frozen on the screen.

When he pressed *play,* two gaunt, somber Army aviators in dusty, sweat-stained flight suits stared at the camera, answering questions from an Arab interrogator.

"The guys from the 11th AHR," Jim said. "That captured Apache crew—Ron Young and David Williams."

The two prisoners grudgingly answered the questions, trying not to give any information that would have propaganda value.

At least they're alive, I thought.

"That's not all, Sir," Jim said, fast-forwarding through the tape. "Check this out."

Iraqi Minister of Information, Mohammed Saeed Al-Sahaf—known derisively as "Baghdad Bob" to the international press corps—stood before the smoking ruins of several shops and market stalls in the capital. "The air bombers of the criminal Bush struck this marketplace," he proclaimed. According to Al-Sahaf, "hundreds" of innocent civilians had been killed or wounded.

"If Sahaf weren't so sad, he'd be funny," I said.

"I checked with the CAOC," Jim explained. "We think it was an Iraqi missile, probably an SA-2 they fired two nights ago, unguided.

What goes up, does in fact come down. It hit that marketplace before dawn. There was nobody on the street."

"So," I said, "we've got no problem."

"We might, Sir." Jim handed me more printouts—a batch of Arab newspapers from across the Middle East. There was Baghdad Bob in the smoldering marketplace. "All the headlines feature that line: 'hundreds of dead and wounded.'"

A picture from the Iraqi TV tape showing the two captured Apache pilots appeared near the image of Al-Sahaf. On the Arab street, it would be easy for people to associate the photo of two captured American pilots with the claim that American bombs had killed hundreds of innocent people.

"Draw up a statement, Jim. We have to put out the true story."

"I'm on it, Sir," he said. "But our pals in the BBC are already running with Baghdad Bob's version."

As Donald Rumsfeld would have said, "That's not very helpful."

This was shaping up to be another unpleasant morning.

I RECOGNIZED THE IMPACT OF RECENT BAD NEWS WHEN I ENTERED my office for that morning's staff huddle. Normally, Gene Renuart and Jim Wilkinson competed for the best wisecrack or ironic comment. Not today, though. Everyone at the table looked like he'd just sat down at a funeral service.

"What's up, guys?" I asked.

Renuart shook his head. "Kind of hard to smile this morning, General. The Fedayeen are giving us trouble on the LOCs. The Marines are tangling with more Fedayeen on Highways 1 and 7. The log tails just aren't catching up to the maneuver units."

"And we've got a problem on the Syrian border," Jeff Kimmons added. "Baathist leaders and their families are fleeing into Syria in convoys of Mercedes and SUVs. God knows what they're carrying."

"Got it," I said. "Rats and sinking ships. They're probably taking most of the hard currency and all of the gold in Iraq with them.

Let's get Gary Harrell and Dell Dailey to fly out to the border and meet some of these families."

"And, Sir," Jeff added, "we might have some interesting targets. Overheads indicate that civilian bus convoys full of foreign fighters are coming in from Syria. Arabs from all over. Maybe even some Chechens. These are bad actors, but it's gonna be tough to target them while they're riding on civilian buses."

Another comment on Syria, I thought. A constant thorn in our side. Not our enemies—but certainly not our friends—the Syrians were permitting cross-border traffic into and out of Iraq. "Get Harrell and Dailey to work up at least an aviation screen along that border," I said to Gene Renuart. "We're going to put a crimp in that traffic."

"Okay, Boss," Gene said.

And the conversation around the table stopped dead, leaving a glum silence. I thought a moment. This was not a good situation.

"All right," I said. "Listen up. You guys are tired. We're getting our asses kicked in the media. And every armchair strategist from the E-Ring to the CBS newsroom in South Podunk, Idaho, is reporting we've got big problems. The Fedayeen are still active. The main attack toward Baghdad has slowed with the weather."

A few nods of agreement.

I held up my hand. "But *none* of this shit really matters. We are on-plan. In fact, we're *ahead* of plan. We're killing the Fedayeen day and night. It's better to fight them on the highways than in Baghdad. BDA isn't worth a damn, but we do know the Republican Guard is getting its collective ass kicked from the air. And V Corps is locked and loaded for Baghdad. The Marines will tough it out. The media are chameleons. When things get better, they'll be all sweetness and light."

I wasn't sure if my argument had taken.

"Look," I added. "We've been fighting on the ground for a little over a week. This is early days, guys—*early*. Wars take time. I always said the enemy gets a vote, and he's at the damn polling place right now. Remember, World War II lasted four years for the Americans, six years for the Brits. There are going to be bad days and good days. But we can't lose faith. If *we* stop believing, the troops will stop believing. And then we *will* be in trouble. Let me worry about the press and the strategic issues. We will win this fight."

I saw a few brighter expressions start to break the gloom.

"This ain't complicated, Brothers. It comes down to one thing: You gotta believe."

THE RED SWITCH RANG. MY WATCH SAID 0305 HOURS. WHAT day?

Right—April 1. This had better not be somebody's idea of an April Fool's joke.

"Yeah," I growled.

"Message from Dell Dailey, Sir," Van Mauney reported. "They have the passenger."

Good news. "The passenger" was the female enlisted soldier the Agency had traced to the Saddam Hospital in downtown An Nasiriyah. A friendly Iraqi in the hospital had provided details on her exact location.

Van filled me in on what was known so far. Backed up by Marines, Dell's SMU operators had fought through Fedayeen ambushes and stormed the hospital. No Coalition forces were injured in the rescue. "There's a video of the op, Sir," Van added.

I lay back in bed, feeling sleep well up inside my head. "I'll see the staff at 0700, Van."

"Yes, Sir."

". . . Hey," I said. "What's that soldier's name?"

"Lynch, Sir. PFC Jessica Lynch."

JIM WILKINSON WAS EAGER TO TRANSMIT THE DRAMATIC NIGHT-vision video of Jessica Lynch's rescue to the world.

"It's absolutely great news, General," he said. "Fantastic visuals."

"Not a good idea, Jim," I said. I was about to take away another Christmas bike from under Jim's tree.

"This is the deal," I began. "We got one POW back alive. But there are seven others. There may be more before this is over. Plus, we have to keep an even tone. We never spike the ball in the end zone."

"The reporters already know about the rescue, Sir. They're going to be screaming for facts at the morning brief."

I thought a moment. "Okay," I said. "Let *them* raise the issue. If they ask for the video, release it. But don't lean forward on this. Meanwhile, get on TV and reassure the other POW families that we're doing everything we can to free their loved ones."

Jim did his job. The press got their story. But after PFC Jessica Lynch was Medevaced, the PR machine in Europe and the States put their own spin on the operation. By the time they finished, that young soldier who had endured so much pain and suffering had become a combat hero, and her rescue had become the stuff movies are made of. The whole saga reminded me of the truth of the old saying—*At the end of the day things are never as bad—or as good—as they first appear.*

A DUTY OFFICER CALLED FROM THE FUSION CELL LATE ON THE afternoon of April 1. "General, the J-2 requests that you join him here if you're free for a minute."

Something's up. Jeff Kimmons would have brought any routine intelligence report he wanted me to see to my office.

"David says 1 MEF and the Brits have confirmed this right down to the company level, Sir," Jeff said, handing me a Top Secret single-page summary.

"Thanks." I read the sheet carefully. *This is significant.* Marines clearing out Fedayeen barracks in As Samawah had found a shed with padlocked steel doors that held tons of munitions, many of the crates stamped with the stencil of Special Republican Guard units.

The Marines also discovered more than three hundred chemical-biological protection suits and masks. This wasn't some forgotten load of surplus equipment from the Gulf War twelve years ago. This was brand new gear, state-of-the-art, never used—enough to equip a reinforced company assigned to work with toxic weapons, such as nerve gas. Equally significant, the Marines found several hundred field-syringe injectors, filled with the nerve gas antidote atropine. In the courtyard behind the shed there were two fully equipped field decontamination vehicles, their high-pressure spray tanks loaded with detergent solution. These Iraqis were prepared to operate in a WMD environment.

The Iraqis knew that none of the Coalition forces was equipped with chemical weapons. The United States and all of its partners had renounced the use of such weapons and were destroying the stocks they had remaining from the 1970s. Saddam Hussein's military was gearing up to protect itself not from *our* WMD, but from its own.

Jeff handed me a second sheet. British troops operating around Basra had found a similar cache of masks and protective suits. They had also unearthed cases of field training equipment for chemical warfare, including nerve gas sensor alarms and atropine injector simulators.

More evidence pointing to the same conclusion: The Iraqis were prepared to fight with chemical weapons, probably VX and Sarin nerve gas, the same agents they'd used with such lethal effect on Iranian troops and their own Kurdish villagers in the 1980s.

"Thanks, Jeff," I said. "These are thorough reports, but it sure as hell isn't good news."

"I don't think it's going to be long before the troops get chem'd," Jeff said.

"I'm afraid you're right."

A ND WE DID *NOT* HAVE LONG TO WAIT BEFORE THE NEXT WMD crisis. On the afternoon of April 2, John Abizaid and I were discussing operational plans for the endgame in Baghdad when Jeff Kimmons came to my office.

"Sorry to interrupt, General," Jeff said. "This intercept just came in." He handed me a Top Secret printout.

Our Signals Intelligence had intercepted a voice message from the commander of the Medina Republican Guard Division, relaying orders to his dispersed brigades above the Karbala Gap.

The message was simple—and frightening: "Blood. Blood. Blood."

"This may be the authorization order to begin using WMD, Sir," Jeff said.

I lifted the Red Switch and called David McKiernan. "David, Jeff Kimmons is faxing you a SIGINT intercept from the Medina commander. We're about to get into this WMD thing real soon."

"Understand, General," David said in his normal calm tone. "I've directed every trooper within indirect fire range of the Republican Guard to keep his MOPP gear close."

I knew that wearing MOPP suits in the mounting April heat was a hardship. But we couldn't risk losing thousands of soldiers and Marines to a sudden massive nerve agent attack as our forces closed on Baghdad.

I DIDN'T KNOW ON APRIL 2 WHEN OUR FORCES WOULD BE HIT BY chemicals or biologicals—but I was certain it would be soon. The Iraqis had prepared themselves to fight in a WMD environment, the regime had used chemical weapons before, indications were that they had WMD . . . and we were advancing on their capital. Our best chance was to accelerate the fight—to move even faster than we had in the previous twelve days.

A SINGLE ICON ON THE BLUE FORCE TRACKER SPED NORTH, WITHIN a few miles of Saddam International Airport in the southwest suburbs of Baghdad.

It was 1014 hours on Friday, April 4.

The 3rd ID, supported by a successful deep strike of Apache gunships, had fought through the Karbala Gap. The Division's armored task forces had overwhelmed the remnants of the Medina Division and swept aside their Fedayeen auxiliaries.

Now a solitary company-size troop of the 3-7 Cavalry was racing up Highway 8, about to turn onto the expressway to the airport.

"Those guys are way the hell out front," I told Gene. "I hope they know where they are."

I picked up the Red Switch and called David McKiernan. "Hey, David," I said. "You watching that 3-7 Cav troop going like a bat out of hell?"

"General," David said, actually chuckling. "Open the field on your Tracker screen a notch or two. Those Cav scouts are being followed by about six or seven thousand of their good buddies thirty minutes back."

I clicked the computer mouse. An endless ladder of blue icons— the vanguard of the 3rd ID—was rolling up the highway, about twenty kilometers behind the Cav scouts, just as David said.

"This is great," I said, feeling a grin spread across my face.

"Check out Walter Rogers on CNN," Grinch said.

The embedded reporter was jolting along in a Bradley, doing a live feed with a videophone. In the blurred pixels of the background, I recognized the multilane highways and overpasses of suburban Baghdad . . . and the charred hulks of Republican Guard T-72s and BMPs.

"I'D LIKE TO GIVE YOU AN UPDATE ON OUR SITUATION AROUND Baghdad," David McKiernan explained over the VTC.

I could see on the map that the brigades and task forces of the 3rd ID were arrayed around Baghdad's western and southern outskirts, with the heaviest concentration at the international airport. But one brigade was positioned along Highway 8 several miles to the south.

It was late on Friday night, April 4. We'd spent the last hour discussing the best approach to fracturing organized regime resistance in the capital.

I wanted American tanks in the city the next day. And this would be more than a show of force. In fact, my intent was to probe the enemy defenses to see if any cohesive Republican Guard units had escaped into the city after the pounding they'd taken south of Baghdad.

"Looks to me like a 'Thunder Run,'" I said, recalling reconnaissance-in-force operations of that name I'd seen near the Y Bridge in Vietnam in 1968. *Some things about Vietnam are worth remembering,* I thought. A "Thunder Run" was a unit of armor and mechanized infantry moving at high speed through a built-up area like a city. The purpose was to either catch the enemy off guard *or* overwhelm him with force.

"Understand, Sir," David said. "'Thunder Run' it is."

"Keep me informed," I said.

I was tempted to get down on the map boards with Buff Blount's officers to help plan their tactics. But the 3rd ID had proven their ability to fight in all kinds of terrain, from desert to city. Their tanks and Bradleys had punched through enemy defenses in the desert—and in several towns and cities on the long march up Highways 1 and 8.

The embedded media had often been to the rear of the lead maneuver units, and much of this combat had happened at night. So the public wasn't aware of the intensity and scope of the battles these soldiers had fought. But three of the fights in and above the Karbala Gap had been pitched battles as vicious as ground combat in World War II. If any unit in the U.S. Army could handle the mission, it was the 3rd ID.

A T 0629 HOURS THE NEXT MORNING, I WAS ALONE IN THE WAR Room. A battalion task force was about to cross their line of departure on Highway 8 to drive north into central Baghdad. John

Abizaid and Gene Renuart joined me, and we watched the icons move up the highway through the sprawling outskirts and into the city.

Baghdad Bob, the Iraqi information minister, had been telling reporters at the press center in the Palestine Hotel that the Americans were bogged down in the south. "They are not near Baghdad," he proclaimed. "But if they approach, we shall slaughter them."

Gene switched channels until we found a jumpy TV broadcast from the embedded reporter with the Task Force—1-64 Armor, with twenty-nine Abrams and fourteen Bradleys. The 3rd ID also had a Hunter UAV tracking the action, so we had a sometimes confused and grainy overhead video feed as well.

The speeding column of tanks and Bradleys was under fire, from small arms, machine guns, and RPGs. Yet we all noticed something surprising: There were no enemy tanks to be seen.

"There's a technical," I said.

"There *was* a technical, Sir," Gene said. The pickup truck disappeared in a cloud of smoke as the Bradley's 25 mm chain gun tore it apart.

The fight continued farther north along the highway. Iraqi Republican Guard infantry—fighting in small, disorganized formations—and Fedayeen swarmed along the road. It looked as if every one of them was carrying an RPG, and a number of them scored hits on our tanks and Bradleys. But the task force pushed ahead, fighting through a series of sharp, bloody ambushes. They gave far better than they got.

After almost two and a half hours, the task force—now missing several vehicles that had been disabled by RPGs—rolled up to the division positions near the airport.

Those troopers have got guts—and brains.

"There will be no Fortress Baghdad," John Abizaid said.

We'll know for sure in a day or so, I thought.

As we spoke, the regimental combat teams of the 1 MEF were closing the pincer on the southeast quadrant of the city. The Marines had fought sharp battles with remnants of Republican Guard units that had survived the relentless air attacks.

And they had also encountered several hundred foreign fighters from Egypt, the Sudan, Syria, and Libya who were being trained by the regime in a camp south of Baghdad. Those foreign volunteers fought with suicidal ferocity, but they did not fight well. The Marines killed them all.

I SET THE VIEW ON MY BLUE FORCE TRACKER TO THE NORTHEAST corner of Iraq, the Kurdish Autonomous Zone. Where hours earlier there had been only a few icons marking Special Forces teams and their Peshmerga allies, there were now symbols representing the units of the 173rd Airborne Brigade, as well as more Special Forces ODAs.

Gary Harrell called from his headquarters. "We've just had a good fight up there, Sir," he said. "There were three SF teams and about eighty *Pesh*. They seized a crossroads for the 173rd and then held off a regular army mechanized company."

"Tanks?" I asked.

"A platoon of T-55s with a few BMPs and at least one tracked 57 mm flak gun. The bastards came in on a fake surrender, then opened up. Our guys smashed them."

To Gary Harrell, such an operation was routine. But I wondered how those troopers had pulled it off. "Did they have air?"

"No, Sir," Gary said. "But they had a bunch of *Javelin* antitank missiles."

The Javelin was the latest generation of shoulder-launched "fire-and-forget" antiarmor weapon. It was fortunate the Green Berets had them.

And I was fortunate to have such brave and resourceful troopers. We were winning this war, and it was because of the men and women fighting it.

THERE WAS A DECAL OF THE WORLD TRADE CENTER TOWERS stuck to the bulkhead of the MH-53 Special Ops helicopter. I sat in a sling seat on the port side, watching the desert sail by at

160 knots. We were right down on the deck, heading toward the British 1st Armoured Division headquarters near Basra.

It was almost 1000 hours on April 7, and I was making my first visit to the troops in Iraq. The initial stop would be with the Brits; then I'd head on to the Marines, and up the Euphrates to the 101st Airborne.

The helicopter crew chief at the starboard machine gun listened to a message over his headset, then held up a gloved index finger. "One minute," he yelled.

There was a thick gray Kevlar shrapnel blanket spread on the floor of the chopper, and we were all sitting on flak jackets. The Fedayeen were still active in this area, and a big bird like this made a good target.

We set down in a cloud of gritty sand.

The division commander, Major General Robin Brims, wearing the distinctive tan-striped British desert camouflage uniform, strode forward and snapped off a sharp salute.

"General," he said, "good of you to come."

It was baking hot on the LZ, not unlike Binh Phuoc in the dry season. I could smell diesel fumes. A ring of Challenger tanks and Warrior infantry fighting vehicles surrounded the landing zone.

True to form, Robin Brims had tea ready in his command tent, with real china cups and saucers, small plates of open-faced sandwiches, and "biscuits"—Brit for cookies.

Brims showed me his tactical situation on a large table map. The division had opened the road to Umm Qasr. "Humanitarian supplies are flowing in, Sir," Robin Brims reported.

"How's security, Robin?" I asked.

"Fine during the day, General. A bit dicey at night. But the locals are coming around." He pointed to a detailed map of greater Basra. "They are going into the Baath Party offices and ripping them apart. It looks like looting, but it's actually revenge." That type of spontaneous violence was spreading across Iraq as the regime collapsed.

"Well, Robin, looks like we're winning the war," I said. "But violence like that is going to keep us here a while."

"Right you are, Sir," Robin said. "And we will all be here together. But as the U.K. begins to rotate its troops, our people in London are planning a victory parade. The troops appreciate that type of thing."

"You bet," I said. The Brits deserved it—so did the Americans.

Two hours later we landed at Lt. General Jim Conway's 1 MEF headquarters near An Nasariyah. Instead of tea and cookies, we ate MREs. I had a pouch of barbeque with western-style beans. It wasn't lunch at Johnny's in Midland . . . but it was great to be with the Marines.

Jim Conway's briefing was sharp and complete. "One thing we learned in this fight, General Franks," he said, "is that the enemy, either regular army or Fedayeen, consistently positioned their command posts, heavy weapons, and ammo dumps in schools, hospitals, and mosques."

"It's the same all over the country, Jim."

When we left the tent, I hopped up on the back of a Humvee to congratulate the Marines. "In my entire life," I said, as the vehicle surged forward, "I have never seen anything like you. You're taking care of the mission. You're taking care of each other. You're acting like Marines. I won't make a long speech here. I just want you to know that if I had a son I'd want him to be a Marine."

With that, I got down from the vehicle and started shaking hands. I always like getting up close and personal with the troops, but I had another purpose today. I wanted to look into their eyes, to estimate their level of physical and psychological fatigue. I knew from Vietnam and Desert Storm that tired troops can continue to fight, to take care of themselves and accomplish the mission. Young men and women in uniform are extremely resilient. But they do reach a point of exhaustion. And *exhausted* troops can no longer take combat.

I shook hands, posed for snapshots, told a couple of corny jokes. These Marines were tired, but they weren't exhausted.

After flying to An Najaf, we drove in a Kevlar-skinned "hard shell" Humvee to visit the 101st Airborne Division. On the run-in from the airstrip, we were passed by a regular array of battered sedans, motorcycles, taxis, and buses. There were men honking horns and grinning, flashing V signs; there were kids waving Iraqi flags. It was hard to believe that this city had been the scene of fierce combat less than ten days earlier.

The division commander, Maj. General David Petraeus, met us at a bullet-pocked school. He gave a succinct briefing, much like Jim Conway's: schools, hospitals, and mosques used as weapons caches and command posts.

"We're collecting tons of ordnance, Sir," he said. "Probably *hundreds* of tons."

A tough, tobacco-chewing first sergeant led us to a large pile of broken Kalashnikovs, RPG launchers, and machine guns that the troopers were destroying before the local people could collect them for scrap metal.

This whole country is one big weapons dump, I thought. *There must be thousands of ammo storage sites. It will take years to clear them all.*

I asked Petraeus about enemy prisoners of war. "We don't have a whole lot, Sir. Most of them took off their uniforms and just walked home."

I knew that would be a problem for Jay Garner's Office of Reconstruction and Humanitarian Assistance. Putting Iraqi soldiers to work as soon as possible would be key to stability.

Jay would have to make this a priority before those former soldiers found other—illegal—ways to earn money.

WEDNESDAY, APRIL 9. THE STAFF CROWDED THE CONFERENCE room. It was already standing room only, and they kept piling in.

We were watching CNN as the huge, mud-spattered engineer vehicle crawled forward through the throng of Iraqis surrounding the huge statue of Saddam Hussein in Baghdad's Firdos Square.

Some of the crowd had tried to topple the statue by tugging on ropes attached to the dictator's neck. After a long struggle, they saw the task was impossible. The Marines stepped in to help, using a chain on the vehicle's boom. It didn't take long to rip down the tons of bronze.

As boys and men beat the statue's head with the soles of their sandals—an ultimate Muslim insult—the gang in the conference room cheered.

The media would report the war was won. And the major battles *were* over. But not the war.

"Mr. Secretary," I said to Donald Rumsfeld at the end of our scheduled VTC. "We've been talking about the timing of Phase IV. The British are going to hold a victory parade when their first combat units return from the Gulf. But our soldiers aren't going home yet. I'd like to figure out a way to acknowledge their sacrifice and service. There's a lot of work to be done over here, but major combat operations are over." I wanted the Secretary—or the President—to publicly acknowledge this fact for the troops.

And there was another reason to make a public statement about the end of Phase III. There were Coalition members who didn't want to participate in combat, but had said they would help once that phase was over. "I'd like to see some of them start bringing in their reconstruction and humanitarian assistance troops," I told Rumsfeld.

"What do you have in mind, Tom?"

"It would be good if the President could acknowledge the success of major combat operations, Mr. Secretary." I tried to find the right words. "The troops have accomplished every mission we gave them. There's never been a combat operation as successful as Iraqi Freedom."

"I'll talk to the President," Don Rumsfeld said.

Unintended consequences.

I was grateful on the first of May for the President's words. Little did I know the criticism he would face for doing what I had recommended.

IT WAS LATE. THE STAFF CONTINUED THEIR SHIFTS IN THE ECHOING cave of Building 217. My J-5 Director of Planning, Rookie Robb, had just returned from Kuwait, where he'd conferred with Jay Garner about progress at the Office of Reconstruction and Humanitarian Assistance.

Rookie was discouraged. In several concise sentences, he summarized his concerns about the status of Phase IV, Post-Hostility Operations:

ORHA was understaffed, with fewer than two hundred officers and technical experts on the ground.

They were badly underfunded, and their mission was not clear to everyone on the team.

Ahmad Chalabi and his Iraqi National Congress had finally arrived in Iraq. But the Iraqi people had not "risen up" to take control of their country, as he had predicted. Nor had the smoking gun of weaponized WMD been found.

"Jay Garner is going into this situation badly handicapped," Robb said. "His organization is behind. They haven't gathered the financial support and resources they require. And Jay doesn't have the kind of open checkbook he'll need to immediately rehire the hundreds of thousands of Iraqis put out of work by the Coalition." A key point, I thought. When so many in Iraq's military laid down their weapons and simply walked home, it made ORHA's job much more difficult—and costly.

Before the war had begun, Garner had spent weeks walking the corridors of Washington, hat in hand. He needed people and money. But he could only suggest a hypothetical situation: *If the United States went to war, could your department provide* . . . ?

No experienced bureaucrat would refuse a hypothetical request. They would meet it—with hypothetical resources, vague promises that cost their department nothing in terms of funds or personnel.

But the situation on the ground today was real, not hypothetical.

The Baath Party had so permeated Iraqi institutions—the security forces of course, but also the ministries that controlled electrical power, oil production, public health, education, telecommunications—that with the collapse of the regime, the country's organizational skeleton was broken.

Tens of thousands of policemen had disappeared from the country's cities and towns, fearful of citizens' vengeance.

And rather than surrendering in cohesive units—which would have allowed us to put troops to work on reconstruction—the army had "melted away." More than two hundred fifty thousand former soldiers were now unemployed, looking for some way to feed their families.

In the months leading up to the war, Saddam Hussein had butchered political prisoners, and then emptied his jails of common criminals: thieves, robbers, kidnappers, rapists, and murderers. An estimated fifty thousand of these criminals were now roaming the countryside like wolves.

CENTCOM had many capabilities—engineering skills and equipment, medical teams, and Arabic-speaking civil affairs specialists. But we had neither the money nor a comprehensive set of policy decisions that would provide for every aspect of reconstruction, civic action, and governance.

Listening to Robb's report, I knew it would be necessary to move quickly to accelerate ORHA functions—to identify Iraqis for a transitional government, to fund the hiring of unemployed Iraqis, to clarify the policy of "deBaathification," making it possible for the educated middle class to take part in building the New Iraq. And we would need funding authorization to spend massive amounts of money: Iraqi dinars, U.S. dollars, or Euros—it didn't matter.

As I had said throughout our planning sessions, civic action and security were linked—*inextricably* linked. There was a commonly held belief that civic action would not be possible in Iraq without security. I would continue to argue that there could be no security without civic action.

Penny wise will surely be pound foolish, I thought. *We will spend dollars today . . . or blood tomorrow.* I knew George W. Bush and Don Rumsfeld agreed with me. The trick would be to get an international bureaucracy moving—quickly.

"Dick," I said to the Chairman later that same day. "We need a major donor conference—hosted in Washington—to line up support, money and troops, as rapidly as possible."

"The Brits are working on a conference now, Tom," Dick replied. "I'll see what we can do."

ON APRIL 15, JAY GARNER, MEMBERS OF HIS SMALL ORHA STAFF, and White House envoy Zalmay Khalilzad held talks with an eighty-member delegation of Iraqi tribal, religious, ethnic, and opposition group leaders in the ruins of Ur, the Sumerian city a few kilometers from An Nasiriyah. V Corps Civic Action units had erected a large white marquee tent near the age-worn brick ramparts of the ziggurat, which had already been an ancient monument when the Prophet Abraham was a boy in the city.

Khalilzad, an Arabic-speaking Afghan-American and former senior Defense Department official, was the keynote speaker. In English, he told the assembled Iraqis that the United States and its Coalition partners had "no interest, absolutely no interest in ruling Iraq. We want you to establish your own democratic system based on Iraqi traditions and values."

"A free and democratic Iraq will begin today," Jay Garner added optimistically. It was significant, he noted, that this first meeting on Iraq's future was being held at the ancient site of Ur. "What better place than the birthplace of civilization could you have for the beginning of a free Iraq?"

The delegates, who represented the Sunni, Shiite, and Kurdish communities as well as several exile opposition groups, received these enthusiastic statements with somber caution. Thousands of Shiites were demonstrating in the streets of An Nasiriyah, demanding immediate self-rule and chanting, "No to America and no to Saddam!"

At the conference site, representatives of a Shiite exile group still based in Iran were demanding the immediate establishment of a "democratic" interim government, one that would automatically place the Shiite majority in a dominant position. After decades of brutal repression by Saddam's Sunni Baathist minority, these Shiites were more interested in revenge than constructive accommodation. They avoided the Sunni delegation, and were only lukewarm toward the Kurdish representatives.

For their part, the Kurds were rigidly opposed to any future unified state that would impinge on their prosperous Kurdish Autonomous Zone in the northeast. Further, the Kurds at the meeting advanced their agenda to expand the boundaries of this zone to include the city of Kirkuk and its nearby oil fields.

One exile leader, Hatem Mukhliss, pleaded with the delegations to put aside their traditional ethnic and religious distrust and concentrate on the problems of reestablishing security and restoring public utilities, which diehard Baathist fighters were attempting to sabotage.

The majority of the tribal leaders listened, but they said little. They were wary, watching, uncertain what this sudden freedom meant for them and their people.

A senior Kurdish representative, Hoshyar Zebari, summarized the mood of mutual distrust and anxiety among his fellow delegates.

"They are still nervous," he said. "They don't believe Saddam is gone yet."

As I read Jim Wilkinson's report on the meeting, I was reminded of the months of bickering and backstabbing at the Versailles Peace Conference in 1919 among the ethnic and religious factions from the defeated Ottoman and Austro-Hungarian Empires. We would have to be patient.

But progress was being made. We had seen the first representative meeting in Iraq in more than thirty years. The seeds of democracy had been planted. Jay Garner and his team were in Iraq, and beginning to organize national ministries to assist in running the country. Dick Myers and Don Rumsfeld were having some success at enlarging the Coalition in Iraq. Planning was under way to rebuild an Iraqi military and police force. Hospitals and schools were opening, and electrical power was being restored.

All this is good news, I thought. The task immediately before us is to dampen unreasonable expectations—ours and the Iraqis'—that this would be fast and easy.

I T WAS WEDNESDAY, APRIL 16, 2003—FOUR WEEKS SINCE D-DAY.
That morning, I had authorized the distribution of a "Freedom Message to the Iraqi People," which read in part:

Peace be upon you.

I, General Tommy R. Franks, Commander of Coalition Forces, do hereby proclaim that:

Coalition Forces in Iraq have come as liberators, not as conquerors. We have come to eliminate an oppressive and aggressive regime that refused to comply with UN Security Council resolutions requiring the destruction of weapons of mass destruction.

The Coalition is committed to helping the people of Iraq heal their wounds, build their own representative government, become a free and independent people and regain a respected place in the world. We will ensure that Iraq's oil is protected as a national asset of and for the Iraqi people. Iraq and its property belong to the Iraqi people and the Coalition makes no claim of ownership by force of arms.

Would Iraq make it? I didn't know. But I knew that now, because of what our troops had done, almost twenty-six million Iraqis had a *chance* to build a new nation.

I arrived in Baghdad just before noon. David McKiernan was hosting a component commanders' meeting at one of Saddam Hussein's ornate palaces, west of Baghdad. It was a little battered, compliments of a few well-aimed Coalition strikes—but it was livable. This get-together was less a victory lap than a chance for me to thank my commanders for a job superbly done.

We dragged some of the posh settees into a half-circle and proceeded to dine in splendor: MREs and bottled water.

As I had told the news media in Qatar on March 22, the campaign had in fact been unique in military history. Because of its unprecedented speed, however, the global public was not fully aware of the savage fighting that had taken place. Nor was the world aware of the skill and determination of the Coalition airmen, who had done so much to cripple Iraq's Republican Guard.

But I knew how well the troops, airmen, and my component commanders had performed. I thought of the famous commentary by the Roman general Lucius Paulus:

Commanders should be counseled chiefly by persons of known talent, by those who have made the art of war their particular study, and by those who are present at the scene of action, who see the enemy, who see the advantages that occasions offer, and who, like people embarked in the same ship, are sharers of the danger.

The men around me in this echoing, bomb-damaged palace were cut from the cloth Lucius Paulus was describing. They had shared the danger.

We had won many battles.

Major enemy resistance had been crushed. But the country was still filled with thousands of diehard Baathists, vengeful troops from the decimated Republican Guard, and former *Mukhabarat* agents—as well as foreign fighters who were still finding their way into Iraq.

At least for these few hours, though, we comrades in arms were able to enjoy each other's company, under relatively relaxed conditions. I couldn't remember feeling such pride and affection for the people with whom I served since I'd left Vietnam.

I kidded Buzz Moseley that he was even balder than he had been a month earlier. I told Admiral Tim Keating some retread joke about sailors in a bar. And I tried, in vain, to get David McKiernan to hum a few bars of a Neal McCoy Nashville song.

In this opulent building—part of Saddam Hussein's "oil for palaces" program, I joked—I also shared my thoughts on the nations and bureaucrats who had aided and abetted a despotic regime at the expense of the Iraqi people.

But what I remember most clearly was sitting along a curved wall in a courtyard, smoking a cigar.

Reflecting on Shakespeare's *Henry V,* I tried to recite those famous words about the "Band of Brothers."

But tears came before the words.

I N LATE APRIL, I CALLED SECRETARY RUMSFELD. "MR. SECRETARY, Cathy and I have decided to retire this summer."

"I'll get a vote on that," Rumsfeld said. I waited for him to chuckle.

"We are at an obvious point of 'mission change,'" I said, "moving from major combat to post-hostility operations. This phase will go on for several years, and I can't see myself staying in this job for that long."

It would not be right for me to remain in command another year, only to leave CENTCOM midway through a lengthy and complex Phase IV.

"I'll get back to you," said Rumsfeld.

I N EARLY MAY, DON RUMSFELD CALLED AND OFFERED ME THE position of Chief of Staff of the Army, which had recently become vacant.

I didn't have to think long before responding. "Sir," I said, "I thank you for the compliment. But I have to refuse. I'm a warfighter, not a manager. I wouldn't do well in the Title Ten community."

That was the beginning of a conversation that lasted, off and on, for the next several weeks. Don Rumsfeld and I discussed the Washington bureaucracy, the Army chief's job, Iraq Phase IV, and our grandkids.

Phase IV was actually going about as I had expected—*not* as I had hoped, but as I had expected. Despite sabotage, infrastructure was being slowly rebuilt. The Shiites, Sunnis, and Kurds were contending for key positions in the "new Iraq." Increased numbers of international troops were joining the Coalition; the Poles were establishing a division-size area of operations in the South. Don Rumsfeld and the Service Chiefs were thinking through the questions of troop and equipment levels that would remain in Iraq for the foreseeable future.

On the other hand, it was taking longer than any of us wanted to organize our own bureaucracy and the international community to provide sufficient funding for required Iraqi reconstruction projects. But Don Rumsfeld was pushing, Jay Garner was pushing, I was pushing, and we were making progress, but it was taking too long.

With the announcement that Ambassador Jerry Bremer would replace Jay and head the Coalition Provisional Authority, working directly for the President, I was convinced we were about to bring the appropriate level of attention and authority to the task. Jay had done a hell of a job getting ORHA up and running—now it was time to raise the ante to the level of ambassador. We needed money—and we needed clout.

In the wake of Jay Garner's departure, some tried to claim that he was fired. But that was not the case. Everyone inside the Coalition understood that his assignment was temporary, with an emphasis on meeting a humanitarian crisis that did not arise. The

White House had intended to appoint a presidential envoy as soon as possible. Jay Garner's training and experience had prepared him to get the ball rolling in Iraq. He had done that. Now Bremer would bring a different, more complete set of skills to a much more political environment.

TOWARD THE END OF MAY DON RUMSFELD CALLED. "Okay, Tom, if you want to retire, I'll approve it. But we will miss you."

"Thank you, Sir," I said. "I recommend John Abizaid as my replacement."

Two days later, the Pentagon announced my retirement.

ON JUNE 5, PRESIDENT BUSH AND AMBASSADOR JERRY BREMER visited our headquarters in Qatar. Bremer had just taken over as the Coalition Provisional Authority, and he brought with him a new, larger civilian team—and a great deal of money: several billion dollars and the prospect of much more.

As I met with Jerry and the President that morning, I was struck by the depth of commitment both men brought to the task at hand. As we stood and talked in George Bush's suite at the Ritz-Carlton hotel in Doha, it was obvious that Bremer knew it would take a year just to identify a transitional government for Iraq, and the President displayed no anxiety about the lengthy time horizons before us. We would stay as long as it takes and do what we had to do.

"We are committed to Iraq for the long haul," George Bush told us.

We knew that pockets of Baathists and jihadists would make trouble for the Coalition—and the Iraqis—*every* step of the way. Jerry Bremer would "fight through the problem," as we used to say in Midland.

Provincial teams would be established in each of the eighteen Iraqi provinces—the model that had proven so successful in

Afghanistan. And reconstruction would be managed by these teams in rural areas, just as in Baghdad. Security would be provided by Coalition forces working with Iraqi police and a new Iraqi army. And the Coalition would become even more "international," as additional countries—Poland, Italy, Ukraine, Japan, and nine others—deployed troops for Phase IV operations.

The keys to eventual success remained the same: participation by the Iraqis themselves, the building of Iraqi security forces and an Iraqi military, and broad-based civic action to meet the needs—and expectations—of twenty-six million people who had been terrorized and abused for more than three decades. A formidable task, and one that would require adaptability and flexibility—the same virtues that had carried the day for us in the first three phases.

As the meeting concluded, I was confident in the Phase IV plan—and the players.

THE CENTCOM CHANGE OF COMMAND CEREMONY—IN effect my last day in the Army—took place in Tampa on Monday, July 7. John Abizaid, the man who would now shoulder the burden of command, and Command Sergeant Major Dwight Brown sat beside me.

Secretary Rumsfeld, the featured speaker, was generous in his praise of my tenure as CENTCOM commander, and of the job the troops had done since 9/11.

"What a privilege it is to be able to salute the men and women of U.S. Central Command," he said. "From the Horn of Africa to the mountains of Afghanistan and the heat of Iraq, troops of this command are serving the cause of freedom with dedication and distinction. We thank each of you for all that you do for our country."

In my mind I saw the young 10th Mountain Division troopers slogging up the steep icy ridges in Afghanistan's Shah-i Kot Valley under mortar and RPG fire. I pictured the Predator videos of 1 MEF Marines firing over the heads of terrified human shields, blasting the

Fedayeen out of their technicals in An Nasiriyah and al Kut. I saw again the stubborn courage of those tankers on the first Thunder Run into Baghdad, climbing down from their Abrams to attach a tow bar to a disabled Bradley, the Kalashnikov and machine gun fire chopping holes from the concrete roadway around them.

Dedication and distinction indeed.

"When war comes," Secretary Rumsfeld continued, "you look for certain special qualities in the people you'll be working with. General Tom Franks embodies those qualities: strength, experience, a keen mind, energy, honor, good humor and a deep loyalty to his troops and to his country. Tom Franks is truly a soldier's soldier. . . .

"After the attacks on September 11, General Franks and his team responded. They quickly developed a plan for a new set of challenges, and then skillfully led coalition forces in overthrowing the Taliban regime in their rugged, landlocked stronghold. This year again, Tom Franks crafted an innovative war plan. And again, his team brilliantly led coalition forces, fighting their way to the regime's doorstep in Baghdad in a matter of weeks.

"And even with the large and growing number of forces on the Iraqi border, General Franks achieved something seemingly impossible: tactical surprise. That surprise, and the speed and flexibility of his plan, helped to remove a brutal regime in less than a month, without massive loss of civilian life, without tens of thousands of refugees fleeing their country, without Iraq striking its neighbors with Scud missiles, and without the destruction of roads, bridges, dams, and oil fields. Remarkable accomplishments. . . .

"Tom Franks and his team stand as our nation's—indeed the world's—most joint warfighters. The team in Operation Iraqi Freedom developed joint warfighting in ways that will change how our forces train and fight for many years to come. So General Franks may be leaving the service, but his service will have lasting impact on the U.S. armed forces for many decades.

"General Tom Franks, you have my respect. You have my friendship. We wish you and your lovely Cathy the very best in the years ahead."

I responded with gratitude to Don Rumsfeld.

"Mr. Secretary, thanks for your leadership, thanks for your friendship, thanks for your morality, thanks for caring. . . ."

I braced myself against the emotions I felt coming over me.

"To Cathy Franks," I said, seeking out her eyes in the audience. "Today is the day I make myself an honest man, having told my wife thirty-four years ago that I was going to leave the United States Army. . . .

"Cathy, thanks for your love, your support. And as Secretary Rumsfeld said, thanks for your service to this nation. Man has no greater treasure than family. You're the best. And I'm a lucky guy.

"Today is a very stressful time for me," I said, warming to the moment. "When I woke up this morning, I had a Boeing business jet, several aides, several sedans, and now I'm worrying about how in the hell I'm going to get home."

But I had a serious message I wanted to impart to my audience.

"Twenty-two months ago, the United States of America—in fact, the free world—looked into the face of evil. We came on that day to recognize our vulnerability, and the world came to recognize America—with *attitude*.

"Our nation's changed. We've been blessed with leadership that evidences character and moral courage, depth of resolve seldom seen. We see in our country today the evidence of a core value that, in my view, was dormant for a time: patriotism. Constant, deep patriotism by those who salute the flag, and by those who wave the flag. . . .

"And we see love, we see appreciation, and we see caring. We see support for our men and women in uniform—selfless men and women, who continue today to answer the call. We mourn the loss of those who have given their lives in the cause of freedom. . . .

"I said recently that America stands at a crease in history—two hundred and twenty-five-plus years behind us, we ask ourselves, what will the next two hundred and twenty-five years bring?

"We're reminded every day by the loss of brave men and women who serve in the global war on terrorism that freedom isn't free.

"I'm frequently asked by members of the media, is the prize we seek in the global war on terrorism worth the price that we have to pay for it? And I have answered, and I'll continue to answer, *You bet*. Because the prize we seek in this time in history is a way of life. . . .

"Freedom is worth whatever it takes. Future generations, I predict, will continue to pay the price for freedom, in this wonderful, this *magnificent* experiment we call democracy."

When John assumed command, I left the stage and hugged Cathy, Jacqy, and the grandkids.

As we walked toward the exit, Don Rumsfeld gave me an envelope containing a handwritten note from President George W. Bush:

Dear Tommy,

Congratulations on your retirement from the U.S. Army. You served our nation with distinction and class.

Our nation has been tested over the past two years. We were attacked by ruthless killers who thought we would cower. They were wrong. We had a man named Franks in charge.

Tommy, you led our troops in two major battles in the war on Terror. We prevailed in Afghanistan and Iraq because you commanded brave troops with a sound strategy. Our nation is grateful for your service. It has been my privilege to serve with you. You are a good man. My best to Cathy.

Sincerely,
George Bush

. . . *a good man* . . . and for thirty-eight years a proud American soldier.

EPILOGUE
CREASES IN HISTORY

It feels odd showing my retired-member Defense Department ID card at the main gate of MacDill Air Force Base. I used to roll right through. But it's been a year since I was the four-star general commanding CENTCOM.

Most of the guards recognize me, but the THREATCON requires that they conduct "positive verification," comparing my face with the photo. The global war on terrorism continues, and rigorous security is a necessary habit of discipline.

White egrets stand at the edge of the pond near the flight line—stately birds that move gracefully, but have a raucous croak. Passing them, I remember the small gray owls of Athena that called across the roof of the Kydon Hotel on September 11, 2001, the first night of this long war. Almost three years have passed since that September evening in Greece.

We have won important battles . . . yet the war is far from over.

I'm headed to the CENTCOM History Office, a secure facility holding the thousands of pages of classified messages, transcripts of

VTCs, operational orders, and after-action reports I've reviewed while writing this book.

I drive past the hangars where the old Spar 06 was maintained. On the left, the doublewides of Coalition Village cover an area the size of several city blocks. The flags of the nations represented in the village are a field of color in the humid breeze: the United Arab Emirates, the Kingdom of Saudi Arabia, Pakistan, Yemen, Egypt, the United Kingdom, France, Germany, Australia, Denmark, Canada, Uzbekistan . . .

A young airman in DCUs crosses the parking lot, carrying a stack of messages to the Village. "Good morning, General," she says.

"It sure is, Sergeant." I look at the rows of flags. "How many countries we got over there now?"

"Sixty-five, Sir," she says.

The largest coalition in history. And these are just some of the more than one hundred and thirty countries that have banded together to fight terrorism—some lending direct military support, some financial support, and still others supporting the struggle diplomatically. Many nations, like those represented here in Tampa, have made their role public. Others prefer not to disclose their assistance, but help in vital ways—especially with intelligence, which is always a scarce commodity.

But twenty-one countries, as diverse as Japan and Ukraine, Germany and France, keep more than eighteen thousand troops in CENTCOM's Area of Responsibility. Some have deployed forces to Afghanistan, some to Iraq, some to both. Today they also conduct Humanitarian Assistance and peacekeeping missions. Their sons and daughters have died beside the Americans, British, and Australians who have borne the brunt of the fighting. Polish Special Ops troopers joined U.S. Navy SEALs seizing the oil terminals on the al Faw Peninsula, saving Iraq's natural resources from sabotage and preventing an unprecedented environmental disaster. And French soldiers, Canadians, and so many others, fought beside us in Afghanistan.

I remember that afternoon in September 2001 when I told Colonel Michael Hayes, "I've got a job for you"—a job building the first corner of this village. Since that day, the CENTCOM staff has worked with talented and energetic colleagues in the Pentagon and State Department to enlarge the Coalition.

In my more than thirty trips to the region seeking partners, I used lots of carrots and a few sticks. I drank hundreds of cups of tea—and a few tumblers of vodka. I recall Churchill's words: "The only thing worse than working with allies is working without them." *Churchill was struggling to preserve the unlikely alliance of World War II,* I muse as I watch the multicolored flags snapping in the sea breeze from the Gulf of Mexico. For me, helping to form this Coalition was an honor.

And it was worth the heartburn. German commandos fought beside their Danish, Australian, and British counterparts, as well as Dell Dailey's SMU operators on the snowy ridges above the Shah-i-Kot Valley in Afghanistan during Operation Anaconda. And though the world knew little of Pakistan's military role in that battle, Pervez Musharraf was good to his word, and he remains so today. Tough, battle-wise soldiers of Pakistan's 11th Corps killed and captured hundreds of al Qaeda terrorists that fled the fighting. And they continue to hunt terrorists to this day in the mountains of Waziristan, while Pakistani security forces track them in the cities. The recent arrests of al Qaeda terrorists mark just the latest success in the ongoing campaign. When President Bush observed that the nations of the world would either be with us or against us, Pakistan understood.

The world did indeed move through a crease in history in September 2001. Never again will democracies fight alone. This Coalition represents the way of war for the future.

L EAVING THE BASE, I DRIVE UP BAYSHORE BOULEVARD ON MY WAY home to pick up Cathy for an afternoon flight to California, where I'll speak to a corporate audience on America's future in the age of international terrorism.

A car horn beeps, then another. I see the Bayshore Patriots, waving flags on the corner, as they have every Friday since September 2001. I tap the horn and wave. Tampa is a patriotic town, which is one of the reasons Cathy and I decided to settle here. During our three years at CENTCOM, we grew to love the city's unique combination of multi-ethnic sophistication and down-home friendliness. Tampa is a quintessential American melting pot. It began as a Cuban and Italian cigar-making enclave and evolved into an international banking center, the largest port on the Gulf, and one of the nation's most vibrant sports capitals, with the Super Bowl champion Tampa Bay Buccaneers and the current holders of hockey's Stanley Cup, the Lightning.

In one of life's coincidences, we live a few doors down from Norman Schwarzkopf. I occasionally see him around town; despite knee surgery, he has the upright stature of a soldier. He is one of America's great heroes. We don't always agree on military strategy—he fought his war in his way, and I fought a different operation. But we are both proud of our service. And we both love our country.

I THINK ABOUT AMERICA—THE *UNITED* STATES OF AMERICA—AS the jet sails above the green checkerboard of Alabama farms and over the sparkling bayous of Louisiana. At this speed and altitude, the sun appears stationary. How many times did I sit on the flight deck of Spar 06 talking to the crew on endless afternoon flights back from the eastern longitudes of the AOR? During those three years of command I came to know cities that had never appeared in my high school geography books: Djibouti, at the entrance to the Red Sea; Asmara, in the highlands of Eritrea; Riyadh, Saudi Arabia's capital; Ashgabat in Turkmenistan; Islamabad, with the snowy wall of the Hindu Kush shimmering in the distance; Muscat, Oman's capital on the clear blue water of the Arabian Sea. And many, many others.

The news today is dominated by stories from Iraq. Under the guidance of the United Nations, after months of wrangling and negotiation, the disparate leaders of Iraq's Shiite, Sunni, and Kurdish communities have finally produced interim leaders who will lead a sovereign nation to democratic elections next year. It shouldn't be over-looked that this successful exercise in representative government occurred during a savage campaign of violence directed not only against Coalition forces, but increasingly against the Iraqis themselves.

Since that April 2003 afternoon when I sat with my component commanders in Saddam's palace, hundreds of Coalition troops—Americans, British, Spanish, Italian, Ukrainian, as well as United Nations reconstruction experts and international humanitarian assistance workers—have died, as have thousands of innocent Iraqis. They were murdered by criminals the press has collectively labeled "insurgents." Some have even referred to them as the "resistance." But these armed bands are hardly the resistance fighters we saw in the French Maquis of World War II.

Many of the violent young men on Iraq's streets and high-ways—planting mines and booby traps, firing RPGs at truck convoys, dropping mortar rounds into police stations, driving suicide car bombs, assassinating clerics and aid workers—are leftover Baathists who already had blood on their hands and face a grim future in a free Iraq.

And Iraq after the fall of Saddam Hussein and his sons has also become a magnet for jihadists and terrorists. Until recently, they streamed across the country's leaky borders with Syria and Iran. But now revitalized Iraqi security forces—trained by the Coalition military—are slowly sealing those borders.

This does not mean that the violence will end when the last Baathist diehard or foreign jihadist is captured or killed. Hundreds of thousands of Iraqis—members of Saddam's military, as well as lower and mid-level Baathist bureaucrats—are out of work. Without jobs, and thus without a hope of being able to care for their families, they have become the "angry young men" with whom the new Iraqi government must deal. When there is employment—practical opportunity to build for a better life—peace will follow.

Certainly chaos will continue for a time, as Iraq's interim government assumes authority over a sovereign nation. To the Baathists, this will be the death knell of their aspirations to dominate. And as for the jihadists, a multiethnic Iraq in which religious tolerance allows Shia and Sunni freedom of faith will defeat their dark hopes as well.

In the immediate future we will continue to see violence, much of it aimed at Coalition troops. And Iraq's new leaders, from cabinet members to military officers and soldiers, to police officials—all the way down to school teachers and oil field workers—will continue to be targets of intimidation. International technical experts, humanitarian assistance workers, and foreign business people seeking opportunity in the new Iraq will also be in the assassins' sights.

In these difficult months, the resolve of the United States will be sorely tested. The news media, whose embedded correspondents did such splendid work during the major combat of Operation Iraqi Freedom, will focus almost exclusively on casualties. All of us, especially those who have worn our nation's uniform, will grieve each time we hear of a young man or woman killed in a suicide bombing or mortar attack, or by a roadside mine. And the relentless glare of the media spotlight on casualties will continue to obscure the Coalition's accomplishments since the Baathist regime was removed.

But the man and woman on the hometown streets of America know the truth. Coalition forces have constructed or rebuilt thousands of schools—many that the Republican Guard and Fedayeen used as weapons depots and command posts. And this same pattern prevails for war-damaged and neglected rural clinics and city hospitals. Today, thanks largely to Coalition and Iraqi medical professionals who have bravely cooperated with the Coalition Provisional Authority, health care in Iraq far surpasses that available under the Baathist regime.

There has been steady progress in other areas as well. Despite the continuing violence, more electrical power is available today than there was before Operation Iraqi Freedom. Iraq's long-neglected oil industry—the nation's economic lifeblood—is slowly but steadily being modernized. Despite ongoing sabotage, Iraq has now surpassed prewar production, and the country's oil economy is on the path to becoming a major contributor to world energy production once again.

Yes, America knows the truth—because it is her sons and daughters who have helped Iraq move forward. And virtually every American family has been touched by these wonderful men and women in uniform. There is an inspiring story here, and historians will tell it. Until then, we can expect our headlines to be dominated by assassinations, suicide bombs, Coalition casualties. And, on occasion—though we hope not often—there will be worse, like the shameful chapter that occurred in the early months of 2004, when the crimes committed at Abu Ghraib Prison were revealed. These outrages can never be excused. Millions of men and women have worn the uniforms of America's military with honor and compassion. As has been so often said, it takes but a few to smear the reputation of all. That's unfortunate—but true.

I've seen soldiers give their last pair of socks to enemy prisoners who needed them. I've seen tears in the eyes of troopers helping wounded civilians—an inevitable result of war. Such humanity is not the exception—it is the rule. I am proud of the hundreds of thousands of Americans who serve our country in places and under conditions most of us cannot imagine.

As for the few who defile the service of the many, our criminal justice system—both military and civilian—will do its duty. But, sadly, the images of dogs and naked prisoners have taken the place of the more hideous pictures of Iraq's mass graves. Within the context of his culture and population, the torture and massacre Saddam Hussein's Baathist regime committed over decades approached the atrocities of World War II, the Soviet Gulag, Cambodia under the Khmer Rouge, the Balkans, and the killing fields of Rwanda. There is evidence that a *minimum* of 290,000 innocent Iraqi men, women, and children were massacred on the orders of Saddam and his sons. The number is likely much larger but will never be known for sure.

Yes, America will shoulder the shame of the abuses of Abu Ghraib. But America can also take pride in the fact that the crimes of Saddam Hussein's regime have come to an end.

COALITION FORCES WILL REMAIN A POPULAR TARGET—A FOREIGN army on Iraqi soil. Yet no credible Iraqi leader has asked us to leave the country. Only the entrenched enemies of progress seek to force the Coalition out of Iraq. They seek victory through the "Madrid effect," fomenting dissension and fragmentation of the Coalition by inflicting casualties on its individual members. When al Qaeda-affiliated terrorists killed hundreds on commuter trains in Spain's capital, voters elected a new government running on a platform that pledged to withdraw Spanish troops from Iraq. I expect the future will confirm that this was an unwise decision.

The terrorists at large in Iraq, and around the world, will continue to attack our forces where they're most vulnerable. And with each man or woman killed or wounded, with each crisis, with each investigation, the Washington blame game will be extended a few more innings. *Bush should be booted; Rumsfeld fired.* I am constantly amazed at the shallow thinking that underpins such commentary.

Things go wrong in war. *If war were easy and convenient, there would be too many of them.* Americans fight wars only when we are threatened. I wouldn't want it any other way.

As I reflect on my experience over the past decade, I wish some things had been done differently. I wish Don Rumsfeld and Colin Powell had forced the Defense and State Departments to work more closely together. I wish there had been an Iraqi version of the Bonn Conference, to select and legitimize a leader the way Hamid Karzai was selected for Afghanistan. I wish the international community had infused more money more quickly into Iraq, and that Iraq's military hadn't "melted away" as our troops moved on Baghdad. I wish these angry young men had instead committed themselves to building the New Iraq. I wish President Clinton hadn't pulled out of Somalia in 1993 when we suffered casualties in the alleyways of Mogadishu. And I wish Congress hadn't decimated America's human intelligence capability after the Cold War.

In the difficult days of the postwar, some have asked me to lay blame, to point to guilty parties or condemn perceived misdeeds. I have said, and will continue to say, *There's enough blame to go around*. We live in a democratic society, a free country. We elect our leaders for their proven judgment—and we expect them to use that judgment.

As I remind myself where I was on September 11, 2001, I remember how I felt, the depth of my concern for my family and my country. America is passing through a crease in history—the future will not look like the past. We have seen the exercise of extraordinary judgment during an extraordinary time.

I have not agreed with every decision made over the past three years—as I did not agree with many made before that. I found fault with Don Rumsfeld's centralized management style, and with Doug Feith's impracticality. I chafed at the intellectual arrogance of some in this Administration—as I had chafed at the same phenomenon in the Clinton Administration. And I was often frustrated by the parochial views of our uniformed Service Chiefs.

But I never doubted the loyalty or the motivation of any of these men. They used their judgment in the face of hard decisions, based on the information available.

If we had it all to do over again—armed with what we know today—I'm sure some of the decisions would be different.

I am not at all sure, however, that all the different decisions would be better.

Thanks to the decisions America's leaders made, the people of Afghanistan and Iraq—more than fifty million men, women, and children—are free today. Terrorists no longer plot strikes against America from havens in these counties. And rogue states around the world have been served notice. We need not apologize for these successes. History will record that America's strategy for fighting terrorism was a *good* strategy, that the plan for Operation Iraqi Freedom was a *good* plan—and that the execution of that plan by our young men and women in uniform was unequalled in its excellence by anything in the annals of war.

I am frequently asked what I found to be most surprising during my tenure at CENTCOM. In each case I answer: *The absence of weaponized WMD in Iraq.*

We went to war to remove these weapons. Now some say we were duped into believing they existed—and that, therefore, we were wrong to have toppled Saddam Hussein's regime and freed Iraq.

I do not agree. The critics tend to ignore the January 2004 Senate testimony of Dr. David Kay, the weapons expert who led the U.S. Iraq Survey Group that scoured the country for WMD for six months, beginning in June 2003.

"Let me begin by saying, we were almost all wrong, and I certainly include myself here," Kay told the senate committee. "My view was that the best evidence that I had seen was that Iraq indeed had weapons of mass destruction," he emphasized.

"I would also point out that many governments that chose not to support this war—certainly, the French president, Jacques Chirac, as I recall in April of last year—referred to Iraq's possession of WMD.

"The Germans certainly—their intelligence service—believed that there were WMD."

In October 2003, Kay's Iraq Survey Group reported on their preliminary findings. Their report confirmed that Saddam Hussein's WMD programs "spanned more than two decades, involved thousands of people, billions of dollars." These programs "were elaborately shielded by security and deception operations that continued even beyond the end of Operation Iraqi Freedom." Even as Coalition forces entered Baghdad, Iraqi officers were destroying records and equipment connected with chemical and biological weapons.

"Some WMD personnel crossed borders in the pre-transconflict period and may have taken evidence and even weapons-related materials with them."

The Iraqi Survey Group found a "clandestine network of laboratories and safehouses within the Iraqi Intelligence Service" that successfully hid equipment and research materials on chemical and biological weapons from United Nations inspectors in the early months of 2003. They also found evidence of new research on deadly germ warfare agents.

Kay's group also discovered numerous "dual-use" industrial facilities that had been specially prepared to resume the production of chemical weapons.

Indeed, Coalition military forces searching potential WMD sites found tons of precursor chemicals stored separately from commercial stocks, as if being held in readiness for rapid production.

Kay's report rang loud and clear to me: While we may not have found actual WMD stockpiles, what the Coalition discovered was the equivalent of a disassembled pistol, lying on a table beside neatly arranged trays of bullets.

Anyone who's still skeptical about whether Saddam Hussein's regime posed a threat to international security in this age of global terrorism would do well to read the thousands of pages of evidence that the Iraq Survey Group produced.

Even though Kay's Iraq Survey Group found no stockpiles, he emphasized that Saddam Hussein's ouster was a victory on any number of grounds.

"I think the world is far safer with the disappearance and removal of Saddam Hussein," Kay said. "I think that when we have the complete record, you're going to discover that after 1998, [Iraq] became a regime that was totally corrupt. Individuals were out for their own protection, and in a world where we know others are seeking WMD, the likelihood at some point in the future of a seller and a buyer meeting up would have made that a far more dangerous country."

A ND THE DISCOVERIES CONTINUE: A 155 MM ARTILLERY PROJECTILE filled with four liters of Sarin nerve gas was found in Baghdad in May 2004; certainly that proves that Saddam Hussein was lying when he claimed to have destroyed *every* munition from his stockpile. When this shell was found, in a roadside improvised explosive device, the news media downplayed the discovery, claiming the shell was simply a "forgotten" leftover of Iraq's war with Iran in the 1980s.

It strikes me as important, however, to recognize the significance of weapons like this. The Special Republican Guard, the Republican Guard, and internal security forces were known for tightly controlling the distribution of chemical and biological munitions. That leaves only two conclusions: Either the unexploded Sarin gas shell found in Baghdad was removed by renegades or terrorists from a controlled stockpile, or it was a munition from a larger regime cache. In either case, the discovery of a nerve gas projectile in good condition, filled with viable agents, discredits the regimes' always-dubious claims that all such WMD had been destroyed.

I was surprised that WMD were not used against our troops. And I am surprised that we have not found stockpiles of such weapons in Iraq. But I am gratified by the fact that a regime that used weapons of mass destruction to murder thousands of its own people will never have a chance to use them on America.

It would have been inexcusable for the United States to allow Baathist Iraq to facilitate the nexus between weapons of mass terror and terrorists such as Abu Musab Zawahiri. Tens of thousands of average Americans I have met over the past year have convinced me that the majority of my fellow citizens understand that principle and agree.

I recall the eighteenth-century British philosopher Edmund Burke, who reminded us that "The only thing necessary for the triumph of evil is for good men to do nothing."

T HE UNITED STATES MUST HELP BUILD A SOVEREIGN, REPRESENTATIVE Iraqi government. But the job before us is immense. It will be years before Iraq's rebuilt oil industry turns the corner to profitability.

In the interim, the Coalition, with help from the international community, must continue to grant and loan huge sums of money to rebuild physical and human infrastructure.

Saddam and the Baathists looted Iraq's wealth for personal gain. Now we need to help the people of Iraq until the country can pay its own way. To fail to do so would be all too shortsighted. America is invested in Iraq's future. Guaranteeing the success of an Iraqi democracy in the center of the Middle East promises a significant payoff on our investment.

Despite the daily parade of negative headlines, the Coalition and the people of Iraq are making progress. After the 2004 American presidential elections—when approximately 35 percent of the new Iraqi military and security forces will be trained and fielded—the level of violence and the number of casualties will likely decrease. The appeal of a "Madrid Effect" in America will lose its luster to remaining hard-line Baathists and terrorists, and Iraqis themselves will begin to experience the true blessings of liberty.

Since April 2003, I have flown above the patchwork of irrigation canals in the heartland of Mesopotamia. I've looked down at the ziggurat pyramid at Ur, the reconstructed walls of Babylon. This is a land where time has traditionally been measured in centuries and millennia, not in decades—certainly not in months.

Yet, ironically, the Iraqi people are impatient for progress following the defeat of the Baathist regime. Many had spent their entire lives under cruel repression. And they expected the American-led Coalition, which seemed to have swept aside Saddam's vaunted military so easily, to rebuild their country with equal speed and ease.

A year from now, Iraq will be a different country. Our steady progress in Afghanistan is one factor that gives me confidence that Iraq will be able to provide for its own security in the years ahead.

While the security situation in Afghanistan is far from perfect, the Afghans have fielded a National Army and law enforcement forces necessary to permit a free country to evolve and prosper. Like the Baathists in Iraq, the remnants of the Taliban—and al Qaeda fighters surviving in the rugged frontier mountains of southeast Afghanistan—

are violently opposed to a unified, successful, multiethnic country. And, like the Baathists, neither the Taliban dead enders nor the surviving *araban* terrorists are likely to reform and work with the government of Hamid Karzai to build a new country.

They will have to be crushed. Until that mission is completed, Coalition forces will be needed in Afghanistan and Iraq. In September 2001, when I took the operational concept for Afghanistan to the White House for the President's approval, I anticipated that Phase IV could last as long as five years. That was three years ago. From my perspective, we are still on that timeline in Afghanistan—and we can expect about the same in Iraq.

Indeed, history reveals that wars often end in chaos that continues for years after the last tank shell or artillery projectile is fired. Renowned British military historian John Keegan recently noted that the two world wars of the twentieth century, which ended in armistice or surrender, were followed by decades of confused violence. After World War I, the collapse of the Ottoman and Austro-Hungarian Empires sparked civil wars in central and eastern Europe, the Balkans, and Asia Minor, which lasted for years. And following the defeat of Nazi Germany in May 1945, civil war raged for years in the Balkans. When World War II ended in the Pacific, the anti-colonial uprisings following the Japanese occupation of Southeast Asia continued for a decade.

Today, simply because we fight with JDAMs, UAVs, the Blue Force Tracker, and satellite communications, does not mean that the primitive human emotions of pride, greed, jealousy, and xenophobic hatred have been extinguished. Those negative human characteristics are unfortunately widespread in both Iraq and Afghanistan.

It will take years, but peace and prosperity will ultimately emerge.

ONE OF THE ADVANTAGES OF TRAVELING BY EXECUTIVE JET IS that the FAA often assigns the planes altitudes above 40,000 feet. I enjoy the broad perspective of the terrain from this height.

As we leave the green width of the Mississippi Delta, the irrigated circular cotton fields of northern Texas appear ahead. I remember my father's well-drilling rig in Stratford up there above the northern horizon. Since childhood I've been fascinated by irrigation, the magic of finding water that turns dry land green. Watching the tiny rainbows of irrigation spray miles below, I think of the hundreds of hectares of irrigated desert I saw this spring in Israel.

Cathy and I had landed in Tel Aviv on a clear warm evening in March, traveling with our friends Marty and Nancy Edelman. It was our first trip to Israel. For years I had told my Arab friends that I had "no Israeli visa in my passport," an unofficial way of letting them know I understood their side of the story. Now I had that visa.

Naturally I had long been curious about Israel, both as a soldier and as my country's senior military officer in the region. From the professional military perspective, the Israeli Defense Forces (IDF) were a world-class outfit. Proportionally, they had as many officers and NCOs with successful combat experience as the U.S. Armed Forces. Their troops were disciplined, superbly trained and equipped.

But as a senior American official I was often frustrated that both the Israeli government and the Palestinian Authority under Yasser Arafat had spent years grappling for an accommodation that would allow both peoples to live in peace.

The second Intifada that began in September 2000 has been smoldering and flaring ever since—at a cost of thousands of lives on both sides. And the Israeli-Palestinian conflict remains a constant irritant between the United States and many of the countries in CENTCOM's Area of Responsibility.

I'll never forget the day I called on General Ali bin Muhayya, Chief of the Saudi Arabian General Staff, to discuss our military-to-military relationship. But instead of following our agenda, General Muhayya handed me a copy of a local English-language newspaper. On the front page was a large picture of a Palestinian boy of about eight cowering before a heavily armed Israeli soldier. The child was so terrified that he had wet his pants.

"General Franks," bin Muhayya said, "the policies of your country will *never* succeed in the Middle East as long as we must see such pictures every day."

He was right, of course. But it is equally true that the policies, hopes, and aspirations of the Arab people will never be understood in the United States as long as we see pictures of the mutilated bodies of Israeli school children dangling in the charred wreckage of a Tel Aviv bus destroyed by a Palestinian suicide bomber.

During my career I spent decades training to fight wars predicated on such seemingly intractable conflicts: the Cold War in Europe, the tense standoff with North Korea. I once believed that the Israeli-Palestinian conflict fit such a category.

Then my friend Marty Edelman convinced me to visit Israel.

On the surface, Marty and I are unlikely friends. He is a talented Manhattan lawyer, and a liberal Democrat; we had never moved in the same social circles. We met in the spring of 2002 when I was presented an award from the Intrepid Foundation aboard the decommissioned aircraft carrier of the same name, now a military museum that sits proudly at a midtown pier on the Hudson River in New York. Marty received the Intrepid Salute Award at the same ceremony for his longstanding volunteer service to American service members and their families.

I found his work intriguing. And we hit it off at once.

The purpose of our trip to Israel was to attend the groundbreaking for a new multiethnic university to be built on the border of Israel and Jordan. Young Palestinians, Jordanians, and Israelis will comprise the student body, taught by an international faculty. The institution is sponsored by Cornell and Stanford Universities and the Bridging the Rift Foundation, with which Marty is affiliated.

The goal of the foundation is to create a center of academic excellence and achievement, where the region's next generation can contemplate their mutual future, meet each other as human beings, not as enemies, and perhaps begin to build societies that can live in peace.

Both the Jews and the Arabs have deep roots in this austere land. The conflicts of the last hundred years may not be settled in our lifetimes, but perhaps one day when the children of the students who attend this university meet at their parents' class reunions there will be less hatred and more understanding.

As in so much of the Arab world, Palestinian youth are disillusioned. They see the future as hopeless. Lacking strong moral leadership, and often educated in extremist settings, they are seduced by those who instill a culture of violent fanaticism that lionizes a martyr's suicide.

Saddam Hussein and his regime supported this terrorism by offering $25,000 to the families of each Palestinian suicide bomber—money that could have been used to build schools and hospitals, to provide jobs instead of promoting death and destruction.

I have seen the counterparts of these young people in the medieval alleyways of Yemen and the shantytowns of Karachi, and in the endless miles of government housing projects stretching into the Saudi desert from the palm-lined boulevards of Riyadh and Jeddah. Facing chronic unemployment and societies with no room for meritorious advance, and courted by extremist clerics who have hijacked and distorted the peaceful core of Islam, these young men and women form an army of potential terrorists.

If the cycle of terrorism is ever to be stopped, future leaders of Israel and independent Palestine—and of so many other countries in the region—will have to build a productive future for this "youth cohort," which embraces life not martyrdom, which rewards achievement and tolerance. This is an immense challenge—one that so many see as insurmountable.

Yet as I stood with Cathy at the site of this new university, in the ancient olive groves and vineyards where the prophets of the world's three great monotheistic faiths found inspiration, I found meaningful cause for optimism.

Yes, despite the daily parade of bad news, there's reason for optimism.

On September 11, 2001, America suffered the worst single attack in our nation's history. Since then, we have acted decisively to defend our homeland and to defeat terrorist regimes and groups overseas. Al Qaeda's headquarters—its previously inviolable sanctuary—has been destroyed, most of its senior leaders killed or captured. The fate of Osama bin Laden remains unknown, but he can no longer plot and finance audacious attacks in the safe harbor of Afghanistan . . . and one day he will be "brought to justice."

The international community—including the Saudi government and the Europeans—has made strides in cutting the shadowy transnational web of financial support that once fed the largest terrorist groups. And nations have banded together to share intelligence and cooperate on covert operations that target terrorists before they can strike.

On September 7, 2001, I had expressed concern that a major terrorist attack on American soil might spark such pervasive fear that it would lead to martial law. But my concerns have proven unfounded. The rule of law—civil law—prevails in America. The administration and Congress put aside partisan differences in the aftermath of 9/11 and acted quickly to pass the Patriot Act, which paved the way for the Department of Homeland Security and provided the American people more effective protection than in the past. As this election year ends, I'm hopeful that we will again leave partisan politics behind and focus on one of the most serious threats America has ever faced.

In March 2004, I testified before a panel of the National Commission on Terrorist Attacks—the 9/11 Commission—in closed session. I wanted to speak candidly to discuss substantive issues at the classified level, and I didn't need the publicity that recent self-promoters have found in televised hearings.

"General," one of the panel members asked, "what could have been done to prevent 9/11?"

For the next several hours I offered my honest opinion, beginning with the terrorist bombing of our Marine barracks in Beirut,

Lebanon in 1983. I worked through the truck-bomb attack on the World Trade Center in 1993, the Khobar Towers bombing in Saudi Arabia in 1996, the East Africa Embassy bombings in 1998, and the attack on the USS *Cole* in Aden, Yemen, in October 2000. And then I described the American experience in Mogadishu, Somalia, in October 1993.

"My opinion," I said, "is that terrorists have been killing Americans for more than *two decades.*"

And during that time the budgets and authority for intelligence collection—human intelligence, espionage, good old-fashioned, sometimes reliable spies—have not kept pace with the threat. Even today, the CIA has only about eleven hundred case officers working worldwide, a much smaller Clandestine Service roster than during the Cold War. Certainly the United States saved money cutting back on Human Intelligence. But freedom is not free. It never has been.

America is not responsible for terrorism, I told them—not George W. Bush, not Bill Clinton. Terrorists are responsible for terrorism.

To a terrorist, national weakness—the tendency to cut and run— looks exactly like *national weakness.* The lessons terrorists took away from these earlier attacks on America was simple: *If you kill Americans, they will quit.*

That *was* the prevailing wisdom among terrorists—until October 7, 2001, when JDAMs began dropping into the Taliban barracks in Kandahar and al Qaeda camps at Duranta. Two months later, the terrorists knew they could no longer strike America with impunity. And in March 2002, when European, Australian, and American Special Ops troopers and tough young Rangers and infantrymen fought hand to hand and defeated the terrorists seeking shelter in the snowy ridges above the Shah-i Kot Valley, al Qaeda learned that it was fighting a Coalition, not a single nation.

I am frequently asked, "Do you think the price America is paying in blood in the War on Terrorism is justified?"

"Of course" I always answer. "I defer to no man in my love of troopers; I still consider myself a soldier. But it's often been necessary in our nation's history to fight for our freedoms, and it's never been more necessary than today. It seems to me that fighting terrorism has more to do with our kids and grandkids than with us."

In the wake of the Coalition military victory in Iraq, another lesson was learned: America would use its military decisively to protect itself and the security of the world. The message quickly spread.

One early sign of progress was the sudden turnaround of President Muammar Qaddafi of Libya. A longtime antagonist toward America, Qaddafi admitted late in 2003 that his regime had spent hundreds of millions of dollars developing weapons of mass destruction, and he invited the international community to intervene and surrendered his WMD projects. There are those who claim that he was acting in good faith, at the end of protracted secret negotiations. That may be so. But I would guess that the sight of Abrams tanks rolling through central Baghdad, less than a month after they crossed the line of departure in Kuwait, might have given him a little incentive. And if the CNN images of American armor in Baghdad had not been persuasive enough, the spectacle of a filthy and bearded Saddam Hussein being dragged out of a hole in the courtyard of a farmhouse near Tikrit might also have encouraged President Qaddafi to reconsider his priorities. Saddam survived to face the justice system of a free Iraq. His brutal sons Uday and Qusay were killed by 101st Airborne troopers after one of their former Baathist colleagues betrayed them to collect the Coalition reward money.

And Operation Iraqi Freedom has spurred the work of U.N. weapons inspectors as well. The International Atomic Energy Agency (IAEA)—encouraged by the United States and Great Britain—has begun to lean hard on the Iranians. The mullahs running the government in Tehran have not yet divulged the true nature of their nuclear weapons program. But the world knows what they're doing because the IAEA has issued a detailed report on their uranium-enrichment program. Significantly, the IAEA has also passed a resolution demanding that North Korea readmit international inspectors to survey that rogue state's nuclear weapons facilities.

THE SMALL JET BANKS AND DESCENDS A FEW THOUSAND FEET. OFF the narrow right wing, the rolling plains of central Texas are green from recent heavy rains. Still, I see a line of distant brown dust plumes, one following another. A familiar sight: a column of armored vehicles moving out fast on a dirt road. As the dust plumes form crescents on either side, sun glints off the rotor blades of helicopter gunships nearby. I recognize the terrain—Fort Hood—and I remember the long days and nights we spent packing up the 1st Cavalry Division to ship out for Desert Storm.

Those tanks pounding through the mesquite so far below remind me of the Abrams that Colonel Randy House's brigade sent up the Wadi al Batin in February 1991. But the similarity is superficial. The sergeants and lieutenants commanding the tanks I see today follow the progress of their units on networked computer screens. They communicate voice and data to higher echelons on secure radio links. The tankers are backed up by Army missile and cannon artillery that fires Precision Guided Munitions onto GPS coordinates that are often identified by Special Operations Forces inserted far ahead of the armor and artillery by parachute or helicopter.

At the speed of this jet, the ranges of Fort Hood disappear in a few minutes. But I have seen enough. In a month or so, that outfit will be on the baking sand of the National Training Center at Fort Irwin, California. But the soldiers will not be conducting a purely Army exercise. They will be training with Marines, the Air Force, Navy Hornet pilots, and Green Berets from Fort Bragg. They will be honing their skills together: speed, flexibility, joint firepower. The face of modern war.

The American military is being transformed. And the template for that transformation was forged in the mountains of Afghanistan and the deserts of Iraq.

And as they train—hoping never again to have to cross another berm and speed through a foreign desert toward a distant capital— the troops will have a unique perspective on the effectiveness of America's new joint warfighting doctrine.

This is because we now know, from the Iraqi military themselves, what they thought about Iraqi Freedom. Soon after the end of Phase III in 2003, Secretary Donald Rumsfeld ordered a classified review of "Enemy Lessons Learned." Admiral Ed Giambastiani of the Joint Forces Command and his teams interviewed scores of Iraqi officers and government officials, most of whom were eager to tell their stories. Fifteen of these Iraqi leaders were in CENTCOM's Most Wanted deck of fifty-five playing cards.

What emerged from these debriefings was a picture of a well-equipped and often well-led military, at the brigade, divisional, and even the corps level. But the broader perspective revealed a fragile, top-heavy, and rigidly authoritarian command structure.

As is the case with most totalitarian leaders, Saddam Hussein was obsessed not with the defense of his country, but with his own survival. His subordinates, both civil and military, lived in terror of arbitrary retribution.

Deputy Prime Minister Tariq Aziz summarized this mentality in one remark he made to the American team: "It was not allowed to raise your head above anyone around you. That was too dangerous."

Saddam and his sons' unwillingness to accept bad news made for incredibly flawed decision making in the chain of command. On one occasion in late 2002, as the Coalition was building up its forces in the region, an Iraqi general had the audacity to tell Saddam Hussein during a strategy meeting that the static defenses of Desert Storm would not be effective against the joint, combined arms warfare they might face. In return for his honesty, the officer was executed.

The Enemy Lessons Learned report confirmed that Saddam and his senior military leaders were in fact influenced by our deception work; they remained convinced that the main Coalition attack would not come from the narrow front in Kuwait. Their reasoning was based in part on their belief that the U.S. Marine Corps "never fights far from the sea." So it must have been a bitter surprise when Marine tanks and LAVs rolled into Baghdad and then into Tikrit, almost five hundred miles from the beaches of Kuwait.

Further, Iraqi leaders were certain that Coalition forces would never advance far if they *did* launch from Kuwait but rather would attempt to seize the southern oil fields as a bargaining chip. The Iraqi reasoning was based on the assumption that their forces could inflict unacceptable losses on the Coalition and on the assumption that the "Americans will not tolerate casualties."

And even after the 4th Infantry Division's (ID) ships began to move south through the Suez Canal in late March, ongoing Coalition deception efforts in regional capitals resulted in the Arab news media reporting that the 4th ID would land at the Jordanian port of Aqaba and attack straight through the western desert toward Baghdad. The traditionalist Iraqi military always thought the heavy 4th ID *had* to be our principal invasion force. Our deception operations played on that mind-set.

On April 2—even as the 3rd ID was through the Karbala Gap—the commander of the Republican Guard Corps told his subordinates that Coalition operations in the south were a trick, and instructed them to reposition to defend Baghdad from that threat. The Republican Guard did try to reposition. But the Coalition Air Component pounded them around the clock.

In the early days of the war, Coalition forces moved with such speed and along such unpredictable routes that many Iraqi division commanders had no idea of the advances V Corps and the 1 MEF were making.

And once air operations with precision-guided munitions began, the enemy command and control structure crumbled. When individual tanks and artillery pieces suffered direct hits from JDAMs during the height of the three-day sandstorm, Iraqi morale plummeted. One

Iraqi brigade commander called the PGMs "a bullet that pierces the heart without touching the body."

A pretty fair metaphor for the whole campaign.

A s I THINK ABOUT THE HISTORIC PAST FOUR YEARS, I REFLECT ON the men and women I served with—heroes every one. John Abizaid now commands CENTCOM. He wears four stars, and I call him friend. Rifle DeLong and Dwight Brown retired; both now live in Tampa, and I see them frequently. Chuck Wald is a four-star, serving in European Command in Germany; Buzz Moseley, another four-star, serves in Washington. Willie Moore works in the Pentagon with Tim Keating, who has been nominated for a fourth star and will soon become commander of Northern Command. David McKiernan still commands 3rd Army and ARCENT. Scott Wallace is the commander of the Army's Combined Arms Center at Fort Leavenworth, Kansas; and Dan McNeill, now a four-star, commands Army Forces in the United States.

Tim Conway still commands the 1st Marine Expedition Force. Earl Hailston retired to South Carolina. Dell Dailey works in Special Operations at MacDill AFB; and Gary Harrell, now a two-star, remains the Special Ops commander for CENTCOM. Van Mauney, now a one-star admiral, works on the Navy staff in the Pentagon; Grinch Goedeke is working hard at CENTCOM. Jeff Kimmons is a two-star in Washington. Gene Renuart, now a three-star, is in Hawaii with Pacific Command. Denny Jackson retired to Tampa, Rookie Robb is off to the Navy staff in the Pentagon, and Jim Wilkinson is back in the White House.

Pat Hailey and "Hank" still work for the Agency. Ambassador Marty Cheshes, my original POLAD, has retired to Colorado. Ambassador David Litt, his successor, still works for John Abizaid. Colonel Michael Hayes, who retired last summer, works with me every day.

I am thankful for this band of brothers. They enriched my life.

After giving the speech in California, we stop for a few hours in Midland.

"Got to get gas somewhere along the line," I say. "Might just as well get some of that good barbeque, too."

Cathy and I ride out Big Spring Street for a brief visit to the graves of my folks at Resthaven Memorial Park. It's a warm West Texas summer morning.

The family plots are close together in the sparse shade. My father, Ray. My mother, Lorene. Aunt Mildred and Uncle Bob, Docie, Betty, Johnny and Doris Jean. All of them there, all of them at rest.

Seeing my father's grave, I smile, remembering something he told me when I was a teenager, conflicted over some long-forgotten crisis.

"What do you think you should do about it, Tommy Ray"? He'd asked.

"I dunno," I'd said. "It's all so confusing."

He looked at me with a gentle smile. "Remember this, son. You don't necessarily need to know anything to have an opinion."

Since that day, I've been what you might call opinionated, although as an adult, I like to believe I've earned the opinions I have.

When my friend George Tenet, the Director of Central Intelligence, announced his intention to retire from the CIA after seven hard years' service, it created a firestorm of media speculation.

"He wants to leave before the 9/11 report is published," said one commentator.

"He's doing President George W. Bush a favor," another pundit said.

"His tenure at the CIA will go down in history as a failure unless Osama bin Laden is captured before he leaves," said yet another.

The fact is that George and his Agency worked in a world of uncertainty. And of course it was his right to relinquish power whenever he felt it was the right thing for himself and for his country. Perhaps one day the media will step aside long enough for him to tell his own story.

Colin Powell said recently that he was disappointed that some of the intelligence on Iraq's WMD program was "inaccurate and wrong and in some cases deliberately misleading." That, of course, is the nature of human intelligence. The issue is not whether the source of the intelligence information was telling the truth, but whether George Tenet, Colin Powell, and President George W. Bush *believed* that the information was true. I believe they did. I know I did. And I do not regret my role in disarming Iraq and removing its Baathist regime.

T HE SUN AND PUFFY CLOUDS ALTERNATE GLARE AND SHADOW ON the grass. The graves are silent, peaceful.

Cathy stands with me, as she has for more than thirty-five years. We talk about Jacqy and Patrick and the grandkids, Anne Cathryn and Samuel Thomas. Patrick, now a Lieutenant Colonel, serves with my former mentor and good friend, retired General Gary Luck.

Jacqy, following in her mother's footsteps, is enrolled in graduate school at George Washington University. Anne Cathryn, seven, takes piano lessons and has joined a local swim team as her mother had when we were stationed at the Pentagon in the late 1970s. And Sam, now four years old, passes time on the "jumpaline" as he prepares himself for a life as Spiderman.

We talk about our new house on the Ellis Family ranch in Oklahoma and about Wynnewood and Hobart where we were born. We talk about Cathy's mother, Gaynelle, and her father, Dr. Otto Carley, who died in 1983.

Cathy's family is my family. Her grandpa, Jimmie Ellis, was the only grandfather I ever knew, and her Uncle Don Ellis is as close as my brother. Her brother James and sister Caryn are the brother and sister I never had.

The tears well up as I look at my dad's gravestone: RAY W. FRANKS, 1914–1987, VETERAN WW II.

"The man never owned a rocking chair," I mumble.

Cathy squeezes my hand. "No son ever had a better father."

I nod, overwhelmed by emotion. *That man taught me so much—the value of truth, honor, duty, respect, dignity . . . and unconditional love.*

T HAT OLD CEMETERY HOLDS THE GRAVES OF MANY OLD VETERANS like my father: men who fought at Anzio, Normandy; who flew B-17s into the German flak; who battled Japanese kamikazes off Okinawa; who bled on the snow of Korea and in the rice paddies of Vietnam. And the graves of soldiers like Desert Storm veteran Staff Sergeant Doug Eccleston, an Air Force pararescueman killed in December 2001 on a rescue mission in the Atlantic.

We are still a nation at war. The world itself, not just my former Area of Responsibility, is a "dangerous neighborhood."

As we leave the cemetery, I think for a moment of another period when America was deeply tested: the height of the Iranian hostage crisis in 1979, when I was a young major. Frustrated and irritable one night after watching the television news declare to the world that my country's will was "broken," I sat down and wrote a poem that captured my feelings.

THE PARABLE OF ARMAGEDDON

There was once a land called Free, a plum surrounded by briars of Less. The people there were, in olden times, proud of the Manna of Free—a curious essence known as Will.

Will, it seems, was cherished above all else in the land of Free, as it was the armor that protected Free from the briars of Less. Will, as the story goes, was held in the State of Mind in the land of Free. The true patriots of Free knew if the State of Mind should ever falter, the Will would be Lost and the briars of Less would engulf them all—

And so it was years and years ago.

Twenty-five years later—despite 9/11 and the global war on terrorism—we are still a land called Free. But the briars of envy and terror threaten us.

I hope we never forget the value of Will.

ACKNOWLEDGMENTS

In acknowledging all those without whose help and inspiration I would not have written this book, I first think of our friends Marty and Nancy Edelman and "the kids"—Matthew and Jen, Maggie and Brian. Marty's drive, energy, and intellect and Nancy's unheralded devotion to military families have had a profound impact on Cathy and me. We will be forever grateful for your friendship.

My search for a literary agent ended when I found the very best—Marvin Josephson, the legendary founder of International Creative Management. Marvin guided me through a new world. He prodded as necessary, helped find a collaborator and a publisher, and reminded me many times during the course of writing that "nobody ever said it would be easy." Thanks, Marvin.

My collaborator, Malcolm McConnell, came with exactly the right credentials—a journalist and the author or co-author of more than twenty books, he had served in the Foreign Service in the Middle East and in the military. I liked him the day we met and have since come to respect and admire him. His work, with the help and support of his wife, Carol, has been truly remarkable. Malcolm and Carol—thanks for your hard work, your dedication to this project, and for sharing with us your incredible talent.

Jane Friedman and Judith Regan of HarperCollins and Regan-Books are the most successful publishers in the business for a simple reason—they are the best. Thanks, Jane, for believing in my story, and thanks, Judith, for bringing it to life. The whole team at Regan-Books is extraordinary—there is no better editor than Cal Morgan. He and his staff made this effort doable. Thanks for the support, the professionalism, and the gentle nudges just when I needed them.

My special thanks also to Michael Hayes and his wonderful wife, Kelley. Michael's work on every page and every thought for this book was "value-added." Mike Hayes, a.k.a. "Maverick," has been a friend and confidant since we first served together in Bamberg, Germany in 1981. He not only helped write the story, he helped make it. I'm in your debt, Michael. Jene Hagler Byczek works with Michael and me every day. Thanks for putting up with the cigar smoke, thanks for the wise counsel, and thanks for keeping everything running in our constantly hectic office.

Numerous people assisted with research, background information, and confirmation of facts. Gene Renuart has been worth his weight in gold—the best operator I ever met and the best friend a senior military commander could ever have. My thanks also to John Abizaid, Michael DeLong, Michael "Buzz" Moseley, Gary Harrell, Dell Dailey, Rookie Robb, Jim Wilkinson, Van Mauney, John Mulholland, Jeff Haynes, Chris "Grinch" Goedeke, Dan Fitzgerald, Dutch Holland, Lee Alley, Charles "Chick" Hatton, Larry DiRita, Hugh Shelton, Donald Rumsfeld, Dick Myers, Peter Pace, and Nordie Schwartz.

I have been blessed with great bosses, subordinates, and friends throughout my career. Eric Antila, Bill Bowen, Charlie Gordon, Al Lamas, Ed Vernon, Bill Crouch, Steve Hurst, Mark Burns, Jim Noles, John Hudacheck, Nick Krawciw, Charlie Zipp, John Seigle, Cal Hosmer, Pete Schoomaker, Gordon Sullivan, Carl Vuono, Tug Greer, John Dubia, John Vessey, Shy Meyer, Jack Buffington, Butch Saint, Don Mann, Tom Healey, Larry Budge, Harvey Goff, Gary Luck, Fred Franks, Colin Powell, Leon LaPorte, Dan McNeill, Warren Edwards, Jim Lovelace, Hondo Campbell, Billy Soloman, Dwight

Brown, P. T. Mikolashek, Johnny Rogers, Peggy Beisner, Bill Cohen, Tom Schwartz, Tony Zinni, Keith Alexander, Denny Moran, Rusty Blackman, Steve Whitcomb, Shelley Young, Jay "Rabbit" Campbell, Tim Keating, Jim Schwitters, Willie Moore, Dave McKiernan, Bert Calland, Frank Libutti, Earl Hailston, David Halverson, Michael Fitzgerald, Sandy Sandstrom, John Warner, Carl Levin, Ike Skelton, Paul Wolfowitz, Torie Clarke, Doug Brown, Marty Cheshes, Michael Cope, Barbara Faughn, Jeff Hoon, Tony Blair, George Tenet, David Litt, Karen Ballard, David Kennerly, Israel Villanueva, Al "Banana Bread Man" and Barbara Davis, Mike Corley, Jack Slayton, Jim Sewell, Lawrence Geller, Rudy Giuliani, T. O. Stanley, Jack Kemp, Bill Hickman, Chuck Hamilton, Adrian Nash, Hassan Tatanaki, Sara Marks, Billy White, Richard Fisher, Arnold and Audrey Fisher, Avi and Joyce Arad, Les Huey, Leslie Hinds, Steve Holcomb, and Jerry Robinson.

There are men who have no last names because of the work they do—heaven holds a special place for you: "Coyote," Peter, Bob, Tom, Hank, Pat, Kevin, Jim, Keith, and "April Fool."

Others serve in another way—the great entertainers who give so selflessly to our troops far away from home and many who have become friends: Wayne and Kat Newton, Neal McCoy, Robert DeNiro, Gary Sinise, JoDee Messina, Aaron Tippin, Paul Rodriguez, Billy Crystal, Kevin Spacey, Toby Keith, Charlie Daniels, Lee Greenwood, Harvey Keitel, Robin Williams, the Dallas Cowboy Cheerleaders, Drew Carey, Kid Rock, Leeann Tweden, Jared Franzreb—and others too numerous to mention.

Folks from our new hometown, Tampa: Dick and Linda Greco, George Steinbrenner, Frank Megna, Bill Curry, Danny Lewis, John and Linda Lynch, Vince and Lenda Naimoli, Eddie and Candy DeBartolo, Ron Campbell, Monsignor Laurence Higgins, Tim Marcum, Vivian Reeves, Malcolm Glazer, The Bayshore Patriots, David Mallitz, Pam Iorio, and all who are helping with the CENTCOM Memorial—Al Austin, Bill Edwards, Chris Sullivan, Paul Avery, and many others.

I continue to be blessed by a loving family—Carmal Wilson; Pauline Franks Borjes; David and Debi Foster and children Jared and Devon; my mother-in-law, Gaynelle Carley Gray; James and Rita Carley and children Jason and Erin Carley, Jodie and Andrea Carley Wilson and son Gatlin; Tom and Caryn Carley Maher and daughters Tara and Killian; Don and Janice Ellis and their family, Gary and Tracy Ellis Kincannon and sons Grant and Kade, Nick and Jeralynn Ellis and daughter Alexa.

To our beautiful daughter, Jacqueline Franks Matlock, a dedicated Army wife and a very talented woman, and to her husband, Lieutenant Colonel Patrick Matlock. Thank you both for the gift of our precious grandchildren, Anne Cathryn Matlock and Samuel Thomas Matlock.

And to the love of my life, Cathryn Carley Franks. My wife of thirty-five years—my partner and best friend. My "editor," teacher, trainer, my conscience. Without Cathy there would be no story.

GLOSSARY

A-10	Warthog ground attack jet
A-Day	Beginning of major air operations
AA	Assembly area
AAA	Antiaircraft artillery
ABCCC	Airborne command and control center
AC-130	Spectre four-engine turboprop gunship
ACR	Armored cavalry regiment
AD	Armored division
ADA	Air defense artillery
AK-47, 74, AKM	7.62 × 39 mm Soviet-design Kalashnikov assault rifles
AH-6	Little Bird Special Operations helicopter gunship
AH-64	Apache helicopter gunship
ALO	Air liaison officer
AOI	Area of Interest
AOR	Area of Responsibility
APC	Armored personnel carrier
ARCENT	Army Forces, Central Command; also U.S. 3rd Army
ATACMS	Army Tactical Missile System
AWACS	Airborne Warning and Control System
B-1	Lancer strategic bomber
B-2	Stealth bomber
B-52	Stratofortress strategic bomber
BDA	Battle damage assessment
BDE	Brigade
BDU	Battle dress uniform

BG	Brigadier general
Black Hawk	UH-60 utility helicopter
BMP	Soviet-design infantry fighting vehicle
BN	Battalion
Bradley	M-2 infantry fighting vehicle or M-3 cavalry fighting vehicle
C-17	Four-engine jet USAF Cargo plane
C⁴I, C4I	Command, Control, Communications, Computers, and Intelligence
CA	Civil affairs
CAOC	Combined Air Operations Center
CAS	Close air support
CAT	Crisis Action Team
CAV	Cavalry
CD	Cavalry division
CENTAF	Central Command, Air Forces
CENTCOM	Central Command; one of America's Unified/Joint Commands
CEO	Chief Executive Officer
CEP	Circular error probable
CEV	Combat engineer vehicle
CFACC	Combined Forces Air Component Command
CFLCC	Combined Forces Land Component Command
CFMCC	Combined Forces Maritime Component Command
CFSOCC	Combined Forces Special Operations Component Command
CG	Commanding general
CGSC	U.S. Army Command and General Staff College
Chinook	CH-47 helicopter
CIA	Central Intelligence Agency
CINC	Commander-in-Chief
CINCCENT	Commander-in-Chief, Central Command
COL	Colonel
COMM	Communications
CONPLAN	Contingency plan

CONUS	Continental United States
CP	Command post
CPT	Captain
CSAR	Combat search and rescue
DCU	Desert camouflage uniform
D-Day	Beginning of hostilities
DEROS	Date Eligible for Return from Overseas
DIA	Defense Intelligence Agency
DOD	Department of Defense
DPICM	Dual-purpose improved conventional munitions
Dust Off	GI slang for medical evacuation helicopter
ELINT	Electronic intelligence
EPW	Enemy prisoner of war
F-16	Falcon fighter bomber
F-117	Night Hawk Stealth bomber
F/A-18	Naval/Marine fighter bomber
FAC	Forward air controller
Firefinder	Countermortar, counterartillery radar
"First Team"	Nickname for the 1st Cavalry Division
FIST	Fire support team
FISTV	Fire support team vehicle; a modified M113 APC
FLIR	Forward-looking infrared
FOB	Forward operating base
FORSCOM	U.S. Army Forces Command
FRAGO	Fragmentary order
G-2	Intelligence staff officer/section—division or higher
G-3	Operations and plans staff officer/section—division or higher
G-4	Logistics staff officer/section—division or higher
GBU	Guided bomb unit
G-Day	Beginning of ground phase of a campaign
GEN	General
GPS	Global Positioning System
Grunt	GI slang for an infantryman
HARM	High-speed antiradiation missile
HDR	Humanitarian daily ration

HEAT	High-explosive antitank projectile
Hellfire	Laser-guided antitank missile
H-Hour	The specific hour at which a particular operation commences.
Howitzer	An indirect fire cannon
HQ	Headquarters
Huey	UH-1 Iroquois utility helicopter
HUMINT	Human intelligence
Humvee	High-mobility, multipurpose wheeled vehicle
IADS	Integrated Air Defense System
ICBM	Intercontinental ballistic missile
ID	Infantry division
INTERNAL LOOK	A joint training exercise
J-2	Intelligence staff officer or section at joint headquarters
J-3	Operations staff officer or section at joint headquarters
J-5	Plans staff officer or section at joint headquarters
J-6	Communications staff officer or section at joint headquarters
JCS	Joint Chiefs of Staff
JDAM	Joint direct attack munition
JIC	Joint Intelligence Center
JOC	Joint Operations Center
JSOTF	Joint Special Operations Task Force
JSTARS	Joint Surveillance Target Attack Radar System
JTF	Joint Task Force
K-2	Karshi Khanibad, Uzbekistan
KFIA	King Fahd International Airport
KKMC	King Khalid Military City
Klick	GI slang for kilometer
KM	Kilometers
LAV	U.S. Marine Corps light armored vehicle
LCC	Land component commander
LD	Line of departure
LNO	Liaison officer
LT	Lieutenant
LTC	Lieutenant colonel

LTG	Lieutenant general
M1A1	Abrams tank
M-14	7.62 mm Infantry rifle
M-16	5.56 mm Infantry rifle
M-60	7.62 mm machinegun
M-26	U.S. fragmentation grenade
M-109	Paladin 155 mm self-propelled howitzer
MANPADS	Man Portable Air Defense System—a shoulder-fired missile
MARCENT	Marine Forces, Central Command
MEB	Marine Expeditionary Brigade
MEF	Marine Expeditionary Force
Mech	Mechanized
MEDEVAC	Medical evacuation
METT T	Mission, enemy, troops, terrain, and time available
MEZ	Missile enlargement zone
MG	Major general
MI	Military intelligence
MLRS	Multiple Launch Rocket System
MM	Millimeter
MOPP	Mission Oriented Protective Posture
MP	Military police
MRE	Meals, ready to eat
MSR	Main supply route
NATO	North Atlantic Treaty Organization
NBC	Nuclear, biological, chemical
NCO	Noncommissioned officer—corporal or sergeant
NEO	Noncombatant evacuation operations
NGO	Nongovernmental organization
NSC	National Security Council
NTC	National Training Center, Fort Irwin, California
NVA	North Vietnamese Army
OCS	Officer Candidate School
OPFOR	Opposing force
OPLAN	Operations plan

PAC-3	Improved anti-theater ballistic missile version of Patriot
PGM	Precision-guided munition
PL	Phase line
Polo Step	Classified security compartment
POW	Prisoner of war
PR	Public relations
PSAB	Prince Sultan Air Base, Saudi Arabia
PSYOP	Psychological operations
R&D	Research and development
REFORGER	Return of forces to Germany
RPG	Rocket-propelled grenade
S-2	Intelligence staff officer/section—battalion or brigade level
S-3	Operations and plans officer/section—battalion or brigade level
S-4	Logistics staff officer/section—battalion or brigade level
Sabot	Armor-piercing tank projectile
Sapper	A military engineer; Viet Cong saboteur
SATCOM	Satellite communications
SCIF	Special Compartmented Intelligence Facility
Scud	Soviet-design ballistic missile
SEAD	Suppression of enemy air defenses
SF	Special Forces
Shamal	A Middle Eastern seasonal windstorm often associated with blowing dust and rain
SIGINT	Signals intelligence
SJA	Staff Judge Advocate
SMU	Special Mission Unit
SOCCENT	Special Operations Command Central Command
SOCOM	Special Operations Command
SOF	Special Operations Forces
Spectre	Air Force AC-130 aircraft
T-55, 62, 72	Soviet design main battle tanks
TAA	Tactical assembly area
TAC	Tactical command post
TBM	Tactical ballistic missile

TF	Task Force
TLAM	Tomahawk Land Attack Missile
TOC	Tactical operations center
TOW	Tube-launched, optically tracked, wire-guided anti-tank missile
Track	A tracked vehicle—often an armored personnel carrier
TRADOC	U.S. Army Training and Doctrine Command
UAE	United Arab Emirates
UAV	Unmanned aerial vehicle; remotely piloted vehicle (RPV)
UK	United Kingdom
UN	United Nations
USAF	United States Air Force
USAREUR	U.S. Army Europe
VC	Viet Cong
VISOBS	Visual observation posts
VTC	Video teleconference
VULCAN	20 mm antiaircraft cannon/gun system
WMD	Weapons of mass destruction
WP	White phosphorus
XO	Executive officer
ZSU-14.5, 23, 57 mm	Soviet-design antiaircraft gun

INDEX